2000

Published under licence by
devELop ENGLISH
"Ranmalee", Mahawela Road, Nakulugamuwa, Sri Lanka.
UK Correspondence
c/o ELgazette, Dilke House
London WC1E 7JA
Tel: +44 171 255 1969
Fax: +44 171 255 1972
e-mail: editorial@elgazette.com
Printed by
Sarvodaya Vishva Lekha
41, Lumbini Avenue,
Ratmalana, Sri Lanka.
e-mail: sarvsl01@sri.lanka.net
ISBN 0-9514576-9-1

TENTH EDITION

GW00587663

ELT Guide

Editorial Team David Francis, Gideon Kaltenbacher

Marketing Manager Lisa Thomas

Marketing Assistant Volker Malzahn

Marketing Team Borja Alcocer, Iona Dyson

Publisher John Gorner

Cover Illustration Sarvodaya Vishva Lekha

Acknowledgements

We would like to thank the following for their invaluable help: Association of Recognised English Language Services, The British Council, especially Richard Law, David Mason and Ruth Brander and their colleagues worldwide; International House; English Worldwide, Chris Graham and his colleagues; ACELS especially Jim Ferguson; ELICOS Association, International Association of Teachers of English as a Foreign Language, Teachers of English to Speakers of Other Languages, Trinity College, London, University of Cambridge Local Examinations Syndicate, Voluntary Service Overseas

How to Use the ELT Guide

Notes about the ELT Guide to help you access specific information to suit your needs.

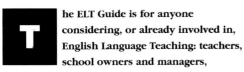

The ELT Guide is for anyone considering, or already involved in, English Language Teaching: teachers, school owners and managers, prospective teachers, language travel agents, publishers, consultants, as well as suppliers needing to know about the profession.

Section One – Becoming a Teacher explores initial teacher training courses, internationally recognised certificates, and lists course details.

Section Two – Finding a Job advises on where to start finding a teaching job, describes and provides details of the major chain schools, voluntary organisations, government and self-funding teaching schemes, and gives details of where to find job adverts in the media and on the Internet. It also gives financial and medical advice.

Section Three – International Job Prospects gives the lowdown on teaching opportunities in over 100 countries worldwide, including the UK, Ireland, the US, Canada, Australia and New Zealand, arranged by geographical region.

Section Four – Further Qualifications covers more involved courses, such as Diplomas and Masters degrees, which can be taken as an initial qualification but are more popular amongst experienced teachers wishing to improve their skills. There are also details of short specialist and refresher courses, including how to fund them. The course grids in Sections One and Four have been designed to help readers sort quickly through the many courses offered so that they can find those that best suit their needs.

The **Reference Section** contains details about organisations and other useful addresses.

Prospective Teachers

Are you considering EFL/ESL teaching as a career? Do you want to be trained so that you can work while you travel around the world? Turn immediately to **Section One.** This section provides clear information on basic teaching courses and qualifications, along with practical information about how to put this training into practice. **Section Two** shows you how to go about getting a job. **Section Three** shows you how to use teaching as a means of seeing the world. It lists hundreds of schools throughout the world. **Section Four** will help you to plan a long-term career strategy with advice on further qualifications and training.

Educational Consultants/ Language Travel Agents

If you are looking for a local English school, including schools in English-speaking countries, look up your country in **Section Three,** where you will find hundreds of schools listed.

To get a real understanding of what you can expect from teachers, read through **Section One** and **Section Four** which show what teaching qualifications actually mean.

Teachers/EFL Professionals

Do you want to improve your career prospects, develop your teaching skills, specialise or refresh your classroom techniques? **Section Four** explains how to achieve your goals.

If you do not have a qualification, turn to **Section One** to assess the initial qualifications on offer. For ideas about teaching, developing your career, associated jobs and starting your own business, turn to **Section Four**.

And, if you are looking for a job anywhere in the world, **Section Three** explores opportunities in over 100 countries.

3

Contents

5

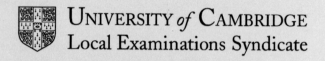

Becoming a Teacher

There are many routes to becoming a teacher of English. Each has its own advantages. The following pages explain how to select the best route for you and provide details of many of the initial training courses which are available throughout the world.

Experienced teachers turn to page 185

Acronyms and Terminology

In common with many other professions, the English Language Teaching world has its own acronyms. This list should help you understand what your colleagues are talking about.

ARELS: Association of Recognised English Language Services.

ATT: Association for Teacher Training, Ireland.

BASELT: British Association of State English Language Teaching.

BC: British Council.

CALL: Computer Assisted Language Learning.

CEELT: Cambridge Examination in English for Language Teachers. An UCLES/RSA exam for non-native teachers of English.

CELTA: Certificate in English Language Teaching for Adults. The newly-developed initial teaching certificate from UCLES/RSA.

CILT: Centre for Information on Language Teaching and Research.

CTEFLA: Certificate in the Teaching of English as a Foreign Language to Adults. One of the many names for the UCLES/RSA teaching training course or examination. This has now been replaced by the CELTA.

DELTA: Diploma in English Language Teaching to Adults. The new version of the DTEFLA. This was introduced in 1997-98.

DOS: Director of Studies.

DTEFLA: Diploma in the Teaching of English as a Foreign Language to Adults. The advanced UCLES/RSA teaching training course/exam, now replaced by the DELTA.

EAP: English for Academic Purposes. The study, or teaching, of English with specific reference to an academic course.

E2L: English as a Second Language (L2).

ECIS: European Council of International Schools.

EFL: English as a Foreign Language. The general UK term. In North America and Australia it is used only to refer to teaching abroad.

ELICOS: English Language Intensive Courses for Overseas Students. The Australian term as well as the name of Australia's main association of ELT schools.

ELT: English Language Teaching or Training. A general international term used by publishers.

ESL: English as a Second Language. The general US term for any English Language Teaching within the country. In the UK and Australia the term refers to teaching English to immigrants.

ESOL: English for Speakers of Other Languages. Another general US term.

ESP: English for Specific Purposes. Teaching or studying English for a specific task.

IATEFL: International Association of Teachers of English as a Foreign Language.

IELTS: International English Language Testing System. Exam for non-native speakers of English developed by UCLES and the British Council.

JALT: Japan Association for Language Teaching.

JET: Japanese Exchange and Teaching Programme.

L1: First Language.

LCCIEB: London Chamber of Commerce and Industry Examination Board.

NATESOL: National Association of Teachers of English for Speakers of Other Languages.

ODA: Overseas Development Agency.

PGCE: Post Graduate Certificate in Education. Main UK teaching qualification - essential for state sector teaching.

QTS: Qualified Teacher Status. State teaching qualification awarded to a teacher who has qualified and gained one year's experience.

RELSA: Recognised English Language Schools Association. Irish organisation of independent language schools.

RSA: Royal Society of Arts. Examination body which, in conjunction with UCLES, has developed some of the key TEFL teacher training exams.

TEFL, TESL, TESOL: The prefix (T) simply stands for Teaching. TESOL is also the name of an American association.

TOEFL: Test of English as a Foreign Language. Key US exam for students of English.

UCLES: University of Cambridge Local Examinations Syndicate. Examination body which, in conjunction with RSA, has developed some of the key TEFL teacher training courses and exams.

USIA: United States Information Agency.

VSO: Voluntary Services Overseas.

Why English?

In the year 2000 it is estimated that more than a billion people will be learning English. Why? Quite simply, English is the international language of business, communication and the media. Nearly 85 per cent of Internet Websites are in English and it has been suggested that more than 80 per cent of the information stored in the world's computers is in English.

With English as the chosen international language of communication, anyone who speaks the language is at an advantage when it comes to looking for a job, especially if they have other skills which are in demand.

What work can I do as an English speaker?

The most obvious work for an English speaker is *teaching*. There is massive demand for English learning and the worldwide English Language Teaching (ELT) industry is worth an estimated £20 billion per year. This means that there are plenty of opportunities at every level, be it in the private, public, corporate or voluntary sectors! For further details see Why EFL, page 10.

It is surprising how many international organisations do not have in-house *translators*. Many organisations end up spending up to a third of their budgets on freelancers. As a translator, you could be working on anything from correspondence and contracts to technical data and sales literature. Most of the work will involve translating from English into the local language so you will need to have bilingual proficiency, with a wide vocabulary and a good feeling for idiom. If you are the only translator in the area, the rewards can be very great, especially when you build up a good network of clients. However, as you will be working freelance, make sure that you are managing your finances and tax payments correctly.

For those who have advanced bilingual proficiency, there might be some demand for *interpreters*. Interpreting rates vary enormously but can be more than £350 per day.

English is the international language of *business, financial and insurance services*, even in countries which do not traditionally speak the language. If a company wants to export its products or services internationally, it will need English packaging, publicity, and probably even complete sales management strategies. An English speaker with knowledge of the local language and legal, financial or marketing experience would have a lot to offer. Some companies offer internships and work experience to undergraduate students and school leavers. Check at your local careers office to see if any links have been established.

The worldwide *travel and tourism* industry is thought to be worth around £1 trillion, employing some 130 million people. Many hotels belong to international chains which need to market themselves internationally so they will need marketing and management personnel with knowledge of English as well as receptionists and tour operators. If you have good communication skills, you might also find short or longer term work as a travel agent or representative.

For more information about developing your career and branching out into related areas such as language travel agency and publishing, see Developing Your Career, page 253.

How well do I have to speak English?

There are three types of English speaker. First-language (L1) speakers have grown up in a country where English is the only or dominant language spoken. Second-language (L2) speakers have grown up in a country where English is a second language. Speakers of English as a foreign language (EFL) learn English although the language is not spoken in their country. The line between L2 and EFL speakers is a difficult one to define and for the purposes of finding a job, the bottom line is how proficient the applicant is.

9

Why EFL?

 E nglish is the international language of business and communication, especially on the Internet. More than 80 per cent of international companies use the language to communicate and it is estimated that three quarters of the world's mail is in English. English is used for international academic papers, diplomatic conventions and even air traffic control.

Why teach?

Given the current and future demand for English learning worldwide, teaching offers stable work for travellers and world explorers. Any tourist can get on a plane and visit a country but as an English language teacher, you will be able to *experience* the country. You will access the country's culture through your students in a unique way and you will be able to contribute to the development of the country in which you teach.

But ELT is much more than a means to fund your travels. It offers an exciting and flexible career with plenty of opportunities for advancement, development and branching out into related professions. A brief look at Developing Your Career, starting on page 253, will show you why many who become English language teachers never leave the profession.

Where can I teach?

Teachers are needed everywhere where English is learnt. English is the most popular modern language studied worldwide and many countries that already have English in their secondary schools and universities have also been introducing the language into their primary schools. However, countries often do not have enough local English language teachers to fill these *public sector* positions and this means that there are many opportunities available for overseas teachers. Recruitment for these positions might be undertaken directly by governments or indirectly through agencies, educational programmes or voluntary organisations.

If incomes in a country are high enough, there will be a *private sector* with language schools offering English to those who can afford it. Schools will offer lessons or courses at all levels covering all kinds of English which might be demanded. English courses for young learners and business English are popular in countries whose economies are expanding or thriving and there might even be demand for English for Special Purposes from learners who want to apply their English in a specific context such as computing, law, journalism or aviation. See Developing Your Career, page 253, and the sections on Business English and Young Learner English for more information.

Many companies looking to enter international markets will need to supply English language training to their employees. They will either send employees to a private language school or hire private tutors. There are many opportunities then in the *corporate sector* and some large multinationals might even have permanent in-house trainers.

In some developing countries, incomes are not high enough to support private language schools. Salaries for public sector teachers tend to be much lower than in more developed countries but many of these developing counties have relationships with international *voluntary organisations and educational programmes* which place overseas teachers in public sector positions. Incomes are often supplemented and such positions offer overseas teachers the opportunity to pick up valuable experience and make a wider contribution to local communities. For further information about working in the voluntary sector, see page 76.

For further information about finding a job in ELT, see Finding a Job, page 67, and International Job Prospects, starting on page 81.

Can I teach EFL?

Don't I have to have a qualification?

No. There are some countries where you can teach English without a recognised qualification (see page 12) Remember, though, that schools will generally offer qualified teachers better salaries and/or more favourable terms and conditions.

Is it better to look for a job once I reach my destination?

It is often easier to get a job if you are already in the country where you want to work. Indeed, in some countries, budget constraints and availability of teachers locally mean that schools will not pay the advertising rates charged by international newspapers.

Check *EL Prospects* and the local English language newspapers and bulletin boards or approach schools individually.

I am already a teacher. Can I teach EFL?

If you want to teach in the state educational system, you must achieve QTS (Qualified Teacher Status), such as a BEd or PGCE in the UK or State Certification in the US. If your qualification is not in the field of English language teaching, you will need a further qualification.

What is the basic TEFL qualification?

There are no standard international TEFL qualifications at present. In recognised schools in the UK, only teachers with externally validated certificates are considered 'qualified'. Such courses are widely recognised throughout the world and last about a month.

There are alternatives, though, and details of these courses can be found in this section of your *ELT Guide*.

Is it possible to do shorter courses in TEFL?

There are various introductory courses which give you a grounding in TEFL. These are well worth considering if you are unsure about committing yourself to a career in TEFL or if you cannot afford to do a full certificate course.

Some schools run their own courses, training less qualified as well as experienced teachers in their own particular methods. Such courses can be very useful and can result in a job.

Where can I train?

You can take TEFL courses throughout the world. The cost of the course usually reflects the state of the local economy and/or popularity of the course. Sometimes, doing a course in the country you would like to work in can help you make contacts and give you an advantage over others when applying for a job afterwards.

Do I need to be a graduate to get on a course?

Most courses require candidates to have some sort of further education qualification but this may not have to be a degree. Non-graduates may be required to do an introductory course first. Some countries only issue work permits to those with a degree.

How can I pay for my course?

In most countries nationals can secure Qualified Teacher Status through government funding. Full time overseas students can often secure visas which will allow them to work legally for a number of hours per week. In the UK, grants are not available for teacher training courses at private institutions, although some further education colleges offer subsidised courses for unemployed candidates. Some governments offer career development loans at preferential rates or offer tax breaks to companies to encourage vocational training.

Starting out

Even if you have no formal TEFL qualifications, as an L1 English speaker you can still find teaching work almost anywhere.

In France and Germany, Business experience is often considered more important than a teaching qualification.

ith a boom going on in Latin America and Central Europe this could be the best time in years for unqualified teachers to find a job. But there are some things to bear in mind.

In many countries teachers are recruited only locally. This means that going over to a country and knocking on doors can be the only way for unqualified teachers to secure a position. When choosing a destination, avoid capital cities and big tourist centres like Paris, Barcelona and Prague, as they attract a mass of English speakers – many of whom will have qualifications.

You should always make sure that it's the right time of year. Try a couple of weeks before the beginning of the academic year or in January when schools might need teachers to cover staff who left after the first term.

The Far East

The JET scheme recruits around 500 teachers a year.

In most countries in the region, qualifying for a work permit means having a degree. Beyond that, schools are not very fussy and chances are multiplied if you have business or primary school/kindergarten experience.

There is also a lot of short-term demand, especially in Thailand and Indonesia where school owners are keen to employ teacher-travellers so, if you head for the very touristy areas, you could get lucky.

Central and Eastern Europe

There is great demand for teachers in Central Europe and the former Soviet Union although you will find yourself in competition with local teachers who are often impressively trained and qualified. In some areas qualifications may not be necessary, but tough climatic conditions and poor wages can be intimidating and discouraging.

The European Union

This is the toughest area to find work in as an unqualified teacher, though it might still be possible off the beaten track. However, unless you are a citizen of an EU country (or already have work rights), you are very unlikely to get a job.

In France and Germany, business experience is often considered more important than a qualification but it is increasingly difficult to get jobs in Italy, Spain or Portugal without qualifications. In Greece, primary or secondary teacher training is often preferred to EFL training.

The rest of the world

In the peak season, usually the summer, when the supply of qualified teachers cannot cover the demand for courses, unqualified teachers will find plenty of opportunities in English-speaking countries. At other times, it's very difficult to find work. If you are a US citizen or have a Green Card, it might be possible to pick up work in a US private school, but the pay is likely to be very poor.

Government programmes

Many governments run programmes which accept untrained graduate L1 speakers. Rates of pay are usually good, but competition is fierce so you should apply early. For programmes in Central and Eastern Europe, wages tend to be set according to local rates and teachers may have to budget carefully.

The Japan Exchange and Teaching programme (JET) employs 500 graduates each year with recruitment in October for the following July. There are new programmes in Korea and China (CIEE) also. Apply through the Council on International Exchange in the UK or your local Japanese, Korean or Chinese embassy or consulate.

Basic Qualifications

A qualification greatly enhances your chances of finding a job but, with more than one type of qualification available, it is important to know what your employers are looking for.

Anyone can teach English once their proficiency in the language reaches a certain level. The courses examined on these pages are open to both L1 and non-L1 speakers, but entry requirements often favour the former who are advantaged through their natural familiarity with the language.

Probably as result of increased student debt, the number of graduates trying to find work in the area has fallen. Interestingly, the percentage of applications for training courses from more mature candidates with experience – such as engineers, bankers or mothers going back to work – has increased dramatically. The objective of most of these people is to find the quickest and cheapest route to a valid teaching qualification that will help them access teaching jobs in the country of their choice.

Beginners courses can vary from a few days to a few years with corresponding variations in coverage and cost, but most employers consider externally validated certificates resulting from courses lasting at least four weeks full-time and including teaching practice to be the minimum qualification.

It is important to remember that most schools only recognise certain qualifications – which ones will vary depending on the school's status and location. Most American teachers will have completed an MA course (see page 195), which will obviously cover much more than a four-week course, although CELTA (see below) is now becoming more popular in the US. However, the MA may not have teaching practice, which is of fundamental importance to many employers and an important component of most certificate courses. For qualifications in Europe to be accepted, they must be externally validated. The Cambridge/RSA and Trinity certificates are generally viewed as standard entry-level qualifications.

Which Qualification?

The qualification you need in order to work in a private sector language school depends primarily on where you want to work. In North America, Central America and most of the Far East the essential qualification is a good first degree though a certificate in TEFL can be a definite advantage. Because these areas have cultural and economic ties to North America, a Masters degree, often taken as a pre-service qualification, has most value.

In the EU, the British Commonwealth, Australasia, the Southern cone of Latin America and increasingly, Central Europe, language schools operate within the British qualification model. This means that the basic requirements to be a qualified teacher are to have passed a 70-hour course (a certificate or otherwise) which includes observed teaching practice, and to be a graduate of any discipline.

Cambridge/RSA Certificate

The Cambridge/RSA Certificate in English Language Teaching to Adults (CELTA) is a pre-service course with a strong pragmatic element and an emphasis on teaching practice. It is probably the most widely recognised and respected basic TEFL qualification internationally. CELTA has replaced the well-established CTEFLA, which was the profession's benchmark qualification for many years, but has now been comprehensively updated to take into account the profession's

In addition to degree and diploma courses, universities also run EFL certificate courses.

development. (Many people still refer to the CTEFLA even though they are actually talking about CELTA.)

Over 8,000 candidates take the Certificate every year, so it certainly has the widest enrolment. The course and the examination are externally validated by the University of Cambridge Local Examinations Syndicate (UCLES).

Most courses are run on an intensive four-week basis but there are some centres offering the course on a part-time basis. Although the UK has the largest number of courses available, CELTA is now available in some 190 validated centres in 40 countries around the world, including a growing number in North America.

There is also an extension course in teaching young learners for those candidates who have gained the CELTA. Successful candidates will receive an endorsement to their CELTA Award. A parallel certificate in teaching young learners in language schools is also available, the CELTYL (Certificate in English Language Teaching to Young Learners).

Certificate courses are open to both native and non-native speakers, though all candidates have to pass a language awareness test and an interview administered at the individual centres. The syllabus is quite strict and observed teaching practice is an integral part of all courses. Wherever you qualify, Cambridge/RSA offers a job placement service to successful candidates.

Trinity Certificate in TESOL

Trinity College London runs the Certificate in TESOL (Teaching English to Speakers of Other Languages). The number of validated centres offering the course has

grown rapidly in recent years and it now has about 4,000 successful candidates a year.

The Trinity syllabus has basic requirements which must be met by all its validated centres. For example, all course trainees are expected to take lessons in a foreign language. However, course designers in individual centres are free to submit their own ideas to supplement requirements. Centres are free to emphasise different course elements and no two courses are exactly the same.

This flexibility has proved popular with both trainees and teacher trainers alike, but if you have specific requirements for your certificate, check before enrolling that the focus of that particular course meets them. Most Trinity centres also offer short, pre-sessional courses as an introduction before the one-month or six-week intensive course begins. Several offer a correspondence module in addition to the 130 tuition hours.

Trinity College has also developed a specialist course in teaching young learners, called CertTeyl (Certificate in Teaching English to Young Learners). As with the Certificate in TESOL, it does not differentiate between L1 native and non-L1 native speakers and is offered at some centres as an add-on to the Certificate in TESOL (see page 225).

Alternatives

There are a number of other certificate courses at roughly the same level as those offered by Cambridge/RSA and Trinity. They may not be as well known at an international level, but they are often very well respected within their own geographical sphere and many employers will consider them on a case-by-case basis. An example of such courses is the RELSA Certificate offered in certain Irish schools (see page 53).

UK Cambridge / RSA Certificate (CELTA) Courses

College	Full or Part Time	Course Length	Fees	Start Dates	Entry Requirements	Contacts	Address/ Advert Page
Amersham & Wycombe College	PT	22 wks	£499	January (provisional)	'A' level English or equivalent	Sheila Tracey	83
Anglo-Continental Educational Group, Bournemouth	FT	20 days	£892 (incl Camb reg fee)	May, August	20 yrs old, 2 A levels or equiv, degree pref	Ms J Manwaring, Co-ordinator of Teacher Training	83
Angloschool. London	FT	4 wks	£820	August, May, February, November	As RSA/UCLES (only 8 students per course)	David Bartlett	83
Barnet College, Herts	Both	FT: 4 wks; PT: 9 months	£774	FT: September, November, January, May, June; PT: September	Age 20+, university degree pref, foreign lang knowledge, interview	S Alberton, Course Organiser	60,83
Basil Paterson College, Edinburgh	FT	4 wks	£999	January, March, May, July, August, October, November	Age 20+, higher ed, Eng competence	Mary Beresford-Peirse	60,83
Bath Spa University College	FT	4 wks	£850	July	Graduate	Ms Joanna Hopkins	
Bedford College, Bedford	PT	15 wks	£725 + UCLES fee	October	As Cambridge/ RSA	Frances Napthine	83
Bell Language School, Cambridge	Both	FT: 4 wks; PT: 27 and 15 wks	On application	Throughout year	University entry level	Head of Teacher Training	59,83
Bell Language School, London	PT	16 wks	£875	On application	University entry level	Enquiries and Registration	59,83
Bell Language School, Norwich	FT	4 wks	£990	Throughout year	University entry level	Enquiries and Registration	59,83
Bournemouth & Poole College of Further Ed	PT	20 wks	£750	October, April	20 yrs of age, 2 A levels	Lorna Wedge	84
Brasshouse Centre, Birmingham	Both	FT: 1mth, PT 6 mths	£900	March, July	Application form, interview	Fiona Copland	84
Bromley School of English	FT	4 wks	Every month	21+, 'A' levels	Robin Summers		84,64
Brooklands College, Weybridge	PT	22 wks/30 wks	£750 + £61.50	On Application	2 A levels, age 20 +, L1 competence	Janet Drysdale	84
College	Full or Part Time	Course Length	Fees	Start Dates	Entry Requirements	Contacts	Address/ Advert Page

UK Cambridge / RSA Certificate (CELTA) Courses

College	Full or Part Time	Course Length	Fees	Start Dates	Entry Requirements	Contacts	Address/ Advert Page
Canterbury Christ Church University College, Canterbury	PT	18 wks	UK: £950, Overseas £1,980	February	As RSA/ Cambridge	CELTA Course Co-ordinator	84,263
Cardiff University, ELSIS	FT	1 mth	£975	Contact for details	Graduate or equiv	Departmental Secretary	84,260
Cheltenham International Language Centre	FT	5 wks	£857.65	September, November, Februry, April, July	Quals sufficient for higher education	Piers Wall	85
City of Bath College, Avon	Both	FT: 4 wks; PT: 6 mths	£950 (incl Camb reg fee)	FT: July; PT: July	20+, 2 'A' levels + 5 GCSEs min, L1 speaker	David Bull	85
City of Bristol College, Bristol	PT	10 wks	£995	September, January	2 'A' levels (pref langs)	Alison Haliburton, Sue Scott	85
Clarendon City College, Nottingham	Both	FT: 5 wks;15 wks	FT: £750; PT: £718	FT: July; PT: September, February	Age 20+, 2 'A' levels or equiv	David Hughes	85
The College of St Mark & St John, Plymouth	FT	4 wks	£1,100	August, March	Age 20+, higher ed entry level, good English	Michael G Hall	85
Concorde International, Canterbury	FT	4 wks	£798	March, May, June, July, September,	20+, sound educational background	Anne Kennedy	85
Croydon English Language Scheme, Sth Norwood CETS Centre	PT	25 wks	£700	September	20+, good speaking * writing skills	Janet Ott	85
Dundee College	FT	4 wks	£795	September, March	Age 20+, higher ed entry level	Alec Edwards, Brian McQueen	85
Eastleigh College	PT	2 terms	£660 + Cambridge fees	September, June	20+, 2 'A' levels	Customer Services	85
Farnborough College of Technology, Farnborough	On application	On application	On application	September - 1 yr courses	On application	Mrs Maria McClure	86
Farnborough College of Technology, Aldershot	PT	30 wks	£620	September	Nr native speaker of English, higher ed entry level	Mr David Constable	86
Filton College, Bristol	PT	2 terms	£825	September	As RSA/ Cambridge	Helen Bowen	86
College	Full or Part Time	Course Length	Fees	Start Dates	Entry Requirements	Contacts	Address/ Advert Page

UK Cambridge / RSA Certificate (CELTA) Courses

College	Full or Part Time	Course Length	Fees	Start Dates	Entry Requirements	Contacts	Address/ Advert Page
Frances King School of English, London	FT	4 wks	£799 (1999 price)	Throughout the year	Univ entrance quals, age 20+	Gerald Kelly, Director of Teacher Training	60,86
GEOS English Academy	FT	4 wks	£870 (incl Cambridge fees)	January, March, May, June, July, August, Sept, Oct, Nov	20+, 2 'A' levels, good spoken/writte n English	Teacher Training Co-ordinator	66,86
Gloscat, Cheltenham	Both	FT: 6 wks; PT: 6 mths	c. £900 + exam fee	FT: April, October, January; PT: January, September	Degree or equiv, recent learning of foreign lang	Paul Burden	60,86
Greenhill College, Harrow	PT	23 wks	£547	September, January	1 'A' level min	Liz Hoten, Administrator	86
Hammersmith & West London College	Both	FT: 4 wks; PT: 20 wks	£695	FT: September, November, January, February, April, July, August; PT: September	Age 20+, 2 'A' levels, good command of English	College Info Centre	63,86
Handsworth College, Birmingham	PT	1 year	£350	September	'A' level or equiv	Ms Brigid Bird	86
Harrow House International College, Swanage	FT	4 wks	£875 (99price)	October, November, January, March, May, July, September, October	20+, qualifications for higher education, interview	Mark Bauer	86
Hilderstone College	FT	4 wks	£912	May November	Contact for details	Teacher Training Dept.	87
Huddersfield Technical College	Flexible	Flexible	Contact for details	Throughout the year	Contact for details	Cath Brownhill	87
Intensive School of English, Brighton	Both	FT: 4 wks; PT: 20 wks	FT: £750; PT: £650	FT: January, July; PT: September. February	Degree + exp	Chris Edge	
International House, Picadilly	Both	FT: 4 wks; PT: 11 wks	FT: £967; PT: £1,127 (inc reg fee)	All year	University entrance req	International House	64,87
International House, Newcastle	FT	4 wks	£899	All year	University entrance req	International House	61,87
International Language Centres, Hastings	Both	FT: 4 wks; PT 22 wks	FT: £799 (incl UCLES fee); PT: tba	FT: monthly, PT: January	Interview	Rose Holmes	87
College	Full or Part Time	Course Length	Fees	Start Dates	Entry Requirements	Contacts	Address/ Advert Page

College	Full or Part Time	Course Length	Fees	Start Dates	Entry Requirements	Contacts	Address/ Advert Page
International Language Institute, Leeds	Both	FT: 4 wks; PT 1 term	4 wk: £875, 1 term £799 (+ CELTA fee)	FT: June, August; PT: January, September	As RSA/ UCLES	The Registrar	87
International Teaching & Training Centre, Bournemouth	FT	4 wks	£999	Every month	2 'A' levels min	Chris Goodchild	62,87
Language Link, London	Both	FT: 4 wks; PT: 12 wks	FT: £750; PT: £850	FT: Monthly; PT: September	Good standard of written & spoken English	McPherson, Academic Director	88
Leeds Metropolitan University	FT	4 wks	£600 - £900	9 mths per yr	Excellent English, uni entry level ed	Sarah Turnbull	88
Mid Kent College	Both	FT: 4 wks; PT: 3 terms	£600 + registration	FT: July; PT: September	Application form + interview	Jo-Ann Delaney	89
Newcastle College	PT	15 wks	£795	September, January	20+, 'A' level education	Sheran Johnson, Course Leader	89
Newnham Lang Centre, Cambridge	FT	4 wks	£1,006 (incl Camb reg fee)	October, January, May, July	20 yrs of age, univ entrance, L1 speaker competence	David Rowson	89
North Trafford College		Contact for details	Contact for details	Contact for details	Contact for details	Admissions Dept	89
North West London College	PT	23 wks	£492 (inc UCLES fee)	January	As RSA/UCLES	Central Admissions	
Nottingham Trent University	FT	4/5 wks	£800 + exam fee	4 wks: July, January; 5 wks: August	Graduates, prof in English	Linda Taylor, Senior Lecturer	61,89
Oxford Brookes University (ICELS), Oxford	PT	10 wks	£1,190	October, April	1st degree or higher education level	Clare McKinley	89,264
Oxford College of Further Education	Both	FT 4 wks; PT 12/20 wks	£775	FT: July, August; PT: January, October	As RSA/UCLES	Steven Haysham	89
Pilgrims Ltd, Canterbury	FT	1 mth	£1085	June, July, August, September	20+, univ entrance level	Gill Johnson, CELTA Course Director	90
Queen's University, Belfast	Both	FT: 4 wks; PT: 1 term	£925	July, August, September, February	As RSA/UCLES	Steve Walsh	90

College	Full or Part Time	Course Length	Fees	Start Dates	Entry Requirements	Contacts	Address/ Advert Page

UK Cambridge RSA Certificate (CELTA) Courses

College	Full or Part Time	Course Length	Fees	Start Dates	Entry Requirements	Contacts	Address/Advert Page
Regent London	FT	4 wks	£750	January, March, April, June, July, September, November	20+, Degree	Julie Trew, Teacher Training Registrar	58,90
St George International, London	Both	FT: 4 wks; PT: 13 wks	FT: £495; PT: £545	FT: Monthly, PT: March	Good educational background	Max Loach	62,90
Saxoncourt Teacher Training	FT	4 wks	£719 - £819	Throughout year except August	'A' levels	Christopher Hart	77.90
Skola Teacher Training	FT	4 wks	£650 - £730	Contact for details	As RSA/UCLES	Cindy Cheetham	90
Solihull College	Both	FT: 4 wks; PT: 8/11 wks	£750	FT: June; PT: 8 wks - April, 11 wks - Sept to December	2 'A' levels, selection procedure	Pat Morris, CELTA Administrator	
South Devon College, Torquay	PT	2 terms	£1,065	January	2 A levels	Charlie Hadfield	91
South Thames College	Both	FT: 4 wks; PT 10/20 wks	£600 + exam fee	FT: July; PT 10 wks - April, 20 wks - September	2 'A' levels or degree	Juliet Birgues (April start), Susan Weird (September start)	91
South Trafford College	PT	30 wks	£695 + exam fee	September	Contact for details	Patrick Bennett	91
St Giles, Highgate, London	Contact for details	Contact for details	£870	Throughout the year	Graduate, good standard of gen education	Principal	90
St Giles, Brighton	FT	4 wks	£870	Monthly	Graduate, good standard of gen education	The Principal	90
Stanton Teacher Training Courses	FT	4 kws	£612 + Camb reg fee	Every month	20+, 2 'A' levels or equiv university matric	David Garrett, Director	59,91
Stevenson College, Edinburgh	Both	FT: 4-5wks PT: 2terms	£750	FT: July/August; PT: September arch	Age 20+, university entry quals	Sarah Woolard	91
Stoke-on-Trent College	Both	FT: 4-5 wks PT: 2 terms	£860	FT: July; PT: September, February	As RSA/ UCLES	Monique Littleton,	91
Studio School, Cambridge	FT	4 wks	£880 + assesment fee	March, May, September	Age 20+, univ entry quals	Lucy Purvey	91
Surrey Language Centre, Farnham	FT	4 wks	£ 720 inc moderation fee	Throughout the year	2 'A' levels, high level of English, 18+	Mrs F Cox	91
College	Full or Part Time	Course Length	Fees	Start Dates	Entry Requirements	Contacts	Address/Advert Page

UK Cambridge / RSA Certificate (CELTA) Courses

College	Full or Part Time	Course Length	Fees	Start Dates	Entry Requirements	Contacts	Address/ Advert Page
Torbay Language Centre, Devon	FT	4 wks	£860+ exam fee	October, March	Degree or equiv	Val Lynas, Director of Studies	91
University College, Chichester	3 Modules of MA Course	3 months	£370 per module (EU); £960 per module (non-EU)	Sept	Degree	Angela Karlsson	92,264
University of Glasgow	PT	4 mths	£900	November	20+, educated to tertiary level	Esther Dunbar	86
University of Strathclyde	Both	FT: 4 wks; PT: 12 wks	£920	FT: February, July, August; PT: September	21+, univ entry qualifications	The Secretary	91
University of Wales, Aberystwyth	FT	4 wks	£800 (99 price)	June, January	L1 speaker competence, degree or equiv	Head of TEFL	
University of Wales College, Newport	Both	FT: 4 wks; PT: 22 wks	£900	FT: April, July, August; PT: October	'A' levels min	J Cann, Languages Co-ordinator	
University of Wales, Swansea	FT	4 wks	£925	tbc	Degree	David Priestley	91
University of Westminster	FT	1 mth	£760	September, June	As RSA /UCLES	Ann Marie Griffin	92
Waltham Forest College	Both	FT: 5 wks; PT: 5 mths	£650	FT: June, July; PT Sept, March	Univ entrance level	Nicole de labouviere, Head of Division	92
Warwickshire College	On application	On application	£850 - £950 (EU); £1400 (non-EU)	No experince req	Diane Mattingley		92
West Cheshire College	Both	FT: 4 wks; PT: 3 mths	£750	September, January, May	As RSA/UCLES	Ms C Weaver	92
West Herts College, Watford	PT	2 terms	£690 + UCLES fee	September	Standard entry criteria	C Romijn/ J Kirsh	
Westminster College	Both	FT: 4 wks; PT: 16 wks	FT: £640; PT: £927 (EU); £1245 (non-EU)	FT: Sept, Nov, Jan, Feb, May, June, July; PT: Sept	Degree or A levels	FT: Martin Brindle; PT: DWilson/ RWilliams	92
Wigan & Leigh College	PT	12 wks	£700	September	2 'A' levels or equiv	Lucy Hale	92
Wigston College	PT	1 year	£528	September	A level	David Harris	92
Woolwich College	Both	FT: 4 wks; PT: 12 wks	£550	FT: October; PT: September	2 A levels or degree	Ms Manj Dhanda	60,92

| College | Full or Part Time | Course Length | Fees | Start Dates | Entry Requirements | Contacts | Address/ Advert Page |

Overseas Cambridge/RSA Certificate (CELTA) Courses

College	Full or Part Time	Length Of Course	Fees	Start Dates	Entry Requirements	Contacts	Address/ Advert Page
American University in Cairo, Cairo	Both	FT : 4 wks; PT :10 wks	$1,000	October, January, May, June	Good standard of education, interview	Magda Laurence, Director	173
Auckland Language Centre, NZ	FT	4 wks	NZ$2,750	January, April, August, November	Written assessment, interview	Jane Hilton	158
Australian TESOL Training Centre, Bondi Junction, Aus	Both	FT: 4 wks; PT: 3 mths	Aus$2,1500	FT: Every month; PT: April, June, September	Degree or tertiary entry quals, sound English knowledge	Eileen Morley	154
Bell Language School, Geneva, Switzerland	Both	FT: 4 wks; PT: 12 wks	SFr3,600	FT: January, July; PT: Sept, March	Interview, pre-course task	Jackie Ecreur	127
Berne University, Switzerland	PT	6 mths	SFr3,500	January	Contact for details	Dr Heather Murray	
BFI Wien, Austria	Both	FT4 wks; PT: 2 months	ATS19,500	FT: July; PT: February	L1 or near-L1 competence, uni degree or equiv	Alexandre Klaus	62,95
BKC- International House Moscow, Russia	FT	4 wks,	On request	July, February, August	20+, L1 level English,	Lena Ovchinnikova	124
British Council, Damascus	FT	4 wks	£850	February, September	Univ degree preferred	Jon Gore, Michael Manser, Tracey White	63,177
British Council, Delhi	PT	2 mths	On request	On request	First degree	Ms Emma Levy	170
British Council, Hong Kong	PT	10 wks	HK$19,600	September, November, February, May		Nick Florent	162
British Council Bahrain, Manama, Bahrain	PT	8/11 wks	645 B Dinars	8 wks: February; 11 wks: September	Contact for details	Nick Baguley, Main Course Tutor	172
British Council, Singapore	PT	Contact for details	$3,150 (Singapore)	March, June, September	Contact for details	Head ITDU	166
British Council, Syria	FT	1 mth	£850	September, February	Univ entrance	Jon Gore & Tracey White	177
British Council, Istanbul, Turkey	PT	4 wks	£950 (tbc)	July, August	Native English speakers or non-native with high competence	Laura Woodward	128

| College | Full or Part Time | Length Of Course | Fees | Start dates | Entry Requirements | Contacts | Address/ Advert Page |

College	Full or Part Time	Length Of Course	Fees	Start Dates	Entry Requirements	Contacts	Address/ Advert Page
British Language Centre, Madrid, Spain	Both	FT: 4 wks; PT: 10 wks	145,000 pts	FT: Every month PT: Jan, April, October	As Cambridge RSA	Alistair Dickinson	109
British Language Training Centre, Amsterdam, Netherlands	Both	FT: 1 mth; PT: 12 wks	fl3,700	September, February, June	20 +, degree	Christabel O'Gorman	106
British School of Udine, Italy	FT	5 wks	LIt2,600,000	June	Standard CILTs	Richard Baudains	104
Cambridge School Verona, Italy	Both	FT: 4 wks; PT: 6 months	LIt2,500,000	FT: June, September; PT: January	Interview	Tracey Sinclair	104
Campbell College, Valencia, Spain	FT	4 wks	150,000 ptas	February, May, July, November	Contact for details	Seamus Campbell	109
Capital Language Academy, New Zealand	FT	4 wks	NZ$2,700	January, May, July, November	20+, univ entrance	Jo Leach, Annie Taylor	158
Capital Language Academy, Wellington, New Zealand	FT	4 wks	NZ$2,700		20+, educated to univ entrance level	Jo Leach, Lead Trainer	158
Columbia College, Canada	Both	FT: 4 wks; PT: 8 wks	C$ 2500 per semester	On application	BA degree	James R. Janz	139
ECC (Thailand), Bangkok, Thailand	FT	1 mth	US$1,200 - 1,400	September, November, January, March, May, July, September,	21+, up to degree level education	Steve Lawrence	169
ELS - Bell School of English, Poland	FT	4 wks	£590 + UCLES entry fee	June	20+, good general education, native speaker competence	Halszka Ziotkowska	
Embassy CES, New York	FT	4 wks	$2,225	Jan, Feb, April, May, June, July, Aug, Sept, Oct	Undergraduate degree, study of a foreign language	Bruce Sharpe	132
Embassy CES, Fort Lauderdale	FT	4 wks	$2,225	June, September	Undergraduate degree, study of foreign language	Steve Cunningham	131
College	Full or Part Time	Length Of Course	Fees	Start Dates	Entry Requirements	Contacts	Address/ Advert Page

Overseas Cambridge/RSA Certificate (CELTA) Courses

COLLEGE	FULL OR PART TIME	LENGTH OF COURSE	FEES	START DATES	ENTRY REQUIREMENTS	CONTACTS	ADDRESS/ ADVERT PAGE
English Centre, Durban, South Africa	FT	4 wks	£1,500 inc airfare, accom, reg fee	October, November, January, July, November	University entrance, high level of English	Dallas Harris, Principal	179
Eurocentres - Virginia, USA	FT	4 wks	US$2050	October, July	Min age 20, first degree, or current undergraduate	Richard Grant	133
Holmes Colleges, Aus	FT	4 wks	Aus$1950	All year	As Cambridge RSA	Ms Judith Boileau	155
Holmesglen Institute of TAFE, Chadstone, Aus	Both	FT: 4 wks; PT: 2 terms	Aus$1,950	Various	Age 20+, interview, higher ed entry level	Larry Foster	155
Institute of Continuing and TESOL Education (ICTE), Aus	FT	4 wks	Aus$2500	February, May, October	CELTA, age 21+	Ms Moya Dew, Enrolments Officer	155
International House, Queensland, Cairns, Aus	FT	4 wks	Aus$2,300	February, June, October	20+, post Cambridge prof level	Simon Bradley	155
International House, Sydney, Aus	Both	FT: 4 wks; PT: 12 wks	Aus$2,350	FT: January, March, May, June, July, November; PT: February, August	Contact for details	Nicola Rendall	155
International House, Prague, Czech Republic	FT	4 wks	CzCr36,500	May, July, November	Contact for details	International House	116
International House, Cairo, Egypt	FT	4 wks	£575	February, June, September, October	Contact for details	International House	173
International House, Paris, France	FT	4 wks	FF9,460	Throughout the year	Contact for details	International House	99
International House, Budapest, Hungary	Both	FT: 4 wks; PT: 12 wks	£670	FT: October, January, May, June, July, August; PT: October, February	Application, Interview	Steve Oakes, Head of Teacher Training	58,119
International House, Dublin, Ireland	FT	4 wks	On application	June	As Cambridge/ RSA	Mark Baker	
COLLEGE	FULL OR PART TIME	LENGTH OF COURSE	FEES	START DATES	ENTRY REQUIREMENTS	CONTACTS	ADDRESS/ ADVERT PAGE

Overseas Cambridge/RSA Certificate (CELTA) Courses

College	Full or Part Time	Length Of Course	Fees	Start Dates	Entry Requirements	Contacts	Address/ Advert Page
International House, Rome, Italy	Both	FT: 4 wks; PT: contact for details	LIt2,400,000	FT: February, July, September; PT: Contact for details	Contact for details	International House	105
International House, Krakow, Poland	FT	4 wks	£640	July, August	Contact for details	International House	62,121
International House, Poznan, Poland	FT	4 wks	£650	June, September	Contact for details	International House	62,121
International House, Wroclaw, Poland	FT	4 wks	£670	August	Contact for details	International House	62,121
International House, Lisbon, Portugal	FT	4 wks	PTE210,000	March, May, July, August	Contact for details	International House	66,107
International House, Cape Town, South Africa	FT	4 wks	R6,600	February, June, October	Age 20, good language ability	Jonathan Tennant	179
International House, Johannesburg, South Africa	FT	4 wks	R6,400	February, June, July	Contct for details	International House	179
International House Barcelona, Spain	Both	FT: 4 wks; PT: 14 wks	180,000 ptas	FT: regularly throughout yr; PT: March	Univ entry level, native level English	Jenny Johnson	65,110
International House, Madrid, Spain	Both	FT: 4 wks; PT: 3 mths	Pts150,000	FT: May, July, August, September; PT: January, October	Contact for details	International House	63,110
International House, Palma, Spain	Both	FT: 4 wks; PT: 4 mths	Pts150,000	FT: July; PT: February	Contact for details	International House	110
International House, Seville, Spain	FT	4 wks	Pts160,000	February, March, May, July, August, September, October	Contact for details	International House,	65,110
International House, Santa Monica, California, USA	FT	4 wks	US$2,200	May, June, September, October	Language Awareness interview	John Myers	

| College | Full or Part Time | Length Of Course | Fees | Start Dates | Entry Requirements | Contacts | Address/ Advert Page |

Overseas Cambridge/RSA Certificate (CELTA) Courses

College	Full or Part Time	Length Of Course	Fees	Start dates	Entry requirements	Contacts	Address/ Advert Page
International House, Portland, Oregon, USA	FT	4 wks	US2,200	January, February, March, May, June, July, September, October	Language Awareness interview	John Myers	
International Language Academies South Pacific, New Zealand	FT	4 wks	NZ$2,950	January, February, May, September, November	20+, 6th form cert or equivalent, L1 competence	Julie van Dyk	158
International Language Institute, Nova Scotia, Canada	FT	4 wks	C$1,900 + $25 application fee	June, July, August, September	20+, proficient in written & spoken English, eligible for higher ed	Raissa Musial, Registrar	139
International Training Institute, Istanbul, Turkey	Both	FT: 4 wks; PT 12 wks	£800	FT: July; PT: October; January	As Cambridge/ RSA	Tom Godfrey	128
Izmir British Council Teachers' Centre, Turkey	FT	4 wks	£950	June	Degree	Steve Darn	128
Kwantlen University College, Canada	Both	FT;4 wks 12 wks, PT	C$2500	FT June, July; PT January, September	As Cambridge/ RSA	Martyn Williams	140
The Language Academy, Florida, USA	FT	4 wks	US$2,150	Monthly	College degree, foreign language	Esme Noakes, Course Director	
Language Centre, Cork	Both	FT: 1 mth; PT: 1 term	IR£850	FT: July, August; PT: Oct, Jan	Graduate status	General Office	93
Language Centre of Ireland, Dublin	Both	FT: 4 wks; PT: 9 wks	IR£950	January, April, June, September	Degree, interview	Registrar	94
Language Link, Russia	Both	FT: 4 wks; PT: 12 wks	$1,200	Jan, July, Aug, June, Septrember October	As Cambridge/ RSA	ELT Department	124
Language Studies Canada, Toronto	FT	4 wks	C$2150	March, April, May, June, July, August, September	Univ entrance qual, 20+ yrs, native speaker or non-native equiv	Alex Rossi, Gerald Bagge	140
Languages International, Auckland, New Zealand	FT	4 wks	NZ$2,750	November, January, February, June, August	Univ entrance level qual, 1st degree pref	Craig Thaine, Director of Teacher Training	158
College	Full or Part Time	Length Of Course	Fees	Start dates	Entry requirements	Contacts	Address/ Advert Page

Overseas Cambridge/RSA Certificate (CELTA) Courses

College	Full or Part Time	Length Of Course	Fees	Start Dates	Entry Requirements	Contacts	Address/Advert Page
Lektor International House, Poznan, Poland	FT	1 month	£590 (incl exam fee)	September	CELTA reqs	TT Department	121
Milner International College of English, Perth, Aus	FT	4 wks	Aus$2,250	November, January, February, May, August	Tertiary entry quals	Linda McLeod	156
Münchner Volkshockschule, München, Germany	FT	5 wks	Dm2,500 approx	April 2000	As all CELTA courses	Briony Beaven, Director of Studies	
NSTS English Language Institute, Malta	Both	FT: 4 wks; PT: 12 wks	£899	FT: August, November; PT: January	As Cambridge/RSA	Louis Grech/Alan Marsh	64,120
Phoenix English language Academy, Perth, Aus	FT	4 wks	Aus$2200	November, January, March, July	Cambridge requirements	Felicity Mason, Teaching Training Co-ordinator	156
Polyglot Institute, Oman	FT	4 wks	£745	Jan, March, May, July, Sept, Nov	Univ entrance level, 20+	Alison Glasier, John Carmichael, John Sutter	176
RMIT Training Centre for Eng Lang Learning, Melbourne, Aus	Both	FT: 4 wks; PT 4 mths	Aus$1,950	FT: January, February, June, November; PT: February, July	Pre-course assessment	Peter Pavan	156
Seafield School of English, Christchurch, New Zealand	FT	4 wks	NZ$2,600	Throughout the year	Contact for details	Director of Studies	158
South Aust. College of English, Adelaide, Aust	Both	FT: 4 wks; PT: 10 wks	Aus$ 1,850	Jan, Feb, March, June, July, Sept, Oct, Nov	12 yrs of schooling	Ms Stephanie Mewett, Admissions	156
St Giles College, San Francisco, USA	FT	4 wks	US$2,695 (incl $150 non-refundable deposit)	Every month	2 yrs higher ed, second lang, teaching exp pref	Maria Brooks -De Dios	136
St Mark's International College, Perth, Aus	PT	12 wks	Aus$2,250	Janaury, April, July, September	Age 20+, L1 competence, tertiary entry level	Deirdre Conway	156
St Mary's University, Halifax, Canada	PT	3 mths	C$650	May	Undergrad degree pref	Maureen Sargent, Director, TESL	140
College	Full or Part Time	Length Of Course	Fees	Start Dates	Entry Requirements	Contacts	Address/Advert Page

Overseas Cambridge/RSA Certificate (CELTA) Courses

College	Full or Part Time	Length Of Course	Fees	Start Dates	Entry Requirements	Contacts	Address/ Advert Page
Tasmanian College of English, Tasmania	Both	FT: 4 wks; PT: 10 wks	Aus$2,000	January, March, August, November	12 yrs of education	Ms Helen Cox	157
TBI, Jakarta, Indonesia	FT	4 wks	US$1,750	May, November	Univ entrance level, high standard of spoken & written English	Rachel Wicaksono, Director	162
University College Cork, Eire	Both	FT: 4 wks; PT: 1 term	IR£850	PT: October, January; FT: July, August	Degree	Director	93
Volkshochschule Zurich, Switzerland	PT	16 wks	SF3,700	May	As RSA/Cambridge	Mrs Margaret Stark	127
Waikato University (Hamilton), NZ	FT	1 month	NZ$3,000	June, November	Age 20+, univ entry level, L1 level Eng, lang task, interview	CELTA Coordinator	159
Winnipeg University, (Continuing Education), Canada	FT	4 wks	C$2000	TBA	As per UCLES	Elizabeth Madrid	140
Wollongong University (Institute for Australian Studies), Dubai, UAE	Both	FT: 20 days; PT: 4-5 mths	8,000 dirhams	FT:November - December; PT: February - May	20+, entry to higher ed, competence in English written & spoken	Philippa Coleman, Director of Studies	178
Yonsei University, Seoul, South Korea	Both	FT: 4 wks; PT: 7 months	1,995,000 won	July, February	Some exp	James Forrest	167

College	Full or Part Time	Length Of Course	Fees	Start Dates	Entry Requirements	Contacts	Address/ Advert Page

27

UK Trinity Licentiate Certificate in TESOL Courses

COLLEGE	FULL OR PART TIME	COURSE LENGTH	FEES	START DATES	ENTRY REQUIREMENTS	CONTACTS	ADDRESS/ ADVERT PAGE
Aberdeen College	PT	1 or 2 terms	£400	September, April	Interview	Anne Bain	83
Basingstoke College of Technology, Hants	Both	FT: 1 mth; PT: 6 mths (1 day or 2 eves/wk)	£565+ £80 reg fee	FT: July; PT: Sept, October, November	Interview, pre-course assignment	Annabel Stone	83
Blackpool and The Fylde College	PT	30 wks	£450	September	'A' level or equiv, 20 yrs of age	Barbara MacDougall/ Zoe Hodgson	
Bolton College	PT	34 wks	£490 + £75 moderation fee	September	2 'A' levels	Nicky Salmon	84
Bracknell & Wokingham College, Berkshire	PT	3 terms	£670	September/ October	1st degree preferred	Colette Galloway	84
Bradford College, W Yorks	Both	PT: 30 wks; FT: 4 wks	£600 (incl exam fee)	PT: October; FT: November, July	Degree or equiv, 'A' level passes, exp	Nancy Hall	84
Brooklands College, Weybridge	PT	22 wks	£680	October	Contact for details	Admissions Registrar	84
Bury College , Lancashire	Both	PT: 2 or 3 terms; FT: 4 wks	£575	PT: September (3 term), January (2 term); FT: October, February, May, June	PT: 2 'A' levels min; FT: Degree, teaching exp pref.	David Marrs	84
Cicero Languages International, Kent	FT	4 wks	£780 + £70 exam fee	January, February, March, May, September, October, November	Advanced level of English	Jenny Bodenham	85
City College Manchester	Both	FT: 2/3 wks + 2 wks teaching); PT: 12 and 16 wks	£680-800 (incl moderation fee)	FT: September, October; PT: Sept, November, January	Higher education qualification or equiv.	Arnold Spencer	85
Colchester Institute, Essex	FT	4 wks distance + 9 wks	£750	October, January, May	Degree	Simon Haines	85
Coventry Technical College	Both	FT: 4 wks; PT: 10 mths	£695 (Coventry); £895 (twin centre course)	Every month	University entrance, degree	Christopher Fry	85
Darlington College of Technology	PT	1 year	On application	January	L1 speaker or equiv, degree	Libby Selman	85
COLLEGE	FULL OR PART TIME	COURSE LENGTH	FEES	START DATES	ENTRY REQUIREMENTS	CONTACTS	ADDRESS/ ADVERT PAGE

UK Trinity Licentiate Certificate in TESOL Courses

COLLEGE	FULL OR PART TIME	COURSE LENGTH	FEES	START DATES	ENTRY REQUIREMENTS	CONTACTS	ADDRESS/ ADVERT PAGE
East Berkshire College	PT	23 wks	£645	September	As Trinity	Chris Hammonds	86
Gateshead College, Tyne & Wear	PT	30 wks	£385	September	'A' level min, degree preferred	Admissions Office	
Golders Green College	Both	FT: 5 wks; PT: 13	£645 + moderation fee	Throughout year	Interview	Dig Hadoke	86
Guildford College	PT	5 mths	£587 (inc moderation fee)	September, February	Contact for details	Marion Mayne	86
Hammersmith & West London College, London	Both	FT: 4 wks; PT: 20 wks	£695	FT: September, November, January, February, April, July; PT: Sept	Age 20+, 2 'A' levels, good command of English		63,86
Hopwood Hall College, Lancashire	PT	1 year	£540	September	Age 21+, 2 'A' levels, proficiency in Eng	Mr Philip Day	87
Hull College	FT	10 wks	£250	September	'A' levels, degree	Doug Kelley	87
Inlingua Teacher Training, Cheltenham	Both	FT: 5 wks; PT: 9 mths	FT: £875 + moderation fee; PT: £899 + moderation fee	FT: Throughout year; PT: Sept	Age 18+, interview	Dagmar Lewis	87
International Training Network, Bournemouth	FT	5 wks	£930 + moderation fee	10 courses a year	Native speaker, 2 'A' levels	Eileen Hobby	62,87
ITS English School, Hastings	Both	FT: 4/5 wks; PT: 20 wks	£495 + TC fee	January, February, March, May, July, September	Contact for details	Paul Power, Director of Teacher Training	87
Joseph Priestley College	PT	7 mths	£550	November	Initial assessment, interview	Jo Mingham, Course Tutor	87
Kent School of English	FT	4 wks	£690 (incl moderation fee)	January, May, September		Chris McDermott	87
Langside College Glasgow	Both	FT: 4 wks; PT: 1 year	£500 + exam fee	FT: various; PT: September	Degree, good English literacy & articulacy	Tony Foster	88
The Language Project, Bristol	FT	5 wks	£900 (inclusive)	January, June, August	Pre-course task, interview	Dr Jon Wright	88
COLLEGE	FULL OR PART TIME	COURSE LENGTH	FEES	START DATES	ENTRY REQUIREMENTS	CONTACTS	ADDRESS/ ADVERT PAGE

UK Trinity Licentiate Certificate in TESOL Courses

College	Full or Part Time	Course Length	Fees	Start Dates	Entry Requirements	Contacts	Address/ Advert Page
Languages Training & Development	FT	8 wks	Fully funded	Throughout the year	Energy and commitment	J West	88
Leeds Metropolitan University	Both	FT: 32 wks; PT: 33 wks	£477	October	Excellent English, good general education	Anne Beigy	88
London Study Centre	Both	FT: 5 wks; PT: 15 wks	Contact for details	Throughout the year	Good standard of English, entry test and interview	Teacher Training Dept	60,88
Luton University	FT	4 wks	£700	July	Excellent standard of English	Andy Russell	88
Manchester Academy of English	FT	4 wks	£799 + Trinity fee	September, November 1999, 2000 contact for details	'A' level, degree pref	Mrs Sandra Kaufman	88
Manchester College of Arts & Technology, Manchester	Both	25 wks	£595	September, October	Degree, high level of proficiency	Louise Matthews	88
Medway Adult Education Centre	PT	31 wks	£750	25/9	Good knowledge of spoken & written English	Teresa Cambell	87
Middlesborough College	PT	1 year	£400 (incl moderation fee)	September	Degree or equiv, native speaker or CPE Grade A/B	Rosemary Smith	89
Northampton College	PT	33 wks	Contact for detail	September	Assessment at interview	Mrs Helen Young	89
Northbrook CDT, West Sussex	Both	FT: 4 wks; PT: 3 mths	EU: £512; non-EU: £1,184	FT: September, October, January, March, May, June; PT: Sept, January, April	Age 21+, interview, tests, exp and degree pref	Susan Scowen	89
Oaklands College, St Albans	Both	FT: 5/10/12 wks; PT: 30/36 wks	£595	FT: September, January, July; PT: Sept, October	Higher Education level	Helen Day, Curriculum Team Leader	89
Oxford House College, London, UK	Both	FT: 4 wks; PT: 13/22 wks	FT: £600 + exam fee; PT: £700 + exam fee	Throughout year	Good educ background	Toby Doncaster	89
College	Full or Part Time	Course Length	Fees	Start Dates	Entry Requirements	Contacts	Address/ Advert Page

UK Trinity Licentiate Certificate in TESOL Courses

College	Full or Part Time	Course Length	Fees	Start Dates	Entry Requirements	Contacts	Address/ Advert Page
Park Lane College, Leeds	PT	1 year	£360 + moderation fee	September	Higher Education level	Anita Taylor, Course Manager	89
Plymouth College of FE, Devon	PT	32 wks	£998	Contact for details	'A' level standard, evidence of lang learning exp	Gill Godfrey	90
Queens University (TEFL Centre), Belfast	Both	FT: 5 wks; PT: 1 year	FT: £795; PT: contact for details	FT: June, August; PT: Sept	Grads pref, must be L1 or CPE level	TEFL Centre	90
Regent Edinburgh	FT	4 wks	£897	Throughout the year	Degree pref	Michelle Sweeney	90
Richmond Adult & Community Centre	PT	1 year	£824	January	Graduate or equivalent	Barbara Beaumont	90
Sheffield Hallam University, TESOL Centre	Both	FT: 4 wks + 16 wks dist; PT: 30 wks	£950	FT: November, January, March, July, October; PT: January, May	Must have training/study experience or first degree	Fran Bellbin, Programme Coordinator	90
Sidmouth International School	FT	1 month	£845	February, May, October	Degree, interview	Vincent Smidowicz	90
South East Essex College	PT	34 days	approx £445 + registration fee	September	Good ed standard	Mr R Hopkins	91
St Andrew's University, Fife	FT	5 wks	£850	June	Graduate or equiv	Alison Malcolm-Smith	90
St Brelade's College, Jersey	FT	4 wks	£750 + £75 exam fee	March, September	Degree (Eng/modern langs pref)	Donald Brown	90
St Giles College, London	FT	4 wks	£650 + moderation fee	Contact for details	Graduate, good standard of gen education	The Principal	90
Stockport College of Further & Higher Education	PT	6 mths	£784.90 (incl moderation fee)	September	2 A levels, 21 yrs+	Ms Jill Cregeen	91
Stranmillis University College, Belfast	FT	4 wks	£795	Contact for details	18+, 'A' level or equiv in English, modern lang or related discipline	Director (External Affairs)	
Students International Ltd, Leics	FT	4 wks	£865	November, February, April, July, August, September	Age 20+, good English	Mrs AL Blythe	63,91
College	Full or Part Time	Course Length	Fees	Start Dates	Entry Requirements	Contacts	Address/ Advert Page

UK/Trinity Licentiate Certificate in TESOL Courses

College	Full or Part Time	Course Length	Fees	Start Dates	Entry Requirements	Contacts	Address/ Advert Page
Surrey Language Centre, Farnham	FT	4 wks	£720 (incl moderation fee)	Throughout the year	Age 18+, 3 GCSE + 2 A levels high level of English	Peter Dransfield	91
Sussex University, Brighton	PT	4 wks	£760	July, August	Univ entrance	R De-Witt, L Gunn	91
Sutton College of Liberal Arts	PT	32 wks	£550	September	Interview, grammar test, teaching exp	Caroline O'Reilly	
Thurrock College, Essex	FT	4 wks	£302.40 + exam fee	September	Degree and/or Cert Ed, interview	John Saunders	91
University College Chichester	PT	1 year	£460	September	Entry into Higher Education, test, interview	Richard Kiely	92,264
Universal Language Training Ltd, Old Woking	Both	FT: 4 wks; PT: 4 months	£695 + £76 moderation fee	Throughout year	Good ed background, interview	Elaine Stafford	91
University of the West of England	FT	5 wks	Contact for details	October, November, February, April	Good level of English and Education	George Mann	59,92
University of Westminster	FT	5 wks	£785 + moderation fee	July, September	Entry test	Ann-Marie Griffin	92
University of Wolverhampton	Both	FT: 2-4 wks; PT: 1 year	£175/wk	FT: July, August; PT: Sept	Contact for deails	Jonathon Richards	92
Windsor Schools TEFL, Berks	Both	FT: 4 wks; PT: 4 mths	£799 (incl VAT) + exam fee	Every month	2 'A' levels	Mrs C Fuller	92

Overseas Trinity Licentiate Certificate in TESOL Courses

College	Full or Part Time	Course Length	Fees	Start Dates	Entry Requirements	Contacts	Address/ Advert Page
CITEC English Language Centre, NZ	FT	5 wks	NZ$2600	Jan, July, October	Interview	Pamela Protheroe	158
Dickens Institute, Montevideo, Uruguay	Both	FT: 9 wks; PT: two 9 month periods	Contact for details	March	Proficiency level, written exam, interview	Monica Leon	152
East Coast College of English, Brisbane, Aus	Both	FT: 4 wks; PT: 15 wks	FT: Aus$2,600; PT: Aus$2,800	FT: November, January, June, November; PT: February, August	20+, interview	Teacher Training Coordinator	155

UK Overseas Trinity Licentiate Certificate in TESOL Courses

College	Full or Part Time	Course Length	Fees	Start Dates	Entry Requirements	Contacts	Address/ Advert Page
Forum Language Centre, Cyprus	PT	18 wks or 24 wks	Cyprus £730	October	Contact for details	Mr Peter Lucantoni	
Grafton International, Dublin, Eire	Both	FT: 4 wks; PT: 12 wks	£900	October	Good general education	Jessica Long	93
International Pacific College, New Zealand	Contact for details	Contact for details	NZ$2,800	Contact for details	Contact for details	Dianna Beatson TESOL Director	158
Lord Byron College, Italy	FT	1 mth	Contact for details	July	Degree, application, interview	Mr John Credico, Director of Studies	105
Native Nation, Barcelona, Spain	FT	1 mth	£650	Contact for details	University entrance level	Barney Griffiths	
Next Training Espana, Barcelona, Spain	FT	4 wks	£767-£793	March, May, June, July, August, September, October, November	Rel quals and exp	Duncan Foord/Barney Griffiths	111
Oxford House College, Barcelona, Spain	FT	4 wks	£550 (inc exam fee)	Throughout the year	Contact for details		111
Oxford House College, Budapest, Hungary	FT	4 wks	£500 (inc exam fee)	June, July, August	Contact for details		105
Oxford House College, Istanbul, Turkey	FT	4 wks	£600	January, June, August	Contact for details		
Oxford House College, Tuscany, Italy	FT	4 wks	£600	January, June, July, August, November	Contact for details		
Professional Training Institute, Al Ain, UAE	PT	7 mths	8,000 UAE Dirhams	October, February	University standard	Jim Macdonald	
Seafield School of English, Christchurch, NZ	FT	4 wks	NZ$2,600	Throughout the year		Director of Studies	158
College	Full or Part Time	Course Length	Fees	Start Dates	Entry Requirements	Contacts	Address/ Advert Page

University Certificate Courses

Universities offer a wide range of certificate courses, from short introductions to specialised modules

Getting qualified in the UK

It is possible to take a university course in most anglophone countries as an alternative to a Cambridge/RSA or Trinity Certificate.

here are so many EFL training courses offered by universities that it would be impossible to describe all the variations here. Below we explore some of the trends in university pre-experience and in-service certificate courses.

Pre-experience certificate courses

The term 'certificate' generally refers to a short course between one and six months in length. Most certificates are initial teacher training courses open to L1 and non-L1 speakers.

In most anglophone countries it is possible to enrol on a university certificate course and in the UK, Ireland, Australia and New Zealand these courses are often viewed as alternatives to Cambridge/RSA or Trinity Certificates. In the US and Canada, where there are fewer Trinity and Cambridge courses, university courses are the most common short, initial pre-experience training courses available.

Recently there has been a growth in advanced certificates for experienced teachers wishing to specialise.

The number of UK universities offering certificates has greatly increased in the last few years, partly due to the abolition of Post Graduate Certificates in Education for EFL teachers. However, an alarming number of UK universities with no previous experience in the English language field are now taking advantage of the demand for teaching certificates and offering new certificate courses as a way of getting in more revenue.

Above all, check that any course you are considering includes teaching practice with foreign students rather than just with fellow trainees. Many employers will not

be willing to accept any initial qualification unless it includes teaching practice.

If you do not have teaching experience, avoid courses which offer distance training only. There are respected hybrid courses, though, which mix distance training with some on-site training and these often offer practice elements.

In-service certificate courses

These are usually called 'advanced certificates' and last three to six months. They are designed for those who have experience but no previous qualifications, or for those who have training and need further qualifications but do not have the time to do a full Masters degree. As these courses are designed for teachers who are already practising, distance training is a well-accepted method of delivery.

In-service certificates are part of a general trend towards offering further qualifications for experienced teachers. These teachers often want to take advantage of the changing ELT market by specialising in defined areas of teaching, such as English for Academic Purposes, Teaching Young Learners or Teacher Training.

Other certificate courses

In English-speaking countries, universities offer state-accredited certificate or diploma courses which lead to Qualified Teacher Status (QTS) – a qualification which enables a teacher to teach in the state sector. In the UK, for example, a Post Graduate Certificate in Education (PGCE) leads to QTS, while in Ireland, it is the Higher Diploma.

These courses leading to QTS offer practical teaching experience but do not allow candidates to specialise in ELT. However, having QTS can be very useful for a TEFL teacher. There is a relative worldwide shortage of primary and secondary English language teachers, so teachers armed with QTS and a TEFL qualification or experience can find themselves in a strong position when it comes to looking for work.

Getting Qualified in the USA and Canada

The rapidly rising demand for **EFL (or ESL) has lead to an increase in both the number and variety of courses currently available for teachers.**

At present, there are no absolute equivalents to the Cambridge/RSA in the US, but the situation is changing. Many states with burgeoning immigrant populations are pressing for more flexible and effective certification programmes at all levels. An increasing number of universities is offering comprehensive, non-degree, certificate programmes that combine theoretical considerations with practical applications, including a student teaching component.

Several certificate programmes (including CELTA) are available across the country, particularly on the West Coast, where at least six are currently on offer. Meanwhile, it is still possible in some states – California is one – to obtain an adult credential or secondary authorisation to teach ESL to adults. A large number of non-profit, community-based organisations offer effective, free training programmes for volunteers who wish to teach English

Hundreds of English teaching positions do not require an advanced degree in the United States, particularly those in private language schools.

and many teachers are ex-Peace Corps volunteers.

The minimum qualification to enter most programmes is a BA or BSc degree. However, university BA and certificate programmes in TESOL and many of the private, intensive teacher training schools or volunteer programmes will accept trainees with a High School Diploma. You do not need any previous teaching experience to enter one of these programmes and programmes tend to encourage, if not require, teaching practice and classroom observation. The fact that you can take the Cambridge CELTA course in places as far apart as Portland Oregon and New York City shows that English language teaching in the United States is changing.

In the past, English language teaching in the United States meant TESL (Teaching English as a Second Language). For decades TESL was conducted primarily at university level with academic students. However, beginning in the 70s, and continuing well into the 80s, there was mass immigration of non-English speakers into the US. Many of these immigrants lacked basic literacy skills, even in their own language and, as they began to enter both schools and the workplace, a strong need for eclectic methodology arose.

Today, as the world becomes more like a 'global village', the importance of teaching English as a foreign language is well recognised.

Most of the better jobs in state-run institutions in the US are for TESL and generally require a Masters degree. However, hundreds of English teaching positions do not require an advanced degree, particularly in private language schools, where overseas experience and a certificate may be more useful than a Masters.

Canada

The very wide variety of training programmes on offer in Canada is a result of continuing demand in the domestic market. Native French speakers account for 24 per cent of the population, average annual immigration is 200,000 and annual numbers of short-term EFL students has grown to an estimated 80,000 per year.

Several universities, including Brock and Winnipeg, offer undergraduate BA and BEd courses which specialise in TESL. Admission requirements vary, but usually involve secondary school graduation. Mature student acceptance can often be facilitated by TESL experience.

Those seeking short courses with certification can choose from five-day intensives to regular Cambridge/RSA CELTA and university certificates. Distance learning options are also available from the ESL Teacher Training Centre, University of Saskatchewan and Vancouver Community college and these programmes include teaching practice. The latter also offers distinct programmes for L1 and non-L1 speaker teachers, as well as a series of 30-hour courses for teachers without qualifications.

Non-L1 teachers have the option of specially tailored non-credit courses at the University of British Columbia, Canadian College of Business and Computers and Humber College. L1 speakers looking to work overseas can consider the Canadian Global TESOL Institute's five-day seminar held at various centres across the country.

Low tuition and living costs coupled with the chance to train while living in a French-speaking environment make Canada a very attractive option.

Low tuition and living costs coupled with the chance to train while living in a French-speaking environment make Canada a very attractive option.

Getting Qualified in Australia and New Zealand

The EFL sector has experienced steady growth in Australasia with cross-cultural skills training being integrated into innovative teaching methodology.

There are schools in both Australia and New Zealand offering Cambridge or Trinity qualifications. There is also a variety of home-grown training programmes approved under official accreditation schemes.

Australia

EFL courses for adults are mainly taught in accredited ELICOS (English Language Intensive Courses for Overseas Students) institutions. The National ELICOS Accreditation Scheme (NEAS) has set minimum standards for teacher qualifications within such institutions. These guidelines state that teachers must have at least:

EITHER a recognised pre-service teaching qualification (minimum three years) plus or including an appropriate TESOL qualification,

OR a recognised degree or diploma (minimum three years), plus at least 800 hours classroom teaching experience, plus an appropriate TESOL qualification.

It may be possible for teachers to get work with as little as a certificate in TESOL in some institutions, but most colleges require the equivalent to NEAS minimum qualifications

To be deemed 'an appropriate teaching qualification', the course must have a content focus on English language learning and teaching, a practical component including at least six hours supervised and assessed practice teaching, and no less than 100 contact hours. The course must also be accredited by the appropriate accrediting body. For more details of the NEAS policy, contact: NEAS, Locked Bag 2, Post Office, Pyrmont, NSW 2009.

Recently the Australian government relaxed its rules to allow students from some countries to study on tourist visas and on such 'Study Tour' courses teacher qualifications are unregulated. It may be possible for teachers to get work with as little as a certificate in TESOL in some institutions. However, most colleges require the equivalent to NEAS minimum qualifications.

A wide range of teacher training courses, from introductory level upwards, are available. In Sydney, the Australian TESOL Training Centre offers RSA Certificate and Diploma courses, as well as an introductory one-week course. The Australian Centre for Languages has an intensive four-week and part-time RSA Cambridge certificate courses. The Insearch Language Centre, part of the University of Technology, Sydney, also offers a four-week full-time or five-month part-time RSA Cambridge certificate.

The University of Southern Queensland offers courses from graduate certificate level upwards, some pre-service and some for practising teachers. Also in Queensland, Bond University offers a Graduate Certificate in TESOL. The

University of South Australia offers a graduate certificate for trained teachers with at least one year's experience. In Western Australia, Cambridge Certificate courses are provided by the Milner International College and in Victoria by the Holmesglen Institute of TAFE.

EFL in Australia was entering a growth period with more opportunities for teachers wishing to get higher level teaching positions in ELICOS centres, but this has been hit hard by falling numbers of Asian students due to regional economic difficulty.

Generally, employers would expect a coordinator or head teacher to have a qualification at RSA Diploma level or above, and there are many courses available at the level of graduate certificate or diploma and Masters which prepare teachers for a senior teaching position.(See page 223 for details.)

New Zealand

The export of education has been the fastest growing industry in New Zealand, and this growth in demand has led to the increased popularity of short, intensive teacher training courses. A certificate along with a degree is the accepted qualification for NZQA (New Zealand Qualification Authorities) accredited . schools. As with Australia, demand from Asian students has been reduced.

Languages International in Auckland was the first school to offer the RSA Cambridge Certificate, now also run by the Capital Language Academy in Wellington, Dominion English Schools in Auckland and ILA South Pacific in Christchurch

UK University Certificate Courses

College	Course Title	Course Length	Fees	Start Dates	Entry Requirements	Contacts	Address/ Advert Page
Aston University, Birmingham	Advanced Certificate in Principles of TEFL	Dist: 6 months	£1,200	October, January	Teaching Qual, 2 yrs exp.	Secretary, Language Studies Unit	83,259
	Certificate in TEFL	FT: 4 wks	£745	July	Graduates	Secretary, Language Studies Unit	83,259
British Institute, Paris	British Institute Cert TEFLA	PT: 9 months	FFr12,000	October	Native speaker or L1 competence	Mme Schwarz	97
Eastbourne College of Arts & Technology, UK	ARELS One-to-One Certificate	PT: 11 wks	£295		Cert in TEFL pref + 1:1 exp	Bob Hustwayte	85
Edinburgh University	Advanced Certificate in ELT	10 wks	tba	October	Degree + 3 -5 yrs exp	Registration Secretary	85,264
	Advanced Certificate in Teaching ESP	FT: 10 wks	£1,550	January	Degree, 3 yrs exp	Registration Secretary	85,264
Essex University (EFL Unit)	Certificate in TEFL	FT: 10 wks	Contact for details	October	Graduate, 2 yrs teaching exp	Dilly Meyer	58,86
	Certificate in English for Language Teaching (inc CEELT	FT: 10 wks	£1,675	January	Good pass at FCE or above	Dilly Meyer	58,86
Exeter University	Certificate in Advanced Professional Studies (ELT)	FT: 1 year	On application	October	Degree and experience	Marion Williams	86
Lancaster University, Institute for English Language Education	Certificate of Advanced Studies Course - Teaching English for Specific Purposes	FT: 10 wks	Contact for details	October, January, April	Contact for details	Institute for English Language Education	88
College	Course Title	Course Length	Fees	Start Dates	Entry Requirements	Contacts	Address/ Advert Page

UK University Certificate Courses

College	Course Title	Course Length	Fees	Start Dates	Entry Requirements	Contacts	Address/ Advert Page
Lancaster University, Institute for English Language Education	Certificate of Advanced Studies Course - The Communicative Teaching of English	FT 10 wks	Contact for details	October, January, April	Contact for details	Institute for English Language Education	88
	Certificate of Advanced Studies Course - Development & Management of English Language Education	FT: 10 wks	Contact for details	October, January, April	Contact for details	Institute for English Language Education	88
	Certificate of Advanced Studies Course - Principles and Practice of Language Testing	FT: 10 wks	Contact for details	October, January, April	Contact for details	Institute for English Language Education	88
	Certificate of Advanced Studies Course - British Studies in ELT	FT: 10 wks	Contact for details	October, January, April	Contact for details	Institute for English Language Education	88
	Certificate of Advanced Studies Course - Special Groups	FT: 10 wks	Contact for details	October, January, April	Contact for details	Institute for English Language Education	88
Leeds Metropolitan University	Postgraduate Certificate in Language teaching Both	FT: 4 wks; PT: 1 year	£531	Throughout the year	Degree or equiv	Sarah Turnbull	88
Leeds University, School of Education	Access Certificate course to TESOL Certificate Both, Distance	8 mths	£400/module	January, May, September	Initial teaching qualification, first degree or equiv, 2 yrs relevant experience, 5.5+ on IELTS test	Higher Degrees & Diplomas Office	88,260

College	Course Title	Course Length	Fees	Start Dates	Entry Requirements	Contacts	Address/ Advert Page

UK University Certificate Courses

College	Course Title	Course Length	Fees	Start Dates	Entry Requirements	Contacts	Address/ Advert Page
Liverpool University, (AELSU)	Cert in TEFL/ESP	FT: 6 wks, PT: 8 mths	£950	FT: July, August; PT: October	First degree	Dr S Thompson	88
Manchester University	Foundation Certificate in TESOL	FT: 4 wks	Contact for details	June	Degree	CELSE	89,260
University College, Chichester	English Language Teaching (Minor Route BA Arts & Humanities)	FT: 3 yrs	EU: £1,000/yr; non-EU: £6,700/yr	September	Contact for details	Dr Mich Randall	92,264
University of Wales, Swansea	Cert in TEFL to Adults	FT: 4 wks	£925	Summer	Grad level of education, pref with first degree	Karen Frith	92
Westminster College	RSA/CFLA Certificate in TFL to Adults	FT: 16 wks	EU: £924	September, February	Age 21+, degree or equiv, native speaker level of English	Course Information Unit	92
Wigston College	Access to Teaching	PT: 1 year	£91	September	21 yrs +	David Harris	92

USA/Canada University Courses

College	Course Title	Course Length	Fees	Start Dates	Entry Requirements	Contacts	Address/ Advert Page
Alabama University, Huntsville	Graduate TESOL Certificate	Both: FT/PT 3 semesters	In-state: $1,674 / sem; Out-of-state: $3,332 / semester	Fall, Spring	Undergrad record of B (3.0), GRE 1500, TOEFL 500	Dr Madeleine Youmans	137
Algonquin College of Applied Arts and Technology, Canada	Cert TESOL	Both: FT/PT 2 semesters	$2,626.25/ semester	Fall, Winter	First degree	Sophie Beare, Coordinator	139
American University TESOL Prog, Washington, USA	American University Certificate	FT: 2 terms; PT: 5 terms	$2,061 - $6,183/ semester	September, January, May	TOEFL 600	Brock Brady, TESOL Programs	131
American University, Paris, France	TEFL Certificate	FT: 6 wks	FF13,750	October, January, March, May	Degree, essay, refs, interview	Ms Severine Ducet	97
Biola University, CA	Undergrad minor/ certificate in TESOL	2 semesters, upper division	$7,143/ semester	Any semester	TOEFL 600+, GPA 2.5, students from Christian evangelical community	Chair, Dept of TESOL & Applied Linguistics	131
College	Course Title	Course Length	Fees	Start Dates	Entry Requirements	Contacts	Address/ Advert Page

COLLEGE	COURSE TITLE	COURSE LENGTH	FEES	START DATES	ENTRY REQUIREMENTS	CONTACTS	ADDRESS/ ADVERT PAGE
Biola University, CA	Certificate in TESOL (graduate level)	Both: FT/PT 2 semesters + 1 interterm	$307/sem unit	Fall	BA degree, GPA 3.0, transcripts, letters of recommendation, TOEFL 600+, students from the evangelical Christian community	Chair, Dept of TESOL & Applied Linguistics	131
Brigham Young University	BA in TESOL	Both: FT/PT 4-5 semesters	Latter Day Saints:$1,066/ sem; Other: $1.596/sem	Fall, Winter	Contact for details	TESOL Program Division Chair	131
	Certificate in TESL	Both: FT/PT 2 semesters	Latter Day Saints: $1,550; Other: $2,325/sem	Feb 1- application deadline; enrol spring, summer, fall terms	First degree GPA 3.6, GRE, TOEFL 580	TESOL Program Division Chair	131
Brock University, Canada	BA (hons) with TESL Specialisation	Both: FT/PT 4 years	$1,885/course	Fall	Contact for details	Department of Applied Language Studies, Brock University	139
California University, Berkeley, USA	TEFL/TESL Certificate	Both: FT/PT 1.5 years	TEFL: approx $3,000; TESL: approx $3,000	Any semester	Contact for details	TESL/TEFL Program Director	137
California University, Irvine ext, USA	Certificate in TESL	Both: FT/PT 3 quarters	$60-90/quarter unit	Any quarter	TOEFL 530	Haley Dawson, Academic Advisor	137
California University, Riverside, USA	TESOL Certificate	Both:FT/PT 4 quarters	$2,500/program	Any quarter	High school dip, TOEFL 500, TSE 200, writing proficiency	Dr Sheila Dwight	137
California University, San Diego, USA	Certificate in TESOL	FT: 6 mths	$4,950 + $170 application	January, March, June, September	525 TOEFL, 195 Computer TOEFL	Peter Thomas, Director	137
California University, Santa Barbara	TESL/TEFL Certificate	Both: FT/PT 1 year approx	$150-$250	Any quarter	2 yrs of college course work, associate's degree or equiv. TEOFL 550	Brice Taylor, Certificate Adviser	137
California Polytechnic State University	TESL Certificate	Both: FT/PT 3 quarters	In-state: $743 for 6 units +; Out-of-state: $164 / qtr unit in addition	Any quarter	Matriculating students	Dr John Battenburg, Coordinator	131

| COLLEGE | COURSE TITLE | COURSE LENGTH | FEES | START DATES | ENTRY REQUIREMENTS | CONTACTS | ADDRESS/ ADVERT PAGE |

College	Course Title	Course Length	Fees	Start Dates	Entry Requirements	Contacts	Address/ Advert Page
California State University, Fullerton	Certificate in TESL	Both: FT/PT 3 semesters	In-state: $640.50/0-6 units; Out-of-state: $246/unit in addition	Contact for details	Bac degree, GPA 3.0, TOEFL 575, TSE 55-60	TESOL Coordinator	131
California State University, Los Angeles	Certificate in ESL/EFL	Both: FT/PT Contact for details	In-state: $1,754/yr; Out-of-state: $5,900/yr	Summer, Fall	GPA 2.75, 1 yr college level foreign language study or equiv, TOEFL 600	Coordinator, TESOL Program	137
California State University, Northridge	BA in Linguistics	Both: FT/PT 8 semesters	In-state: $990/sem; Out-of-state: $246/sem in addition	Any semester	Contact for details	Dr Sharon Klein, Coordinator	131
Carleton University, Canada	TESL Certificate	Both: FT/PT 2 semesters	C$3,527 (domestic); C$9,157 (international)	Any semester	BA degree	Prof Lynne Young, Assistant Director	139
Carroll College, MT	BA TESOL	Both: FT/PT 8 semesters	$5,745/sem	Any semester	High school graduation with GPA 2.5, recommendations, writting assessment, interview	Linda Lang, Director	131
Central Connecticut State University	Certification in TESOL (graduate level)	Both: FT/PT Variable	In-state: $1,252/sem; Out-of-state: $3,490/sem	Any semester	Bac degree, GPPA 2.7+, TOEFL 550	Dr Andrea G Osburne, Dept of English	131
Central Missouri State University	Certificate in TESL	Both: FT/PT Contact for details	In-state: $132/sem hr; Out-of-state: $264/sem hr	Any semester	Bac degree, GPA 2.5, TOEFL 565+	Graduate Coordinator, MA-TESL Program	151
Central Washington University	BEd TESL	Both: FT/PT 4-5 quarters	In-state: $168.40/cr hr; Out-of-state: $597.40/cr hr	Any quarter	GPA 3.0, California Achievement Test scores, letters of recommendation	Minerva L Caples, Director	131
Clarke University, USA	Certificate in Teaching ESL to Adults	PT Varies - 3.5 semesters min	$900 per course	Any semester	First degree, beginning college level language, TOEFL 600+ for non native speakers	Director, ALCI	132
	Graduate Certificate in Teaching ESL in Grades 5-12	PT Varies - 6 semesters min	$900 per course	Any semester	First degree (in arts and sciences), TOEFL 600+	Director, ALCI	132
College	Course Title	Course Length	Fees	Start Dates	Entry Requirements	Contacts	Address/ Advert Page

College	Course Title	Course Length	Fees	Start Dates	Entry Requirements	Contacts	Address/ Advert Page
Concordia University, Canada	University Certificate in TESOL	Both: FT/PT 8 months FT; no limit PT	Contact for details	September, January	Teacher certification (any subject) &/or 2nd lang teaching exp, excellent English	Ms B. Barclay, Coordinator, or Dr L Morris (Director)	132
	BEd TESL	4 yrs FT; no limit PT	Contact for details	September, January	Good junior college (Quebec), or equivalent (13 yrs of prior education), excellent English and good French language skills	Ms B. Barclay, Coordinator, or Dr J. White (Director)	132
Columbia University in the City of New York	Certificate of Professional Achievement in TESOL	Both: FT/PT 1 semester	$368/cr	Any semester	BA degree, TOEFL 600	Coordinator of Student Services	132
Eastern Kentucky University	BA in English/ teaching with TESL Endorsement	Both: FT/PT 8 semesters	In-state: $1,970/yr; Out-of-state: $5,450/yr	Any semester	Open admissions, GPA 2.5, writing proficiency exam, computer literacy	Dominick J Hart	132
Eastern Mennonite University,	Minor in TESL	Both: FT/PT 1 year	$12,600/sem	Any semester	GPA 2.0,	Dr Ervie L Glick	132
Eastern Washington University	Certificate in TESOL	Both: FT/PT 3 quarters	In-state: $2,430/yr; Out-of-state: $8,616/yr	Any quarter	15 high school units,	Mark Brooks, Minor Program Director	132
Fairfield University,	Certificate of Advanced Study in TESOL	Both: FT/PT 4 semesters	$335/cr		GPA 2.6, non native TOEFL 550	Sr M Julianna Poole	133
Florida University,	TESL Certificate (grad or postbac)	Both: FT/PT 2 semesters	In-state: $3,096/yr; Out-of-state: $10,428/yr	Any semester	Contact for details	TESL Coordinator	132
Florida Atlantic University	BA in Elementary Education with ESOL Endorsement	FT 4 semesters after completion of 2 yrs of university	Contact for details	Any semester	Contact for details	Gloria M Pelaez, Coordinator	132
College	Course Title	Course Length	Fees	Start Dates	Entry Requirements	Contacts	Address/ Advert Page

College	Course Title	Course Length	Fees	Start Dates	Entry Requirements	Contacts	Address/ Advert Page
Florida International University	BA Certification	Both: FT/PT Contact for details	In-state: $60/cr (undergrad); $115/cr (grad); Out-of-state: $385/cr (grad)	Contact for details		TESOL Coordinator	133
Fresno Pacific University	TESOL Certificate	Both: FT/PT 2 semesters	$240/sem unit	Any semester	Bac degree, letters of recommen dation, GRE or MAT scores	Dr David Freeman, Director	133
George Mason University	Certificate in TESL	Both: FT/PT 2 semesters	In-state: $139/cr hr; Out-of-state: $358.50/cr hr	Any semester	Bac degree, GPA 3.0+, TOEFL 575	Charles Jones	133
Georgetown University, USA	Certificate in TESL	Both: FT/PT 2 semesters	$751/cr hr	Any semester	Bac degree with B+, TOEFL 600	Director, MAT Program	133
	Certificate in Bilingual Education	Both: FT/PT 2 semesters	$751/cr hr	Any semester	Bac degree with B+, TOEFL 600	Director, MAT Program	133
Goshen College, USA	Certificate in TESOL	Both: FT/PT 1 year	$5,725/sem	Aug 22, Jan 5	High school graduation in top half of class, GPA 2.0, SAT 920+, TOEFL 500+	Carl Barnett	134
	BA with a minor in TESOL	Both: FT/PT 1 year	$5,725/sem	Any semester	High school graduation in top half of class, GPA 2.0, SAT 920+, TOEFL 500+	Carl Barnett	134
Hamline University, USA	Certificate in TEFL	Both: FT/PT 1 mth, 10 wk, 6 mth courses available	$1,960/1 mt intensive; $2,280/6 mth and 10 wk program	Contact for details	First degree preferred, teaching experience pref, knowledge of languages pref	Betsy Parrish, Assoc Prof/TEFL Coordinator	134
	Certificate for Teachers of Adult ESL PT	Contact for details	$225/course	Any term	BA degree	Betsy Parrish, Coordinator	134
Hawaii Pacific University, USA	Certificate in TESL	Both: FT/PT 2 semesters minimum	$3,750/sem or $13 /cr	Any semester	BA Degree, TOEFL 550	Edward F Klein	134
	BA with major in TESL Both	8 semesters	$3,750/semest er or $135/cr	Any semester	High school diploma or equivalent, GPA 2.5	Dr Edward Klein PhD, Associate Dean	134
College	Course Title	Course Length	Fees	Start Dates	Entry Requirements	Contacts	Address/ Advert Page

USA/Canada University Courses

COLLEGE	COURSE TITLE	COURSE LENGTH	FEES	START DATES	ENTRY REQUIREMENTS	CONTACTS	ADDRESS/ ADVERT PAGE
Hobe Sound Bible College	BA in TESOL	Both: FT/PT 8 semesters	$1,970/12-17 hrs	Any semester	SAT or ACT score, graduation from high school	Admissions Director	134
Illinois State University	BA Minor in TESOL	Both: FT/PT 3-4 semsters	In-state: $98.40/cr hr; Out-of-state: $295.20/cr hr	Any semester	All aspects of high school academic record	Ronald Fortune, Chair	134
Indiana University, USA	Certificate in Applied Linguistics	Both: FT/PT 3 semesters	In-state: $147/cr hr; Out-of-state: $428/cr hr	Fall, Spring	Bac degree, GRE score, TOEFL 573+	Karla Bastin	134
Jersey City State College	ESL - Initial Certification, Second Certification	Both: FT/PT 3 semesters	In-state: $170/cr; Out-of-state: $213/cr	Any semester	Undergrad cum average 2.75, letters of recommen-dation, GRE or MAT score	Mihri Napoliello	135
Kansas University	BA in Linguistics	Both: FT/PT Contact for details	In-state: $97.80/cr; Out-of-state: $321.75/cr	Any semester	GPA 3.0, GRE score, TOEFL score	Chair, Linguistics Dept	135
McGill University, Faculty of Education, Canada	Certificate in TESL	Both: FT/PT 3 semesters	Contact for details	September, January, July	Teaching permit, completion of English Language Proficiency Exam	Tia Habib, Student Affairs Assistant	140
	BEd Major in TESL	FT 8 semesters	Contact for details	Fall	GPA 2,8, 80%+ EPE	Joyce Gaul	140
Memphis University	BA in English with ESL Concentration	Both: FT/PT 4 years	In-state: $96/cr hr; Out-of-state: $282/cr hr	Any semester	Contact for details	Director of Undergraduate Programs	135
Montana University	Certificate of Accomplish ment in ESL Teaching	Both: FT/PT 1 year	In-state: $1,500/term; Out-of-state: $3,400/term	Any semester	Undergrads, graduates, non-degree graduate students	Robert B Hausmann	136
Montclair State University	BA in Linguistics	Both: FT/PT 8 semesters	In-stat: $117.58/sem hr; Out-of-state: $166.33/sem hr	Fall, Spring	High school dip, SAT score, GPA 3.0 in Linguistics	Coordinator of Teacher Education	136
	Postbac Certification in TESL	Both: FT/PT 2 semesters	In-state: $186.30/sem hr; Out-of-state: $236.10/sem hr	Any semester	Undergrad transcripts, certification in another content area, interview	Coordinator of Teacher Education	136
COLLEGE	COURSE TITLE	COURSE LENGTH	FEES	START DATES	ENTRY REQUIREMENTS	CONTACTS	ADDRESS/ ADVERT PAGE

USA/Canada University Courses

College	Course title	Course length	Fees	Start dates	Entry requirements	Contacts	Address/Advert page
Mount Vernon College	Certificate in TESOL	Both: FT/PT Contact for details	$378/cr	Any semester	BA with GPA 3.0, TOEFL 600	Sharon Ahern Fechter, MA TESOL Program	136
Northwestern College, MN	BA/BS in ESL Education with/without state licensure	FT: 4 years	$4,640/12-18 qtr cr	Fall preferred	Contact for details	Feng-Ling Margaret Johnson	136
Our Lady of the Lake University of San Antonio	BA with ESL Endorsement, BA with Bilingual Certification	Both: FT/PT 8 semesters	$261/sem hr	Any semester	Contact for details	Dr Hugh B Fox III	136
Portland State University, Department of Linguistics,	Certificate in TESL	FT: 1 year	$1,746-$3,771/quarter	September, January, March, June	550 TOEFL; contact PSU for further details	Karin Tittleback-Goodwin	136
Quebec University at Trois Rivieres, Canada	BA in ESL	FT: 4 years	C$1,500/term	Fall	College diploma or relevant experience	Egan Valentine PhD	140
Queens College of the City University of New York	BA in Linguistics	Both: FT/PT 4 semesters	In-state: $1,600/sem; Out-of-state: $3,400/sem	Fall	B+ average in high shool, GPA, SAT score recommended	Prof R Vago	137
Queen's University, School of English, Canada	Additional qualifications courses in ESL	PT 3 semesters	C$750/course	Contact for details	Contact for details	Office of the Faculty Registrar	140
St Cloud State University	BS minor in ESL & ESL Licensure	Both: FT/PT 4 semesters	In-state: $90/cr; Out-of-state: $110/cr	Any semester	Graduation from high shool in upper half of class, ACT 25+	James H Robinson	136
St Michaels College	Diploma in TEFL/TESL	FT: 8 weeks	$2,300	June	High school diploma only, TOEFL 550+	Mahmoud T Arani	136
San Diego State University	Basic & Advanced Certificates in Applied Linguistics & ESL	Both: FT/PT 2 semesters	Contact for details	Any semester	Contact for details	Jeffrey P Kaplan, Adviser	136
College	Course title	Course length	Fees	Start dates	Entry requirements	Contacts	Address/Advert page

USA/Canada University Courses

College	Course Title	Course Length	Fees	Start Dates	Entry Requirements	Contacts	Address/ Advert Page
San Jose State University, CA	TESOL Certificate, Graduate & Undergraduate	Both: FT/PT 2 semesters	Contact for details	Contact for details	Undergraduate high school dip, Graduate: Bac degree, GPA 2.5+, TOEFL 570	TESOL Coordinator	137
Saskatchewan University (Extension Division), Canada	University Certificate in TESOL	PT: 1-3 years	C$470.55/course	Fall, Spring, Winter	Secondary school diploma, native speaker of English or TOEFL, 21+	CERTESL Program, Extension Credit Studies	140
School for International Training, Vermont	SIT Tesol Certificate (in New England, Japan, Brazil)	FT: 4 wks	$2,000	Contact for details	Eligible for tertiary education, written application, interview, TOEFL 550/213	Lani Wright, Certificate Co-ordinator	137
School of TESL, Seattle,	Certificate in Teaching English as a Second or Foreign Language	FT: 1 mth; PT: 1 yr (1 course per quarter)	$2,280 for 12-credit cert course	Monthly	BA Degree	Dr Nan Tulare, Director	137
Shenandoah University	Professional Certificate in TESOL	Both: FT/PT 2 summer institutes or year-round	$450/cr	Any trimester	Bac degree, TOEFL 500+	Chair, TESOL Dept	137
	EFL Certificate	Both: FT/PT yr-round or 3 summers	$450/cr	Fall, Winter, or summer institute	Bac degree, TOEFL 500+	Chair, TESOL Dept	137
Simon Fraser University, Canada	Postbac Diploma in TESL	Both: FT/PT FT: 4 - 5 sems; PT: varies	approx C$80 per credit	C$231 / cr hr	First degree in a related field, native fluency in English	Rita Parmar	140
	Certificate in TESL	PT: 4 - 5 semesters	Can$231/cr hr	Any semester	General admission requirements to the university, 1 year of undergrad study	Rita Parmar	140
Sonoma State University (Dept of Anthropology and Linguistics)	Certificate in TESL	FT: 2 terms; PT: 4 terms	In-state: $1,065/term; Out-of-state: $246/unit	August	Contact for details	Richard J Senghas, Asst Prof/TESOL Co-ordinator	137
College	Course Title	Course Length	Fees	Start Dates	Entry Requirements	Contacts	Address/ Advert Page

College	Course Title	Course Length	Fees	Start Dates	Entry Requirements	Contacts	Address/Advert Page
South Carolina University, USA	Certificate in TEFL	Both: FT/PT 2 semesters + 1 summer	In-state: $1,862/sem; Out-of-state: $3,817/sem	Summer, Fall	Contact for info	Carol Myers-Scotton, Linguistics Program	137
Southeast Missouri State University	BA in English, language option	Both: FT/PT 8 semesters	In-state: 93.30/hr; Out-of-state: $173.30/hr	Any semester	Contact for details	Dr Adelaide Heyde Parsons	137
St Mary's University, Canada	TESL 100 - An overview to TESL / TEFL	FT: 4 wk;, PT: 3 mths	C$650	FT: August; PT: August, September, March	Undergraduate degree pref	Maureen Sargent, Director, TESL Centre	140
St Michael's College, Vermont	The Diploma Course in TEFL	FT: 8 wks	$2,300		High school diploma, TOEFL 550	Mahmoud T Arani	136
Texas University, Arlington	Certificate in TESOL	Both: FT/PT Contact for details	In-state: $1,115.25/9 sem hrs; Out-of-state: $3,131.25/9 sem hrs	Any semester	Contact for details	Graduate Adviser	138
Texas University, Pan American	BA with ESL and/or Linguistics concentration	Both: FT/PT 4 semesters above sophomore level	In-state: $615/12 cr hrs; Out-of-state: $2,331/12 cr hrs	Any semester	Graduation from high school or GED dip, transcripts, ACT scores	Dr Lee Hamilton, Chair	138
Toronto University, Woodsworth College	Certificate in TESL	Both: FT/PT 1 year	C$1,600/ course	May, September	Contact for details	Professional & International Programs	140
United States International University	BA in TESOL	Both: FT/PT 4 years	$3,600/qtr for 12-16 units	Any quarter	GPA 2.5, SAT or ACT scoress, personal essay, TOEFL 550	Dr Linda J Swanson, Chair	137
Utah, University of	Certificate in TESOL	Both: FT/PT 6 quarters	In-state: $1,150/sem; Out-of-state: $3,118/sem	Any semester	High school or GED dip, GPA and SAT or ACT score, TOEFL 600+	Coordinator, Linguistics Program	138
Vancouver Community College, Canada	International TESL Certificate	FT: 10 months	C$6,000	September, January	University degree	Jennifer Pearson Terell, Senior Programme Coordinator	140
College	Course Title	Course Length	Fees	Start Dates	Entry Requirements	Contacts	Address/Advert Page

USA/Canada University Courses

COLLEGE	COURSE TITLE	COURSE LENGTH	FEES	START DATES	ENTRY REQUIREMENTS	CONTACTS	ADDRESS/ ADVERT PAGE
Vancouver Community College, Canada	CERTESL Certificate	PT: 9 months	C$2,350	January, May, September	Academic English Secondary School	Jennifer Pearson Terell, Senior Programme Coordinator	140
	Tutoring ESL Certificate	PT: 6 months	C$1100	September, January, May	University degree	Jennifer Pearson Terell, Senior Programme Coordinator	140
	TESOL Certificate	FT 6 months; PT 10 months	C$2900	January, April, September	University degree	Jennifer Pearson Terell, Senior Programme Coordinator	140
	TESL Inservice Qualification Certificate	PT: 6 mths	C$1700	October, March	University degree + 600 hours ESL/EFL teaching experience	Jennifer Pearson Terell, Senior Programme Coordinator	140
Victoria University, Dept of Linguistics, Canada	Diploma in Applied Linguistics/TESOL	FT: 1 year	C$2,543	September	First degree or equiv including 2 yrs of English and 2 yrs of a 2nd language	Dr L Collins	140
	BA Applied Linguistics	Both: FT/PT Contact for details	Approx C$2,000/yr	Any semester	BA or BS, GRE score	Graduate Advisor	140
Waterloo Centre for Applied Linguistics, Canada	TESL Certificate	FT: 8 months	C$5,000	September	First degree	Janet Stubbs, Director	140
West Chester University PA	Certificate of Preparation in ESL Teaching	Both: FT/PT 2 semesters	In-state: $187/sem hr; Out-of-state: $336/sem hr	Any semester	Bac degree	Cheri Micheau, Director	138
Western Ontario University	Cert in Second Language Teaching	PT: 2-3 years	C$ 4,400/program	September	Contact for details	Diploma and Certificate Programs	140
	Professional Training for Teachers: ESL	PT Three 125-hour sections	C$630/course	Summer, Fall	Practice teaching	Ruth Heard	140
Wheaton College, IL	Graduate Certificate in TESL	Both: FT/PT 2 semesters	$350/cr hr	Any semester	BA degree, GPA 2.75+, TOEFL 600+	Dr Alan Seaman	138
COLLEGE	COURSE TITLE	COURSE LENGTH	FEES	START DATES	ENTRY REQUIREMENTS	CONTACTS	ADDRESS/ ADVERT PAGE

USA/Canada University Courses

COLLEGE	COURSE TITLE	COURSE LENGTH	FEES	START DATES	ENTRY REQUIREMENTS	CONTACTS	ADDRESS/ ADVERT PAGE
Wichita State University, USA	BA in Elementary Education with TESL state teching endorsement	Both (FT last 4 semesters) 8-9 semesters	In-state: $81.50/cr hr; Out-of-state: $286.85/cr hr	Any semester	High School dip, TOEFL 570+	Peggy Anderson, Director, TESOL Program	138
	Undergraduate /Graduate Certificate in TESOL	FT 1 year	In-state: $81.50/cr hr; Out-of-state: $286.85/cr hr	Any semester	High school diploma for undergrad cert	Peggy Anderson	138
Wisconsin University of, Madison,	Certificate in TESL	Both: FT/PT 2-3 semesters	Contact for details	Any semester	Undergraduate/ graduate entry	Prof. charks Scott	138

Australia/New Zealand University Certificate Courses

COLLEGE	COURSE TITLE	COURSE LENGTH	FEES	START DATES	ENTRY REQUIREMENTS	CONTACTS	ADDRESS/ ADVERT PAGE
Canberra Institute of Technology, Aus	Certificate in English for Academic Purposes	FT: 10 wks	Aus£240/wk	Monthly intakes	Contact for details	Dr C Juodvalkis	154
Deakin University, Melbourne, Aus	Graduate Certificate of TESOL	FT: 1 semester; PT Two semesters	Aus$6500	February	3 years tertiary study, inc teacher training	Dr Alex McKnight	155
Griffith University, Brisbane, Aus	Graduate Diploma in Applied Linguistics	FT: 1 year	Australian students: Aus$650 per 10 credit points; Overseas students: Aus$1,250 per 10 credit points	Contact for details	Degree, 3 yrs exp	Gary Birch	155
	Post Graduate Certificate in Second Language Teaching	Dist 6 months	Australian students: Aus$650 per 10 credit points; Overseas students: Aus$1,250 per 10 credit points	January, June	Degree, 3 yrs exp	Dr Shirley O'Neill	155
	Post Graduate Certificate in Language Assessment	Dist 6 months	Contact for details	January, June	Contact for details	Dr Shirley O'Neill	155
COLLEGE	COURSE TITLE	COURSE LENGTH	FEES	START DATES	ENTRY REQUIREMENTS	CONTACTS	ADDRESS/ ADVERT PAGE

Australia/New Zealand University Certificate Course

COLLEGE	COURSE TITLE	COURSE LENGTH	FEES	START DATES	ENTRY REQUIREMENTS	CONTACTS	ADDRESS/ ADVERT PAGE
Griffith University, Nathan, Aus	Post Graduate Certificate in Language Assessment	Dist FT: 6 mths; PT 1 year	Contact for details	January, June	Contact for details	Dr Shirley O'Neill	155
La Trobe University, Melbourne, Aus	Post Graduate Certificate in Second Language Teaching	Dist FT: 6 mths; PT 1 year	Contact for details	January, June	Contact for details	Dr Shirley O'Neill	156
	Graduate Diploma in TESOL	FT: 1 yr; PT: 2-3 years	Local: Aus$6,900; International: Aus$12,000	March, July	BA degree, teaching qual, Eng proficiency	Ms Marion Sargeant	156
	Graduate Certificate in TESOL	FT: 6 mths; PT: 1year	Local: Aus$6,900; International: Aus$12,000	March, July	BA degree, teaching qual, Eng proficiency	Ms Marion Sargeant	156
Macquarie University, Dept of Linguistics, Sydney, Aus	Postgrad Dip in Language & Literacy Education	FT: 2 sems; PT/dist: 3-6 mths	Aus$7,200 (less for Aus/NZ applics)	March, July	First degree, 1 yr rel exp	Linguistics Distance Learning Office, Linguistics Postgraduate Office	156
Macquarie University, NCELTR, Sydney, Aus	Postgrad Cert in TESOL	FT: 1 sem; PT: 2-4 sems	Contact for details	March, July	Degree, rel exp, strong TESOL motivation	NCELTR Professional Development Section	156
New Zealand College of Studies, Auckland	Dip ELT & Learning for Overseas Teachers	FT: 41 wks	NZ$13,150 (incl reg, mats, etc)	August, February	Age 20+, IELTS 5.5, experience, overseas teacher	Lisa Bieleski	158
Northern Melbourne Institute of TAFE, Aus	ELICOS	FT: 5-40 wks	Aus$200/wk	Various	18+	John Michaels	156
Queensland Uni of Technology, Brisbane, Aus	Graduate Certificate in Education (TESOL)	FT: 19 wks or 1 term	Aus$5,950	20/7, mid-Feb	Rel deg or quals, work exp, IELTS 6.5	Student Affairs Officer	156
	Advanced Certificate in International Business & Trade	FT: 31 wks	Aus£9,200	March, June, October	IELTS 5.5 or TOEFL 525	The Registrar	156
COLLEGE	COURSE TITLE	COURSE LENGTH	FEES	START DATES	ENTRY REQUIREMENTS	CONTACTS	ADDRESS/ ADVERT PAGE

Australia/New Zealand University Certificate Courses

College	Course title	Course length	Fees	Start dates	Entry requirements	Contacts	Address/ Advert Page
UNITEC Institute of Technology, Auckland, NZ	Certificate in Intensive English	Both: FT/PT 10 wks	FT: NZ$315 per wk; PT: NZ$190 per wk	October, November	Contact for details	Frances Little	159
University of Waikato Language Institute, Hamilton, NZ	Diploma in TESOL	Contact for details	NZ$9,900 approx	Contact for details	Successful tertiary study	international@ waikato.ac.nz	159
	Postgrad Diploma in Second Language Teaching	Both: FT/PT 8 mths	Contact for details	March	Degree, teaching exp	Rhonda Robertson	159
Victoria University, School of Linguistics and Applied Language Studies, N Z	Diploma in TESOL	FT: 9 months; PT: 18-36 months	NZ$15,000 (international students)	March, July	First degree, 2 yrs teaching exp	Dr Elaine Vine	159
	Certificate in TESOL	FT: 4 months; PT: 1 year	NZ$7,500 (international students)	March	First degree, teaching exp	Dr Elaine Vine	159
Woollongong, University, Aus	Diploma in TESOL	Both/Dist FT: 1 yr; PT: 4 years	On application	On campus: February, July; Dist: Any time	3 yr degree or equiv	Ms Kim Roser, Executive Officer	157
	Graduate Certificate in TESOL	Both/Dist FT: 6 mths; PT: 1 year	On application	On campus: February, July; Dist: Any time	3 yr degree or equiv	Ms Kim Roser, Executive Officer	157
	Certificate in Second Language Teaching	Both/Dist FT: 6 mths; PT: 1 year	On application	On campus: February, July; Dist: Any time	NSW high school certificate or equiv	Ms Kim Roser, Executive Officer	157
College	Course title	Course length	Fees	Start dates	Entry requirements	Contacts	Address/ Advert Page

Initial Qualifications in Ireland

Although many UK qualifications are acceptable in Ireland, domestic qualifications are gaining international acceptance and becoming increasingly standardised.

Ireland could be the first English speaking country to have a national recognition scheme for teacher training.

RELSA and ATT offer qualifications accepted by ACELS and, increasingly, by employers overseas.

If the current proposals to introduce a TEFL accreditation scheme goes ahead, Ireland will be the first English speaking country to have a national recognition scheme for teacher training. Plans for the scheme are being spearheaded by ACELS, the body which administers the Inspection/Recognition Scheme for Language Schools under the aegis of the Department of Education and Science.

Ireland probably produces more TEFL teachers per capita than any other English speaking country. While the economic situation is not bad, the lack of readily available jobs and the terms and conditions in relation to those elsewhere has encouraged many of the very large graduate population to seek employment abroad. Prospects have not been helped by the reputation of Irish teacher training courses, in the past they have often been short, with little teaching practice and run by unqualified trainers with no background in English Language Teaching.

Staff teaching in schools recognised by the Education and Science Department must now have a first degree and a TEFL qualification from a programme lasting a minimum of 70 hours. Qualification criteria in Irish recognised schools are now among the toughest in the world and, apart from some summer school jobs in the unrecognised sector, it is virtually impossible to get a job without a qualification. Most newly-qualified teachers should expect to work overseas.

RELSA

The Recognised English Language Schools Association is the main association of Irish EFL schools, and it introduced its own teacher training certificate in in 1992. The course, known as the RELSA Preparatory Certificate lasts 70 hours and involves teaching practice, observation and a project. The cost is about IR£250 and schools usually offer students the choice of either an intensive full-time or part-time course of study.

ATT

The Association for Teacher Training in TEFL has nine member schools and runs a full 106-hour International Certificate, as well as a 40-hour Preliminary Certificate and a 40-hour refresher courses for both L1 and non-L1 teachers.

The Preliminary Certificate is designed to entice trainee teachers away from the less reputable short courses, while the International Certificate is set up as an equivalent to the RSA and Trinity College certificates. Course fees range from IR£150-450 Irish punts and standards are assured and maintained by the ATT's own panel of moderators.

University and State Courses

Most Irish universities now offer a TEFL training course which meets ACELS requirements, but there is some course variation. The University of Cork, for example, runs RSA courses, while the University of Limerick offers a one-year pre-service diploma course, which can be also taken as part of a two-year Masters. Trinity, University College Dublin (UCD), and Galway Universities also offer training programmes.

Both Trinity and UCD run TEFL add-ons as part of their HDips, the postgraduate courses which confer Qualified Teachers Status (QTS). The HDip at University College Dublin, for example, offers a well-established add-on option in EFL which lasts 100 hours and fulfils ACELS criteria.

Irish/ATT/RELSA Certificate Courses

College	Course Title	Course Length	Fees	Start Dates	Entry Requirements	Contacts	Address/Advert Page
Bluefeather School, Dublin	ATT Diploma Both	FT: 6 wks; PT: 12 wks	TBA	TBA	Degree, Good TEFL cert	Tony Penston	93
	ATT Dip by Distance	PT: 100 study hrs	IR£250	Any time	Good Leaving Certificate/A Levels	Tony Penston	93
	ATT Initial Cert	FT: 4 wks; PT: Depends on centre (106 hrs)	From IR£450	Depends on centre	Degree	Tony Penston	93
	ATT Preliminary Cert	FT: 5 days; PT: 12 days (40 hrs)	From IR£180	Normally monthly	Good ed standard	Tony Penston	93
	ATT Foundation Cert	FT: 3 wks; PT: 6 wks (70 hrs)	From IR£250	Depends on centre	Degree or equivalent	Tony Penston	93
	ATT Teacher Refresher for Foreign Teachers	FT: 60 hrs	Closed groups only, negotiable	Any Monday	Practising teachers, student teachers	Tony Penston	93
Centre for English Studies, Dublin	RELSA	FT: 2 wks	IR£280	January, March, April, May, September, November	Degree	Director of Studies	93
Dublin School of English	RELSA	FT: 2 wks; PT: 4 wks	IR£585	January, February, March, May, July, September, November	Degree or diploma	Barry Crossen	93
Excel International Language Institute, Cork	ATT Preliminary Cerwtificate in TEFL	FT: 5/10 days	IR£180	Fortnightly	Good educational background	Martin Murray	93
	ATT Foundation Certificate in TEFL	FT: 5/10 days	IR£130	Twice per year	Good educational background	Martin Murray Director	93
Language & Activity Holidays	RELSA Prep Cert	FT: 2 wks; PT: 4 wks	IR£245	October, December, March, April, June, September,	Degree	Barbara Connelly	93
Language Centre of Ireland, Dublin	RELSA	FT: 4 wks; PT: 1 term	IR£250	September, October, March, April, May	Primary degree	Mary Shepherd	93
Language Centre of Ireland Dublin	RELSA Certificate	FT: 3 wks	IR£290	January, May, June, August, November	Degree	Tom Doyle	94
TEFL Training Institute, Dublin	ATT Refresher Course	FT: 2-4 wks; PT: 4-10 wks	IR£265-1,200	Monthly	Degree	Dr K McGinley	
Westlingua Language School, Galway	RELSA	FT: 3 wks	IR£350	August,	21 + Degree	Eoghan Garvey & Sandra Bunting	94
College	Course Title	Course Length	Fees	Start Dates	Entry Requirements	Contacts	Address/Advert Page

Introductory Courses

If you are unsure if TEFL is the job for you or if you simply cannot afford the time and money for full-time training, an introductory course can be a good way to test the water.

The basic aim of these courses is to provide you with a taste of EFL teaching, not to qualify you to teach.

Introductory courses aim to provide you with a taste of EFL teaching, not to qualify you to teach. Most of these courses are only one week long and few provide supervised teaching practice with real students - something that most employers require. Unless you already have teaching experience, TEFL or otherwise, you will still be considered 'unqualified' after the course.

During the peak summer season the number of students can double in the UK, Ireland, USA, Canada, Australia and New Zealand. This surge in demand cannot be met by qualified teachers and the experience of an introductory course would give you an advantage over applicants with no experience or qualifications.

A number of large school chains offer the opportunity to be trained without worrying about job-hunting afterwards

For longer term work, some schools running introductory courses might be able to use their relationships with employers overseas to organise jobs for trainees. Otherwise, opportunities exist in the Far East and Latin America where a short introductory course will give you an edge over unqualified applicants.

It's worth noting that certificate courses are often open only to graduates or those who have successfully completed an introductory course.

Cowboy operators

Beware of introductory courses which claim that after a week or so you can get any ELT job anywhere in the world. Also, avoid any course claiming to be 'recognised', 'accredited' or 'validated'. Schools and colleges can be recognised or accredited, but teacher training courses cannot (although, of course, many recognised schools do run introductory courses).

In-house courses

Some large school chains train teachers so that they can be placed in one of their schools upon completion of the course. Having a specific training may be a disadvantage later if you want to find work elsewhere, but the opportunity to be trained without worrying about job-hunting afterwards can be very attractive. Here are some of the major chains.

Berlitz (320+ schools worldwide): With branches in Latin America, Europe and the Far East, Berlitz offers introductory courses in the Berlitz Method. Courses last for one to two weeks and are only open to native English speakers, especially language graduates with some ELT experience abroad.

Contact: Berlitz Inc, 400 Alexander Park Drive, Princeton NJ 08540-6306 USA or Berlitz UK, 9-13 Grosvenor Street, London W1A 3BZ.

GEOS (250+ schools in Japan): GEOS Corporation provides teacher training courses for native English speakers recruited for its chain of schools in Japan.

Contact: GEOS Language Corporation Ontario, Simpson Tower 2424, 401 Bay Street, Toronto, Ontario M5H 2Y4, Canada or GEOS Corporation, 55-61 Portland Road, Hove, Sussex, BN3 5DQ, UK.

inlingua (270+ schools worldwide): Using specially designed coursebooks, inlingua adopts the 'direct' method of teaching. The organisation prefers British or Irish applicants with a university degree.

Contact: inlingua Teacher Training and Recruitment, Rodney Lodge, Rodney Road, Cheltenham, GL50 1XY, UK.

Distance Training in TESOL

For those who are unable to spare either the time or the money for a full-time teacher training course, distance learning may be attractive.

Although distance diplomas are widely accepted, distance certificates have not been traditionally popular with employers.

ecause of their convenience and relative cost, certificates by distance training have always been popular with aspiring teachers, especially those already in full-time jobs. However, although distance diplomas are widely accepted, distance certificates have not been traditionally popular with employers in the UK though acceptability abroad is fairly widespread.

Employers look for two things in an initial teacher training programme: quality assurance (preferably through external validation) and the provision of supervised teaching practice with real students.

In the US and Canada, there are a number of distance certificates run by respected universities, such as the University of Scotdale, which include observed teaching practice. Elsewhere they are more difficult to find.

Quality assurance

Some distance courses offer a period of on-site training and supervised teaching practice

There have, historically, been a lot of poor quality UK operators running distance programmes. However, the small number of reputable UK distance training providers have during recent years made a lot of progress in the area of quality assurance. The College of Teachers is a respected institution, which is empowered by Royal Charter to offer professional qualifications by distance learning in the UK and overseas. The College externally validates a 250-hour distance programme leading to the Associateship of the College of Teachers in TESOL. It also validates an Advanced Certificate in TESOL a hybrid combination of distance training and supervised teaching practice; a 450 hour DipCoT (TESOL) by distance only as a hybrid programme leading to an Advanced Diploma in TESOL and Fellowship of the College, a qualification at MPhil level.

Another important development is the establishment of ACTDEC - the Accreditation Council for TESOL Distance Education Courses, a non-profit making quality control body. ACTDEC has introduced a code of practice covering a range of areas including course evaluation and quality assurance. It aims to establish an accreditation scheme for courses involving four distance education and training qualifications at four separate levels from introductory to diploma level.

Teaching practice

Outside North America, there are some hybrid courses, mostly validated by Trinity College or the College of Teachers, which offer part or all of the teaching theory by distance learning, plus a period of supervised teaching practice. Other distance training providers working with schools abroad have set up 'apprenticeships', so new certificate teachers work with an experienced teacher mentor.

Many distance courses do, however, lack teaching practice. At diploma level, lack of teaching practice presents little difficulty as diplomas tend to be open to experienced teachers only.

Where can I work?

In many countries in the Far East and Latin America teaching practice is valued less highly than a good degree and a solid theoretical knowledge of EFL. However, the English-speaking countries which run recognition schemes are likely to continue to view you as 'unqualified'.

✠◉ Linguarama

LANGUAGE TRAINING FOR BUSINESS

Linguarama is Europe's largest wholly-owned language training organisation specialising in training for business and professional people. With over 40 centres in 13 countries Linguarama offers professional training for international client organisations.

RECRUITMENT

Due to our continued expansion Linguarama is continuously recruiting people for teaching positions. Last year we filled over three hundred vacancies. Candidates should have a degree, a recognised qualification and an interest in business.

Contact Mr D Coughlan, Linguarama, 89 High Street, Alton GU34 1LG
Tel: 01420 80899 Fax: 01420 80856 Email: personnel@linguarama.com

TRAINING

AN INTRODUCTION TO TEACHING ENGLISH AS A FOREIGN LANGUAGE

Intensive one-week courses in Birmingham and Manchester provide a stimulating introduction to teaching TEFL. Linguarama courses are well known and accepted by many employers throughout the world. Suitable for those considering entry into the profession or trained teachers who need orienting towards TEFL.

Contact TEFL Dept Linguarama, 16 Waterloo Street, Birmingham B2 5UG
Tel: 0121 632 5925 Fax: 0121 643 9295 Email: birmingham@linguarama.com

CAMBRIDGE DIPLOMA IN TEACHING ENGLISH FOR BUSINESS AND PROFESSIONAL PURPOSES

An eight-week programme for teachers with at least two years' experience who wish to focus on teaching English for business and professional purposes. Courses are held in London and Stratford.

Contact Anne Laws, Linguarama, 89 High Street, Alton GU34 1LG
Tel: 01420 80899 Fax: 01420 80856 Email: annelaws@linguarama.com

www.linguarama.com

BPP
PART OF THE BPP
TRAINING GROUP

61

Finding a Job

Whether you are looking for an International Teaching Career or a just away of funding a year abroad you need to be properly organised. This Section gives advice on the essential questions.

How to find a job

Whether taking your first steps or exploring ways to further your career, here are some of the most effective recruitment media and some reliable first ports of call.

1 Chain schools

his will be the first port of call for many newly-qualified teachers looking for a job. Chain schools tend to have one central office and 'branches' around a country or around the world. There are chain schools with only one other branch in a town near the central office and there are others, like International House, with more than 200 schools worldwide.

Advantages

Recruitment for all branches of a chain school is often dealt with at the central office. This is very attractive to job seekers because, in effect, one application letter will cover all job openings for all branches. A chain with 150 schools can have as many as 70,000 students at any one time, with as many as 350 full time opportunities annually. These opportunities will be at all levels, so applying to a chain can also be attractive to teachers with more experience.

Applying

Each chain will have its own application procedure and you would be advised to talk to the staffing unit at the central office before applying. You will probably be required to supply a CV and copies of any relevant qualifications. You should also write a letter introducing yourself, outlining any specific requirements you may have with respect to location, specialised teaching and so on.

It might be worth mentioning a region or selection of countries to help the staffing unit explore as many possibilities as possible for you. Explain what experience you have had and try to show how specific experience you might have had might be relevant to a specific country or region. If you have some knowledge of Spanish, for example, and are looking for a position in Latin America, mention this in your letter and CV.

Some chain schools, AEON Corporation, ELT Banbury, inLingua and International House, also offer training courses and place trainees in their chain and affiliate schools. Some chain schools, including Berlitz, place all their trainees in its schools. See the directory of chain schools on page 281 and refer to the training grids in their Sections One and Two for further information.

2 Recruitment agencies

Another way to cut down on the leg work when looking for your first job is to register with a recruitment agency. Schools often contact agencies to help them recruit and agencies will either match up the school's requirements with teachers they have on file or they will seek suitable teachers by advertising. A recruitment agency will either specialise in a country or region, or it will recruit for schools worldwide.

The essential advantage of applying through and agency is that it allows you to offer yourself to a number of schools in a number of locations at the same time. For more qualified teachers, registering through an agency can allow you to match up your specific qualifications to schools' requirements without wasting time applying to those schools which have no need of your skills.

Requirements

Although agencies are often willing to take on newly-qualified teachers, many will not want to get your hopes up. Recruiting through an agency can be an expensive way for a school to recruit, so schools often have strict specifications.

Many agencies will want teachers who have a certificate minimum, although for recruiters operating in the Asia Pacific Rim, a degree and a US MA might be preferred. Some agencies will not register teachers without diplomas and at least one year's teaching experience. Some agencies will consider applicants with certificates obtained by distance but only if the applicants have had some teaching experience.

Nationality

Nationality is often an important factor too. Schools recruiting through agencies tend to favour L1 speakers but this is not exclusively the case. The standard of teacher training in non-L1 speaker countries is becoming increasingly well-regarded and international recruitment agencies are taking on teachers from Italy, the Gulf, Germany, Spain and Argentina among others.

And just because you are an L1 speaker, it doesn't mean that you will automatically be eligible for a job. Some countries have cultural and trade ties with the US, for example, rather than the UK and US applicants will be more favoured. These biases operate especially where there are visa restrictions. For example, it is almost impossible for a non-EU teacher to obtain a work visa for EU countries so US teachers, for example, will be very much disadvantaged when applying for a position in an EU country.

Applying

You can apply directly to the recruitment manager at an agency (see the directory on page 281) although you should call to make sure that the agency can help someone with your qualifications and experience.

3 British Council and USIA

The British Council promotes Britain around the world and is the largest international ELT employer. Its Central Management of Direct Teaching recruits 300 teachers each year for its ever-increasing network of more than 80 key teaching centres in over 50 countries. Applicants must be L.1 speakers with an ELT Certificate and an ELT Diploma, along with 18 months' post-qualification experience. Contracts are usually for two years and can often be renewed. Teachers are encouraged to move to other centres at the end of their contracts giving plenty of opportunity for career progression.

Contact: Information Assistant, The British Council (CMDT), 10, Spring Gardens, London SW1A 2BN, UK. Tel: 44 171 389 4914, Fax: 44 171 389 4140.

The British Council also acts for overseas government agencies via its Overseas Appointment Services. Much of the recruitment here is done for the Overseas Development Administration (ODA), recruiting professionals, including those involved in English language, for projects funded under the British government aid programme in developing countries. Applicants should have a certificate, a diploma and even an MA with considerable experience.

Contact: OAS, Medlock Street, Manchester M15 4PR, UK Tel: 44 161 957 7755.

The US Information Agency (USIA) is the US equivalent of the British Council and has binational centres worldwide. Short-term projects are available in ESP, teacher training and development but each centre coordinates its own recruitment. The USIA has a resource centre and can supply addresses of its binational centres.

Contact: English Programs Division, E/AL, Room 304, 301 4th Street, SW, Washington. DC 20547, USA. Tel: 1 202 619 5869. Fax: 1 202 406 1250.

4 Educational, government and self-funding ELT programmes

These programmes tend to place teachers in public sector schools at primary (elementary), secondary (high school) and university (college) levels for six months or more. Programmes place at various levels from conversation teachers to teacher trainers and salaries are paid at local rates although it is common to receive an additional supplement. For Central and Eastern Europe, the Central European Teaching Program and Soros Professional English Language Teaching Program are the major programmes while the CIEE JET Programme places 550 teachers in Japan each year. CIEE's Teach in China Programme will be placing 100 teachers in China this year.

A number of self-funding programmes, including Students Partnership Worldwide and Teaching Abroad, which respectively place 160 and 750 teachers worldwide, are open to applicants at university entrance level. This can be a good way for 'gap-year' students who are taking a year between school and university to get valuable experience.

For self-funding programmes, teachers have to pay for travel, accommodation and at least some living expenses.

Requirements

Applicants will need an undergraduate degree and probably one year's teaching experience. Applicants for the JET programme do not need any experience while those applying for the Soros programme should have a certificate and three years of teaching experience.

The self-funding programmes are less strict. If applicants are at university entrance level and have the ability to fund themselves, they are eligible.

Nationality

As with recruitment agencies, nationality is often a factor and programmes tend to favour applicants from the country in which the programmes are based. In addition, L1 speakers are favoured although some programmes will place non-L1 applicants, including French. The Teach in China programme places 15 non-L1 teachers of any nationality each year.

Applying

Applications can be made directly to the organisation operating the programme. Always call first to make sure that someone with your skills and experience can be accommodated.

5 Voluntary programmes

Voluntary organisations operate programmes for countries, often in Africa or the Asia Pacific region, which are keen to develop their educational infrastructure. Voluntary Service Overseas places 150 teachers while WorldTeach places 250-300. Other organisations include the Peace Corps and East European Partnership. There are a number of religious organisations, including Christians Abroad, who have contracts for English language teachers.

Volunteers are generally paid local salaries although supplements may be made available. Some programmes expect the teachers to pay for their airfare. Contracts are generally for one year.

Requirements

Voluntary organisations have stricter requirements than they used to have. A university degree is generally a standard minimum and, although no ELT experience is necessary, there are more options for experienced teachers. Voluntary Service Overseas (VSO), for example, has openings also for teacher trainers and resource centre managers. Many teachers find that volunteering is a good way to get a taste of responsibilities which might be slower to come in other sectors.

Some organisations run programmes for younger teachers. For example, undergraduates can participate in WorldTeach's summer teaching programme at a language camp for Chinese high school students in Shanghai.

Non-L.1 speakers are often made welcome on voluntary programmes. German, Japanese,

Mexican, Swedish, Dutch, Israeli, French and Brasilian have all been placed recently. VSO accept applicants from any country who have unrestricted right of re-entry to the UK or Canada.

Applying

Apply directly to the organisation (see the directory on page 282). Always call first to make sure that the programme can accommodate your skills and experience.

6 International media

There are a number of international and local newspapers, journals and bulletins which will help you in your job search.

EL Prospects is the first step for anyone looking for an ELT position, whether unqualified, newly-qualified, in-service teacher or director of studies. It contains more than 250 current positions monthly and offers valuable career development advice and features.

EL Prospects is available with EL *Gazette,* the international ELT newspaper, or separately. EL *Gazette* contains ELT news, features, interviews, discussion forums, book reviews and photocopiable teachers' materials. Subscriptions to EL Gazette (including EL *Prospects*) - Priced £30 (UK), £30.00 (EU) can be obtained from: Subscriptions Coordinator, Dilke House, 1 Malet Street, London WC1E 7JA. Tel: +44 (0) 171 255 1969. Fax: +44 (0) 171 255 1972. Email: elgazette@compuserve.com. (Payment can be made through Visa Mastercard or UK cheque.)

Other international media can be found in the directory on page 280. ELT job adverts also appear in local newspapers around the world. Details of these can be found by country in the International Job Prospects section starting on page 81.

Applying

Job advertisements which appear in international or local media are placed directly by schools and organisations looking to recruit or by agencies recruiting on their behalf. Different schools have different application requirements depending on the position advertised, where the school is, and so on. Follow the instructions carefully. If you have any doubts about what is required, contact the advertiser before applying.

In the first instance you might be asked to supply any number of items: a CV, a letter of introduction, copies of qualifications, copies of degree transcripts, photographs, copy of the front page of your passport, etc. Where possible, do not send original forms as this might stop you from applying for other positions.

7 Websites

The number of ELT websites is expanding rapidly and there are now some good recruitment sites, although trawling through them can be quite time-consuming and frustrating. See page 280 for our selection of the best sites.

Always check that the application date has not passed as some site editors do not clear expired jobs often enough. Remember also that although websites try to research all the companies which post job information, strict checks do not generally exist. Try to do your own research about a school or speak to its director of studies before applying.

8 Jobshops

Some of the big teachers' associations run 'jobshops' at their conferences where job information is made available on a huge noticeboard or at an information centre. The biggest of these jobshops are at the TESOL international conference in March, the IATEFL international conference in August and the JALT international conference in November.

Survival List

Essential books for the English language teacher going overseas.

 nce you have your job offer or have decided to pack your bags in search of that exciting position overseas, you ought to consider the materials that may not be available locally. Below is a selection of teachers' books, which can help you as you study for TEFL qualifications and that are practical when teaching. Take at least a grammar reference and a resource book. We also recommend that you have a stock of pictures: of objects, places, famous people and family, and a slab of blu tac.

The Practice of English Language Teaching (Longman)
Jeremy Harmer
A complete guide to the theory, techniques and materials for teaching EFL or ESL. This book provides guidance in analysing student needs and developing approaches to presenting language for essential elements of lessons: grammar, vocabulary, skills and pronunciation.

Learning Teaching (Heinemann) *J Scrivener*
This is a guide for English language teachers during their training and when they reach the classroom. It includes ideas on how to survive the first lesson, and then develop skills with lesson ideas.

About Language (CUP) *S Thornbury*
A guide to test the teacher's own understanding of how the English language works and therefore teach it better. There are 28 units with 10 tasks in each to help people training to be teachers, or aid their preparation for the classroom.

Teaching Aids
English Grammar in Use (CUP) *Raymond Murphy*
Grammar and practice book for use by students on their own, or in class, up to First Certificate level. A book of supplementary exercises is also available.

Practical English Usage (OUP) *Michael Swan*
Popular reference book for teachers and students. Alphabetical listings of common problems of usage with explanations and examples.

Grammar Practice Activities
A Practical Guide for Teachers(CUP) *Penny Ur*
A collection of 200 activities practising a wide range of important grammar points for all levels, with lesson procedure and preparation explained in full. Includes a detailed introduction to grammar teaching in the EFL classroom and guidelines for designing additional activities.

Keep Talking
Communicative Fluency Activities for Language Teaching (CUP) *Friederike Klippel*
A practical guide to more than a hundred communication and role-play activities covering all levels. Provides notes on level, time, preparation, procedure and language aims for each activity. Accompanying worksheets are supplied at the back of the book to aid understanding.

Essential Grammar in Use (CUP) *R Murphy*
An ideal first grammar book, which is specifically aimed at elementary students. Spanish and Italian versions are also available.

Learner-based Teaching (OUP)
Colin Campbell & Hana Kryszewska
Contains over 70 adaptable activities (with variations) for all levels, and covers grammar, integrated skills, writing, translation, games and examination practice. Intended as a resource when no other materials are available.

1000 Pictures for Teachers to Copy - New Edition (Longman) *Andrew Wright*
Invaluable resource of 1000 simple drawings for teachers to present or elicit language. Introduces basic techniques, as well as ways of using pictures in the classroom. Covers basic vocabulary, verbs, adjectives, scenes, settings and sequences.

Teaching Tenses
Ideas for Presenting and Practising Tenses in English (Longman) *Rosemary Aitken*
A resource book with ideas for presenting tenses and verb patterns. Analyses form and function of each tense and includes a review of common errors, suggestions for presentation and practice of structures in context.

Additional Recommendations
A Source Book for TEFL (Heinemann)
Anti-Grammar Grammar Book (Longman)
Vocabulary Games & Activities for Teachers (Penguin)
Recommendations supplied by Bournemouth English Book Centre and Keltic International.

DICTIONARIES

You are bound to need a dictionary no matter how wide your vocabulary is and over the past few years a new breed of ELT dictionary has appeared, which is much easier to use and is packed with examples. The most popular examples are:

Cambridge International Dictionary of English
Collins Cobuild English Dictionary
Longman Dictionary of Contemporary English
Oxford Advanced Learners Dictionary

Financial Advice

Although financial reward may not be the key motivation when working abroad, it is important to make sure that your finances are in order and you are not losing money.

The idea of being able to find work wherever you fancy is one of the most attractive benefits of teaching English. However, such a lifestyle has inherent financial disadvantages unless relatively simple arrangements are made prior to departure. Always consult an authorised Financial Advisor before coming to any final decisions. Below are the main areas which could affect your financial well-being. Much of this information applies to teachers of all nationalities, but for specific details teachers should ensure that they consult the relevant authorities in their home country.

Financial reward may not be the first objective when considering a career in ELT. If you are starting your first job abroad, the chances are that you will not be earning a fortune.

However, many teachers find that they can save considerable sums of money, be it through working in a country with low rate of income tax, having very low living expenses, or because on completion of their contract they are entitled to a surprisingly generous bonus payment – especially common in the Middle East. These payments may be taxed in the country where they are earned, or they could be taxed on the teacher's return to their native country, even if the bonus is tax-exempt in the country in which it was earned.

Taxation

Even if your starting salary is relatively low, you still need to be aware of the taxation system both in your home country and in the country in which you are intending to work. Without care, it is possible to find yourself liable for tax in both countries.

For teachers to avoid unnecessary tax payments on income earned abroad, they must establish their personal status. First, see if the country where you are going to work has a reciprocal agreement with your country by contacting your local tax office. If this is not the case the intricacy of tax laws could mean that some expert advice is advisable in this complex field.

US Citizens for example are in very general terms taxed for being citizens, rather than for their residential status, and have to file tax information home for assessment of rates and exemptions.

Australians have to file their own tax returns, so also need to be able to convey the information of whether they are overseas in a given period. Generally, if Australians work abroad for less than a tax year, when they return home they should declare their overseas earnings and tax, and are either credited back excess tax they have paid, or charged for a shortfall under Australian assessment. If Australians leave for a longer period, then a break is made in the tax returns, to be resumed on returning home. It is advisable to check what will happen to your pension rights if you are away for some time, as social security subscriptions paid elsewhere cannot be repatriated or credited in the same way as income tax.

Canadians need to determine whether they are factual residents, deemed residents or non-residents. If you work outside of Canada temporarily and retain your ties, then you are a factual resident and have to report all of your incomes, from within and outside of Canada, paying federal taxes, and have all of the normal deductions and allowances. 'Relevant ties' to Canada can include such things as a Canadian driver's licence or bank account. To be a non-resident there must be some permanence in the stay abroad and a cutting of ties. If this is done then income earned in Canada is taxed differently.

If you a factual resident of Canada then you can generally claim tax credits for deductions made in the country where you worked. The credit will equal the lower of the following sums: the

73

foreign tax paid, or the tax you owe on the income earned abroad if assessed under Canadian rules. Information is available in a form 'Overseas Employment Tax Credit' IT-497. Canada has tax conventions (treaties) with many countries to eliminate double payment or liability in the first place, which will influence what local social security payments you might make whilst working abroad.

Under **UK law,** if you are away for at least 365 days, and visits to the UK are for less than 62 consecutive days (or one-sixth of the total period abroad), you are eligible for relief, which can be up to 100%. This does not qualify you for non-resident status, which is obtainable only if you work full-time abroad for more than a whole tax year (ie from April to April) without visiting the UK for more than six months within a tax year, or three months on average in each year if you straddle the tax year.

The difference between non-resident status and exemption is that non-residents are not liable for tax on unearned income arising overseas (such as interest on offshore bank accounts) and capital gains. However, non-resident status does not exempt you from all UK tax by any means. Court rulings have determined that most non-residents are still considered to be domiciled in the UK. This means that incomes obtained in the UK are still taxable, and that your estate (your assets worldwide) is liable to UK inheritance tax.

Teachers should retain documentation of what they earn and contracts of employment, as the Inland Revenue will often question whether your job abroad was full time. Remember also to keep a record of any taxation payments you have made whilst abroad – this will help to ensure you are not taxed again on your return home.

Many countries have taxation treaties to prevent the double payment of tax on the same income. In relation to the UK if there is not an agreement with a given country, credit is given against the UK tax liability that has already been paid abroad. See the Inland Revenue leaflet IR6 – Double Taxation Relief.

National Insurance/Pensions

While you are working abroad, you may lose your entitlement to social security if you fail to keep up your contributions. To qualify for a full UK state retirement pension, you must have paid the minimum contribution each year for at least 90% of your whole working life.

If you miss some payments, then you will generally receive a reminder from the Department of Social Security. This will not be a demand for money, but will simply point out that you have not made your full year's quota of payments. You are then offered the opportunity of making up the payments, so that you are still on course to receive a state pension. It is then up to you to decide whether to make up the missing amount – depending on your future career plans and other pension arrangements.

If you are from the UK, obtain leaflet NI39 (SA29 if you will be working within the EU) from the Overseas Branch of the Department of Social Security (Tel: 0191 213 5000). This explains the effect on benefits of working abroad.

If you are working in a country which has a reciprocal agreement with the UK for a certain period of time, you will be subject to the UK social security scheme for that period, and will have to pay Class 1 contributions. After this period you can pay Class 2 (self-employed) or three (voluntary) contributions to the UK scheme and remain eligible for benefits.

If you are working in a country with a permanent reciprocal agreement with the UK, you must pay contributions to that country's scheme – which could be substantially higher than in the UK. Check these figures before you go.

Medical Advice

Part of the enjoyment of teaching abroad is the sense of adventure. Like every adventure, however, it is best to be prepared for the unexpected.

 Teaching abroad is stimulating and exciting, but coping with different climates and social environments can put people under great stress as well as exposing them to physical risk.

Pre-departure check-ups

You must take some general health precautions before going to work abroad. Some countries will insist on this before granting you a visa. The required check-up may be just an overall medical or may include specific tests, such as HIV.

Even if a health check is not a prerequisite, it makes sense to have one, as any problems that can be sorted out at home could save you a lot of time and trouble later. A visit to an optician for an eye test or a change of glasses is also advisable. Don't leave vaccinations to the last minute. Vaccination programmes should be started at least six weeks prior to departure.

European Union

If you are an EU citizen, you and your family are entitled to the same level of medical cover as the nationals of any EU country in which you are staying. In order to take advantage of this reciprocal cover, you must obtain the relevant form prior to departure. In the UK, it is known as form E111 and is available from the Department of Health and Social Security.

Social Security Services

If you are staying for more than a few months in a country, then it is likely that you will start paying taxes and/or making social security contributions. Find out if you are making such contributions (and if your employer is also contributing to the scheme) and what your contributions entitle you to. Once you are clear what you are entitled to within the state system, you must then assess the standards of care and efficiency that the system offers before deciding

whether they are sufficient to give you complete peace of mind, or whether you would be happier investing in a private health care scheme.

Travel Insurance Packages

If you are not intending to be a long-term resident in a country, then there are a number of 'extended stay' travel insurance packages available. Although these are adequate for essential needs, you may find yourself with better cover at a lower premium under a tailor-made policy.

Private Medical Insurance

Having private medical insurance can take the worry and uncertainty out of health care abroad. It gives you control over where you are treated and ready access to treatment when you need it. Some employers will offer medical insurance as part of your job package. If your employer offers this benefit, check the scheme to ensure that it provides adequate cover.

If you are taking out private medical insurance, make sure that you understand what you are paying for and make sure that you are sufficiently covered for your circumstances. Most schemes provide a generous annual maximum for the costs of hospital stays, specialists' fees, in-patient charges, such as X-rays, drugs and dressings, and out-patient consultations and treatment.

An important service that can also be provided is evacuation cover with 24 hour emergency service. Many people think of this service as one of helicopters and air ambulances flying to hospitals from remote areas. But it has other features, such as the fact that the subscriber is never more than a telephone call away from multi-lingual medical help. This can be of great importance if you, a child or a partner are seriously ill in a country whose language and culture you are still unfamiliar with.

Volunteering

Teaching English is a good way to become involved in voluntary work, especially since learning English helps spark economic development.

Voluntary Service Overseas (VSO)

Each year VSO places around 1,870 volunteers covering a wide range of skill areas in 59 countries throughout Africa, the Pacific, the Caribbean and Eastern Europe (with East European Partnership). Volunteers are paid local salaries, but receive flights, accommodation, insurance and maybe a supplement, if the salary is considered too small to live on. Teachers are expected to have a degree, a TEFL certificate and a minimum of two years' experience. To apply you can come from any country, but you must have unrestricted right of entry to the UK or Canada and must be able to finance a trip to the UK for interviews and training. Contracts are usually for two years.
Contact: 317, Putney Bridge Road, London SW15 2PN. Tel: 44 181 780 1331. Fax: 44 181 780 1326

East European Partnership

EEP was set up by VSO to contribute to the development of Central and East European countries. There are more positions for ESP/EAP volunteers than straight EFL ones and applicants are expected to have a TEFL certificate, at least two years' teaching experience and, preferably, some specialist experience. Volunteers are paid a local salary and provided with accommodation and insurance. Posts are generally for two years.
Contact: Carlton House, 27A Carlton Drive, London SW15 2BS. Tel: 44 181 780 2841. Fax: 44 181 780 9592

Peace Corps

The Peace Corps has English language programmes in more than 70 countries and, although its presence has diminished in Central and Eastern Europe over the last five years, it still has active programmes in the Russian Republics. Placements are usually for two years and returning volunteers are well-positioned to move into state sector teaching jobs in the US while they study for Masters degrees.

Contact: 1990 K St NW, (Box 941), Washington DC. Tel: 1 202 606 3780, or 1 800 424 8580 (toll free within the US).

WorldTeach

WorldTeach is a non-profit programme within Harvard University's social service organisation, which places more than 270 volunteers in nine countries worldwide, including Costa Rica, Lithuania, South Africa, Thailand and China. Volunteers pay a fee of around $3,500 to cover insurance, air fares and support services and, once teaching, receive a local salary and accommodation. Applicants do not have to be US citizens, but they should have a BA degree and a TEFL qualification or 25 hours' TEFL experience.
Contact: Harvard Institute for International Development, 1 Eliot Street, Cambridge USA. Tel: 1 617 495 5527. Fax: 1 617 495 1599

The Project Trust

This educational charity sends over 200 British school leavers, aged 17 to 19, to projects in schools all over the world. Volunteers need to fundraise about £3,000 to help cover the cost of the project. Applicants are usually processed a year prior to departure.
Contact: St John Street, London EC1M 4AA. UK. Tel: 44 171 490 8764. Fax: 44 171 490 8759

Other Voluntary Organisations

Christians Abroad, 1 Stockwell Green, London SW9 9HP.UK. Tel: 44 171 737 7811.
Fax: 44 171 737 3237
Christian Vocations, Holloway Street West, Lower Gornal, Dudley, West Midlands DY3 2DZ. UK. Tel: 44 1902 882836.
Concern Worldwide, 248 Lavender Hill, London SW11 1LJ. UK. Tel: 44 171 738 1033.
Fax: 44 171 738 1032
Global Routes, 1814 7th Street, Suite A, Berkeley, CA, 94710 USA. Tel: 1 510 848 4800. Fax: 1 510 848 4801
ICD, Unit 3, Canonbury Yard, 190a New North Road, London N1 7BJ. UK. Tel: 44 171 354 0883. Fax: 44 171 359 0017
Teaching Abroad, 46 Beech View, Angmering, Sussex BN16 4DE. UK. Tel: 44 1903 859911. Fax: 44 1903 785779
Volunteer Service Abroad, VSA House, 31 Pipitea Street, Thorndon, Wellington, New Zealand

English is a tool. Pass it on.

TEFL opportunities overseas

Develop yourself & the people you work with.

English language is a valuable development tool. That's not just VSO's opinion. It's shared by the many countries that ask us to send them TEFL teachers. In 1999-2000 we have had requests from China, Ethiopia, Vietnam, Bangladesh, Bulgaria, Cambodia, Cameroon, Eritrea, Ghana, Guinea Bissau, Guyana, Kenya, Kiribati, Laos, Indonesia, Malawi, Maldives, Mongolia, Mozambique, Namibia, Nepal, Nigeria, Pakistan, Rwanda, Uganda and Zambia.

As the world's largest independent volunteer sending agency, we support a wide range of development initiatives. As one of our volunteers, you could be involved in projects such as upgrading language at secondary or tertiary level... or teacher training... or curriculum development... or resource centre management.

Requirements vary from placement to placement, but, at the very least, you will need a degree backed by a relevant teaching qualification. The more classroom experience you can offer the better.

We will provide return airfare, full medical cover, NI contributions, pension scheme, various training courses and grants on application. Your overseas employers will provide accommodation and a local wage.

Our main departure times are January/February, May/June and August/September, but since it takes time to process applications, don't delay. Apply now.

For further details and an application form, please contact, quoting reference EG/10. VSO Enquiries Unit, 317 Putney Bridge Road, London SW15 2PN. Tel: 020 8780 7500. Fax: 020 8780 7207. E-mail: enquiry@vso.org.uk Website: http://www.vso.org.uk Or contact your local VSO group.

Charity number 313757

International Job Prospects

Armed with a qualification and, sometimes, some teaching experience, many teachers of EFL set their sights on working abroad. The following pages give details on working conditions in more than 100 countries, along with the addresses of local schools.

European Union

Although demand has tailed off and immigration restrictions have tightened for non-EU nationals, there are still many opportunities for European Union citizens.

Under current European legislation, citizens of EU member states have the right to work in other member states who have QTS status and to be afforded the same opportunities as citizens of that state, though in practice it is difficult to get a job. The situation is more difficult for native speakers as the UK and Eire do not have state qualifications in EFL, though some state teacher training courses do include a TEFL option. It is still necessary to apply for residence visas and tax numbers but, although there can be long queues, the process is a minor headache compared with the inability to work a few years ago. Teachers who are not citizens of the Union need a work permit and because the process is often lengthy and expensive, employers are reticent to employ them.

Non-EU teachers are required to apply for work permits at home, so coming out to look for a position on spec is difficult. As traditional markets like Spain and Italy have become saturated with native speaking teachers, local employers have no need to recruit overseas. It's not surprising that teachers from North America, Australia and New Zealand tend to try their luck outside the EU in the expanding markets of Central and Eastern Europe.

Readers of European descent outside the EU should pursue the possibility of claiming residency rights on the strength of their family origins. For instance, ethnic Greeks now living in Australia will be pleased to hear that they can apply for a Greek identity card, which enables teachers to work in Greece and as an additional bonus, throughout the EU. This is also true of teachers with grandparents from Great Britain.

Western Europe is an extremely rewarding place to teach. The demand for English language learning has matured in the last five years to incorporate a lot of Business English courses and in some countries, including France and Germany, teachers will find it just as important to have commercial experience as a TEFL qualification.

Because of an abundance of teachers in major cities such as Paris, Madrid and Rome, competition is great. Teachers may find greater opportunities in smaller, provincial towns. If you do decide to work in a capital city, don't expect to get a full-time contract for the first year or two. Most teachers survive through a series of part-time contracts at various language schools and potentially highly-paid private classes. It can take a while to build up enough work to live on, so it does help to save money beforehand.

The Norwegian population voted in a referendum against joining the EU. Even so, EU citizens are allowed to work in Norway without a permit. If you are not an EU citizen then a very specialised skill, such as EAP, will help to secure a permit. High unemployment means fierce competition for jobs. In Iceland opportunities are especially scarce.

United Kingdom

English Language Teaching has been an important industry in the UK since the 1950s.

During the summer, towns like Oxford, Cambridge and Hastings are flooded with foreign students, who are studying English and living with host families. This summer demand means that there are a lot of temporary positions for teachers, who have only recently finished a certificate course or who have returned from teaching positions overseas.

However, it can be quite difficult for a newly-qualified teacher to find permanent work. The British Council recognition scheme has strict rules on staff qualifications, so recognised schools tend to prefer teachers with diplomas. Newly-qualified teachers who are keen to work in the UK often get their first job with schools outside the Council's accreditation scheme or as freelancers.

Visas and work permits: Work permits are extremely difficult for non-EU citizens to obtain. Employers must apply on behalf of teachers before they enter the country and prove that the job is not one which can be performed by an EU citizen. As a result, opportunities only exist for those with very specialist skills.

Members of the EU are entitled to work in Britain, but they must arrange a National Insurance number before starting work. Europeans cannot receive unemployment benefit while looking for work unless they have lived in Britain before. Many private schools require L1 speakers of English as teachers.

Citizens of Commonwealth countries who are 17-27 years old can come to Britain on a working holiday. They are allowed to work part-time or casually, work which includes teaching in summer schools.

Spouses of non-nationals who have work permits or who are studying full-time at a British university may work in the UK. Full-time students can work part-time, if they gain permission from the Department of Employment. Study must continue to be independently funded.

Cost of living: Expensive in London and popular tourist towns, but cheaper elsewhere.

Salaries and taxes: Rates vary considerably. Schools in Oxford and Cambridge pay well, while rates in London are relatively low. You should get around £10 per hour in the private sector and double that in the state sector or if you have a specialist skill. The basic tax rate is 23 per cent.

Accommodation: Expect to pay around £50 per week for a room in a shared house in London or the south of England. Rents rise sharply according to centrality in London, but are much cheaper in the north of England and outside the major cities. A standard deposit is one month's rent and most leases are for six or 12 months. It is possible to find nine month leases in student areas.

Health insurance: Health care is free for everybody on the National Health Service. There are long waiting lists for non-urgent operations, so private health care is becoming increasingly popular.

Newspapers: Look for teaching jobs in EL *Prospects* and EL *Gazette*, Tuesday's Guardian and the Times Education Supplement.

List of Schools in the United Kingdom

The Abbey College, Wells Road, Malvern Wells, Hereford and Worcester WR14 4JF

Aberdeen Centre For English, 66/68 Polmuir Road, Aberdeen, Scotland AB1 2TH Tel: 01224 580968 Fax: 01224 575855 Email: info@acescotland.co.uk. Contact: Mrs Pervis Reid. Teacher Refresher Courses, All Levels all year round, Exciting social and cultural programme, Friendly learning environment, IELTS test centre

Aberdeen College, Galles Gate, Aberdeen, AB9 1DN

Aberystwyth, University of Wales, Language and Learning Centre, Llandinam Building, Penglais Campus, Aberystwyth SY23 3DB

Academy English Programmes, 2A Boileau Parade, Ealing, London W5 3AQ

Academy School of English Central London, 3 Queens Gardens, Bayswater, London W2 3BA

Accent, 9 Mill Street, St. Peter Port, Guernsey, Channel Islands

Accent Courses Ltd, 30/32 Station Road, Liphook, Hampshire GU30 7DR

Accent International Language Consultancy, Bicton College, East Budleigh, Devon EX9 7BY

Alba, English in the Highlands of Scotland, PO Box 11, Kingussie, PH21 1YB

Alexanders International School, Bawdsey Manor, Bawdsey near Woodbridge, Suffolk IP12 3AZ

Amersham & Wycombe College, Spring Lane, Flackwell Heath, High Wycombe, Bucks HP10 9HZ

Anglia Polytechnic University, Cambridge Campus, East Road, Cambridge CB1 1PT

Anglian School of English, 77-83 Norfolk Road, Cliftonville, Margate, Kent CT9 2HX

Anglo-Continental, 29-35 Wimborne Rd, Bournemouth BH2 6NA

Anglo European School of English, 77 Lansdowne Road, Bournemouth BH1 1RN

Anglo European Study Tours Ltd, 8 Celbridge Mews, London W2 6EU

Anglo World Bournemouth, 130-136 Poole Road, Bournemouth BH4 9EF

Anglo World Cambridge, 75 Barton Road, Cambridge CB3 9LJ

Anglo World Central London, 3-4 Southampton Place, London WC1A 2DA

Anglo World Education (UK) Limited, Head Office, 130-136 Poole Road, Bournemouth BH4 9EF

Anglo World North London, 8 Queen's Road, Hendon, London NW4 2TH

Anglo World Oxford, 108 Banbury Road, Oxford OX2 6JU

Anglo-Continental School for Juniors, 29-35 Wimborne Road, Bournemouth BH2 6NA

Anglo-Continental School of English, 29-35 Wimborne Road, Bournemouth BH2 6NA

Anglo-Continental Vacation Centres, 29-35 Wimborne Road, Bournemouth BH2 6NA

Anglolang (Scarborough) Ltd, 20 Avenue Road, Scarborough North Yorkshire YO12 5JU

Angloschool, 146 Church Road, London SE19 2NT

Anglo World Education (UK) Ltd, Head Office, 130-136 Poole Road, Bournemouth BH4 9EF

Anniesland College, Hatfield Drive, Glasgow G12 0YE

Ardmore Language Schools, 11-15 High Street, Marlow, Buckinghamshire SL7 1AA

Armagh School of English, 13 Upper English St, Armagh BT61 7BH

Aston University, Language Studies Unit, Aston Triangle, Birmingham B4 7ET

Avon Language Centre, St Peter's Building, Dorset Close, Bath BA2 3RF

Bailbrook College, 39 London Road West, Bath BA1 7JD

Barnet College, Wood Street, Barnet, Herts EN5 4AZ Tel: 0181 440 6321 Fax: 0181 441 5236 Email: stsbys@barnet.ac.uk Website: http://www.barnet.ac.uk Full and part time general English, Business English. Easter and Summer Schools. Groups by arrangement. Cambridge EAL all level and LCCI exams

Basil Paterson Edinburgh Language Foundation, 22/23 Abercromby Place, Edinburgh EH3 6QE

Basingstoke College of Technology, Worthing Road, Basingstoke, Hants RG21 8TN

The Bath School of English, 6, Lyncombe Hill, Bath BA2 4PG

Bedford College, Enterprise House, Old Ford End Road, Queens Park, Bedford MK40 4PF

Bedford School Study Centre, 67 De Parys Avenue, Bedford MK40 2TR Tel: 44 (0) 1234 362300 Fax: 44 (0) 1234 362305 Email: bssc@bedfordschool.beds.sch.uk Director of Studies: Jonathan McKeown Prepare boys and girls (aged 11 - 17) for boarding school in the UK. English, Science, Maths and Computing. Very small classes

BEET Language Centre (also known as ALPHA Language Centre), Nortoft Road, Charminster, Bournemouth BH8 8PY

The Bell Language Schools (Headquarters), Hillcross, Red Cross Lane, Cambridge CB2 2QX Tel: 01223 212333 Fax: 01223 410282 Email: info@bell-schools.ac.uk Website: www.bell-schools.ac.uk CELTA and DELTA courses.Extensive programme of short courses for teachers and teacher trainers. Excellent on-site facilities, residential or homestay

The Bell Language School, Bath, Henley Lodge, Weston Road, Bath BA1 2XT

The Bell Language School, Cambridge, 1 Red Cross Lane, Cambridge CB2 2QX

The Bell Language School, London, 34 Fitzroy Square, London W1P 6BP

The Bell Language School, Norwich, Bowthorpe Hall, Bowthorpe, Norwich NR5 9AA

83

The Bell Language School, The Old House, Norwich, 49 Church Lane, Eaton, Norwich NR4 6NW

The Bell Language School, Saffron Walden, South Road, Saffron Walden, Essex CB11 3DP

The Bell Language Schools, Young Learners' Courses, Lancaster House, South Road, Saffron Walden, Essex CB11 3DP

Beltring Language Centre, Beltring House, Beltring, Paddock Wood, Kent, TN12

Berkshire Languages, 14-18 Rose St, Wokingham

Bidbury House for English, Bidbury Lane, Havant, Hampshire PO9 3JG

Birkbeck College, Dept of Applied Linguistics, 3 Gordon Square, London WC1H 0PD

Birmingham, University of, Centre for English Language Studies, Edgbaston, Birmingham B15 2TT

Blackburn College, Feilden Street, Blackburn, Lancs BB2 1LH

Blackpool and Fylde College, Ashfield Road, Bispham, Blackpool FY2 0HB Tel: 44 (0) 1253 352352 Fax: 44 (0) 1253 356127 Email: BMA@Blackpool.ac.uk Website: http://www.Blackpool.ac.uk Associate College of Lancaster University, Beacon College and Accredited College. Thriving EFL/ESOL department. CertTESOL (Trinity College) provider

Bolton Metropolitan College, Manchester Road, Bolton BL2 1ER

The Bournemouth & Poole College of Further Education, Lansdowne Centre, Bournemouth, Dorset BH1 3JJ

Bournemouth Business School, 4 Yelverton Road, Bournemouth BH1 1DF

Bournemouth International School, 711-713a Christchurch Road, Bournemouth BH7 6AF

Bournemouth International Language College, Royal London House, Christchurch Road, Bournemouth, Dorset BH1 3LT Tel: 01202 318269 Fax: 01202 318269 Email: efl@bilc.co.uk Website: http://www.bilc.co.uk/index.htm Full member of the Association of Language Excellence Centres. LCCIEB Registered Centre

Bracknell and Wokingham College, Montague House, Broad Street, Wokingham RG40 1AU

Bradford College, English Language Centre, Old Building, Great Horton Road, Bradford, West Yorkshire BD7 1AY Tel: 01274 753 207 Fax: 01274 741 553 Email: elc@bilk.ac.uk Website: http://www.bilk.ac.uk Contact: Nancy Hall. Well-established centre; experienced, highly qualified staff; students of over forty nationalities. Excellent pass rate, superb facilities. Value for money.

The Brasshouse Centre, 50 Sheepcote Street, Birmingham B16 8AJ

Bridge International School of English, 3 Bennett Street, Bath BA1 2QQ

Brighton College of Technology, Pelham Street, Brighton BN2 2BP

Brighton, University of (Language Centre), Falmer, Brighton, E Sussex BN1 4QG

The Bristol Centre of English, 45 Queen's Road, Clifton, Bristol BS8 1QQ

Bristol City College, (formerly Brunel College of Arts and Technology), Ashley Down Road, Bristol BS7 9BU

Bristol University, 35 Berkeley Square, Bristol BS8 1JA

British Association of Boarding School Summer Courses (BABSSCo), The Bursary, Harrow School, Harrow-on-the-Hill Middlesex HA1 3HP, UK Tel: 44 (0) 181 426 4638 Fax: 44 (0) 181 864 7180 Email: babssco@har-rowschool.org.uk Website: http://summerschool.babssco.org.uk Residential Easter and summer courses for children at top UK boarding schools such as Eton and Harrow

Bromley School of English, 2 Park Road, Bromley,Kent, BR 1 3HP

Brooklands College, Heath Road, Weybridge, Surrey KT13 8TT

Broxtowe College, High Road, Chilwell, Nottingham NG9 4AH

Buckingham University, Hunter Street, Buckingham UK, MK18 1EG Tel: 01280 820377 Fax: 01280 820391 Email: gerry.loftus@buckingham.ac.uk Website: http://www.buckingham.ac.uk Contact: Gerry Loftus. TEFL/TESOL courses; small group tuition in small, friendly town near Oxford, with safe, attractive campus.

Buckswood Grange, Uckfield, East Sussex TN22 3PU

Bury College, Teacher Education, Parliament Street, Bury BL9 0T3

Burlington School of English, 1/3 Chesilton Road, London SW6 5AA

Cambridge Academy of English, 65 High Street, Girton, Cambridge CB3 0QD

The Cambridge Centre for Languages, Sawston Hall, Cambridge CB2 4JR

The Cambridge Centre for Languages Summer Courses for Young Learners, Sawston Hall, Cambridge CB2 4JR

Cambridge Language and Activity Courses, 10 Shelford Park Avenue, Great Shelford, Cambridge CB2 5LU

The Cambridge School of English, 7-11 Stukeley Street, London WC2B 5LT

The Cambridge School of Languages, 119 Mill Road, Cambridge CB1 2AZ

Camden College of English, 61 Chalk Farm Road, London NW1 8AN

Campana International College, Moor Park House, Moor Park Lane, Farnham, Surrey GU9 8EN

Canning, Bath, 1 Brock Street, Bath BA1 2LN

Canning, London, 4 Abingdon Road, London W8 6AF

Canterbury Christ Church University College, North Holmes Road, Canterbury, Kent CT1 1QU Tel: 01227 458459 Fax: 01227 781558 Email: ipo@cant.ac.co Website: http://www.cant.ac.co Contact: Susan Rhodes-Molden. A modern University campus in the centre of historic Canterbury. Within easy reach of London and ports to mainland Europe.

Canterbury Language Training, 73 Castle Street, Canterbury, Kent CT1 2QD

Cardiff, University of, Elsis, 53 Park Place, Cardiff, Glam CF1 3AT

Carrick Language Courses, 29 Verona Avenue, Glasgow G14 9EB

Central Lancashire, University of, Dept of Languages, Preston, Lancashire PR1 2HE

Central School of English, 1 Tottenham Court Road, London W1P 9DA

Centre for Academic & Professional Development (CAPD), Roman House, 9-10 College Terrace, London E3 5AN

Centre for English Language Teaching (CELT), 3 Foster Drive, Penylan, Cardiff CF3 7BD

Centre for International Education Oxford, 5 Worcester Street, Oxford OX1 2BX

Channel School of English, Bicclescombe Park, Ilfracombe, Devon EX34 8JN

Cheltenham International Language Centre, Cheltenham and Gloucester College of Higher Education, Francis Close Hall, Swindon Road, Cheltenham, Gloucestershire GL50 4AZ

Cheltenham School of English, 87 St George's Road, Cheltenham , Gloucestershire GL50 3DU

Chichester College of Arts, Science & Technology, Westgate Fields, Chichester, West Sussex PO19 1SB

Chichester Institute of Higher Education, The Dome, Upper Bognor Road, Bognor Regis, West Sussex PO21 1HR

Chichester School of English, 44 North Street, Chichester, West Sussex PO19 1NF

Churchill House School of English, 40-42 Spencer Square, Ramsgate, Kent CT11 9LD

Cicero Languages International, 2 Upper Grosvenor Road, Tunbridge Wells, Kent TN1 2ET

City College Manchester, 141 Barlow Moor Road, West Didsbury, Manchester M20 2PQ

City of Bath College, Avon Street, Bath, Avon BA1 1VP

City of Bristol College (Faculty of Humanities), Ashley Down, Bristol BS7 9BU

Clarendon International Language Centre, Languages and International Development Directorate, 11 Queen Street, Nottingham NG1 2BL

Clark's International Summer School, 13 Friern Park, London N12 9DE

The Clock Tower English Language Centre, 218 Leicester Road, Wigston, Leicestershire LE18 1DS

Colchester English Study Centre, 19 Lexden Road, Colchester CO3 3PW

Colchester Institute, Sheepen Road, Colchester, Essex CO3 3LL Tel: 44 (0) 1206 518186 Fax: 44 (0) 1206 518186 or 763041 Email: efl@colch-inst.ac.uk Website: http://www.colch-inst.ac.uk General English to Proficiency. Higher level options including Business English and exam preparation. Accommodation and full access to college facilities

---

The College of North West London, Kilburn Centre, Priory Park Road, London NW6 7UJ

College of St Mark and St John, Derriford Road, Plymouth PL6 8BH

Concord College, Acton Burnell Hall, Shrewsbury SY5 7PF

Concorde International Study Centre, 22/24 Cheriton Gardens, Folkestone, Kent CT20 2AT

Concorde International Business Centre, Arnett House, Hawks Lane, Canterbury CT1 2NU

Concorde International Summer Schools, Arnett House, Hawks Lane, Canterbury, Kent CT1 2NU

Coventry International English Studies Centre, 9 Priory Row, Coventry CV1 5EX

Coventry Technical College English Centre, Coventry Technical College, Butts, Coventry CV1 3GD

Croydon English Language Scheme, South Norwood, CETS Center, South Norwood, Croydon SE25 4XE

Darlington College of Technology, Cleveland Avenue, Darlington, Co Durham DL3 7BB

The Devon School of English, The Old Vicarage, 1 Lower Polsham Road, Paignton, Devon TQ3 2AF

Devonish Language School, Corralea Activity Centre, Corralea, Belcoo BT93 5DZ

Direct Learning, 71 High Street, Saltford, Bath BS31 3EW

Dorset English Language Institute, Wessex House, 9-11 Gervis Place, Bournemouth BH1 2AL

Dundee College, Blackness Road, Dundee DD1 5UA

Durham Language Services, The Old Rectory, Church Lane North, Old Whittington, Chesterfield S41 9QY

Durham, University of, Dept of Linguistics & English Language, Elvet Riverside 2, New Elvet, Durham DH1 3JT

Eagle International School, Tiami House, 55 Elms Avenue, Lilliput, Poole, Dorset BH14 8EE

East Anglia, University of, School of Modern Languages and European Studies, Norwich, Norfolk NR4 7TJ

East Berkshire College, EFL Unit, Station Road, Langley SL3 8BY

Eastbourne College of Arts and Technology, Centre for Languages and Academic Studies, Grove House, Cross Levels Way, Eastbourne, Sussex BN21 2UF

Eastbourne College of Arts and Technology, St Anne's Road, Eastbourne BN21 2HS

Eastbourne School of English, 8 Trinity Trees, Eastbourne, East Sussex BN21 3LD

Eastleigh College, Chestnut Avenue, Eastleigh SO5 5HT

The East Sussex School of English, 19 Reynolds Road, Hove, East Sussex BN3 5RJ

Eaton Language Centre, York House, 32 York Road, Sale , Manchester M33 6UU

Ebury Executive English, 132 Ebury Street, London SW1W 9QQ

The Eckersley School of English, 14 Friars Entry, Oxford OX1 2BZ Tel 44 1865 721268 Fax: 44 1865 791869 Email: carolynBlackmore@eckersley.co.uk Website: http://www.eckersley.co.uk Contact: Carolyn Blackmore. For teachers of secondary and adult students who want to widen their knowledge of English and extend their teaching skills

---

ECS Scotland, 3a Eton Terrace, Edinburgh EH4 1QE

Edinburgh School of English, 271 Canongate, The Royal Mile, Edinburgh EH8 8BQ

Edinburgh, University of, Dept of Applied Linguistics, 14 Buccleuch Place, Edinburgh EH8 9LN

Edinburgh, University of, Institute for Applied Language Studies, 1 Hill Place, Edinburgh EH8 9LN

Educare College, 'Santaidd', Burnage Lane, Manchester M19 1DR

Edwards Language School, 38 The Mall, Ealing, London W5 3TJ

EFA International School, Seadown House, Farncombe Road, Worthing, West Sussex BN11 2BE

EF Executive Centre, Romsey House, 274 Mill Road, Cambridge CB1 3NG

EF International School of English, 1-2 Sussex Square, Kemptown, Brighton BN2 1FJ

EF International School of English, 221 Hills Road, Cambridge CB2 2RW

EF International School of English, 74-80 Warrior Square, St Leonards-on-Sea, Hastings, East Sussex TN37 6BP

EF International School of English, 74 Roupell Street, London SE1 8SS

The Elizabeth Johnson Organisation, West House, 19-21 West Street, Haslemere, Surrey GU27 2AE

ELS Language Centre (UK) London, 3-5 Charing Cross Road, London WC2 0HA

ELS Language Centre (UK) Summer School, 3-5 Charing Cross Road, London WC2 0HA

ELT Banbury, 49 Oxford Road, Banbury, Oxfordshire OX16 9AH

Embassy CES, London, Arbury Road, Cambridge CB4 2JF

Embassy Language and Training Centre, 5-7 Wilbury Villas, Hove, East Sussex BN3 6GB

Embassy Language and Training Centre, 7 Warrior Square, St Leonards-on-Sea, Hastings, East Sussex TN37 6BA

English and Cultural Studies Centres (ESC), 40 Village Road, Enfield, Middlesex EN1 2EN

The English Centre Eastbourne, Gordon Lodge, 25 St Anne's Road, Eastbourne, East Sussex BN21 2DJ

English Country School, Lillesden, Hastings Road, Hawkhurst, Kent TN18 4QG

English For You, 25 Wellington Square, Hastings, East Sussex TN34 1PN

English in Chester, 9-11 Stanley Place, Chester CH1 2LU

English in Exeter, 42 Longbrook Street, Exeter, Devon EX20 1QY

The English Language Centre, 33 Palmeira Mansions, Hove, East Sussex BN3 2GB

The English Language Centre Bristol, (incorporating Abon Language School), 44, Pembroke Road, Clifton, Bristol BS8 3DT

English Language and Cultural Organisation, 'Lowlands', Chorleywood Road, Rickmansworth, Hertfordshire WD3 4ES

English Language Institute, Guildford, University of Surrey, Guildford, Surrey GU2 5XM

English Language Institute, Royal Waterloo House, 51-55 Waterloo Road, London SE1 8TX

English Language in the Lakes, Nab Cottage, Rydal, Ambleside, Cumbria LA22 9SD

English Language Training, 18 Old Town, London SW4 0LB

Essential English Ltd, 124, High Street, Old Woking, Surrey GU22 9JN, Tel/Fax: 44 (0) 1483 750278 Email: pamelaparry@essenglish.demon.co.uk General and Business English, one-to-one and small groups with accommodation in teachers' comfortable homes in Surrey and Hampshire, near London.

Essex, University of, Dept of Languages & Linguistics, Wivenhoe Park, Colchester, Essex CO4 3SQ

Essex, University of, EFL Unit, Wivenhoe Park, Colchester, Essex CO4 3SQ

Eurocentre Bournemouth, 26 Dean Park Road, Bournemouth BH1 1HZ

Eurocentre Brighton, Huntingdon House, 20 North Street, Brighton BN1 1EB

Eurocentre Cambridge, 62 Bateman Street, Cambridge CB2 1LX

Eurocentre Lee Green, 21 Meadowcourt Road, Lee Green, London SE3 9EU

Eurocentre London Victoria, 56 Eccleston Square, London SW1V 1PQ

Eurocentres Summer Centres, 21 Meadowcourt Road, London SE3 9EU

Europa House Language School, 1 Imperial Avenue, Westcliffe-on-Sea, Essex SS0 8NE

European Language Studies International, Commonwealth Hall, Cartwright Gardens, London WC1H 9EB

Evendine College, 34/36 Oxford Street, London LO1N 9FL

Excel Communications Ltd, 51 Tweedy Road, Bromley, Kent BR1 3NH

Excel English Language School, North Bank House, 28 Pages Lane, London N10 1PP

Exeter Academy, 64 Sylvan Road, Exeter EX4 6HA

Exeter, University of (School of Education), University of Exeter, Heavitree Road, Exeter EX1 2LU

Exlingua International, International House, 16 Ulsterville Avenue, Belfast, Antrim BT9 7AQ

Expression International, 50 Shore Road, Tostrevor BT48 3AA

Farnborough College of Technology, Boundary Road, Farnborough, Hants GU14 6SB

Filton College, Filton Avenue, Bristol BS34 7AT

Foyle Language Centre, 73 Clarendon St, Londonderry BR48 7ER

Frances King Teacher Training Centre, 5 Grosvenor Gardens, London SW1W 0BB, Tel: 0171 630 8055. Fax: 0171 630 8077. Email: gerald@frances-king.co.uk Website: www.frances-king.co.uk Contact: Gerald Kelly. High quality training from a very experienced team. Central London location. Courses throughout the year. Post-course jobs advice given.

Frances King School of English, 195 Knightsbridge, London SW7 1RE

Frances King School of English, 18 Dunraven Street, London W1Y 3FE

Functional English, 5 Chubb Hill, Whitby, North Yorkshire YO21 1JU

Gateshead College, Durham Road, Gateshead, Tyne & Wear NE9 5BN

GEOS English Academy, 55-61 Portland Road, Hove, East Sussex BN3 5DQ

Glasgow University, Hetherington Bldg, Bute Gardens, Glasgow G12 8RS

The Globe English Centre, 1 St Davids Hill, Exeter EX4 4DA

Gloscat - The Language Unit, 73 The Park, Cheltenham, Gloucestershire GL50 2RR

Gloucestershire College of Arts and Technology, 73 The Park, Cheltenham, Gloucestershire GL50 2RR

Golders Green College, 11 Golders Green Road, London NW11 8OX

Goldsmiths College, English Dept, New Cross, London SE14 6NW

Greenhill College, (Temple House Campus), 21-225 Station Road, Harrow, Middlesex HA1 3AQ

Greenwich School of English, 259 Greenwich High Road, Greenwich, London SE10 8NB

The Greylands School of English, 315-317 Portswood Road, Southampton SO17 2LD

The Griffin Language Centre, 28 Bank Road, Matlock, Derbyshire DE4 3NF

Grove House International Language Centre, Carlton Avenue, Greenhithe, Kent DA9 9DR

Guildford College, Stoke Park, Guildford GU1 1EZ

Hamilton School of English, Capielaw, Near Rosewell, Midlothian EH24 9EE

Hammersmith and West London College, Gliddon Road, Barons Court, London W14 9BL

Hampstead Garden Suburb Institute, Central Square, London NW11 7BN

Hampstead School of English, 553 Finchley Road, London NW3 7BJ

Handsworth College, Soho Road, Handsworth, Birmingham B21 9DP

Harrogate Language Academy, 8A Royal Parade, Harrogate, North Yorkshire HG1 2SZ

Harrogate Tutorial College, 2 The Oval, Harrogate, North Yorkshire HG2 9BA

Harrow House International College, Harrow Drive, Swanage, Dorset BH19 1PE

Harrow House, London, 103 Palace Road, Hampton Court, London KT3 9DU

Hart Villages Centre, Robert Mory's School, West Street, Odiham, Basingstoke, Hampshire RG29 1NA

Harven School of English, 'The Mascot', Coley Avenue, Woking, Surrey GU22 7BT

Hastings College of Arts and Technology, Archery Road, St Leonards-on-Sea, East Sussex TN38 0HX

Hastings English Language Centre, St Helens Park Road, Hastings, East Sussex TN34 2JW

Heathfield Summer School, London Road, Ascot, Berkshire SL5 8BQ

Hendon College, Grahame Park Way, Colindale, London NW9 5RA

Henley College Coventry, Henley Road, Bell Green, Coventry CV2 1ED

Hertfordshire, University of, Wall Hall, Aldenham, Watford, Herts WD2 8AT

Highland Language Centre, 12 Marine Terrace, Rosemarkie, Ross and Cromarty IV10 8UL

Hilderstone College, St Peter's Road, Broadstairs, Kent CT10 2AQ

Home Language International, 17 Royal Crescent, Ramsgate, Kent CT11 9PE

Hopwood Hall College, St Mary's Gate, Rochdale, Lancs OL12 6RY

House of English, 24 Portland Place, Kemp Town, Brighton BN2 1DG

Huddersfield Technical College, New North Road, Huddersfield HD1 5NN

Hull College, Park Street Centre, Park Street, Hull HU2 8RR

Hull Grammar School, Cottingham Rd, Kingston Upon Hull HU5 2DL

Hull, University of, EFL Unit, University of Hull, Hull HU6 7RX

Hurtwood House, Holmbury St Mary, Near Dorking, Surrey RH5 6NU

inlingua Teacher Training, Rodney Lodge, Rodney Road, Cheltenham, Gloucestershire GL50 1JF

inlingua, Torquay, 30 Moorlane Close, Torquay TQ2 8PL

Institute of Education, University of London, 20 Bedford Way, London WC1H 0AL

Institute of International Education in London, Regent's College, Inner Circle, Regent's Park, London NW1 4NS

Interlingua Jersey, Sunnyfield, La Rocque, Grouville, Jersey JE3 9SG

Interlink School of English, 126 Richmond Park Road, Bournemouth BH8 8TH

International Community School, 4 York Terrace East, Regent's Park, London NW1 4PT

International House, 5 Trim Street, Bath BA1 1HB

International House, Folkestone, Living Language Centre, Highcliffe House, Clifton Gardens, Folkestone, Kent CT20 2EF Tel: 44 (0)1303 258 536 Fax: 44 (0)1303 851 455 e-mail: ilc@compuserve.com Website: http://www.ilcgroup.com British Council recognised. General English, Business English and summer courses. Part of ILC Group.

International Language Centres Hastings, White Rock, Hastings, East Sussex TN34 1JY

International House London, 106 Piccadilly, London W1V 9FL

International House Newcastle, 14-18 Stowell Street, Newcastle upon Tyne NE1 4XQ

International House Torquay, 13 Castle Road, Torquay TQ1 3BB

International Language Academy, Bournemouth, Hinton Chambers, Hinton Road, Bournemouth BH1 2EN

International Language Academy, Cambridge, 12-13 Regent Terrace, Cambridge CB2 1AA

International Language Academy, Edinburgh, 11 Great Stuart Street, Edinburgh EH3 7TS

International Language Academy, London, 4 Russell Gardens, London W14 8EY

International Language Academy, Oxford, 7 Norham Gardens, Oxford OX2 6PS

International Language Academy, Torquay, Castle Circus, Union Street, Torquay TQ1 3DE

International Language Centre, Calderdale College, Francis Street, Halifax, West Yorkshire HX1 3UZ

International Language Centres, White Rock, Hastings, East Sussex TN34 1JY

International Language Holidays, 19 Lexden Road, Colchester CO3 3PW

International Language Institute, Country House, Vicar Lane, Leeds LS1 7JH

i to i International Projects Ltd, One Cottage Road, Headingley, Leeds LS6 4DD

The International School, 1 Mount Radford Crescent, Exeter EX2 4EW

International Teaching and Training Centre, 674 Wimborne Road, Winton, Bournemouth BH9 2EG

International Training Network, Exchange Buildings, Upper Hinton Road, Bournemouth, Dorset BH1 2HH

InterNexus Centre for Language Studies Ltd, Regent's College, Inner Circle, Regent's Park, London NW1 4NS

InTuition Languages, International House, 106 Piccadilly, London W1V 9FL

Irwin College, 164 London Road, Leicester LE2 1ND

The Isca School of English, PO Box 15, 4 Mount Radford Crescent, Exeter EX2 4JN

ISI Language Courses Limited, Belgrave House, 2 Winner Street, Paignton, Devon TQ3 3BJ

ITC Intensive TEFL Courses, Jabel House, Hurworth, Co. Durham DL2 2AJ Tel: 01325 721066 Fax: 01325 720766 Email: tefl@compuserve.com T.E.F.L. practical 20 hour weekend courses held in cities throughout England & Scotland for basic TEFL qualification with optional follow-up course for further certificate

ITS English School, 43-45 Cambridge Gardens, Hastings, East Sussex TN34 1EN

Joseph Priestley College, Alec Beevers Centre, Off Burton Avenue, Leeds LS11 5ER

Kensington and Chelsea College, Marlborough Centre, Sloane Avenue, London SW3 3AP

Kent School of English, 3 Granville Road, Broadstairs, Kent CT10 1QD

Kent University, School of European Culture and Languages, Cornwallis Bldg, Canterbury, Kent CT2 7NF

Kettley Institute of Language Teaching, 57 Spottiswoode Rd, Edinburgh, EH9 1DA

King's College of Further Education, 31 Poole Road, Bournemouth BH4 9DL

King's College London, English Language Centre, Strand Campus, Strand, London WC2R 2LS Tel: 0171 848 1844 Fax: 0171 836 1799 Email: elc@kcl.ac.uk Website: http://www.kcl.ac.uk/kis/schools/hums/ELU/top.html Cambridge/RSA DELTA courses and a Masters in ELT & Applied Linguistics with a fast-track for those who have DTEFLA/DELTA.

King's St Joseph's Hall Oxford, Junction Road, Cowley, Oxford OX4 2UJ

King's Junior School, 282 Iford Lane, Tuckton, Bournemouth BH6 5NQ

King's School of English, London, 25 Beckenham Road, Beckenham, Kent BR3 4PR

King's School of English, 58 Braidley Road, Bournemouth BH2 6LD

Kingsway College, Regents Park Centre, Longford Street, London NW1 3HB

Kingsway College, Vernon Square Centre, Penton Rise, London WC1X 9EL

Kingsway English Centre, Northwall House, 11 The Butts, Worcester WR1 3PA

Lake School of English, 14 Park End Street, Oxford OX1 1HW

Lancaster University, Dept Linguistics Modern English Language, Bowland College, Lancaster LA1 4YT

Lancaster University, Institute for English Language Education, George Fox Building, Lancaster LA1 4YJ

Langside College Glasgow, Prospecthill Road, Glasgow, Strathclyde G42 9LB

Language Link, 181 Earls Court Road, London SW5 9RB

Language-Link Limited, 21 Harrington Road, South Kensington, London SW7 3EU

The Language Project, 78-80 Colston Street, Bristol BS1 5BB

Language Specialists International, Elizabeth House, 13-19 Guildhall Walk, Portsmouth PO1 2RY

Language Studies International, 41 Tenison Road, Cambridge CB1 2DG

Language Studies International, Heath House, 13 Lyndhurst Terrace, London NW3 5QA

Language Studies International, 13 Ventnor Villas, Hove, East Sussex BN3 3DD

Languages Training and Development, 116 Corn Street, Witney, Oxon OX8 7BU

Leeds Metropolitan University, Centre for Language Study, Beckett Park Campus, Leeds LS6 3QS Tel: 44 113 283 7440 Fax: 44 113 2745 966 Email: cls@lmu.ac.uk Website: http://www.lmu.ac.uk/cls Full range of EFL and teacher development courses from beginner to masters level; short and long term courses. University campus.

Leeds, University of, School of Education, Leeds LS2 9JT

Leicester Square School of English, 22 Wardour Street, London W1V 3HH

Leicester, University of, School of Education, 21 University Road, Leicester LE1 7RF Tel: 44 (0) 116 252 5782 (24 hrs) Fax: 44 (0) 116 252 3653 Email: hw8@lc.ac.uk Website: www.le.ac.uk/education MA Applied Linguistics & TESOL Full Time, Part Time or Distance Learning

Lewes Tertiary College, Mountfield Road, Lewes, East Sussex BN7 2XH

Lewis School of English, 33 Palmerston Road, Southampton SO14 1LL

Lewisham College, Lewisham Way, London SE4 1UT

Linguarama, Oceanic House, 89 High Street, Alton, Hampshire GU34 1LG Tel: 44 (0) 1420 80899 Fax: 44 (0) 1420 80856 Email: personnel@linguarama.com Website: http://www.linguarama.com Contact: Daniel Coughlan. Over forty centres around Europe specialising in language training for business. Career opportunities available for new and experienced teachers.

Linguarama London - City, Head Office, Queen's House, 8 Queen Street, London EC4N 1SP Tel: (0) 171 236 1992 Fax: (0) 171 236 7206 email: london@linguarama.com

Linguarama London - West End, 37 Golden Square, London W1R 3AA Tel: (0) 171 434 9261 Fax: (0) 171 734 0938 email: londonwestend@linguarama.com

Linguarama Alton, Oceanic House, 89, High Street, Alton, Hants GU34 1LG Tel: (0) 1420 80899 Fax: (0) 1420 80856 email: alton@linguarama.com

Linguarama Birmingham, New Oxford House, 16 Waterloo Street, Birmingham B2 5UG Tel: (0) 121 632 5925 Fax: (0) 121 643 9295 email: birmingham@linguarama.com

Linguarama Ditteridge, Box, Corsham, Wiltshire SN13 8QF Tel: (0) 1225 743557 Fax: (0) 1225 743916 email: cheney-court@linguarama.com

Linguarama Manchester, 28-32 Princess Street, Manchester M1 4LB Tel: (0) 161 228 3983 Fax: (0) 161 236 9833 email: manchester@linguarama.com

Linguarama Stratford-upon-Avon, 1 Elm Court, Arden Street, Stratford-upon-Avon, Warwickshire CV37 6PA Tel: (0) 1789 296535 Fax: (0) 1789 266462 email: stratford@linguarama.com

Liverpool Community College, Aulis House, Riversdale Centre, Riversdale Road, Liverpool L19 3QR

Liverpool Hope University, Hope Park, Liverpool L16 9JD

Liverpool, University of, Applied English Language Studies Unit, English Dept, Liverpool L69 3BX

Living English, New Oak House, Stevenage Road, Little Wymondley, Herts SG4 7JA

London Guildhall University, English Language Centre, Old Castle Street, London E1 7NT

London House School of English, 51 Sea Road, Westgate-on-Sea, Kent CT8 8QL

London Meridian College, 67-83 Seven Sisters Road, London N7 6BU

The London School of English, 15 Holland Park Gardens, London W14 8DZ

London Study Centre, Munster House, 676 Fulham Road, London SW6 5SA

Loughborough College, Radmoor Road, Loughborough, Leicestershire LE11 3BT

LTC International College, Compton Park, Compton Place Road, Eastbourne, East Sussex BN21 1EH

LTS Training and Consulting, 5 Belvedere, Lansdowne Road, Bath BA1 5ED

Luton, University of, Dept of Linguistics, Vicarage Street, Luton, Bedfordshire LU1 3AJ

Lydbury English Centre, The Old Vicarage, Lydbury North, Shropshire SY7 8AU

Making Training Work, 26, Links Yard, Spelman Street, London

MLS International College, 8/9 Verulam Place, Bournemouth , Dorset BH1 1DW

ManCAT (Manchester College of Arts and Technology), EFL Unit, The John Unsworth Building, Lower Hardman Street, Manchester M3 3ER

Manchester Academy of English, St. Margaret's Chambers, 5 Newton Street, Manchester M1 1HL Tel: 0161 237 5619 Fax: 0161 237 9016 E-mail: english@manacad.co.uk Website: http://www.manacad.co.uk City centre language school, British Council accredited, offering 4 week intensive courses all year leading to Trinity Certificate in TESOL.

Manchester College of Arts & Technology, Dept of Language Studies, Hardman Street, Manchester M3 3ER

Manchester Language School, Moor Cottage, Grange Lane, Didsbury, Manchester M20 6RW Tel: 0044 161 448 8372 Fax: 0044 161 448 9343 Email: mls@isite.co.uk Website: http://www.isite.co.uk/mls Contact: Bill Godfrey. Business English, General English, Teacher Training and adult language plus programmes: Revolution, Literary Landscapes & English Garden Tours.

Manchester, University of, Centre for English Language Studies in Education, School of Education, Oxford Road, Manchester M13 9PL

Marble Arch Intensive English, 21 Star Street, London W2 1QB

Margate Language Centre, 38 Hawley Square, Margate, Kent

Marymount International School, George Road, Kingston-Upon-Thames, Surrey KT2 7PE

Mayfair School of English, 45 Oxford Street, London W1R 1RD

Mayfield Academy of English, 24 Holland Road, Hove, East Sussex BN3 1JJ

Mayfield College of English, 24 Holland Road, Hove, East Sussex BN3 1JJ

Mayflower College of English, 36 Pier Street, The Hoe, Plymouth PL1 3BT

Meads School of English, 2 Old Orchard Road, Eastbourne, East Sussex BN21 1DB

Melton College, 137 Holgate Road, York YO2 4DH

Mercator Language School, 31 High Cross Street, St Austell, Cornwall PL25 4AN

Meridian School of English, 9 Yarborough Road, Southsea, Hampshire PO5 3DZ

Merrion House Centre for English Studies, 60 Penn Road, Beaconsfield, Buckinghamshire HP9 2LS

Middlesborough College, Kirby Campus, Roman Road, Middlesborough, Cleveland TS5 5PJ

Middlesex University (Tottenham), White Hart Lane, London N17 8HR

Mid Kent College, Oakwood Park, Tonbridge Road, Maidstone, Kent ME16 8AQ

Millfield English Language School, Millfield School, Street, Somerset BA16 0YD

Milner School of English, 32 Worple Road Mews, Wimbledon, London SW19 4DB

MM Oxford Study Services Ltd, 44 Blenheim Drive, Oxford OX2 8DQ

Moray House College of Education (The English Language Centre), Holyrood Road, Edinburgh, East Lothian EH8 8AQ

Multi Lingua, Abbot House, Sydenham Road, Guildford, Surrey GU1 3RL Tel: 01483 535118 Fax: 01483 534777 Email: mail@multi-ligua.co.uk Websit: http://www.multi-lingua.co.uk Multi Lingua is an international language services organisation. The teacher training division offers TEFL courses at Preparatory, Certificate, Business and Diploma levels. Job placement service.

Nene - University College, Northampton, English Dept, Moulton Park, Northampton NN1 7AL

Netherhall International College, 18b Netherhall Gardens, Hampstead, London NW3 5TH

The New School of English, 52 Bateman Street, Cambridge CB2 1LR

Newcastle College, Rye Hill Campus, Scotswood Road, Newcastle upon Tyne NE4 7SA

Newcastle Upon Tyne, University of, Language Centre, Newcastle upon Tyne NE1 7RU

Newnham Language Centre, 8 Grange Road, Cambridge CB3 9DU

Nord Anglia International Ltd, 10 Eden Place, Cheadle, Cheshire SK8 1AT

Northampton College, Military Road, Northampton NN1 3ET

Northbrook College, Modern Language Centre, Littlehampton Road, Goring by Sea, West Sussex BN12 6NU

North East Surrey College of Technology, Reigate Road, Epsom, Surrey KT17 3DS

North London, University of, 166-22 Holloway Road, London N7 8DB

North Trafford College, Talbot Road, Stretford, Manchester M320XH

Northumbria House, Churchill Business Centre, 12 Mosley Street, Newcastle-upon-Tyne NH1 1DH

Northumbria University, School of Modern Languages, Lipman Building, 21 Ellison Place, Newcastle Upon Tyne NE1 8ST

Norwich Institute for Language Education (NILE), PO Box 2000, Norwich, Norfolk NR2 1LE

Nottingham, University of, Oaklands College, St Albans City Campus, St Peters Road, St Albans, Hertfordshire AL1 3RX

Nottingham Trent University, Nottingham Language Centre, Burton Street, Nottingham NG1 4BU Tel: 44 (0) 115 948 6526 Fax: 44 (0) 115 948 6513 Email: nlc@ntu.ac.uk Website: http://www.nlc.ntc.ac.uk/nlc.html Contact: Gillian Nanson. British Council recognised. English for Academic Purposes, General English, Courses for Teachers (CEELT, CELTA, DELTA and MA) and summer courses.

NOVA Group UK, Carrington House, 126/130 Regent Street, London W1R 5FE

Oaklands College EFL/TESOL St Albans City Campus, St Peters Road, St. Albans AL1 3RX Tel: 01727 737000 Fax: 01727 737273 Email: EFL@oaklands.ac.uk British Council recognised. General English, English Plus, Summer courses and teacher training. 30 minutes from Central London

Oliver English Language School, 50-52 Norfolk Square, Brighton, East Sussex BN1 2PA

The Oxford Academy, 18 Bardwell Road, Oxford OX2 6SP

Oxford Brookes University, International Centre for English Language Studies, Gipsy Lane Campus, Headington, Oxford OX3 0PB

Oxford College of Further Education, Oxpens Road, Oxford OX1 1SA

The Oxford English Centre, (Formerly UTS Oxford Centre), Wolsey Hall, 66 Banbury Road, Oxford OX2 6PR

Oxford House College, 3 Oxford Street, London W1R 1RF

Oxford House School of English, 67 High Street, Wheatley, Oxford OX33 1XT

Oxford Intensive School of English, Youth Language Schools, OISE House, Binsey Lane, Oxford OX2 0EY

Oxford Intensive School of English, Bristol, 1 Lower Park Row, Bristol BS1 5BJ

Oxford Language Training, 9 Blue Boar Street, Oxford OX1 4EZ

Oxford Study Centre, 17 Sunderland Avenue, Oxford OX2 8DT

Padworth College, Padworth, Near Reading, Berkshire RG7 4NR

Park Lane College, Park Lane, Leeds LS3 1AA

The Park Language Centre, 2nd Floor, 141 West Street, Sheffield S1 4ES

Parkland International, Leighton Park, Reading , Berkshire RG2 7DH

Passport Language Schools, 37 Park Road, Bromley BR1 3HJ

Perth College, Language School, Faculty of Arts, Chieff Road, Perth PH1 2NX

Peterboroough Regional College, Park Crescent, Peterborough PE1 4DZ

Pilgrims Ltd, Pilgrims House, Orchard Street, Canterbury, Kent CT2 8AP

Plymouth College of FE, Goschen Centre, Saltash Road, Plymouth, Devon PL2 2BD

Polyglot Language Centre, 214 Trinity Road, London SW17 7HP

Portsmouth, University of (Language Centre), Park Building, King Henry I Street, Portsmouth, Hampshire PO1 2DZ

Princes College, School of English and Computer Studies, 217-218 Tottenham Court Road, London W1P 9AF

Queen Mary and Westfield College, Learning Development and Continuing Education, Mile End Road, London E1 4NS

Queen's College, Trull Road, Taunton, Somerset TA1 4QS

Queen's College Junior School, Trull Road, Taunton, Somerset TA1 4QR

Queen's University of Belfast, TEFL Centre, University Road, Belfast, County Down BT7 1NN, Northern Ireland

Reading University (CALS), Whiteknights, P O Box 241, Reading, Berkshire RG6 6WB

The Regency School of English, Royal Crescent, Ramsgate, Kent CT11 9PE

Regent Brighton, 18 Cromwell Road, Hove, East Sussex BN3 3EW

Regent Capital Executive Centre, 12 Buckingham Street, London WC2N 6DF

Regent Edinburgh, 29 Chester Street, Edinburgh EH3 7EN

Regent Fitzroy, (formerly Fitzroy College), Northdown House, Margate, Kent CT9 3TP

Regent Language Holidays, 12-14 Buckingham Street, London WC2N 6DF

Regent London, 12 Buckingham Street, London WC2N 6DF

Regent Oxford, 90 Banbury Road, Oxford OX2 6JT

Regent Park House, Hyssington, Montgomery, Powys SY15 6DZ

Regent Summer Schools, 14 Buckingham Street, London WC2N 6DF

Richard Language College, 43-45 Wimborne Road, Bournemouth BH3 7AB

Richmond Adult and Community College, Burney, Clifden Road, Twickenham TW1 4LT

Richmond Upon Thames Tertiary College, Egerton Road, Twickenham TW2 7SJ

St Andrews Tutorial Services Ltd, 2A Free School Lane, Cambridge CB2 3QA

St Andrews, University of, Butts Wynd, St Andrews, Fife KY16 9AL

St Bede's School, The Dicker, Hailsham, East Sussex BN27 3QH

St Bede's Summer School, The Dicker, Hailsham, East Sussex BN27 3QH

St Bede's Preparatory School, Duke's Drive, Eastbourne, East Sussex BN20 7XL

St Brelade's College, Mont Les Vaux, St Aubin, Jersey, Channel Islands JE3 8AF

St Clare's, Oxford, 139 Banbury Road, Oxford OX2 7AL

St Edmund's College, Old Hall Green, near Ware, Hertfordshire SG11 1DS

St George International, English Language Centre, Language House, 76 Mortimer Street, London W1N 7DE

St Giles College, Regency House, 3 Marlborough Place, Brighton BN1 1UB

St Giles College, 13 Silverdale Road, Eastbourne, East Sussex BN20 7AJ

St Giles College, 51 Shepherds Hill, Highgate, London N6 5QP

St Giles College, London Central, 154 Southampton Row, Bloomsbury, London WC1B 5AX

St Hilary School of English, 2 & 4 Midvale Road, Paignton, Devon TQ4 5BD

St John's Wood School of English, 126 Boundary Road, London NW8 0RH

St Mary's University College, Dept. of Language & Literature, Strawberry Hill, Twickenham TW1 4SX

St Michael's College, Oldwood Road, St Michael's, Tenbury Wells, Worcestershire WR15 8PH

St Patrick's International School, 24 Great Chapel Street, London W1V 3AF

St Peter's School of English, 4 St Alphege Lane, Canterbury, Kent CT1 2EB

Salford, University of, International Institute, University of Salford, The Crescent, Salford, Manchester M5 4WT

Salisbury College, Southampton Road, Salisbury, Wiltshire SP1 2LW

Salisbury School of English, 36 Fowlers Road, Salisbury, Wiltshire SP1 2QU

Sandwell College, Crocketts Lane, Smethwick, West Midlands B66 3BU

Saxoncourt Teaching Training, 59 South Molton Street, London W1Y 1HH

Scanbrit School of English, 22 Church Road, Bournemouth BH6 4AT

Scarborough College, Filey Road, Scarborough YO11 3BA

Scarborough International School, 'Cheswold Hall', 37 Stepney Road, Scarborough, North Yorkshire YO12 5BN

School of English Studies Folkestone, 26 Grimston Gardens, Folkestone, Kent CT20 2PX

School of Oriental and African Studies, English Language Unit, 4 Gower Street, London WC1E 6HA

Scot-Ed Courses, 6 Blinkbonny Gardens, Edinburgh EH4 3HG

Select English, 2 Kings Grove Barton, Cambridge

Selly Oak College, Birmingham B29 6LQ

Sels College, 64 Long Acre, Covent Garden, London WC2E 9JH

Severnvale Academy, 25 Claremont Hill, Shrewsbury, Shropshire SY1 1RD

Shane English School, 59 South Molton Street, London W1Y 1HH

Shane English School, 5 Cambridge Terrace, Oxford OX1 1UP

Shane Junior Vacation Courses, 59 South Molton Street, London W1Y 1HH

Sheffield College, Granville Road, Sheffield, South Yorkshire S2 2RL

Sheffield Hallam University, University TESOL Centre, Collegiate Campus, Sheffield S10 2BP

Sheffield, University of, Dept of English Language & Linguistics, 5 Shearwood Road, Sheffield, South Yorkshire S10 2TD

Sidmouth International School, May Cottage, May Terrace, Sidmouth, Devon EX10 8EN

Skola Teacher Training, 21 Star Street, London W2 1QB

SLS/English in York, 38-40 Coney Street, York YO1 1ND

Solent Language Centre, 54 The Avenue, Southampton SO1 2SY

Southampton, University of, Faculty of Educational Studies, Highfield, Southampton, Hampshire SO17 1BJ

Southbourne School of English, 30 Beaufort Road, Bournemouth BH6 5AL

South Chelsea College, 4 Tunstall Road, London SW9 8BZ Tel: 44 (0)171 738 4660 Fax: 44 (0) 171 738 4750 e-mail: southchelseacollege@btinternet.com Contact: Mrs Tina Kinsella, Principal. ABLS recognised University of Cambridge English Examinations. Classes: Beginner to Advanced/Proficiency + Summer Courses. Friendly college. Modern, attractive premises. Qualified Teachers

South Devon College, The Language Centre, Newton Road, Torquay, Devon TQ2 5BY

South East Essex College, Carnarvon Road, Southend on Sea, Essex SS2 6LS

South Thames College, 50-52 Putney Hill, London SW15 6QX Tel: 020 8918 7305/7354 Fax: 020 8918 7347 Email: Student Services@south-thames.ac.uk Strong emphasis on language awareness. Enthusiastic student volunteers. Excellent FEFC Inspector's report. Good networking among former students. Part-time/Full-time Courses.

South Trafford College, EFL Section, Manchester Road, West Timperley, Altrincham, WA14 5PQ

Southgate College, EFL Unit, EFL/ESOL School, High Street, London N14 6BS

Southwark College, EFL Section, Waterloo Centre, The Cut, London SG1 8LE

Stafford House School of English, 68 New Dover Road, Canterbury, Kent CT1 3EQ

Stafford House Study Holidays, 68 New Dover Road, Canterbury CT1 3EQ

Stanton School of English, Teacher Training Courses, 167 Queensway, London W2 4SB

Stevenson College, Bankhead Avenue, Sighthill, Edinburgh EH11 4DE

Stirling, University of, Centre for English Language Teaching, Stirling, Central Scotland FK9 4LA

Stockport College of Further & Higher Education (ESL Section), Wellington Road South, Stockport SK1 3UQ

Stoke-on-Trent College, Stoke Road, Shelton, Stoke-on-Trent, Staffordshire ST4 2DG

Strathclyde, University of, English Language Teaching Division, Jordanhill Campus, Southbrae Drive, Glasgow G13 1PP

The Stratford-upon-Avon School of English Studies, 8-9 Tiddington Road, Stratford-upon-Avon, Warwickshire CV37 7AE

Students International Limited, 158 Dalby Road, Melton Mowbray, Leicestershire LE13 0BJ

Studio School of English, 6 Salisbury Villas, Station Road, Cambridge CB1 2JF

SuperStudy UK, 1-3 Manor Parade, Sheepcote Road, Harrow HA1 2JN

Surrey Adult Education Service - Elmbridge Area, Esher Green Centre, 19 Esher Green Esher, Surrey KT10 8AA

Surrey Language Centre, 39 West Street, Farnham, Surrey GU9 7DR

Surrey, University of, English Language Institute, Guildford, Surrey GU2 5XH Tel:01483 259910 Fax: 01483 259507 Email: efl@surrey.ac.uk Website: www.surrey.ac.uk/ELI/eli.html Contact: Tammy Hughes Distance Learning Postgraduate Degrees for EFL Teaches. Year round English Language courss. IELTS teaching centre. Business English. English Language Consultancy

---

Sussex, University of, The Language Centre, Falmer, Brighton BN1 9QN Tel: 01273 678006 Fax: 01273 678476 EMail: R.De-Witt@sussex.ac.uk Website: www.sussex.ac.uk/Lange/ General/academic/specialist/ BALEAP-accredited pre-sessional courses; Introduction to TEFL/TCL Cert. TESOL/Refresher/MA; Summer School; South Coast location

Suzanne Sparrow Plymouth Language School, 72-74 North Road East, Plymouth PL4 6AL

Swan School of English, 111 Banbury Road, Oxford OX2 6JX

Swandean School of English, 12 Stoke Abbott Road, Worthing, West Sussex BN11 1HE

Swandean School of English, 2nd Floor, Broadway House, 112/134 The Broadway, Wimbledon, London SW19 1RL

Swansea, University of, English Language Institute, Singleton Park, Swansea SA2 899

Tara Language Services (TLS), 145 Lowry Park, Limavady, Co Londonderry BT49 0NX

TEFL Training, Freepost, Stonesfield, Witney, Oxford OX8 8BR

Thames Valley Cultural Centres, 15 Park Street, Windsor, Berkshire SL4 1LU

Thames Valley University, Grove House, 1 The Grove, Ealing, London W5 5AA

the really useful english company, Rushton Court, 16 Rushton Crescent, Bournemouth, Dorset BH3 7AF

Thurrock College, Woodview, Grays, Essex RM16 4YR

Torbay Language Centre, Conway Road, Paignton, Devon TQ4 5LH Telephone (01803) 558555

Torquay International School, 15 St Marychurch Road, Torquay TQ1 3HY Telephone (01803) 295576/298854

Totnes School of English, Gate House, 2 High Street, Totnes, Devon TQ9 5RZ Telephone (01803) 865722

Training Link International, 21 Wessex Gardens, Dore, Sheffield S17 3PQ

The Trebinshun Group, Trebinshun House, Near Brecon, Powys LD3 7PX

Tresham Institute of Further and Higher Education, St Mary's Road, Kettering, Northants NN15 7BS

Trinity College English Language Centre, Trinity College, Stoke Hill, Stoke Bishop, Bristol BS9 1JP

Trythall English Language Centre, The Duchess of Albany Building, Ox Row, Salisbury SP1 1EU

Ulster, University of, Coleraine, Northern Ireland BT52 1SA

Universal Language Training, Woking College, Woking.

Universal Language Training, The Old Forge, Oakham Lane, Oakham, Surrey GU23 6NP

University of Brighton, The Language Centre, Falmer, Brighton BN1 9PH

University of East Anglia, School of Education and Professional Development, Norwich NR4 7TJ Tel: 44 (0) 1603 592855 Fax: 44 (0) 1603 593446 Email: e.chapman@iea.ac.uk Website: http://www.uea.ac.uk/edu MA in Professional Development for ELT Practitioners. Full-time/Part-time/Distance learning

---

University of Luton, 75 Castle Street, Luton, Bedfordshire LU1 3AJ

University of Manchester, EFL Section, Oxford Road, Manchester M13 9PL

University of Portsmouth, The Language Centre, Park Building, King Henry I Street, Portsmouth PO1 2DZ

University of Sussex, The Language Centre, Falmer, Brighton, Sussex BN1 9QH Tel: 01273 678006 Fax: 01273 678476 Email: R.De-Witt@sussex.ac.uk Website: www.sussex.ac.uk/lange Contact: Raymond de Witt. General/academic/specialist/BALEAP-accredited. Pre-sessional courses; Introduction to TEFL/TCL Cert. TESOL/Refresher/MA; Summer School; South Coast location

---

University of Ulster, Centre for English Language Teaching, Coleraine, Co Derry, Northern Ireland BT52 1SA

University of York, EFL Unit, Language Training Centre, Heslington, York YO10 5DD Tel: 44 (0) 1904 432480 Fax: 44 (0) 1904 432 481 Email: efl2@york.ac.uk Website: http://www.york.ac.uk/inst/ltc/efl/mateyl.htm A distance MA in Teaching English to Young Learnes. A unique MA catering for this specialist area of EFL.

University College Chichester, The Dome, Upper Bognor Road, Bognor Regis, West Sussex PO21 1HR

University College London, UCL Language Centre, 136 Gower Street, London WC1E 6BT

University College of Ripon and York St John, Lord Mayor's Walk, York YO3 7EX

University College of St Mark and St John, Derriford Road, Plymouth PL6 8BH

Vacational Studies, Pepys' Oak, Tydehams, Newbury, Berkshire RG14 6JT

Victoria School of English, 28 Graham Terrace, Sloane Square, London SW1W 8JH

Wales, University of (Bangor), Dept of Linguistics, School of English & Linguistics), Bangor, Gwynedd, Wales LL29 7ED

Wales, University of (Cardiff), Cardiff, Wales

Wales, University of (Swansea), Centre for Applied Language Studies, Singleton Park, Swansea

Waltham Forest College, Forest Road, London E17 4JB

Warwickshire College, Warwick New Road, Leamington Spa, Warwickshire CV32 5JE

Warwick, University of (CELTE), Coventry CV4 7AL

Wessex Academy School of English, 84-86 Bournemouth Road, Parkstone, Poole, Dorset BH14 0HA

Westbourne Academy, 31 Alumhurse Road, Westbourne, Bournemouth BH4 8EN

West Cheshire College, The International Study Centre, Eaton Road, Handbridge, Chester CH4 7ER

West Kent College, Brook Street, Tonbridge TN9 2PW

Westminster College School of Languages, Peter Street (near Piccadilly Circus), London W1V 4HS Tel: 44 (0) 171 436 8536 Fax: 44 (0) 171 287 0711 Email: barabara_worms@westminster-cfe.ac.uk Website: www.westminster-cfe.ac.uk Two central London sites. General and vocational English Teacher training. Summer school. British Council recognised. Full social programme. Excellent facilities.

Westminster College, School of Languages, Castle Lane, London SW1E 6DR

Westminster, University of, 9-18 Euston Centre, London NW1 3ET

West of England University of, Coldharbour Lane, Bristol BS16 IQY

The West Sussex School of English, 7 High Street, Steyning, West Sussex BN44 3GG

Wigan & Leigh College, P O Box 53, Parsons Walk, Wigan WN1 1RS

Wigston College of Further Education, Station Road, Wigston Magna, Leicestershire LE8 2DW Telephone 0116-288 5051

Wimbledon School of English, 41 Worple Road, Wimbledon, London SW19 4JZ

Winchester School of English, Beaufort House, 49 Hyde Street, Winchester, Hampshire SO23 7DX

Windsor English Language Centre, 51 Albany Road, Windsor, Berkshire SL4 1HL

Windsor English Studies, 89 Arthur Rd, Windsor, Berkshire SL4 1RU

Windsor Schools TEFL, 21 Osborne Road, Windsor, Berkshire SL4 3EG

Wirral Metropolitan College, The English Language Unit, IBMC, Europa Boulevard, Conway Park, Birkenhead, Merseyside L41 4NT

Wolverhampton, University of, Stafford Street, Wolverhampton, West Midlands WV1 1SB

Woolwich College, Villas Road, London SE 18 7PN

YES Educational Centre, 12 Eversfield Road, Eastbourne, East Sussex BN21 2AS

Young English Studies (SKOLA), 21 Star Street, London W2 1QB

Young English Studies (SKOLA), 4 York Terrace East, Regents Park, London NW1 4PT

Youth Service Schools/EuroAccents, 16/20 New Broadway, Ealing, London W5 2XA

Ireland

Work in Ireland is very seasonal, with the vast majority of students coming to Dublin in July and August. Schools usually cope with this by having a skeleton staff of experienced teachers working all year-round and then hiring large numbers of additional teachers for two to four months.

Summer work in Ireland is extremely popular with Irish teachers on short contracts overseas. Large numbers of British and American teachers apply for summer school work but, without a mailing address in Ireland, you should expect to go to the bottom of the pile. Schools are unlikely to hire somebody they haven't interviewed and they also realise that students coming to Ireland expect to be taught by Irish teachers.

With such a large number of highly qualified teachers looking for work in Dublin during the summer, unqualified teachers will find work hard to come by. Indeed, unqualified teachers will not find work in recognised schools. There has been some decentralisation of the industry recently, though, and the number of schools in tourist towns, such as Cork, Kerr, Limerick and Galway, has increased dramatically.

Visas and work permits: UK citizens do not need a work permit. For other nationalities, employers must arrange permits, convincing the authorities that no Irish citizen is qualified to do the job.

Cost of living: Many visitors are surprised at how expensive Ireland is. Expect standard West European prices. A two-bedroom flat will cost £600 a month, more in Dublin.

Salaries and taxes: A good hourly wage during the summer would be Ir£12-14, but many schools pay less. An average teacher's salary Ir£17.000-18.000 p.a. The basic tax rate is about 24 per cent.

Accommodation: Short-term accommodation is primarily targeted at business visitors, so it can be expensive.

List of Irish Schools
The Academy of English Studies, 33 Dawson Street, Dublin 2

Achill School of English, School Rd, Dooagh, Achill Island, Co Mayo

Aisling Ireland, 137 Lower Rathmines Road, Dublin 6

Allihies Language Centre, 6 Rue Arthur Rozier, 75019 Paris, France

Alpha College of English, 4 North Great George's Street, Dublin 1

American College Dublin, 2 Merrion Square, Dublin 2

Applied Language Centre, Daedalus Building, University College Dublin, Belfield, Dublin 4

Barkley Language School, 366 Sundays Well, Naas, Co Kildare

Berlitz Language and Technology Centre, 15-16 Georges Place, Dun Laoghaire, Co Dublin Tel: 353 1 202 1200 Fax: 353 1 202 1299 Email: lingua@berlitz.ie Website www.berlitz.ie Wide range of courses to suit all needs. Homestay accommodation arranged

Bluefeather School of Languages, Montpelier House, 35 Montpelier Parade, Monkstown, Co Dublin

Bray Language Centre, 23 Rectory Slopes, Herbert Rd, Bray, Co Wicklow

The Bristow School of English, Strand House, Fairview Strand, Dublin 3

Brook House School, Brook House, Herbert Rd, Bray, Co Wicklow

Butler School of Languages, Monument Cross, Shannon, Co Clare

Carraig Linguistic Services, Abbey House, 4 North Abbey Street, North Mall, Cork

CELT Ltd, 16 Longford Terrace, Monkstown, Co Dublin

Centre of English Studies, 31 Dame Street, Dublin 2

Clare Language Centre Ltd, Market Street, Corofin, Co Clare

Connemara Language & Activity Centre, Roundstone, Connemara, Co Galway

Cork Language Centre International, Wellington House, Wellington Rd, Cork

Cork School of English, 13 Bruach na Laoi, Union Quay, Cork

Dalmac Language Institute, North Beach, Rush, Co Dublin

De Sales School, St Catherine's St, New Campus, Maynooth, Co Kildare

Donegal Language School, Clemenstown, Ballylar, Letterkenny, Co Donegal

Dublin City University Language Services, Dublin City University, Dublin 9

Dublin English Language Foundation, 7 Herbert Place, Dublin 2

Dublin International Language Institute, 'The Brambles', Newtownpark Ave, Blackrock, Co Dublin

Dublin Language Centre, Camp Ireland, ATC Language & Travel, Rockford House, Deansgrange Rd, Blackrock, Co Dublin

Dublin Language Institute, 38 Harrington St, Dublin 8

Dublin School of English, 10/11/12 Westmoreland St, Temple Bar, Dublin 2 Tel: 353 1 6773322/6799872 Fax: 6718451/6795454/6264692 e-mail: Admin@des.ie. Website: http://www.dse.ic/dse TEFL Teacher Training Courses leading to the Prep.RELSA Cert. in TEFL operated on a regular basis throughout the year for native and non native speakers of English. Courses in English for all ages and interest groups. Work Placement and Au Pair Programmes.

Dublin Summer Language School, 29 Rossmore Park, Templeogue, Dublin 6W

Dublin Summer School, P O Box 2659, Dublin 6

Eden Hill, Navigation Road, Mallow, Co Cork

Education Through English, 68 Merrion Square, Dublin 2

Elians International Language Institute, Jubilee Hall, Ballyman Rd, Bray, Co Wicklow

Emerald Cultural Institute, 10 Palmerston Park, Rathgar, Dublin 6

English in Tipperary, Southpark, Ballingarry, Roscrea, Co Tipperary

English Language Centre, National University of Ireland, Galway

English Language Institute, 99 St Stephen's Green, Dublin 2

English Language Professionals, Brunswick House, Brunswick Place, Dublin 2

Euro-Irish Summer Schools, Lingua Club, 7 bis rue Degres, 75014 Paris, France

Eurocentre Dublin, Monagae, 41 Barnhill Rd, Dalkey, Co Dublin

European Education Centre, Ashfield College, Main St, Templeogue, Dublin 6W

Executive Language Teaching Service, The Old School, Ratharoon Bandon, Co Cork

Excel International Language Institute, I D A Enterprise Centre, North Mall, Cork

Fr Altabella Summer School, Carmichael House, 60 Lower Baggot St, Dublin 2

Galway Cultural Institute, Lowstrand House, Flood St, Galway

Galway Language Centre, The Bridge Mills, Galway

Grafton Tuition Centre, Clifton House, Lower Fitzwilliam St, Dublin 2

Greenhills College, 29 Templemanor Grove, Walkinstown, Dublin 12

Griffith College, South Circular Rd, Dublin 8

Hibernia English Language Programmes, The Glenroyal Centre, Maynooth, Co Kildare

Homefield Language Centre, Bayview Avenue, Bundoran, Co Donegal

The Horner School of English, 40 Fitzwilliam St Upper, Dublin 2

Hughes House Cultural Institute, Thomas St, Castlebar, Co Mayo

ICON International, 3 Abbey St, Howth, Co Dublin

Imaal Tutorials, Ballinabarny, Knockanarrigan, Dunlavin, Co Wicklow

Inlingua Dublin - Psmatic Language Centre, Kilmarnock, Military Rd, Killiney, Co Dublin

Institute of Education, English Language Unit, Portobello College, South Richmond St, Dublin 2

International Study Centre, 67 Harcourt St, Dublin 2

International Summer Schools, 91 Hillside, Greystones, Co Wicklow

Ireland West English Language Holidays, Baile Eamon, Spiddal, Co Galway

Irish College of English, 6 Church Rd, Malahide, Co Dublin

Key Institute, Knockvicar, Boyle, Co Roscommon

Kilfinane Education Centre, Kilfinane, Co Limerick

Kilkenny Language Centre, 6 Cashel Crescent, Waterford Rd, Kilkenny

Killala School of English, Crosspatrick, Killala, Co Mayo

KLS Language Centre, Collis Sandes House, Oakpark, Tralee, Co Kerry

Lakeland Language & Training, Kilnahinch, Moate, Co Westmeath

Land of Scholar Tours, 3 Bushfield Terrace, Donnybrook, Dublin 4

Langtrain International, Torquay Rd, Foxrock, Dublin 18

Language & Activity Holidays Ltd, 31/32 St Patrick's Quay, Cork

Language & Leisure Ireland, 1 Clarinda Park North, Dun Laoghaire, Co Dublin

Language Centre, Alfred O'Rahilly Building, UCC, The National University of Ireland, Cork

Language Centre of Ireland, Kildare St, Dublin 2

Language Development Programme, St Paul's College, Sybil Hill Rd, Raheny, Dublin 5

Language Holidays Ireland, The Old Courthouse, Timoleague, Co Cork

Language Institute of Ireland, Seaview, Forth Commons, Wexford

Language Learning Concepts Ltd, Oaklands, Putland Road, Bray, Co Wicklow

Language Training, 17 Dromore Rise, Raheen, Limerick

Language Vacations Ireland Ltd, 32 Leesdale Court, Ballincollig, Co Cork

The Linguaviva Centre, 45 Lower Leeson St, Dublin 2

Limerick Language Centre, 16 Upper Mallow St, Limerick

LSB College, 6/9 Balfe Street, Dublin 2

Lucan Language Centre, Student and Language Trvel, 18 Barton Rd, Rathfarnham, Dublin 14

Malahide Language School, 31 Seafield Ave, Clontarf, Dublin 3

Marian English Language College, Lansdowne Rd, Ballsbridge, Dublin 4

Mayoralty College, Mayoralty House, Flood St, Galway

Midland Language School, 6 Retreat Rd, Athlone, Co Westmeath

Midleton Camp International, Jonik Ireland Ltd, 52 Merrion Court, Montenotte, Cork

Monaghan English Language Centre, Latlurcan House, Monaghan

Monkstown Park Language & Activity Centre, Christian Brothers College, 12 Longford Tce, Monkstown, Co Dublin

Morehampton Language Institute, 74 Morehampton Rd, Donnybrook, Dublin 4

Moyle Park English Language College, Clondalkin, Dublin 2

Munsboro Language School, Munsboro Lodge, Roscommon

Nations Language Training Centre, Nations House, 14 Parnell Place, Cork

Nenagh Summer Language School, 22 Villier's Rd, Rathgar, Dublin 6 Newpark, Ballymote, Co Sligo

Newpark House Language School, Newpark, Ballymote, Co Sligo

North Monastery Language Institute, North Monastery Road, Cork

O'Farrell Summer School, Wohlertstr 11, 10115 Berlin, Germany

OISE, 7 Herbert Place, Dublin 2

Our Lady's Bower Preparatory School, Killashee, Naas, Co Kildare

Outdoor Education Centre, Roscrea Rd, Birr, Co Offaly

Pace Language Institute Ltd, 30 Dublin Rd, Bray, Co Wicklow

Parlez Pronto, Market Square, Castlebar, Co Mayo

Portobello College, Institute of Education, Portobello House, 5 Richmond Street, Dublin 2

Portmarnock School of English, 60 The Dunes, Portmarnock, Co Dublin

Psamtic Language Centre, Kilmarnock, Military Rd, Killiney, Co Dublin

Rectory Language Centre, Old Rectory, Portumna, Co Galway

Regards Linguistic School, Rampart Rd, Newport Rd, Westport, Co Mayo

St Gerard's School, Thornhill Rd, Bray, Co Wicklow

Salesian English Language Centre, Salesian College, Celbridge, Co Kildare

Sandycove Language Centre, Sandycove, Kinsale, Co Cork

Shannonside Language Centre, Coolbawn, Nenagh, Co Tipperary

Siemens English Language Competence Centre, Leeson Close, Dublin 2

S O M Languages International, 52 Lower Leeson St, Dublin 2

South of Ireland Language Centre, 71 Wilton Court, Wilton, Cork

Summer Educational Courses, Travel Ireland ltd, 23 Grand Parade, Cork

Swan Training Institute, 110 Grafton St, Dublin 2

Tara English Language Centre, 9 Stradbrook Ln, Blackrock, Co Dublin

Travel Ireland Ltd, Summer Educational Courses, 23 Grand Parade, Cork

U-Learn, 205 New Street Mall, Malahide, Co Dublin

University of Limerick Language Centre, Dept of Languages & Cultural Studies, University of Limerick, Limerick

Waterford English Language Centres, 31 St John's Hill, Waterford

Waterford School of English, Leoville, Dunmore Rd, Waterford

West of Ireland Schools of English (WISE), Old Bond Store, Dillon Terrace, Ballina, Co Mayo

Westlingua Language School, Cathedral Building, Middle St, Galway

West Waterford Language School, West St, Tallow, Co Waterford

WestWords Language School, Athry House, Recess, Connemara, Co Galway

Woodlands Academy, Wingfield, Kilcroney, Wicklow

Words Language Services, 70 Baggot St, Dublin 2

YES Language Institute, Abbey House, 4 North Abbey Street, North Mall, Cork

Youghal International College, Centra Afuera, Plaza de Santa 13, Madrid, Spain

Austria

Knowledge of German is a basic requirement for working in Austria and there is stiff competition for teaching jobs from the ex-patriate community. Now that Austria is in the EU, British and Irish teachers can apply for teaching jobs in state schools, although the most commonly available work is part-time and company-based. See our list below for language schools able to recruit locally and overseas. In the summer, there is always the chance of working in a summer camp. Apply to Young Austria or Village Camps. Unqualified teachers might be able to find private classes.

Visas and work permits: EU nationals can now compete with Austrians to apply for teaching jobs in the state sector. However, teaching positions in state schools are normally only available to Austrian and EU citizens. Exceptions for non-EU nationals are possible if you are highly qualified. Teaching positions are restricted to 1 year. Although there are no longer work permits, EU citizens must apply for an identity card after three months in the country. Non-EU nationals require visas and work permits, which must be applied for outside Austria. Together with a work permit you will need a residence permit. These are very difficult to secure and teachers are generally allowed to work for under ten hours per week without a permit.

Cost of living: Food is expensive, but restaurants and drinks can be relatively cheap. Otherwise, costs are high, especially in Vienna.

Salaries and taxes: Expect AS230-400 per hour depending on qualifications. This is often paid cash-in-hand and can be less if lessons are shorter than an hour. On contract, expect AS15,000 per month, with income tax and social security deductions of around 40 per cent, depending on where you work. Discuss this with your employer before you accept a job

Accommodation: A one-bedroomed flat in Vienna or Salzburg will cost around AS6,000 per month but they are difficult to find.

Health insurance: Advisable.

English language newspapers: The Vienna Reporter, Austria Today, ELT News.

List of schools in Austria
American International School, Salmannsdorferstrasse 47, A-1190 Vienna.
Amerika-Institut, Operngrasse 4, 1010 Vienna
Austro-British Society, Wickenburgasse 19, 1080 Vienna
Berlitz Sprachschule, Rotenturmstrasse 1-38, 1060 Vienna
Berufsforderungsinstitut, Kinderspitalgasse 5, 1090 Vienna
Business Language Centre, Trattnerhof 2, 1010 Vienna
Danube International, Guderunstrasse 184, A-1100 Vienna
Didactica Akademie Fur Wirtschaft Und Sprachen, Schottenfledgasse 13-15, 1070 Vienna
English For Kids, A-Baumgartnerstr 44 A/7042, 1230 Vienna
English Language Centre, In der Hagenau 7, 1130 Vienna
Graz International Bilingual School, Klusemannstrasse 25, A-8053, Graz
inlingua Graz, Rechbauerstr 23/2, A-8010 Graz
inlingua Innsbruck, Sudtiroler Platz 8/2, A-6020 Innsbruck
inlingua Linz, Landstrasse 24, (Ecke Spittelwiese), A-4020 Linz
inlingua Salzburg, Linzer Gasse 17-19, A-5020 Salzburg
inlingua Vorariberg, Bahnhofstr. 18, 1-6800 Feldkirch
inlingua Wien, Kamtner Strasse (Eingang Neuer Markt 1), A-1010 Wien
Innsbruck International Highschool, Schonbeg 26, A-6141, Innsbruck
Institut CEF, Garnisongasse 10, 1090 Vienna. Tel: 42 04 03
International House Vienna, Schwedenplatz 2/55, 1010 Vienna
The International Montessori Preschool Vienna, Mahlerstrasse 9/13, A-1010 Vienna
Jelinek & Jelinek, Privatlehrinstitut, Rudolfsplatz 3, 1010 Vienna
Kindergarten Alt Wien, Am Heumarkt 23, A-1030, Vienn

Linguarama Vienna, Concordiaplatz 2, 1010 Wien Tel: (0) 1 533 08 79 Fax: (0) 1 533 08 76 email: vienna@linguarama.com
Lizner International School, Aubrunnerweg 4, A-4040 Linz
Mini Schools & English Language Day Camp, Postfach 160, 1220 Vienna
Salzburg International Preparatory School, Moosstrasse 106, A-5020, Salzburg
Sight & Sound Studio Gesmbh, Schubertring 12, 1031 Vienna
Spidi (Spracheninstitut Der Industrie), Lotringer Strasse 12, 1031 Vienna
Sprachstudio J-J Rousseau, Untere Viaduktgasse 43, 1030 Vienna
Sprachinstitut Vienna, Universitatstr. 6, 1090, Vienna
Super Language Learning Sprachinstitut, Florianigasse 55, 1080 Vienna
Verband Wiener Volksbildung, Wiener Volkshochschulen, Hallergrasse 22, 1150 Vienna
Young Austria, Alpenstrasse 108a, A-5020 Salzburg

Belgium

As the bureaucratic centre of the EU, Brussels has a strong demand for English and other European languages. However, when it comes to opportunities, there is competition from expatriate spouses and Belgian nationals who speak excellent English. Unqualified teachers will find it hard to get work in Belgium.

Young learner courses are increasingly popular and it might be possible to find work at one of the many summer camps. Teachers generally begin work on a freelance basis and will need to supplement this with private lessons. Qualified teachers can be included on the British Council register and earn more than those who go it alone.

Visas and work permits: Non-EU nationals should apply to their local embassy with proof of employment.

Cost of living: High, but food is relatively cheap. Clothes and entertainment are very expensive.

Salaries and taxes: Teachers earn between BF550 and BF800 per hour depending on qualifications.

On a contract, expect to earn between BF45,000 and BF50,000. Employers pay tax and health insurance only if you are on a contract. Rates vary for freelancers and some freelancers who are staying in the country for a short period get away with not declaring earnings.

Accommodation: Outside Brussels, rent costs a minimum of BF10,000 per month, while in the capital it costs BF15,000. A 3-room furnished flat will cost a minimum of BF28,000, while a single room in a hotel will cost BF12,000 Schools rarely assist in finding accommodation.

Health insurance: Advisable for self-employed teachers.

English language newspapers: The Bulletin (weekly) and Newcomer (biannually).

List of schools in Belgium
Access bvba Taalbureau, Abdijstraat 40, 2260 Tongerlo
Antwerpse Talenakademie, Karei Govaertstraat 23/25, 2100 Deume
Berlitz Language Centre, Avenue de Tervuren 265, 1150 Brussels
Berlitz Language Centre, Avenue des Arts 36, 1040 Brussels
Berlitz Language Centre, Place Stephanie 10, 1050 Brussels
Berlitz Language Centre, rue du Pont d'Avroy, 2/4, 4000 Liege
Berlitz Language Centre, Meir 21 (1st floor), 2000 Antwerpen
Berlitz Language Centre, Britselei 15, 2018 Antwerpen
Berlitz Language Centre, Kouter 177, 9000 Gent
Berlitz Language Centre, rue de la Station 112, 7700 Mouseron
Berlitz Language Centre, Westinform, Monnikenwerve 17/19, 8000 Brugge
Berlitz Language Centre, Leuvenselaan 17, 3300 Tienen
Bilingua, rue Renier Chalon 6, 1060 Brussels
British Commission, rue de la Charité 39, 1040 Brussels
Crown Language Centre, rue de Beguinage 13, 1000 Brussels
EPFC (Enseign Promot Soc & Form Cont), ULB Batiment H A, CP 220, Campus de la Plaine du Triomph, 1050 Brussels
inlingua Antwerpen, Frankrijklei 39, B-2000 Antwerpen

inlingua Gent, UCO Building - 6de verdieping, Bellevue 9/10, 9050 Gent (Lederberg)

Institut Pro Linguis SC, Place de l'Eglise 19, 6717 Thiamont

Kamer voor Handel & Nijverheid, VUB, Room 3B/208, Pleinlaan 2, 1050 Brussels

May International, rue Lesbroussart 40, 1050 Brussels

Mitchell School of English, rue Louis Hap 156, 1040 Brussels

Peters School, rue des 2 Eglises 87, 1040 Brussels

Practicum, Reep 24, 9000 Gent

The British School of Brussels, Leuvensesteenweg 19, 3080 Tervuren

Denmark

With local unemployment running at an average of 11 per cent, the prospects of finding a teaching post in Denmark are poor. In addition, the number of children of school age is decreasing and schools and universities are cutting back on staff.

Accustomed to free education, the private school sector continues to be small and the difficulty of finding posts in the Danish public sector is exacerbated by the need for foreign teachers to possess a sound knowledge of Danish. Some opportunities may be found in institutes running part-time courses and evening classes, particularly in Business English, and it is in this area that job-hunting efforts should be concentrated.

Visas and work permits: Very difficult for non-EU nationals.

Salaries and taxes: Salaries vary according to teachers' qualifications and the type of institution they work for. Expect a minimum of 175 kroner per hour. The tax rate is about 50 per cent, one of the highest in the world.

Accommodation: In and around Copenhagen, the cost of accommodation averages out at 8,000-10,000 kroner per month. Elsewhere it can be considerably less, and standards are high.

Other useful information: Danish state teachers enjoy some of the highest salaries in the EU, primarily because they are expected to be able to teach any subject to students of any age. As a result, the majority of Danish teachers have a very high standard of proficiency in English and there is little need in schools for native English speakers.

List of schools in Denmark

Access, Hamerensgade 8, 1267 Copenhagen K - branches in Odense & 4 other cities

Activsprog, Rosenvµgets Alle 32, 2100 Copenhagen - also Odense, Arhus & Aalborg

Babel Sprogtrµning, Vordingborggrade 18, 2100 Copenhagen

Berlitz International, Vimmelskaftet 42a, 1161 Copenhagen

Bis Sprogskole, Rolfsvej 14-16, 2000 Frederiksberg

Cambridge Institute Foundation, Vimmelskaftet 48, 1161 Copenhagen

Center for Undervisning, arhus amt, Ulla Sørensen, Vesterskovvej 4, 8660 Skanderborg.

Elite Sprogcentret, Hoffmeyersvej 19, 2000 Frederiksberg.

Erhvervs Orienterede Sprogkurser, Betulavej 25, 3200 Helsinge

European Education Centre Aps (Inlingua), Lyngbyvej 72, 2100 Copenhagen

FOF, Sønder Allⱴ 9, 8000 Arhus C

Frit Oplysningsforbund, Vestergrade 5000 Odense C

Linguarama, Hvilevej 7, 2900 Hellerup

Master-Ling, Sortedam Dossering 83, 2100 Copenhagen

MS University A/S, Raadhustorvet, 3, Farum DK-3520 Tel: 0045 44 99 22 45 Fax: 0045 44 99 22 46 Email: info@msuniversity.com Website: www.msuniversity.com Contact: Soren Stuhde. Technology-based distance learning language training centre. University graduates only.

Finland

More than 90 per cent of Finnish children learn English at school and English is taught to adults in universities, technical colleges and commercial colleges. It should be relatively easy to find work in one of these educational institutions. Younger children are sent to private kindergartens where it is often possible for less qualified L1 native speakers with young learner experience to find work.

Private and state-sponsored schools tend to recruit locally. The best time to look for work is in the spring when schools start recruiting for the following

September. Contracts are usually for the nine months which make up the academic year. If teachers are lucky enough to find work before they leave their home country, the package might include flights and accommodation.

Visas and work permits: Finland, now in the EU applies community rules concerning working rights. Non EU nationals have to apply for the necessary work permits, leaving Finland to do so if they find a job on spec. Papers can take two to three months to come through. Although there are US-operated schools in the country, some teachers applying on spec from a North American address might find that responses are not very forthcoming.

Cost of living: High; eating and drinking out are very expensive.

Salaries and taxes: Freelance teachers can earn anything from 70 to 125 markka per lesson. Contracted teachers can expect to earn up to 10,000 markka per month depending on experience. Tax is approximately 30 per cent. Schools pay statutory deductions but tend to leave teachers to make their own arrangements for payment of tax.

Accommodation: It's easy to find somewhere to live and schools often arrange it. Expect to pay 1,000 markka per month for a room in a shared flat, with one or two months' rent as a deposit. For a small apartment in the capital 2,000 markka is more realistic. Rent often includes heating, a real bargain during the long, cold winters.

Health insurance: There is a good healthcare system, which is free for EU citizens.

List of schools in Finland

AAC-Opisto, Kauppaneuvoksentie 8, 00200 Helsinki

The Federation of Finnish-British Societies, Puistokatu 1bA, 00140 Helsinki

International House, Mariankatu 15 B 7, 00170 Helsinki

IWG Kieli-Instituutti, H'meenkatu 25 B, 33200 Tampere

Kielipiste Oy, Kaisaniemenkatu 4A, 00100 Helsinki.

Linguarama Helsinki, Head Office and School, Annankatu 26, 00100 Helsinki Tel: (0) 9 680 32 30 Fax: (0) 9 603 118 email: helsinki@linguarama.com

Linguarama Lahti, Mariankatu BA, 15110 Lahti Tel: (0) 3 881 14 45 Fax: (0) 3 881 14 46 email: lahti@linguarama.com

Linguarama Turku, Yliopistonkatu 24A 1,8, 20100 Turku Tel: (0) 2 251 90 25 Fax: (0) 2 251 21 28 email: turku@linguarama.com

Lingua - Forum Ky, Fredrikinkatu 61 A 36, 00100 Helsinki

Lansi-Suomen opisto, Loimijoentie 280, 32700 Huittinen

International House (Habil Oy), Kieliopisto, Mariankatu 15B 7, 00170 Helsinki 17

Richard Lewis Communications, It'tuulenkuja 10 B, 02100 Espo, Helsinki

France

French companies are required by law to spend more than one per cent of their salary budget on vocational training. Computer and English language training are the most popular areas for this imposed investment, so many private schools are able to get by on commercial sector contracts alone, while the best paid jobs are often found at the Chambres de Commerces, which do a lot of the training for smaller firms. Interestingly, because of the great demand for Business English and English for Specific Purposes, TEFL qualifications do not count as much as commercial experience and most schools will expect a good knowledge of French.

France can be very protective towards its national workforce. However EU legislation is forcing developments within the French public teaching sector, opening up posts to non-nationals. There are also a good many private schools in the country.

English language teachers are split into two groups: contract workers (salariés) and self-employed workers (travailleurs indépendants). Status imparts different rights and obligations. If you are employed as a salarié, your employer has to make social security contributions equivalent to around 20 per cent of your salary. In turn you are entitled to sick leave, holiday pay and certain other advantages. Travailleurs indépendants are paid hourly fees (honoraires) and employers do not deduct social security in the context of the employee's work. As a result, honoraires tend to be significantly higher than contracted salariés but indépendants may not

be covered by the French social security system. Because schools can make great savings not paying social security, they are increasingly taking on freelancers rather than contracted teachers. Although the pay is better as a freelancer, it can be a hard life, especially in Paris and the major cities where there are not nearly enough teaching hours to go round.

Anyone thinking of teaching in France should look at Teaching English as a Foreign Language in France, available from the British Council in Paris. For those wishing to keep in touch with political developments, it is advisable to obtain the Bulletin Officiel du Ministère de l'Education Nationale. An additional source of useful information on working and teaching in France is the Centre d'Information et Documentation Jeunesse (CIDJ).

Visas and work permits: EU nationals need a carte de séjour, which should be applied for within three months of arrival in France, or as soon as you find work. It can take several months to be issued with a carte and if you apply before you have found a job, you will need to show that you have some savings to live on.

Non-EU nationals will find it difficult to secure a work visa and application should be made before leaving your home country. American English is popular in France however, and there are student exchange programmes, including those organised by the Council on International Educational Exchange and the Fulbright Commission, so US students can get hold of six-month work permits. Some North American teachers seem to get away with teaching on a visitor's visa although risk heavy fines and deportation.

Salaries and taxes: Salaries for teachers vary immensely in France and will usually be considerably lower in the provinces than in Paris, due to the lower cost of living. Ironically, pay in Paris can also be low due to the sheer numbers of language teachers seeking work. Contracted teachers can expect between F7,000 and F8,000 per month, while freelancers in schools can expect between F80 and F120 per hour with the possibility of earning up to F220 in universities. Many schools require RSA TEFL qualifications, often on top of a degree. Many of the

Chambers look for EC teaching accreditation, which is a nine month course. The British Council recruits in the UK for its new Young Learners Centre, paying £12,000 to £17,000 for teachers with a diploma and 2-3 years experience. Income tax is progressive, you should pay the equivalent of about one month's salary per annum (perhaps F10,000). Local and health related tax is about 30 per cent on top of this.

Accommodation: Costs from around F4-5,000 per month for a one-bedroomed flat in Paris, though rooms and studios would be nearer F3,000. Living outside the capital in rural areas would be cheaper, unless you chose to live along a commuter route.

English language newspapers: International Herald Tribune, Paris Passion.

List of schools in France
AC3, 38 rue du Temple, 75004 Paris
Access Langue Speakwell, 35 rue de Ponthieu, 75008 Paris
Action Formation, 4 bis rue Mertens, 92270 Bois-Colombes
ADELE, 5 rue St-Philippe du Roule, 75008 Paris
Alexandra School, les bois de Grasse, 1 Avenue de Louison Bobet, Boulevard Emmanuel Rouquier, 06130 Grasse
American University of Paris, 102, rue st. Dominique, 75007, Paris
Anglesey Language Services (ALS), 1 bis Avenue du Marechal Foch, 78400 Chatou
Aquitaine Service Linguistique, 199 Avenue Louis Barthou, 33200 Bordeaux
Audio-English, 44 allee de Tourny, 33000 Bordeaux
AVL, 28 Bd Sébastopol, 75004 Paris
BLITS, 41 rue Dauphine, 75006 Paris
BLS, 4 rue de l'Abreuvoir, 92415 Courbevoie
British Institute, 11 rue de Constantine, 75007 Paris
Business & Technical Languages, 82 bld Haussmann, 75008 Paris
Business English Service & Translation, 91 route de Chateaurenault, 41000 Blois
CEL, 2 rue Vade, 80017 Amiens CEDEX 01
CEL, 8 bld du Roi Rene, BP 626, 49006 Angers CEDEX
CEL, Campus - Allee des Fenaison,s BP 660, 84032 Avignon CEDEX 3
CEL, 26 rue Etienne Dolet, 89015 Auxerre

CEL, 50/51 allees Marines, BP 215, 64102 Bayonne CEDEX

CEL, 16 bld Maine de Brian, 24100 Bergerac

CEL, 46 avenue Villarceau, 25000 Besancon

CEL, 8 rue de l'Azin, 41018 Blois CEDEX

CEL, 2 place de la Bourse, 33076 Bordeaux

CEL, rue Professeur Joseph Rousselot, BP 5036, 14022 Caen CEDEX

CEL, Parc d'activité des Bellevues, BP 69 Epargny sur Oise, 95612 Cergy Pontoise CEDEX

CEL, 18A avenue Georges Corneau, 08000 Charleville Mezieres

CEL, Route de Campo dell'Oro, 20000 Ajaccio, Corse

CEL, 7 rue Hoche, 38000 Grenoble

CEL, 7 avenue des Platanes, 72100 Le Mans

CEL, Immeuble Interconsulaire, 16 bld Bertrand, BP 127, 43004 Le Puy en Velay CEDEX

CEL, 7bis rue Max Linder, BP 194, 33504 Libourne CEDEX

CEL, 58 rue de l'Hopital Militaire, 59800 Lille

CEL, 43 rue Sainte Anne, BP 834, 87105 Limoges CEDEX

CEL, 14 rue Gorge de Loup, 69337 Lyon CEDEX 09

CEL, 35 rue Sainte Victoire, 13292 Marseille

CEL, rue de General Lapasset, 57070 Metz

CEL, 38 bld de l'Ayrolle, BP 145, 12101 Millau CEDEX

CEL, Avenue Pierre-Mendes France, 76290 Montivilliers

CEL, 325 avenue du Professeur Blayac, BP 3100, 34034 Montpellier CEDEX 1

CEL, 15 rue des Freres Lumieres, BP 2333, 68069 Muhlouse

CEL, 4 rue Bisson, BP 90517, 44105 Nantes

CEL, 74 rue Faidherbe, BP 232, 58002 Nevers CEDEX

CEL, Nice Leader Apollo, 62 route de Grenoble, 06200 Nice

CEL, 1 ter avenue du General Leclerc, 30000 Nimes

CEL, 23 place du Martroi, 45044 Orleans

CEL, 9/100 rue de la Petite Pierre, 75011 Paris

CEL, 3 rue de l'Union, 2400 Perigueux

CEL, Route de Thuir - Orle, BP 2013, 66011 Perpignan

CEL, 145 avenue de Meradennec, BP 410, 29330 Quimper

CEL, 2 rue Robert d'Arbrissel, 35065 Rennes CEDEX

CEL, 7bis rue Jeanne d'Arc, 76000 Rouen

CEL, 51 bld de la Paix, 78100 Saint Germain en Laye

CEL, Immeuble de la Concorde, 4 quai Kleber, 67055 Strasbourg CEDEX

CEL, Avenue Azeirex, 65000 Tarbes

CEL, 3 rue Hippolyte Duprat, 83000 Toulon

CEL, 1 rue Schiller, BP 537, 37005 Tours

CEL, 160 bld Harpignies, immeuble Philippa du Hamault, 59300 Valenciennes

CEL, CEL de Versailles, 18 rue Mansart, 7800 Versailles

European Executive Services, 2-6 rue de Strasbourg, 93110 Rosny sous bois

Euro-teclangues, 48 bld Voltaire, 75011 Paris

Executive Language Services, 20 rue Sainte Croix de la Bretonnerie, 75004 Paris Tel: 01 44 54 58 88 Fax: 01 48 04 55 53   Email els@club-internet.fr Leader in French, English Executive courses, Groups and Individuals, Business, General and Exams. Recognised: UNOSEL, UNDP/United Nations for French speakers.

Forum Accord, 52 rue Montmartre, 75002 Paris

IAL (Franco-Britannic Chamber of Co.), 41 rue de Turenne, 75003 Paris

I.E.L.P., 95 bld de Sebastopol, 75002 Paris

IFERP, Berkeley Building, 92903 Paris Cedex

ILC/International House, 20 passage Dauphine, 27 rue Mazarine, 75006 Paris

---

ImpaQt, Téléport IV- Futuropolis IV - BP 186, 86960 FUTUROSCOPE Cedex Tel: 33 5 49 49 63 80 Fax: 33 5 49 49 63 81 Email HQ@ImpaQt.net (Branch offices in Abingdon (near Oxford) UK, and Paris, Poitiers, Tours, Angoulême. Leading provider of learning solutions in the field of international business.

---

inlingua Aix-en-Provence, 115 rue Claude Nicolas Ledoux, F-13854 Aix-en-Provence CEDEX 03

inlingua Amiens, Rue des Jacobins, %-80000 Amiens

inlingua Belfort, 28 Faubourg des Ancetres, F-900000 Belfort

inlingua Besancon, 138 rue de Belfort, F-25000 Besancon

inlingua Bourdeaux-Merignac, Parc du Chateau Rouquey, F-33700 Bordeau-Merignac

inlingua Boulogne sur Mer, 50 bld de la Liane, F-62200 Boulogne sur Mer

inlingua Caen, 10 rue Colonel Remy Bt M18, Parc d'Activites de la Folie Couvrechet, F-14000 Caen

inlingua Colmar, 12 rue Berthe Molly, F-68000 Colmar

inlingua Compiegne, Les Tertiales Bat A, SAC de Mercieres 1, F-60200 Compiegne

inlingua Dijon, 10 Allee A Bourland, BP 176, F-21005 Dijon CEDEX

inlingua Dunkerque, 88 rue Pierre et Marie Curie, F-59760 Grande Synthe (Dunkerque)

inlingua Epinal, 7 rue de Lormont, F-88000 Epinal

inlingua Evreux, 13 rue de la Mairie, F-27000 Evreux

inlingua Haguenau, 44 bld de Lattre de Tassigny, F-67500 Haguenau

inlingua Hazebrouck, 41 Avenue du Marechal de Lattre de Tassigny, F-59190 Hazebrouk

inlingua Le Havre, 19 Quai George V, F-76600 Le Havre

inlingua Lille, Chateau Rouge, 278 Avenue de la Marne, F-59708 Marcq-En-Baroeul (Lille)

inlingua Lyon, 74 rue de Bonnel, F-69003 Lyon

inlingua Metz, 19 en Nouvellerue, Espace Serpenoise, F-57000 Metz

inlingua Mulhouse, 17 bld de l'Europe, F-68200 Mulhouse

inlingua Nancy, 10 rue Mazagran, F-54000 Nancy

inlingua Orleans, 2 rue de Palay, F-45000 Orleans

inlingua Paris la Defense, World Trade Center 2; BP 451 CNIT, 2 Place de la Defense, F-92053 Paris la Defense

inlingua Paris Bastille, 28 bld de la Bastille, F-75012 Paris Bastille

inlingua Paris Rive Gauche, 109 rue de l'Universite, F-75007 Paris

inlingua Pau, 52 Av des Lilas, F-64000 Pau

inlingua Rennes, 31 rue Marechal Joffre, F-35000 Rennes

inlingua Rouen, 8 rue Jean Rostand, BP 156, F-76143 Le Petit Quevilly CEDEX

inlingua Saverne, 34-36 Grand Rue, F-67700 Saverne

inlingua Strasbourg, 8 rue Hannong, F-67380 Lingolsheim

inlingua Toulouse, 13 rue Paulin Talabot, F-31100 Toulouse

inlingua Valenciennes, Espace Mercure, Ave Henri Barbusse, F-59770 Marly-les-Valenciennes

Institut Franco-Americain, BP 2599, 7 quai Chateaubriand, 35000 Rennes CEDEX

International House, Centre d'anglais d'Angers, 16 rue des Deux Haies, 49000 Angers

International House, Centre de langues Riviera, 62 rue Gioffredo, 06000 Nice

International House, 20, Passage Dauphine, 27, Rue Mazarine, 75006, Paris

International House, 152 alles de Barcelona, 31000 Toulouse

Isform Champs-Elysées, 19 rue de Berri, 75008 Paris

Language Forum, 20 Place de l'Iris, 92400 Paris la Defense

Language Plus Services, 37 Quai de Grenelle, 75015 Paris

Lingua Formation, 61 rue d'Anjou, 75008 Paris

Linguarama Paris - La Défense, 7e Etage, Tour Eve, La Défense 9, 92806 Puteaux Cedex Tel (enquiries): (0) 1 47 73 00 95 (school): (0) 1 47 74 66 63 Fax: (0) 1 47 73 86 04 email: defense@linguarama.com

Linguarama Paris - Champs Elysées, 6 rue de Berli, 75008 Paris Tel: (0) 1 40 76 07 07 Fax: (0) 1 40 76 07 74 email: paris@linguarama.com

Linguarama Dijon, Amphypolis, 10 rue Paul Verlaine, Rond Point de l'Europe, 21000 Dijon Tel: (0) 3 80 78 77 30 Fax: (0) 3 80 78 77 35 email: dijon@linguarama.com

Linguarama Grenoble, Mini Parc Alpes Congrés, 6 rue Roland Garros, 38320 Eybens Tel: (0) 4 76 62 00 18 Fax: (0) 4 76 25 89 60 email: grenoble@linguarama.com

Linguarama Lyon, Tour Crédit Lyonnais, 129 rue Servieni, 69003 Lyon Tel: (0) 4 78 63 69 69 Fax: (0) 4 78 63 69 65 email: lyon@linguarama.com

Lingua Formation, 57 rue d'Amsterdam, 75008 Paris

Metropolitan Languages, 151 rue de Billancourt, 92100 Boulogne

Nouvelles Frontieres, 166 bld Montparnasse, 75014 Paris

Reed-OIP, 11 rue du Colonel Pierre Avia, 75726 Paris Cedex 15

Sterling International, 12 rue Hippolyte Lebas, 75009 Paris

Studylang, 96 rue Lafayette, 75010 Paris

Télélangues Systems, 9 rue Grandcoing, 94200 Ivry S/Seine

Transfer Formation Conseil, 18-20 rue Godot de Mauroy, 75009 Paris

Unilangues, La grande Arche-Paroi Nord, 1 le Parvis, 92911 Paris la Defense

Universal Communication, 20 rue de Mogador, 75009 Paris

Wall Street Institute, 21 avenue Victor Hugo, 75016 Paris

We would like to thank Angela Baker, Franco-British Chamber of Commerce, for help in compiling this listing.

Germany

Despite the advanced level of English language teaching in state schools there is still considerable demand for General English in Germany. Oversubscribed courses at 'Volkshochschule' (Adult education and community colleges) cater for General English, even though those who need a refresher course sometimes prefer to go to the UK.

As in France, the commercial and professional sectors dominate demand for English courses and there are government incentives for companies to train their employees, which take the form of one or two week training holidays. The majority of these take place near home, for those requiring general skills, whilst only around one quarter of such courses include Business English.

TEFL qualifications will help employment prospects, as can some commerical experience. If you know something about futures, minimum reserve ratios or floating exchange rates, then you could be in a strong position. An education in English is more important than being an L1 native-speaker alone. Being able to speak German also helps.

It is also possible to secure work through educational programmes. The Central Bureau organises UK students and graduates to work as classroom assistants in universities and the USIA Fulbright Program organises for US graduates to work as teaching assistants in high schools.

There are many private language schools, with Linguarama, Inlingua and Berlitz being particularly well-represented. It's possible to find work speculatively if you have plenty of time. Try getting in touch with the English Language Teachers Association in the region where you most want to work for advice and lists of

schools on our list of ELTAs below. The British Council recruits on contract from London and takes on a few people from the freelance sector in Germany.

Visas and work permits: All EU citizens are able to work in Germany, but within three months have to register with the local authority for a residence permit and ID card. Like German citizens, they will need their landlord or their employer to countersign as proof that they live or work locally.

Other nationalities should arrange employment and apply for a work permit before they leave their home country. It may take a couple of months or more but is generally considered easier than in other EU countries.

Cost of living: High.

Salaries and taxes: German schools can be divided into three main groups: private language schools paying between DM20-30 per 45-minute lesson, night schools from DM35-40, and in-company work from about DM35-50. Freelance teachers can earn up to DM80 per hour.

Freelance teachers are responsible for their own social security payments (about 13%) which cover health costs, and although technically they should pay around 20% for old age provision, rarely do so. Freelancers should remember, however, that no matter what tax arrangements they choose, tourist emergency health cover does not continue indefinitely. EU nationals have a period of 100 days' grace, when they can pay their home tax rates before transferring to the German system. The general tax rate is around 30 per cent on earnings over DM12,096 p.a. If careful financial advice is taken, much work-related expenditure can be claimed back against tax. ELTA in Berlin holds an advice workshop on this every two years.

Accommodation: A one-bedroomed flat will cost upwards of DM1,000 in any of the big cities. Three months' rent is payable as a deposit, but landlords will normally accept double rent for three months if you can't afford to pay that much up-front. Many schools will assist in finding accommodation.

Health insurance: Essential for freelance teachers.

SECTION 3 International Job Prospects

English language newspapers:
Spotlight and World Press.

Other useful information: Phone numbers for the main ELTAs in Germany:
Berlin: 030 454 2604
Dresden: 351 2210 172.
Frankfurt: 6131 479 915.
Hamburg: 40 796 7996.
Munich: 89 692 4670.
Ravensburg: 751 222 109.
Rhine: 220 313 266.
Stuttgart: 70 238 084.

List of schools in Germany
Administration Office for
Examinations Ltd, Platanestr 5, 07549 Gera
American Language Academy, Charlottenstr. 65, 10117 Berlin
Anglo-German Institute, Christopherstr 4, 70178 Stuttgart
ASK Sprachenschule, 1 Kortumstr 71, 44787 Bochum
Bansley College, Str Des Friedens 35, 03222 Lubbenau, Brandenburg
Benedict School, Gurzenichstr 17, 50667 Koln
Berlitz, Friedrich-Willhelm-Strasse 30, 47051 Duisburg
British Council: Hardenbergstr 20, 10623 Berlin
Carl-Schurz Haus, Kaiser Joseph Str 266, D-79098 Freiburg
Christopher Hills School of English, Sandeldamm 12, 63450 Hanau.
Collegium Palatinum, Adenauerplatz 8, 69115 Heidelberg
Didacta, Hohenzollernring 27, 95440 Bayreuth
English Language Centre, Bieberer Strasse 205, 63071 Offenbach am Main
English Language Institute,
Sprachenschule 4, Ubersetzer Am Zwinger 14, 33602 Bielefeld
Europa-Universitat Viadrina, Sprachenzentrum, Grosse Scharrnstr 59, 15230 Frankfurt (Oder)
FBD Schulen, Katharinenstr 18, 70182 Stuttgart
German-American Institute, Sophienstr 12, Heidelberg
German-American Institute, Gleissbuehlstr 13, Nurenberg
German-American Institute, Berliner Promenade 15, 66111 Saarbruecken
German-American Institute, Karlstrasse 3, 72072 Tuebingen
GLS Sprachenzentrum, B Jaeshke, Pestalozzistr 886, 10625 Berlin

Hallworth English Centre, Frauenstrasse 118, 89703 Ulm-Ponau
inlingua Aachen, Markt 29-31, D-52062 Aachen
inlingua Augsburg, Burgermeister-Fischer-Str 9, D-86150 Augsburg
inlingua Bad Godesberg, Koblenzer Strasse 36, D-53173 Bonn (Bad Godesberg)
inlingua Berlin, Ludwigkirchstr 9A, D-10719 Berlin
inlingua Bielefeld, Niedernstrasse 28, D-33602 Bielefeld
inlingua Bochum, Kortumstrasse 17, D-44787 Bochum
inlingua Bonn, Markt 10-12, D-53111 Bonn
inlingua Braunschweig, Munzstrasse 15, D-38100 Braunschweig
inlingua Bremen, Obernstrasse 14, D-28195 Bremen
inlingua Bremen Business Center, Bremen World Trade Center, D-28195 Bremen
inlingua Chemnitz, Annaberger Str 231, D-09120 Chemnitz
inlingua Dessau, Ferdinand von Schill Strasse 5, D-06844 Dessau
inlingua Detmold, Hermannstrasse 45, D-32756 Detmold
inlingua Dortmund, Westenhellweg 66-68, D-44137 Dortmund
inlingua Dresden, An der Mauer, D-1067 Dresden
inlingua Duisburg, Konigstrasse 61, D-47051 Duisburg
inlingua Dusseldorf, Graf-Adolf-Strasse 41, D-40201 Dusseldorf
inlingua Essen, Flachsmarkt 1, D-45127 Essen
inlingua Erlangen, Sudliche Stadtmauerstr 2, D-91054 Erlangen
inlingua Frankfurt, Kaiserstrasse 37, D-60329 Frankfurt
inlingua Friedrichshafen, Allmandstrasse 8, D-88045 Friedrichshafen
inlingua Fulda, Mardostrasse 2, D-36037 Fulda
inlingua Giessen, Ludwigsplatz 11, D-35390 Giessen
inlingua Gutersloh, Alte Verler Strasse 11, D-33332 Gutersloh
inlingua Halle, Talamtstrasse 1 2, D-06108 Halle
inlingua Hamburg Spitalerstrasse, Spitalerstrasse 1, D-20095 Hamburg
inlingua Hamburg Pulverteich, Kleiner Pulverteich 9, D-20099 Hamburg

inlingua Hannover, Andreaestrasse 3, D-30159 Hannover
inlingua Heidelberg, Im Breitspiel 11, Eingang C, D-69126 Heidelberg
inlingua Heilbronn, Karlstrasse 37, D-74072 Heilbronn
inlingua Herford, Backerstrasse 31, D-32052 Herford
inlingua Ingolstadt, Ludwigstrasse 12, D-85049 Inglostadt
inlingua Iserlohn, Nussstrasse 5, D-58636 Iserlohn
inlingua Kaiserslautern, Eisenbahnstrasse 51, D-67655 Kaiswerslautern
inlingua Karlsruhe, Kaiserstrasse 231-233, D-76133 Karlsruhe
inlingua Kassel, Konigstor 35, D-34117 Kassel
inlingua Kempten, Bodmanstrasse 7-9, D-87435 Kempten
inlingua Kiel, Alter Markt 1-2, D-24103 Kiel
inlingua Koblenz, Markenbildchenweg 34, D-56068 Koblenz
inlingua Koln, Grosse Sandkaul 19, D-50667 Koln
inlingua Konstanz, Wollmatinger Strasse 22, D-78467 Konstanz
inlingua Krefeld, Hochstrasse 114, Schwanenmarkt, D-477987 Krefeld
inlingua Leipzig, Konradstrasse 52, D-04315 Leipzig
inlingua Lubeck, Amimstrasse 4, D-23566 Lubeck
inlingua Ludenscheid, Knapper Strasse 38, D-58507 Ludenscheid
inlingua Ludwigsburg, Schillerstrasse 8, D-71638 Ludwigsburg
inlingua Ludwigshafen, Ludwigstrasse 49, D-67059 Ludwigshafen
inlingua Magdeburg, Goethestrasse 1, D-39108 Magdeburg
inlingua Mannheim, T6, 26, D-68161 Mannheim 1
inlingua Moers, Xantener Strasse 15-17, D-47441 Moers
inlingua Monchengladbach, Hindenburgstr 161-163, D-41061 Monchengladbach
inlingua Munchen, Sendlinger-Tor-Platz 6, D-80336 Munchen
inlingua Munster, Berliner Platz 2a, D-48143 Munster
inlingua Nurnberg, Sandstrasse 7, D-90443 Nurnberg
inlingua Offenburg, Hauptstrasse 81, D-77652 Offenburg
inlingua Oldenburg, Wallstrasse 15, (Julius-Mosen-Platz), D-26122 Oldenburg

inlingua Osnabruk, Georgstrasse 4, D-49074 Osnabruk

inlingua Paderborn, Schildern 8, D-33098 Paderborn

inlingua Pforzheim, Zerrennerstr 18, D-75172 Pforzheim

inlingua Ravensburg, Meersburger Str 8, D-88213 Ravensburg

inlingua Recklinghausen, Wickingstrasse 13, D-45657 Recklinghausen

inlingua Regensburg, Kumpfmuhler Str 8, D-93047 Regensburg

inlingua Reutlingen, Nikolaiplatz 3, D-72764 Reutlingen

inlingua Saarbrucken, Viktoriastrasse 30-32, D-66111 Saarbrucken

inlingua Schwerin, Gadebuscher Str 153G, D-19057 Schwerin

inlingua Singen, Ekkehardstrasse 16a, D-78224 Singen

inlingua Stuttgart, Tubinger Strasse 21, D-70178 Stuttgart

inlingua Trier, Brotstrasse 1, D-54290 Trier

inlingua Tuttlingen, Konigstrasse 3, D-78532 Tuttlingen

inlingua Uberlingen, Hofstatt 8, D-88662 Uberlingen

inlingua Ulm, Neue Strasse 72, D-89073 Ulm

inlingua VS-Villingen, Bickenstr 17, D-78050 VS-Villingen

inlingua Wiesbaden, Friedrichstrasse 31-33, D-65185 Wiesbaden

inlingua Wuppertal, Neumarkt 2, D-42103

Intercom Lang Services, Muggenkampstr 38, 20257 Hamburg.

International House, Poststrasse 51, 20354 Hamburg Tel: 00 4940 35 20 41 Fax: 00 4940 35 26 25 Contact: Patrick Woulfe. Providing communicative English courses to employees of national and multinational companies. Flexible programmes for small groups and one-to-one.

International House, LGS Sprachkurse, Werderring 18, D-79098 Freiburg

Kennedy-Haus, Holtenauerstr 9, D-2300 Kiel 1

Knowledge Point, Nymphenburgerstr. 86, 80636 Munchen

Language Link, Germany, Recruitment Section, 21 Harrington Road, South Kensington, London, UK, SW7 3EU

Linguarama Berlin, Atrium Friedrichstrasse, Friedrichstrasse 60, 10117 Berlin Tel: (0) 30 203 00 50 Fax: (0) 30 203 00 515 email: berlin@linguarama.com

Linguarama Cologne, Marzellenstrasse 3-5, 50667 Kπln, Tel (0) 221 16 09 90 Fax: (0) 221 16 099 66 email: cologne@linguarama.com

Linguarama Düsseldorf, Steinstrasse 30, 40210 DŸsseldorf Tel: (0) 211 13 20 83 Fax: (0) 211 13 20 85 email: dusseldorf@linguarama.com

Linguarama Frankfurt, Linguarama Haus, Goetheplatz 2, 60311 Frankfurt/Main Tel: (0) 69 28 02 46 Fax: (0) 69 28 05 56 email: frankfurt@linguarama.com

Linguarama Hamburg, Hopfenburg, Hopfensack 19, 20457 Hamburg Tel: (0) 40 33 50 97 Fax: (0) 40 32 46 09 email: hamburg@linguarama.com

Linguarama Leipzig, Lipsia Haus, Barfussg˘sschen 12, 04109 Leipzig Tel: (0) 341 213 14 64 Fax: (0) 341 213 14 82 email: leipzig@linguarama.com

Linguarama Munich, Rindermarkt 16, 80331 MŸnchen Tel: (0) 89 260 70 40 Fax: (0) 89 260 98 84 email: munich@linguarama.com

Linguarama Stuttgart, Leuschnerstrasse 3, 70174 Stuttgart Tel: (0) 711 22 19 36 Fax: (0) 711 22 61 882 email: stuttgart@linguarama.com

Lingotek Institut, Schlueterstrasse 18, 20146, Hamburg

Neue Sprachschule, Rosastrass 1, 79098 Freiburg

NSK Language and Training Services, Comeniusstr 2, 90459 Nurnburg

Sprachstudio Lingua Nova, Thierschstrasse 36, 80538 Munich

Stevens English Training, Ruttenscheider Strasse 68, 45130 Essen

Vorbeck-Schule, 77723 Gengenbach

Wirtschaftwissen-schaftliche Fakultat Ingolstadt, Auf der Schanz 49, 85049 Ingolstadt

Yes Your English Services, Altonaer Chaussee 87, 22559 Schenefeld, Hamburg

Greece

There is a huge demand for English in Greece. Of all the candidates worldwide for the Cambridge First Certificate and Cambridge Proficiency exams, one quarter are in Greece.

In many parts of the country, parents pay for their children to attend private language schools (frontisteria), in order to supplement the English language teaching they receive in state schools. There are estimated to be more than 5,000 frontisteria in the country. Recruitment normally happens locally in May/June or September, although posts are also regularly advertised overseas. You must be a graduate to teach.

Until recently language schools could be opened only by Greek nationals if they had passed the Cambridge Proficiency exam. A large expatriate community in Athens, coupled with new legislation allowing non-Greek nationals to open language schools has increased competition and pushed up standards. Less reliable schools have found it hard to survive and the necessity for teachers to have qualifications to gain employment has increased. Those less qualified may well have more success finding work in January as there are fewer native speakers in the country during the winter. The British Council has pointed out that many language schools are reporting a drop in student numbers, as state school provision has improved and the number of small classes and personal tutors has increased.

Whilst the state sector only employs Greek nationals, there are many openings in the private arena. Foreign teachers are sometimes contracted for one year and often share classroom responsibility with a Greek colleague. Recruitment takes place locally and overseas. The British Council recruits locally. Opportunities exist in the corporate sector for in-house training, usually from the local freelance pool. Non L1 speakers have a hard time finding work, as they have to compete with many able Greeks.

Visas and work permits: For a residency permit, EU citizens must first obtain a teacher's licence. Applicants for the licence will need to have their degree certificate translated into Greek and, once in Greece, are required to go for an X-ray to receive a health certificate. Residency permits take about a month to come through.

Non-EU citizens can receive a work permit by producing an employment offer from a Greek school at their local Greek consulate. Permits take at least two months to be granted, and must be applied for before their arrival.

Cost of living: Relatively cheap, but clothes and furniture are expensive.

Salaries and taxes: An English language teacher employed in the private sector or by the British Council earns about dr2,000 if inexperienced, and up to dr2,500 for those teaching examination classes. Freelancers can make around dr5,000 for private lessons, depending on their experience and origin, and the age of the client. Taxes are around 20 per cent on declared earnings with national insurance contributions around 16.5%.

Accommodation: Prices can be high, especially around Athens, but most schools assist or provide accommodation. If not, expect to pay around one third of your salary, with two months' rent as a deposit. A decent flat can cost dr80,000 a month. Bills can be a big shock, especially in winter when it gets surprisingly cold. There is a ten-year waiting list for phone installation, so look for somewhere with a phone if you want to give private classes.

Health insurance: Advisable. EU citizens no longer require a health check.

English language newspapers: Athens News.

Other useful information: Remember you can claim residency rights if you are of Greek descent, before moving on to teach elsewhere in the EU.

List of schools in Greece

A Trechas Language Centre, 20 Koundouriotou St, Keratsini

Alpha Abatzolglou Economou, 10 Kosma Etolou St, 54643 Thessaloniki

A Andriopoulou, 3, 28 Octobrio, Tripolis

Athens College, PO Box 65005, 15410 Psychico, Athens

British Council, Ethnikis Amynis 9, PO Box 50007, 54013 Thessalonika

English Tuition Centre, 3 Pythias Street, Kypseli 1136, Athens

Enossi Foreign Languages (The Language Centre), Stadiou 7, Syntagma, 10562 Athens

Eurocentre, 7 Solomou Street, 41222 Larissa

Featham School of English, Mrs A Featham, PO Box 12, 50 Ep. Marouli St, Rethymnon 74100. Tel: +30 (0)831 23428, Fax: +30 (0)831 23922. A reputable, modern school in custom-built premises. The school has been at the forefront of EFL since 1976.

Hambakis Schools of English, 1 Filellinon Street, Athens

Hellenic American Union, 22 Massalias Street, GR-106 80 Athens

International Language Centre, 35 Votsi Street, 26221 Patras

Institute of English, French, German and Greek for Foreigners, Zavitsanou Sophia, 13 Joannou Gazi St, 31100 Lefkada

Institute of Foreign Languages, 41 Epidavrou St, 10441 Athens

ISIAA 93, Lamia 35100

Kakkos School of English, Constantine Kakkos, A'Par. Papastratou 5, Arginio 30100.

Makris School of English, 2 Pardos G Olympion St, 60100 Katerini

G Michalopolous School of English, 24E Antistasis, Alexandria, 59300 Imathias, Thessaloniki

New Centre, Arkarnanias 16, Athens 11526

Omiros Association, 52 Academias St, 10677 Athens

Peter Sfyrakis School of Foreign Languages, 21 Nikiforou Foka St, 72200 Ierapetra, Crete

Profile, 4 Frantzi & Kallirois Street, Athens 11745

Protypo English Language School, 22 Deliyioryi Street, Volos 38221

School of English, 8 Kosti Palama, Kavala 65302

School of Foreign Languages, 12 P Isaldari St, Xylokastro, 20400 Korinth

SILITZIS School of Languages, 42 Koumoundourou, 412 22 Larissa

Skouras Language School, 7 G. Miltiadi St, 67100 Xanthi

Strategakis Schools, 24 Proxenou Koromila St, 54622 Thessaloniki

Study Space, 86 Tsimiski, 54622 Thessaloniki

Universal School of Language, 66 M Alexandrou St, Panorama, Thessalonika 55200

Zoula Language Schools, Sanroco Square, 49100 Corfu

Italy

The recent recession in Italy seems to have levelled off, and the demand for English language learning continues. Economic problems have been caused by Italy attempting to meet the joining demands of the single European currency. This could spell out ongoing

uncertainties. The popularity of the country as a destination means that it can often be hard to find work, especially in the major cities. Teachers generally need to be native speakers with at least a TEFL certificate. With schools trying to save money, overseas recruitment is increasingly rare.

Legal freelance work is very difficult to find, but in the unofficial sector teachers often find work. The existence of compulsory social security contributions for employees encourages some companies to take on more freelancers. This independence may suit short-term workers, but disadvantage those who in the longer term do not have access to the option of health and severance pay.

Some organisations employ British teachers on a UK contract and then send them over to Italy, for instance English Worldwide. This allows the lower UK tax laws to sidestep compulsory Italian deductions which include reciprocal social security agreements. Teachers should beware of Italian schools without significant ties to the UK offering this kind of deal; they may find themselves without social security cover or employment protection.

Visas and work permits: All EU citizens have the right to work in Italy, and should obtain a residency permit from local police. Non-EU citizens will find it very difficult to get work. Generally, the authorities overlook EU teachers finding jobs before applying for permits. Other nationalities will experience difficulties and should apply from their home country with a definite job offer.

Cost of living: Roughly the same as the UK. Italy is no longer a cheap country.

Salaries and taxes: After tax, salaries average around 1.4-1.9 million lira. Higher rates, occasionally reaching 2 million lira, are more likely in the cities. The tax rate is volatile, something around 20 per cent should be read as a rough indication, with a further 10 per cent social security deduction. It should be noted that although the exchange rate of the lira to other major currencies may make potential wages seem low, the spending power of the income is reasonable in Italy. Schools pay return flights.

Accommodation: It is easy to find but tends to be expensive (500,000 - 650,000 lira). Schools sometimes assist in the search and might sort out cheaper rents. A one-roomed flat could cost as much as one million lira per month in the major cities and two or three months' rent is usually required as a deposit. Teachers with English Worldwide often share digs, and pay 4-500,000 lire per month.

Health insurance: Advisable for non-EU teachers.

Other useful information: Italian machismo is notorious, especially in the south, and women should be prepared. If advertising in a local newspaper, it's a good idea not to betray your gender and you should arrange your lessons in a public place.

List of schools in Italy

Academia Britannica, Via Bruxelles 61, 04100 Latina

American Language Center, 1 Via Brunelleschi, 50123 Firenze

American Studies Center, 36 Via Andrea d'Isernia, 80122 Napoli

American Studies Center, 32 Via Michelangelo Caetani, 00186 Rome

Anglo American School, Piazza S. Giovanni in Monte 9, 40124 Bologna

Anglocentre, Via A de Gasperi 23, 70052 Bisceglie (BA)

Arlington Language Services, cp99, 29100, Piacenza

Associazione di Cultura/Studio Italo-Americana "Amica della Johns Hopkins", 11 Via Belmeloro, 40126 Bologna

Bari Poggiofranco English Centre, Viale Pio XII 18, 70124 Bari

Benedict School, Via Sauro 36, 48100 Ravenna

Berlitz, Via delle Asole 2, Milano

The British Council, Via Manzoni 38, 20121 Milan

The British Council, Palazzo del Drago, Via Quattro Fontane 20, 00184 Rome

British Institute, Fontane 109, Rome

British Institute of Milan, via Marghera 45, 20149 Milan

British Institute of Florence, Palazzo Feroni, Via Tornalbuoni 2, Florence

British Institute of Rome, Via IV Fontane 109, 00184 Rome

The British Language Centre, Via Piazzi Angolo Largo Pedrini, 23100 Sondrio

The British Language Centre, Via Piazza Roma 3, 20038 Serengo

The British School, Via A De Gasperi 2, Arzano (Na)

The British School, Via A De Gasperi 2, Asti

The British School, Via Celenono 27, 70121 Bari.

The British School, Via C Rasalba 49, Bari

The British School, Piazzale Codama 22, Bassano del Grappa

The British School, Via delle Poste 39, Benevento

The British School, Via Coltolengo 9, Biella (VC)

The British School, Via L Zamboni 1, Bologna

The British School, Piazza Vargas 29, Boscoreale

The British School, Via L Einaudi 11/A, Brescia

The British School, Via De' Terribile 9, Brindisi

The British School, Via Bruscu Onnis 6, Cagliari

The British School, Via L Pirandello 30, Campobasso

The British School, Via Gramsci 25, Carbonia (CA)

The British School, Via Roma 10, Caserta

The British School, Via E De Nicola 102, Cassino (FR)

The British School, Via Eduic 12, Castellamonte (TO)

The British School, Via Montesanto 116, Cosenza

The British School, Via Di Borbao 1, Firenze

The British School, Corsa Roma 110, Foggia

The British School, Via C Sforza 5, Forli'

The British School, Via Vitruvio (Traversa Lucciola), Formia (LT)

The British School, Piazza Picccapietra 76, Genova

The British School, Via de' Barberi 108, Grosseto

The British School, Via XXIV Maggio 86, Isernia

The British School, Corso Trento e Trieste 43, Lanciano (CH)

The British School, Via XXIV Maggio 178, La Spezia

The British School, Via Eugenio di Savoia 5, Latina

The British School, Via 140¡ Regg Fanteria 16, Lecce

The British School, Via Grande 82, Livorno

The British School, Via Della Libert^ 2/2, Lugo (RA)

The British School, Via GB La Salle 1, Massa

The British School, Via P Saroi 28, Mestre (VE)

The British School, Via Montenapoleone 5, Milano

The British School of Monfalcone, Via Duca d'Aosta 16, 34074 Monfalcone

The British School, Via Zucchi 38, Monza

The British School, Via Roma 148, Napoli

The British School, Via XX Marzo, Parma

The British School, Via Ugo Fosculo 11, Pavia

The British School, Corso Vittorio Emanuele 58, Piacenza

The British School, Via Rigattieri 37, Piza

The British School, Galleria Nazionale 21, Pitoia

The British School, Via Tasco Romagnolo 100, Pontedoro (PI)

The British School, Via Rosico 58, Potenza

The British School, Via della Republica 171, Prato

The British School, Via Zirordini 5, Ravenna

The British School, Via S Caterina 145, Reggio Calabria

The British School, Vei Dei Correttori 6, Reggio Calabria

The British School, Via dei Mille 2, Reggio Emilia

The British School, Viale Ceccanni 109, Riccione (FO)

The British School, Viale Andre Doria 6/E, Rimini (FO)

The British School Company Services, Salita S, Nicola da Tolentino 1/B, Roma

The British School, Via Serchio 7, Roma

The British School, Via Rhodesia 16, Roma

The British School, Lungorivere Ripa 6, Roma

The British School, Via Cassia 536, Roma

The British School, Circonvallazione Tuscolana 32, Roma

The British School, Via G A Senna 9, Sassari

The British School, Piazza A da Scio 14, Schio

The British School, Via Dante 217, Taranto

The British School, Via Roma 49, Telese terme (BN)

The British School, Vico Umberto 1,1, Termoli (CB)

The British School, Via Giolitte 55, Torino

The British School, Via Manin 54, Treviso

The British School, Vicolo Pulesi 4, 33100 Udine

The British School, Via IV Novemgre 9, Valdagno (VI)

The British School, Via V Veneto 6, Vercelli

The British School, Galleria Pelliciai 11, Verona

The British School, Viale Roma 8, Vicenza

Cambridge Centre of English, Via Campanella 16, 41100 Modena

The Cambridge School, Via S Rochetto 3, Verona

Cambridge School, M La Camera, Via Mercanti 36, 84100 Salerno

Canning School, Via San Remo 9, 20133 Milano

Centro di Lingue, Via Pozzo 30, Trento

Centro Internazionale di Linguistica Streamline, Via Piave 34/b, 71100 Foggia

Centro Lingue di Vinci Antonella, Via San Martino 77, Pisa

Centro Lingue Moderne - The Bell Educational Trust, Via Canella 14, 38066 Riva del Garda

Centro Lingue Moderne - The Bell Educational Trust, Viale Dante Alighieri 1, 38057 Pergine Valsugano

Centro Lingue Tradint, Via Jannozzi 8, S Donato Milanese (N1). Chandler, Viale Aventino 102, 00153 Roma

CLM-Bell, Eugen Joa, Via Pozzo 30, 38100 Trento

English Centre, Via Promis 8, 11100 Aosta

The English Centre, Via P Paoli 34, 07100 Sassari, Sardinia.

The English Connection, Via Ferro 1, 30027 San Dona di Piave

English For Business Snc, Via Magnani Ricotti, n.2, 28100 Novara.

The English Institute, Corso Gelone 82, 96100 Siracusa

English House, Via Roma 177, 85028 Rionero, Potenza

English Language Centre, Viale Milano 20, 21100 Varese

The English Language Studio, Via Antonio Bondi 27, 40138 Bologna

English School, Via dei Correttori 6, 89127 Reggio Calabria

Eurolingue, Via Chiana 116, 00198 Roma

European Language Institute, Via IV Novembre 65, 55049 Viareggio (LU)

European Language School, International House, Piazza Degli Artisti 38, 80128 Naples

Filadelfia School, Via L. Colla 22, 10098 Rivoli

Home School, Via F. Malvotti 8, Conegliano (TV)

inlingua Albano Laziale, Matteotti 178, I-00041 Albano Laziale

inlingua Ancona, Via Menicucci 1, I-60121 Ancona

inlingua Ascoli Piceno, Corso Mazzini 237, I-63100 Ascoli Piceno

inlingua Avellino, Via Roma 154, I-83100 Avellino

inlingua Avezzano, Via B Croce 26, I-67051 Avezzano

inlingua Bari, Via Amendola 201-1, I-70126 Bari

inlingua Bergamo, Via XX Settembre 58, I-24122 Bergamo

inlingua Bologna, Via Testoni 2, I-40123 Bologna

inlingua Brescia, Via Moretto 42, I-25122 Brescia

inlingua Cassino, Via Cellini 9, I-03043 Cassino

inlingua Civitavecchia, Torre Europa, Via Annovazzi, I-00053 Civitavecchia (Roma)

inlingua Civitanova Marche, Piazza XX Settembre 36, Civitanova Marche (MC).

inlingua Ferrara, Via Mascheraio 17, I-44100 Ferrara

inlingua Firenze, Via J Nardi 13, I-50132 Firenze

inlingua Foggia, Via Bari 72, I-71100 Foggia

inlingua Foligno, Via Oberdan 49, I-06034 Foligno

inlingua Frosinone, Marconi, Viale Marconi 12, I-03100 Frosinone

inlingua Frosinone, Piave, Via Piave 65, I-03100 Frosinone

inlingua Genova, Viale Brigate Partigiane 4/19, I-16129 Genova

inlingua Imola, Via Fratelli Bandiera 12, I-40026 Imola (Bo)

inlingua Latina, Piazza Mercato 11, I-04100 Latina

inlingua Messina, Viale S Martino 62, I-98123 Messina

inlingua Milano, Fitzi, Via Fabio Fitzi 27, I-20124 Milano

inlingua Milano, Leopardi, Via Leopardi 21, I-20123 Milano

inlingua Milano, Morgagni, Via G B Morgagni 5, I-20122 Milano

inlingua Modena, C so Canalgrande 9, I-41100 Modena

inlingua Monza, Via Italia 39, I-20052 Monza (M)

inlingua Centro Direzionale SRL, Centro Direzionale Isola G7, I-80143 Napoli

inlingua Napoli, Cimarosa, Via Cimarosa 66, I-80100 Napoli

inlingua Ortona, Corso Vittorio Emanuele II 3, I-66026 Ortona (Ch)

inlingua Pavia, Via Cavallotti 9, I-27100 Pavia

inlingua Pesaro, Via S Francesco d'Assissi 44, I-61100 Pesaro

inlingua Pesaro, Via Giolitti 159, I-61100 Pesaro

inlingua Pescara, Piazza della Rinascita 24, I-65100 Pescara

inlingua Recanati, Via Calcagni 19, I-62019 Recanati

inlingua Rimini, Piazza Ferrari 22-Scala B, I-47037 Rimini

inlingua Roma, Colombo, Via C Colombo 436, I-00145 Roma

inlingua Roma, Salandra, Via Antonio Salandra 6, I-00186 Roma

inlingua Salerno, Via Pietro da Eboli 18, I-84100 Salerno

inlingua S Benedetto del Tronto, Via Mazzocchi 4, I-63039 San Benedetto del Tronto

inlingua Terni, Via Cesare Battisti 7, I-05100 Terni

inlingua Torino, Corso Vittorio Emanuele 68, I-10121 Torino

inlingua Trieste, Via Valdirivo 21, I-34132 Trieste

inlingua Vasto, Corso Garibaldi 41, I-66054 Vasto

inlingua Velletri, Viale Roma 7, I-00049 Velletri

inlingua Venezia, Via Monte Piana 42, Venezia.

inlingua Verona, Via Leoncino 35, I-37121 Verona

inlingua Vicenza, Via Edmondo de Amicis 25, I-36100 Vicenza

inlingua Vigevano, Piazza IV Novembre 11, I-27029 Vigevano

International British School, Via Santacaterina 146, 89100 Regio Calabria

International House, Via Zurlo 5, 86100 Compobasso

International House La Spezia, Via Manzoni 64, 19100 La Spezia

International House - Accademia Britannica, Via Bruxelles 61, 04100 Latina

International House, Via Jannozzi 6, 20097 San Donato Milanese

International House Livorno, Piazza Folgore 1, 57128 Livorno

International House, Via Como 27, 22055 Merate (Lecco)

International House Language Centre, Via Gaetano Daita 29, 90139 Palermo

International House Pisa, Via Risorgimento 9, 56126 Pisa

International House - Accademia Brittanica SAS, Via Marco Roncioni 116, 50047 Prato

International House Roma, Viale Manzoni 22, 00185 Roma

International House - DILIT, Via Marghera 22, 00185 Roma

International House Roma, Via San Godenzo 100, 00189 Roma.

International House - Accademia Brittanica, Viale Etiopia 8/A, 00199 Roma

International House, Via Pietro Gori 32, Sarzana

International House - Accademia Britannica, Via Gozzano 4/6, 20038 Seregno

International Language School, Via Tibullo 10, 00193 Rome

Italo American Association of the Region Friuli Venezia Giulia, 15 Via Roma, 34132 Trieste

Language Centre, Via Milano 20, 21100 Varese

Language Centre, Via G Daita 29, 90139 Palermo

Lb Linguistico, Centro Insegnamento, Lingue Staniere, Via Caserta 16, 95128 Catania, Sicily

Lingua Due Villa, Pendola 15, 57100 Livorno

Linguarama Milan, Via S Tomaso 2, 20121 Milano Tel: 02 89 01 16 66 Fax: 0 89 01 16 51 email: milano@lin guarama.com

Linguarama Rome, Via Tevere 48, 00198 Roma Tel: 06 85 35 57 07 Fax: 06 85 35 57 13 email: roma@linguarama.com

Linguarama Turin, Via E de Sonnaz 17, 10121 Torino Tel: 011 562 03 35 Fax: 011 562 21 63 email: torino@linguarama.com

Living Languages School, Via Magna Grecia, 89100 Regio Calabria

London School, International House, Viale Emilia 34, 90144 Palermo

Lord Byron College, Via Sparano 102, 70121 Bari

Managerial English Consultants, Via Sforza Pallavicini 11, 009193 Rome

Modern English Study Centre, Via Borgonuovo 14, 40125 Bologna

Multimethod, I Go Richini 8, 20122 Milan

Oxford School of English, Via S Pertini 14, Mirano, 30035 Venice

Oxford School, San Marco 1513, Venice

The Professionals, Via F Carcona 4, 20149 Milan

Regency School, Via dell' Arcivescovado 7, 16121 Turin

Regent International, V.U. Da Pisa 6, Milano

Regent International, Corsa Italia 54, 21047 Saronno

RTS Language Training, Via Tuscolana 4, 00182 Rome

Scuola The Westminster, Via Tevere 84, Sesto Fiorentino (FI)

Spep School, Via della Secca 1, 40121 Bologna

Studio Linguistico Fonema, via Marconi 19, 50053 Sovigliana-Vinci (Fl).

Studio professionale Apprendimento Linguistico Programmato, Via Ferrarese 3, Bologna

Summer Camps, Via Roma 54, 18038 San Remo

Unimoney, Corso Sempione 72, 20154 Milano

Victoria Language Centre, Viale Fassi 28, 41012 Capri.

Wall Street Institute, Piazza Combattento 6, 4100 Ferrara

We would like to thank Chris Burdett, English Worldwide for help in compiling this listing.

Netherlands

With very high levels of English in the state school system, most work available to foreign teachers tends to be in Business English. Native speaker teachers should have a teaching qualification and commercial experience to have a chance.

Schools rarely offer contracts, depending instead on long-term freelance teachers. Self-employed teachers typically work for a number of schools or agencies and their incomes can fluctuate considerably. To find work, go through the list of language schools below as well as those in the Dutch Yellow Pages (look under Talen Institut). Expect to give an observed lesson before you are hired.

Visas and work permits: British and Irish nationals need to obtain a tax number from the police when they arrive. There are complex rules for other nationalities and it can take three months to arrange a work permit. Some teachers do work on tourist visas, but it is hard to find work in reputable schools without a tax code.

Cost of living: Expensive, but it is possible to live well.

Salaries and taxes: Qualified freelance teachers with commercial experience tend to get paid between 30 and 50 guilders per lesson. Schools pay around 35 guilders. The tax rate is about 30 per cent.

Accommodation: It is expensive, especially in and around Amsterdam. A one-bedroomed flat would typically cost around 500 guilders a month, with a month's rent as a deposit.

Health insurance: Not necessary if you pay tax.

List of schools in theNetherlands
Amerongen Talenpraktikum, De Kievit 1, 3958 Dd Amerongen

Asa Studiecentrum, Kotterstraat 11, 1826 Cd Alkmaar

Asco, Nassauplein 8, 1815 Gm Alkmaar

AVC, Oringerbrink 43, 7812 Jr Emmen

Avoc Teleninstituut, Heugemerweg 2d, 6229 As Maastricht

Bell College, Afd English LanguageTraining, Stationsstraat 17, 6221 Bm Maastricht

Berlitz Language Centre, Rokin 87-89, 1012 Kl Amsterdam

Bltc, Keizersgracht 389, 1016 Ej Amsterdam

British Language Training Centre, N.Z. Voorburgwal 328e, 1012 RW Amsterdam. Contact:Christabel Gorman Tel: 31 20 622 3634 Fax: 31 20 622 4962 Email: bltc@bltc.nl Website: http:/www.xs4all.nl/bltc. Teacher Training - CELTA, 4 & 12 weeks. English and Dutch - all levels, Cambridge exams, Business, Specialist, Academic & IELTS

Boerhave Opleidingen, Hoogstraat 118, 801 Bb Zwolle

Bressler's Business Language, Buiksloterdijk 284, 1034 Zd Amsterdam

Class International, Bijlwerffstr 28b, 3039 Vh Rotterdam

Dinkgreve Handelsopleiding, Wilemsparkweg 31, 1071 Gp Amsterdam

Dutch College, P Calandlaan 42, 1065 Kp Amsterdam

EBC Taleninstituut, Stationstraat 40, 4611 CD Bergen op Zoom

Educational Holidays, Beukstraat 149, 2565 Xz Den Haag

Eerste Nederlandse Talenpraktikum, Kalverstr 112, 1012 Pk Amsterdam

Elseviers Talen, Jan Van Galenstraat 335, 1061 Az Amsterdam

Elseviers Talen, Westelijke Parallelweg 54, 3331 Ew Zwijndrecht

Erasmus College, Planetenlaan 5, 2024 Eh Haarlem,Hendrik Ido Ambacht

Europa Talenpraktikum, Vosselmanstraat 400, 7311 Cl Apeldoorn

Fikkers Handelsinstituut, Anna Paulownastr 37a, 2518 Bb Den Haag

Gouwe College, Turfsingel 67, 2802 Bd Gouda

Instituut Meppel, Tav Dhr J G Rijpkema, Postbus 263, 7940 Ag Meppel

Instituut Schoevers, Markt 17, 5611 Eb Eindhoven

Instituut Schoevers, Postbus 10486, 5000 Jl Tilburg

Interlingua Taalsupport Bv, Wijnhaven 99, 3011 Wn Rotterdam

Interlingua Talenpraktikum, Burg van Royensingel 20 - 21, 8011 ct Zwolle

International Studiecentrum, voor de Vrouw Concertgebouwplein 17, 107 LM Amsterdam

Interphone Opleidingen, St Jorisstraat 17, 5361 Hc Grave

Language Partners - Rotterdam, Wtc Beursplein 37, 3011 A Rotterdam

Leidse Onderwijsinstelling,Tav Mr Wirtz, Leidsedreef 2, 2352 Ba Leiderdorp

Linguarama Nederland, Bleijenburg 1, 2511 VC Den Haag Tel: 00 3170 364 58 38 Fax: 00 3170 365 43 81 Email: den-haag@linguarama.com Website: www.linguarama.com Contact: Nicola Courtney. Centres in Amsterdam, Den Haag, Utrecht. Part of Linguarama International. Specialises in training language for business and government. Excellent teacher support

Linguarama Amsterdam, Nieuwezijds Voorburgwal 120-126, 1012 SH Amsterdam Tel: (0) 20 428 05 28 Fax: (0) 20 428 06 28 email: amsterdam@nl.linguarama.com

Linguarama Hoofddorp, Kantorencentrum, De Reitlanden 2, Polderplein 166, 2132 BG Hoofddorp Tel: (0) 23 565 22 11 Fax: (0) 23 565 22 14 email: hoofddorp@nl.linguarama.com

Linguaphone Instituut, Peperstraat 7, 6127 As Grevenbicht, Huis Van Bewaring, de Koepel Afd Onderwijs, Harmenjansweg 4, 2031 Wk Haarlem

Notenboom, Kerkakkerstraat 34, 5616 Hc Eindhoven

Onderwijsinstituut Netty Post, Haverstraat 2, 1447 Ce Purmerend

Scholengem. G K Van Hogendorp, Postbus 290725, 3001 Gb Rotterdam

School of English, Eerste Wormenseweg 238, 7331 Nt Apeldoorn

Stichting Volwasseneducatie Deventer, Afd English Language Training, Postbus 639, 7400 Ap Deventer

Talenpraktikum Twente, Tav Dhr P De Wit, Ariensplein 2, 7511 Jx Enschede

Zeeuwse Volksuniversiteit, Afd English Language Training, Postbus 724, 4330 As Middleburg

Portugal

The general level of English tends to be high in Portugal since it is very well taught within the state school system, but it is still relatively easy to find a job, especially if you decide to teach young learners.

There are a number of foreign school chains firmly established in the country and there is a lot of recruitment overseas, especially by schools outside the major tourist cities which cannot rely on native

speakers just turning up. Work which is advertised abroad usually involves some kind of contract while local recruitment is more likely to be paid on an hourly basis.

It is far easier to find work away from Lisbon, and teaching Business English in-company can be very lucrative.

Visas and work permits: EU citizens need a residence permit, which can be obtained on production of a letter of confirmation from your employer to the authorities. For non-EU citizens a lot of paperwork and waiting around is involved and contracts should be in place before coming to the country. Schools are less likely to hire non-EU teachers.

Cost of living: It's not as cheap as many people assume, but salaries are getting better and costs are not increasing as much.

Salaries and taxes: The going rate is between 2,000 and 2,500 escudos per hour. Salaries vary, from around 125,000 at the lower end of the market, to between 150,000 and 225,000 escudos per month in reputable schools. The higher amounts are to be found in Lisbon. If you are on a contract, you are often entitled to a bonus after 12 months. International House and the British Council pay some in Porto and Coimbra.

The income tax rate is about 20-25 per cent, and national insurance about 8 or 11 per cent.

Accommodation: Some schools provide accommodation for their teachers, or help in finding some. Otherwise, expect to pay about quarter of your salary in the small towns for a shared flat or upwards of 60,000 escudos per month in Lisbon, 70,000 to 80,000 in Porto and Coimbra. Two months' rent is expected as a deposit.

Health insurance: Employers are required to insure all employees in the workplace but you should make arrangements for outside.

English language newspapers: The Anglo-Portuguese News, The Post.

List of schools in Portugal
American Language Institute, Rua Jos/ Falcao 15-5† Esq, 4050 Oporto

Berlitz, Av Conde Valbom 6-4, 1000 Lisboa

Big Ben School, Rua Moinho Fanares 4-1, 2725 Mem Martins

Bristol School Group, Trav. Dr Carlos Felgueiras, 12-3†, 4470 Maia

British Council, Rua De Sao Marcal 174, 1294 Lisbon Codex

British Council, Rua Do Breyner 155, 4050 Oporto 200 5577

Cambridge School, Avenida da Liberdade 173-4, 1200 Lisboa

Casa de Inglaterra, Rua Alexandre Herculano 134, 3000 Coimbra

CENA-Cent. Est. Norte Americanos, Rua Remedios 62 c/v, 1200 Lisboa

Centro de Estudos IPFEL, Rua Edith Cavell 8, 1900 Lisboa

Centro de Instrucao Tecnica, Rua Da Estefania 32-10 Dto, 1000 Lisboa

Centro Internacional Linguas, Av Fontes P de Melo 25-1Dto, 1000 Lisboa

Centro de Linguas de Alvide, Rua Fonte Nino, Viv Pe Americo 1, Alvide, 2750 Cascais

Centro de Linguas Estrangeiras de Cascais, Av Marginal BI A-30, 2750 Cascais

Centro de Linguas Intergarb, Tv da Liberdade 13-1, 8200 Albufeira

Centro de Linguas de Quarteira, Rua Proj 25 de Abril 12, 8125 Quartiera

Centro de Linguas de Queluz, Av Dr Miguel Bombarda 62-1E, 2745 Queluz

Centro de Linguas de Santarem, Lg Pe Francisco N Silva, 2000 Santarem

CIAL-Centro De Linguas, Av Republica 14-20, 1000 Lisboa

Class, Rua Gen Humberto Delgado 40-1, 7540 Santiago Do Cacem

Clube Conversacao Inglesa 3M, Rua Rodrigues Sampaio 18-3, 1100 Lisboa

Communicate Language Institute, Praceta Joao Villaret 12B, 2675 Povoa de Sto Adriao

Curso de Linguas Estrangeiras, Rua Dr Miguel Bombarda 271-1, 2600 Vila Franca De Xira

Ecubal, Lombos, Barros Brancos, Porches, 8400 Lagoa

ELTA, Av Jose E Garcia 55-3, 2745 Queluz

Encounter English, Av Fernao De Magalha, 4300 Porto

English at PLC, Praca Luis de Camoes 26, Apartado 73, 5001 Vila Real

English Institute Setubal, Av 22 Dezembro 88, 2900 Setubal

The English Language Centre, Rua Calouste Gulbenkian 22-r/c C, 3080 Figueira Da Foz

The English School of Coruche, Rua Guerreiros 11, 2100 Coruche

English School of Loule, Rua Jose F Guerreiro 66M,Galerias Do Mercado, 8100 Loule

Escola de Linguas de Agueda, Rua Jose G Pimenta, 3750 Agueda

Escola de Linguas de Ovar, Rua Ferreira de Castro 124-1 A/B, 3880 Ovar

Eurocenter Instituto de Linguas, Av de Bons Amigos 4-1, 2735 Cacem

Gab Tecnico de Linguas, Rua Hermenegildo Capelo 2-2, 2400 Leiria

GEDI, Pq Miraflores Lt 18-lA/B, 1495 Alges

Greenwich Instituto de Linguas, Rua 25 de Abril 560, S Cosme, 4420 Gondomar

IF Ingles Funcional, Rua Afonso Albuquerque 73-A, 2460 Alcobaca

IF Ingles Funcional, Rua Com Almeida Henriques 32, 2400 Leiria

IF Ingles Funcional, Ap 303, 2430 Marinha Grande

INESP, Rua Dr Alberto Souto 20-2, 3800 Aveiro

inlingua Lisboa, Rua Rodrigo da Fonseca, 60-2 Dto, P-1250 Lisboa

inlingua Porto, Rua Goncalo Cristovao 217-12¡, P-4000 Porto

INLINGUA, Campo Grande 30-1A, 1700 Lisboa

INPR, Bernardo Lima 5, 1100 Lisboa

Instituto Britanico, Rua Conselheiro Januario 119/21, 4700 Braga

Instituto Britanico, Rua Municipio Lt B - 1 C, 2400 Leiria

Instituto Britanico, Rua Dr Ferreira Carmo, 4990 Ponte De Lima

Instituto Franco-Britanico, Rua 5 de Outubro 10-1Dto, 2700 Amadora

Instituto Inlas do Porto, Rua S da Bandeira 522-1, 4000 Porto

Instituto de Linguas, Rua Valverde 1, 2350 Torres Novas

Instituto de Linguas do Castelo Branco, Av 1 Maio, 39 S - l E, 6000 Castelo Branco

Instituto de Linguas de Faro, Av 5 de Outubro, 8000 Faro

Instituto de Linguas do Fundao, Urb Rebordao Lt 17-r/c, 6230 Fundao

Instituto de Linguas de Oeiras, Rua Infante D Pedro 1 e 3-r/c, 2780 Oeiras

Instituto de Linguas de Paredes, Av Republica, Casteloes Cepeda, 4580 Paredes

Instituto Nacional de Administracao, Centro de Linguas, Palacio Marquus de Oeiras, 2780 Oeiras

Instituto Sintrense de Linguas, Rua Dr Almeida Guerra 26, 2710 Sintra

Interlingua, Lg 1 de Dezembro 28, 8500 Portimao

Interlingua, Rua Dr Joaquim Telo 32-1E, 8600 Lagos

International House, Rua Domingos Carrancho 1-1 DT, 3800 Aveiro

International House, Avenida Alfredo da Silva 57, 2830 Barreiro

International House Braga, Rua dos Chaos 168, 4710 Braga

International House, Rua Antero de Quental 135, 3000 Coimbra

International House, Rua Macario de Castro No 70, 5100 Lamego

International House Lisbon, Rua Marques Sa Da Bandeira 16, 1000 Lisboa

International House Porto, Rotunda da Boavista 99-4¡ andar, 4100 Porto

International House, Rua Miguel Bombarda 3-1, 2560 Torres Vedras

International House, Rua dos Casimiros 33, 3510 Viseu

International Language School, Av Rep Guine Bissau, 26-A, 2900 Setubal

ISLA, Bo S Jo de Brito, 5300 Bragan A, Manitoba,C Com Premar, l 72, 4490 Povoa De Varzim

Know-How, Av Alvares Cabral 5-300, 1200 Lisboa

Lancaster College, Rua C Civico, Ed A Seguradora 2, 6200 Covilha

Lancaster College, Pta 25 Abril 35-1E, 4400 Vila Nova De Gaia

Language School, Rua Alm Candido Reis 98, 2870 Montijo

Linguacoop, Av. Manuel da Maia 46-10 D, 1000 Lisboa

Linguacultura, Rua Dr Joaquim Jacinto 110, 2300 Tomar

Linguacultura, Lg Sto Antonio 6-1 Esq, 2200 Abrantes

Linguarama Lisbon, Edificio Liberdade, Avenida da Liberdade 49, 1250 Lisboa Tel: (0) 1 342 63 50 Fax: (0) 1 342 63 51 email: lisboa@linguarama.c

Lisbon Language Learners, Rua Conde Redondo 33-r/cE, 1100 Lisboa

Mundilingua, Rua Dr Tefilo Braga, Ed Rubi-1, 8500 Portimao

Mundilinguas, Rua Miguel Bombarda 34-1, 2000 Santarem

The New Institute of Languages, Urb Portela Lt 197-5B-C, 2685 Sacavem

Novo Instituto de Linguas, Rua Cordeiro Ferreira 19 C-1D, 1700 Lisboa

PEC, Rua SA Bandeira 5385, 4000 Operto

PROLINGUAS, Rua Saraiva Carvalho, 84 - Pt2, 1200 Lisboa

Royal School of Languages, Av Dr Lourenco Peixinho 92-2, 3800 Aveiro

Tell School, Rua Soc Farmaceutica 30-1, 1100 Lisboa

Tjaereborg Studio, Av Liberdade 166-4F, 1200 Lisboa

Wall Street Institutes Avenidas, Av Praia de Vitoria, 71 3rd, Lisbon 1000

Wall Street Institutes Oporto, Rua do Campo Alegre 231, 3†, 4100 Oporto

Weltsprachen-Institut, Qta Carreira 37 r/c, 2765 Sao Joao do Estoril. Tel: 4684032. Branch: Rua Dr Brito Camacho 22-A-1, 7800 Beja

Whyte Institute, Lg das Almas 10-2E/F, 4900 Viana Do Castelo

World Trade Centre - Lisbon, Av Brasil 1-5e8, 1700 Lisboa

Spain

With the 1992 Olympics in Barcelona demand for English language learning soared, but the recent economic climate has slowed things down. Most activity now focuses on the young learner market and the continued attraction of the country means that teachers are plentiful.

Opportunities for unqualified L1 native speakers are very slim and even qualified teachers who apply on the off-chance from overseas are likely to be disappointed. Most recruitment is done on the spot. September is the best time to look as this is after the summer holidays and before the beginning of the academic year, but there might be opportunities in January when contracted teachers fail to turn up after a perhaps unexpectedly cold winter.

Schools usually only offer part-time work and, because statutory employee entitle-

ments start operating only after 12 months work, nine-month contracts tend to be the norm unless you are a director of studies. The maximum number of teaching hours per week allowed by law is 33, but contracted teachers can expect a punishing schedule with close to this number of hours, often at inconvenient times.

Private work is also an option and because it is better paid than working in schools, even contracted teachers compete for hours.

Visas and work permits: With a copy of their contract, EU-nationals can easily obtain a residence card. Employer help with the paperwork is variable. Non EU nationals will find it expensive and time-consuming (about two years) to secure the necessary permit, so schools are reluctant to take them on.

Cost of living: Moderate to fairly expensive in the major cities.

Salaries and taxes: These vary a lot. Initial salaries for the state sector in Catalonia are 180,000 pesetas per month for primary teachers and 210,000 pesetas for secondary. Private sector schools (including the British Council) pay from 1,500 to 2,000 pesetas per hour in Catalonia, and 2,500 pesetas in Bilbao, and contracts often provide flights and baggage allowance. Freelancers can earn between 1,500 and 2,500 pesetas per hour in the Valencia region and from 2,000 to 5,000 pesetas in Catalonia.

The British Council office in Valencia maintains a register for freelance teachers to join.

Residents pay 15 per cent tax in arrears with 6 per cent social security.

Accommodation: Rents often take up more than a quarter of a teacher's salary, especially in cities, although lower salaries in smaller towns might include accommodation. Expect to pay between 65,000 and 100,000 pesetas a month if you want to live on your own. For shared accommodation, standard rents are around 30,000 pesetas per month. Up to two months deposit is essential. If you find accommodation through an agency,

you will pay an extra month's rent on top.

Health insurance: Essential.

Important cultural differences: The Spanish start work early and leave late, with a long break for lunch.

Other useful information: After two years on contract, employees should become full members of staff, which makes it almost impossible to be fired. Therefore after two years some companies sack employees and hire someone cheaper. The rules on contracts are continually changing in Spain, so you should check you own situation.

List of schools in Spain

Academia Andaluza de Idiomas, Crta El Punto 9, Conil, Cadiz

Academia Benedict Idiomas, Av Tirajana 37, 35100 Playa Del Ingles, Gran Canaria

Academia Britanica, Rodriguez Sanchez 15, 14003 Cordoba

Academia Lacunzia, International House, Urbieta 14-1, 20006 San Sebastian

Academia Saint Patricks, Calle Caracuel 1, 17402 Girona

Academia Wellington House, Guiposcoa 79, 08020 Barcelona

Acento - The Language Company, Ruiz De Alarcon 7, 21, 41007 Sevilla

Afoban, Alfonso Xii 30, 41002 Sevilla

CIM, Loramendi 7, Apartado 191, Mondragon Guipuzcoa

Alce Idiomas, Nogales 2, 33006 Oviedo

Aljarafe Language Academy, Crta Castilleja-Tomares 83, Tomares, Sevilla

American British College, Guillem Tell 27, 08006 Barcelona

American Institute, El Bachiller 13, 46010 Valencia

Apple Idiomas, Aben al Abbar 6, 46021 Valencia

Ard Escuela de Idiomas, Alejandro del Castillo, 35100 Play del Ingles, Gran Canaria

Audio Jeam, Pza Ayuntamiento 2, 46002 Valencia

Augusta Idiomas, Via Augusta 128, 08006 Barcelona

Aupi, Jesus 43, 46007 Valencia

Avila Centre of English, Bajada de Don Alonso 1, 05003 Avila

Benidorm Int College, Partida de Sanz s/n, 03500 Benidorm, Alicante

Berlitz, Gran Via 80, 4°, 28013 Madrid

Berlitz, Edif Forum 1 Mod, 3 Av Luis Morales, S/N 41018 Sevilla

Big Ben College, Plaza Quintiliano 13, Calahorra 26500 La Rioja

Brighton, Rambla Catalunya 66, 08007 Barcelona

Bristol English School, Fundacion Jado 10 Bis 6, 48950 Erlandio, Vizacaya

Britannia School of English, s 9, Bl 2 41010 Sevilla

Britannia School, Leopoldo Lugones 3-1B, 33420 Lugones, Asturias

Britannia School, Raset 22, Barcelona 08021

The British Centre, Amezqueta 17 trasera, San Sebastian

British Council, Bravo Murillo 25, 35003 Las Palmas De Gran Canaria

British Council, General San Martin 7, 46003 Valencia

British Language Centre, C/Bravo Murillo 377, 28020 Madrid

British School Children's Garden, Avda. Peris y Valero 57-59, 46006 Valencia

Business Classes, International House, Calle Zurbano 8, 28010 Madrid

Business & United Schools, Genova 4, 1D 41010 Sevilla

Callan Method School of English, Calle Alfredo Vicenti 6 bajo, 15004 La Coruna

Cambridge House, Primary School: Campo Olivar-Godella, 46110 Valencia

Cambridge House, c/ Bravo Murillo 153, IC, 28020 Madrid

Cambridge School, Placa Manel Montanya, 4, 08400 Granollers

Campbell College, Teacher Training Centre, Pascual y Genis 14-4, 46002 Valencia Tel/Fax: 00 34 96 3524217 Email: campbell@cpsl.com Website: http://www.cpsl.com.campbell Cambridge/RSA CELTA February/May/July/November. Personalised individual attention. Pleasant learning environment. Accommodation office. Job placement service. Spanish courses

---

Caxton College, Ctra de Barcelona s/n, 46530 Puzol, Valencia

CEE Idiomas, c/ Carmen 6, 28030 Madrid

Centro Atlantico, Villanueva 2 apdo, 28001 Madrid

Centro Britanico, Republica De El Salvador 26-10m, (Edificio Simago), 15701 Santiago De Compostela, La Coruna

Centro Britannico, Alfereces Provisionoles 1 1°B, 23007 Jaen

Centro Cooperativo de Idiomas, Clavel 2, 11300 La Linea, Cadiz

Centro Estudios Norteamericanos, Aparisi y Guijarro 5, 46005 Valencia

Centro de Estudios de Ingles, Garrigues 2, 46001 Valencia.

Centro de Idiomas Concorde, c/ Gral Moscardo 12, 28020 Madrid

Centro De Idiomas Liverpool, Libreros 11-1°, 28801 Alcala de Henares, Madrid

Centro de Idiomas Sagasta, c/ Sagasta 27, 28004 Madrid

Centro De Ingles, Tejon Y Marin, S/N 14003 Cordoba

Centro de Ingles Luz, Passage Luz 8 bajo, 46010 Valencia

Centro Linguistico del Maresme, Virgen De Montserrat (Jenifer Grau).

Centro Superior de Idiomas, Tuset 26, 08006 Barcelona

Chatterbox Language Centre, Verge de l'Assumpcio 21, Barbera del Valles

Chester School of English, c/ Jorge Juan 125, Madrid

CIC Escola d'Idiomes, Via Augusta 205, 08021 Barcelona

CIM-Idiomas, Avenida de Alava 4, Arrasate-Mondrag—n 20500, Guipezcoa

CLIC (Centro de Lenguas e Intercambio Cultural), International House Seville, Calle Santa Ana 11, 41002, Sevilla

Collegium Palatinum, Calle de Rodriguez San Pedro 10, 28015 Madrid

Colon, Gran Via 55, Madrid

Eastview School, Edif Puerta Este, junto Continente, Sevilla

The English Academy, Cruz 15, 11370 Los Barrios, Cadiz

English 1, c/ Santa Maria Mozzarello s/n, Sevilla

English Activity Centre, Pedro Frances 22a, 07800 Ibiza

The English Centre, Apdo de Correos 85, 11500 El Puerto De Santa Maria, Cadiz

English Institute, Carrer La Mar 38, 03700 Denia

English Language Centre, Jesus Maria 9-1d, 14003 Cordoba

English Language Centre, Mtra Sra de Los Colcanes 38, 35500 Arrecife, Lanzarote

English Language Institute, c/ Larra 1, Sevilla

The English School Los Olivos, Avenida Pino Panera 25, 46110 Godella, Valencia

English Studies, SA Avenida de Arteijo 8-1, 15004 La Coruna

English Way, Platero 30, San Juan De Aznalfarache, Sevilla

EPI Center, Niebla 13, 41011 Sevilla

Escuela Oficial de Idiomas, Av Drassanes s/n, 08001 Barcelona

Escuela Oficial de Idiomas, c/ Jesus Maestro s/n, 28003 Madrid

Eurocentre, Puerta De Jerez 3-1, 41001 Sevilla

Eurocentres, pa Castellana 194, 28046 Madrid

Eurolingua, San Felipe 3, 14003 Cordoba

Eurolog Idiomes, Plaza Lesseps 4, 08023 Barcelona

European Language Schools, Regueiro 2, 36211 Vigo

European Language Studies, Edificio Edimburgo, Plaza Nina, 21003 Huelva

Fiac School, Mayor 19, 08221 Terrassa, Barcelona

FLAC, Escola De Idiomes Moderns Les Valls, 10 2/0, 08201 Sabadell, Barcelona

Glossa English Language Centre, Rambla De Cataluna 9, 78 20 2A 08008 Barcelona

ICL, Av Josep Tarradellas 106 2° 3a, 08029 Barcelona

Idiomas Blazek, Llinas 2, 07014 Palma de Mallorca

Idiomas Oxford, Calvo Sotelo 8-1, 26003 Logrono

Idiomas Progreso, Plaza Progreso 12, 07013 Palma De Mallorca

Idiomaster, c/Juan Rico 6, 14900 Lucena, Cordoba Tel: 957 59 16 78 Fax: 957 59 16 78 Email: idiomaster@jet.es Three centres in the province of Cordoba. English for young learners and adults. Qualified and experienced teachers. Trinity College examinations centre.

---

inlingua Albacete, Tesifonte Gallego 20, Apdo 14, E-02002 Albacete

inlingua Almeria, Cl General Segura N° 13-Bajo, E-04004 Almeria

inlingua Barcelona, Placa Tetuan, 40-41 2 pl, E-08010 Barcelona

inlingua Benedorm, Alameda 5-2°, E-03500 Benidorm

inlingua Bilbao, Colon de Lareategui 38-1°, E-48009 Bilbao

inlingua Blanes, c/ la Fe 11, E-17300 Blanes (Gerona)

inlingua Burgos, Martinez, Plaza Alonzo Martinez 8-3°, E-09003 Burgos

inlingua Burgos, Perlado, Avda Eladio Perlado 31-1°, E-09005 Burgos

inlingua Calella, C Bruguera 172, E-08370 Calella

inlingua Castellon, Calle Vera 4, E-12001 Castellon de la Plana

inlingua Gijon, Menendez Pelayo 2, E-33202 Gijon (Asturias)

inlingua Huesca, Avda Juan XXIII, 15-bajos, E-22003 Huesca

inlingua Irun, c/ Joaquin Gamon 2-1°, E-20302 Irun

inlingua Las Palmas, c/ Francisco Gourie 67-3°, E-35002 Las Palmas de Gran Canaria

inlingua Lleida, Alcalde Rovira Roure 9, E-25006 Lleida

inlingua Logrono, Portales 47-1°, E-26001 Logrono

inlingua Lorca, Avda Juan Carlos I 47, Apdo 28, E-30800 Lorca

inlingua Madrid, Arenal 24, E-28013 Madrid

inlingua Malaga, Plaza de las Flores 7-3°, E-29005 Malaga

inlingua Manresa, Passeig Pere II 68-bis, E-08240 Manresa

inlingua Marbella, Avenida Ricardo Soriano 4-2°, E-29600 Marbella

inlingua Molina de Segura (Murcia), Plaza Region Murciana 1, E-30500 Molina de Segura (Murcia)

inlingua Murcia, Plaza Hernandez Amores 4 1°, E-30001 Murcia

inlingua Ordizia, Elcano 8-1°, Izq, E-20240 Ordizia

inlingua Palma de Mallorca, c/ 31 de Diciembre 7, E-07003 Palma de Mallorca

inlingua Reus, c/ Saint Joan 24 bis 1, E-43201 Reus

inlingua San Sebastian, Hernani, Hernani 29-1°, E-20004 San Sebastian

inlingua San Sebastian, Larramendi, c/ Larramendi 23, E-20006 San Sebastian

inlingua Santander, Avenida de Pontejos 5, E-39005 Santander

inlingua Tarragona, Rambla Nova 3, E-43202 Tarragona

inlingua Valencia, c/ Colon 18-3B, E-46004 Valencia

inlingua Valladolid, Gregorio Fernandez 6, E-47006 Valladolid

inlingua Vitoria, Postas 6-2°, E-01001 Vitoria

inlingua Zaragoza, Cost 2-1° izda, E-50001 Zaragoza

inlingua Idiomas, Maestro Falla 5, 2,12, Puerto del Rosario, 35600 Fuerteventura, Canary Islands

inlingua Idiomas, Tomas Morales 28, 35003 Las Palmas de Gran Canaria

The Institute of English, Santiago Garcia 8, 46100 Burjasot

Institute of North American Studies, Via Augusta 123, 08006 Barcelona

Institutos Mangold, Rambla Catalunya 16, 08007 Barcelona

Interlang, Pl Padre Jean de Mariana 3-2, 45002 Toledo

International House, Trafalgar 14 entlo, 08010 Barcelona. Tel: 34 3 268 4511, Fax: 34 3 268 0239, e-mail: training@bcn.ihes.com, Website: http://www.ihes.com/bcn. Long-established and successful centre for Teacher Training, English and Spanish courses with a worldwide reputation for excellence.

International House, Avinguda Diagonal 612 entlo, 08021 Barcelona

International House, Rodriguez Sanchez 15, 14003 Cordoba

International House, C/Hernan Cortes 1, 21001 Huelva

International House, Calle Zurbano 8, 28010 Madrid

International House, Calle Serrano 19 2a, 28001 Madrid

International House, Juan XXIII 9, Chaminade, 28040 Madrid

International House, Carrer Balmes 29, 08301 Mataro

International House, Bonaire 9, Esc 2.1°, 07012 Palma de Mallorca

International House, Calle Llovera 47-2, 43201 Reus

International House, Escola Industrial 12, 08201 Sabadell

International House, Rambla Nova 99, 43001 Tarragona

International House, Bonaire 9, Esc 2.1°, 07012 Paluade Mallorea

International House, Albarda 19, Sevilla 41001

International House, La Rasa 50, 08221 Terrasa

International House, Cortes de Aragon 50, 50005 Zaragoza

John Atkinson School of English, Isaac Peral 11 y 13, 11100 San Fernando

JD Ray Idiomas, Antonio Lopez 47 1°b, 28019 Madrid

Kensington Centros de Idiomas, Avda Pedro Mururuza 8, 20870 Elgoibar

King's College, Serrano 44, 28001 Madrid

Lacunza SA - International House, Main School, Business English Dept, Open Learning Centre, Urbieta 14-1°, 20006 San Sebastian

Lady Elizabeth School, Apartado de Correos 298, 03730 Javea, Alicante

Langage, c/ Enrique Granados 149, pral, 08029 Barcelona

Language Studies International, Luchana 31, 1°, 28010 Madrid

Language Study Centre, Corredera Baja 15 Bajo, Chiclana De La Frontera, Cadiz

Lawton School, Cura Sama 7, 33202 Gijon, Asturias

The Lewis School, Gran Via de Carlos III 97, bajos K, 08028 Barcelona

Lexis, Avenida de la Constitucion 34, 18012 Granada

Linguacenter, c/ Rafael Calvo 8, 28010 Madrid

Linguarama Madrid, Edificio Iberia Mart 11, Orense 34, 28020 Madrid Tel: 96 394 00205 Fax: 96 394 4127 email: madrid@linguarama.com

Linguarama Barcelona, Edificios Trade, Torre Norte, Gran Via de Carlos II 98 -2, 08028 Barcelona Tel: 93 330 16 87 Fax: 93 330 80 13 email: barcelona@linguarama.com

Linguarama Pamplona, Avenida Pio XII 26 - 1 - 1, 31008 Pamplona Tel: 948 26 50 19 Fax: 948 26 50 42 email: pamplona@linguarama.com

Linguarama Seville, Edificio Forum, Calle Luis de Morales 32 - 196, 41018 Sevilla Tel: 95 453 45 34 Fax: 95 453 47 54 email: sevilla@linguarama.com

Linguarama Valencia, Centro de Negocios Paz, Plaza Alfonso el Magnanimo 1-1, 46003 Valencia Tel: 96 392 3646 Fax: 96 392 3646 email: valencia@linguarama.com

Linguasec, Malaga 1, 14003 Cordoba

Listen and Learn, c/ Narvaez 14, 28009 Madrid

London Centre, c/ Asuncion 52, Sevilla

London House, Baron de S Petrillo 23 bajo, 46020 Benimaclet

Madrid Plus, c/ Arenal 21 6°D, Madrid

Manchester School, San Bernado 81, 33201 Gijon, Alicante

Merit School, Campo Florida 54, 08027 Barcelona

Modern School, Gerona 11, 41003 Sevilla

Nelson English School, Jorge Manrique 1, Santa Cruz, Tenerife

Next Training Espana, Rocafort 241-243, 6o-5o, Barcelona 08029

Ten Centro de Ingles, Caracuel 24, Jerez de la Frontera.

The New School, Calle Sant Joan 2, 2a Reus Tarragona

Newton College, Camino Viejo Elche-Alicante Km 3, Partida de Maitido, 03295 Elche, Alicante

Number Nine English Language Centre, Sant Onofre 1, 07760 Ciutadella De Menorca, Baleares

Onoba Idiomas, Rasco 19-2, 21001 Huelva

Oxford Centre, Alvaro de Bazan 16, 46010 Valencia

Oxford House, San Jeronimo 9-11, Granada

The Oxford School, Maron Feria 4, 41800 Sanl·car La Mayor, Sevilla

Piccadilly English Institute, Los Chopos 8, 14006 Cordoba

Plantio International School of Valencia, Calle 233 n 36, Urb El Plantio, La Canada, 46182 Paterna, Valencia

Preston English Centre, Edif El Carmen Chapineria 3, Jerez De La Frontera, Cadiz

Principal English Centre, Aptdo 85, Puerto De Santa Maria, Cadiz

SALT Idiomes, Prat De La Riba, 86 08222 Terrassa (Barcelona)

San Roque School, Plaza San Roque 1, Guadalajara

Sierra Bernia School, La Caneta s/n, San Rafael, 03580 Alfaz del Pi

Skills, Trinidad 94, 12002 Castellon.

The Smiths' School, Maestro Guridi s/n, 20008 San Sebastian

Stanton School of English, Colon 26, 03001 Alicante

St Patrick's Caracuel, 1 Jerez De La Frontera, Cadiz

TELC, Av Andalucia 8, 6o, 11006 Cadiz

Thamesis, c/ Castello 24, 28001 Madrid

The Tolkien Academy, Juan Bautista Erro 9, 20140 Andoain

Trafalgar Idiomas, Avda Castilla 12, 33203 Gijon, Asturias

Trinity School SL, C/ Golondrina (Plaza Jardines) 17 Bajo, 11500 Puerto De Santa Maria, Cadiz

Universidad de Barcelona, Escola d'Idiomes Moderns, Gran Via 585, 08007 Barcelona

Universidad Autonoma de Barcelona, Servei d'Idiomes Moderns, Edifici C, 08193 Bellaterra, Barcelona

Universidad Complutense, c/ Donoso Cortes 65, 28015 Madrid

Universidad Autonoma de Madrid, Ciudad Universitaria de Contoblanco, 28049 Madrid

Universidad del Pais Vasco, Asociacion de Estudios para Extranjeros, Plaza de Onati 2, 20009 San Sebastian

Universidad de Sevilla, Instituto de Idiomas, c/ Palos de la Frontera s/n, 41004 Sevilla

Wall Street Institute, Gutenberg 3-13, 1o 8a, 08224 Terrassa (Barcelona)

Wall Street Institute, Centro Comercial Cuesta Blanca, Local 12, 2a Planta, la Moralega, Alcobendas, 28100 Madrid

Wall Street Institute, Av Republica Argentina 24 P12 D, 41011 Sevilla

Warwick House Centro Linguistico Cultural, Lopez Gomez 18-2, Valladolid 47002

Westfalia, Chapineria 3, Edificio El Carmen, Modulo 310, 11403 Jerez de la Frontera

William Halstead School of English, Camilo Jose Cela 12, 11160 Barbate de Franco

Windsor School, Av Diagonal 319, pral 4a, 08009 Barcelona

Windsor School of English, Virgen De Loreto 19-1, 41011 Sevilla

York House, English Language Centre, Muntaner 479, 08021 Barcelona

Sweden

Most English teachers are employed by the Folk University, a kind of public university, similar to the Open University in the UK. It places teachers in its network of five adult education centres (Kursverksamheten), formerly called British Centres, throughout the country. A wide range of English programmes are required but there has been increasingly strong demand for Business English courses. At the Folk University specialisms on top of basic English teaching are sought and rewarded according to skill. The university runs a week long induction course which puts TEFL into a Swedish context.

The Folk University offers full-time contracts for nine months. For details of this scheme, contact the Folk University, Nina Saevig, PO Box 26152, S-100 41 Stockholm, Sweden. Tel: 46 8 679 29 60, Fax: 46 8 678 15 44.

Visas and work permits: Sweden joined the European Union in 1995, making it easier for other EU members to find work. Teachers from non-EU countries will need to be studying in Sweden or be married to somebody who works there since the Folk University only recruits British nationals.

Cost of living: Expensive but the standard of living is very high.

Salaries and taxes: The Folk University offers a basic rate of SKr11,500 per month, but most teachers are on higher rates, up to SKr15,000, depending on the type of teaching task given. Initially some tight budgeting may be required. Tax is deducted from pay at around 30 per cent, with some variation according to the municipality. The trend in Sweden is for people to have individual pay rates and personal contracts, which will make general conditions harder to judge.

Accommodation: Teachers often spend between 25 and 35 per cent of their salaries on accommodation, but deposits are often not required. One person can pay between SKr2,500 and SKr3,500 per month for a place including hot water and heating costs. Away from Stockholm lower rates of around SKr1,500 may be possible.

Health insurance: Advisable.

List of schools in Sweden
British Institute, Stockholm, Hagatan 3, 511348 Stockhom

Folkuniversitetet, Box 26152, 100 41 Stockholm.

We would like to thank Olla Miasen, Folkuniversitetet for help with this listing.

The Rest of Europe

Exciting opportunities are available throughout the former Soviet Bloc states with cultural programmes allowing teachers to work in both state and private sectors.

 European countries which are not yet part of the EU are excellent places to look for work. English is big business in the former Communist countries of Central and Eastern Europe and there are at least as many opportunities in the region as there were in Spain, Italy and Greece in the Seventies. Indeed some places offer similar salaries to those being offered in Italy and Spain now. This is very good when the lower cost of living is considered.

Many of these countries have their eyes set on EU membership so governments are focusing on bringing stability to their economies. This, coupled with recent growth in tourism, means that these are increasingly popular teaching destinations despite the sometimes difficult living and teaching conditions. Competition means that teaching qualifications are more necessary, especially in major cities.

A number of Central and East European countries are served by voluntary and cultural organisations, including the East European Partnership (EEP), Central Bureau for Educational Visits and Exchanges, Teaching Abroad and Travel Teach, based in the UK and the Peace Corps and Soros Foundation, based in the USA. These organisations tend to offer teachers salaries at local rates along with supplements, accommodation and other benefits.

There is still considerable voluntary, as well as some commercial, ELT activity in the Ukraine, Uzbekistan and Kazakhstan but standards of living can be modest and conditions harsh.

English is an official language in Malta and attracts a lot of students but most English language teaching is undertaken by Maltese nationals and it is extremely

hard to get a work permit. Macedonia has a volatile economy which cannot support much of an English language industry.

Recent troubles in Albania with many refugees crossing to Italy and continuing uncertainty in some areas of the former Yugoslavia, such as Bosnia - still patrolled by NATO and, Serbia - Montenegro (Yugoslavia) - still under autocratic rule, mean that teaching needs while existing, are harder to exploit and may be impossible or unwise to seek. The recent war in the ethnic Albanian area of Serbia, Kosovo, makes it unwise to try to travel to this part of te country.

Andorra

List of Schools in Andorra

Inlingua Andorra, Rebes, Placa Rebes 4, AND-Andorra la Vella

Inlingua Andorra, Les Canals, Les Canals 12, AND-Andorra la Vella

Inlingua Andorra, Encamp, Carretera de Vila, Casa Jaumet, AND-Encamp

Inlingua Andorra, Escaldes, Placa Co-Princeps 4, 1er, AND-Escaldes-Engordany

Bulgaria

Despite having economic and political troubles, Bulgaria has quite a well developed English Language Teaching structure.

In the private sector, teaching loads are notoriously heavy with some teachers having to travel between two or three schools to deliver 30 contact hours per week, often in the evenings and on Saturday mornings. In the state sector, a week's teaching is likely to consist of about twenty 40-minute lessons.

Because many students make great sacrifices to pay for their courses, a Bulgarian

teaching experience can be very inspiring and rewarding.

The well-developed English Language Teaching structure includes a local IATE-FL and a nascent Association of Quality Language Providers. The British Council has a Teaching Centre which employs native speakers with a first degree and RSA Cert/Dip TEFL.

Visas and work permits: It is quite easy to get work in Bulgaria. All non-Bulgarian citizens need an entry visa which can be obtained from the Bulgarian Consular Service in any country. Your school should help you to organise the work permit paperwork. It is important to carry your documentation as foreigners are regularly stopped and checked by police. No entry visa is required for stays of up to 30 days if you are from an EU country, Canada, the USA Australia or New Zealand. Bulgaria is an Associate member of the EU.

Cost of living: Very cheap in the provinces, reaching western levels in Sofia, but conditions are still extremely tough. Living expenses per person = 300,000 - 350,000 levs p.a.

Salaries and taxes: Most contracted teachers are paid at local rates the equivalent of $150 per month. Paid airfares, furnished accommodation and holiday are generally included and there might also be a supplement paid in pounds or dollars. A highly-paid Bulgarian teacher might be paid the equivalent of $125 per month. native speaker teachers can earn $10 per hour giving private lessons.

Accommodation: Usually provided by employers.

Health insurance: Essential. UK passport holders with an NHS card have access to hospital treatment, medical treatment and dental treatment. Bulgarian medical staff are well trained but often lack necessary supplies.

Inoculations: Hepatitis A and B recommended, Polio, Tetanus, Typhoid.

Important cultural differences: Nodding your head means no, shaking your head means yes. In economically difficult times foreigners should be aware that their belongings can be targeted, especially at airports.

English Language Newspapers: The Sofia Echo, The Sofia City Guide, BTA News

List of schools in Bulgaria

Alliance, Centre for Teaching of Foreign Languages, 3 Slaveikov Square, 1000 Sofia

American College, Tsar Osvoboditel Blvd, Sofia

Avo-3 School of English, House of Culture Sredets, 2a Krakra Street, Sofia

ANDRA, 1 Ch Smirnenski Blvd, Sofia 1421

BELS & BELIN Centre, PO Box 37, 1421 Sofia

British Council, 7 Tulovo Street, 1504 Sofia

Bulgarian Dutch College for Commerce, Trudovets Botebgrad, Sofia

Business Private High School, Kosta Lulchev Street, Sofia

Centre for Language Qualification, National Palace of Culture, Administrative Bldg, 2nd Floor, Room 131, Sofia

ELIT, 14 GM Dimitrov Boulevard, Sofia

ELS, PO Box 16, Sofia 1404

English Language Club, 143 Kniaz Boris 1 St, Entr 2, Sofia

ESPA, Darwin Street, Sofia

Europe Schools, 25 Gladston St, Sofia

FAROS, 2 Sofroni Vrachanski St, Sofia

First Private English Language Medium School, Stara Planina Street, Sofia

ICO Intellect, Kostur Street, 1618 Sofia

Institute of Tourism, Park Ezero, 8000 Bourgas.

INTERED, 3 Saborna St, Sofia

Language Schools of Europe, 82 Tsar Simeon Stret, entr 3, fl 3, Sofia 1000

MEL, First Primary School, 24 Vessela Street, Plovdiv 4000

Meridian 22, Alabin Street, Sofia 1000

Meridian, Macedonia Boulevard, Sofia 1606

New School of English, 13 Serdika Street, Sofia

Pharos Ltd, 2 S.Vrachanski Street, Vasrazhdane Square, Sofia

Private High School for Law & Management, D Dimov Street, Sofia

Private High School for Management & Business Admin, Raiko Alexiev Street, Complex Iztok, Sofia

Private High School for Management & Stock Trade, Velikoknyazhevska Street, Sliven

Yanev School, bl 147 ap 38, Complex Liulin, Sofia

Croatia

By 1997 the political situation in Coatia had much improved from the immediate post war instability, with economic restructuring underway. Inflation is quite low at 4 per cent but unemployment is high, at 18 percent in 1997. English is in demand, being the principle foreign language, especially for the young, taught at all levels in the education system. As the economic situation improves ordinary Croatians have proved willing to spend money on additional education for their children. Inter-university links between Croatia and Britain are increasing and the standard of Croatian school examinations has been recognised as acceptable for entry to British universities. American English is popular due to films and the media.

The Education Ministry has shown some hostility to foreign language learning, fearing that those with such skills will join the "brain drain". While this has restricted opportunities for foreigners in the state sector, HUPE (Croatian Association of Teachers of English) is very international in focus.

Private schools operate in Zagreb, Karlovac and Varazdin, some having been established for 50 years. There are plenty of opportunities for English teachers, especially L1 speakers, with schools

recruiting locally and abroad. Because the English language industry is so long-standing, schools are less likely to employ unqualified teachers. Jobs are advertised abroad, but local job hunting on spec is possible. Full-time contracts are normal and there are opportunities for private lessons.

Visas and work permits: British or Irish citizens do not need an entry visa for up to 90 days as a tourist and can research available jobs in this time. Other nationalities should check their situation with a local Croatian embassy. To actually work an entry permit must be applied for in your home country, showing a contract for employment in Croatia. This is sent to the Internal Affairs Ministry in Zagreb for approval. On arrival in Croatia, you have to register with the police and within three months your employer has to apply to the Ministry of Labour and Social Welfare for a permit.

Cost of living: Cheap.

Salaries and taxes: The local currency is the kuna, which is pegged to the value of the Deutschmark. Salaries are usually paid in Deutschmarks with tax deducted by the employer. The pay rate is between DM1,000 and DM1,200 per month, in private language schools. More experienced teachers may earn more. In Primary schools the pay is DM600 par month, in Secondary schools, DM700, and in Tertiary schools DM900-1000.

Accommodation: Rooms tend to be expensive and hard to find. A bedsit can cost 400 DM per month, paid for in hard currency. If you share it works out much cheaper. A flat with two or three rooms will cost around 500 DM per month. There is usually a deposit of a month's rent, although landlords can ask for up to six months' rent in advance. Employers often help teachers to find accommodation.

Health insurance: Advisable. UK nationals have access to hospital treatment, other medical care and some dental treatment.

Inoculations: Hepatitis A, Polio, Typhoid.

List of schools in Croatia

Agencija F, Trg Frane Petrica 4, 51557 Cres

Barbic p o Skola Stranih Jezika, Dioklecijanova 1, 21000 Split

Byron, Giardini 11, 52100 Pula

The British Council, Ilica 12, Zagreb

Centar Stranih Jezika STARA VLASKA, Vlaska 26/11, 10000 Zagreb

Centar za Strane Jezike, Vodnikova 2, 10000 Zagreb

Centar za Strane Jezike, Trg Republike 2/1, 21000 Split

Class, Jankomirska 1, 10000 Zagreb

ELC-English Language Center, Kralja Tomislava 9, 40000 Cakovec

Eurolingua Multimedia, A Starcevica 2, 44000 Sisak

Gloria, Strossmayerova 9, 43000 Bjelovar

Hello English Language Club, A Senoe 4, 48000 Koprivnica

Ilmo, Pontovcak 9, 10000 Zagreb

Interlang, Krizaniceva 7, 5100 Rijeka

Kolag-Trade d o o, L Bezeredija 41, 40000 Cakovec

Lancon, Mukiciceva 10, 10000 Zagreb

Langlia, A Starcevica 19b, 23000 Zadar

Linguae, Radiceva 4, 51000 Rijeka

Linguapax, Vatrogasna 1, 32000 Vinkovci

Octopus, Branimirova 25, 100000 Zagreb

Open University, L. Jagera 6 Osijek

Poliglot, Wenzelova 2, 51000 Rijeka

Pucko Sveuciliste (Skola Stranih Jezika), L Jagera 6, 31000 Osijek

Skola stranih jezika, Varsavska 14, 10000 Zagreb

Skola stranih jezika LANCOS, Vukovarska 2, 34000 Pozega

Skola stranih jezika NIKA, Sidonije Rubido 7, 48260 Krizevci

Skola stranih jezika JEKA, P Zrinskog 12a, 43000 Bjelovar

Skola stranih jezika Sever, Park Rudolfa Kropeka 2, 40000 Cakovek

Skola stranih jezika SIMUNIC d o o, Trenkova 23, 4200 Varazdin

Skola stranih jezika Ziger, Ivana Trankog 19, 42000 Varazdin

Skola za stranih jezike, Varsavska 14, 10000 Zagreb

Stara Vlaska, Vlaska 26/11, 10000 Zagreb

Svjetski Jezici, Varsavska 13, 10000 Zagreb

Vern, Trg Bana Jelacica, 10000 Zagreb

Cyprus

There are few private language schools or institutes in the Turkish sector of Cyprus. Considering the great demand for English language learning in Turkey itself this is surprising and probably due to the relative unpopularity of Turkish Cyprus as a tourist destination for English speakers.

In Greek Cyprus, however, English is the second language. It is taught from an early age in school and there are strong links between Britain and the former colony through families, business, tourism and entertainment.

Because English is a high priority on the Greek Cypriot school curriculum, the number of private language schools (frontisteria) are fewer per capita than in Greece. This situation, coupled with immigration policies that protect Cypriot nationals in the employment market makes it hard for foreigners to find teaching positions.

There is little overseas recruitment and almost no entry into the state sector unless you speak Greek and have skills that no Cypriot has. There are a number of private schools, especially those preparing young children for overseas exams but, again, they tend to require skills not available locally. Positions which do become vacant tend to be full-time. There is some scope to take private classes and L1 speakers are often pre-ferred.

Visas and work permits: It is illegal to work in Greek Cyprus on a tourist visa and work permits are difficult to secure. To qualify for a work permit a teacher will need a degree in English Language, Literature or Linguistics. Immigration policies are strongly enforced to protect local teachers.

Cost of living: Relatively cheap.

Salaries and taxes: Salaries and taxes vary considerably but you might expect to be paid about C£8-9 per hour, and C£9-10 is possible, especially for private lessons. Income tax is 20% on a salary of up to C£8,000 (the first C£5,000 is tax free).

Accommodation: Flats cost US$3-400 per month and up, but it's difficult to rent just a room. Deposits are not always necessary although one month's rent is sometimes expected.

Health insurance: Good health care available.

English language newspapers: Cyprus Mail, Cyprus Weekly.

List of schools in Cyprus

AISC International School, 11 Kassos Street, Ay Omoloyitea, PO Box 3847, Nicosia

American Academy, PO Box 112, Larnaca

American Academy, Despinas Pattichi Street, PO Box 1867, Limassol

American Academy, 3A Michalaki Paridi Street, P O Box 1967, Nicosia

Ashley Janice, Arch. Makarios III Avenue, Kanika Street, CDA.

British Council, 3 Museum Street, (PO Box 5654), 1387 Nicosia

Centre of Advanced Studies, Amohostou, PO Box 6738, Limassol

Centre of Higher Studies, PO Box 545, 2 Evagorou Street, floor 6, Nicosia

Centre of Technical and Commercial Studies (KTEE), 9-11 Katellari Street, Nicosia

Coaching Centre, 5 Akritas Street, Larnaca.

The English School, PO Box 3575, Nicosia

Europa Language Centre, 3 Kypranoros Street, Nicosia.

Falcon School, Corner of Stavrou and Antistasios Street, PO Box 3640, Nicosia

Foley's Grammar School, Homer Avenue, Ayios Nicolas, Limassol

Forum Language Centre, 47a Prodromou Street, Strovolos, Nicosia.

GC School of Careers, 96 Stadiou Street, PO Box 5267, Nicosia

The Grammar School, Katinas Paxious Street, PO Box 1340, Limassol

The Grammar School, PO Box 2262, Nicosia

Heritage School, 25 Stradigou Makriyianni Str, Limassol

International Language Institute (ILI), 12 Richard & Verengaria Street, Limmassol

International School of Paphos, 22 Hellas Avenue, PO Box 218, Paphos

KES College, Kallipoleos Corner, Nicosia

King Richard School, BFPO 58, Dhekelia

Language Centre, 49 Kennedy Avenue, Nicosia.

Lebanese Green Hill, 76 Nicou Patihi Street, PO Box 5044, Limassol

Limasol International School, 121 Costa Palama Street, Limassol

Linguaphone Institute, 21 P Katelari Street, Nicosia.

Logos School, 33-35 Vialousa Street, PO Box 1075, 3501 Limassol

Massouras Private Institute, 1 Liperti Street, Flat 103, Paphos

Melkart College, 340 St Andrews Street, PO Box 4874, Limassol

Melkonian Educational Institute, PO Box 1907, Nicosia

Pascal English School, 3 Costaki Panteli Street, PO Box 4746, Nicosia

Pascal Institute, 3c Pantelides Street, Strovolos, Nicosia.

Proodos Institute, 2 Asopios Street, Nicosia.

Richmond Institute, 9 Chr Kannaouros Street, Dasoupolis, Nicosia.

St John's School, BFPO 53, Episkopi

St Joseph's School - Nicosia, 7 Favieros Street, Nicosia

Saint Mary's School, Grivas Dighenis, Limassol

Terra Santa College, 12 Lyceourgos Street, PO Box 1546, Nicosia

Themis Tutorial, 6a Einar Gzerstad Street, Larnaca.

Thomas Michaelides, 52 Golgon Street, Limassol.

Zahf al Ahdar, 7 Koritsas Street, Makedonitissa, Nicosia

Czech Republic

Since the 'Velvet Divorce' which separated the Czech Republic and the Slovak Republic in January 1993, the English language industry in both republics has taken off dramatically. With the popularity of Prague as a tourist destination many private schools have opened, backed by both western companies and local operators.

Schools do not tend to specify preferred nationalities for teachers but qualifications are increasingly important. The Czech Republic is a haven for qualified teachers, with opportunities in both the state and private sectors. The Academic Information Agency coordinates opportunities for foreign teachers in primary and secondary schools, often in smaller towns. The minimum qualification for such work is a university degree in English and a recognised TEFL certificate.

Although English is booming, most teachers have part-time contracts. It is easy to find private lessons and there are opportunities for non-qualified teachers. Non-L1 speakers will find it harder to find work. Companies do require English courses but usually hire a language school to run them.

In Prague, jobs can be found through word of mouth and the Prague Post. Otherwise, British Council noticeboards are useful. Other noticeboards can be found in cultural centres. The capital is over subscribed with EFL teachers, which has driven pay rates down, and accomodation costs up.

Visas and work permits: All nationalities need a work permit and no one is allowed to teach without one. Your employer can fix up the paperwork before you come, but must ensure that the job cannot be taken up by a Czech national, and it will take about two and a half months to secure the visa. You can apply for a work permit after browsing for a job in the Republic, but residency papers must be secured from the embassy in the teacher's home country. Applying from within the Republic takes as long as from outside so this is not a good option if you are going to run out

of savings. All documents with the exception of the travel and registry documents must be not older than 180 days.

Cost of living: Low but increasing, especially in Prague. You can live reasonably on a teacher's salary but you won't be able to afford much travel. When assessing costs it can be better to have a lower salary if some food and accomodation is included, than a seemingly higher wage.

Salaries and taxes: In the state sector, teachers can earn about 5,000-9,000 crowns per month after tax. Private language schools have varying terms and conditions but a good contract might earn you 8,000-12,000 crowns per month. Private classes yield about 200 crowns with business classes earning as much as 300 crowns per hour. The tax rate is between 25 and 30 per cent. Freelance teachers by law should be registered as sole proprietors to pay income tax.

Accommodation: It is very difficult to find accommodation, especially in Prague, where sharing is usual at 5,000 crowns per month. Elsewhere 3,000 crowns per month is more likely with one month's rent expected as a deposit. Some employment contracts provide full accommodation while others do not even help in the search.

Health insurance: Essential. UK passport holders have access to hospital treatment and other medical care.

English language newspapers: The Prague Post.

Other useful information: Czech nationals pay lower prices for hotels and transport.

List of schools in the Czech Republic

Accent Language School, Bitovska 3, Praha 4, 14000 Tel: 004202 420123 Fax: 004202 422845 Email: brian@akcent.cz Website: www.akkcent.cz Contact: Brian O Heithir. Large, established school. Owned and run by teaching staff. Strong emphasis on teacher development including DELTA courses (CELTA planned 2000)

Aesop - The American English School of Prague, M Horakove - Prasny most, Praha 6

Agentura Gulliver, Dlouha 4309, Zlin

Agentura Klic, Krnovska 69, 746 01 Opava

Agentura Vika, Masarykova 31, Brno

AHA Jazykova Agentura, Kourimska 11, Vinohrady, Praha 3

AIDA - JS, Cajkovskeho 18, 787 01 Sumperk

AJACK Su, nam Miru 4, 787 01 Sumperk

Akademie JAK, Nadrazni 120, 702 00 Moravska Ostrava

Akademie J A Komenskeho, Brozikova 40, 738 02 Frydek-Mistek

ALKA School, Pluku 8-10, Karlin, Praha 8

J A Amadeus, Schweitzerova 50, 779 00 Olomouc

Anglictina Expres, Zahrebska 32, Praha 2

Anglo American College in Prague, Na Jeteice 2, Praha 9

AUREUS, Antonina Tragra, 370 10 Ceske Budejovice

The Bell School - Prague, Nedvezska 29, Praha 10

Berlitz Schools of Languages (Head Office), Hybernska St 24, 110 00 Praha 1

Berlitz, Starobmenska 3, Brno

Berlitz, Praha 2 Jecna 12, Praha

The Boland School, Palackeho 148a, Brno

British Council, The English Language Teaching Centre, Narodni 10, 125 01 Praha 1

Brno English Centre, VUT Kravi Hora 13, 602 00 Brno

The Caledonian School, Vitavska 24, 150 00 Praha 5

California Sun School, Na Bojisti 12, 3rd Floor, Praha 2

Cloverleaf s r o, Puchmajerova 8, 702 00 Moravska Ostrava

Corfix Brnp, trida kpt Jarose 3, Brno

Cosmolingua International, Zdarila 8, 140 00 Praha

Cosmolingua International, Dominikanske Nam 4/5, 602 00 Brno

Cyrilometodejska fak, Univerzitni 22, 771 11 Olomouc

D and D jazykova skola, Komenskeho 372, Modrice

Detska jazykova skola, Prazska 1114, Pelhrimov

Easy English s r o, Botanicka 13, Brno

EDUCA - vzdelavaci centrum, Jungmannova 8, Jablonec n Nisou

EDUCO - J Capek, Pekarenska 55, 370 04 Ceske Budejovice

English House, Vysehradska 2, Praha 2

English Language Teaching, Na Valech 36, Litomerice

English Link, Na Berance 2, Praha 6

English Studio, Komenskeho 10, Blansko

ETC Jazykova Skola, Dusni 17, 110 00 Praha 1

Fak telesne kultury, tr Miru 115, 771 40 Olomouc

Faktum, Nadrazni Okruh 27, 746 01 Opava

Filozoficka fak - katedra anglistiky a amerikanistiky, Krizkovskeho 10, 771 80 Olomouc

Fishnet ACA v o s, Polska 1542, 708 00 Ostrava

Grapa, Nadrazni 2a, Brno

Gymnazium, Cajkovskeho 9, 775 00 Olomouc

Gymnazium Hejcin: anglicka sekce, Dolni Hejcinska 8, 776 00 Olomouc

Gymnazium Zlin, Lesni ctvrt 1364, 761 37 Zlin

IEC s r o, Rantirovska 9, Jihlava

ILC The English School, International House - Brno, Sokolska 1, 602 00 Brno

Informatorium Linguae, 28 Rijna 1495, 738 01 Frydek-Mistek

INTACT, Namesti 84, Velke Mezirici

Inter-contact, Husitska 11, Praha 3

International Language Centre Prague, Lupacova 1, 130 00 Praha 3 Tel: 420 2 6975618 Fax: 420 2 2318584 Email: ilc@lupacovka.cz Website http://www.ilcgroup.com One of Prague's longest established language school offering General, Business, Examination and Young Learners courses. Part of the ILC Group

---

International Training Solutions Ltd, Thamova 24, 186 00 Praha 8

Irbess Agentura, Lannova 53, 370 01 Ceske Budejovice

Kursy Dr Jilka, Stefanikova 2, Brno

Jazykova agentura a skola, Zaluzanska 361, Chlumec

Jazykova agentura Choteborsky, Skolni 2429, Louny

Jazykova Skola ALBA s r o, Bavorovska 329, Netolice

Jazykova Skola, Ulrychova 83, Brno

Jazykova Skola, Sobotkova 24, Brno

Jazykova skola, Smetanova 10, Jihlava

Jazykova Skola P Tomaskove, Karafiatova 49, 779 00 Olomouc

Jazykova Skola Lingua, nam TGM 2433, 760 01 Zlin

Jazykova Skola Kovalsky, Cejl 93, Brno

Jazykova Skola MKM, Ceska 1, Brno

Jazykova skola SLON, Udolni 11, Brno

Jintes, Husova 45, 370 05 Ceske Budejovice

Jitka Jureckova, Urxova 2, 772 00 Olomouc

J - Service, Jazykova agentura a Skola, Revolucni 8, Usti n Labem

Junior College Laros, Lihovarska 10, 716 00 Ostrava - Radvanice

Junior Language School, Michelska 1487, Stare Mesto

Languages at Work, Na Florenci 35, 110 00 Praha 1

The Language House, Skretova 8, Praha 2

Language Link, Czech Republic, Recruitment Section, 21 Harrington Road, South Kensington, London, UK, SW7 3EU

Latal Foreign Languages, Rooseveltova 26, 779 00 Olomouc

Lekarska fak, tr Sovobody 8, 771 26 Olomouc

Lingua, Janska 6, Jablonec nad Nisou

Lingua, Homi Nam 55, 746 01 Opava

Lingua - jazikova szkola, nam T G Masaryka 2433, 760 01 Zlin

Lingua Centrum H E, Anenska 10, Brno

Lingua Centrum, Krizikova 5, 772 00 Olomouc

Lingua Pro, Vinohradska 28, Praha 2

Linguarama Prague, Srobarova 1, 130 00 Praha 3 Tel: (0) 2 74 48 89/(0) 2 73 04 60 Fax: (0) 2 71 73 55 77 email: praha@linguarama.com

Lingua Service, Husovo nam 17, Chabarovice

Lingua Servis, Chvalkovicka 63, 773 00 Olomouc

Lingua - soukroma jazykova skola, Ruzova 4, Rumburk

London School, Diouha 6, Usti n Labem

London School of Modern Languages, Slezska 13, 120 00 Praha 2

London School of Modern Languages, Francouzska 30, 120 00 Praha 2

Majda Agency, Heinrichova 41, Brno

Matthews Language School, Jindricha z Lipe 124, Ceska Lipa

M K Service, Masna 8, 702 00 Moravska Ostrava

MN s r o, Topolova 584, Most

Mor Realne Gymn. and Jazykova Skola, Nesverova 1, 771 00 Olomouc

OA & JS, Masarykova 101, 751 01 Val Mezirici

O A & JS, Hlavni tr 31, 787 01 Sumperk

Obchodni akademi, tr Spojencu 11, 771 00 Olomouc

Pedagogicka fak, Zizkovo nam 5, 771 40 Olomouc

Perfect English, Josefska 25, Brno

Podnikovy Institut, Rooseveltova 79, 779 00 Olomouc

Polyglot, Komenskeho 50, 370 01 Ceske Budejovice

Polyglot, Mecislavova 8, 140 00 Praha 4

Prague Language Centre, Navratilova 5, 110 00 Praha 1

Pravnicka fak, tr 17 listopadu 8, 771 00 Olomouc

Prirodovedecka fak, tr Svobody 26, 771 46 Olomouc

Richard Language, Kourimska 303, Kutna Hora

ROLINO - Jazykove Studio, Bratri Capka 10, Praha 10

TILIA, Ludmila Tvrdonova, Josefska 5, Brno

Till English Academiy, Cs Armady 10, 710 00 Sleszka Ostrava

Secretarial and Language Institute, Brandlova 4, Brno

Sidia - vzdelavaci institut, Jeremenkova 36, 772 00 Olomouc

Slovanske gymnazium, J z Podebrad 13, 772 00 Olomouc

Soukrome gymnazium, Ceske armady 481, 738 01 Frydek-Mistek

Statni Jazykova Skola, Vranovska 65, Brno

Statni Jazykova Skola, J S Baara 2, 370 01 Ceske Budejovice

Statni Jazykova Skola, Palackeho 123, 738 00 Frydek-Mistek

Statni Jazykova Skola, 1 Maje 18, Liberec

Statni Jazykova Skola, J z Podebrad 13, 772 00 Olomouc

Statni Jazykova Skola, Jizdarenska 4, 709 00 Ostrava

Statni Jazykova Skola, Skolska, 15, 116 72 Praha 1

Statni Jazykova Skola, Buresova 1130, Praha 8

Statni Jazykova Skola, Parizska 15, Usti n Labem

Statni Jazykova Skola, Mostni 51 32, 761 47 Zlin

Statni Jazykova Skola, Bezrucova 19, Znojmo

Universum, Korenskeho 23a, Brno

Ventas - jazykova skola, Prameny, 733 01 Karvina

Vyuka Jazyku, Palackeho 6, 772 00 Olomouc

WorkPlus - Interstaff, Vodickova 33, 110 00 Praha 1

We would like to thank Roman Kacin, IPG Prague, for help in compiling this listing.

Estonia

With 27 universities and private schools in Estonia, there are a range of opportunities for teachers. Estonia is progressing quickly and becoming more discerning, so a certificate will give you the edge. Arrive before the onset of winter in November.

Visas and work permits: It is advised that any traveller to Estonia should have a valid EU passport or they may have difficulties. It is relatively easy to obtain a work permit once you have found a job, but it can take a long time. No entry visa is required for nationals of UK, USA, Australia or New Zealand. All other nationalities require an entry visa. Work permits must be applied for by your employer once you are in Estonia.

Cost of living: Fairly cheap.

Salaries and taxes: Local rates. Teachers need to take private classes to make ends meet.

Accommodation: The average rent for a two-bedroom flat in the dormitory suburbs is around US$200, but lower outside Tallinn. Most flats are arranged through agencies, which charge a month's rent.

Health insurance: Advisable.

Other useful information: The people of the Baltic States are business-minded and keen to build links with the EU.

The seasons are very clearly defined: expect snow from November to March and hot summers.

List of Schools in Estonia

ALF Training Centre Ltd, Ravala pst 4, Tallinn EE0001

Concordia International University, Kaluri tee 3, Viimsi veld, Harjumaa EE3006

EM International, Sutiste tee 21, Tallinn EE0034

Estonian Business School, Lauteri 3, Tallinn EE0001

Folkuniversitet, Lai 30, Tartu EE2400

HEDI, Tina 16a, Tallinn EE0001

International House Tallinn, Pikk 69, Tallinn EE 0001

Ko-Praktik, Tondi 1, Tallinn EE0013

Kullerkupp, Parnu mnt 57, Tallinn EE0001

Language Learning Service, Tonismagi 3, Tallinn EE0001

LEX, Uus 19, Tallinn EE0001

Lingo Ltd, Vaike-Kuke 16, Parnu EE0001

Mainor Language Centre, Kuhlbarsi tn 1, Tallinn EE0001

Multilingua, Endla tn 6-4, Tallinn EE0001

Old Town Language Centre (helo), Puhavaimu 7, Tallinn EE0001

Sugesto, Narva mnt 6-8, Tallinn EE0001

Taavi Koolitus, Lai 1, Rakvere EE2100

TEA, Lijvalaia 28, Tallinn EE0001

Tallinn Language School, Endla 22, Tallinn EE0001

Valentine and Rain Language School, Vene 13, Tallinn EE0001

Georgia

English is fast becoming the second language in Georgia and nearly everybody seems to be learning it. At the moment, there are few L1 English speakers, but thousands of Georgian teachers. The British Council Resource Centre in Tbilisi has 600 members and estimates that these are only a quarter of the English teachers in the capital.

International Job Prospects

SECTION 3

L1 speakers, qualified or not, should be able to find work by going out to Georgia on spec. International House has one school in Tbilisi but only recruits about three well qualified teachers at present, on 9 to 12 month contracts. The Georgian Pipeline Company has recruited from abroad and locally.

Visas and work permits: At the moment, it is easy to work in Georgia and the authorities have been quite flexible. Many do not bother with work permits and it is not certain that such a document exists. Institutions simply ask for regular visa extensions on their teachers' behalf. However, in order to work in Georgia, you need a business visa. You also need a letter of invitation from your school. Do not apply for your visa earlier than three months before your departure to Georgia. Visas can easily be obtained on arrival for $75. Teachers should check with their local Georgian embassy for the exact working visa requirements before leaving.

Cost of living: Extremely cheap. The standard of living is improving.

Salaries and taxes: Private language schools pay around US$500-600 per month. The fee for private classes is generally negotiable: you can charge up to US$10 per hour or more. If you work with a reputable organisation, such as International House then you can expect significantly more and have accommodation and flights added in. There is not enough money in the state sector for a westerner to maintain their basic standard of living. Salaries are taxed at source but the rates have been low.

Accommodation: Flats with two or three bedrooms cost US$250 per month. The school will pay two months' rent. Deposits are not usually expected.

Health insurance: Essential.

Inoculations: Hepatitis A, Polio, Typhoid.

Important cultural differences: Most Georgians are very hospitable and can be compared to Latin peoples.

Other useful information: The war has quietened down but Georgia should still be considered dangerous.

English Language Newspapers: Georgian Times and Resonance

List of schools in Georgia
Centre for Applied Language Studies, International House, 26 May Square, 380015 Tbilisi

Hungary

Favourable economic conditions mean that English language learning is in great demand in Hungary, especially since it is a prerequisite for university and college entrance. There is a growing demand for General English and Business English. There is a plentiful local supply of English teachers but a demand for L1 English speaker teachers continues, albeit at a lower level than a few years ago. It can be a good place for a qualified teacher to find a first job and some opportunities exist for unqualified teachers in Hungarian-owned schools.

Teachers should be aware that lack of regulation means that the quality of school can vary greatly. Schools which require a CELTA are recommended.

Visas and work permits: Visa requirements vary so check with your embassy. British citizens do not need one, but must have a valid work permit on entry into the country. Hungary is very strict about work permits and everybody needs to apply for one if they are going to teach in the country. Permits must be arranged before leaving your country of residence and the applicant has to produce a labour permit sent from the employer in Hungary, stating that no Hungarian is available to do the job.

Cost of living: Fairly cheap. One of the cheapest countries in Europe.

Salaries and taxes: Teachers in the state sector earn from 25,000 forints per month for the less qualified, up to between 40,000 and 50,000 forints per month after tax, for more experienced staff. Private schools pay up to about 45,000 forints

per month after tax and private lessons can earn you 1,000-2,000 forints for a 45-minute lesson.

Accommodation: It is very hard to find accommodation, even with the variable help from schools. Rents must be assessed against your earnings to judge value. For a one bedroom flat around 30,000 forints should be expected, but costs can reach 60,000 forints. Larger flats that can be shared will cost 100,000-125,000 forints. A month's rent is payable as a deposit. Service charges can be high. Find accommodation through the local Express newspaper.

Health insurance: Advisable. Local health insurance is available but it does not cover repatriation. Make sure that the school covers you at an equivalent level to the state health scheme.

Inoculations: Tetanus.

English language newspapers: Budapest Sun, Budapest Week, Budapest Business Week Journal.

List of schools in Hungary
While there are numerous private schools in Hungary offering employment, the sector is fluid with exact addresses and institution names changeable. The list below is as per the 8th edition and has not been updated.

American International School of Budapest, 1121 Kakukk u.1-3, Budapest

Atalanta Business and Language School, Budapest, 1132, 9 Visegradi Utca Tel: 0036 1 339 8913 Fax: 0036 1 339 8549 Email: nyelv.atalanta@qwertynet.hu Website: www.qwertynet.hu/atalanta Accredited language school. 600/400 superintensive and in-company courses. Professional support including mentoring scheme, workshops and extensive library

Avalon '92 Agency, Erzsebet Krt 15, 1/19, 1073 Budapest
Bell Iskolak, Tulipan u. 8, 1022 Budapest
Belvarosi Tanoda Foundation, 1056 Molnar u.9, Budapest

Britannica International School, 1114 Villanya ut 11-13, Budapest

Buda Drawing School, 1126 Marvany u. 23, Budapest

Budenz Jozsef High School Foundation, 1021 Budenz ut 20-22, Budapest

Budapest Pedagogical Institute, Horveth Mihaly Ter 8, Budapest 8

Business Polytechnic, 1096 Vendel u. 3/b, Budapest

Central European Teaching Program (CETP), Beloit College, Box 242, 700 College Street, Beloit, Wisconsin 53511-5595, USA

English Teachers' Assoc. of the National Pedagogical Institute, Bolyai u.14, 1023 Budapest

Helle Studio, 1084 Deri Miksa u. 18, Budapest

Interclub, Hungarian Language School, 1039 Szent Janos u. 16, Budapest

International Business School Budapest, 1115 Etele u. 68, Budapest

International House Budapest, Bimbo ut 7, 1022 Budapest

International House, Mecset utca 3, Eger 3300

Karinthy Frigyes Gimnazium, Thokoly utca 7, Pestlorinc, 1183 Budapest

Kulvarosi Tankor, 1158 Dregelyvar u. 6, Budapest.

Living Language Seminar, Fejer Gyorgy u 8-10, 1053 Budapest

Linguarama Budapest, 1065 Budapest, Bajcsy Zsilinszky ut 25 Tel: (0) 1 311 94 66/(0) 1 312 30 37 Fax: (0) 1 311 53 94 email: budapest@linguarama.com

London Studio, 1114 Fadrusz u. 12, Budapest (PO Box 167, 1518 Budapest)

Mentor Nyelviskola, 1094 Ferenc krt. 37, Budapest

Novoschool Language School, H-1091 Ulloi ut 63, Budapest

Oxford Nyelviskola, Ikva u. 52, Gyor

RLC International, 27-28 George Street, Richmond, Surrey. T9 1HY, UK

Western Maryland College Budapest, 1114 Villanyi ut 11-13, Budapest

Latvia

This Baltic state is still in the process of reasserting its identity from the Soviet past. An increasing demand for English is part of this new direction with many people, from six years old upwards, learning the language.

Generally English speakers should be able to find a teaching position. Nationals of non-English speaking countries may find it harder to do so. People considering this region should know their motivation for going. The pay is likely to be low, especially in the state sector, and the accommodation affordable on local earnings at the bottom end of the market. Several English teachers with families have left, unable to make enough to support them.

The work is necessary however, being genuinely useful in the local society and part of the reward is the enthusiasm of the students and fellow teachers who choose to be in Latvia.

There are few places at present that could be counted as language schools, but positions exist in the state schools and higher education. Banks and other companies take teachers on for in-house training and there are many freelance and private class opportunites.

Visas and work permits: British citizens do not require a visa and work permits can be organised after arrival. The employer should make all of the arrangements. Once work is arranged, an invitation by the State Labour Depatment must be added. You must be able to provide proof of your qualifications and training as a teacher, including a letter from a previous employer.

Salaries and Taxes: Some organisations only pay 5 lats per hour, state schools about 60 lats per month and banks up to around 350 lats per month. Freelancers can charge about 10 lats per hour, more for business English. Tax is 25 per cent but not levied on freelance or private classes.

Accommodation: Relatively expensive, can be of poor standard on local salary.

Health Insurance: Advisable.

List of schools in Latvia

English Language Centre 'Satva', Office 8, 79/85 Dzlmavu Str, Riga; LV-1011

International Centre 'R&V', 10, Meistaru Str, Riga; LV-1050

Jurmala Language Centre, 4, Ogres Str, Jurmala; LV-2000

Language Centre 'Meridian', 9-210, Juras Str, Ventaplla; LV-3600

Public Service Language Unit, 3/1 Smilieu Str, Riga; LV-1838

'Mirte', 23 Raina Bulv, Riga; LV-1050

Lithuania

Qualified teachers should contact the Ministry of Education. There are few opportunities for the untrained or less experienced. The country's currency problems mean that materials and foreign expertise are hard to come by. Organisations which place instructors in Lithuania include Teaching Abroad and the Soros Professional ELT Program (SPELT).

Visas and work permits: UK passport holders do not require a visa though the situation varies for other EU citizens. Americans, Australians and Canadians also can enter without a visa. Obviously it is advisable to check the latest rules with a Lithuanian consulate before you go. For most nationalities the procedure to obtain work permits is relatively straightforward once a teaching position has been secured. Work permits are issued by the local Labour Exchanges in Lithuania upon application by the employer.

Salaries and taxes: Salaries vary according to experience and can be as low as $75 per month.

List of schools in Lithuania

American English School, P.O. Box 731, 2038 Vilnius

Klaipeda International School of Languages, Zveju g. 25800 Klaipeda

Siauliai Pedagogical Institute, P. Visinskio 25, 5419 Siauliai

Soros International House, Gedimino 47, 3000 Kaunas

Soros International House, Ukmerges 41, 2662 Vilnius

Malta

Visas and work permits: No entry visa is required for nationals of the British Commonwealth, the USA, Canada, the Council of Europe and most Eastern

European countries. Non-Maltese nationals may work in Malta provided the employer has been issued with an employment licence. These are restricted to a certain period, normally one year, but may be extended. Jobs are available, mainly in the summer period.

Cost of living: The average weekly wage is Lm70-80 (1LM = £1.56 approx). A 2-bedroom furnished apartment costs LM80-100 a month, a meal in a mid range restaurant cost LM5 approx. Public transport is cheap.

List of schools in Malta
NSTS Language Study Institute, 220 St. Paul Street, Valleta, VLT 07

Poland

The demand for English continues to be strong. The country has progressed greatly since the collapse of Communism in 1990, introducing a new currency in 1995 that has helped stablise inflation. Poland has one of the greatest range of opportunities for English language teachers in the world with positions in both the state and private sectors.

State sector English teachers are placed mainly through voluntary and educational organisations including the Soros Foundation and WorldTeach. Teachers can expect a tough workload in schools but a lighter one in universities. University teachers are expected to be well-qualified, experienced L1 English speakers.

The private industry is now well established with schools owned locally as well as by foreign operators. School-owners are quick to hire native speakers and it is now quite common to find several in one school.

As the Cambridge First Certificate has now replaced local exams in state schools, employing native English-speaking teachers has become more desirable. There are many young learner and Business English opportunities and private tutoring is common. If you go to Poland on spec, it can be beneficial to take an interpreter to your interview.

Visas and work permits: Foreign language teachers do not need a work permit to work in Poland. They have to prove that they are employed as 'foreign language teachers' or 'teachers conducting classes in foreign languages'. Residence visas are required and must be obtained before entering the country. They are usually granted for 12 months. If you go to Poland on a tourist visa to find a job on spec, you will have to leave the country to complete the paperwork.

Cost of living: Quite cheap but rising. Fruit and vegetables cost as much as in the UK.

Salaries and taxes: Average salary is 600 Polish zloties per month in the state sector and from 1,000 to 2,400 zloties per month in the private sector, before tax. (UK£1 is approximately 5.9 zloties.) Some schools may offer overtime rates. Expect to teach up to 24 contracted 45-minute lessons per week or as few as 15 lessons per week in a university. Freelancing is possible at all levels, paying from 20 to 50 zloties per hour. The higher rates are in the cities and could go higher if you get work with business people. Salary packages can include accommodation and airfares. The basic tax rate is 20 per cent.

Accommodation: Your employer will pay for your flight and accommodation. It can be difficult to find accommodation and the cost varies enormously depending on location. Schools in the smaller towns and private schools in the bigger towns may help teachers to find somewhere and might even provide hostel accommodation as part of the package. Living with a family in exchange for English lessons is a popular option.

Health insurance: It is advisable to get it before you go. Those with a UK NHS medical card have access to hospital treatment, other medical care and some dental treatment. Private insurance is advisable.

English language newspapers: The Warsaw Voice is weekly and the Warsaw Insider a monthly guide available on the street.

Important cultural differences: Be prepared to answer quite personal questions. As with other Central and Eastern Europeans, Poles can be very direct.

List of schools in Poland
ABC Szkola Jezykow Obcych, ul Wiktorska 30, Warszawa 02 587

Ability Training Centre, ul Mazowiecka 12, Warszawa 00 048

Academic Worldwide, ul Popieluszki 21 PAW 24, Warszawa 01 595

Agenca 'ET', ul Sokolicz 3a m 85, Warszawa 01 508

Agencja 'MOJE Dziecko', ul Lewicka 9/11 m 31, Warszawa 02 547

AJM-Improve, Ul Gwiazdzista 33 m 8, Warszawa 01 651

Akademos, ul Jagiellonska 5A/14, Warszawa 03 721

American English School, ul Foksal 3/5, Warszawa 00 366

American English School, ul Kryniczna 12/14, Warszawa 03 934

Amerykanskie Centrum Jezykowe, ul Sekocinska 11/39, Warszawa 02 313

Anglomer, ul Panska 5/18, Warszawa 00 124

Angloschool, ul Popieluszki 7, Warszawa 01 786

Ara, Nauka Jezykow Obcych, ul Warszawska 31/45, Warszawa 02 495

Archibald, ul Szpitalna 8/19, Warszawa 00 031

B A T Group Poland, ul Mrzywickiego 34, Warszawa 02 078

B & Q Centrum Jezykow Obcych, ul Agawy 4 m 6, Warszawa 01 158

Berlitz, ul Wiejska 12a, Warszawa 00 490

Berlitz, ul Nowogrodzka 56, Warszawa 00 695

Brams, ul Koncertowa 8, Warszawa 02 784

Britannia Centre, ul Bagatela 14 POK 111, Warszawa 00 585

British & American English School. ul Novakawskiege 24, Warsawa 00 668

B S A Prywatna Szkola Jezykowa, ul Krakowskie Przedmiescie 62, Warszawa 00 322

Business Worldwide, ul Danilowwiczowska 9/21, 00-84 Warsaw

Cambridge School of English, ul Zakroczymska 6, Warszawa 00 225

Cambridge School of English,
ul Wasilkowskiego 6, Warszawa 02 776

Cambridge School of English,
ul Wiertnicza 26, Warszawa 02 952

Challenge, ul Chlodna 11 m 516,
Warszawa 00 891

College of Foreign Languages 'Lexis',
ul Marszalkowska 60/34, Warszawa 00
545

Compact School of English, ul
Nowogrodzka 78/24, Warszawa 02 018

Discovery, ul Sobczaka 49, Warszawa 01
149

EF English First, Smolna 8, P18, 00375
Warsawa

Eibisi, ul Dantego 7/243, Warszawa 01
914

Elmar International, ul Mokotowska
15/13, Warszawa 00 640

Empik, ul Foksal 11, Warszawa 00 366

English Academy, ul Malejlaki 1,
Warszawa 02 793

The English Language Academy,
ul Krakowkie Przedmiescie 6 Mp,
Warszawa 00 325

The English Language Academy,
ul Czestochowska 24/2, Warszawa 02 344

English Language College, ul
Mokotowska 12, Warszawa 00 561

English Language Studio, ul
Jadzwingow 1 m 34, Warszawa 02 692

**English Unlimited, Podmlynska 10,
80-885 Gdansk Tel/Fax: 48 48 301 33
73 Email: kamila@eu.com.pl Contact:
Kamila Anlink. Well established language centre. Comprehensive package for qualified GE/ESP candidates at
teacher and management level.
Applications always welcome.**

Europatent, Native Speaker, ul
Swietokrzyska 1, Warszawa 00 360

Falaland, ul Margerytki 52, Warszawa 04
906

Fast, ul Mickiewicza 74/58, Warszawa 01
650

Firma 'Yes', ul Franciszkanska 1/7,
Warszawa 00 227

Get It - Centrum Szkoleniowe, ul
Szeligowska 2 M 11, Warszawa 01 319

Godiva, ul Wysockiego 20/167,
Warszawa 03 388

Greenwich School of English,
ul Zakrzewska 24, Warszawa 00 737

inlingua Olsztyn, ul Morska 55, PL-10-
145 Olsztyn

**International House Wroclaw, ul
Ruska 46a, 50 079 Wroclaw Tel: 00 48
(0) 71 7817 290 Fax: 00 48 (0) 71
735889 Email wrocdos@id.pl
Websitesite:
http://www.silesia.top.pl/~ihih/katow
ice. Contact: Elisa Jaroch on email
etcentre@id.pl. IH Wroclaw, Opole,
Katowice & Bilesko-Biala - Adult,
Young Learner, Exams, Year-round
Teacher Development Programme, In-
house DELTA, CELTYL.**

**International House Bielsko-Biala, ul
Krasinskiego 24, 43 300 Bielsko-Biala
Tel/Fax: 00 48 33 81179 27 Email:
ihbb@silesia.top.pl Website: www.sile
sia.top.pl/~ihih/english Contact:
Director of Studies. Adults, young
learners, in-company, exam courses,
teacher training. Free flight, accommodation and medical cover. Year
round in-house teacher development
and great career opportunities.
Reductions available on Training
Courses: DELTA, YL extension,
Teaching Business English, ELT
Management**

International House, ul Dworcowa 81,
85-009 Bydogszcs

**International House, ul Sokolska
78/80, 40-128 Katowice Tel/Fax: 00 48
32 253 88 33 Email: ihih@silesia.top.pl
Contact: Director of Studies. Adults,
young learners, in-company, exam
courses, teacher training. Free flight,
accommodation and medical cover.
Year round in-house teacher development and great career opportunities.
Reductions available on Training
Courses: DELTA, YL extension,
Teaching Business English, ELT
Management**

International House, ul Targowa 18 1p
108, 25-520 Kielce

International House, ul Zwyciestwa
7/9, 75-028 Koszalin

International House, ul Pilsudskiego 6,
31-110 Krakow

International House, ul Zielona 15, 90-
601 Lodz

**International House, ul Kosciuszki 17,
45 075 Opole Tel/Fax: 00 48 77 454 66
55 Email: sekret@pol.pl Contact:
Director of Studies. Adults, young
learners, in-company, exam courses,
teacher training. Free flight, accommodation and medical cover. Year
round in-house teacher development
and great career opportunities.
Reductions available on Training
Courses: DELTA, YL extension,
Teaching Business English, ELT
Management**

International House, 'Lektor', ul Sw
Marcin 66/72, 61-807 Poznan

International House, ul Legionow 15,
87-100 Torun

**International House, ul
Leszczynskiego 3, 50-078 Wroclaw
Tel/Fax: 00 48 71 372 36 98 Email:
ttcentre@id.pl Contact: Elisa Jaroch
Adults, young learners, in-company,
exam courses, teacher training. Free
flight, accommodation and medical
cover. Year round in-house teacher
development and great career opportunities. Reductions available on
Training Courses: DELTA, YL extension, Teaching Business English, ELT
Management**

Junior Art & Language Studio, ul
Gwardzistow 8 m 5, Warszawa 02 422

Kajman, ul Felinskiego 15, Warszawa 01
513

Kern's School of English, ul Symfonii 4
m 35, Warszawa 02 786

Konwersatorium, ul Grojecka 40a m
13, Warszawa 02 320

Labor, ul Przemyska 11a, Warszawa 02
361

Language House SP Z.O.O., ul Nowy
Swiat 57/4, Warszawa 00 042

Language Link, Poland, Recruitment
Section, 21 Harrington Road, South
Kensington, London, UK, SW7 3EU

Language Training Centre, ul
Sniadeckich 17, Warszawa 00 654

Langus, ul Skrzetuskiego 42, Warszawa
02 725

Limes, Firma Oswiatowa, ul Wolna 36,
Warszawa 04 908

Linguae Mundi, ul Zlota 61, Warszawa 00 819

Linguarama Polska SP z.o.o., Warsaw, Krakow, Poznan, ul Sniadeckich 17, 00-654 Warszawa Tel: 48 (0) 22 628 72 91 Fax: 48 (0) 22 628 72 93 Email: warsaw@linguarama.com Website: http://www.linguarama.com Contact: Simon Thompson, Manager. Qualified and experienced teachers for Business English throughout Poland. Excellent salary/benefits package. Part of the Linguarama group

Linguarama Warsaw, ul Sniadeckich 17, 00 654 Warszawa Tel: (0) 22 628 72 91/2 Fax: (0) 22 628 72 93 email: warsaw@linguarama.com

Linguarama Poznan, ul Gwarna 5/2A, Poznan 61737 Tel: (0) 61 852 9455/(0) 61 851 0179 Fax: (0) 61 851 0181 email: poznan@linguarama.com

Linguarama Krakow, ul Florianska 13, 31-019 Krakow Tel: (0) 12 422 93 82 Fax: (0) 12 429 12 48 email: krakow@linguarama.com

Lingwista, ul Kopernika 6, Warszawa 00 367

Lingwista Turystyka Wyjazdowa, ul Marszalkowska 83, Warszawa 00 583

Maart Language College, ul Nowy Swiat 1, Warszawa 00 496

Marvit, ul 17 Stycznia 34b/37, Warszawa 02 148

Mateusz International, ul Panska 61 m 10, Warszawa 00 830

Meridian, ul 1-Go Sierpnia 38a/46, Warszawa 02 134

Modern English, ul Juliana Bruna 22/25, Warszawa 02 594

New People, ul Cybisa 4 m 17, Warszawa 02 784

OK! School of Languages, ul Krolewska 19/21, Warszawa 00 064

"O'Kay" Studio Uslug Jezykowych, ul Katalonska 5 m 75, Warszawa 02 763

Oxford Study Centre, ul. 25 Czerwca 60, Radom, Radom 26-600 Tel/Fax: 00 48 48 360 2166 Email: oxford@radom.medianet.pl Contact: Stephen Smith. Professional, supportive language school seeks qualified, energetic teachers who are serious about developing their skills and ideas. Adults, children, business.

Perfekt, ul Kaden-Bandrowskeigo 2/16, Warszawa

Perfekt, ul Meander 18, Warszawa 02 791

Peritia, ul Bednarska 2/4, Warszawa 00 310

Peter Pol, ul Korotynskieg 40/33, Warszawa 02 123

Polanglo, ul Nowowifjska 1/3, Warszawa 00 643

Poliglota, ul Dzialdowska 6, Warszawa 01 184

Premiere Training Company, ul Zurawia 2/20, Warszawa 00 503

Prymus, ul Jasna 2/4, POK 209, Warszawa 00 950

Pygmalion, ul Saska 78, Warszawa 03 914

Semper Bonus, ul Tyniecka 26 m, Warszawa 02 615

Soeto, ul Hoza 50, Warszawa 00 682

Spiker, ul Inzynierska 7 m 8, Warszawa 03 410

Studio Jezyka Angielskiego, ul Zelazna 58/62 Nr 904, Warszawa 00 866

Studio Troll, ul Wrzeciono 1/22, Warszawa 01 951

Studium Jezykow Obcych 'Bakalarz', ul Rakowiecka 23, Warszawa 02 517

Success, ul Agawy 5/9, Warszawa 01 158

Sunny American School, ul Zlota 58, Warszawa 00 824

Sunny Language Studio, ul Krasinskiego 40a/40, Warszawa 00 824

Szkola Jezyka Angloamerykansklego, ul Noakowskiego 24, Warszawa 00 668

Szkola Jezyka Angloamerykanskiego, ul Sienna 53, Warszawa 00 820

Szkola Jezykow Obcych, ul Powstancow Slaskich 67a, Warszawa 01 355

Target School of English, ul Polna 50 7p, 00-644 Warszawa Tel: 00 48 (0) 22 6607027/28 Fax: 00 48 (0) 22 6607029 Email: targeted@it.com.pl Contact: Mike Gardom. Expanding, well-established central Warsaw school teaching general English to adults of all levels. Visas, flats, flights and extensive support

Target Professional English Consultants, ul Polna 50 7p, 00-644 Warszawa Tel: 00 48 (0) 22 6607030 Fax: 00 48 (0) 22 6607029 Email: targeted@it.com.pl Contact: Mike Gardom. Join our large team providing language tuition for the Polish corporate market. Mature applicants especially welcome. Full package, INSETT programme.

Top School, Prywatna Szkola Jezyka Angielskiego, ul Okrezna 89, Warszawa 02 933

Troll, Nauczanie Jezykow Obcych, ul Smolna 40, Warszawa 00 375

Twin Schools of English, ul Afrykanska 6, Warszawa 03 966

TWP, Pl Defilad 1, PKiN, Warszawa 00 901

Universal English College - Bell, Pl Trzech Krzyzy 4/6. Warszawa 00 499

Universal Language Centre, Pl Hallera 5, Warszawa 03 464

Uslugi Jezykowe ABC, ul Zwm 6 m 29, Warszawa 02 786

Warsaw Study Centre, ul Raszynska 22, Warszawa 02 026

Warsaw Study Centre, ul Ursynowska 34/1, Warszawa 02 605

Zak, Niepubliczna Placowka, ul Sierakowskiego 9, Warszawa 03 709

Romania

Private enterprise accounts for nearly one third of Romania's economy and English is the most popular foreign language. However the long, slow, recovery from the Ceaucescu era, has not yet seen investment stretch to the English language industry.

Some opportunities are to be found in the state sector through organisations including the British Council, EEP, the Soros Foundation and the Central European Teaching Programme. The Central Bureau for Educational Visits and Exchanges (CEVE) in London is a government system which appoints some foreign teachers. Only International House Timisoara has contracted overseas teachers, in its language schools, other openings will be ad hoc. There are about 4,200 qualified teachers of English in the country and 3,700 unqualified, for 1.47 million learners. Schools and universities are often poorly equipped so teachers would be advised to pack lots of materials.

Companies do have in-house English programmes, but ironically in regards to the law, recruit locally. Freelancing is very difficult, as private work is done by contracted teachers to make up their income, using the contacts they have from the inside. If a freelance teacher finds work with a company there is no guarantee that work papers will be arranged.

Romania is certainly not a place to make money. Most teachers are paid at local rates, perhaps with a small supplement, and could find that much of this is taken up by rent. Take savings or be prepared to search hard for richer students who can afford private lessons.

Visas and work permits: Tourist visas can be gained at the point of entry. It is not legal to search for work on a tourist visa but is often done. Your prospective local employer will have to get permission to hire you from the local school inspectorate. They will pass on your application to the Ministry of Education.

Cost of living: Romanian products are cheap but treating yourself to imported goods will rapidly deplete your salary. Restaurants are cheap, and cheaper in summer.

Salaries and taxes: Teachers earn local salaries at the equivalent of about £50 to £100 per month in the private sector if they are university graduates. Private classes can bring in £3-5 per hour. In the state sector wages are from £50-70 per month. The average salary is $95 a month.

Accommodation: Flats tend to be expensive and not too good. A one-bed-roomed flat can take up all of a teacher's local salary. Schools and volunteer programmes generally provide accommodation or an extra allowance.

Health insurance: Essential. UK passport holders have access to hospital treatment, other medical care and some dental treatment.

Inoculations: Hepatitis A, Polio, Typhoid.

English language newspapers: Bucuresti, Nine O'Clock, In Review, Romanian Business News.

Other useful information: Romania is a welcoming country with attractive countryside but conditions are not easy. Bring very warm clothes for the winter.

List of schools in Romania
ACCESS Language Centre, Str Tebei nr 21, 3400 CLUJ-Napoca

CLASS (Constanta Language Association), Str Mircea cel Batran nr 103, 8700 Constanta

International House Language Centre, Bd Republicii nr 9, 1900 Timisoara

International Language Centre, Str Moara de Foc nr 35, Et 8, 6600 Iasi

Linguarama Bucharest, 51 Delea Veche Str, B1 46, 9th floor, Sector 2, Bucharest Tel: (0) 1 320 61 56 Fax: (0) 1 320 61 59 email: oppromania@aol.com

PROSPER - ASE Language Centre, Suite 4211, et 2, Calea Griveti 2-2A, Bucharest

PROSPER - Transilvania Language Centre, Str Carpilator 15/17 (ICIM), 2200 Brasov

RALEX Linguistic Centre, Str Buna Vestire nr 35, 1000 Ramnicu Valeca

Russia

Demand for English in Russia continues to expand, with excellent opportunities in the oil cities of Siberia and cities along the Volga, as well as in the more established centres of Moscow and St Petersburg. With a conservative estimate of 150 private English language schools in Moscow alone, the private language industry is flourishing.

Getting a job is probably less easy than a few years ago, but unqualified L1 English-speaker teachers should be able to find work, especially outside the major cities in more rural areas.

Many universities and schools are seeking qualified L1 speaker teachers but salaries offered tend to be low. Teachers prepared to stay for some time often start off working for a school and then when they can afford to, go freelance to earn better rates. Having established contacts obviously makes this easier.

Teachers are also placed by voluntary and cultural organisations including EEP, Central Bureau and GAP Activity Projects.

The main market is for General English. Business English seems to be becoming more important, but at the moment the demand for young learner teaching is small.

Visas and work permits: Everyone needs a tourist visa to enter the country but it makes more financial sense to go looking for jobs on a business visa. For this, your company or school must contact the Ministry of Foreign Affairs. This takes about six weeks. This requires an invitation from a Russian contact or agent but it allows you to make purchases at lower prices.

Although work permits do not exist as such, you need to get hold of a Multiple Entry Visa. This can only be secured by receiving an invitation from a Russian company in your home country which must subsequently be presented at the nearest Russian consulate. The company does not need to employ you: it need only invite you for a two-month consultation trip. Once you are in Russia, there can be a lot of paperwork involved in changing employer.

Cost of living: Rents have now become expensive in Moscow. Public transport is reasonable and very good.

Salaries and taxes: Employers normally pay people in dollars but declare a low salary in roubles to avoid the 40 per cent hard currency tax. In schools, foreign teachers earn US$600 per month, US$13-20 per hour. For private classes you can

SECTION 3   **International Job Prospects**

expect around US$20 per hour. In Moscow or St Petersburg this can increase to US$30 per hour. Ensure that your salary is paid in US$.

Accommodation: The unregulated rental market is chaotic and means that accommodation is expensive, particularly in Moscow. There a bedsit might be as much as US$300 per month and for a one-bedroomed flat, you could end up paying $500 per month. Deposits tend to be one month's rent. If you don't speak Russian or have local friends, an agency can help but will charge a fee of around $200. Flights are paid for by the employer.

Health insurance: Essential. Get it before you go. Those with a UK passport have access to treatment in state hospitals. HIV test results are required for those staying for more than 3 months.

English language newspapers: Moscow Times, Moscow Tribune, Moscow News, St Petersburg Press, Neva News, The Vladivostock Times.

Important cultural differences: A long time is taken to do many things, from shopping to processing paperwork. This is generally accepted as normal.

Other useful information: As schools set up and close quickly, it is vital to have your contract before you arrive, with conditions, school facilities, etc., specified. Take a decent supply of warm clothing for the cold winters.

List of schools in Russia

American Academy of Foreign Languages, Moscow, St Petersburg, Kiev

American Academy of Foreign Languages, 17A, Bolshaya Cheremushkinskaya, St, Moscow 11347

American Academy of Foreign Languages, 11A Pervaya Krasnoarmiskaya Office 52, St Petersburg

Anglo-American School, Penkovaya ui. 5, St. Petersburg

Benedict School, Chapligina 92, Novosibirsk 630099

Benedict School, 23 ul, Pskovskaya, St Petersburg, 190008

BKC International House, Vsevolozhsky per d 2, Moscow 1 19034

BKC International House, Building 4, 9a Tverskaya St, Moscow 103009

BKC International House (Moscow, Molodezhnaya, Zheleznodorozhny), Starovagankovskiy Per 15, 121019 Moscow

BKC International House Zelenograd, Dom 8A, YBK 1806 Rodnik, Berezovaya Alleya, Zelenograd, 103498 Moscow

Breitner Language School, Leninsky Prospekt 29, Britner Ltd, Tatyana, Karmanova

British Council English Study Centre, Library of Foreign Literature, U1 Nikoloyamskaya, 1 Moscow 109189

Centre for Intensive Foreign Language Instruction, Sparrow Hills, Building 2, Moscow 119899

Courses in Foreign Languages Dip Academy (MID), ul Ostozhenka 53/2 fl 102, 119021 Moscow

EF English First, 1st Brestskaya St 15, 5th floor Moscow

Institute of Business Studies (IELTS preparation), Academy of National Economy, 82, Vernadsky Prospect, 117571 Moscow

International Education Centre, School no 807, Pr Vernadskogo 101-6 Moscow

International Language Academy, Naberezhnaya kania Griboedova 5, Rm 527/6, St Petersburg. Also: POL 260, PO Box 289, Weybridge, Surrey KT13 8WJ, UK.

Language Link, Novoslobodskaya ul. 5/2, 101030 Moscow. Tel: 007 095 232 0225 4889. Fax: 007 095 234 0703. e-mail: jobs@language.ru Websitesite: http:www.language.ru. Contact: Robert Jensky 30 teaching centres throughout Russia, competitive salaries, accommodation, visa, academic and pastoral support. Internships & work/study programme available

Linguarama, 2nd Floor Rm 62, Maly Ziatoustinsky per 6, Moscow 101863

Link School of Languages, 15/81 pl Lenina, 394000 Voronezh

Marina Anglo-American School, Leninsky Prospekt 39a, Moscow 117313

Moscow-Cambridge Project Management, Academy of National Economy, 82 Vernadsky Prospect, 117571 Moscow

Moscow International School, 2nd Ulitsa Maryinoy Roshchi 2a, Moscow

Moscow MV Lomonosov University, Sparrow Hills, Moscow 117234

Moscow State Linguistic University, Rm 135, Ostszhenka 38, Moscow 119384

Polyglot International School, 22 Volkov Pereulok, Flat 56, Moscow

Polyglot ILA, Block 5, 19 Novoyasenevsky Prospekt, Moscow 117593

RISC Language School, Ulitsa Dmitri Ulyanova 26, Room 110, Moscow 117036

Russian-American Center, Tomsk Polytechnic University, Room 319, Lenin Ave 30, 634004 Tomsk

St Petersburg University, Universitetskaya, Naberezhnaya 7/9 B-164, St Petersburg 199164

St Petersburg University of Humanities & Social Sciences, Dept. of Foreign Languages, 15 Fuchika Str, 192238 St Petersburg

School of Linguistics, Institute for International Law and Economics, Spartakovskaya St, 2/1, Moscow 107066

Sunny School, PO Box 23, 125057 Moscow

System-3 Language & Communication, Kantemirovskaya Street 16 #531, Moscow 115522

The Headway Fund, Office 70, Ul Vavilova 30/6, Moscow

Slovak Republic (Slovakia)

Since the 'Velvet Divorce' which separated the Czech and Slovak Republics in January 1993, the English language industries in both republics has taken off dramatically. Slovakia is the poorer of the two and has not benefited from tourism in the same way as its neighbour, so growth in the private sector is not comparable. English has become more popular than German as a foreign language and there is a shortage of qualified teachers.

Positions in state schools are not available on spec and tend to be organised through agencies, cultural organisations and the Slovakian Academic Information Agency which is supervised by the Ministry of Education. Most jobs require a teaching qualification and contracts are for full-time work. These state sector jobs are poorly paid and extremely bureaucratic to arrange alone. In the private language schools there are openings at all levels, particularly for Cambridge exam preparation.

Visas and work permits: Foreigners may work in the Slovak Republic only after they have been granted a residence permit. Application for a residence permit must be made at least 60 days prior to departure. Residence permits are granted by the local police. Applicants are not allowed to start work before being granted an entry visa. Foreigners granted an entry visa must register with the police within 3 days of arrival.

Cost of living: Extremely low, but increasing at present.

Salaries and taxes: Teachers are paid at local rates and can expect to earn the equivalent of about $300 per month. The British Council only takes on experienced teachers, recruited abroad for 2 year contracts, paying about £600 per month, with a flight, insurance and housing package. Freelance teachers can earn between £7 and £12 per hour.

Accommodation: Schools often provide accommodation for teachers.

Health insurance: Essential. Those with a UK passport have access to hospital treatment and other medical care.

Inoculations: Hepatitis A, Polio, Tetanus, Typhoid.

English language newspapers: Slovak Spectator.

Other useful information: There isn't much crime and it's easy to escape into the countryside for skiing and hiking.

List of schools in the Slovak Republic

Akademia Vzdelavania, Druzstevna 2, 831 03 Bratislava

Akademia Vzdelavania, Gorkeho 10, 815 17 Bratislava.

Albion, Jazykova skola, Skuteckeho 8, 974 00 Banska Bystrica

American Language Institute, Drienova 34, PO Box 78, 820 09 Bratislava

Bakschool, Independent Language School, Postova 1, 040 01 Kosice

BEA English Studio, Anglicka Jazykova skola, Hlavna 17, Trnava

Berlitz, Jazykova skola, Na vrsku 2, 811 01 Bratislava

Effective Language Centre, Biela 3, 040 01 Kosice

E-Ku, Jazykova skolaPiaristicka 25, 949 01 Nitra

The English Club, Pri Suchom mlyne 36, 811 04 Bratislava

English Learning Centre, Dr Kalaposova Silvia, Zuzkin park 2, 040 01 Kosice

English Teaching Centre, Skuteckeho 11, 974 00 Banska Bystrica

Esperlingvo, Sukromna jazykova skola, Obchodna 42, 811 06 Bratislava

Eurolingua, Jazykova skola sro, Drienova 16, 821 03 Bratislava

Europe House, Jazykova skola, Mikoviniho 1, 831 02 Bratislava

Eurotrend, Starohorska 2, 801 01 Bratislava

Fan Action Language Studio, PhDr Brigita Wallova, Juzna trieda 13, 040 01 Kosice

Flosculus, Chris Elston, Drevny trh 5, 040 01 Kosice

Foundation for a Civil Society, V Zahradach 29A, 811 03 Bratislava

Ivega Learning Center, Moldavska 8, 040 01 Kosice

Jazykova skola EURO, Nabrezna 30, 940 75 Nove Zamky

Jazykova skola MTD, Metodova 2, 821 08 Bratislava

Jazykova skola VAGES, Piaristicka 1, 849 01 Nitra

Language Link, Slovakia, Recruitment Section, 21 Harrington road, South Kensington, London, UK, SW7 3EU

Lengua Agency: Jazykova skola, Galbaveho 3, 841 01 Bratislava

Lingua Centrum, Szakkayho 1, 040 01 Kosice

Lingua Jazykova skola, Zahradnick 2, 931 01 Samorin

The Logos Center, Karpatska 2, 811 05 Bratislava

London House, Krusovska 2093, 955 01 Topolcany

Mestske Kulturne Stredisko, Nam slobody 11, 909 01 Skalica

Nevequelle, Mgr Jolana Masikova, Maurerova 18, 040 01 Kosice

New Life Center, Zuzkin park 4, 040 01 Kosice

Perspektiva, Ursulinska 11, 812 93 Bratislava

Pro Sympatia, Centrum Studia Cudzich Jazykov, Pribinova 23, 810 11 Bratislava

PTK Echo Slovakia sro, Presovska 39, 821 02 Bratislava

Quentin, Magurska 13, 040 01 Kosice

RK Centrum Universa sro, Skuteckeho 30, 974 00 Banska Bystrica

S-Klub, Vojenska 28, 934 01 Levice

Sophist, Juzna trieda 50, 040 01 KosiceTop School of Languages - Pistek, Galandova 2, 811 06 Bratislava

VSMU, Katedra Jazykov, Venturska 3, 813 01 Bratislava.

VSZ VaPC as, Watsonova 1, 040 01 Kosice

Vzdelavacia nadacia ASPEKT, Akademicka 4, 949 01 Nitra

The World Company, Alzbetina 47, 040 01 Kosice

Slovenia

This former region of Yugoslavia managed to stay out of the recent Balkan conflicts, focusing instead on getting its economy up to EU membership standards. The English language industry is well established and the number of private schools continues to grow.

Only a small number of schools offer full-time contracts, but it is quite easy to find private classes. After General English, the main markets are Business English, young learners and exam courses.

Visas and work permits: All foreign national need a work permit and a work visa. The work permit is obtained by the employer in Slovenia prior to an application for a work visa in the employee's country of residence. Processing of visas usually takes about two months. Unofficially, some teachers work on tourist visas.

Cost of living: High for Central Europe but cheaper than Western Europe..

Salaries and taxes: Generally paid in local currency but also in Deutschmarks. Expect DM15-20 per hour after tax depending on experience and qualifications.

Accommodation: This is not usually provided by the employer. Expect to pay about DM800 per month for a small, furnished flat. One month's rent is usually expected as a deposit but sometimes six months' rent is demanded.

Health insurance: Advisable. Those with a UK passport have access to hospital treatment, other medical care and some dental treatment.

List of Schools in Slovenia

Accent On Language d.o.o., Ljubljanska c. 36, 1230 Domzale

Ambra d.o.o., Pobeska 18, 6000 Koper

Andragoski Zavod Maribor/Ljudiska Uni, Maistrova ul 5, 2000 Maribor

AS Asistent d.o.o., Glavni trg 17B, 2000 Maribor

Athena d.o.o., Kolodvorska c 17, 6320 Postojna

Bled, Sola za Tuje Jezike, Breda Vukelj sp, Kajuhova c 11, 4260 Bled

Candor Dominko kd, Turnovse 19, 1360 Vrhnika

Cenca p.o., Masarykova c 18/Ribnisko selo, 2000 MariborDialog d.o.o. Jezikovna Sola lingua, p.o. Terceva ul 39, 2000 Maribor

Dude d.o.o. English Language Centre, Slamnikarska 1, 1230 Domzale

Ekocept d.o.o. Sola za Tuje Jezike, Prezihova 8, 2230 Lenart v Slovenskih, Goricah

Eurocenter, Lilijana Durdevic sp, Kidriceva ul 46, 6000 Koper

Europa Bled d.o.o., Alpska 7, 4260 Bled

Flamingo d.o.o., Pod Gonjami 44, 2391 Prevalje

Forum Center d.o.o., Markova pot 8, 5290 Sempeter pri Gorici

G A P, Belokriska 22, 6320 Portoroz

Hello Sempeter d.o.o, Sempeter v Savinski dolini 34, 3311 Sempeter v Savinski dolin

ISCG Domzale, Kolodvorska c 6, 1230 Domzale

Jasna Dzumhur, sp Jamex, Malgajeva 10, 3000 Celje

Jezikovna Sola Tabula Rasa, Trg svobode 12, 3325 Sostanj

Jezikovni biro Lindic, Cankarjeva ul 10, 2000 Maribor

Jezikovni Studio Kotar Sonja sp, Cesta na Svetino 10, 3270 Lasko

Lingua/Carman Cilka sp, Cesta Zasavskega batljona 27, 1270 Litija

Lingva d.o.o., Ograde 7, 1386 Stari trg pri Lozu, Cerknica

Lingva p.o., Vetrinjska ul 16, 2000 Maribor

Little England Club d.o.o., Medvedova ul 6, 1241 Kamnik

Ljudiska Univerza Kranj, Cesta Staneta Zagarja 1, 4000 Kranj

Ljudiska Univerza Nova Gorica, Cankarjeva ul 8, 5000 Nova Gorica

Ljudiska Univerza Ptuj, Mestni trg 2, 2250 Ptuj

Ljudska Univerza Celje, Cankarjeva ul 1, 3000 Celje

Ljudska Univerza Koper, Cankarjeva ul 33, 6000 Koper

Ljudska Univerza Ravne Na Koroskem, Prezihova ul 24, 2390 Ravne na Koroskem

Ljudska Universa Sezana, Bazoviska c 9, 6210 Sezana

Most d.o.o., Kovinarska ul 9, 8270 Krsko

Multilinga d.o.o., Ulica bratov Hvalic 16, 5000 Nova Gorica

New College d.o.o., Med ogradami 11A, 5000 Nova Gorica

Niansa Jezikovna Sola, Cesta Talcev 4, 1230 Domzale

Ontario d.o.o., Miklosiceva ul 5, 2250 Ptuj

Pharmagan d.o.o., Straziska ul 7, 4000 Kranj

Poliglot d.o.o., Ljublianska c 110, 1230 Domizale

Prevajanje (Translation), Kalinskova ul 31, 4000 Kranj

Progress Jezikovni Tecaji d.o.o., Seljakovo n 33, 4000 Kranj

Rossana d.o.o., Trzaska 30, 1370 Logatec

Samba d.n.o., Bresterniska ul 225, 2351 Kamnica

Selih Kozelj d.n.o., Studio za Ucenje, Miklosiceva 9, 3000 Celje

Sibon, Center za Tuje Jezike, Ljubljanska c.76 11, 1230 Domzale

Speak It, Heintzman and Heintzman, Trubarjeva ul 4, 1230 Domzale

Sports Life Pevc d.o.o., Cesta talcev 6, 4220 Skofja Loka

Tecal d.o.o., Kraigherjeva ul 19A, 2230 Lenart v Slovenskih, Goricah

Tonson Posrednistvo in Storitve d.o.o., Velike Brusnice 13, 8321 Brusnice

Unique d.o.o. , Gabrsko 69, 1420 Ttrbovlje

Vox Vidrih Trebnje kd, Simonciceva ul 10, 8210 Trebnje

Yurena d.o.o., Ulica Marjana Kozine 49A, 8000 Novo mesto

Zavod za Izobrazevanje, Kopitarjeva 5, 2000 Maribor

Zavod za Izobrazevanje BSA, Grajski trg 1, 2000 Maribor

Switzerland

Although Switzerland is in the European Economic Area, it is not a member of the EU. EU nationals are therefore in the same boat as non-EU nationals when it comes to getting a work permit.

Switzerland has a great demand for both Business and General English and there is a very strong bias in favour of qualified teachers. There is a good supply of teachers in and around Basel so schools are unlikely to search further afield. Opportunities that do arise tend to be vacation work.

Visas and work permits: All non-nationals need a work permit to teach. Permis A can be secured for seasonal employment, where the local workforce is deemed too small to cope with the demand. A Permis B might be granted for a specific one-year placement in a Swiss company but the employer must be able to guarantee a minimum number of hours and prove that no Swiss national could do the job. The employer must apply for a work permit prior to the employee's departure. If the permit is granted then an 'Assurance of a work permit' is sent to the employee's address outside Switzerland.

Cost of living: High.

Salaries and taxes: It depends enormously on the school, the hours and the teacher's qualifications but salaries are generally high, maybe up to SF40 per hour. The tax rate is around 15 per cent.

Accommodation: It is relatively easy to find but expensive. Schools often help teachers to find accommodation and might arrange cheap rent or board and lodging. When renting, one months' deposit is usually required.

Health insurance: Essential.

English language newspapers: There are no Swiss-based English language papers, but all British papers are readily available.

Important cultural differences: Lots of kissing, shaking hands and regulations.

List of schools in Switzerland

ASC International House, 72 rue de Lausanne, 1202 Geneva

Basilingua Sprachschule, Birsigstrasse 2, 4054 Basel

Bell Language School, 12 Chemin des Colombettes, 1202 Geneva

Berlitz, 14 rue De L'Ancien-Port, 1202 Geneva

Berlitz, Munzgasse 3, 4001 Basel

inlingua Basel, Heuberg 12, 2 Stock, CH-4051 Basel

inlingua Bern, Waisenhausplatz 28, CH-3011 Bern

inlingua Biel, Silbergasse 32, CH-2502 Biel

inlingua Fribourg, Rue St Pierre 4, CH-1700 Fribourg

inlingua Geneve, Rue du Leman 6, CH-1201 Geneve

inlingua Lausanne, Grand Pont 18, CH-1003 Lausanne

inlingua Luzern, Weinmarkt 15, CH-6004 Luzern

inlingua Neuchatel, 18 Av de la Gare, CH-2000 Neuchatel

inlingua Olten, Dornacherstr 7, CH-4600 Olten

inlingua Sion, 5 Av des Mayennets, CH-1950 Sion

inlingua Zurich, Badener Str 15, CH-8004 Zuric

Institute Le Rosey, Camp d'Etz, Route des Quatre Communes, CH-1180 Rolle

International House, St Gallen, Lindenstrasse 139, 9016 St Gallen

International House Regensdorf/ZH, Althardstrasse 70, 8105 Regensdorf

Leysin American School, CH-1854 Leysin

Markus Frei Sprachenschulen, Neugasse 6, 6300 Zug

Village Camps, 1296 Coppet

Volkschohschule, Slugenstrasse 10, Zurich 8002

Turkey

Expansion of the tourism industry and a focus on meeting EU membership requirements has greatly expanded the demand for English language learning. General English remains the main market, but Business English, EAP and young learners courses are all becoming increasingly popular.

Many language schools recruit overseas and offer full-time contracts including enough to live on, airfare and accommodation. Having a native speaker teacher is a selling point. State schools by law cannot employ foreign teachers directly. They get round this by sub-contracting from a language school, or asking parents to pay for an "unofficial" teacher. In private secondary schools non-L1 native English speakers may be able to get work, added to teaching French or German as well. In the universities recruits tend to have specialist skills, but some openings for English alone may come along. For this level work a degree and CELTA type qualifications are needed. These positions are filled from local advertising.

The corporate sector is expanding, in all types of business. Teachers are recruited from language schools or casually. The law on such workers is unclear so teachers have to be careful to understand their status and rights .

There are plenty of opportunities for private classes too although, strictly speaking, a permit is granted on the basis of a contract set up with a specified employer. Freelance work is illegal without a work permit, but does happen. Contracted teachers will often take private classes to supplement their income.

Visas and work permits: The regulations often change. British nationals need a visa to enter Turkey and all nationalities need a work permit to teach. A permit will be granted only to teachers with a degree and a teaching qualification. It is better to apply for a visa and work permit in Turkey. Many people work on tourist visas although it is strictly prohibited. It is legal to search for work on a tourist visa, but a teacher has to leave the country to collect work papers from a Turkish consulate once permission to hire is granted to the employer. Many employers conduct visa applications but the legal obligation is with the teacher. While the authorities seem to have been ignoring the practise of some to maintain their tourist status by leaving Turkey for a day every 3 months, our latest information is that the checking process on teachers is becoming stricter.

Cost of living: Relatively cheap, but inflation is high.

Salaries and taxes: Salaries vary enormously. Language schools pay US$300-450 per month, while private secondary schools give US$1200. A well qualified teacher in a select school can earn around £1,000 per month. Private classes can earn between US$40 and $60 per hour. An on spec freelancer can make US$20 per hour. No tax is deducted. Often pay is in dollars as local inflation is problematic. If you are offered a Turkish lira salary, it is best to ensure that a mid-year salary adjustment is going to be forthcoming or that there is some foreign currency component.

Accommodation: Schools tend to provide shared accommodation for full-time contracted teachers, but plenty of private rented accommodation is available. The average rate for the suburbs is the equivalent of about US$200, but flats tend to be unfurnished. One month's rent is usually required as a deposit.

Health insurance: Advisable. Private health care is infinitely preferable to the state service.

Inoculations: Hepatitis A, Polio, Typhoid, Malaria in some areas.

English language newspapers: Turkish Daily News.

Important cultural differences: Turkey is a very masculine society. Outsiders, particularly females, should be aware of their novelty value. While the political system is secular, a big debate is continuing between Islamic factions as to the direction of the country. Large conflicts continue in the east, related to the status of the Kurds.

Other useful information: Check contracts very carefully and talk to teachers who already work at the school. Many schools are small, owner-directed operations which try to spend as little as possible on resources, training and administration. Bureaucracy can be frustrating with tasks such as paying bills, getting money from the bank or even getting paid potentially very time-consuming.

List of schools in Turkey

Active English, ybrahim Gokcen Bulvari No 50/1, Manisa

Akademi School of English, PK 234, 21001 Bahar Sokar No 2, Diyarbakir

Anadolu Dershanelery, 859 Sokak No 3, Saray y hani B Blok, Konak - Yzmir

Ankara University, Rektorlugu, Beslevler, Ankara

Best English, Mesrutiyet Caddesi no 2/8, Ankara

Bilkent University, School of English Language, (BUSEL), Bilkent, Ankara 06533

British Academy, 1717 Sokak No 81/4, Egem y hani, 35530 Kar iyaka - Yzmir

British Council, 251-253 Istiklal Cadessi, 80060 Beyoglu, Istanbul

Cambridge English, Kazim Ozalp Sok. No. 15, Kat. 4, Saskinbakkal, Istanbul

Cinar School of English, 860 Sokak No. 1, Kat. 4, Konak, Izmir

Dilko English Centres, Hatboyo Caddesi No. 16, 34720 Bakirkoy, Istanbul

Dilmer LTC, Unlu Cad. 7, Keykel, Bursa

Elissa English, Ihsaniye Mah 41, Sokak 48, Bandirma, Balikesir

The English Centre, Rumeli Caddesi. 92, Zeki Bey Apt. 4, Osmanbey, Istanbul

English Academy, 1374 Sokak No 18, Selvili y Merkezi Kat 4, Cankaya - Yzmir

English Academy, 858 Sok. Tarancilar y hani No 5 K4, Konak - Yzmir

English Club, Cumhuriy et Bulvari 36/5, Konak - Yzmir

English Centre, Cumhuriyet Bulvari No 125 K1, Heykel - Yzmir

English Fast, Burhaniye Mah. Resmi Efendi Sok. No. 4, Beylerbeyi, Istanbul

English Fast, 440 Sokak No 5, Konax - Yzmir

English House, Kemalpa a Caddesi 90/3, Kar iyaka - Yzmir

English Lab, 1720 Sokak No 26/2, Kar iyaka - Yzmir

English Star, Pehit Fethibey Caddesi, y hani No 79/7, Pasaport - Yzmir

English West, Cumhuriyet Bulvari 36/3, Konak - Yzmir

Evrim, Cengiz Topel Caddesi 8, Camlibel, 33010 Mersin

Euro Center, M. pa a Cad, Akif Pahin y h No 102 K4, Salihli

Interlang, Russell Baulk, Zuhtu Pasa Mah, Recep Peker Cd, Sefikbey Sok No 17, Kiziltoprak, Istanbul

Internatinoal House Istanbul,
Nispetiye Caddesi, Erdolen Ismerkesi
No: 38, Kat: 1 1. Levant, Istanbul Tel:
090 212 282 90 64/090 212 282 90 65
Fax: 090 212 282 32 18 Email: karizma
ltd@turk.net Website: http://www.ihis
tanbul.com General English, Business
English, Group and individual cours-
es. Dynamic, professional school situ-
ated in vibrant, historical city.
Committed to quality teaching.

International School, Eser Apt.A Blok Kasap, Sokak 1617, Esentepe, Istanbul

International Training Institute, Istiklal Cad, Kallavi Sakak 7/9 Kat 4, Galatasary, Istanbul

Istanbul Turco-British Association, Suleyman Nazif Sokak 68, Nisantasi, 80220 Istanbul

Istanbul University, Rektorlugu Beyarzit, Istanbul

Izmir British Council Teachers Centre, 1374 SO-kak 18,Selvili 15, Merkezi, kat, Cankaya, Izmir 35210

Karizma/International House Istanbul, Nispetiye Cad Erdolen Ishani No 38 Kat 1, 1 Levent 80660, Istanbul

Kent English Ankara, Mithatpasa Caddesi No. 46 Kat. 3/4/5, 06420 Kizilay, Ankara

Kumlu Dersanerleri, Bursa Merkez, Basak Caddesi, Bursa. Tel: 241 20465.

Kent English, Mithatpasa Cad. 46/3, Kizilay, Ankara

London Languages International, Abide-i Hurriyet Caddesi, Kat. 1, Mecidiyekoy, Istanbul

New Kent English, 1472 Sokak No 32, Alsancak

Practical English, Necatibey Bulvari, Uz y Merkezi 1 No 19 K2, Cankaya - Yzmir

The Sandwich Method, Mustafa Bey Cad No 13 D14, Alsancak - Yzmir

Swissotel Training Centre, Suite Tower, Bayildim Cad. No. 2, Macka 80680, Istanbul

SyTA, Kibris Pehitleri Caddesi, No 125 Karal Apt, Alsancak - Yzmir

TOMER, Kibris Pehitleri Caddesi No 55, Alsancak - Yzmir

TURKENG Teacher Recruitment
(Turkey), 3 Peck Close, Norwich NR5
9NF, UK Barbara Livesey,
Tel/Fax: 44 (0) 1603 747042 Email:
turkeng@angelfire.com. Year-round
TEFL jobs all over Turkey,
professional schools, flight and
accommodation expenses paid!
Arranged free! Summer jobs available.
Visit http://
www.angelfire.com/biz/turkeng

Turkish-American Association, Cennah Caddesi No 20, 06690 Kavaklidere, Ankara

Turkish-American Association, Resat bey Mahallesi, 5 Yeni Yarbasi Karakolu Sokagi No 27, Adana

Turkish-American Association, 1379 Sok No 39, Alsancak, Izmir

The Turco-British Association, Ankara
Tel: 90 (312) 419 18 44 Fax: 90 (312)
418 54 04 Email: tba@tba.ord.tr
Website http://www.tba.org.tr
Contact: Peter Schooley. Ankara's
most prestigious language and cultur-
al centre requires qualified profes-
sional EFL teachers, 2 year contract,
return air fare, furnished
accommodation

Video English, Cumhuriyet Bulvari 36/2, Konak - Yzmir

Video English Karpiyaka, Kernalpa a Caddesi No 7/202, Kar iyaka - Yzmir

Ukraine

As with the rest of east central Europe, the demand for L1 English speakers able to teach English is high. English is the first foreign language of the Ukraine. There are at least sixty language schools registered in Kiev alone, and many others in places such as Odessa, Kharkiv and Donetsk. Not all of these specifically recruit only native speakers. TEFL, CELTA or TESOL qualifications are necessary in many schools, especially those organised by, or associated with, the British Council, International House and the American Academy of Foreign Languages. Elsewhere, being an L1 speaker or fluent in English may be enough to land you a teaching role if you have some teaching experience. Work contracts generally last between 9 and 11 months.

Teachers are required at all levels of the education spectrum, including to help teach the local teachers of English.

Work is available in private schools and through these in companies wishing to expand the language skills of their staff. Demand for young learners teachers is growing, alongside the requirements of students and young professionals.

Many schools report a waiting list of people wishing to join English language courses and have found it problematic to recruit enough L1 speaker teachers, or local teachers, with internationally recognised TEFL qualifications. They recruit locally and overseas. If it is the experience of the Ukraine, rather than to earn money as such, it is possible to volunteer with such organisations as the Ukraine National Association INc (New Jersey, USA, PO Box 17a, 30 Montgomery Street).

Some teachers do find work in university teaching labs, which advertise positions on their internal noticeboards, but the rates of pay for this would be local, which could mean between US$100-$200 per month. Unofficial extras or bonuses may be paid to foreign teachers, but it is probably not advisable to rely on these. The state sector does not recruit or place foreign teachers generally.

If you wish to work with an organisation such as International House, you have to apply and be recruited in London. While the rates of pay will be local, help is given by the school that you go to to find accommodation, and in many cases is provided at cheaper rate by the school. With the international organisations flights to and from the Ukraine are usually included in the employment contract, as is medical insurance.

Visas: Schools linked with International House or the British Council will arrange all of the visa details and work permit requirements for their own teachers. Otherwise the procedure is that for a work permit you must be invited to work by one of the schools. It is possible to travel to the country on a tourist permit and perhaps wise to assess the schools that might recruit you before seeking permission to work. As elsewhere, some teachers do work illegally as tourists on a cash in hand basis, but in official terms it is not permitted to work without a contract and impossible to be in the Ukraine with a multi-entry visa if you do not have a letter of invitation to take up a job. Employers must be registered companies and must produce invites to work. While it is possible to apply to change the status of your visa from tourist to work from inside the country, it can often cause bureaucratic problems, so it may be easier to leave and apply from abroad.

Rates of pay: This varies according to your experience, responsibility and where you work. Local rates are low. Some contract jobs would typically offer US$350-$1000 per month, plus extras in accommodation and the return flights.

In other private schools the pay can be between US$5 and $10 per hour, and usually you would work between 20 and 30 hours per week. This is regarded as sufficient to live in reasonable comfort locally, but would not be enough to support dependants.

Cost of living: The cost of accommodation varies with size and location, but you could expect to pay between US$100 and $200 per month for a small apartment on the outskirts of KIev, but perhaps between US$1000 and $2,000 for good quality city centre flats. It is very cheap to use public transport, with a month's metro pass costing around US$10. Using private cabs is also very cheap, costing between 3 and 10 Hryvnias within the city area (4 Hryvnias = US$1).

English Language Newspapers: The Kiyiv Post, The Odessa Post.

List of Schools in the Ukraine
1&1 English Language Training Course, Kiev
American Academy of Foreign Languages, Office 9, 89 Chervonoarmeiyskaya St, Kiev
INTERLINGUA, Kiev State Foreign Language Training,
International Business Communication Language School, 84 Bozhenko Str, rm 221, Kiev 252022
International House Kharkiv, 7 Marshala Bazhanova St, 31002 Kharkiv
International House Kyiv, 7 V Vasilevskoy St, P O Box 64121, Kyiv 252 055
International House Lviv, 1 109 Zelena Street, 290035 Lviv
International House Odessa, 27a Shevchenko Street, 270058 Odessa
London School of English, Kiev Polytechnic University Bldg 19, Room 530, Kiev
Language Link, Ukraine, Recruitment Section, 21 Harrington Road, South Kensington, London, UK, SW7 3EU
Lingvist Education Centre, Kiev
Monarch International Language Academy, Vorovskogo 8, appt 1/2, Kiev 252 200

The Americas

United States of America

Although government cuts have drastically affected state-funded English language programmes for immigrants, there are still two large markets in the US. Adults learn English in the private sector, which includes the universities, and children learn English in the state-owned public schools.

Before you can teach children, you must have state certification from an American university and to teach adults, a Master's degree is often the minimum qualification. The RSA Diploma might be accepted as an equivalent to an MA, but it is much harder for non-North Americans to find work.

Adult education is broken up into various sectors, including intensive English programmes in universities and private language schools and longer courses at universities. To find work, contact the schools in the area you are interested in or approach TESOL. (Fax: +1-703-836 7864) asking about their placement and resume-holding services.

Trade schools and semi-professional training schools also hire English teachers to train an increasing number of foreign students enrolling on programmes designed for native English speakers. Neither credentials nor MA's are required.

Visas and work permits: To teach, you should have a Green Card, permanent residence or a work permit, although those on student or cultural visas are often eligible for a restricted number of work hours per week. It is unwise to work illegally, as there are stiff penalties. It helps to be qualified before applying for the necessary permit.

If you are participating in a government exchange programme, you can qualify for a J-1 visa entitling you to work legally. Alternatively, an H-1B working visa can be obtained if you are sponsored by a US company. The company will have to show that you have qualifications and skills which cannot be found locally.

Cost of living: More expensive in major centres. Food is relatively cheap elsewhere.

Salaries and taxes: Expect to earn $15-$34 per hour. Tax depends on the state and the salary level, but can be as high as 50 per cent.

Accommodation: Apartments are easy to find, but tend to be expensive. A small apartment will probably cost more than $600 per month, more in California and the East Coast. Rooms in shared houses are cheaper: expect to pay around $400 per month. Three months' rent is usually expected up-front. One month is a non-returnable deposit and the other two months are for the first and last months of the lease.

Health insurance: Essential.
*AAIEP 1997-98 Members, As of April 3, 1998

List of Schools in the USA

*Academia Language School, 1600 Kapiolani Blvd, Suite 1215, Honolulu, HI 96814

*ACE Language Institute, Seattle Pacific University, 3307 3rd Ave West, Seattle, WA 98119

*ACE Language Institute, Pacific Lutheran University, 12002 Park Ave S, Tacoma, WA 98447

*ACE Language Institute, North Seattle Center, 10303 Meridian Ave N #102, Seattle, WA 98133

Adelphi University, Linen Hall, Room 5, Garden City, NY 11530

AESL International, 5930 Preston View Blvd, Dallas, TX 75240

Alabama, University of, Dept of English, 211 Morgan Hall, P O Box 870244, 2nd Street at Ridgecrest, Tuscaloosa, AL 35487 0244

Albert Magnus College, 811a Winchester Ave, Weldon, New Haven, CT 06511-1189

*ALPS - American Language Programs, 1 West Campbell Ave, #77, Campbell, CA 95008-1040

Ame Graduate School, Glendale, AZ 85306

Ame School of International, Training, Intensive English Progs, Two Union Square, Suite 530, Seattle, WA 98101

American English Academy, 1641 W Main St, Suite 222, Alhambra, CA 91801

*American English Academy, 111 N Atlantic Blvd, #112 Monterey Park, CA 91754

American English Institute, Calif State U-Fresno, 2450 E San Ramon Ave, Room 138, Fresno, CA 93740-8032

American English Institute, Box 11000 Oklahoma City, OK 73136-1100

*American Language Academy, Southern Oregon University, 1250 Siskiyou Blvd, Ashland, OR 97520

*American Language Academy, Baldwin-Wallace College, 275 Eastland, Berea, OH 44017

*American Language Academy, 2105 Martin Luther King, Jr Way, Berkeley, CA 94704

*American Language Academy, 29 Winter Street, Boston, MA 02108,

*American Language Academy, Beaver College, Glenside, PA 19038

*American Language Academy, Butler University, 750 West Hampton, Schwitzer Hall/B1, Indianapolis, IN 46208

*American Language Academy, Lake Forest Academy, 1500 W Kennedy Road, Lake Forest, IL 60045

American Language Academy, *Florida Southern College, 111 Lake Hollingsworth Drive, Lakeland, FL 33801-5698

American Language Academy, *Rider University, 2083 Lawrenceville Rd, Lawrenceville, NJ 08648

American Language Academy, *Merrimack College, MS A-26; Merrimack College; 315 Turnpike St, North Andover, MA 01845

*American Language Academy, Oakwood Friends School, 515 South Road, Poughkepsie, NY 12601

*American Language and Culture Institute, California State University, San Marcos, San Marcos, CA 92096-0001

*American Language Academy, University of Tampa, Box 39F, Tampa, FL 33606-1490

*American Language Academy, Nicholls State University, Peltier Hall, P O Box 2112, Thibodaux, LA 70310

*American Language and Culture Institute, California State University, Chico, Center for Regional and Continuing Education, Chico, CA 95929-0250

*American Language and Culture Program, University of Idaho, 209 Morrill Hall, Moscow, ID 83844-3012

*American Language & Intercultural Studies, National University, 4121 Camino del Rio South, Suite 22, San Diego, CA 92054

*American Language Center, UCLA Extension, UCLA Extension, 10995 Le Conte Ave #224, Los Angeles, CA 90024-1327

American Language Institute, A Clive Roberts, SDSU, San Diego, CA 92182-1914

*American Language Institute, San Francisco State University, 1600 Holloway Avenue, San Francisco, CA 94132 (415) 338-1438

American Language Progs, 1 West Campbell Ave 43, Campbell, CA 95008

American University TESOL Program, Department of Language and Foreign Studies, American University, Washington D.C. 20016 Tel: 1 202 885 2582 Fax: 1 202 885 1076 EMail: tesol@american.edu Website: http://www.american.edu/tesol. Contact: Brock Brady. Programs: MA in TESOL, MAT:TESOL (K-12), Joint Masters with Peace Corps, TESOL Certificate, Intensive Summer Institute

Anglo-Continental School of English Boston, 1972 Massachusetts Ave, Cambridge/Boston, MA 02140

Anglo-Continental Boston, Tufts University, 108 Packard Ave, Medford/Boston, MA 02155

Anglo-Continental Los Angeles, Pitzer College, 1050 North Mills Ave, Claremont, CA 91711

Anglo-Continental New York, Monmouth College, 400 Cedar Ave, West Long Branch, NJ 07764

Arapahoe Community Coll, 5900 Sth Santa Fe Drive, Littleton, CO 80120

*Arizona State University, American English and Culture Program, Box 873106, Tempe, AZ 85287-3106

*Arkansas State University, Center for English as a Second Language, P O Box 2910, State University, AR 72467-2910

*ASPECT - Boston, 126 Newbury St, 6th fl, Boston, MA 02116

*ASPECT - Brookville, Long Island University, C W Post Campus, Life Science 148, Brookville, NY 11548

*ASPECT - La Jolla, 1111 Torey Pines, La Jolla, La Jolla, CA 92037

*ASPECT - Orlando, University of Central Florida, P O Box 163610, PC620 #102B, Orlando, FL 32816,

*ASPECT - San Francisco, 26 Third St, San Francisco, CA 94103,

*ASPECT - Whittier, c/o Whittier College, Redwood Hall, P O Box 634, Whittier, CA 90608

Azusa Pacific University - 901 East Alosta Av. Azusa CA 91702-7000

Babson College, P O 57460, Wellesley, MA 02157

Ball State University - 2000 West University, Muncie, IN 47306

Baldwin-Wallace College, 300 Front St, Berea, OH 44017

Barry University, 11300 Ne 2nd Ave, Miami Shores, FL 33161

Bellevue College, Galvin Road At Harvell Drive, Bellevue, NE 68005

*Berkeley English Academy, 2161 Shattuck Ave #313, Berkeley, CA 94704

Biola University, Dept of TESOL & Applied Linguistics, Marshburn Hall, 13800 Biola Ave, La Mirada, CA 90639-0001

Boston University - 605 Commonweatlh Avenue, Boston, MA 02215

Bowling Green State University, Dept. of English, 301 Modely Hall, 1001E, Wooster St., Bowling Green, OH 43403

*Brandon College, English as a Second Language, 830 Market Street, 7th Floor, San Francisco, CA 94102

Brigham Young University, Dept of Linguistics, 2129 JKHB, Provo, UT 84602-6278

Butler University, 4600 Sunset Ave, Indianapolis, IN 46208

*California English Academy, Inc, 870 Market St, Suite 1185, San Francisco, CA 94102

*California State Polytechnic University, Pomona, English Language Institute, 3801 W Temple Ave Bldg 86, Pomona, CA 91768-4030

*California State University - Fullerton, American Language Program, MH 63, P O Box 6850, Fullerton, CA 92834-6850

California State University - Fresno, American English Institute, 5240 N Jackson Ave, Room 127, Fresno, CA 93740-0074

California State University - Hayward, Harward, CA 94542

California, University of, Irvine ext, P O Box 6050, Irvine, CA 22616-6050

*California State University - Northridge, Linguistics Program, 18111 Nordhoff St, Northridge, CA 91330-8306

*California State University - San Bernardino, American Culture and Language Program, 5500 University Parkway, San Bernardino, CA 92407

Caroll College, 161 North Benton Av. Helena, MT 59625

Cardinal; Stritch University, 6801 North Yates Rd, Milwaukee, WI 53217

Carson-Newman College, P O Box 7000215, Jefferson City, TN 37760

Case Western Reserve University, 10900 Euclid Ave, Cleveland, OH 44106

CELCIS, *Western Michigan University, 22-B, Ellsworth Hall, Kalamazoo, MI 49008-5182

Center for Adult Life & Learn, Laura Peskin, 92nd St Y, 1395 Lexington Ave, New York, NY 10128

Center for English as a Second Language, *Xavier University, 3800 Victory Parkway, Cincinnati, OH 45207-2511

Center for English Studies, 330 Seventh Ave, New York, NY 10001

Central Ct State University, 1615 Standley St, New Britain CT 06050

Central MIssouri State University, Warrensbourg, MO 64093-5046

Central Piedmont Community Coll, P O Box 35009, Charlotte, NC 28235

*Central Washington University, University ESL Program, 400 E 8th Ave, Ellensburg, WA 98926-7562

*CES - Center for English Studies, International House, Corporate Headquaters & Office of Admissions, 901 E. Las Olas Blvd, Suite 203, Fort Lauderdale, FL 33301

*CES - Center for English Studies, International House, 888, Las Olas Blvd, 6th floor, Fort Lauderdale, FL 33301

*CES - Center for English Studies, International House, 330 Seventh Avenue at 29th Street, 6th floor, New York, NY10001

*CES - San Francisco, 450 Sansome St ^8F, San Francisco, CA 94411

Christian Missionary Educators, P O Box 1734, Lake Oswego, OR 97035

Cincinnati University, P O Box 210002,Cincinnati, OH 45221-0002

CLA -Coast Language Academy, International House, 200 SW Market St., Suite 11, Portland, Oregon 97201

CLA - Coast Language Avademy, International House, 320 Wiltshire Blvd, 3rd Floor, Santa Monica, CA 90401

Clarke University, American Language and Culture Institute, 950 Main Street, Worcester, MA 01610

City College of San Francisco, 50 Phelan Avenue, Box A71, San Francisco 94112

Coll Prep English Language Institute, 4175 Fairmount Ae, San Diego, CA 92105

*College of English Language, International Educational Systems, Inc, 3580 Wilshire Blvd, #3, Los Angeles, CA 90010

*College of English Language, 625 Broadway, 5th fl, San Diego, CA 92101

College of English Language, 1510 Front St, Suite 100, San Diego, CA 92101

College of International Language, 611 Shatto Place, Suite 200, Los Angeles, CA 90005

*College of Lake County, Intensive English Program, 19351 West Washington Street, Grayslake, IL 60030-1198

College of Mount St Vincent, 6301 Riverdale Ave, Riverdale, NY 10471

*College of Notre Dame, IEI - Intensive English Institute, 1500 Ralston Ave, Belmont, CA 94002

*The College of St Rose, English Language Study Center at St Rose, 432 Western Ave, Albany, NY 12203

*The College of Staten Island - CUNY, English Language Institute, 2800 Victory Blvd, North Admin Bldg, 2A-207, Staten Island, NY 10314

College of Staten Island, 30 Bay St, 2nd Floor, Staten Island, NY 103012

*Colorado International Education and Training Institute, P O Box 9087, Grand Junction, CO 81501

*Colorado School of English, 1325 S Colorado Blvd, Suite 101, Denver, CO 80222

Colorado University, Woodbury 308, Boulder CO 80309-0295

Columbia University, 505 Lewisohn Hall, New York, NY 10027

Concordia University, 7400 Augusta, River Forest, IL 60305

*Converse International School of Languages, 636 Broadway, Suite 210, San Diego, CA 92101

*Cornell University, Intensive English Program, 305 Morrill Hall, Ithaca, NY, 14853-4701

*Creighton University, Intensive English Language Institute, 2500 California Plaza, Omaha, NE 68178

*Cultural Center for Language Studies, 3181 Coral Way, Miami, FL 33145

Doane College, 1014 Boswell Ave, Crete, NE 68333

*Dominican College, Language Institute for English, 50 Acacia Dr, San Rafael, CA 94901

Donelly College, 608 N 18th St, Kansas City, KS 66102

Drexel University, Drexel University 96-015, Philadelphia, PA 19104

East Carolina University, Gcb 2201, Greenville, NC 27858-4353

Eastern Kentucky University, English Language Instruction Program, Case Annex 270 - 3140, Richmond, KY 40475

Eastern Mennonite University, Harrisburg, UA 22802

Eastern Michigan University, 219 Alexander, Ypsilanti, MI 48197

*Eastern Washington University, English Language Institute, Mailstop #34, Dept of Modern Lang, Cheney, W, 99004

*Edgewood Language Institute, 660 Monterey Pass Rd, Monterey Park, CA 91754

Edmond Language Institute, *University of Central Oklahoma, 100 N University Dr, P O Box 341881, Edmond, OK 73034-5209

*EF Institute, 1 Education Street, Boston, MA 02116

EF International School of Business English, 1 Memorial Drive, Cambridge, MA 02142

*EF International School of English, 200 Lake St, Boston, MA 02135

*EF International School of English, Florida International University, 3000 NE 145th St TR 110, N Miami, FL 33181

*EF International School of English, Los Angeles, 7950 Lassen Building 12, Ste 112, Northridge, CA 91330-8363

*EF International School of English, Mills College, White Hall, 5000 MacArthur Blvd, Oakland, CA 94613

*EF International School of English, Evergreen State College, Seminar Building Room 4154, Olympia, WA 98505

*EF International School of English, United States International University, 10455 Pomerado Road, M-4, San Diego, CA 92131

*EF International School of English, 1421 Chapala Street, Santa Barbara, CA 93101

*EF International School of English, Marymount College, 100 Marymount Avenue, Tarrytown, NY 10591

*ELS Language Centers, 400 Alexander Park, Princeton, NJ 08558

*ELS Language Center/Atlanta, 3355 Lenox Road, Suite 300, Atlanta, GA 30326

ELS Language Center/Bay, 631 Howard Ave, 30 Bay, NY 10301

*ELS Language Center/Boston, Emmanuel College, 400 The Fenway, Boston, MA 02115

*ELS Language Center/Chicago, Concordia University, 7400 Augusta St, River Forest, IL 60305

*ELS Language Center/Cleveland, Case Western Reserve University, Yost Hall, 421; 10900 Euclid Ave, Cleveland, OH 44106

ELS Language Center/Culver City, 5761 Buckingham Parkway, Culver City, CA 90230

*ELS Language Center/Denver, Regis University, 3333 Regis Blvd, M-4, Denver, CO 80221

*ELS Language Center/Houston, University of St Thomas, 3800 Montrose Blvd, Houston, TX 77006

*ELS Language Center/Indianapolis, Marian College, 3200 Cold Spring Road, Indianapolis, IN 46222

ELS Language Center/Melbourne, *Florida Institute of Technology, 150 West University Blvd, Melbourne, FL 32901

*ELS Language Center/New Haven, University of New Haven, Bethel Hall, 300 Orange Ave, West Haven, CT 06516-1999

*ELS Language Center/New York—Riverdale, College of Mt St Vincent, 6301 Riverdale Ave, Riverdale, NY 10471

ELS Language Center/San Francisco, 301 Mission St, 2nd Floor, San Francisco, CA 94105

ELS Language Center/San Diego, 635 C St, San Diego, CA 92101

ELS Language Center/Santa Monica, 154 Pico Blvd, Santa Monica, CA 90405

*ELS Language Center/New York—Staten Island, Wagner College, 631 Howard Ave, Staten Island, NY 10301

*ELS Language Center/Oakland, Holy Names College, 3510 Mountain Boulevard, Oakland, CA 94619-9989

*ELS Language Center/Oklahoma City, Oklahoma City University, 1915 NW 24th, Harris Hall, Oklahoma City, OK 73106

ELS Language Center/Orange, *Chapman University, 333 North Glassell Street, Orange, CA 92866

*ELS Language Center/Philadelphia, St Joseph's University, 5414 Overbrook Avenue, Philadelphia, PA 19131

*ELS Language Center/St Paul, University of St Thomas, Mail ALB #404, 2115 Summit Ave, St Paul, MN 55105-1096

*ELS Language Center/St Petersburg, Eckerd College, 4200 54th Avenue South, St Petersburg, FL 33711

*ELS Language Center/San Diego, 1200 Third Avenue, Suite 100, San Diego, CA 92101

*ELS Language Center/San Francisco, 301 Mission Street, 2nd fl, San Francisco CA, 94105

*ELS Language Center/Santa Monica, 1357 2nd Street, Santa Monica, CA 90401

*ELS Language Center/Seattle, Seattle University, 914 E Jefferson, Suite B-24, Seattle, WA 98122

*ELS Language Center/Washington, DC, 2129 S St North-West, Washington, DC 20008

Emmanuel College, 400 The Fenway, Boston, MA 02115

*Embassy Language Training Centers - San Francisco, 1460 Pine Street, San Francisco, CA 94109

English as a Second Language Institute, *St Norbert College, 100 Grant St, De Pere, WI 54115-2099

*English Center for International Women, Mills College, 5000 MacArthur Blvd, P O Box 9968, Oakland, CA 94613

*English Connection, 480 Broadway PO Box 1054, Saratoga Springs, NY 12866

English International, 655 Sutter St, (Suite 200), San Francisco, CA 94102

English Language Center, 29 Commonwealth Ave, Boston, MA 02116

English Language Center, *Concordia College, 171 White Plains Rd, Bronxville, NY 10708

*English Language Center, 29 Commonwealth Avenue, Boston, MA 02116 Kingsville, TX 78363

*English Language Center, Drexel University, 229 North 33rd Street, Philadelphia, PA 19104

*English Language Institute, Diplomatic Language Services, Inc, 1117 N 19th St, Suite 800, Arlington, VA 22209

English Language Institute, *Bellevue Community College, 3000 Landerholm Circle SE, Bellevue, WA 98007-6484

*English Language Institute, SUNY - Buffalo, 320 Christopher Baldy Hall, Buffalo, NY 14260-1000

English Language Institute, *University of Utah, 2202 Annex Building, Salt Lake City, UT 84112

English Language Institute, University of Delaware, 189 W Main St, Newark, DE 19716

*English Language Institute, 4 West 4th Ave, #403B, San Mateo, CA 94402

English Language Specialist, 2600 S Gessner, Suite 225, Houston, TX 77063

English Language Study Center, Southern Utah University, 351 West Center, GC 410, Cedar City, UT 84720

English Language Study Center, 1840 Sth 1300 East, Salt Lake City, UT 84105

English Language Study Center, *Abraham Baldwin Agricultural College, ABAC 40, 2802 Moore Hwy, Tifton, GA 31794-2601

*The English Language and Multicultural Institute, The University of Dayton, 117 Alumni Hall, Dayton, OH 45469-0319

*ESL Department/International Center, Snow College, 150 College Ave, Ephraim, UT 84627

ESL Program, *North Park University, 3225 West Foster Avenue, Chicago, IL 60625

*Eurocentres Inc, Intensive Language Program, 101 N Union St, Suite 300, Alexandria, VA 22314

Evergreen State College, Seminar Building Room 4154, Olympia, WA 98505

Experiment In International Living, Box 676, Kipling Road, Brattleboro, VT 05302

Experiment In International Living, Jacksonville University, Jacksonville, FL 32211

Fairfield University, Fairfield, CT 06430

Fairleigh Dickenson University, 217 Montross Av, Rutherford, NJ 07070

*Ferris State University, Intensive English Program, Center for Int'l Ed, Bishop Hall 300, Big Rapids, MI 49307-2737

*Florida International University, English Language Institute, University Park, LC 204, Miami, FL 33199

Florida International University, EF International School of English, 15101 Biscayne Blvd, TR 110, N Miami, FL 33181

Florida Southern College, 111 Lake Hollingsworth, Lakeland, FL 33801

Florida State University, 918 West Park Ave, Tallahassee, FL

FLS Language Centers/Alhambra, 317 W Main St Suite 328, Alhambra, CA 91801

*FLS Language Centers/Oxnard, 4000 South Rose Avenue, Oxnard, CA 93033

FLS Language Centers, *Citrus College, 101 E Green St, Suite 14, Pasadena, CA 91105

Fort Hays State University, 600 Park St, West Hall, Hays, KS 67061

*Francis Marion University, IEI - Intensive English Institute, FH 220-C, Florence, SC 29501

Fresno Pacific University, 1717 South Chestnut, Fresno, CA 93702

George Mason University, 4400 University Drive, Fairfax VA 22030

Georgetown University, 37th and Q 'Street, NW, DC 20057

*Georgia Institute of Technology, The Language Institute, O'Keefe South Wing, Atlanta, GA 30332-0374

Global Language Institute, Hamline University, 1536 Hewitt Ave, St Paul, MN 55101

Global Village Honolulu/Intercultural Communications College, 1601 Kapiolani Blvd, Suite 100, Honolulu, HI 96814

*Golden Gate Language Schools, Inc, 591 W Hamilton Ave, Suite 101, Campbell, CA 95008-0521

Gonzaga University, Spokane, WA 99258

Goshen College, 1700 S Main St, Goshen, IN 46526

Grand Canyon University, 3300 West Camelback Rd, Phoenix, AZ 85308

*Haggerty Institute, SUNY-New Paltz, Humanities 116, New Paltz, NY 12561

Hamline University, 1536 Hewitt Ave, ST Paul, MN 55104

*Harcum College, English Language Academy, Academic Center, Rm 219, Bryn Mawr, PA 19010-3476

Hawaii Pacific University, English Foundation Programs, 1188 Fort St, Honolulu, HI 96813

Hays Language Institute, *Fort Hays State University, 600 Park St, Picken Hall Rm 200, Fort Hays, KS 67601-4099

Hobe Sound Bible College, P O Box 1065, Hobe Sound, FL 33275

Hofstra University, Hempstend, NY 11549

Holy Names College, 3510 Mountain Boulevard, Oakland, CA 94619

Husson College, One College Circle, Bangor, ME 04401

Illinois State University, Eli-Hudelson Building, Normal, IL 61761-6901

*ICLS-Husson College, Husson College, One College Circle, Bangor, ME 04401

*IEI - Intensive English Institute, School for International Training, P O Box 676, Kipling Rd, Brattleboro, VT 05302

*IEI - Intensive English Institute, Saint Thomas University, 16400 NW 32 Avenue, Miami, FL 33054-9988

*IEI - Intensive English Institute, Portland Downtown Center, 506 SW 6th Avenue, Suite 200, Portland, OR 97204

IEI - Intensive English Institute, *California Baptist College, 8432 Magnolia Avenue, Riverside, CA 92504-3297

IEI - Intensive English Institute, *Texas A&M - Kingsville, Campus Box 137,

IEI - Intensive English Institute, Bentley College, Linden Hall, 175 Forest Street, Waltham, MA 02154-4705

*IELS Language School, 1501 W 5th St, Suite D, Austin, TX 78703 (512) 476-3909

*IEP-Special Programs & Community Services, Hawaii Community College, 200 W Kawili Street, Hilo, HI 96720-4091

Illinois State University, Eli-Hudelson Building, Normal, IL 61761-6901

*Immaculata College, English Proficiency for International Students, Box 694, Immaculata, PA 19345-0694

*Indiana University, Center for English Language Training (CELT), CELT - IU - Memorial Hall 313, Bloomington, IN 47405

Indiana University - Pennsylvania, Eicher 214, Indiana, PA 15705

*Indiana University - South Bend, South Bend English Institute, 902 South Twyckenham Drive, South Bend, IN 46615

Institute for International Students, City College of San Francisco, 50 Phelan Avenue, Box A71, San Francisco, CA 94112

*Institute for the Study of American Language and Culture, Lewis and Clark College, 0615 SW Palatine Hill Road, Box 125, Portland, OR 97219

Institute of Intensive English, Marlanne Hall, 2717-B Pamoa Rd, Honolulu, HI 96822

*Integrated Skills English Training Program, NACOS International Institute, 765 Amana St #507, Honolulu, HI 96814

Intensive English as a Second Language Program, International Language Institute of Massachusetts, Inc, 17 New South St, Sullivan Square, Northampton, MA 01060

Intensive English Language Center/148, University of Nevada, Reno, 1, 27 Mackay Science, Reno, NV 89557

*Intensive English Center (IEC), SUNY at Stony Brook, E5320 Melville Library, Stony Brook, NY 11794-3390

Intensive English Course, Lado International College, 2233 Wisconsin Ave, NW, Washington DC 20007

*Intensive English Institute, University of Maine, 5723 Hannibal Hamlin, Orono, ME 04469-5732

*Intensive English Language Programs, University of Findlay, 1000 North Main Street, Findlay, OH 45840

*Intensive English Language Program, The Center for English Studies, 330 Seventh Avenue, New York, NY 10001

*Intensive English Language Program, Temple University, 211 Seltzer Hall, Philadelphia, PA 19122

*Intensive English Programs, International Center for American English, 1012 Prospect St #200, La Jolla, CA 92037

Intensive English Program, English Language Center, 10850 Wilshire Blvd, Suite 210, Los Angeles, CA 90024,

Intensive English Program, Texas Tech University, Box 42071, Lubbock, TX 79409-2071

*INTERLINK Language Centers, Colorado School of Mines, 1500 Illinois St, Golden, CO 80401

*INTERLINK Language Centers, University of North Carolina at Greensboro, 1000 Spring Garden Street, Greensboro, NC 27412-5001

*INTERLINK Language Centers, Indiana State University, Erikson Hall 630, Terre Haute, IN 47809

*INTERLINK Language Centers, Valparaiso University, Valparaiso, IN 46383-6493

International Center for American English, 1012 Prospect St, #200, La Jolla, CA 92037

International Center for Language Studies, 2640 Fountainview, Suite 140, Houston, TX 77057

International Education Programs, *University of California/Riverside, 1200 University Avenue, Dept AA, Riverside, CA 92507-4596

*International Education Programs, Seattle Central Community College, 1701 Broadway, Seattle, WA 98122

*International English Institute, 2743 E Shaw Ave, Fresno, CA 93710

*International English Institute, 1226 16th Ave South, Nashville, TN 37212

*International Language Institute, Transemantics, Inc, Van Ness Center, 4301 Connecticut Ave, NW, Washington, DC 20008

International English Language Services, 1501 W, 5th St Suite D, Austin, TX 78703

International Language Academy, 621 King St, Alexandria, VA 22314

International Language Institute of Massachusets, P O Box 516, Sullivan Square, Northampton, MA 01060

Intrax English Institute, *Menlo College, 1000 El Camino Real, Atherton, CA 94027

Intrax English Institute, *Bryant College, Hall #7, 1150 Douglas Pike, Smithfield, RI 02917

Iowa State University, Ames, IA 50011

Ise-California, 1500 Ralston Ave, Belmont, CA 94002

JAIMS, 6660 Hawaii Kai Drive, Honolulu, HI 96825

Jersey City State College, 2039 Kennedy Bvd, Jersey City, NJ 07305-1577

Kansas University, Lawrence, KA 60045-2140

Kaplan Berkeley, 2000 Center St, Suite 100, Berkeley CA 94704

Kaplan Birmingham, 1900 28th Ave South St, 100 Birmingham, AL 35209

Kaplan Boulder, The Hilltop Bldg, Upper level, 1310 College Ave, Suite 400, Boulder, CO 80302

Kaplan Davis, 132 E Street, Davis CA 95616

Kaplan Denver, 720 S Colorado, Suite 140-A, Denver, CO 80222

Kaplan Encino, 17167 Ventura Blvd, Plaza de Oro, 2nd level, Encino, CA 91316

Kaplan Fresno, 2763 E Shaw Ave, Suite 104, Fresno, CA 93710

Kaplan Little Rock, Centremark Bldg, 10220 Markham St, Suite 220, Little Rock, AR 72205

Kaplan Los Angeles, Arco Plaza Level C, 505 S Flower St, Los Angeles , CA 90071

Kaplan Orange County, 125 E Baker St, Suite 130, Costa Mesa, CA 92626

Kaplan Palo Alto, California Avenue, Suite 210, Palo Alto, CA 94306

Kaplan Phoenix, Hayden Square, 310 South Mill Avenue, Suite A-103, Tempe, AZ 85281

Kaplan Riverside, UCR-Bannockburn Village, 3637 Canyon Crest Dr, Suite J-115, Riverside, CA 92507

Kaplan Sacramento, 701 Howe Avenue, Suite B20, Sacramento, CA 95825

Kaplan San Diego, 4350 Executive Dr, Suite 305, San Diego, CA 92121

Kaplan San Francisco, 50 First Street, Suite 201, San Francisco, CA 94105

Kaplan San Jose, 100 Park Center Plaza, Suite 112, San Jose, CA 95113

Kaplan Santa Barbara, 6464 Hollister Ave, Suite 7, Goleta, CA 93117

Kaplan Santa Cruz, 740 Front Street, Suite 130, Santa Cruz, CA 95060

Kaplan Tucson, 903 East University Blvd, Suite E, Tucson, AZ 85719

Kaplan Westwood, Village Square, 1133 Westwood Blvd, Suite 201, Los Angeles, CA 90024

***Keystone Intensive English Program,** Keystone College, P O Box 50, La Plume, PA 18440-0200

Lado International, Jesuit College, Washington Ave, Wheeling, WV 26003

Lado International College, 2233 Wisconsin Avenue, NW, Washington, DC

Lake Forest Academy, 1500 West Kennedy Road, Lake Forest, IL 60045

***The Language and Culture Institute in Oregon,** P O Box 1734, Lake Oswego, OR 97035-0510,

***Language Institute for English,** c/o Simmons College, 415 Commonwealth Ave, Boston MA 02215

***Language Institute for English,** Adelphi University, Linen Hall, Room #5, Garden City, NY 11530

***Language Institute for English,** c/o Fairleigh Dickinson University, 285 Madison Avenue, Madison, NJ 07940-1099

***Language Institute for English,** c/o Barry University, 11300 NE 2nd Avenue, Miami Shores, FL 33161

Language Institute for English (LIFE), *Rosary College, 7900 W Division St, River Forest, IL 60305

***Language Institute for English,** San Diego-City Center, 225 Broadway, Suite 200, San Diego, CA 92101

Language Resource Institute, 1336 Polk St, San Francisco, CA 94109

***Language Studies International,** 2015 Center Street, Berkeley, CA 94704

***Language Studies International,** 39-45 Newbury Street, suite 444, Boston, MA 02116

***Language Studies International,** 1706 Fifth Avenue, 3rd flr, San Diego, CA 92101

***Language Systems,** International College of English, 100 E Huntington Drive, Suite 209, Alhambra, CA 91801

***LCP International Institute - Highline,** Highline Community College, 2400 South 240th Street, Des Moines, WA 98198-9800

LCP International Institute, *Irvine College Center, 8001 Irvine Center Dr, #930, Irvine, CA 92718

LCP International Institute, *MiraCosta College, One Barnard Drive, Oceanside, CA 92056-3899

LCP International Institute, *California State University, Sacramento Center, 965 University Ave, #200, Sacramento, CA 95825

Lewis and Clark College, Box 125, 1615 Palatine Hill Road, Portland, OR 97219

***Lewis and Clark State College,** IEI - Intensive English Institute, 8th Avenue & 6th Street, Lewiston, ID 83501-2698

Long Island University, Brooklyn Campus, University Plaza, New York, NY 11201

***Louisiana State University,** English Language and Orientation Program, 397 Pleasant Hall, Baton Rouge, LA 70803

***Loyola Intensive English Program,** Loyola University, Box 205, 6363 St Charles Avenue, New Orleans, LA 70118

***Manhattanville College,** English Language Institute, 2900 Purchase Street, Purchase, NY 10577

Mankato State University, Campus P O 87, Mankato, MN 56002-8400

Maryland University, Baltimore, MD 21250

Marymount College, 100 Marymount Ave, Tarrytown, NY 10591

Maryville College, Center for English Language Learning, MC CELL Int'l House, Maryville, TN 37804

Massachusetts University, School of Education, Amhurst, MA 01003

Memphis State College, Dunn Building, Rm 300, Memphis, TN 38152

Memphis University, Memphis, TN 38152

Meredith College, 3800 Hillsborough St, Raleigh, NC 27604-5298

Mesa State College, P O Box 2647, Grand Junction, CO 81502

***Michigan Language Center,** 309 South State Street, P O Box 8231, Ann Arbor, MI 48107

Michigan State University, Dept of English, East Lansing, MI 18864

*Midwest Institute for International Studies, c/o Doane College, 1014 Boswell Avenue, Crete, NE 68333

Mills College, 5000 Macarthur Blvd, Oakland, CA 94613

Minnesota University, Minneapolis 55455

Missouri State University, MA-TESL Program, Dept of English and Philsophy, Martin 336, Warrensburg, MO 64093-5046

Montana University, Missoula, MT 59812

Monterey Institute of International Studies, 425 Van Buten St, Monterey CA 93940

Montclair State University, Normal Av. Upper Montclair NJ 07043

Mount Vernon College, 2100 Foxhall Road, NW, DC 20007

Murray State University, P O Box 9, Murray, KY 42071

National-Louis University, 1000 Capital Drive, Wheeling, IL 60090

Nazareth College of Rochester, 4245 East Av. Rochester, NY 14618-3790

New Hampshire University, Durham, NH 03824

New Mexico, University of, Albuquerque, NM 87131

New Rochelle College, 29, Castle Place, New Rochelle, NY 10805-2339

New York State University, Buffalo, Buffalo, NY 14260

New York State University, Stony Brook, Stony Brooke, NY 11776-4376

New Age College, Park, 9625 Garden Grove Blvd, Suite A, Garden Grove, CA 92644

*New College of California, English as a Second Language Institute, 450 Chadbourne Avenue, Millbrae, CA 94030

*The New England School of English, Harvard Square, 36 JFK Street, Box 12, Cambridge, MA 02138,

*New York University, American Language Institute, 48 Cooper Square, New York, NY 10003

*Norman English Institute, 730 Asp Avenue, Suite 212, Norman, OK 73069

North Carolina University, 9201 University City Rvd, Charlotte, NC 28223-0001

Northeastern Illinois University, 5000 North Saint Louis Avenue, Chicago, IL z60625-4699

Northern Arizona University, Flagstaff, AZ 86011-6032

Northern Illinois, University of, Dekalb, Dept of English, DeKalb, IL 60155

North Seattle Community College, 9600 Coll Way N, Seattle, WA 98103

*North Texas, University of, Intensive English Language Institute, P O Box 310739, Kendall Hall Rm 259, Denton TX 76203-0739,

Northup University, 5800 Arbor Vitae, Los Angeles, CA 90045

Northwestern College, 3003, Snelling Av S, St. Paul, MN 55113

Oakland Community College, 27055 Orchard Lake Road, Farmington Hills, MI 48334

Ohio University, Gordy Hall, Athens, OH 45701

Oklahoma City University, 1915 N W 24th, Harris Hall , Oklahoma City, OK 73106

Oklahoma State University, Dept of English, 205 Morrill Hall, Stillwater, OK 70478

Old Dominion University, Norfolk, VA 23529-0078

Oregon University, Eugene, OR 97403

*Oregon State University, English Language Institute, Snell Hall 301, Corvallis, OR 97331-1632

Ottawa University, 1001 S Cedar, 58, Ottawa, KS 66067-3399

Our Lady of the Lake University, 411 SW 24th St. San Antonio TX 78207-4689

*Pace University, English Language Institute, Pace Plaza, New York, NY 10038

*Pacific English Academy, 760 Market Street, Suite 824, San Francisco, CA 94102

*Pacific English Language Institute, Cuesta College, 1050 Foothill Blvd, San Luis Obispo, CA 93405

Pacific International Language School, 1451 S King St, Suite 301, Honolulu, HI 96814

Pacific Language Assocs, 5150 SW Griffith Drive, Beaverton, OR 97003

Pacific Lutheran University, Tacoma, WA 98447

*Pacific Rim Language Institute, 1719 Fullerton Road, Rowland Heights, CA 91748

Palomar College, 1140 W Mission Road, San Marcos, CA 92069-1487

Pennsylvania State University, Room 301 Boucke Bldg, University Park, PA 16802

Pennsylvania, University of, Language in Education Division, 3700 Walnut St, Suite A-10, Philadelphia, PA 19104

Pine Manor College, 400 Health Street, Chestnut Hill, MA 02167

Pittsburgh University, 2816 Cathedral of Learning Pittsburg, PA 15260

*Pitzer College, Program in American College English, 1050 North Mills Ave, Claremont, CA 91711

Portland State University, Dept of Applied Linguistics, 124 SW Harrison, Neuberger Hall 467, Portland OR 91201

*Point Loma English Institute, Point Loma Nazarene College, 3900 Lomaland Drive, San Diego, CA 92106

Queen's College New York, Flushing, NY 11367

Radford University, 707, Norwood St. Radford, VA 24142

Rhode Island College, 600 Mount Pleasant Av. Providence, RI 02908

Regis University, W 50th & Lowell Blvd, Denver, CO 80221

*Rennert Bilingual, 216 East 45th St 17th Floor, New York, NY 10017

*Rochester Institute of Technology, English Language Center, 28 Lomb Memorial Drive, Rochester, NY 14623-5604

*Rockford College, English Language Study Center, 5050 E State St, Rockford, IL 61108-2393

*Rosemead College of English, 8705 E Valley Blvd, Rosemead, CA 91770

St. Cloud State University, 720, 4th. Av. South, St.Cloud MN 56301-4498

St Giles Language Teaching Center, One Hallidie Plaza #350, San Francisco, CA 91402

St Joseph's University, 2490 N 54th St, Philadelphia, PA 19131

Saint Michael's College, SIS, One Winooski Park, Colchester, VT 05439

St Thomas University, 16400 N W 32 Ave, Miami, FL 33-54-9988

San Diego City Center, 225 Broadway, Suite 200, San Diego, CA

San Diego State University, American Language Institute, 5814 Hardy, San Diego, CA 92182

School for International Training, King Rd, Brattleboro, VT 05302

San Francisco State University, 1600 Holloway Ave, San Francisco, CA 94132

*San Jose State University, Studies in American Language, One Washington Square, San Jose, CA 95192-0135

Santa Fe College, 1600 St Michael's Drive, Santa Fe, NM 87505

The School of Teaching ESL, 2601 N W 56th St, Seattle, WA 98107

Seattle Pacific University, Seattle, WA 98119

Seattle University, 914 E Jefferson, Room 217, Seattle, WA 98122

Selwyn School, 3333 University Drive West, Denton, TX 76201

Seton Hall University, 400, South Orange Av. South Orange, NJ 07079

*Skagit Valley College, American Cultural Exchange Language Institute, 2405 College Way, Mount Vernon, WA 98273

Snow College, 150 College Ave, Ephaim, UT 84627

*Sonoma State University, American Language Institute, 1801 East Cotati Avenue, Rohnert Park, CA 94928

Shanandoah University, 1460, University Drive, Winchester, VA 227601

Simmons College, 300, The Fenway, Boston, MA 02115

SOKA University of America, 26800 West Mulholland Highway, Calabasas, CA 91302

Southern Illinois University, Carbondale, IL 62901

Southern Maine University, Gorham, ME 04038

Southern Mississippi University, Hattiesburg, MS 39406

South Carolina University, Columbia, SC 29208

*Southeast Missouri State University, Intensive English Program, One University Plaza—MS 2000, Cape Girardeau, MO 63701

Southern Oregon State College, 1250 Siskiyou Blvd, Ashland, OR 97520

*South Seattle Community College, Intensive English Language Program, 6000 16th Avenue Southwest, Seattle, WA 98106

*Spring Hill College, Intensive English Language Institute, 4000 Dauphin Street, Mobile, AL 36608

*Spring International Language Center, Auroria Higher Education Center, 900 Auroria Pkwy, Suite 454, Denver, CO 80204

Spring International Language Center, *University of Arkansas - Fayetteville, 300 Hotz Hall, Fayetteville, AR 72701

*Spring International Language Center, Arapahoe Community College, 5900 South Santa Fe Drive, Littleton, CO 80120

Stanley Kaplan Center, 131 W 56th St, New York, NY 10019

Sunny-Stony Brook, 108 Central Hall, Stony Brook, NY 11794-2700

Suny-Buffalo, 320 Christopher Baldy Hall, Buffalo, NY 14260

Suny-New Paltz, Haggerty Inst, Humanities 116, New Paltz, NY 12561

SW Ohio Council for Higher Education, 2900 Acosta St, Suite 140, Dayton, OH 45420

*Syracuse University, English Language Institute, 230 Euclid Ave, Syracuse, NY 13244-5130

Temple University, 303 Mitten Hall, Broad & Berks, Philadelphia, PA 19122

*Tennessee Intensive English Program, University of Tennessee at Martin, 144 Gooch Hall, Martin, TN 38238,

*Texas Intensive English Program, Texas International Education Consortium, 1103 W 24th Street, Austin, TX 78705-4603

Texas Tech University, Box 42071, Lubbock, TX 79409-2071

*Texas Wesleyan University, Dept of Intensive English Language, 1201 Wesleyan Street, Fort Worth, TX 76105

Tokyo Honolulu International College, 1149 Bethel St, 7th Fl, Honolulu, HI 96813

*Tulane ESL Institute, Tulane University, TESL P O Box 5015, 1326 Audubon Street, New Orleans, LA 70118

*Tulsa English Institute, 3115 S Winston, Tulsa, OK 74135-2058

*UC-Berkeley Extension, English Language Programs, 1995 University Ave, #7022, Berkeley, CA 94720-7022

*UC-Irvine Extension, Program in ESL, P O Box 6050, Irvine, CA 92716-6050

UC-Riverside Entension, 1200 University Ave, Riverside, CA 92507

*UC-San Diego Extension, English Language Programs, UCSD Extension 0176; 9500 Gilman Drive, La Jolla, CA 92093-0176

UCLA, 10995 Le Conte Ave, Unex 224, Los Angeles, CA 90024

*UCSB Extension, International Program, 320 Storke Road, Goleta, CA 93117

*United States International University, English as a Second Language Program, Bldg M11, 10544 Pomerado, San Diego, CA 92131

University of Alabama, Huntsville, AL 35899

*University of Arizona, Center for English as a Second Language, CESL Building, P O Box 210024, Tucson, AZ 85721-0024

*University of Arkansas - Little Rock, Intensive English Language Program, 2801 S University Avenue, Little Rock, AR 72204

University of Arkansas, Fayetteville, 330 Hotz Hall, Fayetteville, AK 72701

University of California, Berkeley, 2223 Fulton St, Berkeley, CA 94720

*University of California, Davis, Univ Extension-ITEC, International English Programs, Davis, CA 95616-8727

University of California, Irvine, P O Box 6050, Irvine, CA 92716-6050

University of California, Santa Barbara Ext, Santa Barbara, CA 93106-1110

University of Cincinnati, P O Box 210002, Cincinnati, OH 45221-0002

*University of Colorado at Boulder, Int English Center, 1333 Grandview Avenue, Boulder, CO 80309-0463

*University of Colorado, Economics Institute English Program, 1030 13th St, Boulder, CO 80302

*University of Delaware English Language Institute, 189 W Main Street, Newark, DE 19716

University of Findlay, 1000 North Main St, Findlay, OH 45840

University of Georgia, Continuing Education Center, Athens, GA 30602

University of Hartford, 200 Bloomfield Ave, A220, West Hartford, CT 06117

University of Hawaii, Hawaii English Language Program, Moore Hall, Honolulu, HI 96822

University of Hawaii-Manoa, 1395 Lower Campus Rd, Mc 13-1, Honolulu, HI 96822-0000

*University of Houston-Downtown, One Main Street, English Language Institute, Houston, TX

*University of Houston, Language and Culture Center, 4800 Calhoun, Houston, TX 77204-3012

University of Idaho, Moscow, ID 83844-1102

*University of Illinois-Chicago, UIC-Tutorium in Intensive English (M/C 324), 601 S Morgan St Room 820, Chicago, IL 60607-7180

University of Maine, 11 Fernald Hall, Orono, ME 04469

*University of Miami, Intensive Language Institute, Allen Hall-P O Box 248005, Coral Gables, FL 33124-1612

*University of Missouri - Rolla, Applied Language Institute, 1870 Miner Circle, 209 Norwood Hall/VMR, Rolla, MO 65409

University of Nevada, 127 Mackay Science Bldg, Reno, NV 89557

University of Northern Iowa, 115 Baker, Cedar Falls, Iowa, 506147-0502

University of Nth Texas, P O Box 13258, Kendall Hall, Denton, TX 76203

*University of Oregon, American English Institute, 5212, Eugene, OR 97403-5212

*University of Pennsylvania, English Language Programs, Room 21 Bennett Hall, 34th & Walnut Sts, Philadelphia, PA 19104-6274

*University of Portland, American Language Academy, 5000 N Willamette Blvd, Portland, OR 97203-5798

*University of Redlands, ELS Language Center, 1200 East Colton Ave, Redlands, CA 92373

University of Saint Thomas, 3800 Montrose Blvd, Houston, TX 77006

*University of San Francisco, Department of ESL/IEP, 2130 Fulton St, LM 142, San Francisco, CA 94117-1080

*University of South Carolina, English Programs for Internationals, Byrnes 310, Columbia, SC 29208

*University of Southern Colorado, American Language Academy, 2200 Bonforte Blvd, Pueblo, CO 81001-4901

*University of Southern Mississippi, English Language Institute, Box 5065, Hattiesburg, MS 39406-5065

*University of South Florida, English Language Institute, 4202 E Fowler Ave, CPR 107, Tampa, FL 33620-5550

University of Tampa, Box 39 F, Tampa, FL 33606-1490

University of Tennessee, 144 Gooch Hall, Martin, TN 38238

*University of Tennessee at Knoxville, English Language Institute, 907 Mountcastle St, Knoxville, TN 37996-3505

*University of Texas - Arlington, English Language Institute, Box 19560, UTA, Arlington, TX 76019

University of Texas - Austin, P O Box 7667, Austin, TX 78713

University of Texas - El Paso, El Paso, TX 79968

*University of Texas - Pan American, English Language Institute, 1201 West University Drive, Edinburgh, TX 78539-2999

University of Toledo, English Dept, Tolded, OH 43606-3390

University of Utah, 255, 5th Central Campus Drive, Salt Lake City, UT 84112

*University of Washington Educational Outreach, English as a Second Language Programs, Box 354232, Seattle, WA 98195

University of Western Kentucky, 1 Big Red Way, Bowling Green KY 42101

University of Wisconsin, 366 Jackson St, Suite 403, St Paul, MN 55101

University of W-Stevens Point, 1 Nelson Hall, Stevens Point, WI 54481

*Utah State University, Intensive English Language Institute, Logan, UT 84322-0715

Valparaiso University, Valparaiso, IN 465831

Vanity International School, 2617 S King St, 3-D, Honolulu, HI 96826

Wartburg College, 222 9th St, N W Waverley, IA 50677

*Washington Academy of Languages, Intensive English Program, 98 Yesler Way, Seattle, WA 98104-2524

Washington State University, 108 Bryan Hall, Pullman, WA 99164-5110

Wayne State University, 351 Manoogian Hall, Detroit, MI 48202

*WESL Institute, Western Illinois University, Memorial Hall, Macomb, IL 61455

WESL Institute, 19 N Pinckney St, Madison, WI 53703

West Chester University, West Chester, PA 19383

Western Illinois University, Memorial Hall, Macomb, IL 61455

*Western Oregon University, Internexus - English Language Study Center, 300 North Stadium Drive, Monmouth, OR 97361

*Western Washington University, Intensive English Program, 530 Old Main, Bellingham, WA 98225-9048

*Westminster College, English Language Study Center, 1733 S 1100 E, Salt Lake City, UT 84105 67260-0122

*West Virginia University, Intensive English Program, P O Box 6297, Morgantown, WV 26506-6297

Wheaton College, Wheaton, IL 60187-5593

*Wichita State University, Intensive English Language Center, Wichita, KS 67209-1595

William Paterson University, 300 Pompton Rd, Wayne NJ 07470

*Wisconsin English Second Language Institute, 19 North Pinckney Street, Madison, WI 53703-2829

Worldwide Teachers' Development Institute, 266 Beaacon, Boston, MA 02116

Wright State University, 438 Millet Hall, Dayton, OH 45435

WVU, Chitwood Hall, Morgantown, WV 26506

*Yazigi Language Study Center, Yazigi International, USA, 5500 34th St W, Suite YLSC, Bradenton, FL 34210

Yokohama Academy, 5401 Wilkens Ave, Baltimore, MD 21228

Youngstown State University, 1, University Plaza, Youngstwon, OH 44555

Canada

The demand for ESL teachers in Canada continues to soar, fuelled by the requirements of seven million French-speaking citizens, an additional 200,000 immigrants and refugees per year, and increasing numbers of foreign students following dedicated courses.

Although state-sector schools can meet much of this demand, the private sector continues to grow, particularly in British Columbia. According to one report, 26 new schools opened in Vancouver last year alone.

Ordinarily, immigrants may choose to take free ESL courses in all jurisdictions except Quebec, which is 75 per cent French-speaking and English courses are not readily available. Education budgets have recently been cut and this has had particularly adverse effects on Ontario's public sector English language programmes.

Although there are a number of training courses available, many newly-qualified teachers go overseas in search of valuable experience and lenient tax rates. This means that there might be some good opportunities for foreign teachers. There is also demand for private and in-company tutoring. A native speaker teacher with French language ability might get responses to advertisements placed around French universities or in student newspapers. Similarly, a capable teacher with Mandarin or Cantonese ability might be able to pick up students from the large Chinese communities in Toronto or Vancouver.

Visas and work permits: Teachers must obtain a work permit to teach. This is difficult since it is necessary to demonstrate that a suitable qualified Canadian is not available for the position. Getting a permit is not impossible, though, especially if the applicant has qualifications which are not common in Canada. RSA/Cambridge Certificate might be such a qualification. To stay permanently in Canada, a valid passport and proof of immigrant status are required. Work must be offered by an Employment Centre in Canada. Exchange professors do not need a job validated by a Human Resource Centre.

Cost of living: Highest in Vancouver and Toronto.

Salaries and taxes: Expect Cdn$25-45 per hour in public sector schools or $12-25 per hour in a private school. Tax rates are very high - higher even than in the US.

Accommodation: A studio apartment can cost as much as Cdn$650 per month in Vancouver or Toronto.

Health insurance: Medical care is free for citizens, residents and those with work permits. Private insurance is available through universities or from a number of companies.

Other information: Foreign students are allowed to work on the campus where they are studying. This means that applying to an institute where you are studying is legal.

List of Schools in Canada

Academie Linguistique Internationale, 5115 Rue de Gaspe, Suite 300, Montreal, Quebec, H2T 3B7

Alberta Vocational College - Calgary, English as a Second Language, 332 - 6 Avenue SE, Calgary, AB, T2G 4S6

Alberta, University of, English Language Program, Rm 4-10 University Extension Centre, Edmonton, AB, T6G 2T4

Algonquin College, International Education Centre, 1385 Woodroffe Avenue, Ottawa, ON, K2G 1V8

Berlitz Canada Inc, 130 Bloor St West, Suite 603, Toronto, Ontario, M5S 1N5

Bishop's University, English Language Studies, Lennoxville, QC, J1M 1Z7

British Columbia, University of, English Language Institute, 5997 Iona Drive, Vancouver, BC, V6T 1Z1

Brock University, Intensive English Language Program, Dept of Applied Language Studies, St Catharines, ON, L2S 3A1

Burnaby College Ltd, 101-1199 West Pender St, Vancouver, BC, V6E 1B5

Calgary, University of, English Language Program, CH C-302/Continuing Education, Calgary, AB, T2N 1N4

Canada Language Centre, 200-549 Howe St, Vancouver, BC, V6C 2C2

Canadian As a Second Language Institute, 88 - 1155 Robson St, Vancouver, BC, V6E 2R1

Canadian Business English Institute, Suite 400, 1130 West Pender Street, Vancouver BC, V6E 4A4

Canadian College of Business & Language, 16 Bastion Sq, Victoria, BC, V8W 1H9

Canadian College of English Language, 1477 W. Pender St, Vancouver, BC, V6G 2S6,

Canadian Co-operative for Language and Cultural Studies, 635 Markham Street, Suite 200, Toronto ON, M6G 2M1

Canadian English Language Centre Ltd, 35 Euclid Avenue, Toronto, ON, M6J 2J7

Capilano College, ESL Dept, 2055 Purcell Way, North Vancouver, BC, V7J 3H5

Carleton University, Applied Language Studies (ESL), PA 215, 1125 Colonel By Drive, Ottawa, K1S 5B6

Centennial College, International Education, P O Box 631, Scarborough, ON, M1K 5E9

Centre Linguista, 802-500 Rene Levesque, Montreal, Quebec, H2Z 1W7

College of the North Atlantic, St. John's District, International Program Office, P O Box 1693, St John's NF, A1C 5P7

Columbia College, English Language Centre, 500-555 Seymour St, Vancouver, BC,

Columbia College, 6037 Marlborough Avenue, Burnaby, BC, V5H 3L6,

Concordia University, Continuing Education, Language Institute, 1455 de Maisonneuve Blvd W. Montreal, QC, H3G 1M8

Douglas College, P O Box 2503, New Westminster, BC, V3L 5B2

Eastern Canada College of Languages, 550 University Avenue, Charlottetown, PE, C1A 4P3

Fanshawe College, International Edueation, 1460 Oxford Street East, London, ON, N5V 1W2

George Brown College, International Centre, P O Box 1015, St. B, Toronto, ON, M5T 2T9

Global English College, 3rd Floor, 530 Hornby St, Vancouver, BC, V6C 2E7

Grande Prairie Regional College, International Education Centre, 10726-106 Avenue, Grande Prairie, AB, T8V 4C4

Grant MacEwan Community College, English as a Second Language, 7319-29 Avenue, Rm 207, Edmonton, AB, T5J 2P2

Hansa Language Centre of Toronto, 2160 Yonge St, Toronto, Ontario, M4S 2AB

Humber College, English Language Centre, 250 Humber College Blvd, Etobicoke, ON, M9W 5LV

International Language Centre of Canada, 5233 Dundas St West, Suite 300, Toronto, Ontario, M9B 1A6

International Language Institute, 5151 Terminal Road, 8th Floor, Halifax, Nova Scotia, B3J 1A1

International Language Learning Centre, 78-1667 West Broadway, Vancouver BC, V6J 1X2

International Language School of Canada, 510 West Hastings, 2nd Floor, Vancouver BC, V68 1LB

IPO Educational Centre, 1819 Rene Levesque West, Montreal, Quebec, H3H 2P5

Kwantlen University College, 12666 72nd Ave, Surrey, BC V3W 2M8

Language Connection International, 60 Bloor St West, Suite 500, Toronto, Ontario, M4W 3B

Language Studies Canada Montreal, 1450 City Councillors Street, Montreal QC, H3A 2E6

Language Studies Canada Toronto, 124 Eglington Avenue West, Suite 400, Toronto, ON, M4R 2G8

Language Studies Canada Vancouver, 200-535 Howe St, Vancouver, BC, V6C 2Z4,

Language Studies International, 101-808 Nelson St, Vancouver BC, V6Z 2H2

Language Workshop, The, Global Village, 180 Bloor St West, Suite 202, Toronto, Ontario, M5S 2V6

Languages International Inc, 330 Bay St, Suite 910, Toronto, Ontario, M5H 2S8

Lethbridge Community College, English Language Centre, 3000 College Drive South, Lethbridge, Alberta, T1K 1L6

Lethbridge, University of, Language Centre (EAP/ESL programs), 4401 University Drive, Lethbridge, AB, T1K 3M4

LSC Language Studies Canada, 124 Eglinton Avenue West, 4th Floor, Toronto, Ontario, M4R 2G8

Malaspina University College, International Education, 900 Fifth St, Nanaimo, BC, V9R 5S5

Manitoba, University of, Intensive English Program, 166 Continuing Education Complex, Winnipeg, MB R3T 2N2

McGill University, Languages & Translation, 770 Sherbrooke Street West, Montreal, QC, H3A 1G1

McMaster University, 1280 Main St W, Hamilton, Ontario L7F 1B1

Medicine Hat College, International Education, 299 College Drive, S.E. Medicine Hat, AB, T1A 3Y6

Mohawk College, International Department, P O Box 2034, Hamilton, ON, L8N 3T2

Mount Royal College, Languages Institute, 4825 Richard Road SW, Calgary, AB, T3E 6K6

New Brunswick, University of, English Language Programme, P O Box 4400, Fredericton, NB, E3B 5A3

Niagara College, International Education & ESL, 300 Woodlawn Road (Box 1005), Welland, ON, L3B 5S2

Okanagan University College, International Education, 1000 KLO Road, Kelowna, BC, V1Y 4X8

Omnicom School of Languages, Sheppard Avenue East, Suite 1002, Willowdale, Ontario, M2N 5Y7

Ottawa, University of, Second Language Institute, 600 King Edward Avenue, Ottawa, ON, K1N 6N5

Pacific Gateway International College, 303-1155 Robson St, Vancouver, BC, V6E 1B5

Pacific Language Institute, 3rd Floor, 755 Burrard St, Vancouver, BC, V6Z 1X6,

Quebec, University of, at Trois Rivieres, P O Box 500, Trois Rivieres, Quebec G9A 5H7

Queen's University, School of English, Kingston, ON, K7L 3N6

Regina, University of, ESL Centre Language Institute, Rm 211, Regina, SK, S4S 0A2

Saint Mary's University, TESL Centre, Burke Building 110, Halifax, NS, B3H 3C3 Saskatchewan, University of, Centre for Second Language Instruction, 33 McLean Hall, Saskatoon, SK, S7N 5E6

Saskatchewan University, Sasktratoon, SK 57N SC8

Selkirk College, English Language Program, 301 Frank Beinder Way, Castlegar, BC, V1N 3J1

Seneca College, English Language Institute, 1750 Finch Avenue East, North York, ON, M2J 2XS

Sherbrooke University, Sherbrooke, Quebec J1K 2R1

Sheridan College - International Ed, English Language Program, 1430 Trafalgar Road, Oakville, ON, L6H 2LI

Simon Fraser University, Dept of Linguistics, 8888 University Drive, Burnaby BC, V5A 1S6

Sir Sandford Fleming College, International Education Office, Brealey Drive, Peterborough, ON, K9J 7B1

Southern Alberta Institute of Technology, International Academic Upgrading, 1301 - 16 Avenue NW, Calgary, AB, T2M 0L4

Studies Canada, 124 Eglinton Avenue West, Suite 400, Toronto, Ontario M4R 2G8 Tel: (416) 488 2200 Fax: (416)488 2225 Email tor@lsc-canada.com Website: www.lsc-canada.com Contact: CELTA Department

---

Tamwood Language Institute Ltd, 909 Burrard St, Suite 300, Vancouver BC, V6Z 2N2

Toronto, University of, Intensive ESL Program, 158 St George Street, Toronto, ON, M5S 2V8

University College of the Fraser Valley, International Education, 33844 King Road, Abbotsford, BC, V2S 7M9

Vancouver Community College, International Education, 1155 East Broadway, Vancouver, BC, V5N 5T9

Vancouver English Centre, 200-840 Howe St, Vancouver, BC, V6Z 2L2

Vancouver Maple Leaf Language College, 250-815 West Hastings St, Vancouver BC, V6C 1B4

VanWest College, 200 - 1215 West Broadway, Vancouver, BC, V6H 1G7,

Victoria, University of, English Language Centre, P O Box 1700, Victoria BC, V8W 2Y2

Waterloo, University of, English Language Institute, Renison College, Waterloo, ON, N2L 3G4

Westcoast English Language Centre, 220 Cambie St, Vancouver, BC, V6B 2M9

Western Ontario, University of, English Language Institute, Continuing Studies, London, ON, N6A 5B8

Windsor, University of, English as a Second Language, Sunset Blvd, Windsor, ON, N98 3P4

Winnipeg University, 346 Portage Avenue, Winnipeg, R3C 0C3

York University, 4700 Keale St. North York, ON M3J 1P3

Latin America and the Caribbean

The economies of this vast continent are much more stable than they were at the beginning of the decade and the region now has a wide range of ELT opportunities.

The economies of Latin America are under greater control than they have been in the past and therefore have a greater range of teaching opportunities. Demand for English learning is strongest in the commercial sector and in many countries, companies encourage their employees to learn, often arranging in-company courses.

With strong economic and cultural ties to the US Latin Americans unsurprisingly prefer to learn American English. Indeed, there are USIA Bi-National Centers all over the continent. Nevertheless, the presence of Culturas Inglesas (cultural associations with close links to the British Council) means that qualified teachers from the UK are finding it easier to get work.

Inflation is still an issue in Latin America and overseas recruitment often viewed as an unnecessary expense. This is especially true in countries where high standard state teaching produces local, non-L1 English speaker teachers, at near-L1 level. However, even in these countries, prestigious, often English medium schools are willing to pay premium rates for L1 speaker teachers.

Opportunities in Belize, Dominican Republic, the eastern Caribbean, Guatemala, Guyana, Haiti, Honduras, Nicaragua and Panama are generally for qualified teachers through aid programmes. Salaries tend to be paid in local currency and might not cover living costs but some include foreign currency supplements.

Teaching in El Salvador is not recommended unless it is arranged by an aid agency.

Argentina

The days when backpackers could pick up a little teaching work in Argentina as they travelled around Latin America have ended. Nowadays there is plenty of competition from English language graduates and English-speaking immigrants. English is big business and there are increasing numbers of schools.

To teach in state schools a local qualification is necessary. Foreign degrees are accepted by private schools but not to teach the national curriculum. There are always vacancies for qualified teachers and private classes are not difficult to find. It is best to start writing application letters in October. This gives employers enough time to arrange a work permit for a March or April start. If you want to look for work on spec, the best time to go is in late January.

While the British Council does not recruit teachers for Argentina, they maintain an informal register of freelance teachers, and can supply a list of bilingual schools in Buenos Aires and Culturas (EL teaching institutes) in provincial areas.

Visas and work permits: UK passport holders do not need a visa. Many teachers work on tourist visas which they renew every three months and institutes pay on an hourly basis. Technically it is illegal to look for work on a tourist visa, but usually overlooked. For a longer-term contract, you need a work permit, which is arranged by your employer. Securing the correct permit can take up to eight months, so look for work months before you intend to arrive.

Cost of living: Fairly high, especially in Buenos Aires. The economy suffered badly in the Eighties and despite government efforts in the recovery process, inflation remains a problem.

Salaries and taxes: Pay depends on qualifications and experience. For contract work, you can earn about US$1,000 per month with return flights and accommodation often included. The going rate for private classes in Buenos Aires is US$30-35 per hour and around $15-$25 per hour elsewhere, depending on whether you teach one to one, or a class. The tax rate is around 15 per cent for those registered with the tax office.

Accommodation: If you are paying for accommodation yourself, a one-bedroomed flat costs US$400 per month and usually requires a two-month deposit. Teachers often live in family-owned *pensiones* until they have saved enough money for a flat.

Health insurance: Local medical care is expensive. Private medical insurance is recommended.

Inoculations: Hepatitis A, Polio, Typhoid, Malaria (in some areas).

List of schools in Argentina

Asociacion Argentina de Cultura Inglesa, Suipacha 1333, (1011) Buenos Aires

Asociacion Comodoro Rivadavia de Intercambio Cultural Argentino Norteamericano (ACRICANA), Escalada 1567, 9000 Comodoro Rivadavia

Asociacion Litoralense de Intercambio Cultural Argentino Norteamericano (ALICANA), San Martin 2293, 3000 Sante Fe

Asociacion Mendocina de Intercambio Cultural Argentino Norteamericano (AMICANA), Chile 987, 5500 Mendoza

Asociacion Paranense de Intercambio Cultural Argentino Norteamericano (APICANA), Cordoba 256, 3100 Parana

Asociacion Rosarina de Intercambio Cultural Argentino Norteamericano (ARICANA), Buenos Aires 934, 2000 Rosario

Asociacion Santiaguena de Intercambio Cultural Argentino Norteamericano (ASICANA), 24 de Septiembre 382, 4200 Santiago del Estero

Asociacion Surea de Intercambio Cultural Argentino Norteamericano (SURICANA), Comandante Salas 119, 5600 San Rafael, Mendoza

Asociacion Tucumana de Intercambio Cultural Argentino Norteamericano (ATICANA), Salta 581, 4000 San Miguel de Tucuman

British Council, Marcalo T De Alvera 590 (4th Floor), 1058 Buenos Aires

Capacitacion en Idiomas y Traducciones (CAIT), Av. Pte. Roque Saenz Pena 615, Piso 6o, 1393 Buenos Aires

English Studies, Catalina Hansen, Rodriguez Pena 232 40 A - 1020, Capital Federal, Buenos Aires. Tel: 54 1371 5352, Fax: 54 (21) 720393. An agency in Buenos Aires, Argentina, working for small, reliable first class schools.

English Language Institute, 25 De Mayo 3773, 7600 Mar Del Plata

The Franklin Institute, Vicente Lopez 54, Salta 4400

The Greenfield Institute, Roca 3660, 8401 Bariloche, Rio Negro

IELI, Alberti 6444, San Jose de la Esquina, Santa Fe 2185

Instituto Cultural Argentino-Britanico, Calle 12, No 1900, La Plata

Instituto Cultural Argention Norteamericano (ICANA), Maipu 672, 1006 Buenos Aires

Instituto Dean Funes de Intercambio Cultural Argentino Norteamericano (IDFICAA), 9 de Julio 177, 5200 Dean Funes, Cordoba

Instituto de Intercambio Cultural Argentino Norteamericano (IICANA), Dean Funes 726, 5000 Cordoba

Instituto ELT, Isabel Gonzalez Bueno, Soler 458 (1714) Ituzaingo, Buenos Aires. Tel/Fax: (541) 624 0148. Courses for children, adolescents and adults. International exams: PET, First Certificate, CAE, Proficiency, Conversation and Business English. Multimedia Laboratory.

Instituto Nacional Superior Del Profesorado En Lenguas Vivas, Carlos Pellegrini 1455, 1011 Buenos Aires

Instituto Pampeano de Intercambio Cultural Argentino Norteamericano (IPICANA), Lisandro de L Torre 674, 6300 Santa Rosa, La Pampa

Instituto San Francisco de Intercambio Cultural Argentino Norteamericano (ISFICANA), Cabrera 1958, 2400 San Francisco, Cordoba

Instituto Salteno de Intercambio Cultural Argentino Norteamericano (ISICANA), Santiago del Estero 865, 4400 Salta

International House, IH Belgrano, Arcos 1830, 1428 Capital Federal, Buenos Aires.

International House, J A Pacheco de Melo 255, (1425) Capital Federal, Buenos Aires

International House, Cosme Beccar 225, (1642) San Isidro, Provincia de Buenos Aires

ITESL Foundation Malaver 1586-PC (1602) Florida, Buenos Aires Tel: 541 796 2534 Fax: 541 797 2775 e-mail: jdewey@satlink.com.ar Contact: Mrs Alicia Ghiorzi, Principle. Courses offered: RSA Cambridge, PE/CAE, T College. Advanced Language, Methodology, Syllabus Design. CVs from teachers holding RSA Diplomas and Certificates welcome.

Instituto Villamarinense de Intercambio Cultural Argentino Norteamericano (IVICANA), 25 de Mayo 143, 5900 Villa Maria, Cordoba

Instituto Ushuaia de Intercambio Cultural Argentino Norteamericano (USH-ICANA), San Martin 1135, 9410 Ushuaia, Tierra del Fuego

Liceo Superior de Cultura Inglesa, Italia 830, Tandil, 7000 Pica de Buenos Aires

Northside School of English, G W Seminario, Velez Sarsfield 56, 1640, Martinez, Buenos Aires. Tel/Fax: 798 5150/793 5469. In Northern BA suburb, General English/Special Purpose courses. Centre: Trinity College London examinations. UCLES examinations. Representatives of King's group.

St John's School, Recta Martinoli 3452, V Belgrano 5417 Cordoba, Pica de Cordoba

Bolivia

This country has suffered from political mismanagement of the economy but there is still demand for English language learning and travelling teachers are often attracted by its low living cost.

Visas and work permits: All nationalities, except UK passport holders, need a tourist visa to enter. A long-term work permit can be secured by the employer for contracts of at least one year. A job should be arranged before you leave for Bolivia.

Cost of living: Very low.

Salaries and taxes: These can be as low as $2 per hour in a language school or $6 per hour for private classes.

Accommodation: Between US$50 and %70 for a one-bedroom apartment, Approximately US$350 for a three-bedroom apartment.

Health insurance: Recommended.

Inoculations: Hepatitis A, Polio, Tetanus, Typhoid, Malaria, Yellow Fever.

List of schools in Bolivia

Centro Boliviano Americano, Calle 25 de Mayo N-0365, Casilla 1399, Cochabamba

Centro Boliviano Americano, Parque Zenon Iturralde No 121, Casilla 12024, La Paz

Centro Boliviano Americano, Calle Cochabamba No 66, Casilla 510, Santa Cruz de la Sierra

Centro Boliviano Americano, Calle Calvo No 331, Casilla No 380, Sucre, Chuquisaca

Colegio Ingles Saint Andrews, Av. Las Relamas, La Florida, La Paz

Colegio San Calixto, C/Jenaro Sanjines 701, La Paz. Tel: 355278

Colegio San Ignacio, Av. Hugo Ernest 7050, Seguencoma, La Paz

Pan American English Center, Edificio Avenida, Avenida 16 de Julio 1490, 7o piso, La Paz

Brazil

Many parents are keen to send their children to private schools to learn English. However, teachers from overseas find it difficult to get through the complicated red tape to get a visa. There are plenty of well-qualified Brazilian teachers, so schools are reluctant to spend money on overseas recruitment. If you are keen to pursue contracted work with a private school in Brazil, some of the more prestigious ones continue to recruit speakers from overseas.

There is great disparity between schools so contact reputable organisations like LAURELS, LABCI, USIA for a list of their institutes. The British Council also has such lists, but often refers EL teachers to the CBEVE (Central Bureau for Educational Visits and Exchanges) which operates a scheme to place 3rd and 4th year undergraduates and recent graduates at Culturas Inglesas on 9 month 'assistantships.'

There are a number of foreign chains who have opened up schools. If you decide to go out on spec, intensive courses start throughout the year. Otherwise, it is best to contact the national headquarters of organisations with schools in Brazil. In the larger cities, one-to-one Business English teaching is readily available.

Visas and work permits: UK and most EU citizens do require a visa. It is the employer's responsibility to arrange a work visa with the Ministry of Labour, which can take up to two months to get. You need to be qualified and have at least two years experience to qualify. The Brazilian employer has to apply on the foreign national's behalf for a temporary work visa, valid for two years and renewable for a further two.

It is possible to arrive, find a job, apply for a visa and pick it up in a neighbouring country, although this is not popular with the bureaucrats. Otherwise, the process should be initiated through the Brazilian consulate at home. Working without papers is forbidden.

Cost of living: Food is cheap but rent is moderately expensive and consumer products are more expensive than in the UK or US. The currency is now stable but not convertible into foreign currencies. There have been sharp falls in inflation and the economy seems to be more stable following mass privatisation.

Salaries and taxes: Teachers are paid for 13 months and salaries are higher in language centres. Full-time salaries start at around US$350 per month. Incomes can be supplemented with private classes at US$15 per hour. This could rise to as much as US$45 if you are well qualified with a diploma. The CBEVE assistantship scheme pays US$350 per month. Tax varies from 12.5 to 25 per cent or higher if you earn a lot. The statutory social security deduction for health and old age cover is 8 per cent.

Accommodation: Better schools will either provide it free or offer a subsidy. It is free on the assistantship scheme, where you live with a host family or another teacher. If you organise accommodation yourself, expect to pay between a third and half of your salary. In Brasilia, an apartment can cost the equivilent of US$250, so it would be hard for a teacher to get by in the city. Apartments are likely to be unfurnished.

Health insurance: Can be taken out locally but does not cover dental treatment.

Inoculations: Cholera, Hepatitis A, Polio, Typhoid, Malaria, Yellow Fever. An International Certificate is required for children from 6 months to 6 years of age.

English language newspapers: Brazil Herald.

Important cultural differences: There are two semesters, one starting after Carnaval in February, the other in August. A knowledge of Portuguese is an advantage.

Other useful information: Internal flights are expensive but some airlines offer special deals on air passes which you can only buy outside Brazil. Bus travel is cheap and efficient but takes a long time. Brazil is very large and three time zones operate.

List of schools in Brazil

Associacao Laumni (ALUMNI), Rua Visconde de Nacar 86, Real Parque Morumbi, 05685-903 Sao Paulo - AP

Associacao Brasil-America (ABA), Avenida Malaquias 171 Aflitos, 52050-060 Recife - PE

Associacao Cultural Brasil-Estados Unidos (ACBEU), Rua Braz Bernardino 73, 36010-320 Juiz de Fora - MG

Associacao Cultural Brasil-Estados Unidos (ACBEU), Avenida Sete de Setembro 1883, 40080-002 Salvador - BA

Britannia Schools, Rua Garcia D'Avila 58, Ipanema, Rio De Janeiro RJ, 22421-010

Britannia Special English Studies, Rua Dr Timoteo, 752 Moinhos De Vent, Porto Alegre RS

Britannia Juniors, Rua. Barao da Torre 599 - Rio de Janeiro, CEP 22411-003,

Britannia Executive School, Rua Barao De Lucena 61, Botofogo, Rio de Janeiro 22260

Britanic International House Recife, Rua Hermogenes de Morais 178, Madalena 50 610-160, Recife-PE

Britanic International House, Rua Viscande Jequitinhonha, 872

British House, Rua Tiradentes 2258, Centro, Pelotas RS 96060-160

Cambridge Sociedade Brasileira de Cultura Inglesa, Rua Piaui 1234, Londrina 86020-320 PR

Casa Branca, Rua Machado De Assis 37, Boqueirao, Santos SP.

Casa Thomas Jefferson (CASA), SEP/Sul 706/906 Conjunto B, Caixa Postal 07-1201, 70390-065 Brasilia - DF

Centro Cultural Brasil-Estados Unidos (CCBEU), Travessa Padre Eutiquio 1309, Batista Campos, 66020-710 Belem - PA

Centro Cultural Brasil-Estados Unidos (CCBEU), Avenida Julio de Mesquita 606, 13025-061 Campinas - SP

Centro Cultural Brasil-Estados Unidos (CCBEU), Rua Jorge Tibirica 5/7, 11055-250 Santos - SP

Centro Cultural Brasil-Estados Unidos (INTER), Rua Amintas de Barros 99, Edifico Itatiaia Centro, Caixa Postal 3328, 80060-200 Curitiba - PR

CEBEU, Av Marechal Rondon, 745, Centro, Ji-Paraná RO. Tel: +55 69 422 3100, Fax: +55 69 422 3100. English classes for children, adolescents and adults. In existence since 1982 in a town in the Amazon region.

CEL-LEP, Av. dos Tajuras 212, Sao Paulo SP 05670-000

Centro Britanico, Rua Joao Ramalho 344, Sao Paulo SP 05008-011

Centro Cultural Brasil Estados Unidos, Avenida T 5, No. 441, 74230-040 Goiania GO

Central Cultural Brasil-Estados Unidos (CCBEU), Avenida T-5 qd 125 Lt 05, Setor Bueno, 74230-040 Goiania - GO

Centro Cultural Brasil-Estados Unidos de Joinville (CCBEUJ), Rua Tijucas 370, Centrol, Caixa Postal 1301, 89204-020 Joinville - SC

Centro de Enseñanza PLI, Rua de Octubro, 1234 Conj 4, Porto Alegre, RS 90000

Centro De Cultura Inglesa, Av Guapore 2.236, Cacoal RO, CEP 78 975-000

Centro De Cultura Inglesa, Rua 12 De Outubro 227, Cuiaba Mt

Cultura Inglesa, Rua do Progresso 239, Recife PE 50070-002

Cultura Inglesa, Av. 17 de Agosto 233, Recife PE 52060-090

Cultura Inglesa, Rua Visconde Albuquerque 205, Recife PE 50610-090

Cultura Inglesa, Rua Visconde de Inhauma 980, Ribeirao Preto SP 14010-100

Cultura Inglesa, Rua Paul Pompeia 231, Rio de Janeiro RJ 22080-000

Cultura Inglesa, R. Plinio Moscoso 945, Salvador BA 40155-020

Cultura Inglesa, Av. Sao Sebastiao 848, Santarem PA 68005-090

Cultura Inglesa, Rua Sao Sebastiao 1530, Sao Carlos SP 13560-230

Cultura Inglesa, Av. Tiradentes 670, Sao Joao del Rei MG 36300-000

Cultura Inglesa, Rua Maranhao 416, Sao Paulo

Cultura Inglesa, Av. Brig. Faria Lima 2000, Sao Paulo SP 01452-002

Cultura Inglesa, R. Joao Pinheiro 808, Uberlandia MG 38400-58

Cultura Inglesa, Praca Rosalvo Ribeiro 110, Maceio AL 57021-57

Cultura Inglesa, R. Eng Mario de Gusmao 603, Maceio AL 57035-000

Cultura Inglesa, Rua Natal 553, Manaus AM 69005-000

Cultura Inglesa, Av. Rio Branco 741, Maringa PR 87015-380

Cultura Inglesa, Rua Acu 495, Natal RN 59020-110

Cultura Inglesa, R. Silvio Henrique Braune 15, Nova Friburgo RJ 28625-050.

Cultura Inglesa, R. Eduardo de Moraes 147, Olinda PE 53030-250

Cultura Inglesa, Av. Bernardo Vieira de Melo 2101, Jaboatao dos Guararapes PE 54410-010

Cultura Inglesa, Rua Paula Xavier 501, Ponta Grossa PR 84010-430

Cultura Inglesa, Rua Quintino Bocaiuva 1447, Porto Alegre RS 90570-010

Cultura Inglesa, Rua Mamanguape 411, Recife PE 51020-50

Cultura Inglesa, Alameda Julia da Costa 1500, Curitiba PR 80730-070

Cultura Inglesa, Rua Ponto Grossa 1565, Dourados MS 79824-160

Cultura Inglesa, Rua Conde de Porto Alegre 59, Buque de Caxias RJ 25070-350

Cultura Inglesa, Rua Rafael Bandeira 335, Florianapolis SC 88015-450

Cultura Inglesa, Rua Ana Bilhar 171, Fortaleza CE 60160-110

Cultura Inglesa, Rua Marechal Deodoro 1326, Franca SP 14400-440

Cultura Inglesa, Rua 86 No. 7, Golania GO 74083-330

Cultura Inglesa, Rua 20 778, Ituiutaba MG 38300-000

Cultura Inglesa, Av. Rio Grande do Sul 1411, Joao Pessoa PB 58030-021

Cultura Inglesa, Rua Dr. Joao Colin 559, Joinville SC 89204-004

Cultura Inglesa, Av. dos Andras 536, Juiz de Fora MG 36036-000

Cultura Inglesa, Av. Barao de Maruim 761, Aracaju SE 49015-020

Cultura Inglesa, Rua Almeida Campos 215, Araxa MG 38180-00

Cultura Inglesa, Rua Virgilio Malta 1427, Bauru SP 17040-440

Cultura Inglesa, R. Fernandes Tourinho 538, Belo Horizonte MG 30112-011

Cultura Inglesa – Santa Catarina, Rua Marechal Floriano Peixoto 433, Blumenau,Santa Catarina 89010-500 Tel/Fax: 55 47 326 7272 Email:mike@bnu.zaz.com.br Contact: Mike Delaney. Schools in Blumenau, Florianopolis, Itajai. General English – all ages. Cambridge examination centre. In-company teaching. Teacher training unit

Cultura Inglesa, SEPS 709/908 Conjunto B DF 70390-89

Cultura Inglesa, Rua Piaui 1234, Londrina 86021-320 PR

Cultura Inglesa, Av. Guapore 2236, Cacoal RO 78975-000

Cultura Inglesa, Rua Lino Gomes da Silva 53, Campina Grande PB 58107-613

Cultura Inglesa, R. Humberto de Campos 419, Campo Grande MS 79020-060

Cultura Inglesa, Av. Agamenon Magalhaes 634, Caruaru PE 55000-000

Cultura Inglesa, Rua Antonio Ataide 515, Vila Velha ES 29100-290

Cultura Inglesa, Av Tiradentes 670, 36300 Sao Joao Del Rei MG

Cultura Inglesa de Londrina, Rua Goias 1507, Centro, Londrina PR 86020-340

ELC, Rua Sa e Souza 655, Boa Viagem, Recife PE, 51030-350

English Forever, Rua Rio Grande Do Sul 356, Pituba, Salvador-BA 41830-140

Independent British Institute, SHCGN 703 Area Especial, s/no Brasilia DF 70730-700.

Inlingua, Rua Prim de Marco 23-2° Andar, Centro, 20010-000 Rio de Janeiro RJ

Instituto Brasil-Estados Unidos (IBEU), Av N Sra de Copacabana 690/6 11 andar, Copacabana, Caixa Postal 12.154, 22050-000 Rio de Janeiro - RJ

Instituto Brasil-Estados Unidos no Ceara (IBEU-CE), Rua Noguera Acioly 891, Aldeota, 60100-140 Fortaleza - CE

Instituto Brasil-Estados Unidos de Vitoria (IBEUV), Rua 7 de Setembro 135, Centrol, 29100-300 Vila Velha - ES

Instituto Britanico, Rua Deputado Carvalho Deda 640, 49025-070 Salgado Filho, Aracaju SE, Brazil

Instituto Cultural Brasil-Estados Unidos (ICBEU), Avenida Joaquim Nabuco 1286, Caixa Postal 61, 69020-030 Manaus - AM

Instituto Cultural Brasil-Estados Unidos (ICBEU), Rua da Bahia 1723, Lourdes, 30160-011 Belo Horizonte - MG

Instituto Cultural Brasil-Norteamericano (CULTURAL), Rua Riachuelo 1257, Centro, 90010-271 Porto Alegre - RS

Instituto da Lingua Inglesa, Av. do CPA 157, Cuiaba MT 78008-000

International House Goiania, Rua 4 no 80, Setor Oeste, Goiania GO 74110-140

International Training Solutions, Julie Pratten, 35 Rua Fonseca Guimaes, Rio De Janeiro. Email: gringa@int-solutions.co.uk Specialise in intensive financial and business training programmes, train-the-trainer, ESP publications and CD production for ELT purposes.

Liberty English Centre, Rua Amintas De Barros 1059, Curitiba PR

Sharing English, Rua Souza de Andrade 56, Recife PE 52050-300

Soc Bras de Cultura Inglesa, Rua Fernandes Tourinho, 538 - Savassi BH-MG 30112.000

System 2000, Rua Deputado Jose Lajes 491, Ponta Verde, Maceio AL 57035-330

St. Peter's English School, Rua Berilo Guimaraes, 182 Centro Itabuna, Bahia

Uniao Cultural Brasil-Estados Unidos (UNIAO), Rua Colonel Oscar Porto 208, Paraiso, Caixa Postal 7197, 04003-000 Sao Paulo - SP

Universitas, Rua Goncalves Dias 858, Belo Horizonte MG 30140-091

Upper English, Rua 09 de Julho 2143, Sao Carlos SP 13560-590

Chile

After severe economic decline in the Eighties under Pinochet, Chile has recovered through a bilateral trade agreement with the US. Since then the country has achieved nearly ten per cent growth. It is a popular destination for foreign investment as well, which means that there is great demand for English, especially in the business and young-learning sectors.

Although it is impossible to work in state schools without a qualification from a Chilean university, there are many private schools and in-company opportunities, especially in Santiago.

Foreigners coming to Chile with the intention of teaching English preferably should have both qualifications and experience. Teachers are trained to a high standard in Chile and competition is tough.

Visas and work permits: Applications for visas and work permits should be made before you leave for Chile It is possible to obtain a work permit after arrival but you have to show that you intend to stay for at least a year. Working on a tourist visa is illegal. No visa is required for British citizens.

Cost of living: Low but generally higher than the rest of Latin America. Most prices are comparable with the UK, but public transport, eating out, alcohol and tobacco are cheap.

Salaries and taxes: For contracted teaching positions, a minimum wage for overseas teachers is set by the government at $400 per month. Rates vary from US$8-11 per hour for qualified teachers. The tax rate is around 10 per cent. VAT is 18%.

Accommodation: Schools offer little help but it is easy to stay in hostels which offer long-term accommodation with good facilities. Rooms can cost as little as US$130 per month but average around US$250. Flats can cost up to US$400 per month and landlords expect a month's rent as deposit and a month in advance. Hotels cost up to US$200

Health insurance: Essential.

Inoculations: Hepatitis A, Polio, Typhoid, but no certificates are necessary.

Important cultural differences: The academic year runs from March to December.

List of schools in Chile

Anglo-American International School, San Sebastian 2975, Santiago

Antofagasta British School, Pedro Leon Gallo 723, Casilla 1, Antofagasta

British Council, Eliodora Yanez 832, Casilla 115-Correo 55, Santiago

British School, Waldo Seguel 454, Casilla 379, Punta Arenas

British High School, Los Gladiolos 10281, Santiago.

Colegio Charles Darwin, Manantiales 0314, Punta Arenas

Colegio Dunalastair, Av. Las Condes 11931, Santiago.

Colegio Ingles George Chaytor, Callejon Ingles 4B, Temuco

Colegio Ingles de Talca, 12 Norte 5/6 Oriente, Talca

Colegio St George, Av. Americo Vespucio Norte 5400, Santiago

Colegio del Verbo Divinio, Av. Presidente Errazuriz 4055, Santiago

Colegio Villa Maria Academy, Av. Presidente Errazuriz 3753, Santiago

Craighouse, El Rodeo 12525-La Dehesa, Casilla 20007-Correo 20, Santiago

Grange School, Av. Principe de Gales 6154, Casilla 51-Correo 12, Santiago

Greenhouse School, Ines de Suarez 1500, Temuco

Instituto Chileno-Britanico De Cultura, Baquedano 351, Casilla 653, Arica

Instituto Chileno-Britanico De Cultura, San Martin 531, Casilla 260, Concepcion

Instituto Chileno-Britanico De Cultura, Santa Lucia 124, Casilla 3900, Santiago

Instituto Chileno-Britanico De Cultura, Dario Urzua 1933, Providencia, Santiago

Instituto Chileno-Britanico De Cultura, Americo Vespucio 631, Las Condes, Santiago

Instituto Chileno-Britanico De Cultura, 3 Norte 824, Casilla, Vina del Mar 929

Instituto Chileno Norteamericano - Antofagasta, Carrera 1445, Casilla P, Antofagasta

Instituto Chileno Norteamericano - Arica, San Marcos 581, Casilla 793, Arica

Instituto Chileno Norteamericano - Chillan, Dieciocho de Septiembre 253, Chillan

Instituto Chileno Norteamericano - Concepcion, Caupolican 315, Casilla 612, Concepcion

Instituto Chileno Norteamericano - Curico, Estado 563, Casilla 258, Curico

Instituto Chileno-Norteamericano De Cultura, Moneda 1467, Santiago.

Instituto Chileno Norteamericano - Osorno, Los Carrera 770 - 2ndo Piso, Osorno

Instituto Chileno Norteamericano - Santiago, Moneda 1467, Holanda esq Pio X, Casilla 9286, Santiago

Instituto Chileno Norteamericano - Temuco, General Mackenna 559, Temuco

Instituto Chileno Norteamericano - Valparaiso, Esmeralda 1069, Casilla 1297, Valparaiso

International Preparatory School, Pastor Fernandez 16001, El Arrayan, Santiago

Iquique English College, Jose Joaquin Perez 419, Iquique

Let's Do English, Villa Vicencio 361, Office 109, Santiago

Lincoln International Academy, Camino San Antonio 55- Las Condes, Santiago

Mackay School, Vicuna Mackenna 700, Casilla 558, Vina del Mar

Mayflower School, Las Condes 12167, Santiago

Nido de Aquilas School, Nido de Aquilas 14515, Casilla 16211-Providencia, Santiago

Redland School, Camino El Alba 11357, Las Condes, Santiago.

St Gabriel's School, Av. Bilbao 3070-Providencia, Santiago

St John's School, Pedro de Valdivia 1783, Casilla 284, Concepcion

St Margaret's School, 5 Norte 1351, Casilla 392, Vina del Mar

St Peter's School, Calle Libertad 575, Vina del Mar

Santiago College, Los Leones 584, Casilla 130-D, Santiago

Thewhla's English School, Las Camelias 2854, Santiago

Wenlock School, Carlos Pena Otaegui 10880, La Foresta, Los Dominicos, Santiago

Wessex School, Colo-Colo 222-Clasificador 43, Concepcion

Windsor School, Av. Francia Esq. Simpson, Casilla 530, Valdivia.

Colombia

Some teachers are scared off by Colombia's reputation for violence. In reality, foreigners are unlikely to get involved in any trouble. In spite of the recent economic recession, there is a huge demand for English especially from companies. The state has expanded the requirement for English to be taught in schools. Many universities require their graduates to have completed at least two terms of English instruction.

The best prospects for teachers come from the big cities. North Americans are in great demand as American English is the first choice for most Colombians. Many of the private schools are American-owned and place people at all levels. There are also English Medium International Schools, Centros Americanos and British Council centres in Bogota and Cali. The number of companies setting up English language classes is increasing too.

This means that most EFL teachers, including unqualified ones looking for a stop-gap while travelling, can get a job fairly easily. You might have to settle for a low wage initially and it may not be enough to live on. If you want to stay

more than a few months it is advisable to get qualified first, so that you can build up contacts more readily to secure more lucrative private classes. There are some opportunities in the state sector at the tertiary level. These would require high qualifications, such as an MA or Ph.D.

Visas and work permits: Teachers must have a work permit before they travel and unusually, a private language school cannot intervene directly with the Ministry of Foreign Affairs to secure this visa. Only those employed by approved institutions can secure the necessary work visa. The application process is associated with red tape and expense and can take two months, so make sure that your potential employer is approved. It is illegal to search for work on a tourist visa and this is investigated quite thoroughly on entry.

Cost of living: The cost of living is expensive in Medellin although due to the recssion inflation is now relatively low. However, once established, teachers can have a good standard of living. Electrical equipment is cheap.

Salaries and taxes: Many schools offer no more than 2,500 pesos per hour and unqualified teachers can expect to earn as little as 1,600. Average monthly salaries are 825,000-1,120,000 pesos and it is possible to find salaries of 1.5 million pesos. The British Council pays $20 per hour for a qualified (CELTA) teacher. Full time teachers can earn US$2,000-2200 a month. Many institutions pay teachers 14 times per year. With a normal work visa, teachers will pay from about 10 per cent tax. Because of the country's inflation, schools which offer (portions of) salaries in other currencies might be more attractive.

Accommodation: Expensive. In Bogota and most other cities, a one-bedroomed flat in a reasonable area can cost US$350 per month and with administration costs this can reach $390.

Health insurance: Advisable as hospital stays can be expensive.

Inoculations: Hepatitis A, Polio, Typhoid, Malaria, Yellow Fever.

English Newspaper:
The Colombian Post.

List of schools in Colombia
Academia Inglesa Para Niños, Calle 106 No 16-26, Bogota

Advanced Learning Service, Transversal 20 No 120-15, Bogota

Aprender Ltda, Calle 17 No 4-68 Ql. 501, Bogota

Aspect, Calle 79a No 8-26, Bogota

Avc, Carrera 45 El Palo 52-59, Cali

BBC De Londres, Calle 59 No 6-21, Bogota

Babel, Avenida 15 No 124-49 Cf. 205, Bogota

Bi Cultural Institute, Avenida 7 No 123-97 Of. 202, Bogota

Boston School of English Ltda, Carrera 43 No 44-02, Barranquilla

Britanico Americano De Idiomas, Avenida 13 No 103-62, Bogota

The British Council, Calle 87 No 12-79, Bogota

Business Language Centre Ltda., Carrera 49 No 15-85, Medellin

California Institute Of English, Carrera 51 No 80-130, Barranquilla

Carol Keeney, Carrera 4 No 69-06, Bogota

Ceico, Calle Siete Infantes, San Diego, Cartagena

Centro Anglo Frances, Carrera 11 No 6-12, Neiva

Centro Audiovisual De Ingles Chelga, Calle 137 No 25-26, Bogota

Centro Colombo Americano, Carrera 14 No 8-62, Apartado Aereo 2216, Armenia

Centro Colombo Americano, Avenida 19 No 3-05, Apartada Aereo 3815, Santa Fe de Bogota

Centro Colombo Americano (North Branch), Calle 109A No 17-10, Santa Fe de Bogota

Centro Colombo Americano, Carrera 22 No 37-74, Apartado Aereo 466, Bucaramanga

Centro Colombo Americano, Calle 13 Norte No 8-45, Apartado Aereo 4525, Cali

Centro Colombo Americano, Calle de la Factoria No 36-27, Apartado Aereo 2831, Cartagena

Centro Colombo Americano, Calle 26 No 21-37, Apartado Aereo 391, Manizales

Centro Colombo Americano, Carrera 45 No 53-24, Apartado Aereo 8734, Medellin

Centro Colombo Americano, Carrera 6 No 22-26, Apartado Aereo 735, Pereira

Centro Colombo Andino, Calle 19 No 3-16 Of. 203, Bogota

Centro Cultural Colombo Americano, Carrera 43 No 51-95, Apartado Aereo 2097, Barranquilla

Centro De Ingles Lincoln, Calle 49 No 9-37, Bogota

Centro De Idiomas Winston Salem, Calle 45 No 13-75, Bogota

Centro De Idiomas Winston Salem, Transversal 74 No C2-33 Laureies, Medellin

Centro De Idiomas Winston Salem, Avenida La Ceste No 10-27, Santa Teresita, Cali

Centro De Idiomas y Turismo De Cartagena, Popa Calle 30 No 20- 177, Cartagena

Centro De Lengua Inglesa, Calle 61 No 13-44 Of. 402, Bogota

Centro De Lenguas Modernas, Carrera 38 No 69 C 65, Barranquilla.

Coningles, Calle 63 No 13-24 Of. 502, Bogota

Easy English, Carrera 45 A No 34 Sur 29 Torre No 4, Portal Del Cerro, A. A. 80511, Envigado, Medellin

El Centro Ingles, El Poblado Carrera 10 A.No 36-39, Medellin

English For Infants (John Dewey), Diagonal 110 No 40-85, Bogota

English Language & Culture Institute (ELCI), Calle 90 No 10-51, Bogota

Esquela De Ingles, Calle 53 No 38-25, Barranquilla

Escuela De Idiomas Berlitz, Calle 83 No 19-24, Bogota

Genelor International, Avenida 78 No 20-49 Piso 20, Bogota

I.C.L., Calle 119 No 9a-25, Bogota

Idiomas-Munera-Cros Ltda, Carrera 58 No 72-105, A.A. 52032, Barranquilla

Ingles Cantando Y Jugando, Calle 106 No 16-26, Bogota

Instituto Anglo Americano De Idiomas, Carrera 16a No 85-34 Of. 204, Bogota

Instituto Bridge Centro De Idiomas, Carrera 65 No 49 A 09, Cali

Instituto De Ingles Thelma Tyzon, Carrera 59 No 74-73, Barranquilla

Instituto De Lenguas Modernas, Carrera 41 No 52-05, Baranquilla.

Instituto Electronico De Idiomas, Carrera 6 No 12-64 Piso, Bogota

Instituto Experimental De Atlantico, "jos Celestino Mutis", Calle 70 No 38-08, Barranquilla

Instituto Meyer, Calle 17 No 10-16 Piso 80, Bogota

Interlingua Ltda., Carrera 18 No 90-38, Bogota

International Language Institute, Carrera 5a No 21-35, Neiva

International Language Institute Ltda, Carrera 11 No. 65-28 Piso 3, Bogota

International Language Institute Ltda, Carrera 13 No 5-79 Castillogrande, Cartagena

International System, Transversal 6 No 51 A 33, Bogota

K.O.E De Columbia, Calle 101 A No 31-02, Bogota

Life Ltda., Transversal 19 No 100-52, Bogota

Oxford Centre, A.A. 102420, Santate de Bogota

Way's English School, Calle 101 No 13 A 17, Bogota

Costa Rica

One of the safest but most expensive Latin American countries. There are many private language schools but often with huge classes of mixed ability and poor facilities. Qualified teachers who speak Spanish can work in private bilingual schools and enjoy a reasonable standard of living in a beautiful, friendly and diverse country.

Visas and work permits: Work visas are very difficult to obtain, even for those who own companies operating in the country. Teachers tend to work on a visitor's visa. UK, Canadian, US, Australian and New Zealand citizens can stay in Costa Rica for up to three months without a visa.

Salary and taxes: The equivalent of US$400-500 per month.

Accommodation: $100-200 a month for a shared flat. Assistance often provided by employers.

List of schools in Costa Rica
Centro Cultural Costarricense Norteamericano, Apartado 1489-1000, Calle Los Negritos, Barrio Dent, San Jose

Centro Linguistico Conversa, PO Box 17-1007, Centro Colon, San Jose

Instituto Anglo Costarricanse de Cultura, PO Box 8184-1000, San Jose

Instituto Internacional Forrester, PO Box 6945-1000, San Jose

Instituto Latinoamericano de Idiomas, PO Box 1001-1050 Sa Pedro, San Jose

Instituto Universal de Idiomas, PO Box 751-2150, Moravia, San Jose

World Education Forum, PO Box 383-4005, San Antonio de Belén, Heredia

Cuba

Cuba is facing economic difficulties now that Russia no longer helps its economy. However, the growing tourism market may cause growth in the demand for English. The Project Trust has links with schools in the country.

Visas and work permits: A restricted immigration policy means it is hard to get a work permit. Apply to your local Cuban embassy.

Salaries and taxes: The state system has a set wage. The private sector pays a small salary in dollars which is convertible on the black market. There is no tax. Foreigners will often be charged for goods and services in dollars, making their stay more expensive.

Accommodation: Difficult to find.

Health insurance: Medical care is free but private cover is advisable.

List of schools in Cuba
Universidad de Cienfuegos, Departamento de Inglés, Carretera a Rodas, Km 4, Cuatro Cam. Cienfuegos 55100.

Dominican Republic

List of Schools in the Dominican Republic
Centro Cultural Dominicano-Americano, Avenida Estrella Sadhala, La Rinconada, Apartado 767, Santiago de los Caballeros

Instituto Cultural Dominico-Americano, Avenida Abraham Lincoln No 21, Santo Domingo

Ecuador

There is a plethora of language schools in Ecuador, making it quite easy for English teachers to find work, whether they are qualified or not. Knowledge of English is more important than being a native speaker. Ecuador is generally considered one of the best starting points for teachers working their way round South America.

Many ex-British Council teachers have set up their own reputable schools but to find work in them it helps to have personal contacts. Other private language schools tend to be less fussy. The demand for business, general and young learner classes is enormous, especially in the cities.

Visas and work permits: It is illegal to work on a tourist visa but some teachers do so nevertheless. Visitors from the UK are entitled to stay for up to six months on a tourist visa, while those from the US get 90 days. Tourist visa 12-X is not required by citizens of the UK and USA. To extend the visa, you have to prove that you have independent income not resulting from work in the country.

If you intend to work legally, you have to produce a return air ticket. A tourist visa cannot be swapped for any other kind of visa once in the country, so if you get a job whilst there, you have to leave the country to get the paperwork sorted out. A work contract is required in order to obtain work visa 12-IV.

Cost of living: Cheap.

Salaries and taxes: The monthly rate for unqualified teachers is US$150, rising to US$250 in more reputable schools. Freelancers earn between US$2 and US$5 per hour. Language schools and organisations such as the British Council pay between £450 and £600, usually only considering qualified teachers. Everyone is taxed at 7 per cent.

Accommodation: A wide range is available. Expect to pay US$40 per month for a room in a shared flat or US$100 for your own place. The usual deposit is two months rent.

Health insurance: Essential. Buy it before you arrive.

Inoculations: Hepatitis A, Polio, Typhoid, Malaria, Yellow Fever.

English language newspapers: Q Magazine, Inside Ecuador.

Important information: Classes are very much geared towards passing exams rather than learning for its own sake.

List of schools in Ecuador

American Language School, Carchi 904 y Velez, Guayaquil

Benedict, 9 De Octubre 1515, Y Orellana, Quito.

Benedict, Datiles y La Primera, CC Urdesa, Guayaquil.

Centro De Estudios Interamericanos, Casilla 597, Cuenca.

Centro Ecuatoriano Norteamericano Abraham Lincoln, Borrero 5-18, P O Box 01.01.1939, Cuenca

Centro Ecuatoriano NorteAmericano, Luis Urdeneta y Cordoba, P O Box 09-01-5717, Guayaquil

---

Experimento De Convivencia International Del Ecuador, Les Embleton, Hernando de la Cruz 218 y Mariana de Jesús, Quito. Tel: 593 2 551937/550179, Fax: 593 2 55 0228. The English department of the Experimento is the most prestigious private English Language institute in Quito.

ELC - The Edinburgh Linguistic Center, Mariana de Jesus 910 y Amazonas, Quito, P O Box 17-21-0405, Quito Tel: 00 593 2 549188 Fax: 00 593 2 549188 e-mail: juliovel@uio.satnet.net Contact: The Director. 'The effective language learning' more than 12 years experience, small groups or 1-1 teaching.

Fulbright Commission, Almagro 961 y Colon, Quito

International Benedict Schools of Languages, PO Box 09-01-8916, Guayaquil

Lingua Franca, Edificio Jerico, 12 De Octubre 2449 y Orellana, Casilla 17-2-68, Quito

Quito Language and Culture Centre, Republica De El Salvador, 639 Y Portugal, Quito

El Salvador

List of Schools in El Salvador

Centro Cultural Salvadoreno, Avenida Sisimiles, Metrocentro

English Language Institute, 79 Avenida Norte y 5A Calle Poniente, San Salvador

Escuela De Idiomas/Universidad CentroAmericana, AutoPista Sur, San Salvador

Extension Program Escuela Americana, Calle y Colonia la Mascota, San Salvador

Guatemala

There is considerable demand for teachers in Guatemala, usually met by candidates from the USA, but available for L1 native speakers from elsewhere to apply for. Some specialist English teaching schools exist and these are the best sources of potential work. Generally, the wage rate for a teacher of English willbe between US$10 and $15 an hour.

Visas: People from the EU, Canada, the USA and Mexico with passports valid for at least six months do not require tourist visas to stay up to 90 days. Citizens of other countries should check their situation with the local Guatemalan consulate. It is possible to look for work on such a visa and then apply to change its status.

The standard route to being allowed to work in Guatemala is to apply to a school or business and get a job offer.

With your confirmation letter you should go to a Guatemalan consulate, and show copies of your last two bank statements for proof of initial funds and supply two photographs. A business visa will then be issued (costing £7 in the UK).

This must be taken to the General Office of Administration on arrival in Guatemala to get a work permit. The process can take up to six months, but you can work in the interim, provided the authorities have been notified and are aware of your situation. A letter of confirmation from your school, in Spanish, will assist with the sorting out of the paperwork.

Tax: Your employer will deduct the tax from your earnings at the relevant rate, which can be anywhere between 25% and 40$. It may be possible to pay your tax returns to your home country if agreements with Guatemala exist. This is something to investigate with the Consulate and your home tax office.

List of Schools in Guatemala

Instituto Guatemalteco-Americano (IGA), Ruta 1, 4-05 Zona 4, Apartado Postal 691, Guatemala City

Haiti

List of Schools in Haiti

Institut Haitiano-Americain, Port-au-Prince. US Mailing: American Embassy Port Au Prince, Department of State, Washington DC 20521-3400

Honduras

There is quite a large demand for English language teaching in Honduras as it is effectively the second language for much of the country. This is in schools, privately, and in the busines sector. It is advisable to have work organised, or contracts that can get you employment, well before arrival in the country, as the employer can get the long process of obtaining residency rights under way.

Visas: There is no such thing as a work permit in Honduras, and the need for a tourist visa depends on which country you are from. You can look for work as a tourist but have to apply for residency

rights in order to take up a post. This can only be done from outside the country, and can take from 4 to 6 months. The type of residency granted depends on how much you are deemed likely to invest in the country. Residency can only be obtained via a job offer presented to the Consulate.

School details in Honduras

Centro Cultural Sampedrano (CCS), 3 Calle, entra 3A y 4A Avenida 20, Apartado Postal 511, San Pedro Sula, Cortes

Instituto Hondureno de Cultura Interamericana (IHCI), 2 Avenida entre 5 y 6 Calles No 520, Apartado 201, Tegucigalpa, MDC Comayaguela, Tegucigalpa

Jamaica

Although Jamaica's first language is English there is some work available teaching EFL to new Jamaican residents plus some Business and Remedial English.

The Jamaican government welcomes qualifying students from the UK and the US to teach in Jamaican schools. British candidates should apply through BUNAC in London while US candidates should apply through the Centre for International Education Exchange in New York.

Visas and work permits: There is no need for an entry visa but you will need a work permit which is best applied for in Jamaica.

Salaries and taxes: Income tax is 25 per cent. There is also a 15 per cent General Consumption Tax. Working in a school you can earn about J$140 per hour or J$100,000 per year. For private lessons you can earn J$200-500 per hour.

Accommodation: Rents vary widely ((J$7,000 - J$20,000 for a studio or one-bedroomed flat). Deposits are usually one or two months rent. Affordable accommodation is very hard to find.

Health insurance: Advisable.

Inoculations: Hepatitis A, Polio, Typhoid, Yellow Fever.

List of schools in Jamaica

Language Training Centre Ltd, 24 Parkington Plaza, Kingston 10

Target English Associates, 9a Duquesnam Ave, Kingston 10

Mexico

When Mexico signed the NAFTA agreement with the US, demand for English in the country soared. Although things have levelled out since then, companies still push employees to learn the language and there are plenty of opportunities in the country for teachers coming from overseas.

Teachers are mainly hired locally because schools find it increasingly difficult to pay recruitment costs, but it is possible to organise things before arrival. If you are coming on spec, you will stand a better chance of finding something if you give the impression that you want to stay in the country for a couple of years. While B.A. and M.A. degrees can be acceptable, a teaching certificate will greatly increase your employability. Most contracts are full-time, for 12 months.

Visas and work permits: The government has clamped down on illegal workers and adopts a strict policy of protection towards its own teachers. Working on a tourist visa is illegal and, unless you are from the US or Canada, work permits are almost impossible to secure.

Cost of living: In Mexico City the cost of living is much higher than you might expect. Elsewhere it is still cheap, but rising steadily. Inflation is still a considerable problem.

Salaries and taxes: Teachers are paid around US$400 per month. This is enough to live on, but do not expect to save much unless you take lots of private classes, which pay around $10 per hour. Expect less in the provinces. The tax rate is around 15 per cent.

Accommodation: There are cheap places to live if you look outside city centres. A small flat will cost around UK£90-100 per month for two people. Most people spend between a quarter and a third of their salary on accommodation. Furnished accommodation is rare.

149

Health insurance: Essential. It is expensive in Mexico.

Inoculations: Hepatitis A, Polio, Typhoid, Malaria, Yellow Fever.

English language newspapers: The Mexico City Times,The News.

Other useful information: Some employers offer foreign currency supplements to counteract inflation.

List of schools in Mexico

Anglo-Mexican Cultural Institute, Rio Nazas 116, Colonia Cuauhtémoc, 06500 Mexico, DF

Centro Mexicano Americano de Relaciones Culturales, Xola No 416, Col de Valle, 03100 Mexico, DF

Colegio Internacional De Cuernavaca, Apartado Postal 1334, Cuernavaca, Morelos

EF English First, Londres 188. Col. Juarez, CP 06600, Mexico DF

Instituto Anglo-Mexicano de Cultura AC, Rio Nazas 116, Col Cuauhtemoc

Instituto Cultural Mexixcano-Norteamericano de Jalisco, Tolsa No 300, 44100 Guadalajara, Jalisco

Instituto Franklin de Veracruz, Azueta 1229 & Diaz Miron, Veracruz, Veracruz

Instituto Franklin de Yucatan, Calle 57 No 474-A, 9700 Merida, Yucatan

Instituto Mexicano Americano de Relaciones Culturales, Blvd Navarrete y Monteverde, Hermosillo, Sonora

Instituto Mexicano-Norteamericano de Relaciones Culturales, P Cardenas No 840 Pte y Purceli, 25000 Saltillo, Coahuila

Instituto Mexicano-Norteamericano de Relaciones Culturales Anahuac, Jose Santos Chocano 606, Col Anahuac, 66450 San Nicolas De Los Garza, Nuevo Leon

Instituto Mexicano-NorteAmericano de Michoacan, Guillermo Prieto 86, 58000 Morelia, Michoacan

Instituto Mexicano-NorteAmericano de Relaciones Culturales de Nuevo Leon, Hidalgo No 768 Pte, 64000 Monterrey, Nuevo Leon

Universidad Autonoma De Aguascalientes, Rio Tamesis 438, 20100 Aguascalientes, Ags

Universidad Autonoma De Baja California Sur, Carr. Al Sur. Km. 5.5, 23080 La Paz, Bcs

Univ. Aut Del Carmen, Fac. De Ciencias Educativas, 24170 Cd. Del Carmen, Camp Alabama 2401, Quintas Del Sol, 31250 Chihuahua, Chih

Universidad Autonoma De Chiapas, Blvd. Belisario Dominguez Km. 1081, 29000 Tuxtla Gutierrez, Chiapas

Univ Autonoma De Coahuila, Depto. De Idiomas, Hidalgo Y Gonzalez Lobo, Col. Republica De Oriente, 25280 Saltillo, Coah

Universidad Autonoma De Guerrero, Av. Lazaro Cardenas 86, 39000 Chilpancingo, Gro

Universidad Autonoma De Guanajuato, Centro De Idiomas, Lascurian De Retana 5, 36000 Guanajuato, Gto

Universidad Autonoma De Hidalgo, Centro De Lenguas, Carr. Pachuca/Tulancingo S/N, 42000 Pachuca, Hgo

Universidad De Guadalajara, Esc Superior De Lenguas Modernas, Apdo. Postal 2-416, 44280 Guadalajara, Jal

Univ Autonoma Del Edo De Mexico, Centro De Ensenanza De Lenguas, Rafael M. Hidalgo No. 401 Pte., 50130 Toluca, Edo De Mexico

Universidad Autonoma Del Edo De Morelos, Centro De Lenguas, Rayon 7b- Centro, 62000 Cuernavaca, Mor

Universidad Autonoma De Neuvo Leon, Fac. Filosofia Y Letras, Apdo. Postal 3024, 64000 Monterrey, Nl, Mil Cumbres

Univ Aut Benito Juarez De Oaxaca, Centro De Idiomas, Armenta Y Lopez 700, Centro, 68000 Oaxaca De Juarez, Oax

Universidad Autonoma De Puebla, Dpto Lenguas, 4 Sur 104, 72000 Puebla, Pue

Universidad Autonoma De Queretaro, Escuela De Idiomas, Cerro De Las Campanas, 76010 Queretaro, Qro

Universidad Autonoma De San Luis Potosi, Centro De Idiomas, Zaragoza No. 410, 78200 San Luis Potosi, S.L.P.

Universidad De Sonora, Idiomas, Rosales Y Blvd. Luis Encinas, 83000 Hermosillo, Son

Universidad Autonoma De Tlaxcala, Depto De Filosofia Y Letras, Carretera A San Gabriel S/N, 90000 Tlaxcala, Tlax

Universidad Veracruzana Udih, Fac. De Idiomas, Fco Moreno Esq Ezequiel Alatriste, 91020 Xalapa, Ver

Universidad Autonoma De Yucatan, Fac. De Educacion, Calle 61 No 525 (Entre 66 Y 68), 97000 Merida, Yuc

Universidad Autonoma De Zacatecas, Centro De Idiomas, Alameda 422, 98000 Zacatecas, Zac

Nicaragua

There is a growing market for teachers of English in Nicaragua, within education institutions and on company in-house training schemes. Pay rates would be local and low. It is best to have work lined up in order to ease the process of obtaining work permits.

The Nicaraguan Consul in London is in the process of setting up an English Teaching programme, most likely to be under the auspices of the British Council, whereby beginner teachers, probably new graduates with some form of TEFL, could go to Nicaragua on a one year contract. The pay would be at the local level and the role to teach the staff of the Nicaraguan Foreign Ministry.

Visas: In order to work a visa must be granted. This is usually done on the strenght of written confirmation of a job from the employer. It is permissible to look for work as a tourist. The necessity for a tourist visa depends on which country you are from, citizens of the UK and USA do not need visas, while Australia, Canada and New Zealand do. Unless you have good Spanish and references that can be easily checked, it can be difficult to obtain work on spec. Officially, you should leave the country to change a tourist visa to a work permit.

School details in Nicaragua

Centro Cultural Nicaraguense-NorteAmericano, Centro Comercial Nejapa (Detras Del Banco Popular), Managua

Panama

Due to the previous American imperial links to this region, with the canal zone, and political and economic involvement, American English schools dominate. It is potentially a hard country to find teaching posts in, as English is widely spoken to native user standard, and there are many Panamanian teachers of English. If you are going, a knowledge of Spanish is very useful.

Visas: You can enter the country as a tourist and look for work, visas are no longer required, but you must have government permission to work. This can involve the hiring of local lawyers and considerable expense. It is recommended that you have a local contact who can help you through the bureaucracy.

List of Schools in Panama

Centro PanUSA - Centro Panameno-Estadounidense, Apartado 4581, Panama 5

Paraguay

As with much of Latin and South America there is a demand for English language skills, for the purposes of economic development and trade, particularly with the USA.

Visas: The need for a tourist visa depends on your country of origin. UK citizens, for example, can be in Paraguay for up to six months without a visa, and are allowed to look for work. It is not recommended that you go to the country to look for legal work on spec, as to get permission to work is a complicated process, involving the need for government departments to analyse original documentation about you. To find out what information you must have and supply, you should approach the Paraguayan representatives in your country.

List of Schools in Paraguay

Centro Anglo-Paraguayo, Artigas 356, Asuncion

Centro Cultural Paraguayo-Americano, Avenida Espana 352, Asuncion

Centro Cultural Paraguayo-Americano, Coronel Bogado 315 Esq Curupayty, Villarrica

Peru

The Peruvian economy has been experiencing considerable growth. Unsurprisingly, the demand for EFL teachers has been rising too and some private schools have been opening. The industry is still in its developing stages however, so ground work is necessary to find positions. Opportunities for teachers giving private tuition are reportedly good, but to work legally individuals have to be attached to an employer in order to get the permits. Some universities and state secondary schools have vacancies for English teachers, but must be contacted directly. The pay they offer will be low.

Visas and work permits: Tourist visas are available for two or three months, renewable up to five months. It is illegal to work on a tourist visa and impossible to switch to a work visa inside Peru. Obtaining a work visa is notoriously difficult and a full-time contract is a prerequisite. The laws concerning visas are strictly enforced.

Cost of living: Living costs are high.

Salaries and taxes: Teachers earn somewhere between US$300 and US$700 per month in private schools. Freelance teaching, if available, pays US$15 - US$20 per hour. English translation work pays US$7 - US$20 per page and interpreting US$100 - US$150 per day. The tax rate is 28 per cent.

Accommodation: The average rent is US$240 - US$320 minimum per month in the capital, Lima, with two months rent as a deposit. Schools generally help teachers find somewhere to live.

Health insurance: Essential.

Inoculations: Hepatitis A, Polio, Typhoid, Malaria, Yellow Fever.

English Language Newspaper: Lima Herald, Lima Times.

List of schools in Peru

Associacion Cultural Peruano Britanico, Av. Arequipa 3495, San Isidro, Lima

CENE Cambridge, Los Abanicos 222, La Encantada de Villa, Chorrillos, Lima 9

Colegio Newton, Av. Elias Aparicio s/n, La Molina, Lima 12

Davy College, Kolometro 3 Carretera al Aeropuerto, Casilla 1, Cajamarca

Hiram Bingham School for Girls, Paseo La Castellana 919, Higuereta, Surco

Inlingua Lima, Av L M Sanchez Cerro 2144-2150, Jesus Maria, Lima 11

Instituto Cultural Peruano Norteamerican de Areguipa (ICPNA Arequipa), Melgar 109, Apartado 555, Arequipa

Instituto Cultural Peruano Norteamerican de Chiclayo (ICPNA Chiclayo), Manuel M Izaga 807, Apartado 34, Chiclayo

Instituto Cultural Peruano Norteamerican de Cusco (ICPNA Cusco), Av Tullumayo 125, Apartado 287, Cusco

Instituto Cultural Peruano Norteamerican de Huancayo (ICPNA Huancayo), Jr Guido 754, Apartado 624, Huancayo

Instituto Cultural Peruano Norteamerican de Lima (ICPNA Lima), Jr Cusco 446, Apartado 304, Lima

Instituto Cultural Peruano Norteamerican de Region Grau-Piura (ICPNA Region Grau-Piura), Apurimac 447, Piura

Instituto Cultural Peruano Norteamerican de Trujillo (ICPNA Trujillo), Av Venezuela 125 esq Husares de Junin, Trujillo

Interaction In English, Manco Capac 649, Miraflores, Lima 18. Markham **College Lower School,** Avda. El Derby Cdra. 3/Esq. Avda El Carmen, Surco

Markham College Upper School, Augusto Angulo 291, San Antonio, Miraflores, Lima 18

Newton College, Av Ricardo Elias, Aparic, Urb Las Lagunas De La Molina, Miraflores, Lima 12

San Silvestre School, Avda. Santa Cruz 1251, Miraflores, Lima 18

Sir Alexander Fleming School, Av. America Sur 3650, Apto. 1310, Trujillo

William Shakespeare Instituto De Ingles, Avenida Dos Mayo 1105, San Isidro, Lima

Uruguay

Qualified English teachers should find work quite easily. Unqualified teachers will probably only be able to find private classes.

Most recruitment is done locally. It is quite easy to find private classes, but most work is found in bilingual schools for children.

Visas and work permits: UK passport holders do not need a visa to stay up to three months. It is impossible to obtain a work permit before you travel. Expect a wait and a trip across the border to pick up your documents.

Cost of living: The standard of living has more in common with Argentina and Chile than with its poorer neighbours.

Salaries and taxes: Schools pay around $95 a month per group, where one teacher can instruct as many as eight groups a month (giving an average income of around $700 per month). Class sizes are generally low at 3 to 8 pupils each. Taxes are at 20-24.5 per cent depending on salary. Teachers can earn more from private classes.

Accommodation: In hard currency, you will probably pay US$300-400 per month, with two months rent as a deposit.

Health insurance: Essential.

Inoculations: Hepatitis A, Polio, Typhoid.

List of schools in Uruguay
Alianza Cultural Uruguay-Estados Unidos de America, Calle Paraguay 1217, Montevideo

British Schools, Maximo Tajes esq Havre, Carrasco, Montevideo

Dickens Institute, 21 De Setiembro 3090, Cp 11300 Montevideo

English Studio Centre, Obligado 1221, Montevideo

Herwood, Avenida Harwood 6235, Montevideo

International Bilingual School, English Lighthouse Institute, Sarandi 1146, Maldonado Tel/Fax: 598 42 33 893 Email: IBSUruguay@yahoo.com Language across the curriculum – Whole language – EFL. Children 2-11/Juniors 12-17/Adults

Instituto Cultural Anglo-Uruguayo, San Jose 1426, Montevideo 11300

International House – London Institute, Av. Brasil 2846, Montevideo

St Andrews, Cavia 2791, Montevideo

St Catherine's School, Rivera 2314, Montevideo

St Patrick's College, Av J.M. Ferrari 1307, Montevideo

Woodlands, Av P Blanes Viale 6399, Montevideo

Venezuela

Venezuela's economic difficulties have levelled out but inflation remains high and is a problem in relation to wage rates. Apply directly the American Binational Centres from your own country or save money first. The British Council will take on teachers with a minimum of an RSA certificate and two years experience. There are small private schools which will take on native speakers, or those with a command of English, whether qualified or not. Such recruitment is done locally.

Visas and work permits: A lot of paperwork is involved. Teachers can job-hunt on a tourist visa, but it is no longer possible to leave the country and re-enter and have documents processed. It is possible to work on a tourist visa, but the authorities are cracking down, and it is not recommended. Work permits must be arranged by the employer.

Cost of living: Extremely high if you are paid at local rates because of inflation.

Salaries and taxes: Expect around $5 per hour, at private language schools. The British Council pays £890 a month and does adjust its rates relative to inflation.

Accommodation: Expensive. Houses are cheaper than flats. Check inflation rates before you go or try to persuade your employer to include it in the package. In Caracas a one bedroom appartment would cost approximately $600 per month, while in the rural areas a rough guide would be $300, fully furnished. The British Council and other reputable schools generally provide help in the hunt for accommodation.

Health insurance: Essential.

Inoculations: Hepatitis A, Polio, Typhoid, Malaria, Yellow Fever.

English language newspapers: The Daily Journal.

List of schools in Venezuela
Academia Jefferson, Calle T con D, Urb. Colinas de Valle Arriba, Caracas

Academia Washington, Calle C, Urb. Colinas de Valle, Arriba, Al lado de Hospital de Dios, Caracas 1060

Berlitz Escuela de Idiomas, Av. Madrid, Urb. Las Mercedes, Caracas 1060

The British Council, Torre La Noria, Piso 6, Paseo Enrique Eraso, Urb. Las Mercedes, Aptdo. 65131, Caracas 1065

The British School, 9a Transversal con, Av. Luis Roche, Urb. Altamira, Caracas

Centro Venezolano-Americano (CVA), Av Principal de las Mercedes, Frente al Automercado Cada, Caracas

Centro Venezolano-Americano, Av. Principal Jose Marti, Urb. Las Mercedes, Caracas 1060-A

Centro Venezolano Americano del Zulia (CEVAZ), Calle 63, No 3-E-60, Apartado 419, Maracaibo, Edo. Zulia

Centro Venezolano Americano de Merida (CEVAM), Prolongacion Ave 2, Esquina Calle 43 No 1-55, Apartado Postal 27, La Parroquia, Merida 5115 A

Children's World, Quinta Santa Ana, Sorocaima, Urb. La Trinidad, Caracas

Christian Day Nursery, United Christian Church, Av. La Arboleda, Urb. El Bosque, Caracas

Colegio Internacional de Carabobo, Apartado 103, Valencia

Colegio Internacional de Caracas, Urb. Las Minutas de Baruta, Apartado 62170, Caracas 1060A

English Lab SRL, Apartado Postal 4004, Carmelitas, Caracas 1101

Escuela Bella Vista, Calle 67 entre Av. 3D y 3E, Maracaibo. Edo. Zulia

Escuela Campo Alegre, Final Calle La Cinta, Urb. Las Mercedes. Apartado 60382, Caracas 1060A

Inlingua Valencia, Avenida Urdaneta, Quinta No 13, Valencia

LEAP, Quinto Blanca, Final 6ta, Transversal, Los Palos Grandes.

Madison Learning Centre, Pre-school: Quinta Amaer, Calle Soledad, El Cafetal

Madison Learning Centre, Primary-HS: Quinta Morelera, Calle Carupano and Calle El Morao, El Cafetal

The Pacific Rim

This has been a very popular destination for teachers, whether in search of holiday money in Thailand or Japanese salaries.

It should be remembered by prospective teachers that the entire Asian Pacific Rim region has suffered major economic turmoil, with financial sector upheaval in Japan and currency collapse in Korea, Thailand, Malasia and Indonesia. Hong Kong has weathered the storm but remains a nervous economy.

Though conditions are now improving, cut-backs on state spending, consumer panic and currency devaluation have accompanied steady increases in regional unemployment rates. Where the problem has been linked to panic in the international currency markets, as in Hong Kong, then the economy will remain internally strong with the local demand and the ability to pay for English language training. Where an economy has serious structural problems, with too much debt or the effects of recession as in Korea and Japan, unemployment has risen. Here private and corporate spending on language classes has been cut. In Indonesia, economic trouble has even led to food riots and looting.

Such a situation has consequences for English Language Teaching opportunities, but should be balanced against the fact that to come out of recession, firms will need educated personnel with the language of global commerce, and demand will continue.

Equally, while currencies have lost relative value to Western rates, this does not necessarily mean that spending power has dropped in the local context. Some might regard the favourable exchange rate of "hard" currencies as good, as foreigners can survive for longer while seeking work. And, with local students less able to go abroad to study English (Australian school enrolment is 60% down) the potential market in the region may well expand.

Competition for work will perhaps become greater as Australian teachers move to find the students that at one time came to them. Pay can still be relatively good and teachers can save quite easily. Expect to spend a lot of time dealing with bureaucracy and paperwork problems.

In Laos, at the moment the only option is to join an aid agency. Please note that volunteer groups cannot normally guarantee successful candidates a place in the country of their choice. At the moment, there is no English language teaching in North Korea, but the Australia Center is rumoured to be moving in.

Vietnam appears to have many potential ELT opportunities, mainly at the low paid, more casual level, typically around US$2 per hour. Qualifications are not so important as fluency in English for many private schools in Hanoi and Ho Chi Minh City. Most teachers find jobs on spec, but some advertisements do occasionally appear in the EL *Gazette* and other papers like it.

The British Council recruits some teachers, requiring experience and preferably an RSA Diploma. Yearly contracts average £11,500 - £12,000 per annum and would also provide flights, medical insurance, accommodation, baggage allowance and vaccinations. VSO also places teachers within Vietnamese institutions.

Teachers should ensure that the organisation for whom they work correctly arranges all working visas (i.e. that they see that the employer doesn't create fake job titles, such as 'appliance salesman') and should push to get accommodation included. It is illegal to work on a tourist visa, and if you are discovered by the authorities the consequences are often severe, entailing large fines or expulsion.

Australia

Australia's TESOL industry is divided into two sectors - ESL and EFL or ELICOS (English Language Intensive Courses for Overseas Students). The ESL sector is government funded and provides English language training for permanent residents from non-English speaking backgrounds. Courses are organised through the Adult Migrant Education Program and the Department of Technical and Further Education.

Government visa statistics indicate that the ELICOS sector grew by a staggering 26 per cent between 1996 and 1997. However, there was an equally dramatic fall in the number of students enrolling in schools from Asia in 1998. (Some Sydney schools down by 60 per cent.) This has been a direct result of the economic crisis in the Pacific Rim region, where 80 per cent of ELICOS students come from. Some students already in Australia have had to cut their study short due to the escalating costs.

Therefore, while ELICOS teachers can be employed on a casual, hourly basis for relief work and short periods of time, there is much less work to do. Some schools are sending teachers out to find work in Asia and 'New Russia' to promote Australian schools to potential Siberian clients.

Teachers employed for more than four and less than 40 weeks must have a sessional contract providing continuity of employment and some provision for sick leave and recreation leave.

If you have an overseas qualification and intend to apply for teaching or Director of Studies positions, it is advisable to have your qualifications formally assessed for equivalence. This can be done through the National Office of Overseas Skills Recognition, Commonwealth Department of Employment, Education and Training (Tel: 61 6 276 8111, Fax: 61 6 276 7636).

Visas and work permits: To work in Australia, you need to have resident status, a working holiday visa or a full-time overseas student visa, which allows you to work up to 20 hours per week. Permanent residents are assessed for immigration on a points system, but English language teaching does not earn any points on the assessment.

British, Irish, Canadian, Dutch and Japanese applicants who are between the ages of 18 and 26 and who do not have children, can obtain a working holiday visa. Those aged 26 to 30 years can get such visas but have to provide a fuller explanation of how they can benefit Australia. This visa is valid for 12 months and allows you to take up temporary or casual employment. This means that you will probably be restricted to working as a relief teacher in the state or private sector.

There is a strong demand for English teachers. With a diploma you have a good chance of getting a job.

Salaries and taxes: Rates for teachers working in ELICOS centres are covered by a union-negotiated pay award. Tax is around 30 per cent with residents receiving significant deductions over non-residents. Those on a working holiday visa are classed as non-residents. There are also automatic contributions to Medicare, the national health insurance scheme, totalling about 1.5 per cent of taxable income. Employees can claim tax deductions on certain expenses, including travel and gifts to approved charities.

Accommodation: Rents are higher in Sydney than elsewhere, but flats are easy to find. A room in a shared flat will cost around A$90-110 per week in Sydney, A$60-70 elsewhere.

Health insurance: Residents of the UK, New Zealand, Sweden, the Netherlands, Finland, Malta or Italy are eligible to enrol on Medicare, which covers 'immediately necessary' medical or public hospital treatment. Medicare covers visitors for the duration of their stay, except those from Italy or Malta, who are covered for a maximum of six months. To be eligible, enrol at any Medicare in Australia, making sure you have your passport with an appropriate visa and proof that you are enrolled in your own country's national health care scheme. Other nationals should take out private insurance.

Inoculations: Yellow fever, if coming from an infected area.

Schools in Australia

A G Mate Academy, Level 12, 33 Bligh Street, Sydney NSW 2000

ABC College of English, PO Box 10, Flinders Lane Post Office, Melbourne VIC 3000

ACACIA College, PO Box 14668, Melbourne City Mail Centre, Melbourne, VIC 3001

Access Language Centre, Level 7, 28-36 Foveaux Street, Surry Hill NSW 2010

Achievers International College, GPO Box 2985, Brisbane QLD 4001

Adelaide Institute of TAFE English Language Centre, GPO Box 1872, Adelaide, SA 5001

Adelaide Institute of TAFE English Language Centre, Torrens Valley Branch, GPO Box 1872, Adelaide SA 5000

Adelaide, University of South Australia, SA 5005

Alexander Language School, Level 5, 95 St George's Terrace, Perth WA 6000

Alpha Beta Colleges, PO Box A222, Sydney South NSW 2000

AMES, Elicos Centre, Myer House, 250 Elizabeth Street, Melbourne VIC 3004

Anutech Education Centre, PO Box 4, Canberra, ACT 2601

Applied Scholastics Training Centre, 44 Smith Street, Balmain NSW 2041

Aspect International Language Schools, Level 18, Tower 1, Bondi Junction Plaza, 500 Oxford St, Bondi Junction, Sydney, NSW 2022

Australia World College, PO Box 36, Katoomba NSW 2780

Australian Academy, 28 Margaret Street, Sydney NSW 2000

Australian Cambridge Language Academy, PO Box 234, Surfers Paradise QLD 4217

Australian Catholic University ELICOS Centre, 251 Mt Alexander Road, Ascot Vale, VIC 3032

Australian Catholic University QLD, ELICOS Unit, McAuley Campus, 53 Prospect Road, Mitchelton, QLD 4053

Australian Catholic University, ELICOS Unit, McKillop Campus, PO Box 968, North Sydney, NSW 2059

Australian Centre for Languages, 420 Liverpool Road, South Strathfield, NSW 2136

Australian Centre for Languages, 157 - 161 Gloucester Street, The Rocks, Sydney, NSW 2000

Australian College of English, PO Box 82, Bondi Junction, Sydney, NSW 2022

Australian College of Language, PO Box 583 D, Melbourne, VIC 3000

Australian Institute for University Studies, Shenton Avenue, Joondalup WA 6027

Australian International College, Level 12A, 3 Spring Street, Sydney NSW 2000

Australian International College of Language, AICOL, Stradbroke Plaza, 66 Marine Parade, Southport, Gold Coast, QLD 4215

Australian National University, Canberra, ACT 2601

Australian Pacific College, GPO Box 5188, Sydney NSW 2001

Australian Premiere College, PO Box 1234, Strathfield NSW 2135

Australian TESOL Training Centre, PO Box 82, Bondi Junction, NSW 2022

Avalon College, 480 Avalon Road, Lara VIC 3210

Ballarat Institute of TAFE, PO Box 668, Ballarat, VIC 3350

Ballarat, University of, PO Box 663, Ballarat, VIC 3353

Barton Institute of TAFE, Private Bag 19, Moorabbin VIC 3189

Bendigo Regional Institute of TAFE, PO Box 170, Bendigo, VIC 3550

Billy Blue English School, PO Box 728, 124 Walker Street, North Sydney, NSW 2059

Bond University English Language Institute, Bond University, Gold Coast, QLD 4229

Box Hill Institute of TAFE, 416 Elgar Road, Box Hill, Melbourne, 3128

Bridge Business College, Level 3, Imperial Arcade, 83-85 Castlereagh St, Sydney NSW 2000

Buckingham College of English, 21 Hindmarsh Square, Adelaide SA 5000

Business Institute of Victoria, PO Box 1225, South Melbourne VIC 3205

Cairns College of English, PO Box 6210, 67 Lake Street, Cairns, QLD 4870

Cairns Language Centre, 91-97 Mulgrave Road, Cairns QLD 4870

Cambridge Academy of English, PO Box 1859, Toowong Business Centre, Brisbane QLD 4066

Cambridge English Language Centre, Suite 16, Level 3, 2-4 Cross Street, Hurstville, NSW 2220, Australia

Cambridge International College, Level 3, 297 Hay Street, Perth WA 6000

Cambridge International College, GPO Box 12481, Melbourne VIC 8006

Canberra Institute of Technology, Bruce Campus, GPO Box 826, Canberra, ACT 2601

Canberra, University of, School of TESOL & International Education, PO Box 1, Belconnen, ACT 2616

Canning College, Marquis Street, Bentley WA 6102

Careers Business College, PO Box 126, Darlinghurst NSW 2010

Casey Institute of TAFE, PO Box 684, Dandenong VIC 3175

Central Queensland University Language Centre, Queensland University, Rockhampton, QLD 4702

Centre for Language Education, Gold Coast Branch, GPO Box 5547, Gold Coast Mail Centre QLD 4217

Charles College, 14 First Avenue, Canley Vale NSW 2166

Charles Sturt University, English Language Centre, Bathurst, NSW 2795

CHEC English Language Centre, Coffs Harbour Education Campus, Hogbin Drive, Coffs Harbour NSW 2547

City College, PO Box 6 Flinders Lane, Melbourne VIC 8009

Curtin University of Technology, Centre for International English, GPO Box U1987, Perth, WA 6001

Curtin University, Centre for International English, GPO Box U 1987, Perth WA 6001

Deakin University, 336 Glenferrie Road, Malvern, Victoria 3144

East Coast College of English, GPO Box 95, Level 1, 295 Ann Street, Brisbane QLD 4001

Edith Cowan University, Claremont Campus, Goldsworthy Road, Claremont, WA 6010

Edith Cowan University, 2 Bradford Street, Mt Lawley, WA 6050

Edwards English Language Centre, Locked Bag 3, PO Melville WA 6158

EF International Language Schools, Ground Floor, 5-7 Young Street, Sydney NSW 2000

ELS International Australia - Sydney Branch of ELS - Wagga Wagga, Level 3, 93 York Street, Sydney NSW 2000

ELS Language Centres, Charles Sturt University, Locked Bag 669, Wagga Wagga, NSW 2678

Embassy Language Training Centre, Sydney Campus, PO Box 126, Darlinghurst NSW 2010

Embassy Language Training Centre, Cairns Campus (Branch Brisbane Campus), Level 2, 20-32 Lake Street, Cairns QLD 4870

Embassy Language Training Centre, Gold Coast Campus, PO Box 198, Surfers Paradise QLD 4217

Embassy Language Training Centre, Brisbane Campus, GPO Box 2923, Brisbane QLD 4001

Embassy Language Training Centre Sydney, Sydney CBD Campus, Level 3, 28 Margaret Street, Sydney NSW 2000

English College of Adelaide, 4th Floor, 97 Pirie Street, Adelaide SA 5000

English Language Program (ELICOS), Carseldine Branch QUT (Branch Kelvin Grove Campus), Victoria Park Road, Kelvin Grove QLD 4059

Excelsior College, Locked Bag Q4001, QVB Post Office NSW 1230

Eynesbury College, 5-19 Franklin Street, Adelaide 5000, SA, 5000

Flinders University of South Australia, Intensive English Language Institute, GPO Box 2100, Adelaide SA 5001

GEOS Melbourne College of English, Level 1, 277 Flinders Lane, Melbourne VIC 3000

Global Skills, 19 Lemongrove Road, Perth NSW 2750

Gold Coast College of Business, PO Box 7045, Gold Coast Mail Centre, QLD 4217

Gordon Institute of TAFE, Private Bag 1, Mail Centre, Geelong, VIC 3221

Griffith University English Language Institute, PO Box 3491, Southport, QLD 4215

Griffith University, Centre for Applied Linguistics & Languages, Faculty Asian/International Studies, Griffith University English Lang. Institute, Nathan QLD 4111

Hales College, GPO Box 29, Flinders Lane Post Office, Melbourne VIC 8009

Hilton International College, PO Box 1433, Fortitude Valley 4006, Brisbane, QLD Tel: 0061 73257 1984 Fax: 0061 73257 1985 Email: enrol@hic.com.au. Contact: Glynne Hilton. ELICOS all levels. Adult migrant English Program. High School Preparation. IELTS, Cambridge exams. Holiday Programs. Homestay, Hostel, Apartment accommodation

---

Holmes College Cairns, 18 Lake Street, Cairns QLD 4870

Holmes College Sydney, 1st Floor, 580 George Street, Sydney, NSW 2000

Holmes Colleges, Gold Coast, (Branch of Holmes College Cairns), Level 2 Oasis Shopping Ctre, Victoria Ave, Broadbeach QLD 4218

Holmes English Language Centre, 185 Spring Street, Melbourne, VIC 3000

Holmesglen College of TAFE, PO Box 42, Chadstone VIC 3148

ICET (Bankstown) (Branch of ICET Davidson), Bankstown Grammar School, Georges Crescent, Georges Hall NSW 2198

ICET (Davidson), Box 1039, Mona Vale NSW 2103

ILA Perth, PO Box 300, West Perth, WA 6872

Insearch Language Centre, UTS, Level 3, 187 Thomas St, Sydney, NSW 2000

Insearch Language Centre, University of Technology, Level 2, 10 Quay Street, Haymarket, NSW 2000

Institute of Continuing & TESOL Education (ICTE), The University of Queensland, Jelico St, St Lucia, QLD 4072

International College of Queensland, PO Box 1002, Spring Hill QLD 4004

International English Centre, Edith Cowan University, Claremont Campus, Goldsworthy Road, Claremont, WA 6010

International English Centre, Churchland Campus, Edith Cowan University, Churchlands, Pearson Street, Churchlands, WA 6018

International House Queensland English Language College, Box 7368, Cairns Mail Centre, Cairns, QLD 4870

International House Queensland Teacher Training Centre, 130 McLeod Street, Cairns, QLD 4870

International House Sydney, 22 Darley Road, Manly, Sydney NSW 2095

International House Sydney, Waratah Education, PO Box 702, Manly, NSW 2095

International Language Academy, 1325 Hay St West, West Perth, WA 6005

International Pacific College, School of International Studies, GPO 2985, Brisbane, QLD 4001

Ivanhoe Grammar School, The Ridgeway, Ivanhoe, VIC 3079

James Cook University of North Queensland, English Language Centre, Townsville QLD 4811

John Paul International College, John Paul Drive, Daisy Hill, QLD 4127

Kangan Batman Institute of TAFE English Language Centre, Brimbank Campus, Private Bag 299, Somerton, VIC 3062

Kangan Batman Institute of TAFE English Language Centre, Hume Campus, Private Bag 299, Somerton, VIC 3062

Kangan Batman Institute of TAFE English Language Centre, Moreland Campus, Private Bag 299, Somerton, VIC 3062

Kent College, 60 Druitt Street, Sydney NSW 2000

Kookaburra College, 74 - 78 Wentworth Avenue, Sydney, NSW 2000

KvB Institute of Languages, 99 Mount St, North Sydney, NSW 2060

La Trobe University, Bendigo Language Centre, PO Box 199, Bendigo, VIC 3552

La Trobe University Language Centre, Kingsbury Drive, Bundoora, VIC 3083

Language Academy, The, 647 Wellington St, Perth, WA 6000

Language Studies International Brisbane, GPO Box 2956, Brisbane, QLD 4001

Lorraine Martin Queensland English Language Centre, 138 Albert St, Brisbane, QLD 4000

Macarthur College of English, PO Box 133, Macarthur Square, NSW 2560

Macarthur English Language Centre, University of Western Sydney, PO Box 555, Campbelltown, NSW 2560

Macleay College, PO Box 433, Paddington, NSW 2060

Macquarie University (NCELTR), **National Centre for English Language Teaching & Research**, School of English & Linguistics, Macquarie University, Sydney, NSW 2109

Maewill English College, Unit 17b, 818 Pittwater Road, Dee Why, NSW 2099

Magill English Language College, PO Box 979, Gosford NSW 2250

Melbourne Language Centre, Carlton, 252 Lygon Street, Carlton, VIC 3053

Melbourne University of, Horwood Language Centre, John Medly Bldg, Grattan Street, Parkville

Melbourne, University of, Parkville, VIC 3052

Metropolitan English College, Level 1, Cnr Church & Macquarie Sts, Parramatta, NSW 2150

Metropolitan English College, PO Box 1136, Queen Victoria Building, Sydney NSW 1230

Metropolitan TAFE, Br of Central Metropolitan, 41 South Terrace Freemantle WA 6160

Milner International College of English, 379 Hay Street, Perth, WA 6000

Milton Language Centre, Level 1, 84 Christie St, St Leonards, Sydney, NSW 2065

Monash University English Language Centre, Normanby House, 100 Normanby Road, Clayton VIC 3168

Murdoch University International Language Centre, South Street, Murdoch, WA 6150

National English Academy, Level 6, 1 Newland Street, Bondi Junction, Sydney, NSW 2022

New England, University of, Language Training Centre, Newling Annexe, Armidale, NSW 2351

New South Wales International College, Level 3, 74 - 78 Wentworth Avenue, Sydney, NSW 2000

New South Wales, University of, Institute of Languages, NSW 2052

North Point Institute of TAFE Language Training Centre, PO Box 2826, Brisbane, QLD 4001

Northern Melbourne Institute of TAFE, 20 Otter Street, Collingwood, VIC 3066

Northern Metropolitan College of TAFE, 20 Otter Street, Collingwood VIC 3066

Northern Territory University, ELICOS Centre, Darwin NT 0909

Notre Dame, University of, PO Box 1225 Fremantle, WA 6160

NSW English College, PO Box 43, Broadway, NSW 2007

Pacific College of English, PO Box 782, Fortitude Valley, Brisbane, QLD 4006

Perth Commercial College, 6 Floor, 160 St Georges Terrace, Perth WA 6000

Phoenix English Language Academy, PO Box 256, Leederville, WA 6007

Phoenix English Language Academy, 223 Vincent St, North Perth, 6006 Perth

Premier Language College, PO Box 5421, Chatswood NSW 2057

Queensland College of English, PO Box 222, Roma Street, Brisbane, QLD 4003

Queensland College of English, Gold Coast Campus, PO Box 567, Surfers Paradise, QLD 4217

Queensland International Business Academy, PO Box 609, Coolangatta, QLD 4225

Queensland International College, Shop 20, Caloundra Central, 11 Bulcock St, Caloundra, QLD 4551

Queensland University of Technology, International Education Program, Locked Bag 2, Red Hill, QLD 4059

Queensland, University of, TESOL Programs, St Lucia QLD 4072

Regent College, 55 Regent Street, Chippendale NSW 2008

RMIT Training Pty Ltd, Centre for English Language Learning, PO Box 12058, A'Beckett St, Melbourne, VIC 8006

RUSSO Institute of Technology, PO Box 2304, Brisbane, QLD 4001

SA Adelaide Language Centre, 48-60 Angas Street, Adelaide, SA 5000

Shafston House International College, 46 Thorn St, Kangaroo Point, QLD 4169

SIS International College, PO Box 735, Bondi Junction, NSW 2022

Skywell College, Level 1, 28 Burwood Road, Burwood, NSW 2134

South Australia, University of, Centre for Applied Linguistics, GPO Box 2471, Adelaide SA 5001

South Australia, University of, CALUSA, Centre for Applied Linguistics, GPO Box 2471, Adelaide, SA 5001

South Australian College of English, 254 North Terrace, Adelaide, SA 5000

Southbank Institute of TAFE, Centre for Language Education, 14 Glenelg Street, South Brisbane QLD 4101

Southern Cross University, PO Box 157, Lismore, NSW 2480

Southern Queensland, University of, ELICOS Centre, Dept of Higher Education Studies, Post Office Darling Heights, Toowoomba QLD 4350

Speciality Language Centre, PO Box A186 Sydney South, NSW 2000

Spelt English College, PO Box 40, Roma Street, Brisbane, QLD 4003

SSTC Perth International College, First Floor, 14-16 Victoria Avenue, Perth WA 6000

St Joseph's College, Nudgee **International Educational Centre**, PO Box 130, Virginia, QLD 4014

St Mark's International College, PO Box 127, Bondi Junction, NSW 2022

St Mark's International College, 375 Stirling Street, Perth, WA 6000

St Paul's International School, 4 Strathpine Road, Bald Hills, QLD 4036

Stella Maris College, 52 Eurobin Road, Manly, NSW 2095

Stott's College of English, Nicholas Building, 37 Swanston Street, Melbourne VIC 3000

Sunshine Coast English College, PO Box 1110, Noosa Heads, QLD 4567

Swan College, Swan College", 2-8 Francis St, Perth, WA 6000

Swinburne English Language Centre, Post Office Box 218, Hawthorn VIC 3122

Swinburne University of Technology, English Language Centre, PO Box 218, Hawthorn, VIC 3122

Sydney College of English, Mail bag 10, PO Broadway, Sydney, NSW 2007

Sydney English Language Centre, PO Box 1900, Bondi Junction, NSW 2022

Sydney Institute of Technology English Centre - SIT English Centre, Level 1, 770 George Street, Sydney, NSW 2000

Sydney International College of English, GPO Box 1711, Sydney, NSW 2000

Sydney Oxford English Institute, 1st Floor, 355 Sussex St, Sydney, NSW 2000

Sydney, University of, Centre for English Teaching, Madsen Building, University of Sydney NSW 2006

Sydney, University of, Ctr for English Teaching, Mallett Street Campus MO2, 88 Mallett Street, Camperdown NSW 2006

TAFE English Language Centre Northern Sydney, Northern Sydney, 213 Pacific Highway, Gore Hill, NSW 2065

TAFE International Education Centre, St George College of TAFE, Cnr Princes Hwy & President Ave, Kogarah, NSW 2217

TAFE International Western Australia, English Language Ctr, Central Metropolitan Coll, Level 7, 190 St Georges Terrace, Perth WA 6000

TAFE Queensland, Centre for Language Education, Locked Mail Bag 2234, GPO, Brisbane, QLD 4001

Tasmania, University of, English Language Centre, P O Box 1214, Launceston, Tasmania 7250

TLCC English Language College, Ground Floor, 97 Pacific Highway, North Sydney NSW 2060

Tuart College, Banksia St, Tuart Hill, WA 6060

Universal English College, Level 12, 222 Pitt Street, Sydney, NSW 2000

University Language Centre, Cairns, 55 - 65 Greenslopes St, Edgehill, Cairns QLD 4870

University of Melbourne's English Language Centre at Hawthorn, 442 Auburn Road, Hawthorn 3122 VIC

University of Newcastle Language Centre, University Drive, Callaghan NSW 2308

University of Technology, P O Box 123, Broadway, NSW 2007

Uniworld English College, PO Box A2278, Sydney South, NSW 1235

Victoria College, Level 4, 232 Flinders Lane, Melbourne, VIC 3000

Victoria University of Technology, PO Box 14428, MMC Melbourne, VIC 3000

Victorian Business College, PO Bx 40, Flinders Lane Post Office, Melbourne, VIC 3001

Vista English Language Centre, PO Box 725N, North Cairns, QLD 4870

Waratah Education Centre, 22 Darley Road, Manly NSW 2095

Wesley Institute for Ministry & the Arts, PO Box 497, Drummoyne, NSW 2047

Western Australia, University of, Centre for English Language Teaching, Graduate School of Education, Nedlands, WA 6907

Western Australian International College, Shenton Ave, Joondalup, WA 6027

Western College, PO Box 251, Middle Brighton, VIC 3186

Western Institute of TAFE, Dubbo Campus, PO Box 787, Dubbo, NSW 2830

Western Institute of TAFE, Wellington Campus, PO Box 92, Wellington, NSW 2820

Western Metropolitan College of TAFE, PO Box 197, Footscray, VIC 3011

Western Sydney, University of, Nepean Languages Centre, Hawkesbury Road, Westmead, NSW 2145

Western Sydney, University of, Hawksbury, Bourke St, Richmond, NSW 2753

Wide Bay Institute of TAFE Language Centre, Urraween Road, Pialba, QLD 4655

Wilcox English College, PO Box 535, Broadway NSW 2007

Wollongong International College, Locked Bag 8812, South Coast Mail Centre, NSW 2521

Wollongong, University of, Centre for Language Education, Northfields Ave, Wollongong, NSW 2522

World English, Level 2, 100 Murray St, Perth, WA 6000

New Zealand

Demand for English learning in New Zealand varies seasonally, with the peak demand during the Japanese and Thai holiday periods, between February and May and between July and October (demand is low in January/February and in July). It is only possible to find work if you are a qualified native speaker or completely fluent.

There are both EFL and ESL opportunities. In addition to General English, there is demand for specialist areas of English teaching, especially in EAP and High School preparation. There is the possibility of getting private classes also, but opportunities are limited. Auckland and Christchurch tend to be the best places to look for work.

Visas and work permits: Australians do not need any documentation to work in New Zealand. People of other nationalities can get a working holiday visa which lasts for nine months. For UK citizens you can be up to 30 years old, for other nationalities this varies. The visa can last for twelve months and has restrictions, including proof of funds to cover your stay in New Zealand. There are only limited numbers of visas given out each year. You should apply to your local New Zealand embassy.

Work permits for older non-Australians are difficult to obtain since the employer has to prove that no New Zealander can do the job. There are temporary work permits which can be obtained by teachers with exceptional qualifications or experience. It is illegal to work on a tourist visa.

Cost of living: Quite cheap, but consumer durables are expensive.

Salaries and taxes: Teachers earn between NZ$25,000 and $40,000 per annum on salary, and between NZ$22 and $32 per hour in the private sector. The tax rate is around 23 per cent and 33% on higher salaries.

Accommodation: Schools do not tend to help teachers find accommodation. However, it should not be too difficult to find accommodation for yourself. A room in a shared flat costs NZ$60-110 per week, while a one-bedroom flat costs NZ$100. NZ$200-$300 per week is

SECTION 3 International Job Prospects

the cost of a full apartment.. Two weeks' rent is generally payable in advance as a bond.

Health insurance: All visitors need private health insurance. An accident compensation levy is paid by employees and employer.

Schools in New Zealand

ABC College of English, PO Box 755, Queenstown

Achievement Institute of Language Ltd, PO Box 25185, Christchurch

Active English Language Academy, PO Box 37102, Parnell, Auckland

Anglo Pacific Languages Ltd, PO Box 105347, Auckland

Aoraki Polytechnic, Private Bag 902, Timaru

Aspiring Language Institute, PO Box 363161 Auckland

Auckland College of Education, P O Box 92601, Auckland

Auckland English Academy, PO Box 11241, Ellerslie, Auckland

Auckland Institute of Studies, PO Box 2995, Auckland

Auckland Institute of Technology, Private Bag 92-006, Auckland 1020

Auckland Language Centre, PO Box 105035, Auckland

Auckland, University of, Private Bag 92019, Auckland

Canterbury Language College, PO Box 4425, Christchurch

Capital Language Academy, PO Box 1100, Wellington

Central Institute of Technology, Private Bag, Wellington Mail Centre, Wellington

Christchurch College of English, PO Box 31212, Christchurch

Christchurch Polytechnic International School of English, 34 Allen St, P O Box 22095, Christchurch

CITEC English Language Centre, PO Box 40-740, Upper Hutt

Coromandel Outdoor Language Center, PO Box 5, Whitianga

Crown English Language Academy, PO Box 1094, Auckland

Dominion English School (Auck.), PO Box 4217, Auckland

Dominion English School (Christ.), PO Box 3908, Christchurch

Dunedin English Language School, PO Box 5707, Dunedin

Dynaspeak, PO Box 106052, Commercial Union House 2nd Floor, 12-14 O'Connell Street, Downtown, Auckland

Eastern Institute of Technology, Private Bag 1201, Taradale, Hawke's Bay

English Language College Ltd, PO Box 28085, Christchurch

Garden City English School, PO Box 2851, Christchurch

Hutt Valley Polytechnic, Private Bag 39803, Te Puni Mail Centre, Petone

---

ILA South Pacific Ltd, PO Box 25-170, 21 Kilmore Street, Christchurch 1 Tel: 00 64 3379 5452 Fax: 00 64 3379 5373 Email: ilachch@ila.co.nz Website: www.ila.co.nz Contact: Mo Killip. Over 20 courses including General English, exam preparation, work experience, vocational training, CELTA centre and Cambridge EFL exam centre

---

inlingua Tauranga, 48 Vine Avenue, Maungatapu

International Academy of Languages, PO Box 10222 Dominion Rd, 26 Wyndham Street, Auckland

International Language Academy, P O Box 25170, Christchurch

International Pacific College, Private Bag 11021, Palmerston North

Key Education, PO Box 105365, Auckland

Kiwi English Academy Ltd, PO Box 9912, Newmarket, Auckland

Language Institute University of Waikato, Private Bag 3105, Hamilton

Language School Aoteara Ltd, PO Box 1170, Taupo

Language Studies International, 10-12 Scotia Place, Auckland

Languages International, PO Box 5293, Auckland

Link Institute of Education, PO Box 36050, Christchurch

Manawatu Polytechnic, Private Bag Palmerston North

Manukau Institute of Technology, Private Bag 94006, Manukau

Massey University, Palmerston North

Modern Age English Language School, PO Box 2137, Tauranga

Mount Maunganui Language Centre, PO Box 5214, Mt Maunganui

Nelson Polytechnic, Private Bag 19, Nelson

New Horizon Language Academy, PO Box 7113 The Mission, Church Road, Greenmeadows, Taradale Napier

New Zealand Education International, PO Box 10500, Wellington

New Zealand English Academy, PO Box 6646, Wellesley Street, Auckland

New Zealand Language Institute, PO Box 2957, Shortland Street, Level 5 125 Albert Street, Auckland

Oceania International College, Private Bag 93239, Parnell, Auckland

Otago Language Centre, PO Box 6061, Dunedin

Palmerston North College of Education, Private Bag 11035, Palmerston North

Queenstown Language School Ltd, PO Box 911 (24 Camp Street), Queenstown

Rotorua English Language Academy, PO Box 2079, Rotorua

Seafield School of English, PO Box 18 516, Christchurch

Shore English School of Language, 2nd Floor NZ Post Bldg, 51 Hurstmere Rd, Takapuna, PO Box 33614, Auckland

Southern Cross Language Institute, 55 Papanui Road, Christchurch

Southern English Schools, PO Box 1300 (69 Worcester Boulevard), Christchurch

Southern Lakes English College, PO Box 405, Queenstown

Sterling Language Foundation, PO Box 105003, Auckland

Supreme English School, Box 2967, Christchurch

Tairawhiti Polytechnic, PO Box 640 290-292, Palmerston Road, Gisborne Tel: 0064 6 8688988 Fax: 0064 6 8672186 Email: Johnc@Tairawhiti.ac.nz Website: www.international-english.ac.nz Contact: John Chemis. Small classes, personalised support, preparation for academic courses, for direct entry. Free email, internet, bicycle. Create your own programme

---

Taranaki Polytechnic, Private Bag 2030, New Plymouth, NZ 4620

Taupo Language & Outdoor Education Centre, PO Box 1234, Taupo

Unique New Zealand Education Centre, PO Box 35212, Browns Bay, Auckland

UNITEC Institute of Technology, Private Bag 92 025, Auckland

University of Canterbury English Language Centre, Private Bag 4800, Christchurch

University of Waikato Language Institute, Private Bag 3105, Hamilton

Victoria University of Wellington, P O Box 600, Wellington

Waikato Polytechnic, Private Bag 3036, Hamilton

Wairarapa Community Polytechnic, PO Box 698, Masterton

Wakatu English Language Centre, PO Box 1217, Nelson

Wanganui Regional Community Polytechnic, Private Bag 3020, Wanganui

Wellington College of Languages, Private Bag 756, Wellington

Wellington Polytechnic, Private Box 756, Wellington

Whitireia Community Polytechnic, Wineera Drive, Private Bag 50910, Porirua City, Wellington

Worldwide School of English, PO Box 1802, Auckland

Brunei

In order to work in this oil-rich, Muslim sultanate in South-East Asia, teachers must have a degree, a certificate or diploma and two years' teaching experience. It is not difficult for teachers who have established themselves in state-sector teaching in Brunei to move into the private sector. Since there is very little public transport and fuel is cheap, a driving licence is essential. Schools usually offer a car loan scheme. CfBT and the Ministry of Education are major recruiters for the country.

Visas and work permits: The Brunei High Commission will supply a visa on proof of a job offer, so do your job hunting before leaving home. Your passport is stamped on arrival for a period at the discretion of the immigration officer. If you are working in the private sector (FEM and Kemuda), your employer must apply for a labour licence once in the country, followed by a work permit.

Cost of living: Similar to Northern Europe, but has fallen..

Salaries and taxes: Teachers must be highly qualified (QTS). Salaries vary enormously in the state sector: it is obviously far less profitable to teach primary school children than post-graduate degree students. Teachers will usually earn B$2,500-7,000 per month. Normally there is no personal income tax.

Accommodation: Apartments are usually provided or subsidised as part of a job package. Because a three-month deposit is often required when renting a flat, make sure that provision is made in your contract. Otherwise, expect to pay about B$1,500 rent per month.

Health insurance: Advisable, but sometimes offered by employers. Have medical and dental check-ups before you go.

Inoculations: Hepatitis A, Polio, Typhoid, Yellow Fever (if coming from an infected country).

English language newspapers: Borneo Bulletin.

Important cultural differences: There is no alcohol in Brunei and split weekends (Friday and Sunday rather than Saturday and Sunday) make travel awkward. Dress modestly.

Other useful information: Shoes are difficult to buy in larger sizes.

Cambodia

English has been in huge demand in Cambodia since the United Nations moved in to restore order after two decades of unrest. With the withdrawal of the United Nations in 1994, the language is still as popular, especially for business, but there is still a certain amount of instability in the country as a result of Khmer Rouge activities.

Teachers can find casual work quite readily but most contracted positions tend to come through aid agencies such as VSO. These are at secondary-school level or involve in-service teacher training and volunteers need to have either a BA degree with a TEFL certificate or an education degree or certificate.

Visas and work permits: Visas will be arranged by the employer if you have a full-time contract. You can also work on a business visa which can be arranged upon arrival at the airport. Working on a tourist visa is strictly sanctioned.

Cost of living: Cheap.

Salaries and taxes: The minimum pay is about US$7 per hour for unqualified teachers. A certificate can earn you more than three times that amount - the usual range being US$12-25 per hour.

Accommodation: The rates have risen dramatically since the United Nations stopped running the country. Rates range from US$400 for a two-bedroomed house or flat.

Health insurance: Essential. Make sure your policy covers evacuation from the country in case of serious illness.

Inoculations: Hepatitis A, Polio, Typhoid, Malaria, Yellow Fever (if coming from an infected area).

Other useful information: There is now a coalition government in place but there are still travel restrictions in parts of the country.

China

English is compulsory in schools for children from the age of nine and it is estimated that more than 200 million are currently learning the language. This means that there are plenty of positions. English teachers from abroad are split into Foreign Teachers and Foreign Experts. The former are normally under 25 and only need a degree, while the latter are experienced teachers with a relevant MA (TESOL, TEFL, Applied Linguistics, etc).

Applications should be made well in advance to voluntary/educational organisations, the Chinese embassy in your country or directly to the institutions in China.

Unqualified teachers should find it quite easy to find work, as the emphasis is on a degree rather than TEFL qualification. There is a small, but growing number of private language schools which recruit from overseas (for details, watch the Guardian Education supplement). It is possible to find fee-paying jobs in the international schools, but not in state-run primary or secondary schools. You can also find teaching work in the commercial sector as there is a large demand for Business English and some companies have in-house English teaching programmes. These often recruit from the ex-pat community or overseas.

The British Council and others employ freelance teachers, and the VSO recruit heavily those seeking teaching experience rather than income alone.

Visas and work permits: In the perfect situation, teachers have their job sorted out whilst their employer notifies the Bureau of Foreign Experts. They in turn send an invitation letter qualifying them for a work visa. Often, though, teachers enter the country on a visitor's visa and the institution processes the paperwork before the tourist visa expires. Foreign Experts require an invitation to work in China before entry and must obtain a visa prior to arrival. Hong Kong and Tibet still count as outside for this purpose.

Cost of living: Cheap compared to the West. Depends on your lifestyle.

Salaries and taxes: The usual salary range is Y1000-Y1,200 per month for a Foreign Teacher. For a Foreign Expert, it is between Y2,500 and Y4,000, with airfares and some baggage costs included. A Foreign Teacher will not normally receive any relocation allowance. No tax is paid.

Accommodation: Should be provided by the employer. Make sure it is, because it can be extremely difficult to find otherwise. If you are employed at a university, it is cheaper.

Health insurance: Essential.

Inoculations: Hepatitis A, Malaria (in some areas), Polio, Tetanus, Typhoid, Yellow Fever (if coming from an infected area).

English language newspapers: China Daily, Shanghai Daily Star.

Other useful information: Salaries may be higher in China's rather polluted cities, and class sizes can be anything up to 100 or more.

List of employers in China
Adult Education Training Dept, Beijing Normal University, 19 Xinjiekouwai, Haidian District, Beijing
Beijing 21 Century American English Training Centre, 4th Floor, China Daily Bldg, 15 East Huixing St, Chaoyang District, Beijing
Beijing Business Management Training Centre, English Dept, Beijing

Foreign Studies Uni, Beijing
Beijing Caledonian International Language School, P O Box 2855, International School Bldg, Xisanqi West, Haidian District, Beijing
Beijing Delter Business English Training Centre, 44 Gaoliangxie St, North Xiaguan, Xizhimen, Beijing
Beijing Epoch-making Senior Talents Training School, Chaoyangmen Primary School, 124 Chaoyangmennei St, 2nd Ringroad, Beijing
Beijing Huijia Private School, East Baifuqiao, Changping County, Beijing
Beijing Jinghua School, Beijing
Beijing Overseas Applied Business Language School, Branch College of Dongchen Education College, 9 Donggong St, East Gulou St, Dongchen District, Beijing
Beijing Self-access University, Di'anmen Middle School, 127 Eastern Di'anmen St, Dongchen District, Beijing
Beijing Sunshine School, Beijing
Beijing USA College of English, No 3 Yuhuili, Xiaoying, Anwai Chaoyang District, Beijing 100101
Beijing Yingdi Economic and Trade College, Beijing
Boying School, Haidian District, Beijing
British Council, c/o British Embassy, Fourth Floor, Landmark Building, 8 North Dongsanhuan Road, Chaoyang District, Beijing 100006
CDI Career Development Institute, 110 Bloor Street West, Suite 202, Toronto, Ontario M5S 2W7, Canada
Changchun Kelian Foreign Languages Training Centre, 80 Tongzhi St, Changchun, Hilin (130021)
China Teaching Program, Western Washington University, Old Main 530A, Bellinham, WA 98225-9047, USA
Chinese Education Association for International Exchange, 37 Damucang Hutong, Beijing
CIBT School of Business, 6th floor, the Main Bldg, Beijing Computer College, 56 Xi Sanhuan Beilu, Beijing 10004
Colorado China Council, 4556 Apple Way, Boulder, CO 80301, USA
Education & Training Centre of the WPCP, The Working People's Cultural Palace, Beijing
EFT International Standard Degree 'Peiqing School, Xinzhonglie Primary

School, opposite the Zhonglie, Stop of the North Gate of the Worker's Stadium, Beijing
Gaode Specialised Foreign Languages School, No 1 Primary School, Fuxingmenwai, Beijing
Huang Po Foreign Languages School, 17 Chunminli Chunyuan Compound, West Renmin Rd, Kunming 650118
Huaqiang School, No 2 Primary School of Xizhimennei, Beijing
Jingdong Night School of 2nd Foreign Language Inst, Rm 017, Fl M, Office Bldg of Baoli Mansion, Beijing
Language Link, China, Recruitment Section, 21 Harrington Road, South Kensington, London, UK, SW7 3EU
Longquan School, East of Yuquanlu Supermarket, Beijing
Modern International Languages Inst, 4th fl, Training Centre Bldg of Beijing, Bureau of Labour, Xizhimen, Beijing
Mozhuang Foreign Languages School, No 33 Middle School, Muxidi, Beijing
New Bridge International Languages Training Inst, Beijing
New China Education Foundation, 1587 Montalban Drive, San Jose, CA 95120, USA
Qunxing School, Yonghegong Primary School, Beijing
Sanyu International Language Inst, Beijing Chemical Industry University, Beijing
Sheng'en Vocational School, 4th fl, Central Primary School, Shuangyushu, Haidian District, Beijing
Shili School, Rm 147, West Hall, Shuangyushu Youth Apartment, Haidian District, Beijing
Teach In China Programme, Council on International Educational Exchange, 52 Poland St, London W1V 4JQ, UK.
Teaching & Training Centre of Capital University, 68 Neixiange, Guang'anmennei, Xuanwy District, Beijing
The Japanese Spec Lang School of Xicheng District, No 28 Middle School, Beijing
Tiancai Foreign Languages School, No 2 Primary School, Xinyuanli, Zhongwaiyundunhaopang (nr Huadu Hotel), Beijing
Training Section of Chaoyang Workers' University, Beijing

Xiangbo School, Ganyu Hutong, Wangfujin, Beijing

Xiangyun Teaching & Training Centre, Xisi Middle School 25 Dahongluochang, Xicheng District, Beijing

Xindongfang School, 50 metres north of the crossroads, Zhongguancun, Haidian District, Beijing

Xinghua University of Capital Economic & Trade, Beijing

Yicheng School of No 96 Middle School, Behind Caishichang, Chongwenmen, Beijing

Yiwen Cultural School, Junyi Private Middle School, Dingfu Zhuang, Chaoyang District, Beijing

Yiquing School, Yuetan Primary School, Xicheng District, Beijing

Yunnan Institute of the Nationalities, Foreign Affairs Office, Kunming 650031, Yunnan, China

We would like to thank Ben Harris of the British Council for his help in compiling this list.

Hong Kong

Hong Hong reverted to Chinese control in June 1997, as a Special Administrative Region in a 'One Country, Two Systems' arrangement. As a continuing economic powerhouse for the region, the need for English language skills remains, with approximately 10,000 teachers for 1 million learners. English, however, has had to sit alongside the Cantonese speaker's need to meet the Mandarin requirements from the motherland.

There are opportunities to teach in English-language schools, English-medium schools and tertiary institutions, initially on 1 and 2 year contracts. While some schools specialising in English as a Foreign Language will employ recent graduates, many do require experienced teachers with diplomas or advanced ELT qualifications. English-medium schools require teachers with specific subject skills as well as English for primary and secondary levels. At the tertiary level, language instructors and lecturers frequently require an MA in Applied Linguistics.

Ensure you have original certificates and qualifications, as most employers do not accept photocopies. The corporate sector does have some demand for in-house

teaching, recruiting locally and overseas. If individuals have work permits, there are good opportunites for freelance teachers, even those with no qualification or experience in 'English Clubs'. Information on them is passed by word of mouth in the travellers hostels on Nathan Road. The Education Department does recruit qualified teachers for the state sector from overseas and plans to continue to expand its 'Expatriate English Teacher Scheme.

Under the new regime and linked to a growing awareness of the need for trained language teachers, will be the difficulty of finding teaching work without a TEFL qualification.

The British Council in Hong Kong is the biggest RSA Certificate and Diploma training centre in Asia with courses running throughout the year. If you plan to study for the Diploma in Hong Kong, you need to apply early in April as competition for places is fierce.

As a teacher, you should be prepared for very short Christmas and Easter breaks. The main holiday is Chinese New Year, usually in February. Many language schools structure the academic year around this with big intakes in September and March. The British Council is a major employer of part-time certificated teachers, running two large summer programmes, and recruits some teachers internationally from January. English-medium schools often recruit in May-June for a September start.

Visas and work permits: Before going to Hong Kong, all foreigners including UK nationals need sponsorship from an employer who can guarantee them full-time work. (In technical terms 'full-time' means a guaranteed 15 hours per week.) They then need to apply to the HK immigration department for work permits covering the duration of the placement. Employers will often help to sort out work papers. Processing a visa extension can take 6-8 weeks. Without a visa UK nationals can travel for up to six months, but must apply for a work permit from outside the territory. Since 1997 it has been strictly illegal to look for work as a tourist. For full details contact the Immigration Department:

Immigration Tower, 7 Gloucester Road, Wanchai, HK.

Cost of living: Higher than most of Europe for almost everything except transport. Eating out and drinking can be very expensive, but there are lots of bargains, particularly if you like the various kinds of Chinese cuisine.

Salaries and taxes: In the private sector pay is from HK$20,000 to HK$45,000 per month. Freelance teachers can earn between HK$200 and HK$600 per hour. Tertiary colleges pay around HK$350-400. In-company work can be very lucrative but is difficult to build up without connections. Tax rates vary according to salary up to a maximum of 15%. All contracted teaching staff can expect to pay the maximum rate.

Accommodation: By far the biggest cost in Hong Hong, though prices have slumped for the last two years. Many teachers live on the out-lying islands of Lamma, Lantau and Cheung Chau where accommodation is cheaper but this does mean up to an hour commuting by ferry to Hong Kong island. Small but comfortable flats range from HK$5000 per month on the out-lying islands to around HK$8,000-14000 on HK island. Public transport is reasonably cheap and very efficient.

Health insurance: Health insurance is important as medical treatment is very expensive. Good employers provide this for full-time employees. Needless to say few private schools do. Have a thorough dental check up and get your inoculations before coming.

Inoculations: Hepatitis A, Polio and Typhoid.

English language newspapers: South China Morning Post, Hong Kong Standard, China Daily - HK edition, HK Magazine (weekly).

Other useful information: Those men who take UK size ten (44 European) or above in shoes should stock up before coming, as big sizes in shoes and clothes are difficult to find. Prepare yourself for culture shock - work in Hong Kong is frenetic! Even so, it's a great place to live and work when you get settled and most teachers end up spending far longer there than they intended. There is a short, cool winter, with some very cold

snaps, a foggy, damp spring, a hot, sticky summer with some typhoons and a dry, sunny autumn. The British Council web site will increasingly hold useful up-to-date information:
http://www.britcoun.org.hk

List of schools in Hong Kong
American International School, 125 Waterloo Rd, Kowloon Tong, Hong Kong
Berlitz, 1 Pacific Place, Central
British Council English Language Centre, 3 Supreme Court Rd, Admiralty, Hong Kong
The Centre for Professional and Business English, 7th Floor, Core B, Hong Kong Polytechnic University, T.S.T
City University of Hong Kong, Personnel Office 4/F Cheng Yick-Shi Bldg, 83 Tat Chee Avenue, Kowloon
Education Dept, Wu Chung House, 213 Queen's Road East, Wanchai
English Language Club, Ka Nin Wah Commercial Building, Hennessy Road
English Schools Foundation, 43B Stubbs Rd, Hong Kong
Expatriate English Teacher Scheme, Hong Kong Education Dept, 13/F Wu Chung House, 213 Queen's Road East, Wanchai
First Class Language Centre, 22a Bank Tower, 351-353 King's Road, North Point
German Swiss International School, 11 Guildford Rd, The Peak, Hong Kong
Hong Kong Association for Applied Linguistics, English Dept, Lingnan College, Fu Tei, Tuen Mun, New Territories
Hong Kong Baptist University, Language Centre 224, Waterloo Road, Kowloon
Hong Kong English Club, Ground floor, 41 Carnarvon Road, Tsimshatsui, Kowloon
HK Institute of Languages, Rm 501 30-32 D'Aguilar St, Central
Hong Kong Polytechnic University, Centre for Professional and Business English, Rm BC721, 7/F Block B, Hung Hom, Kowloon
Hong Kong Polytechnic University, Dept of English, Hung Hom, Kowloon
Island International High School, 20 Borrett Road, Hong Kong.
Open University of Hong Kong, 30 Good Shepherd St, Ho Man Tin, Kowloon
Pasona Education, 2/F One Hysan Ave, Causeway Bay

Secondary Schools English Teachers Assoc (SSETA), Flat H, 5/F Blk 2, Tai Wo Centre, Tai Po, New Territories
University of Hong Kong, The English Centre, 7/F K K Leung Bldg, Pokfulam Rd, Hong Kong
Venture Living Languages Ltd, 1A 163 Hennessy Road, Hong Kong
We would like to thank Nic Humphries, The British Council, English Language Centre, for help in compiling this information.

Indonesia

Indonesia has an established oil industry and over 200 million people. To participate in the international business environment the learning of English has increased. However as in much of South East Asia, currency values have slumped from late 1997-98 with a massive impact on the local economy and the foreign workers in it. From Christmas 1997 to February 1998 the value of the rupiah decreased by 80%. There has been significant social unrest, especially against the wealthy Chinese minority and government crackdown on pro-democracy demonstrators. President Suharto has stepped down and the province of East Timor has voted for independence, though at the time of going to press, this has still to be ratified by the Indonesian government. The situation economically in Indonesia is uncertain. All advice on teaching should be seen in this light.

Certificated teachers have never had trouble securing a contract in Jakarta or Bandung from overseas and, with an abundance of language schools, qualified teachers were able to find work on spec. There are opportunities in small towns as well as major cities but, as with anywhere off the beaten track, schools are likely to be under equipped and lacking up-to-date materials.

Visas and work permits: To be able to work in Indonesia you need to have a sponsor in Indonesia to arrange your work permit. A tourist visa allows you to stay for two months, which should be long enough to find a job. Working on a tourist visa is strictly prohibited and those who are caught are deported and blacklisted from future entry into the country. Teachers going to Indonesia with the intention of finding a job, sometimes

avoid awkward questions by getting an onward ticket, most conveniently to Singapore. This has enabled them to find a job before leaving the country to apply for a work permit.

For a work visa to be issued, teachers must present an employer's sponsorship letter to the Indonesian consulate in your country or, if you arrived on a tourist visa, to the consulate in Singapore.

Cost of living: Very cheap. Teachers tend to eat out most nights and still save money.

Salaries and taxes: Salaries for full-time teachers can exceed $960 per month in the cities. Tax is deducted at about 10 per cent.

Accommodation: Apartments tend to be reasonably priced in Bandung, more expensive in Jakarta. A whole year's rent is often payable in advance but schools tend to offer loans to help out if accommodation is not supplied in the contract.

Health insurance: Advisable.

Inoculations: Hepatitis A, Polio, Typhoid, Malaria, Yellow Fever (if coming from an infected area).

English language newspapers: Indonesian Times, Indonesian Observer, Jakarta Post.

List of schools in Indonesia
American English Language Training (AELT), Jalan R.S. Fatmawati 42a, Keb Baru, Jakarta Selatan 12430
The British Institute (TBI), Plaza Setiabudi 2, Jalan HR Rasuna Said, Jakarta 12920
Centre for Language Training (CLT), Soegijapranata Catholic University, Jl. Menteri Supeno 35, Semarang 50241
EF English Fast, Wisma Tamara Lt 4, Suite 402, Jl Jend Surdiman Kav 24, Jakarta 12920
English Education Centre (EEC), Jalan Let. Jend S.Parman 68, Slipi, Jakarta 11410
Executive English Programs (EEP), Jalan Wijaya VIII 4, Kebayoran Baru, Jakarta Selatan 12160
ELS International, Jalan Tanjung Karang 7 c-d, Jakarta Pusat
English Language Training International (ELTI), Complex Wijaya Grand Centre, Blok F 84A & B, Jalan Wijaya II, Jakarta Selatan 12160

Indonesia-Australia Language Foundation (IALF), Wisma Budi, Suite 503, Jalan HR Rasuna Said Kav c-6, Kuningan, Jakarta 12940 Tel: 62 (0) 21 521 3350 Fax: 62 (0) 21 521 3349 Email: ialf@ialf.edu Website: http://www.ialf.edu Branches in Surabaya and Bali. EAP, IELTS Preparation, Business English. The IALF is the IELTS testing centre for all Australia/NZ bound candidates.

inlingua Jakarta, Sekolah BHK, Jl Rahayu No 22, Daan Mogot, Jakarta Barat 11460

International Language Programs (ILP), Jalan Raya Pasar Minggu No. 39A, Jakarta 12780

International Language Studies (ILS), Jalan Ngemplak 30, Arbengan Plaza B-34, Surabaya 60272

Logo Education Centre (LEC), Jelan H.Z. Arifin 208A, Medan, Sumatra Utara

Oxford Course Indonesia (OCI), Jalan Cempaka Putih Tengah 33C-2, Jakarta Pusat 10510

PPIA - Medan, Jl Dr Manur III No 1-A, P O Box 2617, Medan 20121

Professional Training Services (PTS), Wisma BII, Jalan Permuda No. 60-70, Surabaya 60271

School for International Communication, Jalan Taman Pahlawan 194, Purwakarta

School for International Training (SIT), Jalan Sunda 3, Menteng, Jakarta Pusat 10350

Strive International, Setiabudi 1 Building, Jalan HR Rasuna Said, Jakarta 12920

The British Institute (TBI), Setiabudi Plaza2, Jalan HR Rasuna Said, Jakarta 12920.

The British Institute (TBI), JL Diponegoro No 23, Bandung, 40124

Triad English Centre, Jalan Purnawarman 76 Bandung- 40116

YAYASAN LIA (Lembago Indonesia Amerika), Jl Pramuka 30, Jakarta 13120

YPIA - Surabaya, Jl Dharma Husada Indah Barat 1, No 3, Surabaya 60285

Japan

Unqualified teachers can find work in private schools giving conversation classes or through Japan's Exchange and Teaching (JET) programme (see relevant section in this book). There are also chains of schools, such as GEOS, employing unqualified teachers. A degree is necessary for a work visa and, because Japan has retained its desirability as a place to teach, schools find that they have more and more candidates to choose from. There is no shortage of schools but competition for jobs is quite stiff, especially in the major cities. A teaching qualification will go a long way in helping to secure a more attractive post.

The best times to look for work are March and September before the beginning of terms. Contracts can be set up from outside the country but some teachers prefer to go out on spec because contracts negotiated there can be a bit better. If you choose the latter option, be warned, the cost of living in Japan is very high, but has become easier with the declining value of the Yen. You would need substantial savings to survive while you look for work and wait for your visa to come through. You should probably allow at least £1,500 for a one month job-search period. In 1995 the value of the Yen was approximately Yen160:1 pound, while in mid 1999 it has fallen to about 184:1. This does not effect the situation within Japan, but does reduce any savings you may wish to take home.

However you still can save a great deal in a year or two without living too frugally. If nothing comes up in Tokyo, go to smaller towns which have yet to be saturated with teachers.

Visas and work permits: If you are from Australia, New Zealand or Canada, you can teach in Japan on a working holiday visa, which can be obtained in your own country. All other nationalities need a work visa, which can only be issued if you have a degree and are sponsored by a private citizen or employer in Japan. The sponsor must apply on your behalf to the Ministry of Justice in Tokyo to secure a Certificate of Eligibility. This should be sent to you so that you can take it along with a copy, your passport, a photograph and an application form to your local embassy. Work visas are often issued within a week but may take longer.

Working on a tourist visa is illegal but you are allowed to job-hunt. You cannot obtain a work visa while you are in Japan so if you find a post whilst on a tourist visa, get your sponsoring employer to secure a Certificate of Eligibility and then visit an overseas embassy. Korea is the most popular destination for this change of status.

Cost of living: Expensive, but salaries are high.

Salaries and taxes: The average salary is about 250,000 yen per month with airfares and end-of-contract bonuses offered to more qualified candidates. If you are teaching privately, expect to earn 2,500-5,000 yen per hour. Income tax is progressive, starting at around ten per cent, with the local tax rate at five per cent.

Accommodation: Rents vary enormously and range from 60,000-100,000 yen per month in Tokyo. Landlords can be reluctant to rent to foreigners, so it's worth getting somebody to help. There are agents who can do this, otherwise you might have to pay as much as £3,000 up front as a deposit. Schools which recruit overseas often include accommodation assistance as a perk.

Health insurance: Advisable. It can be purchased locally and larger schools often have a private scheme for their employees. Contributions are expensive up to 30,000 yen per month.

English language newspapers: Japan Times, Kansai Time Out, The Daily Mainichi, The Asahi Evening News.

Important cultural differences: It can take up to six months to get acclimatised to the Japanese way of life. Westerners away from big cities tend to be treated very well and given a lot of attention. Prepare yourself before you go and do not expect high levels of English in rural areas. The Japanese school year runs from April to March, with various short breaks.

List of schools in Japan

Aeon Institute of Foreign Languages, 7f Nihonseimei Building, 1-1, 3 Shimoishii, Okayama-shi 700.

American Academy, 4-1-3 Kudan Kita Chiyoda-Ku, Tokyo 102.

America Eiko Gakuin, Misono-cho 5-2-21, Wakayama City 640.

American School of Business, 1-17-4 Higashi Ikebukuro, Toshima-Ku,Tokyo 170.

Azabu Academy, 401 Shuwa-Roppongi Building, 3-14-12 Roppongi, Minato-ku, Tokyo 106.

Berlitz Schools of Languages (Japan) Inc., Kowa Bldg. 1,5f, 11-41, Alasaka 1-chome, Minato-ku, Tokyo 107.

Bernard Group, 2-8-11 Takezono, Tsukuba City, lbaraki-Ken, 305.

CA English Academy, 2nd Floor Kotohira Building, 9-14 Kakuozan-dori, Chikusa-ku, Nagoya.

Cambridge English School, Dogenzaka 225 Building, 2-23-14 Dogenzaka, Shibuya-ku,Tokyo 150.

Cambridge School of English, Kikumura 91 Building1-41-20 Higashi, Ikebukuro Toshima-ku, Tokyo 170.

Cosmopolitan Language Institute, Yashima B Building 4f, 1-8-9 Yesu Chuo-ku,Tokyo 104.

CIC English Schools, Kawamoto Building, Imadegawaaaru Nishigawa Karasuma-dori, Kamigyo-ku, Kyoto.

DEH, 7-5 Nakamachi, Naka-ku, Hiroshima 730.

David English House, 2-3f Nakano Building, 1-5-17 Kamiyacho, Naka-ku, Hiroshima 730.

EEC Foreign Languages Institute, Shikata Building 2f, 4-43 Nakazald-Nishi 2-chrome, Kita-ku, Osaka 530.

ELEC Eigo Kenkyujo (The English Language Education Council), 3-8 Kanda Jimbo-cho, Chiyoda-ku,Tokyo 101.

Executive Gogaku Centre (Executive Language Centre), 1 Kasumigaseki Building, 12F, 3-2-5 Kasumigaseki, Chiyoda-ku,Tokyo 100.

English Circles/EC Inc., President Building 3rd Floor, South-1, Chuo-Ku, Sapporo 060

FCC (Fukuoka Communication Centre), Dai Roku Okabe Building, 5f, Hakata Eki Higashi, 2-4-17 Hakata-ku, Fukuoka 812.

F L Centre (Foreign Language Centre), 1 Iwasaki Building, 3f, 2-19-20 Shibuya-ku,Tokyo 150.

Four Seasons Language School, Aoyamashorin 2F, 4-32-11 Sanarudai, Hamamatsu-shi 432

Gateway Gakuin Rokko, Atelier House, 3-1-15 Yamada-cho, Nada-ku, Kobe.

GEOS Corporation, Shin Osaki Kangyo Buiding 4F, 6-4 Osaki 1 chome, Shinagawa-ku, Tokyo.

Hearts English School, 2146-3 Shido, Shido-cho, Okawa-gun, Kagawa 769-21

ICA Kokusai Kaiwa Gakuin (International Conversation Academy), l Mikasa 2 Building, 1-16-10 Nishi.

IF Foreign Language Institute, 7f Shin Nakashima Building, 1-9-20 Nishi Nakashima, Yodogawa-ku, Osaka.

inlingua Tokyo, 9F Kyodo Bldg, 2-4-2 Nihonbashi-Muromachi, Chuo-ku, tokyo 103

Kains English School in Gakko, 1-5-2 Ohtemon Chuo-ku, Fukuoka 810.

King's Road School of English, Akasaka 4-3-9, Takaike Bldg 3F, Minato-ku, Tokyo 107

Kyoto English Centre, Sumitomo Seimei Building, Shijo-Karasuma Nishi-iru Shimogyo-ku, Kyoto.

Kobe Language Centre, 3-18 Wakinoharnacho, 1-chome, Chuo-ku, Kobe 651

Language Education Centre, 7-32 chome Ohtemachi Nakaku, Hiroshima-shi 730

Language Resources, Taiyo Bldg 6F, Kitanagasa-dori 5 chome, Chuo-ku, Kobe 650-0012

Matty's School of English, 3-15-9 Shonan-takatori, Yokosuka 234

MIL Language Centre, 3.4F Eguchi Bldg, 1-6-2 Katsutadai, Yachiyo-shi, Chiba-ken 276

Mobara English Institute, 618-1 Takashi, Mobara-shi, Chiba-ken 297

Nova Group, 126/130 Regent Street, London W1R 5FE, UK.

Plus Alpha, (Agency) 2-25-20 Denenchofu, Ota-Ku, Tokyo 145.

Queens School of English, 3f Yuzuki Bldg, 4-7-14 Minamiyawata, Ichikawa 272.

Pegasus Language Services, Sankei Building, 1-7-2 Otemachi Chiyoda-ku, Tokyo 100.

REC School of Foreign Language, Nijojo-mae Ebisugawasagaru Higashihorikawa-dori, Nakagyo-ku, Kyoto.

Royal English Language Centre, 4-31-3-2 Chyo Hakata-ku, Fukuoka 82.

Seido Language Institute, 12-6 Funado-cho, Ashiya-shi, Kyoto.

Sun Eikaiwa School, 6f Cherisu Hachoubori Building, 6-7 Hachoubori Naka-ku, Hiroshima-shi 730.

Shane Corporation, 4f Kimura Building, 4-14-12 Nishi Funa Funabashi Shi, Chiba Ken 273.

Shane Corporation, Yutaka Dai-2 Building 4f, Higashi Kasai 6-2-8, Edogawa-Ku, Tokyo.

Shane English Schools (Head Offices): Kimura Building 4f, Nishifuna 4-14-12, Funabashi-shi, Chiba-ken 273. Maehara Building, Sakuragi-cho, 2-455-2, Omiya-shi, Saitama-ken 331. Fujisawa, 251 Fujisawa Homon Building 6f , Fujisawa 484-25, Fujisawa-shi, Kanagawa-ken 251.

Stanton School of English, 12 Gobancho Chiyoda-ku, Tokyo 102.

Sumikin-Intercom Inc, 7-28 Kitahama 4-Chome, Chou-ku, Osaka 541

Tokyo YMCA College of English, 7 Kanda Mitoshiro-Cho, Chiyoda-ku, Tokyo T-101.

Tokyo Language Centre, Tatsunama Building, 1-2-19 Yaesu, Chuo-Ku, Tokyo 103.

Tokyo English Centre, (TEC) 7-9 Uguisudai-cho, Shibuyaku, Tokyo 150.

Toefl Academy, 1-12-4 Kundankita, Chiyoda-ku, Tokyo 102

Trident School of Languages, 1-5-31 Imaike, Chikusa-ku, Nagoya 464.

World Language School Inc, Tokiwa Soga Ginko Building 4f 1-22-8 Jinnan, Shibuya-ku, Tokyo 171

Malaysia

English is widely used as a lingua franca in Malaysia. While it was once possible for even unqualified and non-native speaker teachers to pick up teaching work, many good private schools now insist on at least a first degree, an ELT certificate and up to three years experience. Malaysia has a protectionist economy which has suffered in the currency crisis. Therefore teachers from overseas have not been as actively recruited, and are usually employed locally. There were opportunities in all markets, including Business English, young learners and ESL but training budgets in the corporate sector are currently frozen and the strictness of the law makes legal freelancing difficult. Much of the work that does exist is part-time but private classes can be picked up quite easily. Available jobs can be found through the Malay Mail and by word of mouth in Kuala Lumpur.

Visas and work permits: Apply for a visa in your home country then go to Malaysia to job-hunt. Many teachers work on tourist visas whilst waiting for their work permits. The government grants permits only to qualified teachers with at least an MA, and the immigration service works closely with schools to ensure that teachers from overseas are qualified for the position offered. You must be able to prove that no Malaysian citizen is available for the post. It is the employer's responsibility to obtain a work permit.

Cost of living: Cheap, with excellent shops and street markets.

Salaries and taxes: Teachers from overseas are no longer offered very high expatriate salaries. Local salaries are quite high and contracted teachers can earn as much as £4.4k per annum on placements which sometimes include housing, flights and other benefits. Non-residents pay 30 per cent tax. Once your papers are in order and you have lived in Malaysia for a certain length of time, you become a resident and pay 15 per cent.

Accommodation: It is quite easy to find accommodation. Expect to pay around 800 ringgits per month to share. You will need to pay a one month general deposit, a smaller deposit for utilities and, two months' rent up front.

Health insurance: Some employers offer a health scheme, but if they do not, it is advisable to organise one yourself.

Inoculations: Hepatitis A, Polio, Tetanus, Malaria, Yellow Fever (if coming from an infected area).

English language newspapers: The Borneo Post (Sabah and Sarawak), The Daily Express (Sabah), The New Straits Times, The Malay Mail, The Sarawak Tribune, The Star, The Sun.(Note that the last two papers are Malaysian not British.)

Important cultural differences: Malaysia is a Muslim country and students come from a very teacher-centred, non-communicative background. It takes a little while to get used to the preferential treatment offered to ethnic Malays over those of immigrant descent.

Other information: Several Malaysian organisations recruit through the UK

press and the Malaysian High Commission in London has an active Education Section. Companies such as CfBT specialise in recruitment for this region. Malaysia is an excellent base if you want to explore South East Asia.

List of schools in Malaysia

Advanced Management College, 2nd Floor, Block A Karamunsing Complex, 88000 Kota Kinabalu, Sabah

British Council Languaghe Centre, 4th Floor, Wisha Hangsan, Box 20, Jalan Hang Setir, Kuala Lumpur

English Language Centre, Fortuneland, Jalan Rock, 93200 Kuching, Sarawak

International English Centre, Kompleks Sunny, Mile 11/2 Tuaran Road, 88100 Kota Kinabalu, Sabah

International Tuition School, Jalan Haji Taha, 93400 Kuching, Sarawak

Inti College, Jalan Stampin Timur, 93350 Kuching, Sarawak

Inti College, Sabah, Lot 17-20 Putatan Point, Jalan Kompleks JKR, 88200 Putatan, Kota Kinabalu, Sabah

Kinabalu College, 3rd Floor Wisma Sabah, 88000 Kota Kinabalu, Sabah

Kinabalu International School, P O Box 12080, 88822 Kota Kinabalu, Sabah

Kolej Ibukota Kinabalu, Jalan Mat Salleh, Sembulan, 88100 Kota Kinabalu, Sabah

Kolej Tuanku Ja'afar, 71700 Mantin, Negeri Sembilan Darul Khusus

Lodge Preparatory School & Kindergarten, Jalan Tabuan Jaya, 93350 Kuching, Sarawak

National College, P O Box 14146, 88847 Kota Kinabalu, Sabah

Stamford College, Bangunan Binamas, Jalan Padungan, 93100 Kuching, Sarawak

Stamford College Sabah, Menara Jubili, Jalan Gaya, 88000 Kota Kinabalu, Sabah

Tunku Putra International School, Jalan Nanas, 93400 Kuching, Sarawak

Universiti Malaysia Sarawak, Jalan Datuk Mohd Musa, 94300 Kota Samarahan, Samarahan, Sarawak

Myanmar
(Formerly known as Burma)

English is taught in state schools from an early age. The country is something of a pariah state, due to the ruling military junta suppressing democratic opponents

and conducting a war against the minority Karenni people. There is the problem of displaced persons, who left Myanmar to work in SE Asia, but have lost their jobs in the economic cut backs.

The English teaching situation is complicated because private enterprise and private education are not legal, but tolerated with ironically some of the demand coming from amongst the ruling military. There are press adverts in Singapore. The best chance is to be recruited by the British Council.

Visas and work permits: Arrange a one-month tourist visa in your own country and then extend it when you are in Myanmar. Schools have to apply for work permits for their foreign staff.

Cost of living: Local produce is very cheap, as are taxis and buses. Supermarkets with imported goods charge 'Asian' prices. Flats cost from US$80-$350 per month, houses and bungalows can be found for under US$500 per month. A minimum of 4-6 months rent is payable in advance.Prices have fallen in the last year.

Salaries and taxes: The usual salary range is from UK£4,000 per annum (with accommodation) to UK£12,000 for extremely well qualified teachers. The tax rate is 15%-18%.

Accommodation: There is not much choice, but acceptable accommodation is available. Schools often help in the search. The average rent is UK£200-350 per month. Refundable deposits tend to be very large and can cost UK£650-13,500.

Health insurance: Essential. Hospital facilities are limited.

Inoculations: Hepatitis A and B, Malaria, Polio, Typhoid, Tetanus, Yellow Fever (if coming from an infected area).

English language newspapers: New Light of Myanmar.

Other useful information: When quoting prices, people in Myanmar tend to jump between different hard currencies.

Useful address: The British Council, 78 Kanna Road (PO Box 268) Yangon. Tel: (951) 254658/256290/256291. Fax: (951) 245345

SECTION 3 International Job Prospects

Philippines

Living costs: Quite cheap generally, especially beer and cigarettes. Eating out depends on where you go. Clothes are cheaper than in Europe with plenty of bargain sales.

Salaries and taxes: Not many, in fact very few opportunities for native speakers due to visa restrictions. Salaries are around £10 per hour maximum with an average considerably lower. Taxes are lower than in Europe.

Accommodation: Comparatively expensive for suitable accommodation (security is an issue) A cheap, one-bedroom apartment would cost £300-£500.

Singapore

English is extremely popular in Singapore. Be aware, however, that much of the demand comes from young learners and business people, so if you are an unqualified teacher trying to pick up travelling money, you might have quite a difficult time locating a school which is prepared to employ you.

The British Council recruits candidates with a full postgraduate teaching qualification plus two years' experience, and schools are keen to see evidence of a commitment to teaching. International House and inlingua also offer such contracts and all provide flights, health insurance and help you to settle in. Minimum one-year contracts are common and it is possible to find lucrative private classes.

Freelancing is only legal if you have a work permit, and many contract teachers also exploit this market using their contacts. Many companies run English language programmes, recruiting locally.

The Ministry of Education recruits overseas for state teaching posts, paying S$3,000-S$5,000 per month, with flights, insurance and cheaper accommodation. The department has a website with more information. http://www1.moe.edu.sg/

Visas and work permits: Visas are not necessary for a tourist visit to Singapore, but all nationalities need work permits. It is not possible to be issued with a permit before you have a job and a sponsoring employer, but once you have secured your position, getting your permit should be fairly straightforward. You can look for a job as a tourist and apply to gain working status from within Singapore.

Cost of living: Similar to the UK or US, as Singapore is wealthy and westernised.

Salaries and taxes: Expect a salary of S$2,000 - S$2,500 per month, in a non-contract post. Rates per hour start at S$20. If you are more experienced and qualified, teaching with a reputable organisation can bring in S$5,000 per month. The tax rate is 2% for the first S$7,500, 15.2 per cent for S$40,000.

Accommodation: Relatively easy to find, but expensive. Most teachers share flats, in which the average rent for a room is S$700 per month. Three months' deposit is usually expected.

Health insurance: Essential.

Innoculations: Hepatitis A, Polio, Typhoid, Yellow Fever (if coming from an infected area).

English language newspapers: Straits Times.

List of schools in Singapore

Advanced Training Techniques (ATT) (International House Singapore), Tanglin Shopping Centre, 19 Tanglin Road, Singapore 1025

American College, 25 Paterson Road, Singapore 0923

The British Council, 30 Napier Road, Singapore 2558509

Canadian International School, 5 Toh Tuck Road, Singapore 2159

Coleman Commercial and Language Centre, Peninsula Plaza, Singapore

Corrine Private School, Selegie Complex 04-277, Selegie Road, Singapore 188350

Dimensions Language Centre, 50 East Coast Road, 0238 Singapore 428769

Dover Court Preparatory School, Dover Road, Singapore 0513

Hua Language Centre, 101 Thomson Road, United Square #B1-35/39, Singapore 307591

ILC Language and Business Training Centre, c/o 545 Orchard Road 11-07, Far East Shopping Centre, Singapore 238882

ILC Language and Business Training Centre, 55 Cuppage Road, 08-21 Cuppage Centre, Singapore 0922

Inlingua School of Languages, 68 Orchard Road, 07-04 Plaza Singapura, Singapore 238839

Inlingua School of Languages, 1 Grange Road 04-01, Orchard Building, Singapore 239683

International School, 21 Preston Road, Singapore 0410

Japanese School, 201 West Coast Road, Singapore 0512

Julia Gabriel Communications, 13 Halifax Road, Singapore

Juliet McCully Speech Training Centre, 277 Orchard Road, Singapore

Language Teaching Institute of Singapore, SEAMEO Regional Language Centre (RELC), 30 Orange Grove Road, Singapore 258352

Linguarama Language Centre, 220 Orchard Road 02-09, Midpoint Orchard Sports, Singapore 238852

Lorna Whiston Study Centre (primary children), 583 Orchard Road, 05-04 Forum Galeria, Singapore 238884

Morris Allen Study Centre, 1 Newton Road 02-07, Goldhill Plaza, Singapore 307943

Nurtureland Language Centre, 195a Thomson Road, Singapore 307634

Overseas Family School, 25F Paterson Road, Singapore 0923

Pave Language Centre, West Coast Recreation Centre, 12 West Coast Walk, Singapore

Seameo Regional Language Centre, 30 Orange Grove Road, Singapore

Secretarial Specialists Training Centre, 277 Orchard Road, 06-01 Specialists Shopping Centre, Singapore 238858

Singapore American School, 60 Kings Road, Singapore 1026.

Stamford City School of Commerce, 192 Waterloo Street, 5th floor Skyline Building, Singapore 0718

Tanglin Junior School, Portsdown Road, Singapore 0513

Translingual Language centre, 3 Coleman St 04-05, Peninsula Shopping Centre, Singapore 179804

United World College, Pasir Panjang PO Box 15, Singapore 9111

South Korea

Demand for ELT has been booming in Korea, comparable to Japan ten years ago. Korea now rivals Japan as a destination for teachers in the Pacific Rim. Teachers should be aware they are entering an economy still trying to recover from the depression of 1997.

Since the Seoul Olympics in 1988, the government has cracked down on illegal workers, including those teaching casually as tourists. Anyone found working without a work permit will be deported and any companies found employing illegal workers risk being closed down.

There are plenty of schools in and outside the cities and a lot of recruitment is done overseas. Finding a job before you go, whether you are qualified or not, is the best way of assessing just how damaging the currency and debt crisis is. The sheer number of native speakers wishing to work in Korea means that schools can do a fair amount of picking and choosing. If there is less money available for the English learning sector, the competition for the remaining positions will be tough. With the right qualifications you can still secure reasonably favourable terms and conditions.

Due to close ties with North America, there is a preference for US or Canadian teachers but even though recruiters are very active in North America, Korean schools are not too fussy so long as you are a native English speaker.

Young Koreans supplement their years of study with conversation classes to help them get into American universities, and the university vacations in July, August, January and February also see huge increases in the number of students studying at private language schools. Some families spend up to $10,000 on extra lessons for their children, so there has been large scope for private tuition. With students perhaps less able to afford to go overseas for language training, the demand could grow at home. If the economy sinks deeper into recession however, then the home market is also likely to contract sharply.

Visas and work permits: North Americans are allowed to stay for up to 90 days on a tourist visa, while British visitors can stay up to 60 days. The visa required is E2. It is illegal to teach on a tourist permit. Obtaining work permits is very complicated but can be done in advance or after finding a job on spec. If done in advance, you must get your employer to send a contract, sponsorship documents and a copy of their Business

Registration Certificate. These should then be sent with your CV, a copy of your degree notarised by a consular official, two photographs and a fee to your nearest embassy. If you apply for a work permit after finding a job on spec, you have to leave the country while the papers are being processed. Work permits are valid for one year.

Cost of living: Don't pack too much, you can buy most things cheaper there than in the West.

Salaries and taxes: Salaries vary enormously but the average is equivalent to about US$1,500 per month. Many schools pay per hour and guarantee minimum teaching hours. If this is the arrangement, expect about $25 per hour. It is possible to earn up to $50 per hour privately, but work visas are issued on the basis of employment by a specified employer. Teaching privately is viewed similarly to teaching on a tourist visa and there are stories of private teachers being deported. Full-time contracts tend to include accommodation, return airfare, bonus and medical insurance. Because of a US-Korea Tax Treaty, US citizens working for colleges or universities are sometimes exempt from paying taxes for up to two years. Income tax for the rest can vary with income levels, ranging from about 10.75% for salaries less than 10 million won, and up to 40% for those above. An additional residency tax of as much as 7.5% is payable.

Accommodation: Traditionally in the Far East, people pay a year's rent up front and the landlord lives off the interest. Korea is no exception. Rents average around US$800 per month for an unfurnished flat, so a year's rent in advance is no mean figure. Fortunately, most schools will pay this "key money" and deduct it from salary at source.

Teachers often share to make the key money tolerable or stay in a boarding house. Expect to pay around $280 for a room in a boarding house. If you might also consider staying with a Korean family.

Health insurance: Essential. Often paid for by the employer.

Inoculations: Hepatitis A, Polio, Tetanus, Typhoid.

English language newspapers: Korea Herald, Korea Times.

List of schools in South Korea
Best Foreign Language Institute, 98-3 Jungang-Dong, Changwon City, Kyungsangnam Province 641-030

Chuncheon National University of Education, Chuncheon 200-703

Dong-A Educational Foundation, 50-10 Jayang-Dong, Dong-ku, Taejon 300-100

Educational Resource Center, Sodaemun-gu, Hongje 1 Dong, 331, Hyundai Apt. 107-201 Ho, Seoul 120-091.

ESS Language Institute, 8, 1-ka Shinchang-dong, Jung-ku, Pusan 600-061

Good Teachers' Center, 271-19, Dongin 3-ga, Jung-ku, Taegu 700-423

inlingua Seoul, 5-6F Mikwan Building, 63 Suhadong, Chunggu, 100-210 Seoul

Keimyung Junior College, 2139 Dae-Myung Dong, Nam-ku, Taegu 705-037

Korea Foreign Language Institute, 16-1 Kwancheol-Dong, Chongro-ku, Seoul

Korea Services Group, Dong-Bang B/D, 4th Floor, 803-3, Mang Mi-Dong, Su Young-ku, Pusan 613-131

Language Arts Testing & Training, Chung Jung-Ro, PO Box 269, Seoul 120-013

Language Teaching Research Center, 60-17, 1-ka, Taepyong-ro, Chung-gu, Seoul 100-101

Mido Foreign Language School, Mido Sang-Ga Bldg, 3rd Floor, 311 Dae-Chi Dong, Kang-Nam Ku, Seoul 135-280

Pacific Language Institute, 1196-6 Guwoi Dong, Namdong-gu, Inchon 405 221

Pagoda Language School, 56-6 2nd Street, Jong-ro, Seoul 110-122

Prime English Language School, 240 Doryang Dong, Kumi, Kyunguk Province

Sogang University, 1 Sinsoo-dong, Mapo-gu, Seoul 121-742

Top Language School, 37-1, 2-Ga, Chung Ang-Dong, Chon-ju City

YBM/ELSI Language Institutes, Yeoksam Heights Bldg, 2nd Floor, 642-19 Yeoksam-dong, Kangnam-Gu, Seoul 135-081

Yonsei Foreign Language Institute, Yonsei University, Sodaemun-ku, Shinchon-Dong 134, Seoul 120-749

Yoido Foreign Language Institute, 54 Yoido-dong, Young-dung-po-ku, Seoul

Taiwan

The days when anybody could pick up teaching work in Taiwan have ended. In 1992 the Taiwanese government clamped down on teachers working illegally. Many schools were visited by the police and some teachers were deported. Nevertheless, there is still great demand for English language teaching and even those with minimal qualifications should find a placement. It is very difficult however to fix up a job before coming to the country, as schools generally do not advertise overseas. Go to Taiwan in the summer after the school year and just in time for the summer school season.

With the economy still essentially healthy, the in-company teaching work should remain available, as well as fervent demand for young learner classes. It is still easy to find work without qualifications. Anyone with a good command of English should be able to find work. Some companies do recruit overseas and some exchange schemes for language teachers, within a university context, are possible.

Visas and work permits: Taiwan has very complicated visa regulations. Teachers must have sponsorship and a degree to obtain a work permit, with a contract of employment and documents of approval from the Ministry of Education. If you enter the country on a tourist visa and find work, you must leave the country to apply for a work permit. You should make arrangements for this well in advance of your tourist visa running out. You are not allowed to work on a visitor visa.

Cost of living: High, especially in Taipei, about NT$30,000 per month.

Salaries and taxes: Schools may pay around NT$500 to NT$800 per hour, depending on qualifications and your ability to speak Chinese. Companies may well pay twice as much. Expect lower rates in the provinces or if you do not have qualifications. A work visa allows you to work for a specific employer and freelance teaching would be considered illegal. People do it though, and as there is a good demand for private lessons, teachers can earn from NT$800 per hour.

Tax is 20 per cent for the first 183 days of a calendar year. After that, it is 10 per cent and, once you have your residency sorted out, you can get a tax rebate for the first six months.

Accommodation: A room in a shared flat in Taipei can cost NT$10,000 per month; less in the provinces. Most landlords will want two months' rent in advance. Many teachers stay in dorms near the central train station and commute to nearby towns where wages may be higher. Dorm beds can cost NT$160-200 per night. Outside Taipei these are 25%-50% cheaper.

Health insurance: Foreigners are entitled (and often required) to join the Taiwanese government health insurance scheme for about NT$230 per month which guarantees very cheap medical cover. Reputable schools offer private schemes to protect teachers who fall seriously ill and require hospital treatment or repatriation.

Inoculations: Hepatitis A, Polio, Typhoid, Yellow Fever (if coming from an infected area), cholera.

English language newspapers: China Post, Taiwan News.

Useful information: See British Council homepage. http://www.britcoun.org.tw

List of schools in Taiwan

Apex English Group, Kwan Chien Rd, #28, Taipei

Big Bird English, Hsin Yi Rd, Sec 4 #181, 2F, Taipei

Chang Chun English, Ji Long Rd, Sec 2, #260 2F, Taipei

Cheng Dan Language Center, Hang Chou Rd, Sec 1, Lane 71, #9 Taipei

Chin Shan English, Hsin Sheng Rd, Sec 3, #98 3F, Taipei

China Youth Service Association, Kwan Chien Road, #45, Taipei

Chuan Mei Kindergarten, Pa Teh Rd, Sec 4, #123, Taipei

Disney English, Hoping East Rd, Sec 2, Lane 96, Taipei

Dong Han English, Hoping East Rd, Sec 2, #100, 4F, Taipei

E Hui English, Roosevelt Rd, Sec 3, #302, B1, Taipei

ELS, 12 Kilung St, Taipei

ELSI, Chung Shan North Rd, Sec 5, #612, Taipei

ELSI, Song Chian Rd, Lane 90, #9, Taipei

ELSI, Nan Jing East Rd, Sec 3, #346, 5F, Taipei

ELSI English, Nan Yang St, #13, 7F, Taipei

Everday English, Chung Hsiao East Rd, Sec 4, #177, 4F, Taipei

GEOS, Chung Hsiao East Rd, Sec 4, #153, 4F, Taipei

Global Village, Min Chuan East Rd, Sec 3, #170, 7F, Taipei

Gram English, Roosevelt Rd, Sec 4, #162, 4F, Taipei

Gram English Institute, 7th Floor, 216 Tun Hwa South Road, Sec 1, Taipei

Great Time English, Min Chuan East Rd, Sec 3, Lane 60, #10, Taipei

Han Bang Language School, Chung Yuan Rd, #17, 2F, Taipei

Happy Maria Kindergarten, Hoping East Rd, Sec 2, Lane 265, #42, Taipei

Harvard Overseas Service Center, Nan Yang St, #24, Taipei

Hess Language School, 83 Po Ai Road, 2F, Taipei

Ho Nan Language School, Chung Shan North Rd, Sec 2, #60, 10F, Taipei

Hsue Du English, Cheng Teh Rd, Sec 7, Lane 188, #2, 2F, Taipei

Hua Language Institute, Fu Hsing South Rd, Sec 1, #390, 4F, Taipei

Hua Ya English, Fu Hsing North Rd, #1, 2F, Taipei

Jian Gong English, Po Ai Rd, #50, 3F, Taipei

Jin Jye English, Chung Shan North Rd, Sec 5, #65, 2F, Taipei

Jordan's Language School, 97 Chuan Chow Street, 1 F, Taipei

Joy Children's English School, Kuling Street, #21, Taipei

Jump Start English, Roosevelt Rd, Sec 3, #190, 4F, Taipei

Jya Ying English, Chuang Ching Rd, Lane 325, #37, Taipei

Jyu Hwei English, Roosevelt Rd, Sec 3, #302, B1, Taipei

Kang Ning English School, PO Box 95, Chutung 310

Kaplan English, Ta Chi St, #69, 7F, Taipei

Lai Hsin Language Center, Hsu Chang St, #42, 7F, Taipei

Language Training & Testing Center, 170 Ilsin-hai Road, Section 2, Taipei.

Lang Wen English Center, Chin Chou St, #16, 3F, Taipei

Lian Hsin English, Fu Hhing North Rd, #92, 7F, Taipei

Liang You Language School, Chung Hsiao East Rd, Sec 4, #76-1, 11F, Taipei

Lingua Language Center, Shi Tung St, #238, Taipei

Luxin Institute, Nanyang St, #12, Taipei
Mei Cheng, Min Chuan East Rd, Sec 3, #7, 2F, Taipei

Mei Ya Language School, Hsin Sheng South Rd, Sec 1, #126-8, 2F, Taipei

Merica English Institute, Nan Yang St, #50, Taipei

Min Sheng English School, Min Sheng East Rd, Sec 5, #226-1, Taipei

Ming Tai Language School, Chung Hwa Rd, Sec 1, #178, Taipei

Overseas Service Corps YMCA, 101 North Wacker Drive, Chicago, IL 60606, USA

Oxford Language & Computer Institute, 8Fl, 240 Chung Shan 1st Road, Kaohsiung

Pioneer Language Institute, Hoping East Rd, Sec 1, #200, 6F, Taipei

The Princeton Review, Chung Hsiao East Rd, Sec 4, #155, 4F-3, Taipei

Rich English, 1F, 27 Lane 222, Tun Hwa North Road, Taipei

Sesame Street English, Cheng Teh Rd, Sec 2, #46, 2F, Taipei

Shane English School, 5F, 41 Roosevelt Road, Section 2, Taipei.

Shane English Center, Hsin Yi Rd, Sec 2, #27, 4F, Taipei

Shang Shang English, Chin Chou St, #311, Taipei

Shang Shang Language School, Ming Teh Rd, #275, Taipei

Shang Yang English, Chung Ching South Rd, Sec 1, #95, 7F, Taipei

Shang Yang Language School, Hsin Yi Rd, Sec 2, #208, 2F, Taipei

Shi Jyou English, Chung Hsiao East Rd, Sec 4, #299, 4F, Taipei

Siao Hong Dou English School, Fu Hsing South Rd, Sec 1, #342, 12F, Taipei
Straight Top Institute, Lian Yun St, #87, 3F, Taipei

Taipei British Institute, Pa Teh Rd, Sec 2, #400, 4F, Taipei

Taipei Language Institute, Kaohsiung Center, 2F, 507 Chuyng Chan 2nd Road, Haohsiung

Taipei Language Institute, Roosevelt Rd, Sec 3, #50, 4F, Taipei

TPR Promotion Center, Jen Ai Rd, Sec 4, #50, 11F, Taipei

Vicker English School, Chung Hsiao East Rd, Sec 1, #11, 3F, Taipei

VIP English, Chung Hua Rd, Sec 1, #192, 3F, Taipei

Wan Guan, Chung Hsiao East Rd, Sec 4, #209, 7F, Taipei

Washington English, Chung Shan North Rd, Sec 3, #39, 2F, Taipei

Washington Language Center, Chung Hsiao East Rd, Sec 5, #510-4, Taipei

Word of Mouth English, 4F-2, 163 Nan King East Road, Sec. 5, Taipei

Yi Hsing English, Nan Jing East Rd, Sec 4, #17, 6F, Taipei

YMCA, Roosevelt Rd, Sec 3, #214, Taipei

We would like to thank Simon Ager, Information Officer at the British Trade and Cultural Office in Taiwan for his help in compiling this information.

Thailand

There is a great demand for English, but relatively little recruitment is done overseas. English-speaking teacher-travellers who want to fund their holidays present school owners with a cheap, readily available and mobile workforce. This means that it is hard to find well-paid and serious teaching work in the country. Qualified teachers have an edge over teacher-travellers but salaries, although very high by local standards, have not increased appreciably and since 1997 are worth much less globally speaking. Busiest times for English language schools are in the holiday period between March and May.

Visas and work permits: All nationalities except New Zealanders require entry visas. All nationalities require work permits to teach legally and these are only issued to teachers with a degree and certificate who are employed at a recognised educational institution. For a work permit a letter of employment from your prospective employer should be sent to the Royal Thai Embassy in your home country. Although illegal, many teachers manage to teach on a tourist visa, which must be renewed every 60 days. The middle road is a non-immigrant visa which allows a teacher to work in the country for up to 90 days at a time. A letter of invitation from an employer or a Thai national is required for a non-immigrant visa.

Cost of living: Cheap, especially outside Bangkok.

Salaries and taxes: Qualified teachers earn B15,000-20,000 per month or B250-450 per hour which provides a comfortable lifestyle. If you get a work permit, the tax rate can be as low as two per cent. In the current economic climate be prepared for constant change in prices, pay rates and tax levels.

Accommodation: It is not that easy to find somewhere to live. You will probably need a Thai speaker to help and schools do not normally assist. Most teachers stay in budget hostels but it is possible to find flats for B2,700-3,500. Three months' rent is payable as a deposit.

Health insurance: Essential.

Inoculations: Hepatitis A, Polio, Tetanus, Typhoid, Malaria (in some areas), Yellow Fever (if coming from an infected area).

English language newspapers: Bangkok Post and The Nation.

Other useful information: Avoid Bangkok if you don't like stress, pollution and noise.

List of schools in Thailand
American University Language Centre, 179 Rajadamri Road, Bangkok 10330

American University Alumni Language Center, 24 Rajdamnern Road, Chiang Mai 50200

ECC, 430/17-24 Chula Soi 64, Siam Square, Bangkok 10330

ELS International, 419/3 Rajavithee Road, Phyathai, Bangkok 10400

English Language Schools, 26/3, 26/9 Chonphol Lane 15, Bangkok 10900

inlingua School of Languages, 7th Floor, Central Chidlom Tower, 22 Ploenchit Road, Pathumwan, Bangkok 10330.

inlingua Silom Branch, 20th Floor, Liberty Sq Bldg, 287 Silom Road, Bangrak, Bankok 10500

inlingua Piklao Branch, 5th Floor, Central Plaza, Pinklao Office Bldg, 7/129 Baromrajchonnee Road, Bangkok 10700

LCC Language Institute, 8/64-67 Ratchadapisek-Larprao Road, Bangkhaen, Bangkok 10900.

Training Creativity Development (TCD), 399/7 Soi Thongloh 21, Sukhumvit Soi 55, Bangkok 10110

The Rest of Asia

There are some private teaching opportunities but most positions are organised by voluntary or educational organisations.

English teachers are in less demand than in the Far East, mainly because many of the countries are too poor to sustain private sector schools. It should be possible to work as a volunteer though and many teachers have found this very rewarding in the past, often taking on challenges, such as teacher training, which they would not have been offered in other, richer countries.

Opportunities are extremely restricted in Mauritius since foreign nationals are rarely granted work permits.

Projects in Bhutan, Mongolia and Pakistan are generally organised through aid agencies as well as through organisations including the British Council and the Bell Educational Trust.

English has been taught in schools for 45 years in Uzbekistan and last year the government initiated a drive to place English language teaching on a par with Russian. This means that the Peace Corps is even more active than before in recruiting for Uzbekistan and its neighbours Kazakhstan, Kyrghystan and Turkmenistan.

Please note that aid agencies cannot normally guarantee volunteers work in the country of their choice.

Bangladesh

English is in great demand but most opportunities are for teachers who can afford to fund themselves. The British Council has a teaching centre in Dhaka and recruits from London for two year contracts. It is possible to find part-time private work in English-medium schools, especially if you are the spouse of an expatriate worker already established there. Qualified teachers often end up in teacher training. Unfortunately, there are no opportunities in the state sector.

Visas and work permits: All nationalities need entry and work permits. Some people work on their three-month tourist visas but it is illegal to do so. Work permits are difficult to secure and can take months to come through. You need a letter from your employer to secure a business visa.

Cost of living: Very cheap.

Salaries and taxes: Salaries are very low and unless on a long-term contract teachers should have other funds. The British Council salary is between £10,000 and £13,000 with flights, baggage, insurance and accommodation included.

Accommodation: It is easy to find accommodation since a lot of new flats are springing up, but a year's rent is generally expected in advance. Flats cost around UK£300 per month so, even if you share, it is expensive. The British Council houses all its teaching staff.

Health insurance: Essential.

Inoculations: Hepatitis A, Polio, Tetanus, Typhoid, Malaria, Yellow Fever (if coming from an infected area, and you must be in possession of a vaccination certificate), Rabies (in some areas), cholera advised.

English language newspapers: The Daily Star, The Bangladesh Observer, The Independent, The New Nation.

Other useful information: Dhaka is very crowded and noisy with poor sanitation.

India

With the liberalisation of the Indian economy, the demand for English language learning is increasing. However, as the language is taught in the state sector, there are very few private language schools in the country. It is possible to arrange an unpaid teaching position at one of these schools but conditions are often difficult. There are some private English-medium schools though, where positions for native speakers are often available. Recruitments can be made through the British Council in London in order to be employed at a teaching centre in New Delhi or Calcutta.

Visas and work permits: A work permit is not easy to obtain but once you have secured a position, you should get a letter of offer from your employer and apply to the Indian embassy before you travel.

Cost of living: Very low but few teachers from overseas find it possible to live on a local salary.

Salaries and taxes: Approximately £100 to £150 per month, up to Rs.1,5000.

Accommodation: Some schools provide furnished accommodation on campus, others offer board and lodging for £50-£100 per month.

Health insurance: Essential.

Inoculations: Hepatitis A and B, Polio, Tetanus, Typhoid, Malaria, Meningitis, Yellow Fever (if coming from an infected area).

English language newspapers: Times of India, The Hindu, The Hindustan Times, The Pioneer, Indian Express

Useful Address: British Council, 17 Kasturba Gandhi Marg, New Delhi 110 001

Nepal

Kathmandu offers the best prospects for EL teachers. However, the many locally-run private schools are notorious for low wages and poor resources. Visitors willing to brave it find work, but for a secure long-term stay only the British Council, the American Language Center and well-established organisations can get you a visa. To maintain what is felt to be a more acceptable standard of living, teachers should not rely solely on their wages.

There is a lot of voluntary work available in Nepal, often in rural secondary schools where duties can include language upgrading, materials design and in-service teacher training. The VSO will provide a top-up in addition to local salaries.

Visas and work permits: A three-month tourist visa is available on entry. Residency visas and work permits have to be arranged by established employers. People do work illegally on tourist visas and these can be renewed twice a year allowing foreigners a maximum stay of three months out of any 12.

Cost of living: Cheap.

Salaries and taxes: Salaries are low with some local schools offering as little as £12 per month. Salaries closer to western rates are paid by the British Council and the American Language Center.

Accommodation: Agents will find you a flat for a small fee. A small, two-bedroomed flat costs US$80-100 per month. Paying a deposit is not common for informal agreements, but if your company finds your accommodation, this can cost anything from US$300 to US$5,000. For volunteers, low-cost accommodation will be provided or found.

Health insurance: Essential.

Inoculations: Hepatitis A, Polio, Tetanus, Encephalitis, Typhoid, Meningitis, Yellow Fever (if coming from an infected area).

English language newspapers: The Rising Nepal, The Kathmandu Post.

Important cultural differences: Nepal is a culturally diverse and challenging place. The religious makeup of Nepal includes Hindu, Buddhist, Christian and Muslim faiths.

Schools in Nepal
American Language Center, USIS - P O Box 58, Kathmandu
Children's Model School, P O Box 4747, Kathmandu
Three Star English School, Dhungin, Faika, Kapan, Kathmandu

Pakistan

Here English Teaching is dominated by the British Council, with three offices around the country and the Pakistan American Cultural Centre, which has seven. There are also some voluntary sector activities, now mainly through VSO since the US-based International Rescue Committee which had been very active, closed down. VSO volunteers can expect to work in North West villages, although there are some posts in Karachi. Some posts require experience in materials and course design but there are also posts for newly-qualified teachers.

List of schools in Pakistan
Pakistan American Cultural Center (PACC) - Head Office, 11 Fatima Jinnah Road, Karachi
PACC - FJR Center, 11 Fatima Jinnah Road, Karachi
PACC - Hyderabad Center, Hospital Road, Hyderabad
PACC - Karimabad Center, 54-C Block 8 Federal B Area, Karachi
PACC - Qasimabad Center, Qasimabad, Hyderabad
PACC - Lahore Center, 25 E-3 Gulberg III, Lahore
PACC - Peshawar Center, c/o St John's School, 1 Sir Syed Road, Peshawar Cantt.
PAC - Quetta Center, Sadiq Shaheed Park, Arbab Mohammad Khair Road, Mali Bagh, Quetta

Papua New Guinea

English is an official language of education. However, with more than 800 language groups, English can only loosely be described as the second language. Jobs are mainly in the secondary sector and few are purely EFL. Teacher training is fairly advanced. Salaries are not high but taxes are.

Visas and work permits: Teachers must secure a job before applying for a work visa. The employer has to lodge an application with the authorities in Papua New Guinea and the prospective employee must apply to the immigration department of Papua New Guinea High Commission.

Other useful information: Although a beautiful country, the PNG High Commission in London says it is not a suitable destination for those of nervous disposition; and some areas are controlled by bandits. VSO and the UN recruit volunteers according to demand.

Sri Lanka

The civil war is largely confined to the north and east of the country where the Tamil minority is. Violence is unpredictable however, so check the situation before you leave and be aware that Colombo is a target for occasional bombings. English is encouraged by the government as a possible way to bridge the gap between Tamils and Sinhalese. Increasing demand for education has encouraged the development of some projects.

Visas and work permits: Employers arrange work permits, leaving the employee to organise the visa. It is not possible to find work on spec.

Cost of living: Cheap.

Salaries and taxes: Most teachers earn UK£2,000 per annum, which is a good local salary. British Council employees with a diploma should earn UK£11,000 - 14,000, about 35% of which is paid in sterling and the rest in rupees. There is no tax in the first year.

Accommodation: A very comfortable three-bedroomed flat will cost UK£250 per month. A year's rent is paid up front. It is advisable to share and to travel to the country with some savings.

Health insurance: Advisable.

Inoculations: Hepatitis A, Polio, Typhoid, Malaria, Yellow Fever (if coming from an infected country).

English language newspapers: The Island, Daily News.

Important cultural differences: There are extremes of wealth and poverty. Most of the Sinhalese population is Buddhist, with an ingrained passive outlook on life. Therefore outsiders should be aware of how offensive and counter-productive it can be to be aggressive and impatient.

North Africa and Middle East

With English as the language of the oil business, there are many lucrative positions available, but the region is not without its cultural challenges and can be dangerous.

Working in the Middle Eastern, oil-rich Gulf states can be lucrative. However, cultural differences between the Middle East and many other regions of the world, combined with civil unrest in some of the Gulf states, means that teaching in these areas is mainly an option for the bold, self-disciplined or married.

The standard package for qualified teachers includes return flights, furnished accommodation and end-of-contract bonuses. It is not really advisable, or even possible to find work on spec in the region. Casual work is available if you are already established in a country. Indeed, teaching English privately, often to children, is the most common profession for an expatriate spouse to take up.

All of the countries of the Middle East, except Israel, are Islamic, but the influence of the religion over state law and social activity varies greatly. Culture shock for a Westerner is common and if you are a single woman you could find yourself at a great disadvantage or even unemployable.

The Middle East can be a dangerous region. Continuing hostility between America and its allies and Iraq overshadows the area. There has been huge unrest in Algeria recently with the rise of Islamic fundamentalism. Mass killings have occurred all over the country with some foreigners being caught up. In Eygpt, tourism has slumped after Islamic groups targeted foreign visitors. Other countries in the area can also be hazardous and volatile, such as Palestinian areas in and around Israel. Check the UK Foreign Office list of countries for those it advises against visiting and consult your Foreign Affairs department before taking a post in the region.

Although teachers should proceed cautiously before looking for work in Libya, oil companies do recruit instructors.

Lebanon is recovering after its turbulent times. English is set to overtake French in popularity and now that the British Council has reopened its teaching operation in Beirut more ELT projects are imminent.

Bahrain

It is possible to work in Bahrain if you organise it in advance by contacting the list of schools below. There are a small number of jobs in the country, but the economic situation is difficult. The only opportunities are for qualified teachers so you will have better prospects if you have a diploma or some experience. Bahrain is probably the most liberal Gulf state and tolerates women in the workplace.

Visas and work permits: British nationals born in the UK do not require an entry visa. Nationals of other countries might have to get their employers to obtain a No Objection Certificate before they can enter, although three or five-day visas can usually be issued on arrival, allowing the employer time to make the necessary arrangements to obtain a work permit.

Work permits and residency permits are required by all nationalities. The employer must get it before the teacher's arrival. New employees must have a medical check-up. Check visa/work permit details with the embassy before departure as requirements are subject to change at short notice.

Cost of living: Higher than in neighbouring Gulf states but with lower salaries.

Salaries and taxes: Salaries are about BD520-580 for those with a certificate and BD580-BD700 for those with a diploma. The rate for part-time work is BD6-8 per hour. No tax is charged.

Accommodation: A flat with one or two bedrooms costs BD180-300 per month.

There is no deposit but three months' rent is required up front.

Health insurance: Essential. Health cover can be obtained locally fairly cheaply.

Inoculations: Hepatitis A, Polio, Typhoid.

English language newspapers: Gulf Daily News.

List of schools in Bahrain
Al Rawasi Academy, PO Box 82110, Riffa
Awal Training Institute, PO Box 28110, Riffa
Bahrain Computer & Management Institute, PO Box 27684, Manama
Bahrain Training Institute, PO Box 33090, Essa Town
The British Council, AMA Centre, (PO Box 452), Manama 356
The Cambridge Institute, , PO Box 224914, Manama
Capital Institute, PO Box 22521, Manama
Child Development, PO Box 11910, Manama
Daar al Merifa, PO Box 3174, Manama
Delmon Academy, PO Box 10362, Manama
Global Institute, PO Box 11148, Manama
Gulf Academy, PO Box 10333, Manama
Gulf College of Hospitality and Tourism, PO Box 22088, Muharraq
Gulf School of Languages, PO Box 20236, Manama
Pitman IPE, PO Box 26222, Manama
Polyglot School, PO Box 596, Manama
University of Bahrain, PO Box 32038, Sakhir-Bahrain

Egypt

Demand for English is still high especially in the commercial sector, as a result of economic growth and privatisation. It was not easy for new teachers to find work in reputable schools and many organisations have minimal requirements.

Following the collapse in tourism and the decline in foreign visitor numbers, some schools may be more willing to employ those prepared to take the risk of going.

There are some very well paid contracts available with oil companies out in the Sinai desert, if you can handle the remote lifestyle. The companies can be contacted locally.

Apart from company classes, one of the largest markets is for young learners. There are English Medium Schools and private schools teaching International GCSEs.

The recruitment season is in March, April and May for a September start. A lot of organisations hire L1 speakers with minimal qualifications. One way to avoid waiting for term to start would be to take a certificate course in Cairo which is cheaper than elsewhere and helps to make useful contacts. The cost of living is low.

Visas and work permits: Most teachers enter the country on a tourist visa, which can be obtained at the airport on arrival. This is valid for one month, which should be long enough to find a job. The school will apply for a work permit from the Ministry of the Interior and this will take around two weeks. All work permit applications must be submitted in the country as permits are not processed by Egyptian representatives abroad.

Cost of living: Cheap.

Salaries and taxes: Expect to earn the equivalent of UK£5-9 per hour in a school, UK£13-£20 privately. In local currency, salaries range from under E£1,000 at less reputable organisations to between E£3,000 and E£6,500 at more established ones, depending on qualifications and specialisation offered. The tax rate is approximately nine per cent.

Accommodation: Do not expect western standards of accommodation. It is quite cheap and generally easy to find, although it is increasingly difficult to do so in Cairo. A decent room in Cairo will cost around UK£100 per month but less elsewhere. A two-bedroom flat in Cairo costs UK£200-£300 per month. Those on a company contract will often get accommodation provided.

Health insurance: Essential.

Inoculations: Hepatitis A, Polio, Typhoid, Malaria (in some areas), Yellow Fever (if coming from an infected area).

English language newspapers: Cairo Times, Maadi Messenger, Egyptian Gazette, Middle East Times.

Important cultural differences: Be respectful in your manner of dress and speech to locals to avoid giving offence.

Other information: Egypt is less liberal than the West but less conservative than the Gulf states. Women will have far fewer difficulties than in neighbouring countries.

List of schools in Egypt

ALS School, Maamoura.

American Cultural Center, 3 El Pharana Street, Alexandria

The American University in Cairo, CACE, ESD P.O. Box 2511, Cairo

AMIDEAST, English Teaching Program, American Cultural Center, 3 Pharana Street, Alexandria

The British Broadcast College, Dokki

The British Council, 192 Nile Street, Agouza, Cairo

The British Council, 9 Batalsa, Bab Shavki, Alexandria

El Kawmeya International School, Horreya Avenue, Bab Sharki

El Manar School, Amin Fikry Street, Ramleh Station, Cairo

El Nasr Boys' College (EBC), Chatby

El Nasr Girls' College (ECC), Chatby

El Pharaana School, El Pharaana Street, Bab Sharki

International Centre for Idioms, (behind Wimpy Bar), Dokki

International House Heliopolis, Cairo, 2 Mohamed Bayoumi St, Off Merghany St, Heliopolis, Cairo Tel: 202 2919295/202 4189212 Fax: 202 4151082 Email: ili@ritsec3.com.eg Contact: Fiona Sibbald. General English courses. Summer courses for young learners. CELTA courses throughout the year. Arabic as a foreign language

International Language Institute, International House, 3 Mahmoud Azmy Street, Medinet El Sahafeyeen, Cairo

International Language Learning Institute, 34 Talaat Harb Street, 5th Floor, Cairo

International Language Learning Institute, Pyramids Road, Guiz

Lycee El Horreya, English Dept., Chatby

October Language Schools, 13, Saad El Ali Street, Mohandesssin

Port Said School, 7, Taha Hussein Street, Zamalek

Ragab Language School, Chatby

Sacred Heart School, Syria School, Roushdy

Schutz American School, Cairo

Victory College, Victoria Tram Station, Victoria

Israel

Because of the large English-speaking community in Israel, there is little need to recruit native teachers from overseas. The British Council has teaching operations in Tel Aviv, Jerusalem and Nazareth which mainly recruit locally.

Some voluntary work is available but this tends to be in the Palestinian West Bank where continuing sporadic violence between Palestinians and Israeli soldiers may make the area unattractive and unsafe.

Visas and work permits: You may enter the country on a tourist visa and must then obtain a work permit, for which you must be sponsored by your school. For Jewish teachers there is always the option of taking up your right of abode, though this will mean you are liable for military service. You should note that to have an Israeli stamp in your passport will deny you entry into several other Middle Eastern states. It is possible to get your entry stamps on removable pages. It is possible to enter Jordan and Eygpt from Israel.

Immigration: Jews from all over the world are encouraged to come to Israel. There are generous incentives, including buying a car without paying tax and help with a mortgage. New immigrants spend three to six months in a government-funded orientation centre, called Ulpan, finding their feet and learning Hebrew.

Cost of living: High.

Salaries and taxes: English teachers can earn US$20-US$28 per hour. Tax rates can be as high as 40 per cent. There are no taxes on tourists for accommodation.

Accommodation: Expensive in Tel Aviv, but cheaper in the suburbs.

Contacts in Israel

British Council, 140 Hayarkon Street, (PO Box 3302)

British Council, 14-706 Al-Nasra Street, (PO Box 355), Al-Rimal, Gaza City

British Council, Ein Sarah Street, (PO Box 277), Hebron

British Council Teaching Centre, Al-Nuzha Building, 2 Abu Obeida Street, (PO Box 19136), East Jerusalem

Jordan

State schools cannot keep up with the demand for English classes and liberalisation means that there is an increasing number of private schools that recruit locally and sometimes overseas. The British Council employs qualified L1 speakers on a part-time basis to teach Jordanian children and teenagers, as does the American Language Centre. There are opportunities for those married to expatriates stationed there to pick up casual work. To get a full-time contract, apply from your home country. The Housing Bank and Royal Jordanian among others have in-house English Language programmes.

Visas and work permits: With a full-time contract obtained at home, your employer will sort out the necessary paperwork. Otherwise, part-time teachers pay an index-linked amount each year for a work permit. Expect to pay around UK£300 per year.

Cost of living: High, but basic necessities and transport are cheap.

Salaries and taxes: A full-time teacher at the British Council can expect to earn around UK£900 per month. The hourly rate is around £10 if you can find a class. Expect to earn between UK£300 and UK£1000 per month if you find work in a good private language school. Some provide flights and accommodation.

Accommodation: One year's rent is often demanded in advance, with the landlord living off the interest. With rents at £300 per month, this up-front payment is large. To avoid paying so much, you can share, sub-let, or try to persuade the landlord to let you pay monthly. The flood of refugees that followed the Gulf War has made it more difficult to find cheap accommodation.

Health insurance: Essential.

Inoculations: Hepatitis A, Typhoid, Polio, Yellow Fever (if coming from an infected area).

English language newspapers: Jordan Times, The Star.

Other information: Jordan is an excellent location for teachers wishing to visit Israel or Lebanon.

List of schools in Jordan

The Ahliyyeh School for Girls, Amman

Amman Baccalaureate School, Amman

American Language Center, P O Box 676, Abdoun 11118, Amman

British Council, First Circle, Jebel Amman, P.O. Box 634, Amman 11118

The National Orthodox School, Amman

New English School, Amman

Yarmouk Cultural Centre, PO Box 960312, Amman

Kuwait

Great efforts have been made to revitalise the English language industry which was very vibrant before the Iraqi invasion. Overall numbers of schools are lower than in the pre-war period and you almost always require qualifications to find work and without exception to maintain a reasonable standard of living. There is a strong demand for English teachers, but Kuwait is not a good place to earn money. As normally male teachers are employed, it is very difficult for women to find teaching position.

Jobs are advertised in the local English language newspapers as well as overseas, making it easier to arrange the necessary visas in advance. Once in Kuwait, there is scope for hourly paid work and opportunities for private lessons. It is illegal to work without an employment permit.

Visas and work permits: All nationalities need entry visas and work permits. Work permits involve notoriously complicated procedures and all applicants must take HIV and TB tests before a permit can be issued.

Salaries and taxes: Annual salaries start at around £13,500, which usually involves a full-time post with about 24 contact hours per week. British Council rates are between £1,000 per month, with medical insurance and a settling-in allowance provided. There is no income tax.

Accommodation: Most schools find and pay for flats because accommodation is expensive. Average rent is UK£400-£520. Usually, one month's rent is required as a deposit.

Health insurance: Advisable. This type of service is usually privately paid for.

Inoculations: Hepatitis A, Polio, Typhoid.

English language newspapers: Arab Times, Kuwait Times.

Important cultural differences: Conditions can sometimes be difficult for single women, although they are allowed to drive. (There are large numbers of single expats of both sexes in Kuwait however.)

Other useful information: Only limited public transport exists and taxis are very expensive, so a driving licence is almost essential. Be prepared for hot summers, when temperatures can rise to 110°C.

SECTION 3 International Job Prospects

List of schools in Kuwait

American International School, Tel: 5318175

British Council, 2 Al Arabi Street, Block 2, PO Box 345, 13004, Safat, Mansourrija

ELU, The Kuwait Institute of Banking Studies, PO Box 1080, Safat 13011

Fahaheel English School, PO Box 7209, Fahaheel 64003

Gulf English School, Tel: 5629216

Kuwait English School, Tel: 5629356

Kuwait University, Tel: 965 483 3655

Institute For Private Education, P.O. Box 6320, 32038 Hawalli

Pitman Secretarial and Business Studies Centre, Tel: 2544840

Language Centre, Kuwait University, PO Box 2575, Safat

Morocco

Morocco is traditionally French-speaking but you will hear Moroccan Arabic, Classical Arabic, various Berber languages and German and Spanish spoken. English has become very popular. It is increasingly a requirement for university entrance and has become a part of state school education. The government has keenly implemented restrictions to prevent the number of foreign teachers in any organisation exceeding 50 per cent.

There are many private schools and despite government restrictions, there are many opportunities for foreign staff. The main markets are in teaching young learners and General English to company-sponsored students.

It is easy to get work with a certificate and experience, possible to get work without experience, and generally impossible without qualifications. Knowledge of French is considered a big asset, especially if you want to stay for a longer period. It is not advisable to come to the country on spec.

Visas and work permits: After you are offered a contract, the school applies for a residence permit. This should happen before arrival in Morocco but often does not. It can take up to three months for your papers to come through. You will need original copies of your birth certificate, degree and teaching qualification.

Cost of living: Cheap, but suffers from high inflation.

Salaries and taxes: Expect low rates of pay, 60-120 dirhams per hour. Taxation is complicated and rises sharply as salary increases. Expect around 25 per cent in deductions. Try to get paid in a hard currency as inflation will erode your local pay.

Accommodation: Flats vary greatly from area to area. In Rabat, a two-bedroomed apartment will cost 2,500-4,000 dirhams a month, more in Casablanca.

Health insurance: Essential.

Inoculations: Hepatitis A, Polio, Typhoid.

Important cultural differences: Morocco takes some adjusting to, but is manageable. It can be difficult for Europeans, especially women who may suffer some harassment.

Other useful information: A knowledge of French is useful.

List of schools in Morocco

American Language Center, 6 Impasse Bagdad, Cite Suisse, Agadir

American Language Center, 10 Place Bel Air, Casablanca

American Language Center, 1 Place de la Fraternite, Casablanca 21000

American Language Center, 2 Rue Ibn Mouaz, BP 2136, Fes - VN.

American Language Center, 2 Bv Al Kadissia, Kenitra

American Language Center, 3 Impasse du Moulain Queliz, Marrakesh.

American Language Center, 21 Rue Antsirabe, 4eme, BP 382, Meknes

American Language Center, 2 Av Mohammed V 1er etage, Mohamedia

American Language Center, 4 Zankat Tanja, Rabat 10000

American Language Center, 35 Ave Al Faks, Souissi, Rabat

American Language Center, 1 Rue El Msallah, Tangiers

American Language Center, 14 Bab Oukla, Ancienne route de Sabta, Tetouan

Benedict School of English, 124 Ave Hassan II, Ben Slimane

British Centre, 3, rue Nolly, Casablanca

British Council, 36 rue de Tanger, B.P. 427, Rabat

British & Professional English Centre (BPEC), 74 rue Jean Jaures, Casablanca

Business and Professional English Centre, 74 rue Jean Jaures, Casablanca

Institut Cegis, 23 Boulevard Ibnou Majid Al Bahhar, Casablanca

International Language Centre, 2 rue Tihama, Rabat

London School of English, 10 ave des FAR, Casablanca

Oman

Oman is a popular destination, but tends to be less well paid than some of its Gulf neighbours. There are a lot of teaching opportunities. It is a nice country to live in. Perhaps its popularity lies in the relatively liberal atmosphere: the buying of alcohol is permitted and there are employment opportunities for women. Positions tend to be for more qualified teachers. Contact CfBT or the English Language Teaching Department., Ministry of Education, PO Box 3, Ruwi.

Visas and work permits: UK, US and EU citizens require a visa to enter the country. Employer sponsorship is required for a permit and the process can often take a long time.

Cost of living: Oman is the most expensive country in the Middle East, prices are comparable to the UK with annual increases. 100 rials per week would secure a moderate, comfortable life.

Salaries and taxes: 550-700 rials per month if you are fortunate. Tax-free.

Accommodation: Often provided. If not, expect to pay between 150 and 250 rials per month, excluding utilities. For 400 rials you would get a very nice apartment.

English Newspapers: Oman Daily Observer, Times of Oman.

Schools in Oman
British Council Muscat, PO Box 73, Postal Code 115, Medinet Al Sultan Qaboos, Sultanate of Muscat

Al Jusr Consultants, PO Box 353, PC 133, Al Khuwair, Muscat, Tel: 968 694681/693906 Fax: 968 696027 Email: aljusrtd@gto.net.om We recruit teachers for the university and the Ministry of Higher Education in Oman

Polyglot Institute, PO Box 221, Ruwi, Oman

Saudi Arabia

English is the acknowledged second language of Saudi Arabia. It is widely used in commerce and with an expatriate labour force outnumbering the domestic population, it is the lingua franca.

Most of the opportunities are in Business English. Companies with training departments for their Saudi staff recruit the most English teachers, whether for EFL or ESL. To find work, look in the EL*Gazette*, EL*Prospects* and the Times Education Supplement. Most contracts are for full-time teaching for 12 months for men. Women are not allowed to work or drive and have to be chaperoned when they go out.

The British Council is now offering regular CELTA courses and are an approved CELTA centre. The centre is able to arrange a visa or extend a visa for those wishing to take a CELTA course.

There are opportunities for unqualified teachers who are doing something else in Saudi Arabia. Moonlighting is common and spouses often take private classes. Parents like their children to study English with L1 speakers.

A contract in Saudi Arabia can be an excellent way of saving money. However it can be an extreme and harsh environment. If you cannot drive it is probably not wise to go to Saudi as the society is car based.

Saudi bureaucracy is very slow, so do not leave your job, let alone book a flight, until you have a signed contract and a visa sorted out.

Visas and work permits: All nationalities need work permits and visas. Teachers must be sponsored by a company in Saudi Arabia, which makes all the applications on behalf of the teacher. There are no tourist visas.

Cost of living: High salaries and all-in packages make it relatively easy for foreign nationals to save money. Accomodation varies between SR2,000 per month for an appartment and SR4,000 per month for a lower priced compound. (The current exchange rate is approximately SR6 = £1.00.)

Salaries and taxes: Most teachers earn between £17,000 and £24,000 per year. Private teaching earns from US$10 to $14 per hour. There are no local taxes. Most packages include accomodation and 1 or 2 flights to the UK per year. Most contracts are single status.

Accommodation: Working for a large employer often includes compound accommodation. If your contract does not include housing, it may not be advisable to accept it. Apartments cost from US$300 per month but rents are going down.

Health insurance: Essential. It is usually part of the contract.

Inoculations: Hepatitis A, Polio, Typhoid, Malaria, Meningitis, Yellow Fever (if coming from an infected area).

English language newspapers: Arab News, Saudi Gazette, Riyadh Daily.

Important cultural differences: There is a strict dress code and many things the West takes for granted - alcohol, women driving, and men and women freely intermingling are prohibited. Schools generally recruit single men or married couples.

Other useful information: For a single person, the right contract in Saudi Arabia can offer an excellent opportunity to make reasonable financial savings. However, it is rarely a career move, unless you work with a global organisation. For a family with children, it is essential to get adequate accommodation and funding for school fees.

If you have a car accident, it will almost certainly be your fault and it is wise not to transgress any local laws, as the legal system can be difficult and stressful to follow for an outsider.

If you plan to make large savings tax free, it is advisable for Britons to obtain a tax office form "working overseas" to avoid a hefty bill on your return to the UK.

List of schools in Saudi Arabia
The British Council, Al Moajil Building, 5th Floor, Dhahran Street, Mohamed Street, PO Box 8387, Daman

Girls College of Arts - General Presidency for Female Institute for Languages and Translation, c/o King Saud University, PO Box 2465, Riyadh 11451

King Abdulaziz University, Jeddah

King Fahd University of Petroleum and Minerals, English Language Centre, Dhahran 31261

Riyadh Military Hospital - Training Division, PO Box 7897, Riyadh 11159

Saudi Airlines, PO Box 167, Jeddah 21231

Saudi Language Institute, PO Box 6760, Riyadh 11575

SCECO - East Central Training Institute, PO Box 5190, Damman 31422

Yanbu Industrial College, PO Box 30436, Yanbu Al Sinaiyah 21477

Syria

Although there is a substantial demand for English teachers, the opportunities are restricted to those with qualifications. The British Council generally favours teachers with a diploma and experience while the American Language Centre is willing to recruit those who are less qualified.

It is essential to sort out a job before heading to the country unless you are the spouse of someone already working there. Part-time local teachers wishing to work for the British Council need a certificate. There is some scope for teaching English privately although only a small proportion of the population would be able to afford it.

Visas and work permits: You need an entrance visa and exit visa, obtainable from the Syrian embassy in your country. Once in the country, teachers can usually secure a residence card by registering on an Arabic course at a university.

Remember you cannot enter Syria with an Israeli stamp in your passport.

Cost of living: General groceries are cheaper than in most Western states, especially those produced locally. Teachers often find it cheaper to eat out than to cook. Part-time local teachers do not earn enough to live on and need to supplement with private lessons or other income. Overseas recruits can live quite comfortably.

Salaries and taxes: For private lessons expect $6-10 per hour. Working as a local-hire teacher should earn you $9-13 per hour while overseas recruits can expect about $450 per month with an annual bonus of $3-10,000 pa.

Accommodation: Flats are expensive but are generally furnished. In the middle of Damascus flats can cost around $4,000 pa. To rent a room with a family in the old city would be around $100 per month.

Health insurance: Recommended.

English language newspapers: Syria Times.

Important cultural differences: The usual differences associated with an Arab/Islamic culture. It is technically illegal to live with someone of the opposite sex who is not your spouse.

Other useful information: Travellers' cheques, credit cards and cheque books are not used in Syria but are useful for travel in the region. Receipts for transactions should be kept.

List of schools in Syria

American Language Center, c/o US Embassy, PO Box 29, Damascus

Al Kindi English Language Centre, 29 May Street, Damascus

Al Kudssi Institute, PO Box 5296, Aleppo

Al Razi English Language Centre, PO Box 2533, Damascus

Alson, Damascus

American Language Center, PO Box 29, Rawda Circle, Damascus

British Council, Al Jala'a, Abu Rumaneh, P O Box 33105, Damascus

Damascus Language Centre, PO Box 249, Damascus

Tunisia

Tunisia remains a Francophone country and English teachers are not in great demand. However, English seems to be replacing French as the language of business, so prospects for teachers are improving. It is best to apply to the ELT institutions in the region before leaving home, and a knowledge of Arabic or French is considered very advantageous.

Visas and work permits: It can take three months or longer to arrange a working visa, but you should receive a temporary work permit or a letter from your employer allowing you to work in the meantime. Original degree and birth certificates are required. The employer must obtain a Resident's Permit endorsed 'Authorised to undertake a remunerated job in Tunisia', and valid for a maximum of two years.

Cost of living: Tourism has driven up the cost of living.

Salaries and taxes: Teachers are paid more than local rates and if fortunate can earn 10 to 14 Tunisian dinars per hour. At the top end, you can expect to earn a minimum of 14,000 dinars per year. The tax rate is around 20 per cent.

Accommodation: It is easy to find somewhere to live. Expect to pay 3-400 Tunisian dinars per month, with at least one month's rent as a deposit. Accommodation is largely unfurnished.

Health insurance: Essential.

Inoculations: Hepatitis A, Polio, Typhoid, Yellow Fever (if coming from an infected area).

English language newspapers: Tunisia News.

Important cultural differences: Tunisia is more open and cosmopolitan than its neighbours, but foreign women need to be streetwise.

Schools in Tunisia

AMIDEAST, English Teaching Program, BP 351, 1002 Tunis-Belvedere

English Language Training Centre, British Council, 47 Avenue Habib Bourguiba, Tunis

Institut Bourguiba des Languages Vivantes (IBLV), 47 Avenue de la Liberte, Tunis

United Arab Emirates

This federation of Arab states, which includes Abu Dhabi, Dubai and Sharjah, has good prospects for EFL teachers, especially on a part-time basis or at tertiary level. Pay is good and contracts usually include accommodation and flights. Teachers with diplomas and experience are rare so these qualifications virtually guarantee work. There is strong demand for English teachers and there are opportunities for women to get jobs. There is a good opportunity to get a job at a College of Technology.

Visas and work permits: Tourist visas are readily issued. To live and work in the UAE, you need an employer to be sponsor unless you are the spouse of someone already working there. Rules concerning visas change at short notice, so contact your local UAE embassy before departure. It is forbidden to work on a tourist visa.

Cost of living: Cheaper than Western Europe, with little inflation. Accommodation is expensive but often comes with the job.

Salaries and taxes: 5-8,000 dirhams per month (£1100), or 100-200 dirhams per hour part-time. No tax for expatriate teachers.

Accommodation: Usually provided, otherwise expensive. A single flat costs 20-35,000 dirhams per year, a double 20,000-50,000.

Health insurance: A Health Card costs about 300 dirhams.

Inoculations: Hepatitis A, Polio, Typhoid, Malaria (in some areas).

English language newspapers: Emirates News, Gulf News, Gulf Today, Khaleej Times.

SECTION 3 International Job Prospects

177

Other useful information: With the growth of tourism, there has been an increasing demand for both male and female EFL teachers. Although the percentage of women in the UAE labour force is still low, both Abu Dhabi and Dubai are cosmopolitan, relaxed cities, without the restrictions normally associated with the Gulf. Dubai is probably the most westernised state, but people should not forget that they are still in a Muslim country and behave accordingly.

List of schools in UAE

Abu Dhabi National Oil Co,
PO Box 898, Abu Dhabi

Al Farabi Language Centre,
PO Box 3794, Dubai

Al-Worood School,
P.O. Box 46673, Abu Dhabi

American University of Sharjah,
PO Box 26666, Sharjah

Arabic Language Centre, (Dubai World Trade Centre), PO Box 9292, Dubai

Dar Al Ilm School of Languages,
PO Box 2550, Dubai

Dubai Aviation College,
PO Box 53044, Dubai

Dubai Cultural and Scientific Institute,
PO Box 8751, Dubai

ELS International, PO Box 2380, Dubai

Higher College of Technology,
Fax: 233 0666.

Institute of Australian Studies,
PO Box 20183, Dubai

International Education Institute,
PO Box 524714, Dubai

International Language Institute (Language Specialists Institute),
PO Box 3253, Sharjah

International Training Solutions,
PO Box 4234, Dubai.

Polyglot School, PO Box 1093, Dubai

Wollongong, University of, Institute for Australian Studies, Dubai Campus, Dubai

Yemen

Yemen is a developing country with economic problems. Funding for English teaching often comes from aid donors. It is a beautiful and fascinating country, perhaps remaining a more traditional Arab society than those with oil-associated development. Potential teachers

should be aware that foreigners have been kidnapped in the past in the northern regions of the country.

Although illiteracy is estimated to be 80 per cent, there is a steady demand for English and it is quite easy for unqualified native and non-native speakers to find teaching work, especially at primary level. Most of the work is associated with EFL but the number of English medium schools is growing in the private sector.

The main markets are in general English and specialist English in the oil and gas industries. Most teachers are on contract with one of the giant oil companies, Canadian-Oxidental being the largest in the country. They recruit mainly from the UK direct. Other work is part-time or paid at an hourly rate, with information available in the local chamber of commerce or by word of mouth.

Visas and work permits: Necessary for all nationalities. Some people do work on tourist visas but it is illegal. An invitation letter issued by a school in Yemen is required for a visa to be issued by Yemeni consulates in the teacher's home country.

Cost of living: Very cheap.

Salaries and taxes: The going rate for teaching is around US$1,000-1,500 per month, or higher at the British Council. Payment in hard currency is essential. There is no tax. Other perks such as flights and insurance are sometimes included.

Accommodation: It is very easy to find accommodation since the market is depressed. The average rent is US$125 per month, with two or three months rent as a deposit.

Health insurance: Essential.

Inoculations: Hepatitis A, Typhoid, Polio, Yellow Fever (if coming from an infected area).

English language newspapers: Yemen Times, Yemen Observer, Daily Chew.

Important cultural differences:
Alcohol is not available and women must wear long-dresses.

List of schools in Yemen

Al Farouq Institute, PO Box 16927, Sana'a

The British Council, PO Box 2157, Sana'a

English Language Centre, PO Box 8984, Sana'a

Faculty of Art, English Department, PO Box 6014, Aden

Faculty of Art, English Department, Sana'a

Faculty of Education, English Department, Sana'a

Faculty of Education, English Department, PO Box 6480, Taiz

Faculty of Education, English Department, PO Box 70270, Ibb

French Culture Centre, PO Box 1286, Sana'a

MALI, PO Box 16003, Sana'a

Madina Institute of Technology (MIT), Aden

The Modern Yemen School, PO Box 13335, Sana'a

Mohammed Ali Othman School, PO Box 5713, Taiz

National Institute for Administrative Science, PO Box 102, Sana'a

Pakistani School, Sana'a

The Pioneer School, Sana'a

Sabaa University PO Box 14400, Sana'a

SAM School, PO Box 19390, Sana'a

Sana'a British School, PO Box 15546, Sana'a

Sana'a International School, PO Box 2002, Sana'a

Spectra Institute, PO Box 16101, Sana'a

University of Al-Ahgaff, PO Box 50341

University of Science Technology, PO Box 15201, Sana'a

YALI - Yemen-America Language Institute, PO Box 22347, Sana'a

Yemen International Language Institute, PO Box 11586, Sana'a

Yemen Language Centre, PO Box 1691, Sana'a

Yemen Sudanese Language Centre, PO Box 13187, Sana'a

Sub-Saharan Africa

The large number of Anglophone countries and a high level of poverty mean that much of the teaching work in this region is limited to voluntary organisations.

Teaching English in sub-Saharan Africa will almost certainly be memorable. As a general rule, there is little work in countries where English is already the official language since teachers can be recruited locally. In those countries teaching opportunities are likely to be limited to secondary and tertiary levels.

Other countries require English language teachers, but their economies cannot support a private language industry. Here overseas teachers are employed through voluntary and educational programmes only. They include: Benin, Burkina Faso, Cape Verde, Central African Republic, Chad, Comoros, Congo, Cote d'Ivoire, Ethiopia, Gabon, Gambia, Ghana, Guinea, Guinea Bissau, Madagascar, Malawi, Mali, Niger, Nigeria, Sao Tome, Senegal, Seychelles, Tanzania, Togo, Zambia.

British voluntary and educational organisations operating programmes in Africa include Voluntary Service Overseas, Project Trust, Teaching Abroad and Concern Worldwide. US organisations include Peace Corps and WorldTeach.

Please note that while teachers may seek to be located in a given region, voluntary groups operate according to demand and cannot guarantee placements in a desired country.

An exception to the above information is South Africa.

South Africa

English is perhaps the most widely used of the 15 official languages of South Africa and since the change in regime the demand for English language learning has rocketed. A major government aim is to extend its education programme to all of the population. This huge increase in demand for teachers is off-set by the other government aim to give employment to South Africans first. If you have citizenship of the country, then English teaching posts abound. If not, then getting a work permit will be much more difficult.

There are no standard qualifications for TEFL taught in South Africa so there is demand for teachers who have qualified abroad, but there are a growing number of RSA courses within the country. Demand is highest in Cape Town, but is growing in Johannesburg. There are several language schools aimed at Europeans seeking a new place to learn English opening up - especially in Cape Town.

Visas and work permits: Most nationalities do not require a visa. All, however, need a work permit which costs around US$110 and is dependent upon having an offer of employment in writing. The employer must show that the position has been advertised locally and this is where the difficulty can arise.

Cost of living: With the country in a period of transition, the rand is quite volatile. Any hard currency you are able to save before travelling to South Africa will greatly multiply when you change it for rands. Local produce is fairly cheap compared with UK or US but imports are very expensive.

Salaries and taxes: Hourly rates range from US£5 to US$13. Income tax is levied at 20% - 30% unless you are registered as a consultant, in which case you pay no tax.

Accommodation: Conditions are good and appartments are large. Furnished appartments are very expensive.

Health insurance: Essential.

Inoculations: Hepatitis A, Polio, Tetanus, Typhoid, Malaria, Yellow Fever (if coming from an infected area).

English language newspapers:
The Star, Weekly Mail.

List of schools in South Africa
Academic Support Programme,
PO Wits, Johannesburg 2050
Academy for English, 14, Rutland Road, Parkwood, Johannesburg
Cape Studies, 100 Main Road, PO Box 4425, Cape Town 8000
Cape Town TEFL School of English and TEFL Training, 1 Draper Square, Claremont, 7708, Cape Town
Cape Communication Centre,
Tel: 27 21 419 1967
Easy English, 46, St Andrews Road, Houghton Estate, Johannesburg
English Centre Durban, PO Box 29016, Maydon Wharf, 4057 Durban
English Language Educational Trust,
6th Floor, Wesley Building, 74, Aliwal Street, Durban 4000
Good Hope Studies, 30, Earrie Road, Newlands 7700
inlingua Language Centre, 27 Dixon Street, Cape Town 8001

inlingua Language Training Ventre, Kinellan, 14 Portswood Road, V + A Waterfront, Cape Town, 8001. Contact Jane Diesel Tel: 00 27 21 419 0494 Fax: 00 27 21 419 0725 Email: info@inlingua.co.za Website: www.inlingua.co.za. General/Business English, EAP, TOEFL/Cambridge examination preparation. Learn English on safari, Homestay and Tours arranged, member of inlingua International.

Interman, P O Box 52621, Saxonworld, Johannesburg 2132
International House Cape Town, Windermere, Portswood Business Park, V & A Waterfront, Cape Town 8001 PO Box 52199

The Language Lab, International House Johannesburg, 4th Floor, 54 De Korte Street, Braamfontein 2001, Johannesburg

Sub-Saharan Africa

Language Travel Africa, PO Box 72361, The Willows, Pretoria 0014

Language Wise, Cargo House, Cnr Jan, Smuts & 7th St, Rosebank, Johannesburg

Magri's Language Institute, 12th Floor, Noswall Hall, Cnr Jan Smuts and Stiemens, Johannesburg 2000

South African Language Labotatory, Cape Town 8001

Studywell College, 102 De Korte Street, Braamfontein, Johannesburg 2000

Botswana

Demand for English language teachers is relatively low as English is the official language. Employers have to give preference to Botswana nationals so work permits can be hard to come by.

Most foreign teachers are recruited through the Teachers for Botswana Recruitment Scheme, administered by the British Council in Manchester and the Department of Teacher Service Management in Botswana. Qualified teachers are recruited throughout Botswana twice a year.

Visas and work permits: An entry permit is required to visit. Visitors can usually get a 30-day permit on production of a return ticket and evidence of sufficient finance. Most EU nationals do not require entry visas for visits of up to 90 days.

Non-nationals in the private sector require work permits from the Department of Labour, valid for a limited period and renewable. These should be obtained by the employer as soon as the employee arrives in Botswana.

Cost of living: Cheap.

Salaries and taxes: A teacher with a degree can earn as much as 2,600 Botswana pula (about £450) per month while a postgraduate can earn more than 3,500 pula (£600).

Accommodation: Subsidised by most state schools. They normally charge a fee of 15 per cent. There is an acute shortage of housing, particularly in Gaborone, and teachers should expect to spend the first

few months in a hotel. A government two-bedroom flat could cost P400-650 per month while a similar private flat could cost P1,500-2,500.

Health insurance: Essential.

Inoculations: Hepatitis A, Malaria (in some areas), Polio, Tetanus and Typhoid.

English language newspapers: Mmegi, Daily News.

Cameroon

English is rapidly becoming the language for business in Cameroon so demand for ELT is increasing. However, the only realistic employment prospects for foreign EL teachers are with the British Council. They demand two years experience and a recognised entry level certificate.

Small, private EL schools in Cameroon do not recruit expatriates due to expense and government schools can only pay low local rates.

Visas and work permits: Visas are granted for up to 12 months, with multiple entry. Foreign teachers require a residence permit, which contains a work clause. These cost around US$750, another reason why there are few freelance teachers in Cameroon.

Cost of living: The cost of living in Yaounde and Dovala is relatively cheap, with local supermarkets, food shops, bars and restaurants offering reasonable prices..

Salaries and taxes: British Council teachers earn about £550 per month, plus £125 housing allowance and £50 transport allowance. They are not liable to any local tax.

Accommodation: Appartments can cost up to £200 per month plus £30 for water and electricity.

Health insurance: Essential.

Inoculations: Yellow Fever essential, Typhoid, Tetanus, Polio, Hepatitis A, Meningitis, Malaria.

English language newspapers: Herald, Cameroon Tribune and Post.

Other useful information: Bring your own teaching materials. There are virtually none on sale locally.

Eritrea

Eritrea's economy is unable to support private language schools, so prospects are few. It is possible to work voluntarily through VSO in rural based junior or senior secondary schools if you have a TEFL certificate and some experience. Be warned that conditions are tough and there can be over 70 pupils in a class.

Cost of living: Cheap.

Salaries and taxes: Salaries are at local rates but top-ups are generally available if they are deemed too low for subsistence.

Accommodation: Provided by local employer.

Health insurance: Essential.

Inoculations: Hepatitis A, Malaria, Polio, Tetanus, Typhoid and Yellow Fever.

Ethiopia

There is little private school activity in Ethiopia. Considerable demand for English language learning exists however, spurred on by a late 1970's literacy campaign, which purportedly increased adult literacy from 4 per cent to 29 per cent by 1987.

VSO recently received its first requests for teachers in the country. These positions are in teacher training colleges where the focus tends to be on language upgrading for undergraduate trainee teachers, who go on to become secondary school English teachers of English. Volunteers need a degree, TEFL certificate/PGCE and at least two years of experience.

Inoculations: Hepatitis A, Polio, Tetanus, Typhoid, Malaria, Meningitis, Yellow Fever, cholera.

Schools in Ethiopia

International Community School, PO Box 70282, Addis Ababa

Sandford English Community School, PO Box 30056 MA, Addis Ababa

University of Addis Ababa, PO Box 1176, Addis Ababa

The Gambia

There are no private language schools. There is some demand for volunteers to teach English language as part of the syllabus in rural secondary schools. Volunteers should have a degree and a TEFL certificate or PGCE but not necessarily teaching experience.

Accommodation: Provided by local employer.

Health insurance: Essential.

Inoculations: Hepatitis A, Polio, Tetanus, Typhoid, Malaria, Meningitis, Yellow Fever.

Ghana

Because of the economic situation there are no private schools even though there is considerable demand for English. Local incomes could not meet fees if a school were set up.

The university may possibly require lecturers soon as current staff near retirement. Otherwise, there are some voluntary positions available in senior secondary schools in quite remote, rural areas of the country.

Visas and work permits: Foreign teachers can secure these by applying to the Ghanaian embassy in their country.

Cost of living: Generally much less than Western Europe.

Salaries and taxes: Salaries at the University of Ghana would range from £1,400 per month for an Assistant Lecturer to £2,100 for a Professor. Expect to receive 240,000 cedis (about £300) per month if on a volunteer programme and employed at local rates.

Accommodation: This is usually arranged by the University or school.

English language newspapers: Ghanaian Times, Graphic, Ghanaian Chronicle.

Inoculations: Hepatitis A, Polio, Tetanus, Typhoid, Malaria, Meningitis, Yellow Fever essential.

Kenya

English is the language of instruction and as in many former British colonies in Africa, there is a shortage of teachers, especially at secondary school level. But, even with this shortage, the government restricts state school work permits to teachers with a certificate and one year of experience. These restrictions do not apply to teachers coming to work in private schools.

Visas and work permits: Officially, anyone who wishes to work needs a work permit before landing in Nairobi. But there is no evidence to suggest that L1 English language teachers looking for work on spec will have their application turned down. You will normally have to prove that no Kenyan citizen is available to fill the post.

Cost of living: Quite high in Nairobi, £250 per month

Salaries and taxes: Generally paid at local rates, which are sufficient for sustaining a basic lifestyle.

Accommodation: Usually arranged by the employer. Can be nothing more than a tin-roofed hut in the more rural areas. Costs in Nairobi are quite high - at least £250 per month for decent rented accommodation. Costs are high because the security situation means that it is not possible to live in cheaper accommodation.

Health insurance: Essential.

Inoculations: Yellow Fever compulsory. Typhoid, Tetanus, Polio, Hepatitis A, Meningitis, Malaria.

Other useful information: You will not save a lot teaching in Kenya and conditions are likely to be tough, with restricted access to running water and electricity common. Teachers should be aware that crime rates are high in Nairobi and that the recent elections saw large scale ethnic violence and intimidation, which spread to the previously safe tourist areas.

Schools in Kenya

American Universities Preparation and Learning Centre, P O Box 14842, Nairobi

The Language Center Ltd, P O Box 14245, Ndemi Close, Off Ngong Road, Nairobi

The British Council Teaching Centre, P.O. Box 40751, Harry Thuku Road, Opposite Norfolk Hotel, Nairobi

Malawi

In Malawi, English is the medium of education but low per capita incomes in the country leave little scope for private schools.

Expatriate teachers tend to be missionaries or volunteers recruited through agencies. Some schools advertise in the Times Educational Supplement, though these are often for subject-related, rather than ELT, positions. Christians Abroad is the main recruiting organisation although there are others, including VSO. Government requirements mean that only certified teachers are likely to be placed.

Visas and work permits: Foreign teachers need temporary work permits, which are obtained for them by their employer.

Cost of living: Local produce is cheap and imported goods very expensive (US$5 for a packet of cornflakes).

Salaries and taxes: Volunteer rates, or US$8,000 to US$17,000 in the private sector. Taxation is up to 35 per cent.

Accommodation: Accommodation with basic furnishings is usually provided by the employer.

181

Health insurance: Essential.

Inoculations: Hepatitis A, Polio, Typhoid, Meningitis, Malaria, Yellow Fever (if coming from an infected area).

Senegal

Qualified native speaker teachers can pick up work informally. However, there are no private language schools and little formal work.

Visas and work permits: EU citizens do not need an entry visa but those from the US and Australia do. They should write a letter of request to the Ministry of Interior, stating how long their stay will be. The visa is stamped on arrival at the airport and on expiry, a request for a carte d'identite should be made to the Ministry. EU citizens must apply for this card if they want to work.

Salaries and taxes: Senegalese teachers of English are poorly paid so the rate offered to native speaker teachers is low also. Expect to be offered 6,000 FCFA (about £6.60) per hour at the top end.

Accommodation: The average rent for a small flat in Dakar is 150,000 - 250,000 FCFA (about £170) per month.

Inoculations: Hepatitis A, Polio, Tetanus, Typhoid, Malaria, Meningitis, Yellow Fever.

List of schools in Senegal
American Culture Centre, BP 49, Dakar

Sierra Leone

This is one of the poorest countries in the world with continuing civil conflict. Consequently there is no market for EFL teaching.

Visas and work permits: Can be obtained from the Sierra Leone High Commissions overseas.

Cost of living: Very cheap.

Salaries and taxes: Very low. Local income per capita is $125 pa. Tax is 50 per cent.

Inoculations: Hepatitis A, Polio, Tetanus, Typhoid, Malaria, Meningitis, Yellow Fever.

English language newspapers: For Di People.

Other information: There is little infrastructure with very limited power and water available.

Sudan

This giant African country has a history of ties to Britain and the English language. However, the country's education system, which was once reputed to be the best in Africa, has suffered as a result of continuing civil war. Government schemes to maintain ELT in schools along side Arabicisation policies have been neglected as a result of budget cuts. The Ministry of Education has suspended its recruitment of teachers overseas. Nevertheless, there is still a good demand for English language teachers in the country and there are many short-term and private teaching prospects available.

Visas and work permits: A tourist visa takes about three weeks to process but, if you are not a national of an Arab country, you will need a work permit. Paperwork should be sorted out before you come to the country.

Cost of living: Cheap, but inflation is rampant.

Salaries and taxes: All salaries are negotiable. The going rate for private work is UK£5-10 per hour. Tax is 10 per cent.

Accommodation: It is fairly easy to find somewhere to live and schools often help. The average rent is only UK£40 per month, but deposits of up to six months are often required.

Health insurance: Advisable. Arrange long-term travel insurance before you leave.

Inoculations: Yellow Fever, Hepatitis A, Tetanus, Typhoid, Polio, Meningitis.

English language newspapers: New Horizon, Sudanow. Newsweek is widely available.

Important cultural differences: Friday is the only non-working day. Islamic laws are strictly enforced and there are restrictions for women and on alcohol consumption. Westerners find there is often a lack of punctuality, privacy and organisation.

Other useful information: In spite of the poor local resources and facilities, the people are generally very warm, hospitable and responsive. Be sure to check the political climate before travelling as the situation tends to fluctuate. The south of the country has suffered enormous persecution for its religious and ethnic make up.

Swaziland

English is the official language of this small rural country and is taught in all schools from lower primary level. This means that most of the opportunities are in government-run schools. There are a few expatriate contracts which are mainly taken by qualified teachers from other African countries.

Opportunities occasionally come up in the small number of private schools. It might be possible for unqualified teachers to find work in the private sector. Qualified non-L1 teachers can find work in Swaziland. The main market is in teaching English as a second language. Jobs are usually advertised in the local press.

Visas and work permits: A visa is not required for Commonwealth citizens, but all nationalities need work permits. It is illegal to work on a tourist visa and a work permit can be obtained by the employer showing that no citizen or resident of Swaziland is able to the job as well as an overseas teacher.

Cost of living: Cheap. The economy is strong for the region.

Salaries and taxes: Salaries vary according to your qualifications and your employer. A secondary school teacher in a government school earns about

UK£200-250 per month plus accommodation. In private schools expect more. The highest rates are for expatriate contracts where you stay in the country for more than two years. You are only taxed if your salary exceeds £220 per month. The maximum rate is 33 per cent.

Accommodation: Cheap rented accommodation is scarce. It is easy to come by flats at the higher end of the scale. A reasonable house with three bedrooms will cost a minimum of £200 per month. One month's rent is expected as a deposit. Government schools generally provide adequate accommodation, especially for teachers on expatriate contracts.

Health insurance: Advisable.

Inoculations: Hepatitis A, Polio, Tetanus, Typhoid, Yellow Fever.

English language newspapers: Times of Swaziland, Observer.

Important cultural differences: Swaziland has a traditional male-dominated culture.

Tanzania

There are only a handful of private language schools in Tanzania but there might be opportunities sometimes in the universities and technical colleges. There are also some private international primary and secondary, English medium schools which might offer positions, especially to those who have a subject/specialisation to offer.

Visas and work permits: Visas required for non-nationals and work permits obtained by the employer areessential for teaching.

Salaries and taxes: About £220 per month. Tax is about 15 per cent.

Accommodation: Should be included with the position.

Health insurance: Essential.

Inoculations: Hepatitis A, Polio, Tetanus, Typhoid, Malaria, Meningitis, Yellow Fever.

Details of school in Tanzania
International Languages Orientation Services, P O Box 6995, Dar es Salaam

Zambia

English is taught in the formal government sector schools and there are no language schools as such. However, as English is the country's official language it commands a high status. There is the occasional private primary school where English is integrated into the normal curriculum.

Visas and work permits: The employing agency must apply for a permit on behalf of a teacher and these are difficult to obtain. The agency must prove that there is no Zambian who could do the job.

Cost of living: Extremely high for this part of Africa.

Salaries and taxes: Private language schools tend to source teachers who are spouses of expatriates already working in the country, so salaries are rarely high enough to cover the cost of living.

Accommodation: Should be provided with the position.

Health insurance: Essential.

Inoculations: Hepatitis A, Polio, Tetanus, Typhoid, Malaria, Yellow Fever.

English language newspapers: The Post, The Times of Zambia.

Other useful information: Because of the high cost of living, ensure that the contract allows for airfare, accommodation, medical cover and education fees for children.

Zimbabwe

Since the country gained its independence in 1980, the government has been trying to balance the education system which had been biased towards the more affluent, white population. English language remains the principal teaching language, so there is a strong demand for teachers. Although the government has set up training colleges, there is a short-

age of trained teachers and the Ministry of Education actively recruits from overseas. Government contracts are secure and usually last for three years. There are also opportunities in private English medium primary and secondary schools.

Visas and work permits: Visitors from the US and UK do not need a tourist visa if staying for less than three months. However, if you want to teach, you will need a residence visa and temporary work permit which should be arranged through the High Commission in your country or through the Department of Immigration in Zimbabwe. Your prospective employer should assist you. Teachers are advised that work permits can take time to issue so it is probably better to sort your job and visa out before you go.

Cost of living: Relatively expensive in Harare but cheap in more rural areas.

Salaries and taxes: Expect to earn up to about Z$3,000 per month in Harare, less in the more rural areas.

Accommodation: Should be provided, otherwise it could be difficult to make ends meet.

Health insurance: Essential.

Inoculations: Hepatitis A, Polio, Tetanus, Typhoid, Malaria, Yellow Fever.

A Word of Warning

Some countries are experiencing cultural, economic or political troubles. At the time of writing, the UK Foreign Office advised its nationals against visiting: Afghanistan, Albania, Algeria, Angola, Burundi, Chechen Republic, Congo, Iraq, Jammu & Kashmir, Kosovo, Liberia, Somalia, Tajikistan and Western Sahara.

At the time of writing it is also advised that only visits on essential business should be made to Angola, Boznia/Herzegovina, Central African Republic, Rwanda, West Bank & Gaza Strip, and Zaire.

SECTION FOUR

Developing Your Career

For experienced teachers keen to improve their skills or move into a specialist sphere of English Language Teaching, there is a vast range of courses on offer from universities, colleges of further education and private language schools. The following section gives details of many of these courses as well as advice on which qualifications might best suit your chosen career path.

Do I need further qualifications?

To stay on the academic side (in Teacher Training or as a Director of Sudies), or to move into management increasingly you do, but in EFL related areas such as publishing you don't, but it helps. There is a wide variety of further qualifications for experienced EFL teachers looking to improve their knowledge and employability.

There is a bewildering variety of in-service courses for experienced teachers. Broadly speaking, courses fall into two main categories. Teacher training courses, such as RSA/Trinity Diplomas, concentrate on teaching practice. Education courses, such as university qualifications, give you a solid grounding in the theory. Which course will suit you, depends on your reason for doing it.

Doing the job better

Any good course should help you to do your job better, even if only because it allows you to take a break and reflect. Indeed, you may choose one of the increasing number of specialist short courses (see pages 224 & 229-248) to explore a particular area of your job, such as teaching literature or the use of technology. These short courses usually provide a good introduction to specialist areas, but if you want to study these areas for a qualification, you might consider a specialist Masters degree.

For a general course covering the whole spectrum of teaching, think about the training you have already done. If your previous training concentrated mostly on language and theory, go for a practical short course or an RSA or Trinity diploma. If your previous training involved teaching practice and methodology, you might prefer the kind of theoretical courses offered by universities.

If you don't have any previous training, you should opt for the kind of course which carries most weight with employers in your home country. For example, in North America this tends to be a university qualification, while in other English-speaking countries a practical course with a teaching practice component often has more value. If you have several years, experience but no qualification, you may be eligible to skip the initial qualification stage and go straight to a further qualification, such as a diploma or Masters.

Getting a better job

For non-L1 speakers, getting a better job means working in your own country, so go for a course with a high status at home. In Brazil, for example, the RSA Diploma is well regarded, while in France, university qualifications in ESP are in demand. As a rule of thumb, choose a course that earns you a qualification, and preferably a course which is validated either externally or by a university.

For L1 speakers teaching General English in the private sector, a practical, validated classroom diploma would probably be your best bet. A diploma is a prerequisite for most jobs in private sector management or teacher training and there is a world shortage of diploma teachers. If you are looking to work in a specialist area, like EAP or Primary English, then look for a specialist qualification. If you want to work in the state sector at university level, you will need a Masters degree.

As there are only a certain number of senior jobs in any given area, getting a better job often means moving. If you are keen to stay where you are, it's probably not worth doing a further qualification unless you are guaranteed a job at the end of it or unless your employer is prepared to pay for the course.

Qualifications by distance training

At this level distance training is a perfectly acceptable form of course delivery. Since you are already an in-service teacher, practice is less of a concern than at certificate level. If you've never done a qualification before, you would probably be wise to opt for a course with a teaching practice component.

If you already have qualifications, then distance-only qualifications should be perfectly acceptable. Choose either an externally validated diploma course or a diploma or masters offered by a well-known university.

Diploma Courses

With a certificate and some teaching experience you can enrol on a diploma course, which will qualify you for a senior job anywhere in the world.

Diploma level teachers are in short supply around the world and this means that anyone with the qualification can get a job in almost any sector in virtually any country. However, diplomas are time-consuming (a year part-time, 8 weeks full-time) and, at over a thousand pounds, an investment. They are only really worth doing if you want to stay in the English language industry, and if you are prepared to move.

Which diploma?

A 'dip-level' teacher is one with a certificate, two or three years experience and a practical, in-service qualification. Employers tend to prefer diplomas from Cambridge/RSA or Trinity, as both include written exams on theory together with graded, observed teaching practice. However, in a market where dip-level teachers are hard to come by, employers will consider alternatives.

Entry requirements for the Cambridge/RSA DELTA (Diploma in English Language Teaching to Adults) are tougher than for the Trinity counterpart and it probably carries a little more weight with some employers. To enrol on a Cambridge/RSA Diploma, you must have at least two years' classroom experience, although most centres will demand more. It is also hard to get in without a certificate. From a teacher's point of view, the advantage of the Cambridge/RSA Diploma is that more centres run it, both in the UK and overseas. Many of these centres offer part-time courses for teachers working locally. A Diploma in English Language Teaching to Young Learners (DELTYL) is also being offered at selected centres during 1999/2000. Cambridge/RSA is also piloting the Diploma in Business and Professional English Language Teaching during 1999/2000.

Trinity requires less classroom experience than Cambridge/RSA (only one year in theory, though most centres ask for more) and is particularly good for experienced teachers without a previous qualification.

International House London is the only school which offers the Cambridge/RSA Diploma partially by distance learning. A distance learning component is a feature of many of the Trinity courses, but there are few overseas centres running them.

Alternatives

Although employers prefer RSA and Trinity diplomas to others, they are not as strict as when selecting teachers at certificate level. This is probably because of the relative short supply of diploma level teachers around the world.

Many employers are willing to accept a full postgraduate course leading to Qualified Teacher Status in ELT along with two years' classroom experience instead of a Cambridge/RSA or Trinity diploma. Most employers will also accept a university diploma, as long as it includes observed teaching practice, or an alternative diploma with entry requirements of a certificate, 200 hours of classroom experience and observed teaching practice.

University postgraduate diplomas

These are usually a year in length, open to L1 and non-L1 English speakers with teaching experience (usually a year minimum). They are generally less practically oriented than the Cambridge/RSA or Trinity Diplomas, though an increasing number do offer teaching practice.

When deciding to choose between a university diploma and an externally validated one, such as those offered by RSA or Trinity, ask yourself what your career aims are. If you are looking to work in the private sector, with an eye perhaps on moving into management, then an externally-validated diploma may be more helpful in getting you there. However, if you intend to work in state education at primary, secondary or tertiary level, a university diploma may equip you better – particularly if you do not want to do a full Masters.

UK Cambridge / RSA Diploma (DELTA) Courses

College	Full or Part Time	Course Length	Fees	Start Dates	Entry Requirements	Contacts	Address/ Advert Page
Bell Language School, Cambridge	Both	PT: 30 wks; FT: 8/10 wks	On application	PT: October; FT: March	2 yrs exp, initial training pref.	Head of Teacher Training	59,83
Bell Language School, Norwich	FT	8 wks	£1,250	March	2 yrs exp, initial training pref.	Enquiries and Registration	59,83
Bell Language School, Saffron Walden	FT	10 wks	£1,450	March	2 yrs exp, initial training pref.	Enquiries and Registration	59,84
Brasshouse Centre, Birmingham	PT	8 mths	£900	September	Experienced practising teachers	Fiona Copland	84
Eastbourne School of English	PT	9 months	£900 tbc	October	1st degree + 2 yrs ELT exp	Dorothy Rippon	85
Edinburgh, Uni of (Inst for Applied Lang Studies)	FT	10 wks	£1,575	April	Degree, 3 yrs exp	Registration Secretary	85,264
English in Chester, Chester	PT	1 year	£950 exc exam fees	October		DELTA Tutor	86
Farnborough College of Technology, Farnborough	On application	On application	On application	September - 1 yr courses		Mrs Maria McClure	86
Gloscat, Cheltenham	PT	9 months	£850 + exam fee	September	EFL/modern lang exp	Language Unit	86,60
Hammersmith & West London College	RSA Dip PT	1 year	£595 + Cambridge fee	September	Age 21+, Degree or teach cert, 2 yrs min teach exp	College Info Centre	86,63
Hilderstone College	FT	9 mths	£1,087+ Cambridge fee	October	Contact for details	Teacher Training Dept	87
International House, Piccadilly	FT	8 wks	£1,495 + Cambridge reg fee	January, March, September	Formal TEFL qual, 2 yrs FT exp	Teacher Training Dept	87,64
International House, Newcastle	FT	8 wks	£1,400	July	2 yrs TEFL min	International House	87,61
International Language Centre, Hastings	Both	FT: 8-9 wks; PT: 9 mths	FT: £1,399/£1,499 inc exam fee; PT: tba	8 wks: September, 9 wks: March; PT: October	CELTA, 2 yrs exp	Rose Holmes	87
Internationl Teaching & Training Centre, Bournemouth	Both	FT: 2 months; PT: 8 mths	£1,600	February, April, October	Univ degree	Chris Goodchild	87,62
College	Full or Part Time	Course Length	Fees	Start Dates	Entry Requirements	Contacts	Address/ Advert Page

UK Cambridge / RSA Diploma (DELTA) Courses

College	Full or Part Time	Course Length	Fees	Start Dates	Entry Requirements	Contacts	Address/Advert Page
King's College London, English Lang Centre	PT	10 months	£850	Sept	2 yrs exp, degree, CELTA pref	Dr Jennifer Jenkins	87
Leeds Metropolitan University, Leeds	Both	FT: 10 wks; PT: 9 mths	EU: £720; non-EU: £1070 + UCLES fee	September	Excellent English, 2 yrs exp, CELTA	Sarah Turnbull	88
Nottingham Trent University	PT	3 terms	£1,130 + exam fee	October	Contact for details	Sheila Spencer, Senior Lecturer	89,61
Oxford College of Further Education	PT	24 wks	£1,050	October	UCLES requirements	Steven Haysham	89
Pilgrims Ltd	PT	2 mths	£1995	July	Practising teachers, 2 yrs exp	Gill Johnson	90
Queen's University, Belfast	PT	2 mths	£1,995	July	2 yrs experience	Course Director	90
Solihull College	Both	FT: 10 wks; PT: 20 wks	£1,295 + exam fee	FT: September; PT: October	ELT experience, 2 'A' levels, selection procedure	Pat Morris, CELTA Administrator	
Stanton Teacher Training, London	PT	8 mths	£605 + reg fee	October	Varied ELT exp, min 1200 hrs	Mr D Garrett, Director	91
University College, Chichester	6 Modules of MA Course	6 months	£370 per module (EU); £960 per module (non EU)		CELTA + exp	Angela Karlsson	92,264
Waltham Forest College	PT	1 year	£650	January	2 years ELT exp	Nicole de la Louviere	92
Warwickshire College	On apllication	On apllication	£850 - £950 (EU); £1400 (non-EU)	2 yrs exp		Diane Mattingley	92
Westminster College	PT	1 year	tba	January	Initial qual - CELTA, TESLA, 2 yrs teaching exp	Course Information Unit	92
Wigan and Leigh College	PT	30 wks	£700	Variable	On application	Lucy Hale	92
College	Full or Part Time	Course Length	Fees	Start Dates	Entry Requirements	Contacts	Address/Advert Page

189

Overseas Cambridge / RSA Diploma (DELTA) Courses

College	Full or Part Time	Course length	Fees	Start dates	Entry requirements	Contacts	Address/ Advert Page
Accent Language School, Prague	PT	28 weeks	£950 + £220 exam fee	October	As RSA/ UCLES		115
Australian TESOL Training Centre, Bondi Junction, Aus	FT	8 wks	Aus$ 3,300	February	1200 hrs exp, Eng competence, tertiary level quals, pre or in-service quals	Eileen Morley	154
British Council, Damascus	PT	Contact for details	£500	October - June	4 yrs experience as TEFL teacher	Jon Gore, Michael Manser, Tracey White	63,177
British Council, Hong Kong	PT	9 months		September 2000		Nick Florent	162
British Institute, Paris	PT	15 months	FFr 16450 + exam fee FFr1,800	October	2 yrs exp + quals	Mme Schwarz	97
British Language Centre, Madrid, Spain	Both	FT: 8 wks; PT: 6 months	On application	FT: April, July, October, January; PT: October	Degree & teaching exp	Alistair Dickinson	109
Columbia College, Vancouver, Canada	FT	8 wks	C$4,000 per semester	October	Relevant BA degree + ELT exp	James R Janz	139
ELS - Bell School of English, Poland	PT	Weekends	£890 + exam fee	October	1200 hrs teaching	Halszka Ziotkowska	121
Holmesglen Institute of TAFE, Chadstone, Aus	PT	8 months	Aus$3,200	Various	As RSA / UCLES	Larry Foster	155
International House, Budapest, Hungary	Both	FT: 9 wks; PT: 17 wks	£1,070	FT: June; PT: January,	2 yrs post-cert exp, application, interview	Steve Oakes, Head of Teacher Training	58,119
International House, Rome, Italy	PT	9 mths	3 million lire	October	CELTA or equiv	The Director, Teacher Training	105
International House, Krakow, Poland	PT	7 mths	£890 + exam fee	November, May	Degree, pref. age 22 yrs +	Danuta Terucka	62,121
College	Full or Part Time	Course length	Fees	Start dates	Entry requirements	Contacts	Address/ Advert Page

Overseas Cambridge / RSA Diploma (DELTA) Courses

College	Full or Part Time	Course Length	Fees	Start Dates	Entry Requirements	Contacts	Address/ Advert Page
International House, Wroclaw, Poland	FT	9 wks	£890 + £181 exam fee	March, July	CELTA, 2 years exp	Elisa Jaroch, TT Administrator	62,121
International House, Lisbon, Portugal	PT	Contact for details	PTE320,000/£1 000	September	As RSA / UCLES	Xana de Nagy	66,107
International House Barcelona, Spain	Both	FT: 8 wks; PT: 6 mths	310,000 ptas	FT: January, February or April, July; PT: October	Degree, CELTA or equiv	Jenny Johnson	65,110
International House, Madrid, Spain	PT	6 months	225,000 ptas	October	CELTA or equiv, 2 yrs exp, completed higher ed	Teacher Training Department	63,110
International Training Institute, Istanbul, Turkey	PT	8 months	£1200	October	As RSA / UCLES	Tom Godfrey	63,128
Language Centre, Cork, Eire	PT	1 year	IR£1,450 - £1,650	October	3 yrs min teaching exp	General Office	93
Language Link, Russia	Both	FT: 9 wks; PT: 18 wks	Contact for details	FT: June; PT: February	TEFL qual + 3 yrs exp	ELT Department	124
Languages International, Auckland, New Zealand	PT	10 mths	Contact for details	February	ELT Cert + 2 yrs teaching exp min	Craig Thaine, Director of Teacher Training	158
University College, Cork, Eire	PT	1 year	IR£1,450 - 1,650	October	3 yrs teaching exp	Director	93
Yonsei University, Seoul, South Korea	PT	7 months	2,950,000 won	October	CELTA + 2 yrs exp	James Forrest	167

UK Trinity Diploma in TESOL Courses

College	Full or Part Time	Course Length	Fees	Start Dates	Entry Requirements	Contacts	Address/ Advert Page
Aberdeen College	PT	2 terms	£680	October, February	2 yrs teach exp	Anne Bain	83
Bracknell & Wokingham College, Berkshire	PT	3 terms	£400 (ex exam fee)	September/ October	2 yrs FT experience or 1 yr + Certificate	Colette Galloway, Course Director	84

UK Trinity Diploma in TESOL Courses

College	Full or Part Time	Course Length	Fees	Start Dates	Entry Requirements	Contacts	Address/ Advert Page
Brooklands College, Weybridge	PT	30 wks	£540	October	Contact for details	Admissions Registrar	84
Bradford College, W Yorks	PT	30 wks	Contact for details	January 2000	Cert TESOL + 2 yrs exp	Nancy Hall, Head of Eng Lang Centre	84
Coventry Technical College	Flexible	Flexible		Any time	Cert TESOL/CELTA + 2 yrs experience		85
Colchester Institute, Colchester	FT	9 wks (+ 4 wks dist)	£750 (inc exam)	October, January, May	Degree or equiv pref	Hannah Piper	85
East Berkshire College	PT	3 Terms	£495	September		Chris Hammonds	85
Golders Green Teacher Training Centre, London	PT	13 wks	£800 + exam fee	September	Interview, University entry level	Dig Hadoke	86
Hertfordshire University, Hatfield	Both	FT: 3 terms; PT: 2 years	£800	September	Cambridge/ RSA Cert TEFL or Trinit Cert TESOL	M Krzanowski	66,87
ITS English School, Hastings	Both	FT: 6 wks; PT: 36 wks	£695 + moderation fee	November, March	2 yrs teaching exp	Paul Power, Director of Teacher Training	87
Kent School of English	Dist	Contact for details	£590	Contact for details	Contact for details	Chris McDermott	87
Langside College Glasgow	PT	1 year	£500 + exam fee	May	Cert-level qual, 2 yrs exp	Tony Foster	88
Language Project, Bristol	Both	Both	FT: £900; PT: £550	March, September	Cert + exp	Dr Jon Wright	88
London Study Centre	Both	1 year	Contact for details	All year	TESOL/CELTA + 2 yrs experience	Nicky Moss	60,88
Northbrook CDT, West Sussex	PT	9 months	EU: £495; Non-EU: £1,490	September	2 yrs FT exp	Susan Scowen	89
Oxford House College, London, UK	PT/Dist	13 wks	PT: £720 - £770; Dist: £670	September	Cert, 2 yrs exp, interview	Fiona Balloch	89
Sidmouth International School	Dist	1 year	£1100	January, August	Cambridge/ Trinity Cert, 2 yrs experience	Vincent Smidowicz	90
College	Full or Part Time	Course Length	Fees	Start Dates	Entry Requirements	Contacts	Address/ Advert Page

UK Trinity Diploma in TESOL Courses

College	Full or Part Time	Course Length	Fees	Start Dates	Entry Requirements	Contacts	Address/Advert Page
Saint George International	Both	From 6 mths to 2 years	£895	Throughout the year	Cert + 2 yrs experience	Teacher Training Manager	90,62
Sheffield Hallam University, TESOL Centre	FT + Dist	4 wks FT + 10 months dist	£1,500 not inc moderators fees	FT: April, July, October; Dist: October, December	Initial teaching qualification, first degree or PGCE, teaching experience	Fran Bellbin, Programme Coordinator	90,63
St Brelade's, Jersey	Distance	9 months	£1060	September	Degree	Donald Brown	90
Students International Ltd, Leics	FT/Dist	No limit	On application	On application	20+ yrs, exp	Mrs A.L. Blythe	63,91
Surrey Language Centre, Farnham	PT	8 wks	£800	Throughout the year	2 'A' levels, high level of English, 18+	Peter Dransfield	91
Windsor Schools TEFL, Berks	PT	8 months	£799 + exam fee	On request	2 A levels + 2 yrs teaching exp	Mrs C Fuller	92

Overseas Trinity Diploma in TESOL Courses

College	Course Title	Course Length	Fees	Start Dates	Entry Requirements	Contacts	Address/Advert Page
Grafton International, Dublin, Eire	Trinity Diploma	PT: 2 years	IR£2,000	October	Trinity reqs	Jessica Long	93
International Pacific College, New Zealand	Trinity Diploma	Contact for details	Contact for details	NZ$3,325	Contact for details	Dianna Beatson, TESOL Director	158
Lord Byron College, Italy	Trinity Diploma	PT: 2 years	Free to in-house teachers	October	Degree, TEFL or TESOL Cert, 1 yr teaching exp	Mr John Credico, Director of Studies	105
Next Teacher Training, Barcelona, Spain	Trinity Diploma	Both/Dist: 4 wks	£767-£793	July, August, September, October, November	Rel quals and exp	Duncan Foord/Barney Griffiths	111
TEC English, Baleares, Spain	Trinity Diploma	6 months or 9 months	Contact for details	October (9 months); January (6 months)	Degree or experience, non-L1 speakers must have CPE	Montserrat Callesa	

UK University Diplomas

College	Course Title	Course Length	Fees	Start Dates	Entry Requirements	Contacts	Address/ Advert Page
Canterbury Christ Church College, Kent	Dip TESOL	FT: 9 mths; PT: 2 years	EU: £1,200; Non-EU: £4,850	October	Degree, teaching exp	Mr Richard Cullen	84,263
Cardiff University	Dip in Applied Linguistics	FT: Dip: 8 mths	EU: £2,675; Non-EU: £6,750	September	Degree or equiv, IELTS 7 or equiv for non-native speakers	Dr Paul Tench	84,260
	Dip in Language and Communication Research	FT: Dip: 8 mths	EU: £2,675; Non-EU: £6,750	September	Degree or equiv, IELTS 7 or equiv for non-native speakers	Dr Paul Tench	84,260
Essex University (EFL Unit), Colchester	Diploma in TESOL	3 terms	Home: £2,610; Overseas: £6,500 (99 fees)	October	Teaching exp, degree or equiv	Dilly Meyer	58,86
Manchester University	Diploma in TESOL	FT: 2 semesters; PT: 2-4 years	EU £2,675 (FT); £1,625 (PT); non EU £6,800 (FT); £4,250 (PT)	September	First degree, 1-2 years' teaching exp, IELTS 7, TOEFL 600	First degree, 1-2 years' teaching exp, IELTS 7, TOEFL 600	89,260
Warwick University, CELTE	Diploma in ELT & Administration	PT: 9 months	Contact for details	October	Degree or training & exp pref	The Secretary, CELTE	92,263
University of the West of England	Postgraduate Diploma/MA in TESOL and Linguistics	FT: Contact for details	October	Contact for details	Contact for details	S George Mann	92,59

UK University Degees

College	Course Title	Course Length	Fees	Start Dates	Entry Requirements	Contacts	Address/ Advert Page
Buckingham University	BA (Hons) in English Language Studies for TEFL	FT: 2 years	Contact for details	January, July	Overseas 'A' level equiv + IELTS 6	Mr Gerry Loftus	84
Exeter University, (School of Ed)	B Phil (Ed) in TEFL	FT: 1 year	On application	October	Teaching qual, 2 yrs exp	Sarah Rich	86
Stirling University	BA in ELT	FT: 3 years	On application	September	Univ entrance quals, IELTS 5	Mrs Stephanie Tytler, Assoc Director	91
Language Centre, Cork, Eire	MA Applied Linguistics	FT: 1 year	EU: IR£1,686; Non-EU: Ir£5,650	October	Honours deg, IIii + in a language subject	Mr W S Dodd	93

College	Course Title	Course Length	Fees	Start Dates	Entry Requirements	Contacts	Address/ Advert Page

Masters Degrees

Masters degrees in EFL-related subjects are offered in all English speaking countries around the world. A wide variety of programmes is on offer appealing to both the career TEFL teacher wishing to further develop their knowledge and expertise in teaching, and those interested in studying in depth the fields of language acquisition and linguistics.

Why do it?

Obtaining a higher qualification in EFL will undoubtedly improve the career-minded TEFL teacher's prospects. The majority of university positions and senior level EFL posts require applicants to hold at least a Masters/Diploma level qualification. In some areas, the Middle East for example, employers are impressed by the professional and academic kudos an MA bestows and frequently specify higher level qualifications when advertising EFL-related posts. As competition for the better jobs becomes more intense, so does the need to become more highly qualified and knowledgeable in the field.

Does the name matter?

Most postgraduate or higher degrees are awarded after successfully completing a taught course, often with a research-based dissertation. There are three main types of Masters programme – Master of Arts (MA), Master of Science (MSc/MS) and Master of Education (MEd/EdM). The title is often historically derived from the department or faculty in which the course is taught, and may indicate a bias in the course content – for example, an MEd is awarded by a Dept/ School of Education and may differ from the MA in that no thesis is required in some institutions; the MSc/MS TESOL and the MA TESOL have virtually identical courses of study. Varying slightly from the above, the American MAT (Master of Arts in Teaching), however, is a second level degree which focuses on the practice of teaching, and is more vocational than the traditional MA – for example, on completion, the candidate is awarded with both a Masters and a public school teaching certificate. Another exception is the UK MPhil, which is primarily a research degree, and can lead on to further PhD study.

Generally speaking, the subject matter of Masters level degrees can be split into two categories: Applied Linguistics, which is a more theoretical subject most suited to those interested in pursuing an academic career, and teaching-oriented Masters degrees, which come under a range of names such as TESOL, TESP, ESOL, ELT. The latter tend to focus more on the study of classroom teaching rather than the study of language or language acquisition. Of course this is a generalisation, and prospective students should read the relevant prospectuses carefully when assessing which course they wish to study. In addition, particularly in the UK, there is a growing number of Master's programmes focusing on specialist areas such as ELT Management, Multimedia, ELT for young learners (such as the MEd in ELT for Young Learners at Leeds University), ESP, and Computing, thus a variety of specialist educational needs are catered for. '

Entry Requirements

It goes without saying that entry requirements vary widely according to individual programmes and institutions. However, as a rule of thumb, outside the US, universities offering teaching orientated Masters degree programmes usually require the applicant to not only have an initial teaching qualification, but also two or three years' ELT experience. More theoretical degree programmes, such as Applied Linguistics, generally admit students having little or no teaching practice behind them, as the focus is quite different. The US, however, differs somewhat from the rest of the English-speaking world: their teaching orientated Masters programmes can be pre-service qualifications. Consequently, applicants are not generally required to have any prior teaching practice (although it is welcome, and sometimes even preferred). A supervised practicum, or teaching practice, is usually offered as a core credit module in contrast to Masters programmes offered in other English-speaking countries where it is quite rare for there to be a practicum. It is worth noting that possessing a UK MA alone, unless it includes supervised teaching practice, will not be enough to qualify you to teach in the classroom.

How long?

Students with prior teaching experience taking a full time Masters can expect to complete it in 9 months to 2 years. North American institutes have traditionally used a flexible modular system based on credits - most Master's programmes comprising 30-36 credits. Previous relevant experience and knowledge are also taken into account. This allows the student to transfer credits thereby making it possible to continue from a certificate programme directly onto a Masters, for example. The duration of the programme therefore depends on a number of factors, and as they are often self-paced, they are usually completed across 1 - 5 years. This modular format is growing in popularity in the rest of the English-speaking world, with a greater number of establishments adopting a more flexible approach. Distance Masters programmes are also being more widely offered in various formats. For example, the MEd in Education Technology and ELT offered at Manchester University can be completed either fully distance, or over one summer in-house, with the remainder by distance learning.

Fees and self funding

In most English-speaking countries, a two-tier fee structure exists which differentiates between national and international students. In the UK and Ireland, the fees for EU nationals are lower than those for non-EU nationals, and tend to be calculated on a yearly basis. It is also worth noting that EU nationals who have lived outside of the EU for more than three years may not be eligible for EU fees and may find themselves having to pay the higher international rates. In the US a three-tier system exists at most universities with different fees charged to students from the following categories: in-state, out-of-state or international. North American fees tend to be calculated according to credit/hour, semester/hour or per semester, thus the system is quite complex as it takes the flexible nature of the programme structures into account. Quite often financial aid is available, but again this varies from university to university. Also, in the US for example, teaching assistantships may be available on a competitive basis, which goes a long way to reducing the final cost of the programme. In Australia, students are permitted to work for a maximum of 20 hours per week, and their spouses are permitted to work up to 40 hours a week.

There are well over 200 TESL-related MA courses in the US and Canada. With such a dazzling array of options available, it is difficult to know which course would best suit your needs.

For further information on US Masters programmes, consult the TESOL director or explore the website at:
http:/www.tesol.edu
For information on UK Masters:
www.britcoun.org/english

UK Masters Degrees

College	Course title	Course length	Fees	Start dates	Entry requirements	Contacts	Address/ Advert Page
Aston University	MSc TESOL/TESP	FT: 1 year; Dist: 2-5 years	FT: EU: £2,850, non-EU: £6,200; Dist: EU: c£500 per 10 credit module; non-EU: c£600	FT: October; Dist: October, January, April, July	Deg, 3 yrs exp	Secretary, Language Studies Unit	83,259
Birkbeck College, Department of Applied Linguistics	MA Applied Linguistics	FT: 1 year; PT: 2 years	£1,320	October	Languages, Social Sciences or Arts degree	Karen Philpott, Department Secretary	84
Birmingham University	MA Translation Studies	FT: 1 year; PT: 2 years	EU £3,500; Non EU £7,000	September	First degree, 2 years' EFL experience, 550 TOEFL/IELTS band 6/Cambridge Proficiency	Jane Gardiner, Administrator	84,263
	MA Applied Linguistics	FT: 1 year; PT: 2 years	EU £3,500; Non EU £7,000	September	First degree, 2 years' EFL experience, 550 TOEFL/IELTS band 6/ Cambridge Proficiency	Jane Gardiner, Administrator	84,263
	MA TEFL/TESOL	FT: 1 year; PT: 2 years; Dist: 30 mths	EU £3,500; Non EU £7,000: Distance - fees depend on the country of residence.	September - in house; Distance April and October, depending on the country of residence	First degree, 2 years' EFL experience, 550 TOEFL/IELTS band 6/ Cambridge Proficiency	Jane Gardiner, Administrator	84,263
Brighton University (Lang Centre)	MA in TEFL or in Media Assisted Language Teaching/ Learning	FT: 1 year; PT: 2 years	FT: £2,600; PT: £1,338/yr (EU), £6,600 (non-EU)	September	Degree, 2 yrs exp	Elspeth Broady	84
Bristol University	MEd Advanced Dip	FT 1 year; PT 2 years	On application	October	First degree or equivalent, 1 yrs teaching exp	Anna Lockett, Administrator	84
Buckingham University	MA TESOL	FT: 1 year	£6,300	January, April, July, October	Degree, IELTS 6.5 min	Gerry Loftus	84
Canterbury Christchurch College, Kent	MA TESOL	FT: 12 mths; PT: 2 years	£2,675 (EU); £6,450 (non-EU)	October	Degree, 3 yrs teaching exp	Richard Cullen	84,263
College	Course title	Course length	Fees	Start dates	Entry requirements	Contacts	Address/ Advert Page

UK Masters Degrees

College	Course title	Course length	Fees	Start dates	Entry requirements	Contacts	Address/ Advert Page
Canterbury Christchurch College, Kent	MA in English Language Education (ELE)	FT: 1 year; PT: 2 years	EU: £2,675; Non-EU: £6,450	September	Degree, 3 yrs experience	Richard Cullen	84,263
Cardiff University, Cardiff	Contact for details	Contact for details	EU: £2,610; Non-EU: £6,510	Contact for details	Contact for details	Dr Paul Tench	84,260
Central Lancashire University	MA Teaching English for International Business	FT 1 year; PT min 2-5 years	Dist: £3,900; FT: EU £2,610, non-EU £6,500; PT £170 per module	Distance: January; FT: September	Relevant degree, 2 yrs teaching	Christopher Barwood	84,260
Durham University (Dept of Linguistics & English Lang)	MA in Applied Linguistics	FT: 9-12 mths; PT: 24 mths (24-36 mths discontinuous)	FT: c. £2,710 (EU); c. £6,850 (non-EU)	October	Degree, IELTS 7.0	Dr Martha Young-Scholten	85
	MA in Applied Linguistics (ELT)	FT: 9-12 mths; PT: 24 mths (24-36 mths discontinuous)	FT: c. £2,710 (EU); c. £6,850 (non-EU)	October	Degree, IELTS 7.0	Dr Martha Young-Scholten	85
	MA in Applied Linguistics (ESOL)	FT: 9-12 mths; PT: 24 mths (24-36 mths discontinuous)	FT: c. £2,710 (EU); c. £6,850 (non-EU)	October	Degree, IELTS 7.0	Dr Martha Young-Scholten	85
	MA in Applied Linguistics (ELT CALL & Education Tech)	FT: 9-12 mths; PT: 24 mths (24-36 mths discontinuous)	FT: c. £2,710 (EU); c. £6,850 (non-EU)	October	Degree, IELTS 7.0	Dr Martha Young-Scholten	85
	MA in Applied Linguistics (ELT & Materials Development)	FT: 9-12 mths; PT: 24 mths (24-36 mths discontinuous)	FT: c. £2,710 (EU); c. £6,850 (non-EU)	October	Degree, IELTS 7.0	Dr Martha Young-Scholten	85
	MA in Applied Linguistics (Translation)	FT: 9-12 mths; PT: 24 mths (24-36 mths discontinuous)	FT: c. £2,710 (EU); c. £6,850 (non-EU)	October	Degree, IELTS 7.0	Dr Martha Young-Scholten	85
	MA in Applied Linguistics (Language Acquisition)	FT: 9-12 mths; PT: 24 mths (24-36 mths discontinuous)	FT: c. £2,710 (EU); c. £6,850 (non-EU)	October	Degree, IELTS 7.0	Dr Martha Young-Scholten	85
East Anglia University	MA ELT and Applied Linguistics	FT: 1 year; PT: 2 years	EU: £2,675; Non-EU: £6,650	September	Degree 2.1 + teaching exp	Keith Harvey, Barbara Betts	85

College	Course title	Course length	Fees	Start dates	Entry requirements	Contacts	Address/ Advert Page

UK Masters Degrees

College	Course Title	Course Length	Fees	Start Dates	Entry Requirements	Contacts	Address/ Advert Page
East Anglia University	MA in Professional Development for ELT Practitioners	FT: 1 year; PT: 2-5 years	EU: £2,675; Non-EU: 6,650	September	Degree, teaching exp	Barbara Betts	85
East London University	MA Linguistics by Independent Study	FT: 1-2 years; PT: 2-4 years	FT: EU: £2,600 per yr; non EU: £6,300 per yr; PT: EU: £750 per yr; non-EU £1500 per yr	September	Degree		
Edinburgh University (Inst for Applied Lang Studies)	MSc in Applied Linguistics	FT: 1 year; PT: 2 years	On application	October	Degree + teach exp	Ms Fay Oliver	85,264
Essex University (Dept of Lang & Lings)	MA in Applied Linguistics	FT: 9/12 mths; PT: 24 mths	EU: £2,610; Non-EU: £6,500	October	2.1 degree or equiv, IELTS 6.0, TOEFL 540	Mrs C White	98,86
	MA in Language Testing & Programme Evaluation	FT: 9/12 mths; PT: 24 mths	EU: £2,610; Non-EU: £6,600	October	2.1 degree or equiv	Mrs C White	58,86
	MA Descriptive & Applied Linguistics	FT: 9/12 mths; PT: 24 mths	EU: £2,610; Non-EU: £6,600	October	2.1 degree or equiv	Mrs C White	58,86
	MA Descriptive Linguistics	FT: 9/12 mths; PT: 24 mths	EU: £2,610; Non-EU: £6,600	October	2.1 degree or equiv	Mrs C White	58,86
	MA English Language and Linguistics	FT: 9/12 mths; PT: 24 mths	EU: £2,610; Non-EU: £6,600	October	2.1 degree or equiv	Mrs C White	58,86
	MA Language Acquisition	FT: 9/12 mths; PT: 24 mths	EU: £2,610; Non-EU: £6,600	October	2.1 degree or equiv, 3 yrsexp	Mrs C White	58,86
Exeter University	MEd TEFL	1 year	On request	October	Teaching qual + 2 yrs exp	Sarah Rich	86
Goldsmiths College (English Department)	MA Applied Linguistics - Sociocultural Approaches	FT 1 year; PT 2 years	EU - FT: £2,675, PT: £1,338; Non EU - £7,040	September	2:1 or above	Dr Hayley Davis	86
Hertfordshire University	MA in ELT and Applied Linguistics	FT: 1 year; PT: 2 years	£2,675 (EU); £6,650(non-EU	September	DELTA or Trinity Dip	M Krzanowski	66,87
Hull University	MA in Applied Language & New Technologies	FT: 1 year; PT: 2 years	FT: EU: £2,675; non-EU: £6,200; PT: £1,230 per year	September	On application	Gertrud Buscher	87
College	Course Title	Course Length	Fees	Start Dates	Entry Requirements	Contacts	Address/ Advert Page

College	Course title	Course length	Fees	Start dates	Entry requirements	Contacts	Address/ Advert Page
Hull University	MEd in ICT for TESOL	PT by distance 2-5 years	£4200	January	Degree, teaching qual, 3 yrs exp	Shirley Bennettt	87
Institute of Education, University of London	MA in TESOL	FT: 1 yearr; PT: 2-4 years	FT: £2,675 (EU), £7,053 (non-EU); PT: £1,338 pa; Email: £1,415 (EU); £2,250 (non-EU) pa	FT: October, January, April, PT: October	Good degree, 2 yrs FT ELT	John Norrish	87,261
International House, London	MSc in TEFL/TESP (jointly with Univ of Aston)	Contact for details	Contact for details	Contact for details	Contact for details	Teacher Training Dept	64,87
Kent University	MA Applied Language Studies (Computing)	FT 1 year; PT 2 years	FT EU £2,675; Non EU £6,860; PT: £1,179	October	Normally: native speaker - degree in foreign language; non-native speaker - degree in English	Dr John Partridge, Course Convener	87
	MA Vocational Techniques for Career Linguists	FT 1 year; PT 2 years	FT EU £2,675; Non EU £6,860; PT: £1,179	October	Degree in foreign language	Dr John Partridge, Course Convener	87
	MA Applied Language Studies	FT 1 year; PT 2-4 years	FT EU £2,675; Non EU £6,860; PT: £1,179	October	Normally: native speaker - degree in foreign language; non-native speaker - degree in English	Dr John Partridge, Course Convener	87
King's College London, English Lang Centre	MA in ELT & Applied Linguistics	FT: 1 year; PT: 2 years	EU: £1.305; non-EU: £3,915	September	Good degree in related subject, 3 yrs exp.	Dr Jennifer Jenkins	87
Lancaster University, Dept of Linguistics & Modern Languages	MA Linguistics for English Language Teaching	FT: 1 year; PT: 2 years	FT: EU: £2,675; non-EU: £6,850; PT: EU: £1,305; non-EU: £3,275 per year	October	Min 3 years full time teaching experience, first degree (2:1); 6.5 IELTS, 580 TOEFL	Marjorie Robinson, Postgraduate Secretary	88
College	Course title	Course length	Fees	Start dates	Entry requirements	Contacts	Address/ Advert Page

College	Course Title	Course Length	Fees	Start Dates	Entry Requirements	Contacts	Address/ Advert Page
Lancaster University, Dept of Linguistics & Modern Languages	MA Language Studies	FT: 1 year; PT: 2 years	FT: EU: £2,675; non-EU: £6,850; PT: EU: £1,305; non-EU: £3,275 per year	October	First degree (2:1), proficiency in English	Marjorie Robinson, Postgraduate Secretary	88
Leeds Metropolitan University	MA Language Teaching	FT: 11 mths; PT: 2 yrs	FT: EU: £2,500; non-EU: c£6,000; PT: £250 per module	October	Excellent language ability, degree level ed, 2 yrs language teaching	Ivor Timmis	88
Leeds University (School of Education)	MEd TESOL (young learners)	FT: 12 months; PT: 2 years	FT: EU: £2,775; non-EU: £6,615; PT: £871	September, February	3 years experience, first degree, initial qualification, IELTS 6.5	Higher Degrees & Diploma Office	88,262
	MEd TESOL	FT: 12 months; PT: 2 years	FT: EU: £2,775; non-EU: £6,615; PT: £871	September, February	3 years experience, first degree, initial qualification, IELTS 6.5	Higher Degrees & Diplomas Office	88,262
Leicester University	MA Applied Linguistics and TESOL	FT: 1 year; PT: 2-5 yrs	EU £2,000; non EU £6,000	September	Degree, ELT exp	Julie Thomson	88,261
Liverpool University (Applied English Language Studies Unit)	MA in Language Teaching and Learning	FT: 1 year	EU: £2,675; non EU £6,600	September	First degree and 2 years' teaching experience	Dr S Champion	88
Luton University	MA Applied Linguistics: TEFL	FT: 1 year	£2,520 (home); £5,400 (overseas)	October	Ist degree	Andy Russell	88
Manchester University	MEd TESOL	FT: 1 year; PT: 2-4 years	EU: £2,675 (FT), £1950 (PT); non-EU: £6,800 (FT), £4950 (PT)	September, January (October/April distance option)	First degree, 3 years' teaching (min), initial teaching qualification, IELTS 7, TOEFL 600	The Administrator	89,260
	MEd ELT	FT: 1 year; PT: max 5 yrs/Dist 3 yrs	£3,620; £495 per module	October, January, April	First degree, 3 years teaching (min), initial teaching qualification, IELTS 7, TOEFL 600	The Administrator	89,260
College	Course Title	Course Length	Fees	Start Dates	Entry Requirements	Contacts	Address/ Advert Page

College	Course Title	Course Length	Fees	Start Dates	Entry Requirements	Contacts	Address/ Advert Page
Manchester University	MEd in Educational Technology and ELT	FT: 1 year; PT: max 5 yrs	£3,620; £495 per module	September, January	First degree, 3 years teaching (min), initial teaching qualification, IELTS 7, TOEFL 600	The Administrator	89,260
	MEd in Educational Technology and TESOL	FT: 1 year; PT: 2-4 years	EU: £2,675 (FT), £1950 (PT); non-EU: £6,800 (FT), £4950 (PT)	September, January	First degree, 3 years teaching (min), initial teaching qualification, IELTS 7, TOEFL 600	The Administrator	89,260
	MA in Applied Linguistics	FT: 1 year; PT: 2-3 yrs	Contact for details	September	Degree, 3 yrs exp	The Administrator	89,260
Moray House, Edinburgh	MEd TESOL	FT: 12 mths, PT: Up to 6 yrs	EU: £2,100; Non-EU: 4,800	FT: October; Dist: Any time	First degree, recognized teaching qual, 3 yrs teaching exp, IELTS or TOEFL score	David Carver	89,262
Nene University College, Northampton	MA Linguistics & Literature	FT: 1 year; PT: 2 years	FT: EU: £2, 675; non EU £5,500; PT: EU: £894 per; non-EU £1,798 per yr	September	First degree pref in English or Soc Sciences, 1st or 2nd class hons	Anne Gilkes, Faculty Registrar	89
Newcastle-upon-Tyne University	MA Media Technology for TEFL	FT: 1 year	EU: £2.675; non-EU: £6,770	September	Degree, teaching qual, 2 yrs exp	Mr W S Windeatt	89
	MA Linguistics for TESOL	FT: 1 year; PT: 2 years	EU: £2.675; non-EU: £6,770	September	Degree, teaching qual, 2 yrs exp	Mr W S Windeatt	89
Nottingham University	MA in ELT	FT: 1 year; PT: 2-4 years	FT: £2,540, 6,885 (non-EU); PT: 900 per yr	October	Contact School of Education for details, MA in Applied Linguistics, TESOL or ELT Education available	Jean Hollingworth	89
Nottingham Trent University, UK	MA in ELT	FT: 1 year; PT: 2-4 years	Contact for details	October	Contact for details	SheilaSpencer, Senior Lecturer	89,61
Oxford Brookes University, (ICELS), Oxford	MA in ELT by Distance Learning	PT 3.5 year	£5,100	January, October	Degree + recent ELT experience	Liz Sayigh	89,264
College	Course Title	Course Length	Fees	Start Dates	Entry Requirements	Contacts	Address/ Advert Page

College	Course Title	Course Length	Fees	Start Dates	Entry Requirements	Contacts	Address/ Advert Page
Portsmouth University, UK	MA in Applied Linguistics	FT: 1 year; PT: 2-5 years	FT: EU: £2,700; non-EU: £6,100; PT: EU: £700 per yr; non-EU: £3,050 per yr	September	Degree, 2 yrs exp	Sandra Smith	90
Queen's University (TEFL Centre), Belfast	MA in ELT	FT: 1 year, PT: 2 years	£2,675 (EU); £6,925 (non-EU)	September	Degree, Eng lang qual	Tony Ridgway	90
Reading University, Dept of Linguistic Science	MA in Applied Linguistics	FT: 12 mths; PT: up to 6 yrs; Dist: up to 5 years	EU: £2,610; Non-EU: £6,462	October	Good 1st degree, 2 yrs professional experience	Ms Kristyan Spelman Miller	90,259
	MA TEFL	FT: 1 year; PT: 2 years	EU & Dist: £4,770; non-EU: £7,710	In-house: October, January; Dist: November, May	Degree, 2 yrs exp	Ms Kristyan Spelman Miller	90,259
Salford University, EFL School of Languages	MA in TEFL	FT: 1 year; PT: up to 5 yrs	£6,400	September	Degree, initial lang teaching qual, 6 mths teaching exp, IELTS 6 if applicable	MA TEFL Enquiries	90
Sheffield Hallam University, TESOL Centre	MA in TESOL	12 wks dist, 6 wks contact, 32 wks research	£2,500	October, March	PGDip or equivalent + several years experience	Fran Belbin	90
Sheffield University	MEd English Language Teaching	PT: 2 years	£1,650 pa	October	1st degree + quals + 2 yrs exp	Mrs C A Worboys	90
Southampton University	MA in Applied Linguistics for Language Teaching	FT: 1 year; PT: 2 years	FT: EU: £2,610; non-EU: £6,500; PT: EU: £875 pa	October	Good first degree, 2 ELT exp or rel exp pref	R Mitchell	90,260
Stirling University	MSc TESOL	FT: 1 year	EU: £2,675; non-EU: £6,350	September	Degree or equiv	Mrs S Tytler	91
	MSc TESOL	FT: 1 year	EU: £2,675; non-EU: £6,350	September	Contact for details	Mrs S Tytler	91
St Mary's, Strawberry Hill	MA Applied Linguistics & ELT	FT 1 year; PT: max 5 yrs	FT: October; PT: October, January, May	On application	First degree (or equiv), teaching practice; applicants without degree considered on merit	Peter Dewar, Director; Kathy Grant, Administrator	90
	MA Linguistics in Education	FT: 1 year; PT: max 5 yrs	FT: October; PT: October, January, May	On application	First degree (or equiv) & teaching practice;	Peter Dewar, Director; Kathy Grant, Administrator	90
College	Course Title	Course Length	Fees	Start Dates	Entry Requirements	Contacts	Address/ Advert Page

UK Masters Degrees

College	Course title	Course length	Fees	Start dates	Entry requirements	Contacts	Address/ Advert Page
Sunderland University	MA Linguistics (TESOL)	FT & Dist: 1 yr	£4,500	January, May, August (DL modules), February (taught semester)	Teaching qual, 3 yrs teacher training	Dr Felicity Breet	
Surrey University, English Language Institute	MA Linguistics (TESOL)	FT: 1 year	£5,400 (in 3 installments)	October, March	1st degree + 2 yrs teach exp	Tammy Hughes	91,266
	MSc ELT Management	Dist: 27 months	£6,760 (in 3 instalments)	October, March	1st degree + 2 yrs ed management/t each exp	Tammy Hughes	91,266
Sussex University	MA in Applied Linguistics	FT: 1 year; PT: 2 years	FT: EU: £2,675; non-EU: £6,870; PT: £1,338	October	2.1 hons degree or degree + rel work exp	Dr A McNeill	91
Thames Valley University	MA in ELT	FT: 1 year	Contact for details	January, October	Qualified teacher status in own country, 3 yrs teaching exp	Dermot Murphy	91
University College, Chichester	MA in ELT Management	FT: 1 year, PT: 3 years	EU: £2,570; Non-EU: £6,700	Contact for details	Degree, 3 yrs teaching exp, IELTS 6.0+	Ian Forth	92,264
	MA Education (International)	FT: 1 year; PT: 2.5 years	No fixed cost		First degree, 3 yrs experience	Ian Forth	92,264
University of North London	MA TEFL	FT: 1 year; PT: 2 years	FT: EU: £2,610; non-EU £6,330; PT: c£155 per module	September, February	On application		9,262
University College London	MA Modern English Language	FT: 1 year; PT: 2 years	EU: £2, 675; non-EU £9,145	September	Degree (1 or 2.1)	Peter Swaab	92
University College of St Mark & St John,	MEd (Exon) in Teacher Training for ELT	FT: 12 months	EU: £3,475; non-EU £6,500	September	ELT exp, teaching qual	Michael G Hall	92
University College of UK	MEd (Exon) in Teaching English for Specific Purposes	FT: 1 year	EU: £3,475; non-EU £6,500	September	ELT exp, teaching qual	Michael G Hall	
College	Course title	Course length	Fees	Start dates	Entry requirements	Contacts	Address/ Advert Page

UK Masters Degrees

College	Course Title	Course Length	Fees	Start Dates	Entry Requirements	Contacts	Address/ Advert Page
University College of UK	MEd (Exon) in English Language Teaching	FT: 1 year	EU: £3,475; non-EU: £6,500	September	ELT exp, teaching qual	Michael G Hall	
University of Greenwich	MA in Management of Language	FT: 1 year; PT: 2 years	£1,625 home, £1,950 overseas	September	Degree + some teaching exp	Dr A Benati	
University of Newcastle Centre for International Studies in Education	M Ed TESOL	FT: 12 months (2 years for non-graduates)	£6770	October	Relevant degree, teaching exp, IELTS 6.5	Dr Paul Seedhouse	89
University of Ulster, Coleraine	MA in TESOL	FT: 9 mths; PT: 18 mths	£6,630 (inc teach practice in Hungary)	September	Degree or equiv + interview	Mrs Joyce Spence	91
University of Wales, Bangor	MA Linguistics	FT: 1 year; PT: 2 years	FT: EU: £2,675; non-EU: £6,450; PT: £1,337 per yr	September	Good first degree	Prof J Thomas	92
University of Wales, Cardiff	MA in Applied Linguistics	FT: 2semesters + dissertation for MA	Contact for details	September	Degree, IELTS 7.0	Mrs Julia Bullough	92
	MA in Language & Communicatin Research	FT:2 semesters + dissertation for MA	Contact for details	Contact for details	Univ degree or equiv	Mrs Julia Bullough	92
Warwick University, CELTE	MA in ELT	FT: 12 months	£3,950 (EU); £7,100 (non-EU)	October	First degree, 3 yrs exp	Thelma Henderson	92,263
	MA in ELT to Young Learners	FT: 12 months	£3,950 (EU); £7,100 (non-EU)	October	First degree, 3 yrs exp	Thelma Henderson	92,263
	MA in ESP	FT: 12 months	£3,950 (EU); £7,100 (non-EU)	October	First degree, 3 yrs exp	Thelma Henderson	92,263
	MA in English LanguageStudies & Methods	FT: 12 months	£3,950 (EU); £7,100 (non-EU)	October	First degree, 3 yrs exp	Thelma Henderson	92,263
University of Westminster	MA in Applied Languages (TEFL)	FT: 1 year; PT: 2 years	UE: £2700; non-UE :£6000	September	Degree + some teaching exp	Admissions Office	92
	MA TESOL	FT: 1 year; PT: 2 years	UE: £2700; non-UE :£6000	September	Degree + some teaching exp	Admissions Office	92
York University	MA in Teaching English to Young Learners	Dist: 2 years	£2,995 each year	August	First degree, teaching qualifications and experience.	MA Secretary	92,262
College	Course Title	Course Length	Fees	Start Dates	Entry Requirements	Contacts	Address/ Advert Page

College	Course Title	Course Length	Fees	Start Dates	Entry Requirements	Contacts	Address/Advert Page
Adelphi University	MA TESOL	Both: FT/PT 3-4 semesters	$470/credit hr, fees $150	Rolling Admission	Bac degree, GPA 2.75+, 3 letters of ref, essay	Prof Eva M Roca, Director	130
Alabama University, Tuscaloosa, AL	MA TESOL	FT: 4 semesters	Contact for details	Fall, Spring	Deg, strong writing samples, references, GPA 3.5+	Vai Ramanathan, Catherine Davies	130
American University, Washington DC	MA TESOL	Both: FT/PT FT: 2 years; PT: 5 years	$655/semester hr	September, January, May	Bac degree, GPA 3.0+, Non-native: TOEFL 600+	Brock Brady	131
	Masters International Program/MA in TESOL	FT: 4 years	$2,061 - $6,183/ semester	September, January, May	3.0 grade point average (on a 4.0 scale), US citizenship	Brock Brady, Co-ordinator, TESOL Programs	131
Arizona, The University of	MA in ESL	Both: FT/PT 4 semesters	In-state: $1,029; Out-of-state: $255/unit, $3,326 max	Fall semester	Bac degree, GPA 3.0+, GRE scores, TOEFL 550+	Director, English Language/ Linguistics Program	137
Arizona State University	Master of TESL; MA in English	Both: FT/PT 4 semesters	In-state: $99+/sem hr; Out-of-state: $942/sem hr	Any semester	BA, GPA 3.0, TOEFL 580+	Roy C Major	131
Azusa Pacific University	MA TESOL	Both: FT/PT 6 terms	$335/unit	Fall, Spring	Deg, GPA 3.0+, TOEFL 550	Director, Graduate TESOL Program	131
	MA in Language Development	Both: FT/PT 6 terms	$325/unit	Fall, Spring	Degree, teaching exp	Director, Language Development Program	131
Ball State University	MA TESOL	Both: FT/PT 3 semesters	In-state: $1,658/semest er; Out-of-state: $4,436	Any semester	GPA 3.0, 2 yrs college study in foreign lang, GRE score, TOEFL score	Director of Graduate Programs	131
	MA TESOL and Linguistics	Both: FT/PT 4 semesters	As MA TESOL	Any semester	As MA TESOL	Director of Graduate Programs	131
Biola University, CA	MA in Applied Linguistics	Both: FT/PT FT usually 4 sem + inter-term; PT max 5 years	$307 per sem unit	Fall	From the evangelical Christian community; First degree GPA 3.0, TOEFL 600	Chair, Dept of TESOL & Applied Linguistics	131
College	Course Title	Course Length	Fees	Start Dates	Entry Requirements	Contacts	Address/Advert Page

US Masters Degrees

College	Course title	Course length	Fees	Start dates	Entry Requirements	Contacts	Address/ Advert Page
Biola University, CA	MA in TESOL	FT: 4 sem + inter-term; PT max 5 years	$307/sem unit	Fall	From the evangelical Christian community; First degree GPA 3.0, TOEFL 600	Chair, Dept of TESOL & Applied Linguistics	131
Boston University	MEd in TESOL (certification program)	Both: FT/PT 3 semesters	$10,985/semester or $344/credit	Any semester	Degree, GPA 3.0, Miller Analogies 50+, TOEFL 600+	Marnie Reed	131
	MEd in TESOL (noncertification program)	Both: FT/PT 2 semesters + one course	As certification program	Any semester	As certification program	Steven J Molinsky, Director	131
	MEd in TESOL - specialisation in EFL/ESL for children	Both: FT/PT 2 semesters	As certification program	Any semester	As certification program	Maria Estela Brisk, Director	131
Bowling Green State University, Bowling Green, OH	MA in English, specialising in TESL	Both: FT/PT 4 semesters	In-state: $7,824/yr; Out-of-state: $14,208	Any semester	First degree GPA 3.2, TOEFL 600	Dr Shirley E Ostler, Coordinator	131
Brigham Young University	MA TESOL	Both: FT/PT Contact for details	Latter Day Saints $1,550/semester; Other $2,325/ semester	Any semester	Application, ecclesiastical endorsement, GPA 3.0	John S Robertson, Chair	131
California University, Davis, CA	MA Applied Linguistics	Both: FT/PT 6 quarters	$1,490/quarter	Fall	First degree, GRE score, TOEFL	Program Director, Dept of Linguistics	137
California, University of Los Angeles	MA Applied Linguistics & TESL	FT: 2 years	Out-of-state: $9,000, fees $4,800/yr	Fall	GRE score 3.0+, TOEFL 625	Lyn Repath-Martos, Student Affairs Officer	137
California State University, Dominguez Hills	MA in English with TESL option	Both: FT/PT 2-4 semesters	In-state: $459/6 units, Out-of-state: $245/unit in addition. Fees: $119		Degree, GPA 2.5+, TOEFL 550+	Vanessa Wenzell, TESL Coordinator	
California State University, Fresno	MA in Linguistics with ESL emphasis	Both: FT/PT 4 semesters	In-state: $901/semester; Out-of-state: $246/unit		BA, GPA 3.0+, GRE 450 (verbal), 430 (quantitative), TOEFL 550	G W Raney, Chair	131
California State University, Fullerton	MS in Education with TESOL concentration	Both: FT/PT 30 semester units	In-state: $640.50 - $973.50; Out-of-state: $246 / unit in addition	Fall	Bac degree, GPA 2.5+, GPA 3.0, TOEFL 575	TESOL Coordinator	131
College	Course title	Course length	Fees	Start dates	Entry Requirements	Contacts	Address/ Advert Page

College	Course Title	Course Length	Fees	Start Dates	Entry Requirements	Contacts	Address/ Advert Page
California State University, Hayward	MA in English with TESOL option	Both: FT/PT 6 quarters	In-state: $590/quarter; Out-of-state: $164/unit in addition	Any quarter	Bac degree, GPA 3.0	Keiko Tanaka	131
California State University, Los Angeles	MA TESOL	Both: FT/PT Contact for details	In-state: $1,754/yr; Out-of-state: $5,900/yr	Summer, Fall	GPA 2.75, Intro to Linguistics B+, TOEFL 600+	Coordinator, TESOL Program	137
California University, Northridge, CA	Master of Arts in Linguistics with a TESOL Emphasis	Both: FT/PT 4 semesters	In-state: $990/semester; Out-of-state: $246/unit in addition	Any semester	First degree GPA 3.0+or GRE; TOEFL 550	Dr Sharon Klein, Coordinator	131
Cardinal Stritch University	MEd in Professional Development with ESL concentration	Both: FT/PT 2 semesters	$260/credit	Any semester	Application, transcripts of previous work, GPA 2.75+	Chair	131
Carson-Newman College	MAT in ESL	Both: FT/PT 3 semesters	$180/credit hr	Any semester	Bac degree, GPA 2.5, GRE score, TOEFL 550+	Dr Mark Brock	131
Central Connecticut State University	MS with TESOL concentration	Both: FT/PT 3-4 semesters	In-state: $1,252/ semester; Out-of-state: $3,490		Bac deg, GPA 2.7+, TOEFL 550	Dr Andrea G Osburne	131
Central Michigan University	MA TESOL	Both: FT/PT 2 semesters	In-state: $35.40/credit hr; Out-of-state: $268.80/hr, fees $480 / yr	Any semester	Contact for details	Dr Clara Lee Moodie	131
Central Missouri State University	MA TESL	Both: FT/PT 3 semesters	In-state: $132/semester hr; Out-of-state: $264/semester hr	Any semester	Bac degree, GPA 2.5+, TOEFL 565	Graduate Coordinator, MA-TESL Program	131
Central Washington University	MA in English: TESL/TEFL	Both: FT/PT 5 quarters	In-state: $1,400/quarter; Out-of-state: $4,260/quarter	Any quarter	GPA 3.0+, GRE score	Graduate Student Coordinator	131
Cincinnati University	MEd TESOL/ Literacy	FT: 1.5 years	$188/credit hr	September	TOEFL, GRE, GPA 3, bac deg	Program Secretary	137
Colorado University, Boulder	MA in Linguistics	Both: FT/PT 4 semesters	In-state: $930/semester; Out-of-state, $3,768/semester, fees approx $200	Fall	Bac degree, GPA 2.75, GRE score	Chair, Linguistics Dept	137
College	Course Title	Course Length	Fees	Start Dates	Entry Requirements	Contacts	Address/ Advert Page

US Masters Degrees

College	Course Title	Course Length	Fees	Start Dates	Entry Requirements	Contacts	Address/ Advert Page
Colorado University, Denver	MA in English, Applied Linguistics (ESL)	Both: FT/PT Contact for details	In-state: $1,284; Out-of-state: $4,182	Any semester	GPA 3.0+, GRE General Test, dept writing exam, TOEFL 580+	Joanne Addison, Ian H G Ying	132
Colorado State University	MA TESL	Both: FT/PT 4 semesters	In-state: $1,300/ semester; Out-of-state: $4,945/ semester	Any semester	Bac degree, GPA 3.0+, GRE score	Karl Krahnke, Coordinator	
Columbia International University	MA in TEFL/ Intercultural Studies	Both: FT/PT 1-2 yrs	$285/semester hr	Fall	Christian, GPA 2.7+, Bac degree, TOEFL 600+	Brian O'Donnell, Admissions Director	132
Delaware University	MA in ESL	Both: FT/PT 3-4 semesters	In-state: $2,060/ semester; Out-of-state: $5,085/ semester	Any semester	GRE 3.0, letters of recommen dation, TOEFL score	ESL Coordinator	137
	MA in Linguistics	Both: FT/PT 4 semesters	In-state: $1,832; Out-of-state: $5,224/ semester	Any semester	GRE 1050+, writing sample, TOEFL 550+	Director of Graduate Studies	137
East Carolina University	MAEd in English with TESL concentration	Both: FT/PT 3 semesters	In-state: $450/semester; Out-of-state: $4,014, fees $466/semester	Any semester	Degree, GPA 2.5+, GRE score	TESL Coordinator	132
Eastern Kentucky University	MA in English with ESL emphasis	Both: FT/PT 2-3 semesters	In-state: $2,150/yr; Out-of-state: $5,990/yr	Any semester	Degree, combined GRE 1000+, GPA 3.0+	Dominick J Hart	132
Eastern Michigan University, Ypsilanti, MI	MA in TESOL	Both: FT/PT 4+ semesters	In-state: $145/cr hr; Out-of-state: $339/cr hr	Fall, Winter	First degree, GPA 2.5, TOEFL 550	TESOL Advisor	132
Fairfield University, CT	MA in TESOL	Both: FT/PT 4 semesters	$335/credit	Any semester	Contact for details	Sr M Julianna Poole	133
Fairleigh Dickinson University, NJ	MAT in ESL (1st & 2nd certification)	Both: FT/PT 3 semesters	$496/credit	Any semester	Degree, GPA 3.0, TOEFL 530+	Director, MAT Program	133
	Multilingual MA	Both: FT/PT Variable	$496/credit	Any semester	As MAT	Chair	130
Findlay University, Findlay, OH	MA in TESOL and Bilingual Education	Both: FT/PT 4 semesters	$227 per semester hr	Any semester	First degree and teaching certificate, TOEFL 550/TSE 230	Director, MA in TESOL	137
College	Course Title	Course Length	Fees	Start Dates	Entry Requirements	Contacts	Address/ Advert Page

College	Course Title	Course Length	Fees	Start Dates	Entry Requirements	Contacts	Address/ Advert Page
Florida International University, FL	MS in TESOL	Both: FT/PT 3-4 semesters	In-state: $60/cr; Out-of-state: $385/credit	Any semester	First degree GPA 3.	TESOL Coordinator	133
	MS in education with TESOL specialisation	Both: FT/PT 1 year	In-state: $120/sem hr; Out-of-state: $300/sem hr	Fall	Degree, GPA 3.0+, GRE 1000	Coordinator	133
Fresno Pacific University	MA TESOL	Both: FT/PT Variable	$240/semester unit	Any semester	Degree, GRE or Miller Analogies Test score	Dr David Freeman, Director	133
Georgetown University, Washington, DC	MAT in TESOL and Bilingual Education	Both : FT/PT 3-4 semesters	$751/cr hr	Any semester	Bac degree with B+ av	Director, MAT Program	133
	MAT in TESOL	Both: FT/PT 3-4 semesters	$751/cr hr	Any semester	As above	Director, MAT Program	133
Georgia University	MEd TESOL	Both: FT/PT 4 quarters	In-state: $1,500; Out-of-state: $4,700	Any quarter	6 cr in English, 6 cr in linguistics, comb GRE of 900+, TOEFL 600+	Linda Harklau	137
Georgia State University, Atlanta, GA	MS in TESL	Both: FT/PT 1.5 - 2 years	In-state: $82.50/cr hr; Out-of-state: $247.5/cr hr	Any semester	Deg, GRE Scores, transcripts, letters of recommendation, TOEFL 600+	Dr Gayle Nelson, Director of Graduate Studies	133
Gonzaga University	MA in TESL	Both: FT/PT 3 semesters	$396/cr	Any semester	Degree, GPA 3.0+, GRE or Miller Analogies Test score, TOEFL 550+	Director, MA-TESOL Program	134
Grand Canyon University	MA with major in TESL	Both: FT/PT 4 semesters	$289/credit	Any semester	GPA 2.8+, GRE or MAT score, teaching cert, TOEFL 575	Prof Bethyl A Pearson	134
Hawaii University, Manoa	MA in ESL	Both: FT/PT 4 semesters	In-state: $2,016/sem; Out-of-state: $4,980/sem	Fall	GPA 3.0, GRE score, TOEFL scor	Dept of ESL	134
Hofstra University	MS in Education: TESL	Both: FT/PT 3 semesters	$429/credit, fees $107	Any semester	Degree, GPA 2.5+, letters of recommen dation	Dr Nancy L Cloud	134
Houston University	MEd in TESL	Both: FT/PT 3 semesters	In-state: $504/9 sem hrs; Out-of-state: $2,214/sem hrs	Contact for details		Kip Tellez	138
College	Course Title	Course Length	Fees	Start Dates	Entry Requirements	Contacts	Address/ Advert Page

US Masters Degrees

College	Course Title	Course Length	Fees	Start Dates	Entry Requirements	Contacts	Address/Advert Page
Houston University	MA Applied Linguistics	Both: FT/PT 4 semesters	In-state: $720/semester; Out-of-state: $2,976/semester	Any semester	Deg, GPA 3.0+, GRE score	Dr Dudley W Reynolds	138
Houston-Clear Lake University	MS in Multicultural Studies with ESL endorsement	Both: FT/PT 2 yrs inc summers	In-state: $240/course; Out-of-state: $744/course		Degree, GRE or MAT score, GPA 3.0+	Dr Judith A Marquez	138
Hunter College of the City University of New York	MA in Education (TESOL)	Both: FT/PT 1-2 years	In-state: $185/credit; Out-of-state: $320/credit	Fall	B average on undergrad work, 12 credits of study in other language	Dr Donald R H Byrd, Head	
Idaho University	MA-TESL	Both: FT/PT 4 semesters	In-state: $810/semester; Out-of-state: $2,690/semester	Any semester	Degree, GPA 3.0+, TOEFL 560	Director of Graduate Studies	138
Illinois University, Chicago	MA in Linguistics with TESOL concentration	Both: FT/PT 4 semesters	In-state: $2,155/semester, Out-of-state: $5,111/semester	Fall	Elliott L Judd, Director	Elliott L Judd, Director	138
Illinois University, Arbana-Champaign	MA TESL	Both: FT/PT 4 semesters	In-state: $1,885/semester; Out-of-state: $5,222/semester		Degree, GPA 3.0+, TOEFL 600, TWE 4	Lawrence F Bouton	138
Illinois State University, IL	MA TEFL/TESOL	Both: FT/PT 4 semesters	In-state: $99.40/cr hr; Out-of-state: $298.2/cr hr	Any semester	Degree, GRE scores, TOEFL 600	Douglas Hesse, Director of Graduate Studies	134
Indiana State University	MA in English with Linguistics concentration	Both: FT/PT 4 semesters	In-state: $137.50/cr hr; Out-of-state: $311.50/cr hr	Any semester	Degree, GPA 3.0	Director of Graduate Studies	134
Indiana University of Pennsylvania	MA in English (TESOL)	Both: FT/PT 1-2 years	In-state: $1,734/semester; Out-of-state: $3,118/semester	Any semester	Degree, letters of recommendation, TOEFL score	Dr Dan J Tannacito, Director	134
Iowa University	MA in Linguistics with TESL focus	Both: FT/PT 4 semesters	In-state: $1,621/semester; Out-of-state: $5,511/semester	Fall	GPA 2.3+, GRE score, TOEFL 600	Prof William D Davis	138

College	Course Title	Course Length	Fees	Start Dates	Entry Requirements	Contacts	Address/Advert Page

College	Course Title	Course Length	Fees	Start Dates	Entry Requirements	Contacts	Address/ Advert Page
Iowa State University	MA in TESL/Applied Linguistics	Both: FT/PT 4 semesters	In-state: $3,048/yr; Out-of-state: $8,974/yr	Fall	Degree, GRE score, TOEFL 600	TESL Coordinator	135
Jersey City State College	MA in Urban Education with ESL concentration	Both: FT/PT 3-4 semesters	In-state: $170/cr; Out-of-state: $213/cr	Any semester	Transcripts for colleges attended, undergrad cum average 2.75, GRE or MAT score	Mihri Napoliello	135
Kansas University	MA TESL	Both: FT/PT 4 semesters	In-state: $125/cr hr; Out-of-state: $325/cr hr	Any semester	Under grad GPA 3.0, Grad GPA 3.5, TOEFL 590	Paul L Markham	135
Long Island University, NY	MS in TESOL	Both: FT/PT 3 semesters	$475/cr hr	Any semester	First degree	Graduate Admissions	135
Manhattanville College, NY	Masters of Professional Studies in TESOL	Both: FT/PT Individualised pacing - PT max 4 years	$406/cr	Any semester	First degree, GPA 3.0+, TOEFL 550+	Dr Laurence Krute, Director - Second Language	135
Mankato State University, Mankato, MN	MA in English (TESL concentration)	Both: FT/PT 4 semesters	In-state: $140/sem hr; Out-of-state: +$21/sem hr	Any quarter	Degree, GPA 3.0+, TOEFL 550	Dr Harry Solo	135
Maryland University, Baltimore County	MA in ESOL/Bilingual Instructional Systems Development	Both: FT/PT 2-3 semesters	In-state: $253/cr hr; Out-of-state: $455/cr hr	Any semester	GPA 3.0, GRE scores, TOEFL 550	Jodi Crandall, Ron Schwartz, Dept of Education	135
	MA in ESOL/Bilingual Instructional Systems Development (with K-12 certification)	Both: FT/PT 4 semesters	In-state: $253/cr hr; Out-of-state: $455/cr hr	Any semester	GPA 3.0, GRE scores, TOEFL 550	Jodi Crandall, Ron Schwartz, Dept of Education	135
Maryland University, College Park	MEd in TESOL	Both: FT/PT 1.5 - 2 yrs with summer courses	In-state: $272/cr; Out-of-state: $400/cr	Any semester	GPA 3.0+, GRE score, TOEFL 600, TWE 4	Dr William E DeLorenzo	000
Marymount University	MEd in TESL, K-12	Both: FT/PT 4 semesters	$445/cr hr	January, May, June, August	Degree, admission to the university master's program, interview	Graduate Admissions Coordinator	000

College	Course Title	Course Length	Fees	Start Dates	Entry Requirements	Contacts	Address/ Advert Page

COLLEGE	COURSE TITLE	COURSE LENGTH	FEES	START DATES	ENTRY REQUIREMENTS	CONTACTS	ADDRESS/ ADVERT PAGE
Massachusetts University, Amherst	MEd with a concentration in ESL	Both: FT/PT 3 semesters	In-state: $1,320/ semester; Out-of-state: $4,476/ semester	Fall, Spring	Degree, GPA 3.0, TOEFL 560+	Chair, Bilingual/ESL/ Multicultural	135
Massachusetts University, Boston	MA in ESL studies	Both: FT/PT Contact for details	In-state: $110/cr; Out-of-state: $368.5/cr	Any semester	Proficiency in a language other than English, TOEFL 575+	Donald Macedo	135
Memphis University	MA in English with ESL concentration	Both: FT/PT 4 semesters	In-state: $147/cr hr; Out-of-state: $348/cr hr	Any semester	12 hrs of upper-division English or related courses	Director of Graduate Programs	135
Meredith College, NC	MEd with an ESL speciality	Both: FT/PT 2 semesters	$250/sem hr	Any semester	Degree, GPA 2.5+, MAT score, TOEFL & TSE scores	Ellen Collie Graden	135
Michigan State University, MI	MA in TESOL/Applied Linguistics	Both: FT/PT 3.4 semesters	In-state: $216/cr hr; Out-of-state: $437/cr hr	Any semester	Strong undergrad record, GRE score, TOEFL 600+	Prof C Polio	136
Minnesota University, Minneapolis	MA in ESL	FT: 2-3 years	In state $2,520 - $4,950	September	GPA 3.2, transcripts of coursework, GRE verbal & quantitative scores of 1,100+, TOEFL score of 600 (non-native)	Dr Andrew D Cohen, Director of Graduate Studies	000
Montana University	MA in English Linguistics and TESOL	FT:1-1.5 years	In-state: $1,500/term; Out-of-state: $3.400/term, fees $350	Degree, GRE score	Any semester	Robert B Hausmann	136
Montclair State University	MA Applied Linguistics, TESL concentration	Both: FT/PT 4 semesters	In-state: $186.3/sem hr; Out-of-state: $236.10/sem hr	Any semester	Undergrad transcripts, GRE score	Graduate Adviser	136
Monterey Institute of International Studies	MA TESOL	Both: FT/PT 3 semesters or 2 semesters + 2 summers	$91,00/ semester	Any semester	Degree, GPA 3.0, TOEFL 600	Admissions Office	136
Mount Vernon College	MA TESOL		$478/cr	Any semester	BA, GPA 3.0, TOEFL 600	Sharon Ahern Fechter, MA TESOL Program	136

COLLEGE	COURSE TITLE	COURSE LENGTH	FEES	START DATES	ENTRY REQUIREMENTS	CONTACTS	ADDRESS/ ADVERT PAGE

US Masters Degrees

College	Course Title	Course Length	Fees	Start Dates	Entry Requirements	Contacts	Address/ Advert Page
Murray State University	MA TESOL	Both: FT/PT 4 semesters	In-state: $1,150/sem; Out-of-state: $4,130/sem	Any semester	GPA 2.75, Undergrad major in English or foreign lang, TOEFL 575	Director, TESOL Program	136
National-Louis University	MEd with ESL Concentration		$490/3-cr-hr	Any semester	Teaching cert, MAT or TOEFL score, BA deg	Dr Darrell Bloom, Coordinator	136
Nazareth College of Rochester	MS in Education, TESOL	Both: FT/PT 4 semesters	$417/cr hr	Any semester	Bac degree with cum index of 2.7 or B	Dr Brett Blake, Dept of TESOL	136
Nevada University, Reno	Inter disciplinary MA TESOL	Both: FT/PT 4 semesters	In-state: $810/sem; Out-of-state: $4,527/sem	Any semester	BA, GPA 3.0, TOEFL 550	MA in TESL Coordinator	138
New Hampshire University	MAT with TESOL concentration	Both: FT/PT 4 semesters	In-state: $2,450/sem; Out-of-state: $6,880/sem	Any semester	BA degree, GRE General Test score, TOEFL 550	Prof Mary Clark	136
New Mexico University	MA in English Language & Linguistics with TESL concentration	Both: FT/PT 4 semesters	In-state: $2,450/sem; Out-of-state: $6,880/sem	Any semester	BA degree, GRE General Test score, TOEFL 550	Prof Mary Clark	136
	MA in Elementary/ Secondary Education with TESOL concentration	Both: FT/PT 4 semesters	In-state: $309.30/3-cr hr; Out-of-state: $4,345.40/sem	Any semester	Application form, letter of intent, 3 letters of recommen, a resume, official transcripts	Coordinator, Division of Language & Literacy	136
	MA in Curriculum and Instruction with TESOL specialization	Both: FT/PT 2 long & 2 short semesters	In-state: $1,176/sem; Out-of-state: $3,672/sem	Any semester	GPA 3.0+, TOEFL 550	Ana H Macias	136
New Rochelle College	MS TESOL	Both: FT/PT 3 academic sessions over 12 mths	$315/cr	Any academic session	BA degree, GPA 3.0, official transcripts	Division Head, Graduate School	136
New York State University, Albany	MS TESOL	Both: FT/PT 1.5 years	In-state: $2,550/sem; Out-of-state: $4,208/sem	Any semester	GPA 3.0, 3 academic letters, personal statement, TOEFL 600+	Chair, Dept of Educational Theory & Practice	136
New York State University, Stony Brook	MA TESOL .	Both: FT/PT 2-3 semesters	In-state: $2,550/sem; Out-of-state: $4,208/sem	Fall	Bac degree, GPA 3.0, GRE score, TOEFL 600	Sandra L Brennan, Graduate Secretary	136
College	Course Title	Course Length	Fees	Start Dates	Entry Requirements	Contacts	Address/ Advert Page

US Masters Degrees

College	Course Title	Course Length	Fees	Start Dates	Entry Requirements	Contacts	Address/Advert Page
New York University	MA TESOL with NY State Certification	Both: FT/PT 3-4 semesters	$610/cr	Any semester	Bac degree, GPA 2.75+, 2 yrs of foreign lang study, TOEFL 600+	Frank L Tang, Director, TESOL Program	136
North Carolina University, Charlotte	MEd	Both: FT/PT 3.4 semesters	In-sate: $859/sem; Out-of-state: $4,436/yr	Any semester	BA degree, GRE or MAT score, TOEFL score	ESL Coordinator	136
North Texas University	MA in English with ESL concentration	Both: FT/PT 3-4 semesters	In-state: $918.65/sem; Out-of-state: $2,844.65/sem	Any semester	BA degree, GPA 3.0, GRE score, TOEFL 575	Chair, Linguistics/ESL Division	136
Northeastern Illinois University	MA in Linguistics with TESL concentration	Both: FT/PT 4 semesters	In-state: $92.75/cr hr; Out-of-state: $278/cr hr	Any semester	Bac degree, GPA 2.75+, TOEFL 600+, TSE 50+	Audrey Reynolds, Linguistics Program	136
Northern Arizona University	MA TESL	Both: FT/PT 4 semesters	In-state: $1,950/yr; Out-of-state: $7,166/yr	Fall	Graduate admission application form, undergrad transcripts	Coordinator, MA-TESL Program	136
Northern Illinois University, IL	MA in English with a focus on TESOL	Both: FT/PT 4 semesters	In-state: $1,150.80/12+ sem hrs; Out-of-state: $3,452/12+ sem hrs	Any semester, Fall preferred	TOEFL 550, GRE, First degree any discipline, GPA 3.0+	Advisor, MA-TESOL	136
Northern Iowa University	MA TESOL	Both: FT/PT 3 semesters + one summer	In-state: $1,583/sem; Out-of-state: $3,902/sem	Any semester	GPA 3.0, 3 letters of recommen	Dr Cheryl Roberts, Graduate Coordinator	138
Nova Southeastern University	MS in Education with TESL concentration	Both: FT/PT 2.5 semesters	$245/cr	Any 8 week session	Bac degree	Director, Graduate Teacher Education Program	
Ohio State University	MA with TESOL concentration	Both: FT/PT 4 quarters	In-state: $1.738/qtr; Out-of-state: $4,500/qtr	Autumn, Summer	BA degree, GRE score, TOEFL 575	Prof Charles R Hancock	136
Ohio University, OH	MA in TEFL/TESOL Applied Linguistics	Both: FT/PT 6 quarters	In-state: 1,708/9-18 qtr hrs; Out-of-state: $3,281/9-19 qtr hrs	Fall	GPA 3.0, (good first degree); TOEFL 600+	Graduate Chair, Dept of Linguistics	136
Oklahoma City University	MEd (MA) with TESOL concentration	Both: FT/PT 3-4 semesters	$300/cr hr	Any semester	BA degree, GPA .0, TOEFL 500	Director, Dept of TESOL	136
College	Course Title	Course Length	Fees	Start Dates	Entry Requirements	Contacts	Address/Advert Page

College	Course Title	Course Length	Fees	Start Dates	Entry Requirements	Contacts	Address/ Advert Page
Oklahoma State University, OK	MA in English with TESL option	Both: FT/PT 4 semesters	Instate: $95.91/cr hr; Out-of-state: $174.50/cr hr	Fall, Spring	First degree, GPA 3.0, TOEFL 600, Test of Written English Score	Graduate Coordinator	136
Old Dominion University, VA	MA in Applied Linguistics	Both: FT/PT 3 years	In-state: $171/cr hr Out-of-state: $453/cr hr	Any semester	BA degree, TOEFL 570	Dr Janet M Bing	136
Oregon University	MA in Linguistics with Applied Linguistics option	Both: FT/PT 6 quarters	In-state: $1,496/qtr; Out-of-state: $3,354/qtr	Any quarter	Graduation, statement of purpose, GRE score, TOEFL score	Dr P L Rounds	136
Our Lady of the Lake University of San Antonio	MEd with a specialization in ESL	Both: FT/PT 4 semesters	$261/sem hr	Any semester	Contact for details	Dr Hugh B Fox III	136
Pennsylvania University, PA	Master's in TESOL	Both: FT/PT 4 semesters	$8,256/ semester	Any semester	Application, transcript, letters of recommen dation, GRE, TOEFL	Keith Watanabe	136
Pennsylvania State University	MA TESL	Both: FT/PT 4 semesters	In-state: $3,151/sem Out-of-state: $6,490/sem	Fall	BA degree, GRE score, 3 letters of reference, TOEFL 600	Sandra J Savignon, Director	136
Pittsburgh University	MA in Linguistics with a TESOL certificate	Both: FT/PT 6 semesters	In-state: $3,855/sem; Out-of-state: $7,937/sem	Any semester	Bac degree, TOEFL 600, GRE score, GPA 3.0+	Admissions Officer	136
Portland State University, OR	MA in TESL	FT: 2 years	$2,034 - $3,482/quarter	September, January, March, June	600 TOEFL, 2 letters of recommen dation, transcripts (GPA 3.0) personal statement	Karin Tittleback-Goodwin	136
Queens College of the City University of New York	MA Applied Linguistics	Both: FT/PT 3 semesters	In-state; $185/cr; Out-of-state $320/cr	Any semester	BA, GPA 3.0+	Prof R Vago	136
	MS in Education: TESOL	Both: FT/PT 3 semesters	In-state; $185/cr; Out-of-state $320/cr	Any semester	BA, GPA 3.0+	Prof R Vago	136
Radford University, VA	MS in Education with TESL concentration	Both: FT/PT 4 semesters	In-state: $1,652/sem; Out-of-state: $3,244/sem	Any semester	GRE, NTE or MAT score, TOEFL 550	Director, English Language Institute	136

| College | Course Title | Course Length | Fees | Start Dates | Entry Requirements | Contacts | Address/ Advert Page |

US Masters Degrees

COLLEGE	COURSE TITLE	COURSE LENGTH	FEES	START DATES	ENTRY REQUIREMENTS	CONTACTS	ADDRESS/ ADVERT PAGE
Rhode Island College	MATESL	Both: FT/PT 4 semesters and 2 summers	In-state: $154/cr Out-of-state: $300/cr	Any semester	Official transcripts, GRE or MAT score, TOEFL 550+	Dr Willis Poole	136
	MEd in TESL	Both: FT/PT 3 semesters and 1 summer	In-state: $154/cr; Out-of-state: $300/cr	Any semester	Official transcripts, GRE or MAT score, TOEFL 550+	Dr Willis Poole	136
Rochester University, NY	MS in TESOL	Both: FT/PT 4 semesters	$672/cr hr	Any semester	BA degree, GPA 2.75+	Coordinator of TESOL Program	136
St Cloud State University, MN	MA in English with TESL concentration	Both: FT/PT 2 years	In-state: $150/cr; Out-of-state: $200/cr	Any semester	BA degree, GPA 2.75+, GRE verbal 480	James H Robinson, Director	136
Saint Michael's College, VT	MA in TEFL/TESOL	Both: FT/PT 3 semesters	$265 - $305/credit hr	Any semester	BA/BS degree, TOEFL 550+, application, official college/univ transcripts, 3 letters of recommen dation	Dr M Arani, Director of Graduate & Professional TEFL/TESL Programs	136
San Francisco University	MA TESL	Both: FT/PT 2 semesters + 1 summer	$627/unit	Fall, Spring	BA degree, GPA 2.7, 2 letters of recommen dation, TOEFL 570+	Dorothy S Messerschmitt	138
	MA in English with TESL concentration	Both: FT/PT 4 semesters	In-state: $459 for 0-6 units, $792/sem for 6+ units; Out-of-state: +$246/unit	Any semester	Degree, GPA 3.0, TOEFL 570+	Coordinator, MATESOL Program	138
San Jose State University, CA	MA in TESOL	FT: 3 semesters	Contact for details	Any semester	Degree, GPA 2.5+, TOEFL 570+	Dr Vanniaragan	137
Santa Fe College	MA with concentration in TESL	Both: FT/PT Contact for details	$237/cr		BA degree	Prof Sandra Rodriguez	139
School for International Training, Vermont	MA in TESOL	FT: 1 yr or 2 FT Summers	$9,466 - $11,073 per semester	1 yr: August, summers: June	Degree or equiv, TOEFL 550/213	Fiona Cook, Admissions Counsellor	137
	MA TESOL + French/ Spanish	Contact for details	Contact for details	Contact for details	Contact for details	Fiona Cook, Admissions Counsellor	137
COLLEGE	COURSE TITLE	COURSE LENGTH	FEES	START DATES	ENTRY REQUIREMENTS	CONTACTS	ADDRESS/ ADVERT PAGE

College	Course Title	Course Length	Fees	Start Dates	Entry Requirements	Contacts	Address/ Advert Page
Seattle Pacific University	MA TESOL	Both: FT/PT Contact for details	$255/qtr cr	Any quarter	BA degree, GPA 3.0+, 2 letters of recommen dation, GRE 950+ or MAT score ,5+ TOEFL 600+	Graduate Coordinator, MA-TESOL	137
	MA TESOL with Washington State K-12 certification	Both: FT/PT Contact for details	$255/qtr cr	Any quarter	BA degree, GPA 3.0+, 2 letters of recommen dation, GRE 950+ or MAT score, 5+ TOEFL 600+	Graduate Coordinator, MA-TESOL	137
Seattle University	MA & MEd TESOL	Both: FT/PT 5 quarters	$329/qtr cr	Any quarter	BA degree, GPA 2.75+, TOEFL score	Brita Butler-Wall, Program Coordinator	137
Seattle Pacific University, Washington	MA in TESOL	FT: 18 mths	$280/credit	September, January, March, June	GRE, GPA 3.0+, 2 letters of recommen dation, TOEFL for non-native speakers	Kathryn Bartholomew	137
Seton Hall University	MA in ESL	Both: FT/PT 4 semesters $472/cr	Any semester		MAT or GRE score, 3 letters of recommendati on, resume	Dr W E McCartan	137
Shenandoah University	MSEd TESOL	Both: FT/PT Year-round or 3 summers	$4,950/ trimester	Any trimester	Bac degree, TOEFL 550+	Chair, TESOL Dept	137
Simmons College	MAT (ESL) Both	2 semesters + 1 summer	$562/cr	Any semester	BA degree, official transcripts, resume, 2 recommen dations, GRE or MAT score, TOEFL 550+	Stephanie Cichon, Staff Assistant	137
SOKA University of America	MA in second & foreign language education with TESOL concentration	Both: FT/PT 3-4 semesters	$200/cr	Fall	GPA 2.75+, 2 references, TOEFL 600+	Director, Graduate Admissions Office	137
South Carolina University, SC	MA in Linguistics	Both: FT/PT 4 semestes	In-state: $1,862/sem; Out-of-state: $3,817/sem	Fall, Summer	2 letters of recommen dation, GRE score, TOEFL 560+	Carol Myers-Scotton	138
South Florida University	MA in Applied Linguistics	Both: FT/PT 4 semesters	In-state: $1,098/sem; Out-of-state: £3,528/sem	Fall, Spring	BA, GRE 1000, TOEFL 600+, TES 55	Director of Graduate Studies in Linguistics	138
College	Course Title	Course Length	Fees	Start Dates	Entry Requirements	Contacts	Address/ Advert Page

US Masters Degrees

College	Course title	Course length	Fees	Start dates	Entry requirements	Contacts	Address/ Advert Page
Southeast Missouri State University	MA TESOL	Both: FT/PT 3 semesters	In-state: $99.30/hr; Out-of-state: $184.30/hr	Any semeste	Official transcript, individual transcripts, TOEFL 550+	Dr Adelaide Heyde Parsons	137
Southern Illinois University, Carbondale	MA TESOL	Both: FT/PT 3-4 semesters	In-state: $98.90/cr hr; Out-of-state: $296.40/cr hr	Fall	Degree, GPA 3.0, letters of recommen dation, TOEFL 570+	Chair, Department of Linguistics	137
Southern Maine University	MSEd in Literacy Education with ESL concentration	Both: FT/PT 3 semesters	In-state: $173/cr hr; Out-of-state: $477/cr hr	Any semester	Undergrad transcripts, 3 references, MAT or GRE score	Donald L Bouchard	137
Southern Mississippi University	MA in the Teaching of Languages (TESOL emphasis)	Both: FT/PT 3 semesters	In-state: $1,259/12-hr load; Out-of-state: $2,669/12-hr load	Any semester	Bac degree, GPA 2.75+, GRE, MAT, NTE or Praxis Series score, TOEFL 560+	MATL Director	137
Syracuse University	MA in Linguistics with ESL concentration	Both: FT/PT 3 semesters	$555/cr	Any semester	GRE score, TOEFL score	Gerald R Greenberg	137
Teachers College, Columbia University	MA TESOL	Both: FT/PT Contact for details	$610/point, fees $250/semester	Fall	2-3 references, personal statement, college transcripts, TOEFL 600+	Patricia Juza, TESOL Program	132
Temple University	MEd (TESOL)	Both: FT/PT 3 semesters	In-state: £308/cr hr; Out-of-state: $429/cr hr	Any semester	Degree, GPA 2.8+, GRE or MAT score, TOEFL 575+	Chair, Dept of Curriculum, Instruction & Technology in Education	137
Texas University, Arlington	MA in Linguistics with TESOL concentration/ certificate	Both: FT/PT 3 semesters	In-state: $1,461/12 sem hrs; Out-of-state: $4,149/12 sem hrs	Any semester	BA degree, satisfactory GPA, GRE score	Graduate Advisor	138
Texas University, Austin	MA in TEFL/TESOL	Contact for details	Contact for details	August, January, June	GPA 3.3, GRE 475 min, BA degree, references, essay	Kathleen Sowash	138
	MA in Foreign Language Education with TESL specialisation	FT: 3 semesters	In-state: $108/sem hr; Out-of-state: $321/sem hr	Fall	Bac degree, GPA 3.25, GRE 1100, essay, letters of recommen dation	Dr Elaine K Horwitz	138
College	Course title	Course length	Fees	Start dates	Entry requirements	Contacts	Address/ Advert Page

US Masters Degrees

College	Course Title	Course Length	Fees	Start Dates	Entry Requirements	Contacts	Address/ Advert Page
Texas University, El Paso	MA in Linguistics	Both: FT/PT 4 semesters	In-state: $650/sem; Out-of-state: $2,576/sem	Any semester	BA degree, satisfactory GPA, TOEFL 550+, GRE score	Graduate Advisor - Linguistics	138
Texas University, Pan American	MA in ESL	Both: FT/PT 1.5 - 2 years	In-state: $72/sem cr hr; Out-of-state: $266/sem cr hr	Any semester	BA degree, GPA 3.0+, GRE 1000+, TOEFL 550	Lee Hamilton	138
Texas University, San Antonio	MA with ESL concentration	Both: FT/PT 3-4 semesters	In-state: $1,191/sem; Out-of-state: $3,117/sem	Any semester	Bac degree, GPA 3.0, GRE score	Dr Robert Milk, Director	138
Texas Tech University	MA in Applied Linguistics	Both: FT/PT 4 semesters	In-state: $32/cr hr; Out-of-state $246/cr hr	Any semester	BA Degree, GRE score, TOEFL score	Graduate Adviser, Applied Linguistics	138
Texas Woman's University	MEd with ESL concentration		In-state: $73/sem hr; Out-of-state: $287/sem hr	Any semester	GRE 700+, GPA 2.75+	Rudy Rodriguez	138
Toledo University, OH	MA in ESL	Both: FT/PT 2 years	In-state: $2,400/sem; Out-of-state: $5,200/sem	Any semester	BA degree, GPA 2.7+, 3 letters of recommen dation, TOEFL score, GRE score	Douglas W. Coleman, Director of ESL	138
	MA- Ed in ESL	Both: FT/PT 3-4 semesters	In-state: $2,400/sem; Out-of-state: $5,200/sem	Any semester	BA degree, GPA 2.7+, 3 letters of recommen dation, TOEFL score, GRE score	Douglas W. Coleman, Director of ESL	137
United States International University	MEd with TESOL concentration	Both: FT/PT 4-6 quarters	$245/quarter unit	Any quarter	3 references, GPA 2.5+, TOEFL 550, TWE 5	Dr Mary Ellen Butler-Pascoe	138
Utah University, UT	Masters in Second Language Acquisition	Both: FT/PT 3 semesters	In-state: $1,150/sem; Out-of-state: $3,118/sem	Fall	First degree, GPA 3.0, TOEFL 600	Coordinator, Linguistics Program	138
Washington University	MAT in ESL	Both: FT/PT 6 quarters	In-state: $1,691/qtr; Out-of-state: $4,158/qtr	Summer, Fall	BA degree, GRE score, 3 letters of recommen dation	MATESL Advisor	138
Washington State University	MA in Literacy Education with ESL concentration	Both: FT/PT 4 semesters	In-state: $2,566/sem; Out-of-state: $6,433/sem	Any semester	GPA 3.0+, GRE score, letters of recommen dation, TOEFL 550+	Dr Gisela Ernst-Slavit, Coordinator	138
College	Course Title	Course Length	Fees	Start Dates	Entry Requirements	Contacts	Address/ Advert Page

US Masters Degrees

College	Course title	Course length	Fees	Start dates	Entry requirements	Contacts	Address/ Advert Page
West Chester University	MA in TESL	Both: FT/PT 4-5 semesters	In-state: $187/sem hr; Out-of-state: $336/sem hr	Any semester	Bac degree, GPA 3.0, 2 recommendations, a resume, 500 TOEFL	Cheri Micheau, Director	138
Western Kentucky University	MA English with concentration in TESOL	Both: FT/PT 4 semesters	In-state: $1,135/sem; Out-of-state: $3,115/sem	Any semester	Diploma, GPA 3.0, GRE 1200, TOEFL 550+	Dr Ronald D Eckard, TESL Director	138
West Virginia University	MA in Foreign Languages (TESOL)	Both: FT/PT 4 semesters	In-state: $941/sem; Out-of-state: $3,499/sem	Any semester	Application form, official transcripts, GRE score, TOEFL 550	Chair, Dept of Foreign Languages	138
Wheaton College, IL	MA in Intercultural Studies with TESL specialization	Both: FT/PT 3 semesters	$350/cr hr	Any semester	BA deg, GPA 2.75, TOEFL 600+	Dr Alan Seaman	138
Wichita State University, KS	Ma in Curriculum & Instruction with TESOL specialization	Both: FT/PT 2 years	In-state: $286.85/cr hr; Out-of-state: $331.85/cr hr		Bac degree, GPA 3.0, GRE 917+ or MAT score 40+, proof of certification, 500 word statement	Peggy Anderson, Director, TESOL Program	138
William Paterson University	MEd with a Bilingual Education/ESL concentration	Both: FT/PT Variable	In-state: $187/cr; Out-of-state: $266/cr	Fall, Spring	BA degree, GPA 2.75+, GRE verbal 450+ or MAT 35, TOEFL 550+	Dr K Kim Yoon, Director	138
Wisconsin University, Madison	MA in Applied Linguistics	Both: FT/PT 2-4 semesters	In-state: $2,346/sem Out-of-state: $7,198/sem	Fall	GRE score, letters of recommendation, statement of purpose, TOEFL score	Prof: Charles Scott	138
Wright State University, OH	MA TESOL	Both: FT/PT 5-7 quarters	In-state: $148/qtr hr; Out-of-state: $263/qtr hr	Any quarter	Departmental requirements; TOEFL 600	Director, Programs in TESOL	138
Youngstown State University	MA in English with TESOL concentration	Both: FT/PT 2 years	In-state: $86/qtr cr; Out-of-state: £182/qtr cr	Any quarter	Contact for details	Dr Steven Brown	138
College	Course title	Course length	Fees	Start dates	Entry requirements	Contacts	Address/ Advert Page

College	Course Title	Course Length	Fees	Start Dates	Entry Requirements	Contacts	Address/ Advert Page
Brock University, Canada	MEd TESOL	FT: 12-15 mths	C$1,700/half credit	Fall	Contact for details	Department of Applied Language Studies, Brock University	139
Carleton University, Canada	MA in Applied Language Studies	Both: FT/PT 3 semesters	C$3,337/term	Any semester	Contact for details	Prof Devon Woods, Graduate Studies Supervisor	139
Concordia University, Canada	MA Applied Linguistics	FT: 2 years; PT: 5 years	Contact for details	May/June, September, January	Good BEd/BA degree including 24 credits of TESL prerequisites. Normally one year of TESL experience	Ms C Parkinson, Dr J White	139
Manitoba University	MEd TESL	Both: FT/PT 2 semesters	C$4,134/program	Fall	4 yr BEd, 2 yrs teaching exp, TOEFL 550	Dr Patrick G Mathews	140
Ontario Institute for Studies in Education of the University of Toronto	MA in Second Language Education	Both: FT/PT 4 semesters	C$7,500/yr	Fall	3 or 4 yr BA degree, TOEFL 580+, IELTS 7, 1 yr teaching experience	Registrar's Office, Graduate Studies	140
	MEd in Second Language Education	Both: FT/PT 3 semesters	C$4,580/yr	Fall	As for MA	Registrar's Office, Graduate Studies	140
Ottawa University	MEd in Second Language Teaching	Both: FT/PT 10 courses	C$2,900/session	Contact for details	BA degree, teaching cert	Richard Chenier	140
St Mary's University, Halifax, Nova Scotia	MEd TEFL/TESOL	FT: 3 years	C$5,000	September	Degree	Maureen Sargent	140
Victoria University, Canada	MA Applied Linguistics	Contact for details of FT/PT	Approx C$2,000/yr	Any semester	BA or BS, GRE score	Graduate Advisor, Dept of Linguistics	140
York University	MA in Theoretical and Applied Linguistics	Both: FT/PT 3 semesters	C$10,800/yr	Any semester	Contact for details	Prof David Mendelsohn, Director	140
College	Course Title	Course Length	Fees	Start Dates	Entry Requirements	Contacts	Address/ Advert Page

Australia/New Zealand Masters Degrees

College	Course title	Course length	Fees	Start dates	Entry requirements	Contacts	Address/ Advert Page
Deakin University, Melbourne, Aus	MA (TESOL)	FT: 1 year; PT: 2 years	Aus$13000	February	4 years tertiary ed inc TT &Grad Cert TESOL	Dr Alex McKnight	155
	M.A. (TESOL)	FT: 1 year; PT: 2 years	Aus$13000	February	4 years tertiary ed inc TT	Dr Alex McKnight	155
Griffith University, Brisbane, Aus	MA in Applied Linguistics	FT: 1 year	Australian students: Aus$650 per 10 credit points; Overseas students: Aus$1,250 per 10 credit points	February	Degree, 3 yrs exp	Gary Birch	155
La Trobe University, Melbourne, Aus	MA in Applied Linguistics	FT: 1 year; PT 2-3 years	Local: Aus$6,900; International: Aus$12,000	March, July	4-yr undergrad degree in rel areas	Ms Marion Sargeant	156
	MA in Education	FT: 1 year; PT 2-3 years	Local: Aus$6,900; International: Aus$12,000	March, July	4-yr undergrad degree in rel areas	Ms Marion Sargeant	156
	Master of Arts	FT: 1 year; PT 2-3 years	Local: Aus$6,900; International: Aus$12,000	March, July	4-yr undergrad degree in rel areas	Ms Marion Sargeant	156
	Master of Adult Education MA in Applied Linguistics	FT: 1 year; PT 2-3 years	Local: Aus$6,900; International: Aus$12,000	March, July	4-yr undergrad degree in rel areas	Ms Marion Sargeant	156
Macquarie University, Dept of Linguistics, Sydney, Aus	(with options in TESOL & Literacy)	FT: 2-3 sems; PT/dist: 4-10 sems	Aus$12,000 (less for Aus/NZ applics)	March, July	First degree, 2 yrs rel exp	Linguistics Distance Learning Office, Linguistics Post Graduate Office	156
Victoria University of Wellington, NZ	MA in Applied Linguistics	FT: 9 mths; PT: up to 4 years	NZ$15,000	March, July	Hon degree or postgrad dip in TESL + 2 yrs teaching experience	Dr J Rond	159
Waikato University Lang Institute, Hamilton, NZ	MA Applied Ling	Both: FT/PT 8 mths	Contact for details	March	Degree/ Diploma of Teaching	Rhonda Robertson	159
Wollongong University, Aus	MEd in TESOL	FT: 1 year; PT: 2 years or Dist.	On application	February, July on campus; Any time by dist	3 yr degree or equiv	Ms Kim Roser, Executive Officer	157

College	Course title	Course length	Fees	Start dates	Entry requirements	Contacts	Address/ Advert Page

Specialising

Teachers seeking to make themselves more attractive to employers, and to make their work more interesting, should consider specialising.

To make the most of a specialisation from both a personal and professional point of view, you are advised to choose an area in which you have a genuine interest.

The world of English teaching is becoming increasingly fragmented or specialised. Although a majority of your teaching is likely to be general English, if you are able to offer a specialisation, then you are likely to find yourself more employable, with more interesting work and better conditions. Some of the key areas of specialisation experiencing significant growth are Teaching Young Learners, ESL and Teaching Business English. These are covered in some depth in the next few pages.

So how do you become a specialist? In some cases your previous experience outside TEFL may be directly relevant to a possible area of specialist teaching. Perhaps you worked in a legal firm or the banking sector. In many cases it may be possible to take a relevant short course to aid specialisation, building on your non-teaching experience or giving insight to the specialist area. However you choose to maximise your specialist potential, remember to choose a specialist area in which you have a genuine interest. There is a very substantial market for Business English, for example, but if the idea of discussing stocks and shares makes your eyes roll, you are unlikely to find it particularly fulfilling.

English for Specific Purposes (ESP)

If you have some general EFL experience, a good way of making the most of your experience is to do a course in teaching ESP, which is teaching English towards a specific objective. A specialist background in banking, for example, will make you specifically suitable for this sphere. If your students want to be doctors or pilots, they will need specialised English, so ESP is job rather than exam-orientated.

Combining English with vocational courses, such as Computing or even Hairdressing, is becoming a popular option, so you can develop virtually any expertise you may have. In some cases the teaching demands can be fairly unusual. You may, as one teacher experienced, find yourself training a group of Algerian engineers, furnishing them with the vocabulary they need to work on the construction of a new power station. It's a challenging and unusual environment but can be very rewarding.

Teaching Business English

Business English is an increasingly popular sector within EFL and also an increasingly demanding one. As with all areas of expertise teaching, students' expectations are becoming more sophisticated and the days when a cursory glance through the Wall Street Journal was all it took to prepare for a Business English lesson are long gone. Results are very closely measured. Fortunately, with the increase in demand has come the development of specialist teacher training courses, particularly from the London Chamber of Commerce and Industry and Trinity College (see page 227 for details of Business English courses).

Working with business people demands special skills, knowledge and interests. Business English is an area that favours more mature teachers, since many business students will be wary of being taught by someone significantly younger than themselves. In those countries where both General and Business English teachers are in demand, Business English is normally better paid.

Students will be highly motivated, but they may feel uncomfortable with any suggestion that they are going back to school. A senior executive might not adapt easily to the role of learner and it is important that the teacher keeps linguistic and professional competence separate. A group from the same company is likely to contain its own hierarchy and some students will be unwilling to risk embarrassing themselves in front of colleagues. All of this requires sensitivity and diplomacy on the part of the teacher.

Cultural Studies

Although some students may be interested only in language learning, others, particularly those who need English in their work, are recognising that an understanding of the history and culture associated with the language is essential for effective communication.

A number of centres now offer courses combining language and cultural studies. But finding the right teachers can be a problem for their directors. Candidates often have a background in history or sociology without having the necessary linguistic and socio-cultural knowledge. If you specialise, you can find yourself standing out in the crowd.

Teaching Young Learners

The skills required to teach children are very specific and very different to those required in teaching adults.

Many teachers' first experience of EFL is in a summer school where students tend to be teenagers or young adults. But the demand for English language teaching continues to explode around the world and parents are keen to give their children a head start by sending them to a language school at a young age, sometimes as low as three.

Teachers of young learners need good classroom management skills and high levels of patience.

Unsurprisingly, more and more teachers are finding that their first experience overseas involves young learners.

Generally speaking, children between the ages of 5 and 16 are regarded as young learners and demand for English courses at this level has been rising sharply. Much of this had been to do with the spread of English language media and the introduction of EFL in primary schools in many countries. There has also been a knock-on effect from the commercial sector, where English has firmly established itself as the international language of business. Parents who are disappointed with the provision in local state schools are enrolling their children in private language schools for extra English lessons.

The country guide in Section Three will help you find the areas where Teaching of Young Learners (TYL) is in most demand. As a rough and ready rule, ask yourself two questions. Does the economic climate in the country enable parents to afford such specific courses? Is there enough exposure to English language media, not only to get adults into the classrooms, but also to motivate them to enrol their children? If the answer is no to these questions, there is likely to be minimal TYL activity.

At the moment teachers of young learners are particularly in demand in Japan, Central Europe and Latin America. In some countries, where there is enthusiasm for early learning, specialist courses have not be set up. English language teachers who have trained to teach adults or secondary level students might suddenly find themselves teaching younger groups without the necessary preparation and specialist materials. Always check what age group you will be teaching.

TYL opportunities exist for L1 and non-L1 English speakers. When it comes to training, although some general teacher training courses do include a TYL element, the TYL will not be tested in the exam. It can be difficult, then, for teachers to provide proof of their TYL ability without some qualification.

Recognised Courses

Cambridge/RSA are running a Certificate in Teaching English to Young Learners (CETYL) focusing on teaching learners from 5-10, 11-16 or 8-13. This includes 100 contact hours, 6 hours supervised teaching practice and 8 hours directed observation of lessons.

Cambridge/RSA also run a Certificate Endorsement course for candidates who have gained the Certificate in English Labguage Teaching to Adults (CELTA) and who wish to 'add-on' an extension course in teaching young learners. The extension course includes 50 contact hours plus 6 hours teaching practice and 8 hours directed observation.

Trinity College offers a Certificate in the Teaching of English to Young Learners (Certificate TEYL) aimed at practising primary teachers. This includes 140 contact hours, teaching practice and lesson observation.

Other Courses

If you are unable to enrol in the Trinity or Cambridge course, there are a number of short courses that will give you some knowledge and, in some cases, experience of TYL. These courses do not lead to teaching qualifications in their own right, but should be considered as a top-up or supplement to a qualification you already have.

Courses for non-L1 Speakers of English

Teacher training courses are usually open to all speakers of English, be it as a mother tongue or as a second language. Anyone who can meet the stipulated English language entry requirements of a course can enrol. This means that non-L1 speakers have a wide variety of courses to choose from.

These are courses primarily aimed at non-L1 speakers or for which non-L1 speakers are advantaged when it comes to enrolling.

COTE

The Cambridge/RSA COTE (Certificate for Overseas Teachers of English) is an in-service course which takes regional conditions into account and uses local classrooms for training. Candidates are at Cambridge First Certificate level by the time they qualify, and require more than 300 hours' teaching experience to enrol.

CEELT

The Cambridge Examination for English Language Teachers is becoming universally available and recognised. The exam relates to tasks which a teacher might perform in the classroom, including correcting students' errors and reading aloud. CEELT courses tend to involve a lot of preparation and even those who do not take the exam benefit from a useful teacher training course.

Short Courses

There are many short courses available exclusively for non-L1 speakers who are already practising teachers. These refresher and language methodology courses are usually from 20 hours to two weeks in length and focus on developing language skills or revising methodology. Some centres, including Language Link in London, offer courses which cover both areas. Sometimes, non-L1 short courses will give candidates the option of studying for a qualification such as CEELT.

Primary/Secondary Courses

There are many specialist short courses available for primary and secondary teachers who want to brush up on their language skills or aspects of methodology. These courses do not exclude L1 speakers but, with as many as 95% of primary and secondary school teachers as nationals of the country in which they are teaching, any such course is likely to be aimed at non-L1 speakers.

College	Course Title	Course Length	Fees	Start Dates	Entry Requirements	Contacts	Address/ Advert Page
Bell Language School, Cambridge, UK	Teaching Business English	FT: 2 wks	£550 to £950	January, June, July, August, September	L1 or non-L1 teachers to secondary or adults	Enquiries and Registration	59,83
Edinburgh University (Inst for Applied Lang Studies), UK	Teaching English for Business Purposes	FT: 2 wks	£480	August	2 yrs exp	Registration Secretary	85,264
English Language Institute, London	LCCI Cert TEB	FT: 2 wks	£510	January, March, July, October	English Teaching Qual + 1 yrs exp.	Tony Evans	86
Eurocentres, Cambridge, UK	LCCIEB Certificate in Teaching English for Business	FT: 2 wks	£505	June, August, September, November	Teaching qualification	Alf Crosby	86
Filton College, Bristol, UK	LCCI Cert	EB FT: 1 wk	£395	Contact for details	Contact for details	Helen Bowen	86
Harrogate Tutorial College	Teaching Business Language and Methodology	FT: 2 wks	£290 per wk	August	Exp teachers	David Herbert	86
International House, Piccadilly, UK	LCCI Cert in Teaching English for Business	FT: 2 wks	£660 + LCCI fee	June, August	Formal ELT training + qual + teaching exp	Teacher Training Dept	87,63
International House, Budapest, Hungary	LCCI Foundation Certificate	PT: 20 wks	Contact for details	October	Teaching exp or some initial training in TEFL	Steve Oakes, Head of Teacher Training	119,58
International House, Wroclaw, Poland	LCCI Cert TEB	FT: 2 wks	£350 + £32 reg fee	January/ February, September	1 years exp, CELTA or equiv	Elisa Jaroch, TT Co- ordinator	121,62
	LCCI Foundation Cert for Teachers of Business English	FT: 5 days	£170 + reg fee	January/ February, September	Camb/RSA CELTA or equiv	Elisa Jaroch, TT Administrator	121,62
International House, Lisbon, Portugal	Teaching Business English	FT: 1 wk	PTE50,000	Contact for details	Contact for details	International House	107,66
International House, Barcelona, Spain	Business English Teachers' Course	FT: 2 wks	Pts45,000	July, August, September	Contact for details	International House	110,65

College	Course Title	Course Length	Fees	Start Dates	Entry Requirements	Contacts	Address/ Advert Page

Teaching Business English

College	Course Title	Course Length	Fees	Start Dates	Entry Requirements	Contacts	Address/ Advert Page
International Language Centres, Hastings, UK	Certificate in Teaching English for Business (LCCI)	FT: 2 wks	£536 + optional exam fee £32	Jan, July/Aug	Contact for details	Rose Holmes	87
Language Link, Russia	LCCI Foundation Cert in Teaching English for Business	FT: 2 wks, PT: 6 wks	Contact for details	FT: January, March, June, PT: January, October	TEFL qual + 1 yr exp	ELT Department	124
	Teaching Business English & ESP	FT: 1 wk	$60-$90	January, March, June, July, August, September, October	Exp teachers and teachers in training	ELT Department	124
Linguarama Alton, UK	Diploma in Teaching Business English and Professional English	FT: 8 wks	£1,800 (1999)	October	3 yrs exp inc 2 yrs business English	Anne Laws	57,88
London Guildhall University, Eng Lang Centre, UK	LCCI Certificate in Teaching English for Business	FT: 2 wks	£550	July, November	Trained teacher, 1 yr exp	Pamela Pickford	63,88
Norwich Institute for Language Education	Courses for Teachers of Business English	FT: 2 wks	£640	February, July	2 yrs exp as EFL teacher	Dave Allan, Penny Miller	89
Oxford English Centre, UK	Oxford English Centre Business English Group Course	FT: Contact for details	Contact for details	April	Pre-intermediate level of English+	Alex Nicholls	89
	Business English (Individual Tuition)	PT: 10-30hrs	£320-£870	Contact for details	Contact for details	Alex Nicholls	89
Pilgrims UK	Teaching Business	2 Wks	£695	From April to June	Contact for details	Sales Dept.	90

Short Courses

College	Course Title	Course Length	Fees	Start Dates	Entry Requirements	Contacts	Address/ Advert Page
Aberdeen Centre for English	Refresher Course	FT: 2-4 wks	2 wks: £380; 4 wks: £760	October, November, February, March, April, May	Intermediate to advanced levels	Perviz Reid	83

Short Courses

College	Course Title	Course Length	Fees	Start Dates	Entry Requirements	Contacts	Address/ Advert Page
Anglia Polytechnic University, Cambridge, UK	Refresher Course	FT: 2 wks	£440	January, July	Non-L1 teachers of English	Teacher Trainer Coordinator	83
Anglo-Continental Educational Group, Bournemouth, UK	Refresher Course	FT: 2-4 wks	2 wks: £470; 3 wks: £655; 4 wks: £840	January, June, July, August	Advanced level English, initial teacher training	Marketing Department	83
Anglolang, Academy of English, UK	Britain Today	FT: 2 wks	£475	June	Intermediate English	Mr G Edner	83
	English in Britain	FT: 2 wks	£475	June, July	Intermediate English	Mr G Edner	83
	Refresher	FT: 2 wks	£475	June, July	Higher Intermediate English, practising teacher	Mr G Edner	83
Angloschool, UK	Teacher Training and Language Development for Foreign Teachers	FT: 2-4 wks	£400-£500	January/ February, July/August	20+, Practising teacher with good English	Dave Bartlett	83
Australian Pacific College	Teaching English as a Foreign Language	FT: 3 wks	Aus$820	Throughout the year	TOEFL 550 or equiv	Amanda Rudge	154
BEET Language Centre, Bournemouth	Refresher	PT: 2 mths	£148/wk	January, February, July, August	Upper Int level of English	Mr Clive Barrow, Director	83
Bell Language School, Cambridge, UK	Multimedia for Self-Access and the Classroom	FT: 2 wks	Contact for details	June	Contact for details	Head of Bell Teacher Training	83
	Multimedia and the Internet	FT: 2 wks	Contact for details	July	Contact for details	Head of Bell Teacher Training	59,83
	Creativity in the Classroom	FT: 2 wks	Contact for details	July	Contact for details	Head of Bell Teacher Training	59,83
	Contemporary English	FT: 2 wks	Contact for details	July	Contact for details	Head of Bell Teacher Training	59,83
College	Course Title	Course Length	Fees	Start Dates	Entry Requirements	Contacts	Address/ Advert Page

College	Course Title	Course Length	Fees	Start Dates	Entry Requirements	Contacts	Address/ Advert Page
Bell Language School, Cambridge, UK	Language & Literature	FT: 2 wks	Contact for details	July	Contact for details	Head of Bell Teacher Training	59,83
	Neuro Linguistic Programming & The Creative Brain	FT: 2 wks	Contact for details	July	Contact for details	Head of Bell Teacher Training	59,83
	Language Development & Methodology	FT: 2 wks	Contact for details	July	Contact for details	Head of Bell Teacher Training	59,83
	Training the Trainer: Skills for Teacher Training	FT: 2 wks	Contact for details	July	Contact for details	Head of Bell Teacher Training	59,83
	Getting the Best from Your Course Book	FT: 2 wks	Contact for details	August	Contact for details	Head of Bell Teacher Training	59,83
	Teaching Techniques & Language Development	FT: 2 wks	Contact for details	August	Contact for details	Head of Bell Teacher Training	59,83
	Teacher Training Plus	FT: 1 wk	Contact for details	July	Contact for details	Head of Bell Teacher Training	59,83
	Language Development & Methodology	FT: 2 wks	Contact for details	July	Contact for details	Head of Bell Teacher Training	59,83
	Creative Teaching & Neuro- Linguistic Programming	FT: 2 wks	Contact for details	January	Contact for details	Head of Bell Teacher Training	59,83
	Recent Developments in Language and Methodology	FT: 2 wks	Contact for details	January	Contact for details	Head of Bell Teacher Training	59,83
	Language Improvement and Methodology	FT: 2 wks	Contact for details	January	Contact for details	Head of Bell Teacher Training	59,83

College	Course Title	Course Length	Fees	Start Dates	Entry Requirements	Contacts	Address/ Advert Page

Short Courses

College	Course Title	Course Length	Fees	Start Dates	Entry Requirements	Contacts	Address/ Advert Page
Bell Language School, Cambridge, UK	British Life and Culture	FT: 1 wk	Contact for details	January	Contact for details	Head of Bell Teacher Training	59,83
	Methodology and Language Awareness	FT: 2 wks	Contact for details	January	Contact for details	Head of Bell Teacher Training	59,83
	British Studies	FT: 2 wks	Contact for details	July	Contact for details	Head of Bell Teacher Training	59,83
	Advanced Language Development	FT: 2 wks	Contact for details	January	Contact for details	Head of Bell Teacher Training	59,83
	Multiple Intelligences in ELT	FT: 2 wks	Contact for details	June	Contact for details	Head of Bell Teacher Training	59,83
	Advanced Language & Culture	FT: 2 wks	Contact for details	August	Contact for details	Head of Bell Teacher Training	59,83
Bell Language School, Norwich, UK	Getting the Best from Your Coursebook	FT: 2 wks	£640 (inc social prog)	August	Inexperienced teachers to secondary or adults	Head of Studies	59,83
	Multimedia & the Internet	FT: 2 wks	£640 (inc social prog)	July	Practising teachers	Head of Studies	59,83
Bell Language School, Saffron Walden, UK	Language Improvement & Teaching Techniques	FT: 2 wks	£753 (inc social prog)	July, August	Practising secondary teachers	Head of Studies	59,84
	Teaching Techniques & Language Developments	FT: 2 wks	£753 (inc social prog)	July, August	Practising primary teachers	Head of Studies	59,84
	Multimedia & Video in the Classroom	FT: 2 wks	£753 (inc social prog)	August	Secondary school teachers	Head of Studies	59,84
	Training the Teacher: Skills for Teacher Training	FT: 2 wks	£753 (inc social prog)	July	Experience teachers	Head of Studies	59,84
Bluefeather School, Dublin, Eire	ATT Refresher for Foreign Teachers	FT: 60 hrs	Closed groups only, negotiable	Any Monday	Practising teachers, student teachers	Tony Penston	93

College	Course Title	Course Length	Fees	Start Dates	Entry Requirements	Contacts	Address/ Advert Page

Short Courses

College	Course Title	Course Length	Fees	Start Dates	Entry Requirements	Contacts	Address/Advert Page
Bradford College, W Yorks, UK	Refresher	FT: 3 wks	£120 per wk	July	Practising teacher of Eng overseas	Nancy Hall, Head of Eng Lang Centre	84
Brasshouse Centre, Birmingham, UK	Training courses for specific purposes, methodology, etc	On application	On application £35/hour upwards	On application	None	Deborah Cobbett	84
Brighton University	Summer Update course for TEFL Teachers	FT: 3 wks	approx $520	July, August	Experienced teacher		84
	Teaching EFL Using New Technologies	FT: 2 weeks	approx £480	June, July	Experienced teacher		84
Bristol University	Pre-sessional course for Masters in TEFL	FT: 4 wks	£600	Contact for details		Arlene Gilpin	84
The British Council, Istanbul, Turkey	ELT Management	PT: 10 wks	tba	tba	L1 speaker or non-L1 with A level competence	Laura Woodward	128
	Teacher Training Diploma	PT: 12 wks	£120	September	Completion of teacher training	Laura Woodward	128
	Drama in ELT	PT: 4 wks	£60	November	FCE competence	Laura Woodward	128
	Aspects of Methodology	PT: 4 wks	£60	October, November	FCE competence	Laura Woodward	128
British Council Teachers Centre, Izmir, Turkey	Language & Methodology	PT: 8 wks	£60	November, February	Non-L1 speaker	Steve Darn	128
	Refresher Course	PT: 6 mths	£180	November	Non-L1 speaker	Steve Darn	128
Cambridge Centre for Languages	Refresher Course	FT: Δ3 wks	£630	July	1 yrs exp at secondary school level		84
College	**Course Title**	**Course Length**	**Fees**	**Start Dates**	**Entry Requirements**	**Contacts**	**Address/Advert Page**

Short Courses

College	Course Title	Course Length	Fees	Start Dates	Entry Requirements	Contacts	Address/ Advert Page
Capital Language Academy, Wellington, New Zealand	Language & Methodology Refresher	FT: 3 wks	NZ$1,200	By arrangement	20+, educated to Univ entrance level	Keiko Calling	158
Centre of English Studies, Dublin	Refresher	FT: 2 wks	IR£410	July, August	None	Director of Studies	93
Chichester Institute of Higher Education	Language Development for English Teachers	FT: 3 wks	£1,080	July	Experienced teacher, English proficiency		85
	Language Skills for English Teachers	FT: 3 wks	£1,140	July	Experienced teacher, English proficiency		85
Chichester School of English	Language Enrichment and Teaching Workshop	FT: 2 wks	£400	July	Post FCE competence		85
The College of St Mark & St John, UK	Teacher Development	FT: 2-4 wks	£420 - £840	July, August, January	xxx	Michael G Hall, INTEC	85
	Teaching English for Specific Purposes	FT: 2 wks	£395	July	Teaching exp	Michael G Hall, INTEC	85
	Trainer Development	FT: 2/4 wks	£395/900	July, January	Teaching exp	Michael G Hall, INTEC	85
	Certificate in Teaching English for Specific Purposes	FT: 11 wks	£2,925	January	Teaching exp	Michael G Hall, INTEC	85
	Certificate in the Principles & Practice of In-service Training for ELT	FT: 11 wks	£2,925	January	ELT exp	Michael G Hall, INTEC	85
	Certificate in Materials Writing	FT: 11 wks	£2,925	January	Teaching exp	Michael G Hall, INTEC	85
College	Course Title	Course Length	Fees	Start Dates	Entry Requirements	Contacts	Address/ Advert Page

Short Courses

College	Course Title	Course Length	Fees	Start Dates	Entry Requirements	Contacts	Address/Advert Page
Colchester English Study Centre	Refresher	FT: 3 wks	£280/wk inc accom	July, August	Practising teacher	Jenny Gray, Registrar	85
Concorde International, Canterbury, UK	Teacher/Refresher Development Course	FT: 2 wks	£207-£256/wk	July, August	Cambridge Proficiency and Advanced level teachers	Anne Kennedy	85
Concorde International, Folkestone, UK	Advanced English Course for Teachers	FT: 2 wks	£184-£256/wk	Monthly	IELTS min 5.5/TOEFL min 550	Anne Kennedy, Director Teacher Training	85
Dundee College, UK	Refresher Course	FT: 2 wks	£380		20+, Higher ed quals	Alec Edwards, Team Leader ESOL	85
Eastbourne School of English, UK	Refresher	FT: 2 wks	£450	January, July, August	Contact for details	Dorothy S Rippon	85
	Communicative Methodology and Advanced Language Management	FT: 2 wks	£450	January, July	FCE level	Dorothy S Rippon	85
	Aspects of British Culture and Advanced Language Management	FT: 2 wks	£450	January, July	Contact for details	Dorothy S Rippon	85
Eastern Mennonite University, Virginia, USA	The English Language	FT: 1 term	Contact for details	September	Contact for details	Dr Ervie Glick, Professor	132
	Grammars of English	FT: 1 term	Contact for details	September	Contact for details	Dr Ervie Glick, Professor	132
	Psycholinguistics	FT: 1 term	Contact for details	September	Contact for details	Dr Ervie Glick, Professor	132
	Methods of Teaching ESL	FT: 1 term	Contact for details	September	Contact for details	Dr Ervie Glick, Professor	132
Eckersley School of English	Courses for Overseas Teachers of English	FT: 3 wks	£600	January, July	Practising teachers		85
Edinburgh University (Inst for Applied Lang Studies), UK	English for TEFL/Applied Linguistics	FT: 4 wks	£790	August	Contact for details	Registration Secretary	85,264
College	Course Title	Course Length	Fees	Start Dates	Entry Requirements	Contacts	Address/Advert Page

Short Courses

College	Course Title	Course Length	Fees	Start Dates	Entry Requirements	Contacts	Address/ Advert Page
Edinburgh University (Inst for Applied Lang Studies), UK	Teaching & Learning English	FT: 2 /3 wks	2 wks: £480; 3 wks: 695	2 wks: September; 3 wks: June, July, August	1 yr exp	Registration Secretary	85,264
	Teaching ESP	FT: 2/3 wks	2 wks: £480; 3 wks: 695	July	2 yrs exp	Registration Secretary	85,264
	Teaching English for Medical Purposes	FT: 2 wks	£480	19 July	2 yrs exp	Registration Secretary	85,264
	Grammar & Communicative Teaching	FT: 3 wks	£695	9 August	2 yrs exp	Registration Secretary	85,264
	Teaching Literature in EFL	FT: 3 wks	£695	19 July	Practising teachers/ trainees	Registration Secretary	85,264
	Drama for TEFL	FT: 3 wks	£695	9 August	Practising teachers	Registration Secretary	85,264
	Pronunciation for Language Teachers	FT: 2 wks	£480	July, August	Practising teachers/ trainees	Registration Secretary	85,264
	Computer Assisted Language Learning	FT: 1 week	£240	July	2 yrs exp	Registration Secretary	85,264
Edinburgh School of English	Language Enrichment and Methodology	FT: 2 wks	On application	July, August	Upper intermediate level		85
Embassy CES, Florida, USA	Teacher Development for Non-Native Speakers	FT: 2 wks	$700	January	550 TOEFL, Cambridge Advanced	Steve Cunningham	131
	Language & Development	FT: 2 wks	$700	January	550 TOEFL, Cambridge Advanced	Steve Cunningham	131
The English Language Centre, Brighton	Refresher for Overseas Teachers	FT: 3 wks	£690		Practising teachers of English	Ms Caroline Mac Andrews	86
	Language Life & Culture in Britain Today	FT: 2/3 wks	2 wks: £492; 3 wks: £690	January, July	Practising teachers of English	Ms Caroline Mac Andrews	86
College	Course Title	Course Length	Fees	Start Dates	Entry Requirements	Contacts	Address/ Advert Page

College	Course Title	Course Length	Fees	Start Dates	Entry Requirements	Contacts	Address/Advert Page
The English Language Centre, Brighton	The International Course for Teachers of English	FT: 2 wks	£492-£546	April, July	Practising teachers of English	Ms Caroline Mac Andrews	86
Eurocentres, Lee Green	Refresher course	FT: 3/4 wks	3 wks: £666; 4 wks: £848	3 wks: July; 4 wks: January, July, August	FCE (or equivalent); experienced teacher of EFL		86
Exeter University, English Language Centre	Refresher course	FT: 2 weeks	£400	July/August	Practising teachers	Bob Weaver	86
Frances King School of English, SW1, UK	Refresher course for overseas teachers	FT: 2 wks	£375 (99 price)	July, August	Advanced level	Gerald Kelly, Director of Teacher Training	86
GEOS English Academy	Teachers' Development Course for Overseas Teachers	FT: 2-4 wks	£210 per wk	July, August, January	Exp teachers/ Interim level of English	January Aram	66,86
Globe English Centre, Exeter, UK	Refresher Course	Both: FT/PT 1-3 wks	£267 per wk	June, July, August	Intermediate to Advanced level English	Catherine Borgen, Director	86
Griffith University, Queensland, Aus	Professional Program in Second language Teaching	FT: 2 wks; PT: 1 wk	Contact for details	Contact for details	Contact for details	Dr Shirley O'Neill	155
Harrogate Language Academy	Methodology Refresher	FT: 2 wks	£450	August	FCE Level	Jackie Godfrey, Director	86
	EFL Methodology	FT: 2 wks	£450	July	FCE Level	Jackie Godfrey, Director	86
	Brush Up Your English	FT: 2 wks	£450	July	Intermediate level	Jackie Godfrey, Director	86
Harrogate Tutorial College	ELT Management	FT: 2 wks	£290 per wk	August	Exp teachers	David Herbert	86
Hastings English Language Centre (HELC)	Refresher course	FT: tba	£220 per week	January; July; August		Clive Pugsley	87
College	Course Title	Course Length	Fees	Start Dates	Entry Requirements	Contacts	Address/Advert Page

Short Courses

College	Course Title	Course Length	Fees	Start Dates	Entry Requirements	Contacts	Address/ Advert Page
Hilderstone College, Kent, UK	Language & Creative Teaching	FT: 1-2 wks	£323-£654 (inc accom)	January, July, August	Advanced level, exp teacher	James Banner	87
	Trainer Development	FT: 2-4 wks	£654-£1,080 (inc accom)	January, July	Advanced level, exp trainer/course director	James Banner	87
	Drama and Literature	FT: 2 wks	£654 (inc accom)	January, July	Advanced level, exp trainer/course director	James Banner	87
	Advanced learners	FT: 2 wks	£654 (inc accom)	January, July, August	Advanced level, exp trainer/course director	James Banner	87
International House, Bath		FT: 2 wks	£500	January, August	Proficient English, qualified teacher		87
International House, London, UK	Language & Teaching Skills	FT: 4 wks	£705	January, July, August, September	Application form	Teacher Training Dept	87,64
	Language Development for Teachers	FT: 2 wks	£410	January, February, June, July, August	Application form	Teacher Training Dept	87,64
	Teaching Literature	FT: 2 wks	£485	July, August	Application form	Teacher Training Dept	87,64
	Current Trends in Language Teaching/ Methodology Refresher	FT: 2 wks	£410	January, June, July, August, September	Application form	Teacher Training Dept	87,64
	Contemporary Britain - Modern English Language & Contemporary Culture	FT: 2 wks	£485	January, July, August	Application form	Teacher Training Dept	87,64
	Educational Management	FT: 2 wks	£720	August	Application form	Teacher Training Dept	87,64
	Teacher Training: Skills & Approaches	FT: 2 wks	£720	August	Application form	Teacher Training Dept	87,64
College	Course Title	Course Length	Fees	Start Dates	Entry Requirements	Contacts	Address/ Advert Page

Short Courses

COLLEGE	COURSE TITLE	COURSE LENGTH	FEES	START DATES	ENTRY REQUIREMENTS	CONTACTS	ADDRESS/ ADVERT PAGE
International House, London, UK	Materials Development	FT: 2 wks	£140	July, August	Application form	Teacher Training Dept	87,64
	Pronunciation	FT: 2 wks	£140	January, July, August	Application form	Teacher Training Dept	87,64
	IH Certificate in TEFL	FT: 4 wks	£895	January, June, July, August, September	IH Application form	Teacher Training Dept	87,64
International House, Newcastle	Refresher course	FT: 2 wks; PT: 4 wks	FT: £850; PT: £420	September, January	Upper intermediate level of English	Trevor Udberg, Director	87,61
International House, Sydney, Aus	IH Certificate in TEFL	FT: 4 wks	£650	September	IH Application form	Teacher Training Dept	155
International House, Poznan, Poland	IH Certificate in TEFL	FT: 4 wks; PT: 12 wks	Aus$2,300	FT: January, May, June, July, November; PT: February, August	IH Application form	Nicola Rendall	121,62
International House, Wroclaw, Poland	ELT Management	FT: 5 days	£190	June, September	CELTA or equiv, 1 yr exp	Elisa Jaroch, TT Administrator	121,62
International Language Academies NZ	Language Improvement & Methodology	FT:2 wks	On application	Monthly	On application		158
International Language Centres, Hastings, UK	Sound Foundations: English Pronunciation and Intonation	FT: 2 wks	Contact for details	January, July	Contact for details	Rose Holmes	87
	The Skills of Academic Management	FT: 2 wks	Contact for details	January	Experienced L1 or non-L1 teachers	Rose Holmes	87
	Becoming a Teacher Trainer	FT: 2 wks	Contact for details	February, July	Exp L1 or non L1 teachers	Rose Holmes	87
	New Trends in ELT	FT: 2 wks	Contact for details	January, February, August	On application Non L1 teachers	Rose Holmes	87
COLLEGE	COURSE TITLE	COURSE LENGTH	FEES	START DATES	ENTRY REQUIREMENTS	CONTACTS	ADDRESS/ ADVERT PAGE

Short Courses

College	Course Title	Course Length	Fees	Start Dates	Entry Requirements	Contacts	Address/ Advert Page
International Language Centres, Hastings, UK	Group Dynamics in Practice	FT: 2 wks	Contact for details	January	Contact for details	Rose Holmes	87
	Modern English Lit & Culture	FT: 2, 3 or 4 wks	Contact for details	January, July, August	On application	Marilyn Bethune	87
	Advanced English	FT: 2 wks	Contact for details	January, February, July/August	Non-L1 teachers preparing for Oxford Arels Diploma	Rose Holmes	87
	Brush Up Your English	FT: 2 wks	£499	June, July, August	Non-L1 teachers	Rose Holmes	87
	ELT methodology refresher	FT: 2 wks	£499	February, June, July	Non-L1 teachers	Rose Holmes	87
	Sound Foundation	FT: 2 wks	Contact for details	January	Contact for details	Rose Holmes	87
International Teacher Training Centre, Bournemouth UK	Refresher	FT: 2-4 wks	£155 per wk	January, February, July, August	Advanced English	Chris Goodchild	62,87
Inter Nexus Centre for Language Studies	Refresher	FT: 4 wks	£450	January, July	Upper Intermediate English	Annette Brolly	87
ITS English School, Hastings	Advanced Conversation & Methodology	FT: 2 wks	£275	July	Practising teachers	John Palim, Principal	87
	English & Methodology	FT: 2-4 wks	£185 - £290 / wk.	Any	Below proficiency level of English	John Palim, Principal	87
Kettley Institute of Language Stuby	Scottish Cultural Study Programme	FT: 2 wks	£495	Easter/ Summer	Non	Richard Kethley	87
Lake School of English, Oxford	Refresher for Overseas Teachers	FT: 2 wks	£499	January, July, August	Practising or trainee teachers of English	Sue Kay, Director	88
Language & Activity Holidays, Eire	Refresher Course	FT: 2 wks	£350	July, August	Upper intermediate level of English, qual teacher		93
College	Course Title	Course Length	Fees	Start Dates	Entry Requirements	Contacts	Address/ Advert Page

COLLEGE	COURSE TITLE	COURSE LENGTH	FEES	START DATES	ENTRY REQUIREMENTS	CONTACTS	ADDRESS/ ADVERT PAGE
Language Centre of Ireland, Dublin, Eire	Refresher course	FT: 2 wks	IR£644 (inc accom)	July, August	In-service teacher	Registrar	93
Language Link, Earls Court	Refresher Course	FT: 2 wks	£450	On application	Teaching experience		88
Language Link, Moscow, Russia	Refresher Course - English Language Development	FT: 1 wk	$60-$90	January, March, June, July, August, September, October	Exp teachers and teachers in training	ELT Department	124
	Language & Methodology - Secondary School Teachers	FT: 1 wk	$60-$90	January, March, June, July, August, September, October	Exp teachers and teachers in training	ELT Department	124
Languages International, Auckland, New Zealand	TESOL Cert Refresher Course	FT: 3 wks	NZ$1,333	January, July	Upper Intermediate level of English	Craig Thaine, Director of Teacher Training	158
Leeds University, The Language Centre	The Language Centre Management Programme	FT: 3 wks	£1,400	June	Teachers/ managers of language centres, professionals with background in ELT	Dr Peter Howarth	88,262
Limerick University, Language Centre, Eire	English for Teachers	FT: 2 wks or 3 wks	IR£530	July	Completed initial training	Caroline Graham	94
London Meridian College	Advanced Language & Methodology	FT: 2/3 wks	2 wks: £600; 3 wks: £750	July	Initial teaching qual		88
Newnham Lang Centre, Cambridge, UK	Refresher for overseas teachers	FT: 2 wks	£440	August	Overseas teacher of Eng, 21 yrs of age	David Rowson	89
Norwich Institute for Language Education (NILE), UK	Intensive Language & Professional Development (ILD 2000)	FT: 4 wks	£1,280	January	Trainee/ recently qualified EFL teachers	Dave Allan, Penny Miller	89
COLLEGE	COURSE TITLE	COURSE LENGTH	FEES	START DATES	ENTRY REQUIREMENTS	CONTACTS	ADDRESS/ ADVERT PAGE

Short Courses

College	Course Title	Course Length	Fees	Start Dates	Entry Requirements	Contacts	Address/Advert Page
Norwich Institute for Language Education (NILE), UK	Language & Literature (LAL 2000)	FT: 2 wks	£640	August	EFL teaching experience, lang level intermediate +	Dave Allan, Penny Miller	89
	Making the Most of Yourself: Being the Best Teacher You Can Be (MMY 2000)	FT: 2 wks	Contact for details	July	EFL teaching experience	Dave Allan, Penny Miller	89
	British Studies: Lang, Literature & Life (BS1 & 2 2000)	FT: 2 wks	£640	July, August	EFL teaching exp, lang level intermediate +	Dave Allan, Penny Miller	89
	Communicative Language Teaching & Testing (CTTI 2000)	FT: 2 wks	£640	July	EFL teaching exp	Dave Allan, Penny Miller	89
	Managing & Creativity in the Language Classroom (MCT 99)	FT: 2 wks	£64	July	EFL teaching exp	Dave Allan, Penny Miller	89
	Lang Materials & Methodology (LMM1 & 2 2000)	FT: 2 wks	£640	February, July	EFL teaching esp	Dave Allan, Penny Miller	89
	Neuro Linguistic Programming in the EL Classroom	FT: 2 wks	£740	February, July	EFL teaching exp, lang level Intermediate +	Dave Allan, Penny Miller	89
	ELT Materials Development	FT: 2 wks	£640	August	EFL teaching exp, lang level intermediate +	Dave Allan, Penny Miller	89
	Advanced Language Courses for Teachers of English (ALC1 & 2 2000)	FT: 2 wks	£640	January, July	EFL teaching exp, advanced lang level	Dave Allan, Penny Miller	89

College	Course Title	Course Length	Fees	Start Dates	Entry Requirements	Contacts	Address/Advert Page

College	Course Title	Course Length	Fees	Start Dates	Entry Requirements	Contacts	Address/ Advert Page
Norwich Institute for Language Education (NILE), UK	Advanced Language Course for Teachers of English (ALC(D) 2000)	FT: 2 wks	Contact for details	August	EFL teaching exp, advanced lang level	Dave Allan, Penny Miller	89
	English Language & Professional Development for Secondary EL Teachers (SLD 1 & 2 2000)	FT: 2 wks	Contact for details	July, August	Secondary EFL teaching experience	Dave Allan, Penny Miller	890
	English Language & Professional Development for Primary EL Teachers (PLD 1 & 2 2000)	FT: 2 wks	Contact for details	July, August	Primary EFL teaching experience	Dave Allan, Penny Miller	89
Oxford Brookes University (ICELS), Oxford, UK	Refresher - Teacher Development for Non Native Speakers	FT: 2 wks	£695	July, August	Experienced teachers, IELTS 6/TOEFL 550	Catharine Arakelian	89,264
Oxford College of Further Education	Refresher	FT: 2 wks	Contact for details	July	Practising teacher of English	Steven Haysham	89
Oxford English Centre, UK	Refresher	FT: 3 wks	£240/wk	January, July	Upper Intermediate + level	Dr Graham Simpson	89
	English for Teachers	FT: 2/3 wks	2 wks: £480; 3 wks £720	2 wks: January; 3 wks: Jul	Contact for details	Dr Graham Simpson	89
Oxford House College, London, UK	Overseas Teachers Course	FT: 1-4 wks	£100 - £125 per wk	January, April, July, August	Qual to teach English in own country	Lax Patel	89
	Language & Methodology	FT: 1 wk	£150	During school holidays	Contact for details	Lax Patel	89
Pilgrims, Canterbury, UK	English for Teachers, The Creative Teacher	FT: 2 wks	£695	April to June	Contact for details	Sales Dept	90
Portsmouth University, UK	TEFL refresher	FT2 wks	£395	January, July	Secondary EFL teaching exp	Yvonne Castino, Programme Manager	90
College	Course Title	Course Length	Fees	Start Dates	Entry Requirements	Contacts	Address/ Advert Page

College	Course Title	Course Length	Fees	Start Dates	Entry Requirements	Contacts	Address/ Advert Page
Queen's University (TEFL Centre), Belfast, UK	Refresher	FT: 2 wks	£270	July, August	Grad, Eng lang qual	Tony Ridgway	90
Regency School of English, Kent, UK	Refresher	FT: 1-4 wks	From £136	Every month	Good level of English	Director of Teacher Training	90
Salisbury School of English, UK	Refresher course for overseas teachers	FT: 2 wks	£450	June, July	Intermediate level English	Barbara Wills	90
Saxoncourt Teacher Training, UK	Overseas Teachers' Course	FT: 2 wks	£400	January, July and on demand	Intermediate level English		77,90
Scarborough International School, UK	Refresher course for overseas teachers	FT: 2 wks	£351-455 (depending on tuition hrs)	August	Must be non-L1	Mrs R Glyde, Principal Director	90
The Shane English Schools, London	Overseas Teachers Course	FT: 2 wks	£400	January, July	Intermediate + English	Andrew Roper	90
Stanton Teacher Training, London	Refresher Course	FT: 2 wks	£235	By arrangement	Camb 1st Cert level of English	Mr D Garrett, Director	59,91
Stevenson College, Edinburgh	Refresher in Methodology	FT: 2 wks	£400	July	Contact for information		91
St Clare's, Oxford	Teacher Methodology	FT: 1-3 wks, PT 1-5 wks	£575 / wk	July, August	Non-L1 teachers	Tessa Richardson, Director of Short Courses	90
St Giles, Brighton	Refresher Course	FT: 4 wks	£641	July, August	Strong intermediate level of English	The Principal	90
St Giles, Eastbourne	Refresher Course	FT: 2/3 wks	2 wks: £356; 3 wks: £528 (1999)	March, July	Strong intermediate level of English	The Principal	90
St Giles Colleges, Highgate, London	Refresher	FT: 2/4 wks	2 wks: £344; 4 wks: 638 (1999)	January, March, July, August	Strong intermediate level of English	The Principal	90

College	Course Title	Course Length	Fees	Start Dates	Entry Requirements	Contacts	Address/ Advert Page

College	Course Title	Course Length	Fees	Start Dates	Entry Requirements	Contacts	Address/ Advert Page
Strathclyde University, Glasgow	Overseas Teachers of English and Very Advanced Learners	FT: 2 wks	£135/wk	July	Advanced level of English		91
Studio School Cambridge	Overseas Teachers Course	FT: 2 and 4 wks	2 wks, July/August; 4 wks, January	£190 per wk	Age 21, Advanced level of English	Nicole Kennedy	91
South Thames College (Putney Centre), UK	Refresher Course	FT: 2 wks	£150	August	Experienced teachers	Gerard McLoughlin	91
Stevenson College, Edinburgh, UK	Refresher in Methodology	FT: 2 wks	£400	July	TEFL exp at adult level secondary school	Information Centre	91
Strathclyde University, Glasgow	Refresher Course	FT: 2 wks	£135 per wk	July	Advanced level of English	Mr Paul Curtis, Academic Manager	91
Sussex University, Brighton	Refresher	FT: 2 wks	£450	July	Contact for details	M Khidhayir	91
	Initial Teacher Training in TEFL	FT: 1 wk	£135	March, June, July, December	Contact for details	Dr A McNeill	91
Suzanne Sparrow Plymouth Language School	Refresher course	FT: 2 wks	From £270	All year	21+, practising teacher of English	Peter Clarke	91
Swan School of English, Oxford, UK	Refresher course for Overseas Teachers of English	FT: 2-4 wks	2 wks: £450, 4 wks: £808	January, June, July, August, September	Qual teacher, high level of English, 20+ yrs	Mrs H A Swan, Principal	91
University College, Chichester	Language Development for English Teachers	FT: 3 wks	£1,080	Summer	Experienced teachers, Eng proficiency	Steve Corcoran	92,264
	Teaching English in Secondary Schools	FT: 3 wks	£1,080	3/7, 24/7	Experienced teachers, Eng proficiency	Steve Corcoran	92
University of Wales, Aberystwyth	Methodology for Teachers 2	FT: 2 wks	£350	August	Practising teacher	Rex Berridge	
College	Course Title	Course Length	Fees	Start Dates	Entry Requirements	Contacts	Address/ Advert Page

Short Courses

College	Course Title	Course Length	Fees	Start Dates	Entry Requirements	Contacts	Address/Advert Page
Volkhochschule, Zurich, Switzerland	Grammar for Teachers	PT: 8 wks	SFr880	October	None	Mrs Margaret Stark	127
Waikato University, Hamilton, NZ	International Teacher Training Program	FT: 3 wks	NZ$1050	August	Teaching exp, 20 yrs+ of age		159
West Cheshire College, Chester, UK	Summer Update, Methodology, Materials and Language	FT: 3 wks	£500	July, August	Practising EFL teachers		92
Westminster University, UK	Refresher course for non-L1 teachers	FT: 4/8 wks	4 wks: £395; 8 wks: £695	July, August	Qualified and practising teachers	Admissions Office	92

Young Learners

College	Course Title	Course Length	Fees	Start Dates	Entry Requirements	Contacts	Address/Advert Page
Bell Language School, Cambridge, UK	Challenging Children & Language Development for Primary Teachers	FT: 2 wks	Contact for details	June	Contact for details	Head of Bell Teacher Training	59,83
Bell Language School, Norwich, UK	Challenging Children and Language development	PT: 2 wks	£550	June, July	Practising primary teachers	Head of Studies	59,83
Bell Language School, Saffron Walden, UK	Practical Vocabulary for Primary Teachers	FT: 1 wk	£369 (incl social prog)	July	Practising teachers	Head of Studies	59,84
	Stories, Drama & Poetry in the Primary Classroom	FT: 1 wk	£369 (incl social prog)	July	Primary teachers	Head of Studies	59,84
	Creativity in the Primary Classroom	FT: 2 wks	£753 (incl social prog)	August	Primary teachers	Head of Studies	59,84
	Teaching Techniques and Language Development	FT: 2 wks	£550	August, September	Practising primary teachers	Head of Studies	59,84
College	**Course Title**	**Course Length**	**Fees**	**Start Dates**	**Entry Requirements**	**Contacts**	**Address/Advert Page**

College	Course Title	Course Length	Fees	Start Dates	Entry Requirements	Contacts	Address/ Advert Page
Bell Language School, Saffron Walden, UK	Teacher Training Plus	FT: 1/2 wks	£380	July, August	Practising primary teachers	Head of Studies	59,84
British Council, Hong Kong	RSA CETYL	PT: 10 wks	HK$19,600	November, May	Contact for details	Mr N Florent	162
	ICTEYL	PT: 6 wks	HK$4,100	September, February	Contact for details	Mr N Florent	162
The British Council, Istanbul, Turkey	Teaching young learners	PT: 4 wks	£60	All year	FCE competence	Laura Woodward	128
British Council, Izmir, Turkey	Young Learners	6 wks	£50	October, December, February	Qualified teacher	Steve Darn	128
Canterbury Christchurch College, UK	Primary International Teachers Course	FT: 2 wks	£410 (£570 inc accom)	July, August	Practising primary teachers		84,263
Chichester School of English, UK	Teachers of English to Young Learners	FT: 5 days	£220	July	Post-FCE	Mike Thomas	85
	Primary Teachers Course	FT: 3 wks	£660	July	Post-FCE	Mike Thomas	85
The College of St Mark & St John, UK	Teaching English to Young Learners Extension	FT: 2/3 wks	£420 (2 wks); £600 (3 wks)	July	Practising teachers	Michael G Hall, INTEC	85
Edinburgh University (Inst for Applied Lang Studies), UK	Teaching Young Learners	FT: 3 wks	On request	July, August	1 yr exp	Registration Secretary	85,264
Hilderstone College, Kent, UK	Language and Teaching Young Learners	FT: 1/2wks	£640 (2 wks); £332 (1 wk)	July, August	Non-L1 teachers	James Banner	87
International House, Bath, UK	Teaching Young Learners	FT: 2 wks	£500	January, August	Contact for details	Mark Appleton	87
International House, London, UK	Classroom Skills for Primary School Teachers	FT: 2 wks	£410	July, August, September	Application form	Teacher Training Dept	64,87
College	Course Title	Course Length	Fees	Start Dates	Entry Requirements	Contacts	Address/ Advert Page

Young Learners

College	Course Title	Course Length	Fees	Start Dates	Entry Requirements	Contacts	Address/ Advert Page
International House, London, UK	Teaching Younger Learners	FT: 2 wks	£410	January, July, August	Application Form	Teacher Training Dept	64,87
International House, Budapest, Hungary	Cambridge Young Learner Extension	FT: 2 wks; PT: 10 wks	Contact for details	FT: February, PT: October	CELTA	Steve Oakes, Head of Teacher Training	58,119
International House, Rome, Italy	CELTYL	FT: 2 wks	L1,200,000	September	CELTA	The Director	105
International House, Wroclaw, Poland	CELTYL	FT: 2 wks; PT: 8 wks	£350 + £71 reg fee	FT: January, February, September; PT: October, February	Camb/RSA CELTA	Elisa Jaroch, TT Administrator	63,121
International House, Lisbon, Portugal	CELTYL	PT: 6 mths	PTE220,000/ £700	January	As RSA/UCLES	Paula de Nagy	66,107
	YL Extension	PT: 3 mths	PTE110,000	October	AS RSA/UCLES	Paula de Nagy	66,107
International House Barcelona, Spain	CELTYL	FT: 4 wks	Pts90,000	July, September	CELTA	Jenny Johnson	65,110
	Cam/RSA Dip Extension YL (pilot)	PT: 7 mths	Contact for details	November	DELTA	Jenny Johnson	65,110
International House, Madrid, Spain	CELTYL	PT: Contact for details	Contact for details	February	Post CELTA	Teacher Training Dept	63,110
International Language Centres, Hastings, UK	Teaching English to Young Learners	FT: 2 wks	£499	January, July, August	Exp L1 or non- L1 teachers	Rose Holmes	87
International Language Institute, Leeds, UK	Overseas Primary Teachers	FT: 3 wks	£515	January, September	Over 18	The Registrar	87
Language Link, Moscow, Russia	Young Learners - Language & Methodology	FT : 1 wk	$60 - $90	January, March, June, July, August, September, October	Exp teachers & teachers in training	ELT Department	124
Lydbury English Centre UK	Primary Teachers Development Course	FT: 2 wks	On request	April, July, August	Non-L1 teachers		88

College	Course Title	Course Length	Fees	Start Dates	Entry Requirements	Contacts	Address/ Advert Page

College	Course title	Course length	Fees	Start dates	Entry requirements	Contacts	Address/ Advert Page
Norwich Institute for Language Education	Language & Methodology for Primary English Language Teachers	FT: 2 wks	£640	July, August	Primary EFL Teacher	Dave Allan, Penny Miller	89
The Percival Centre, Bristol	RSA CELTYL	PT: 5 mths	£985 + UCLES Entrance fee	January	Selection procedure/int erview	The Percival Centre	
Portsmouth University, UK	Primary English Language Teaching (non-native speakers)	FT: 2 wks	£395	July	Intermediate level of English	Yvonne Castino, Programme Manager	90
Saxoncourt Teacher Training, UK	RSA CELTYL	FT: 2 wks	Contact for details	Throughout year	CELTA, exp of working with children	Christopher Hart	77,90
Strathclyde University	Teaching Young Learners	Various	On request	On request	On request		91
University College, Chichester	Teaching English to Young Learners	FT: 3 wks	£1,080	July, August	Experienced teachers, proficient in English	Steve Corcoran	92,264
University of Warwick	Postgraduste Certificate to Teach English to Young Learners	FT: 10 mths	On request	January	Degree, 2 yrs exp		92,263
University of York	British Council Summer School in Teaching English to Young Learners	FT: 2 wks	On request	July, August	3 yrs teaching exp with young learners	Lesley Witts	92,262
	Professional Development Courses in Teaching English to Young Learners	FT: 2-4 wks	£180 per wk	On demand	Practising teachers	Lesley Witts	92,262
College	Course title	Course length	Fees	Start dates	Entry requirements	Contacts	Address/ Advert Page

Cambridge/RSA CEELT Courses

College	Course Title	Course Length	Fees	Start Dates	Entry Requirements	Contacts	Address/ Advert Page
Australian TESOL Training Ctr, Bondi Junction, Australia	FT	5 wks	Aus$2,000	May, July, November	TOEFL 500, IELTS 5.5, Cambridge FCE	Ms Gloria Smith	154
BEET Language School, Bournemouth, UK	FT	3 wks	£595	January, July	Experienced teacher + Cambridge 1st Cert level of English	Mr Clive Barrow	83
Bell Language School, Norwich, UK Birmingham, UK	FT	2 wks	£550	July	Experienced teachers	Malcolm Hebden	59,83
Brasshouse Centre, Birmingham, UK	FT	FT: 1 month; PT: 1 year	£350	July	Cambridge FCE	Deborah Cobbett	84
Cambridge Centre for Languages, Cambridge, UK	FT	3 wks	£630	July	1 yr teaching exp	Dr John Sullivan	84
City of Bath College, UK	FT	4 wks	£640	November	Advanced level of English	Gaby Piou	85
Clarendon City College, Nottingham, UK	FT	2 wks	£550	July	Good level of English	David Hughes	85
Eastbourne School of English, UK	FT	2 wks	£525	August	FCE+	Dorothy S Rippon, Principal	85
Eckersley School of English, Oxford, UK	FT	3 wks	£600	January, July	Teaching exp at secondary or higher level	Richard Side	85
Edinburgh University (Inst for Applied Lang Studies), UK	FT	3 wks	£695	August	CPE or equiv	Stuart Lawson	85,264
ELT Banbury, UK	FT	2/3 wks	2 wks: £630; 3 wks: £795 inc accom	February, July, August	Age 18+	Dr T J Gerighty	86
Essex University (EFL Unit), Colchester, UK	FT	3 wks	£575	July	Good pass at FCE or above	Dilly Meyer	58,86
	FT	10 wks	£1,675	January	Good pass at FCE or above	Dilly Meyer	58,86
College	Course Title	Course Length	Fees	Start Dates	Entry Requirements	Contacts	Address/ Advert Page

Cambridge/RSA CEELT Courses

COLLEGE	COURSE TITLE	COURSE LENGTH	FEES	START DATES	ENTRY REQUIREMENTS	CONTACTS	ADDRESS/ ADVERT PAGE
Hammersmith & West London College, UK	PT	1 year	£195 (home students); £415 (oversea	September	Camb Advanced Level Eng	Course Info Centre	63,86
Hilderstone College, Kent, UK	FT	1-2 wks	£323 - £624	July, August	Advanced level, exp teacher	Teacher Training	87
International House, London, UK	FT	4 wks	£ 705	July, August	Application form	Teacher Training Dept	69,87
International Language Academies South Pacific, New Zealand	FT	4 wks	NZ$1,750	November, March, May	Appropriate level of English, pre-test	Mo Killip, Director of Studies	158
International Language Centres, Hastings,UK	FT (CEELT 2)	2 wks	to be confirmed	January, July/Aug	Post CPE or equiv	Rose Holmes	87
Irwin College Leicester, UK	PT	1-2 terms	£155 per wk (inc accom)	Contact for details	FCE level	Julie Oswald	87
Language and Activity Holidays, Eire	FT	2 wks	IR£350	July, August	Upper int level, qualified teacher		93
Language Centre, Cork Eire	FT	1 mth	CEELT I: IR£660; CEELT II: IR£665; Refresher: IR£585	August	Contact for details	Language Centre	93
Language Link Russia	Both	FT: 3 wks, PT: 10 wks	From $180 + exam fee	FT: January, February, June, July, August, September; PT: February, April, October	Exp teachers & teachers in training, CEELT I - FCE, CEELT II - post CAE	ELT Department	124
Norwich Institute for Language Education (NILE), UK	FT	2 wks	£640	July	EFL teaching exp	Dave Allan, Penny Miller	89
Nottingham Trent Universirty,UK	FT	2/4 wks	£250/£500 + exam fee	4 wk: July; 2 wk: March	FCE or IELTS 6	Linda Taylor, Senior Lecturer	61,89
Phoenix English Language Academy, Perth, Aus	FT	4 wks	Aus$1,380	November, August, March	Intermediate level	Felicity Mason, Teaching Training Co-ordinator	156
COLLEGE	COURSE TITLE	COURSE LENGTH	FEES	START DATES	ENTRY REQUIREMENTS	CONTACTS	ADDRESS/ ADVERT PAGE

Cambridge/RSA CEELT Courses

College	Course Title	Course Length	Fees	Start Dates	Entry Requirements	Contacts	Address/ Advert Page
Queen's University Belfast, UK	FT	4 wks	£ 400	June, July, August	Grad Emglish Lang qual	Steve Walsh	90
Solihull College, UK	Flexible	Flexible	Negotiable	Flexible	Negotiable	Pat Morris, CELTA Administrator	
South Thames College (Putney Centre) , UK	PT	4 wks	£ 250 approx	July	FCE or CAE/CPE	Geraed McLoughin	91
							90
St Giles. Brighton, UK	FT	4 wks	£ 641	July , August	Strong intermediate English		
							90
St Giles. Brighton, UK	FT	2/3 wks	2 wks:£356;3 wks: £528	March, July	Strong intermediate English		
							90
St Giles. Highgate, London, UK	FT	2/4 wks	2 wks: £344; 4 wks: £638	January, March, July, August	Strong intermediate English		
University College Chichester, UK	FT	18 days	£1,140	Summer	Experienced teachers, proficient in English	Steve Corcoran	92,264
Volkshochschule Zurich Switzerland	PT	16 wks	SFr 800	October	Proficiency equiv	Mrs Margaewt Start	127
College	**Course Title**	**Course Length**	**Fees**	**Start Dates**	**Entry Requirements**	**Contacts**	**Address/ Advert Page**

Funding Development Courses

In-service language teachers can get an EU grant to help pay for a short development course.

Lingua funding, is a European Union scheme which provides funding for teacher training and educational exchange between institutions. Although quite complex, the scheme has considerable resources available to help teachers attend development courses overseas.

Lingua is part of Socrates, the EU educational programme, with the aim being to promote language-learning. Its overall budget for 1995-9 was set at ECU850 million and the Commission is currently pushing through an ECU50 million increase. Lingua's **Action B** programme is the one relevant to existing teachers, covering in-service training in the field of foreign language teaching. It provides grants for individuals or institutions to undertake a training activity (normally two to four weeks in duration) in another EU or European Economic Area country.

What qualifications do I need?

Applicants must have been teaching a foreign language for at least six hours per week over a period of more than three years since qualification, if at secondary level. Those involved in higher education are excluded unless they are trainers of teachers.

Which countries are eligible?

Institutions, nationals and associations from EU and EEA countries are eligible: Austria, Belgium, Denmark, Finland, France, Germany, Greece, Iceland (EEA), Ireland, Italy, Liechtenstein (EEA), Luxembourg, Netherlands, Norway (EEA), Portugal, Spain, Sweden and the UK. None of the Baltic states (Estonia, Latvia and Lithuania) are presently involved. Anyone is eligible if they are a permanent resident, registered as stateless or hold refugee status in a participating country.

How do I apply?

Applications are through the National Agency in the country where you are currently working. Deadlines are generally March 1 2000 (for courses after June 1 2000).

Lingua Action C is a European Language Assistantship programme, designed to allow future language teachers the chance to spend 3-12 months as an assistant in another European country.

European Commission, Directorate-General XXIIEd, Training and Youth Directorate A, rue de la Loi 200, B-1049 Bruxelles, Belgium

Socrates & Youth Technical Assistant Office, 70 rue Montoyer 70, B-1000 Bruxelles, Belgium. Tel: 32 2 233 01 11, Fax: 32 2 233 01 50

Austria: National Agencies, BUKA, Minoritenplatz 5, A-1014 Wien, Abteilung III/17, Tel: 43 1 53 120 3462, Fax: 43 1 53 120 3460

Belgium: Ministere de l'Education, Boulevard Pacheco 19-Bte 0, B-1010 Bruxelles. Tel: 32 2 210 55 26, Fax: 32 2 221 89 23

Denmark: ICU, Vandkusten 3, DK-1467 Kobenhavn K. Tel: 45 33 14 20 60, Fax: 45 33 14 36 40, e-mail: icu!post4.tele.dk

Finland: CIMO, Hakaniemenkatu 2, (P O Box 343), FIN-00531 Helsinki. Tel: 358 0 77 47 7033, Fax: 358 0 77 47 7064

France: Agence Socrates, 8 rue Jean Calvin, F-75231 CEDEX 5. Tel: 33 1 40 79 9147, Fax: 33 1 43 37 43 48 (address may change)

Germany: PAD, Nassestrasse 8, D-53113 Bonn. Tel: 49 228 50 1458, Fax: 49 228 50 1500

Greece: IKY, Lysicrates St 14, GR-10558 Athens. Tel: 30 1 325 43 85-9, Fax: 30 1 322 1863

Iceland: University of Iceland, Office of International Education, Neshaga 16, IS-107 Reykjavik. Tel: 354 525 5853

Ireland: ITE, Fitzwilliam Place 31, Dublin 2. Tel: 353 1 873 1411, Fax: 353 1 661 0004

Italy: Bibl di Documentaz, Pedagogica Firenze, Via Buonarotti, 10 I-50122 Firenze. Tel: 39 55 238 0326, Fax: 39 55 24 2884

Liechtenstein: SFL, Herrengasse 2, FL-9490 Vaduz. Tel: 41 75 236 67 58, Fax: 41 75 236 6771

Luxembourg: Ministere de l'Education Nationale, Rue Aldrigen 29, L-2926 Lux. Tel: 352 478 5183, Fax: 352 478 5137

Netherlands: EPNO, Nassauplein 8, NL-1815 GM Alkmaar. Tel: 31 72 511 8502

Norway: OIUC, NCU, Nygaardstaten 8, N-5020 Bergen. Tel: 47 55 54 6700, Fax: 47 55 54 6720/21

Portugal: Gabinete de Assuntos Europeus, Av 5 de Outburo, 107, P-1050 Lisboa Codex. Tel: 351 1 793 1291, Fax: 1 797 8994

Spain: OEI, c/ Bravo Murillo 38, E-28015 Madrid. Tel: 34 1 594 46 82/22, Fax: 34 1 594 3286

Sweden: EU-program, Kingsgatan 8, III, P O Box 7785, S-10396 Stockholm. Tel: 46 8 453 7215, Fax: 46 8 453 7201

UK: Central Bureau, British Council, 10 Spring Gardens, London SW1A 2BN. Tel: 44 171 389 4852, Fax: 44 171 389 4426

Developing Your Career

There is scope for career development in English language teaching and, if you wish to move away from teaching, there are plenty of related jobs.

Although English language teachers often complain about the lack of a clear career path, there are plenty of opportunities in related industries. These offer good second career prospects to language teachers who want to leave the classroom. And, while the teaching careers of L1 and non-L1 speakers are often completely different, these ELT-related job areas are open to most teachers, whatever their mother tongue.

Some teachers organisations, such as IATEFL, also offer special discussion groups on the subject.

Because of the individual character of schools, completing a management course cannot guarantee you a senior position. However, doing such a course, in addition to accepting certain areas of responsibility as they arise, should make you a strong contender when the position does become available.

English Language Teaching

Staffing in schools, whether in the private or public sector, tends to be set up as a pyramid, with a number of teachers at the base, a director or head of department at the top, and maybe a level or two consisting of more senior teachers who have taken on various areas of responsibility.

How do I advance from newly-qualified teacher to senior teacher and then to director of studies? In reality there is a limited number of senior positions available in schools and generalisations about career advancement are not possible. Schools have different requirements depending on their size and where they are operating. Often, getting a senior position may be more a matter of being the right person at the right time than anything else. It is for this reason that English language teachers often complain about the lack of career structure in the ELT industry.

However, it is fair to say that increasing emphasis is being placed on attaining certain management skills and those going into senior positions are finding it necessary to take specialised courses. In some cases, schools might even fund the course.

The number of Masters degrees with management specialisations is growing and the Royal Society of Arts has recently announced plans to introduce its Higher Diploma in ELT Management. MBAs are also becoming popular.

Publishing

ELT publishing is a very large industry. The four main UK publishers alone sell more than £220 million worth of books every year. Outside the US, publishing is not as well-paid as you might have thought and starting salaries are on a par with teaching. However, it is a stable and challenging profession with plenty of opportunities for promotion.

The best time to break into publishing is when you are under 30 and have three or four years of teaching experience. It is a good idea to get yourself known by a publisher while you are still in the classroom and you might do this by getting to know the sales representatives who visit your school.

Most publishing training is done in-house, so you should try to get as much experience as possible while you are still teaching. You can volunteer to pilot material, write reports on publishing proposals, or take part in market research.

Teachers recruited usually go into either publishing, sales and marketing or editorial. Most teachers start out as a sales representative, promoting books in schools, bookshops and at conferences. Interfacing with potential clients means that sales reps should be good communicators with advanced presentation skills. They should be knowledgeable enough about

253

the latest trends in teaching to field probing questions. A driving licence is also essential, as reps often have to travel great distances in a week.

Sales reps need to know a lot about the country in which they are working, so non-L1 speakers are generally more likely to find a job at home. This is not always the case, though.

A position in sales might be the perfect first step into a publishing career. From there, you can move into management, branch out into marketing or move over to the editorial side.

Copy editing, the basic level of editorial work, involves working on manuscripts, checking for errors and inaccuracies. This work requires a neat, organised mind, endless patience and a very good level of English. From copy editing you can move on to working with authors, helping to develop a manuscript, and then on to commissioning, whereby you are responsible for finding the author. From these positions you might move into a more senior management role, supervising a whole project from conception to production.

On the whole, L1 speaker editors tend to work for British or North American publishers, while non-L1 speakers tend to find positions with publishers in their own countries. Again, this is not always the case. One of the most senior publishers in British ELT, responsible for two bestselling coursebooks, Headway and Hotline, is Hungarian and was initially a sales rep in France before moving to the UK to take up an editorship.

Teacher training

The world is crying out for teacher trainers at primary level, at secondary level and in the private sector. As in many other areas, L1 speakers can work all over the world as trainers,

but are usually only employed on short-term contracts. Non-L1 speakers find it easier to secure permanent jobs, but harder to work outside their own country. This is beginning to change, though, particularly in the area of primary teaching, and non-L1 speakers from countries with a strong tradition of teacher training and high English attainment levels are finding it possible to get training placements overseas. In Central and East European countries, for example, it is not so rare to find programmes run by Norwegian or Danish trainers.

Becoming a teacher trainer is difficult. You can not be a teacher trainer until you have trained teachers, but nobody will let you train teachers until you are a teacher trainer. To get that vital training experience, you will need to show that you are serious about teaching. Join your local teachers' group, as well as an international teaching association, such as IATEFL or TESOL. Subscribe to all the right teaching journals and attend the key seminars and conferences, perhaps even making speeches about issues you feel strongly about.

Offering to mentor new teachers or having your classes observed by trainees are other goods ways of showing that you are keen. Soon, you can start putting yourself forward for jobs which involve aspects of training.

If you have tried these avenues and are still finding it hard to get that all-important teacher training experience, consider volunteering. A lot of the international volunteer organisations are desperate for senior teachers, willing to spend two years training teachers in the developing world, and most welcome both L1 and non-L1 speakers. Conditions may be quite difficult, but the training experience would be invaluable.

Teacher trainers may also need a higher qualification as well as extra experience. For L1 speakers the minimum requirement is a Cambridge RSA Diploma or equivalent, a qualification which would be absolutely essential for working with certificate and diploma trainees. For other areas of teaching training, a Masters level qualification is often necessary and an increasing number of Masters degree courses concentrate on teacher education.

Examining

This is a field which you can get involved in while you are still in the classroom. Although some exams are multiple choice and capable of being marked by computers, examination bodies are still dependent on teachers to mark other papers. If you are an experienced teacher, familiar with a particular exam, you might contact the board which runs it. At this level, you can really only expect to work on exams set in your own country and you should be aware that marking is not very well paid. However, if you find you enjoy it, you may consider taking the next step towards item writing.

Item writers set the questions for exams. This is highly skilled work and examination bodies usually provide training. Most item writers specialise in a particular area like grammar or reading comprehension and remain classroom teachers, keeping testing as a sideline. This sideline can be quite lucrative, with one British examination board paying £25 for each multiple choice question.

Many exam boards also employ senior examiners, people who are responsible for teams of markers or item writers. This is well-paid but seasonal work, and few people make a living from it alone.

Full-time positions at examination boards are few and far between. They usually require a Masters degree with a specialisation in the field of testing.

Testing is a growing field of academic study and there are university posts available around the world. A Masters is a minimum requirement for these, and some might also require a doctorate in the field.

Language Travel Agents

These are specialist agents who organise groups of students to go abroad to study languages. They make money either by charging the students (which is illegal in the EU) or by taking a commission from the school, the airlines, the insurance broker and other service providers who might be involved.

Many agents work as teachers, organising groups of students from their own school. Some organise groups on behalf of visiting agents, who pay them a commission or fee, while others work directly with schools. It is important to check out the legalities for your specific country. Some countries, such as Turkey, do not allow any agents who are not insured to take children abroad.

Language schools in English-speaking countries are usually happy to pay a teacher around ten per cent of the student fees for organising a tour, while some North American universities are not allowed to pay commission. In addition to the list in the *Guide* you can usually get lists of schools from embassies, tourist offices or government agencies like the British Council but, unless you know someone who has been there, it is always best to visit the school in person first.

Many teacher agents have gone on to be full-time language travel agents, either working for an existing agency or setting up their own small business. It is one field where non-L1 speakers tend to dominate. There are exceptions though: one of the biggest language travel agencies in Germany is actually British.

Starting Your Own Language Business

Many experienced EFL teachers - as well as a few business entrepreneurs - have seen how lucrative it can be to open their own language teaching business.

Opening a school is an idea that crosses may EFL teachers' minds at some time in their career. Not having to wait for a senior position to become available can be tempting or simply becoming tired of working in someone else's school can be motivation to open your own. Encouragement can be drawn from the fact that there are some very successful, privately-owned schools. However setting up your own business can be daunting and require immense effort. Time has to be spent learning the ins and outs of running an efficient business. The best teacher in the world who does not understand cash-flows is unlikely to run a successful school.

Two difficult years

There are accreditation schemes for language schools in all of the English speaking countries except Canada. In Malta and Australia your school has to be recognised in order to function. Ireland and the UK (British Council) work from the opposite angle, in that they will not recognise a school until it has existed and survived for two years. This can be very difficult in a competitive market when you are trying to become established, as to be accredited is a way potential teachers and pupils judge your reputability. It can take up to two years for a school to break even on costs, so many do fail. For a small school the process of gaining official recognition can be a costly exercise, with demanding criteria, but is generally worthwhile in the long run. For business English schools this tends to be less of an issue.

Ensure that you have enough financial reserves to survive early cash-flow difficulties. Evaluate how much start-up capital will be needed, preferably using professional accounting advice. Initial costs can be large, covering rent, salaries, taxation and bills, as well as market research and advertising. Discipline is vital especially in the early stages as selling courses and receiving payment for them is not simultaneous. Some schools fail despite a lot of interest, as clients may take up to 120 days to pay invoices for courses, which might be three months too late to pay your set-up costs.

Investing for the future

Failure to invest can limit your school's growth potential but you must be clear as to why you are spending money and what benefits will accrue, in the long and short term. A good PC and laser printer, although costly, will help administration and allow you to produce your own professional advertising. Researching carefully for trustworthy suppliers, and negotiating discounts on bulk orders for materials will be beneficial longer term. If you offer excursions or study trips, make sure your tour operator is reliable, realising that this and quality are sometimes more important than financial costs.

The quality of your teaching staff and environment will ultimately determine the success of your school's reputation. Clients judge on the value teachers add to the courses offered and the cost. Recruiting the right people for your school may be frustrating and take time. Plan what your school courses will need and what will attract students before you hire staff. Be aware that to recruit highly-qualified teachers, or those from an English-speaking country, will probably demand that you provide incentives and higher salaries. Careful exploration of job specifications and contract arrangements can help to minimise your staff costs.

Attracting students

Marketing people often refer to the USP (Unique Selling Point) of a product. A school is a type of product and you need to understand what would encourage applications to your school rather than another. Competition can be in terms of cost, quality and location. Assess other schools in the area and try to offer something new, perhaps Business English or classes for younger learners.

Plan a marketing campaign, writing to contacts that you have and try the personal approach by following up with telephone calls or visits. It helps to be flexible and tailor your courses to client requirements. Ensure that your most important clients are taught by your best teachers.

Franchises

One way of potentially avoiding some of the start up problems listed above is to consider the possibility of buying into a franchise. This enables you to utilise the history and expertise of the franchisor, and perhaps spread some of the initial cost and risk. Being under a certain name can give protection by a stronger organisation which will mobilise to defend its reputation more effectively than you could as a single school operator.

The nature of franchises differs according to the organisation involved, so it is important to define exactly what the package entails. Some franchises are little more than loose coalitions or cooperatives, where you take on a name, but have a large degree of autonomy in how you run the school and what you offer over the basic rules of the organisation. Others are quite strict, aiming to achieve as much uniformity as possible, in how the school looks, what it offers and charges and in the standard of teaching. They make much of business format franchising, and seek to make it possible to go to any school in the group and get exactly the same 'product'. In teaching terms this can come with a rigid policy on methodology and materials used. Berlitz is an example of this, while others such as International House, are more relaxed over teaching method, as long as the quality exists.

For a person who is more skilled as a teacher than a manager the help and advice of a franchise operation can be invaluable and make the difference between success and failure in the early period.

Your school can enter the market with the benefit of an established name, and ride on the back of market research experience gained by the franchisor. This can aid competitiveness. Advertising campaigns by a franchise group can be wider reaching for less cost to an individual school than those attempted by single private operations, who may not be able to advertise much at all.

Drawbacks do exist with the system. If your school is successful you may not be fully sure how much this is due to your efforts, or to the franchise. Membership of such a group obviously entails a degree of answerability to it and ongoing fees. While name recognition can be advantageous, if another school in the brand does something unethical or gets bad press, it can reverberate to your school as well. It is worth investigating how easy it is to leave a franchise as well as join.

Educational consultancies

Setting up a school is expensive. If you have an extensive list of contacts, but lack funds to open a school, you could consider setting up an educational consultancy. Businesses or individuals might prefer to learn English from teachers who can come to their premises. Consultancies can retain a number of teachers ' on their books' and deploy them to clients as required. A consultancy operating from a small office has far fewer overheads than a school but sound business principles of research, marketing and recruitment remain true. Your reputation for supplying excellent teachers will be what allows you to expand and perhaps explore new areas of business.

Training for Management

Traditionally those involved with the running and managing of schools have been promoted through the ranks as they have become more experienced. Ironically the more teaching experience gained, the more likely you are to end up less in a classroom, and to become an administrator.

While teachers can and do become good managers of schools or other businesses, the skills and experience do not necessarily coincide. Increasingly the disciplines of marketing and management in the ELT industry are becoming specialisms. Many teachers moving into this area of work feel the need for more and additional training and many schools are starting to require the extra qualification.

Courses

Institutions that have always catered for EFL teacher training are now setting up additional management courses, or are making these a component of their modules. Several options and methods of study (full/part time, distance or open) are available, including ELT Management courses such as the RSA Cambridge Advanced Diploma in Teaching Management or a distance ELT Management Course run by International House. MA courses in ELT Management also exist and some TESOL and TEFL MAs now include management training notably those offered at the University of Surrey and Chichester Institute of Higher Education.

The Right Course

ELT management courses are specifically tailored to training for this field and the issues unique to it. In relation to broader courses it is important to check the syllabus to ensure that it will have content relevant to the ELT field. This includes a balance of the theoretical and practical aspects.

Some institutions are tempted to create new ELT management courses by minor tinkering with general management qualifications. Equally those starting specialist ELT management courses should decide if they provide enough breadth of experience should they wish to move to other industries.

Many teachers who have completed such courses are full of praise for what they have learned, saying it does help them to run a school better and have more confidence and competence.

MBAs

EFL teachers have a record of taking on post-graduate courses and find that these options do help to broaden their employability. A trend is appearing with MBAs becoming more popular than some purely teaching MAs with those of an EFL background. This is partly due to the higher salaries offered to MBA graduates and because it is a surer option should a manager-teacher decide to move to another industry.

Accreditation

With all of the courses caution must be exercised, not just on content, but price levels, which for MBAs are often very high. MBA programmes are unregulated in many countries, including the UK, so employers are looking at where you achieved it as a measure of quality. Many also seem to prefer those who have done full time courses over part-timers. In Britain, the Association of MBAs, AMBA, has its own accreditation scheme which only covers 30 programmes out of 112 in the country. This is a guideline to work with, but does not mean that those not on the list at the moment are all substandard, just that you should examine the institutions carefully. Specialist funding is available through the Natwest MBA Loan Scheme (0171 432 4199).

264

Access a wider world with Trinity TESOL qualifications

Throughout the world, English is the unifying language that overcomes communication barriers.

Teachers of English work in many countries helping students gain the confidence to communicate effectively.

Trinity's qualifications in TESOL (Teaching English to Speakers of Other Languages) give you the training you need to take your first steps in English language teaching.

The Trinity Certificate in Teaching English to Speakers of Other Languages (CertTESOL) is accepted as an initial teaching qualification by many schools in the UK and overseas.

The Trinity Diploma is available for more experienced teachers wishing to broaden their knowledge of language acquisition and learning.

Contact Trinity now for a TESOL information pack

The Information Officer
Trinity College *London*
16 Park Crescent
London W1N 4AP, UK
Tel: +44(0)20 7323 2328   Fax: +44(0)20 7323 5201
e-mail: info@trinitycollege.co.uk
website: www.trinitycollege.co.uk

Trinity
The International Examinations Board

EL*GAZETTE*

Dilke House, 1 Malet Street, Bloomsbury, London WC1E 7AJ
Tel: +44 171 255 1969 Fax: +44 171 255 1972

The Voice of the Industry – that keeps you globally informed

"The only EL newspaper that provides comprehensive, reliable, up to date information in a balanced manner."

ESSENTIAL READING FOR EVERY ELT PROFESSIONAL

- Independently published since 1978, with an established presence as the leading Industry newspaper.

- Monthly colour publication.

- Cutting edge information which details the latest publications, methodologies and developments of relevance to this expanding industry.

- 40,000 readers worldwide.

- Continued research and reviews of topical world issues, debates

EL *PROSPECTS*

- THE JOB SUPPLEMENT SECTION INCLUDED WITHIN THE EL GAZETTE .

- Worldwide job listings, covering all levels of EL experience and positions.

- Additional information on career progression.

SUBSCRIPTION INFORMATION

If you wish to subscribe for one year, please send a cheque made payable to the EL Gazette for the applicable amount. Payments by credit card are accepted either by fax or phone.

Tel: +44 171 255 1969 Fax: +44 171 255 1972

Currency	United Kingdom	Rest of Europe	all other countries
British Sterling	£30.00	£30.00	£40.00
US Dollars		$60.00	$75.00
Australian Dollars			$95.00

REFERENCE SECTION

This section serves as a vital source of information for all teachers, whether experienced or not. These pages contain addresses and information about some of the key ELT organisations, associations and bookshops throughout the world.

If you are serious about your professional career, you need to join TESOL.

English language teaching involves challenges and rewards … like making a difference in the lives of your students, like bringing your best to your work. TESOL tailors benefits to your needs through professional publications, advocacy, career services, and educational opportunities.

Use the career services to find a job teaching English outside your home country. TESOL offers the *Placement Bulletin,* an employment clearinghouse, as well as directories and reference books.

Enjoy discounts on our extensive collection of teacher resource books. For those planning to teach abroad, *More Than a Native Speaker* should be at the top of your packing list. This book covers all the necessary survival skills from adapting to life in a new country and lesson planning to developing professional techniques.

For *the* source in teacher education programs, turn to the recently updated *Directory of Professional Preparation Programs in the U.S. and Canada, 1999-2001.* "Prospective TESOL professionals taking their first step on the career ladder are advised to consult the *Directory.*" —*American Language Review*

TESOL is YOUR professional association. Take action and join TESOL today.

For more information, contact TESOL,
700 South Washington Street, Suite 200, Alexandria, Virginia 22314 USA
Tel. 703-836-0774 • Fax 703-836-6447 • E-mail mbr@tesol.edu • Web http://www.tesol.edu/

Accreditation Schemes

A guide to how accreditation works and an examination of the major schemes and associations in English-speaking countries around the world.

In all English-speaking countries, except the US and Canada, there are government-approved accreditation or recognition schemes. These are run by independent bodies, which set standards for language centres and monitor those centres through inspection.

All national accreditation schemes are open to language schools, state colleges and universities. Universities might have rules preventing them from seeking external accreditation and full-curriculum high school programmes also tend not to be eligible. Standards set by accreditation schemes vary from country to country, but nearly always cover accommodation, language teaching, student welfare, and teacher qualification (although actual courses are not accredited).

Advantages of accreditation

As a student, knowing that a school is accredited by a national, government-backed scheme indicates minimum standards. Some national schemes and most associations of recognised centres also have complaints procedures for dissatisfied clients.

Australia

All language schools, colleges (TAFEs) and university language centres can be accredited by an organisation called NEAS. Centres do not have to be accredited, but student visas are only issued to students enrolled in an accredited school. The controls on NEAS schools are very strict and there is a national complaints procedure. More than half of all the accredited schools in Australia belong to the ELICOS Association.

United Kingdom

Private language schools which have been operating for two years or more, universities and state colleges can all be accredited by the British Council. Although many of the older universities have rules which prevent them from applying for external recognition, some run their own quality assurance scheme through BALEAP. About half of all British schools are not accredited by the British Council, although some may belong to other quality assurance schemes. British Council controls are strict and schools are inspected every three years on average. There are a number of associations for accredited centres. Private schools can belong to ARELS and FIRST, while state colleges and universities can join BASELT.

Ireland

All language schools, state colleges and universities are accredited by the Department of Education, but inspections and recognition procedures are carried out by an independent body called ACELS. Over half of all schools are recognised. Accredited schools and colleges can belong to an association called RELSA.

Malta

Since September 1997 all language centres in Malta have had to be accredited by the Department of Education, the first compulsory ELT recognition scheme in the world. Many private schools also belong to an association called FELTOM.

New Zealand

All institutions working with foreign students can be accredited by NZAAQ. There are a number of associations, of which the biggest are FIELS for private schools and NZEIL for the state sector.

United States

There is, at present, no government-approved national accreditation scheme for language courses in the US. However, all language schools colleges and universities, must, by law, have general educational accreditation, either regulated by individual states, or by a government-approved agency. TESOL, AAIEP and UCIEP are three associations which have federal government backing to set up an accreditation scheme for ELT language courses.

ELT Book Suppliers

A selection of the world's best ELT bookshops where you can buy that crucial book (see page 72).

ALGERIA
Algiers International Study Centre, Villa Baddouche, 54 Route de Beni-Messous, Air de France, Bouzarea

ARGENTINA
Libreria Rodriguez, Sarmiento 835, Buenos Aires

AUSTRALIA
AEE, Antipodean Educational Enterprises, PO Box 5806, Gold Coast Mail Centre, Queensland 9725
AEE, P O Box 455, Cammeray, NSW 2062
The Bridge Bookshop, 10 Grafton St, Chippendale, NSW 2008
Language Book Centre, 555 Beaufort St, Mnt Lawley, Western Australia 6050

BANGLADESH
Karim International, 64/1 Monipuri Para, Tejgaon, P O Box 2141, Yasi Bhavan, Dhaka 1215

BARBADOS
Days Books, Speedbird House, Independence Square, Bridgetown

BELARUS
Lexis Co Ltd, P O Box 507, 220050 Minsk

BOSNIA HERZEGOVINA
BTC Sahinpasic, M Tita 29/2, 71000 Sarajevo, Livanjska 74

BRAZIL
ABC Books, Rua Padre Manuel de Paiva 300, Santo Andre - SP, CEP 09070-230
A e C Book Express, Rua Almirante Protogenes 312, Bairro Jardim, Santo Andre - SP
Boa Viagem Distribuidora de Livros Ltda, Rua Sergipe 314 - Funcionarios, Belo Horizonte - MG, CEP 30130-170
Book Express, Avenida Joao de Barros 326, Recife - PE
Chaves Com de Livros E Papelaria Ltda, Av Dorival Caymmi 110 - Itaoma, Salvador - BA, CEP 40020-050

Disal, Rua Maria Antonia 380, Sao Paulo - SP, CEP 01222-000
Disal, Rua Deputado Lacerda Franco 365, Pinheiros, Sao Paulo - SP, CEP 05418-000
Disal, Rua Amador Bueno 851, Centro, Ribeirao Preto - SP, CEP 14025-010
JL Gomes Comercio de Livors Ltda, Rua Meton de Alencar 803 - Centro, Fortaleza - CE, CEP 60035-160
G Lisboa - Livros Ltda, Rua Princesa Isabel 129-B Vista, Recife - PE, CEP 50050-450
Livraria Cultura, Av Paulista 2073, Conjunto Nacional, Sao Paulo - SP, CEP 01311-940
Livraria do Chain - Aramis Chain, ruya General Carneiro 441 - Centro, Curitiba - PR, CEP 80060-150
Livraria E Distribuidora Curitiba, Av Mal Floriano Peixoto, 1742 - Reboucas, Sao Paulo - SP, CEP 80230-110
Livraria Martins Fontes Editora Ltda, Rua Conselheiro Ramalho 330/340 - Bela Vista, Sao Paulo - SP, CEP 01325-000
Livraria Martins Fontes Editora Ltda, Av Paulista 509, Loja 21, Sao Paulo SP, CEP 04001-080
Livraria Martins Fontes Editora Ltda, Rua da Alfandega 91 - 1j, C - Centro, Rio de Janeiro - RJ, CEP 22780-160
Livraria Nobel SA, Rua de Balso 559, 02910 Sao Paulo
Daniel Mayer, Rua Mal Deodoro 13 - sala 02, Florianopolis - SC, CEP 88010-020
Jose R Pontes & Cia Ltda, Rua Dr Quirino 1223 - Centro, Campinas - SP, CEP 13015-081
Representacoes Paulista Ltda, Av Carlos M Lima, 6l-lj. ed Saint Marie - Bento Ferreira, Vitora - ES, CEP 29050-650
SBS, Alameda Barros 83, 01232-001 Sao Paulo SP
SBS - Special Book Services, Rua Caldas Junior 06, Centro Porto Alegre, RS CEP 90010-260
Sebastian de Miranda, Rua Eugenio Brugger 620 - Centro, Coiania - GO, CEP 74055-120
Sodilvro, Rua Sa Freire 40, CP 3655, 20930 Rio, RJ
Solivros, Sofia Demczuk, SCLS 406-bl Clj 13, Brasilia - DF, CEP 70255-000

BRUNEI
Pansing Distribution Sdn Bhd,
New Industrial Rd 0-01, Singapore 536200

BULGARIA
English Book Centre, 91 Rakovski St, 1000 Sofia

CANADA
Dominie Press, 1316 Huntingwood Drive,
Unit 7, Agincourt, Ontario, M1S 3JL
Librairie Michel Fortin, 3714 St Denis,
Montreal, Quebec H2X 3L7

COLOMBIA
Books & Books, AA 40571, Santafe de Bogota
CME Editorial Ltda, AA 29847,
Santafe de Bogota

COSTA RICA
Textos Educativos SA, Centro Comercial,
San Pedro, Planta Baja, Locales 28-29, San Jose

COTE D'IVOIRE
Edicom SA, 16 BP 466, Abidjan 16

CROATIA
Algoritam doo, P O Box 23, Jurisiceva 1,
10000 Zagreb
Tamris doo, Petrinjska 11, 4100000 Zagreb
IA Interadria doo, Kresimirova 28,
510000 Rijeka
VBZ doo, Dracevicka 12, 100000 Zagreb

CYPRUS
Bridgehouse Bookshop, Byzantiou 24,
P O Box 4527, Strovolos
Soloneion Book Centre, 24 Byzantium St,
P O Box 4527, Nicosia 1300

CZECH REPUBLIC
Bohemian Ventures spol sro, Denicka 13,
170 00 Praha 7
ILC (Czechoslovakia) AS, Kpt Jarose 25,
602 00 Brno
Mega Books International, Rostovska 4/20,
101 00 Praha 10 Vrosvice

DENMARK
Atheneum International Booksellers,
6 Norregade, 1165 Kobenhavn
Bierman & Bierman, Vestergade 126,
7200 Grindsted
DCA Paperbacks, Dansk Centralagentur,
Sluseholmen 6-8, 2450 Kobenhavn K
English Center, Borup Byvej 162, 8900 Randers
Erik Paludan Boghandel, 10 Fiolstraede,
1171 Kobenhavn K
Foriaget Futurum, Mogeimosovej 54,
Rodding, DK 6630

DOMINICAN REPUBLIC
Caribbean Marketing Services, Calle Gaspar
Polanco, Bella Vista, Santo Domingo

ECUADOR
Dimaxa SA, Av Maldonado 366 Y Napo,
Casilia 17-07-9613, Quito
The English Book Centre, Acacias 613 y
Avenida Las Monjas, P O Box 5164, Guayaquil
The English Book Centre,
Geronimo Carrion 117 y 12 de Octobre, Quito

EGYPT
International Language Bookshop,
P O Box 53, Embaba, Giza

EL SALVADOR
ETC Ediciones, Centro Comercial Basilia, Blvd El
Hipodromo 2-502, San Benito, San Salvador

ESTONIA
Allecto Ltd, Juhkentali 32-5, Tallinn EE 0001
AS Lexicon, 20 Vene St, EE 0001 Tallinn

FINLAND
Akateeminin Kirjakauppa, Keskuskatu 1,
SF-00101 Helsinki
Suomaleinen Kirjakauppa, Aleksanterinkatu 25,
SF-00100 Helsinki

FRANCE
Attica, 64 Rue de la Folie, Mericourt, 75011 Paris
Bradleys Bookshop, 32 Pl Gambetta,
3300 Bordeaux
Decitre, 29 Pl Bellecour, 69002 Lyon
English Books, 8 Rue Doree, 30000 Nimes

GHANA
Damas Educational Services, P O Box 10941,
Accra North

GREECE
Kosmos Floras Group, 59 Panepistimiou St,
105 69 Athens
Efstathiadis Group, Olympou 34, 546 30
Thessaloniki

GUATEMALA
Distribuidora General del Libro SA,
10a Calle 1-02, Zona 1, 01004 Guatemala
Instituto Guatemalteco Americano,
91 Avenida 0-19, Zona 4, 01004 Guatemala

HONDURAS
Libreria Inglesa, 3ra Ave 8a Calle,
Frente Farmacia Vida, Comayaguela

HONG KONG
Commercial Press, 9-15 Yee Wo St, Causeway Bay
Commercial Press, 2/f Heng Ngai Jewelry
Centre, 4 Hom Yuen St East, Hunghom

HUNGARY
BELT Bookshop, Bajvivo u 8, H-1027 Budapest
LibroTrade Ltd, Pesti ut 237, H-1173 Budapest

ICELAND
Bokabud Mals og Menningar, Laugavegur 18,
P O Box 392, 121 Reykjavik

INDONESIA
Triad Book Centre, Jl Purnawarman 76,
Bandung
PF Books, Jl dr Setia Budhi no 274,
Bandung 40143
PT Bhratara Niaga Media, Jalan Cipinang,
Bali No 5A, Jakarta Timur

IRAN
Third World Book Services, 101 Mansour St,
Mirzay e Shirazi, Tehran 15969

IRELAND
Fred Hanna Ltd, 27-29 Nassau St, Dublin 2
International Books, 18 South Frederick St,
Dublin 2
Modern Languages Ltd, 39 Westland Row,
Dublin 2

ISRAEL
Eric Cohen Books, ONDA Publications Ltd,
27 Hta'asiya St, P O Box 2325, Ra'anana 43 655
University Publishing Projects Ltd (UPP),
28 Hanatsiv St, Tel-Aviv 67015

JAPAN
Biblos, Fl Bldg 1-26-5 Takadanobaba,
Shinjuku-ku, Tokyo 160

JAMAICA
Times Store, 8-12 King St, Kingston

JORDAN
Jordan Book Centre, P O Box 301 Al-Jubeiha,
Amman 11941
Majdalawi Masterpieces, P O Box 1819,
Amman

KENYA
Book Distributors Ltd, P O Box 47610,
Weruga Lane, Nairobi
Pan-Africa Books, P O Box 96131, Likoni,
Mombasa

KUWAIT
Kuwait Bookshops, Thunayan Al Ghanem Bldg,
P O Box 2942, Safar
Kuwait Family Bookshop, P O Box 20736

LATVIA
Firma 'Janis Roze' SIA, 85a Elizabetes,
Riga, LV 1050
Jana Rozes Gramatnica, K Barona, IELA 3,
Riga LV 1011

LEBANON
Librairie du Liban Publishers,
P O Box 11-9232, Beirut

LITHUANIA
UAB Penki Kontinental, Vilnius g 39,
Vilnius 2001
UAB NETA, Virsuliski 79-66, Vilnius
Humanitas, Donelaicio 52, 3000 Kaunas

MALAYSIA
STP Distributors, SDN BHD 31 Green Hall,
10200 Penang

MEXICO
**Distribuidora American Books sa de cv
(DABSA),** Constituyentes 920, 11950 Mexico DF
Libreria Britanica SA, Serapio Rendon 125,
Col San Rafael, 06470 DF

MOROCCO
American Bookstore, 4 Zankat Tanja, Rabat
Librairie Nationale, 2 Av Mers Sultan,
Casablanca

THE NETHERLANDS
The American Book Centre, Kalverstraat 185,
Amsterdam 1012 XC
W H Smith Amsterdam, Kalverstraat 152,
Amsterdam 1012 XE
**Waterstone's Booksellers, Kalverstraat 132,
1011 HC Amsterdam. Tel: 020-638 3821 Fax:
020-638 4379 e-mail:
BOOKS@AMSTERDAM.WATERSTONES.NL
Contact: Ron de Klerk & Helena Morrison.
Extensive range of ELT materials from all the
main (and some smaller) ELT publishers.
Efficient mail order service, also abroad.**

NEW ZEALAND
Whitecoulls Ltd, 111 Cashel St, Christchurch
University Bookshop, 34 Princes St, Auckland
University Bookshop, 2 Lorne St, Auckland

NIGERIA
Mosuro the Booksellers Ltd, P O Box 30201,
Ibadan

NORWAY
Narvesen Distribusjon, Bertrand Narvesensv 2,
Postboks 6219, Etterstad, 0602 Oslo 6
Norsk Bokirnport,
Postboks 784 S Ovre Vollgate 15, Oslo
Olaf Norlis Bokhandel, Universitersgt
20-24, 0162 Oslo

PANAMA
Distxxsa Panama SA, Calle Alberto Navarro
No 53, Local No 2, El Cangrejo

PARAGUAY
Books SRL, Casilla de Correo 914, Asuncion

PERU
Emilia Books, Atahualpa 390, P O Box 18-1515,
Miraflores, Lima 18
Special Book Services SA, Av La Molina 477,
Lima 3

POLAND
Omnibus Trading, ul Towarow 39/43,
Poznan 61-896

PORTUGAL
Livros Bertrand Lda,
Rua Garrett 73-75, 1200 Lisboa
Livraria Britanica,
Rua de S Marcal 83, 1200 Lisboa
Livraria Britanica,
Rua Jose Falcao 184, 4000 Porto

QATAR
Family Bookshop Ltd, P O Box 5769, Doha

ROMANIA
FIDES, Str Vasile Conta 7-0, sc E, apt 168,
70139 Bucharest

RUSSIA
Anglia British Bookshop, Khlebny per 2/3,
Moscow 121 814
Certercom, 141700 Moscow obl gl Dolgoprdniy,
Institutskii per 9
Digital Universe, 1st Obydensky per 12,
Moscow

Dinternal, 2/3 Khlebny Pereulok, Institute of the USA & Canada, Moscow 121 814
Education Centre, Zubovsky Blvd 5a, Moscow
European Book Company, Volgogradsky pr-t 4, Moscow 109 316
IEC Ltd, ul Pskovskaya 23, 190008 St Petersburg
Relod, ul Khmelova 15/17, Moscow 103051
Rubikon, Kaluzhskaya pl 1, Moscow
Zwemmer's Books, Kuznetsky Most 18, Moscow

SLOVENIA
Zupanciceva 2, 1000 Ljubljana
DZS Solski Epicenter, Mestni trg 23, Ljubljana
Cankarjeva Zalozba, Kopitarjeva 2, 1000 Ljubljana
Markom doo, Prvomajska 9, 1000 Ljubljana

SOUTHERN AFRICA
Book Promotions (PTY) Ltd, P O Box 23320, Clarement 7735, Cape Town

SPAIN
English Book Centre SL, Pascual y Genis 16, Valencia 46002
The English Bookshop, Eduardo Dato 36, Seville 41005
Eurobook Libreria de Idiomas, Fray Luis de Leon 23, Valladolid 47002
Turner, c/ Genova 3 y 5, 28004 Madrid
Come In, c/ Provenza 203, 08008 Barcelona

SWEDEN
Ab Witra Forlag, Engelbrektsgat 19, Box 26056, S-10041 Stockholm
Akademibokhandeln, Box 7634, Mastersamuelsgt 32, 10394 Stockholm
Bokdistribution i Horby AV, Box 73, 242 21 Horby
The English Book Centre, Box 6207, Surbrunnsgatan 51, 102 34 Stockholm
UBS Utbildningsstaden AB, Dr Westrings gata 14, 413 24 Goteborg

SWITZERLAND
Elm Video and Books, 5 rue Versonnex, CH-1207 Geneva

Libraire Centrale et Universitaire SA, 5 Place de la Palud, CH-1003 Lausanne
Librairie Francke, Neuengasse 43/Von Werdt Passage, Bern
Libraire Payot, 4 Place Pepinet, CH-1002 Lausanne
Office du Livre, Z13 Corminboeuf, CH-1701 Fribourg
Staheli's Bookshops Ltd, 'Interlingua' Am Weinplatz 4/5, CH-8021 Zurich
Swiss Book Centre, P O Box 522, CH-4601 Olten

SYRIA
Nour-e-Sham Book Centre, P O Box 249, Damascus

TAIWAN
Bookman Books Ltd, 2nd Floor No 88, Hsinsheng S Rd, Sec 3, Taipei
Caves Books, P O Box 17-66, 103 Chung San N Rd, Sec 2, Taipei
The Crane Publishing Co Ltd, 1F, 59 Chung-Ching S Rd, Sec 2, Taipei
Tung Hua Book Co Ltd, 3F, 147 Chung King South Rd, Sec 1, Taipei

TRINIDAD
RIK Services, 104 High St, San Fernando

TURKEY
ABC Kitabevi, 461 Istiklal Cad, Istanbul
Baris Kitabevi, Koca M Pasa Cad, No 5914, Cerrahoasa, Istanbul

UGANDA
Pan Africa Book Service, P O Box 14197, 152 Kisingiri Rd, Mengo, Kampala

UKRAINE
Evandro Martins Fontes, 1A Hospitalnaya St apt 10, Kiev 252133
I H School - Book Centre, Third Bldg, 7 Vandy Vasilevsky St, 252055 Kiev

UNITED ARAB EMIRATES
All Prints Publishers & distributors, PO Box 857, Abu Dhabi
Al Mutanabbi Bookshop,
PO Box 71946, Abu Dhabi

UNITED KINGDOM
Austick's University Bookshop, 21 Blenheim Terrace, Woodhouse Lane, Leeds LS2 9HJ
BEBC, Charminster Rd, Bournemouth BH8 8UH
BEBC (Mail Order Dept), 15 Albion Close, Parkstone, Poole, Dorset; 106 Piccadilly, London W1
BEBC (London), International House, 106 Picadilly, London W1V 9FL
Blackwells, 89 Park St, Bristol;
University Union, Cardiff;
100 Charing Cross Rd, London;
48-51 Broad St, Oxford OX1 3BQ;
6-12 Kings Rd, Reading
Books Etc Ltd,
120 Charing Cross Rd, London WC2H 0JR
Cambridge International Book Centre,
42 Hills Rd, Cambridge CB2 1LA
Dillons the Bookstore,
82 Gower St, London WC1E 6EQ;
128 New St, Birmingham;
71-74 North St, Brighton;
22 Sydney St, Cambridge;
2-4 St Ann's Square, Manchester;
William Baker House, Broad St, Oxford OX1 3AF
Dillons University Bookshop,
The University of Kent, Canterbury CT2 7NG
The English Book Centre,
31 George St, Brighton, E Sussex BN2 1RH
European Bookshop, 4 Regent Place, Warwick St, London W1R 6BH
W G Foyle Ltd, 113/119 Charing Cross Rd, London WC2H 0EB
Haigh and Hochland, Precinct Centre, Oxford Rd, Manchester M13 9QA
Heffers Booksellers, 31 St Andrew's St, Cambridge CB2 3AR
International Bookshop, Palace Chambers, White Rock, Hastings, Sussex TN35 1JP

KELTIC, 25 Chepstow Corner, Chepstow Place, London W2 4TT
KELTIC Mail Order, 39 Alexandra Rd, Addlestone, Weybridge KT15 2PQ
LCL Benedict Ltd, 104 Judd St, London WC1H 9NF
Practical Books, 14A Western Rd, Hove, Sussex
James Thin Bookseller,
29 Buccleuch St, Edinburgh EH8 9JR
John Smith & Son Bookshops,
57 St Vincent St, Glasgow G2 5TB
Waterstone and Co Ltd,
14-15 The Arcade, Bournemouth BH1 2AH

URUGUAY
Mosca Hnos SA, Av 18 de Julio 1578, Montevideo

USA
Alta Book Center, 14 Adrian Court, Butlingame, CA 94010
Delta Systems Co,
1400 Miller Pkwy, McHenry, IL
Optima Books, 2820 Eighth St, Berkeley, California 94710
Worldwide Teachers Development Institute, 266 Beacon St, Boston, MA 02116

VENEZUELA
The American Book Shop, Ave San Juan Bozco, EDF Belveder L2, Caracas 1060
Read Books, Calle Los Rios, Con Avenida Los Jardines, Quinta Janoco, Urb Prados del Este, Caracas

YUGOSLAVIA
Branka Panic, Yugoslav-British Society Language School, Simina 21, Belgrade, Serbia
Lingua Educo,
Zarka Zrenjanina 65, 23000 Zrenjanin
Milada Sevo, Hello, Arsenija Carnojevica 1599/3, 11070 Novi Beograd

ZAMBIA
Insaka Press Co Ltd, P O Box 50708, Lusaka

ZIMBABWE
Academic Books (Pvt) Ltd,
P O Box 567, Harare

Keeping in Touch

Newspapers, magazines, associations, conferences and other ways of staying in touch while you are overseas.

Stuck in a classroom in rural Romania and putting in 25 or more teaching hours per week? Feeling lonely and lacking in stimulation? Looking for that perfect job that will change your life? Wondering how to invigorate a class full of bored teenagers? Read on.

Professionally and personally teachers need contact as well as new, fresh ideas. ELT is by and large an enthusiast's profession and it is well-serviced with ways in which the classroom teacher can keep in touch with the profession at large. Here are some suggestions for ways in which you can keep your professional awareness and personal motivation alive.

EL*Gazette*

Produced by the sister organisation of the *ELT Guide*, this monthly newspaper can land on your doorstep anywhere in the world. Packed with professional news and surveys, exciting interviews with key industry figures and writers, reviews of the latest ELT books, and photocopiable materials, you can stay up to date no matter where you are.

If you are looking for a job or want to further your career, you will need to read EL *Prospects*. Distributed with EL*Gazette*, but also available separately, every issue has more than 150 select ELT positions worldwide. Specimen copies are usually available at major conferences or from Dilke House, 1 Malet Street, London WC1E 7JA, UK. EL *Gazette* is available from specialist bookshops or by subscription (£30 [UK], £30 [Europe], and £40 [rest of the world]). Visa/Mastercard telephone orders can be made on Tel: +44 171 255 1969, Fax: +44 171 255 1972 or e-mail: editorial@elgazette.com

Research and methodology journals

English Language Teaching Journal is the EFL profession's journal of record. It appears four times a year and is published by Oxford University Press, Walton Street, Oxford OX2 6DP, UK. It contains articles on methodology and linguistics and also reviews courses and teachers' books.

TESOL Matters and *TESOL Quarterly* are the journals of the TESOL association (see page 279). These publications are provided to members of TESOL and reflect on developments in research and methodology.

ELT News and Views provides teachers in the Southern Cone region of Latin America with essays on teaching methodology and educational issues, as well as local association news. For further details write to: ELT News and Views, Uruguay 782-3°, 1015 Capital, Buenos Aires, Argentina.

ELT Review is published by Pearson Education in association with the British Council. For further details, contact: Pearson Education, Edinburgh Gate, Harlow, Essex CM20 2JE, UK

Specialist language journals

There are a number of specialist journals which can help you stay up to date with developments in issues relating to the English Language. One of the most popular and easily approachable is *English Today*, a quarterly review published by Cambridge University Press, The Edinburgh Building, Shaftesbury Road, Cambridge CB2 2RU, UK.

For word buffs, *Verbatim* is the answer. A monthly magazine produced by Lawrence Urdang, former editor-in-chief of the Random House dictionaries.

Language Teaching is the leading abstracting journal in the field. It is published by Cambridge

University Press in association with the British Council. For further details, contact: Cambridge University Press, The Edinburgh Building, Shaftesbury Road, Cambridge CB2 2RU, UK.

There is also *Applied Linguistics* published by the International Applied Linguistics Association.

British Council and USIA

Once you are in a particular country, the British Council and the US Information Agency (through its Bi-National Centers) will be important sources of information. Both organisations have libraries containing ELT materials, have useful advice about the local area and run a number of helpful seminars. There is often a member of staff with special responsibility for English Language activity in British Council offices or contact the Director of Bi-National Center in USIA centres.

The British Council information centre is based at Medlock Street, Manchester M15 4PR, UK (Tel: +44 161 957 7755) and the US Information Agency is located at 301 4th Street SW, Washington, DC 20547-0001, USA (Tel: +1 202 485 2869).

If you are working in a the developing wold, it is worth finding out if there is a Peace Corps or a VSO office in the capital. These can also be a source of support. See page 282 for more information about voluntary organisations.

Associations and Conferences

Ask your colleagues about local EFL organisations who might hold meetings you can attend. There are two major international organisations that you should know about, one British-based and one US-based, as well as several regional ones:

IATEFL: The International Association of Teachers of English as a Foreign Language is a major international organisation, which has it

headquarters in the UK. It publishes its own newsletter four times a year and holds an annual international conference (usually in April) attended by about 1000 delegates from all sectors of ELT. All individual members automatically receive free membership to one special interest group (SIG), of which there are thirteen. These hold their own seminars at various times of the year and publish their own newsletters. Details about the organisation's activities and how to join are available from Jill Stajduhar, Executive Officer, IATEFL, 3 Kingsdown Chambers, Whitstable, Kent CT5 2DJ, UK, Tel: 01227 276528. IATEFL also has 34 branches and 24 affiliates in the following countries, which help maintain international networking in ELT:

TESOL Arabia; ELICOS Australia; TEA Austria; BLENATE Belarus; IATEFL Brazil; BRAZ-TESOL Brazil; TESL Canada; IATEFL Chile; CETRAC China; NFLTAEDSC China; ASOCOPI Columbia; IATEFL Croatia - Hupe; GELI Cuba; ATECR Czech Republic; OATE Czech Republic; ZATE Czech Republic; EATE Estonia' ATEF Finland; ETAG Georgia; HELTA Germany; ELTA Rhine Germany; ELTAF Germany; MELTA Germany; IATEFL Greece; IATEFL Hungary; ATEI (Association of Teachers of English in Iceland) Iceland; ETAI Israel; TESOL Italy; JACET Japan; JALT Japan; KATE Korea; TESOL Korea; TEA Kazakhstan; KOSETA Korea; LATE Latvia; ATEL Lebanon; LAKMIDA Lithuania; MATEFL Malta; VLLT Netherlands; LMS Norway; SPELT Pakistan; PATEFL Palestine; PARATESOL Paraguay; IATEFL Poland; BETA Romania; CETA Romania; TETA Romania; LATEUM Russia; AELT Voronezh Russia; AELT Novosibirsk Russia; NNELTA Russia; SPELTA Russia; TESOL Scotland; SAUA/SATE Slovakia; IATEFL Slovenia; TESOL Spain; LMS Sweden; ETAS INGED Turkey; NATECLA United Kingdom; IATEFL Ukraine; URUTESOL Uruguay; UzTEA Uzbekistan; ELTAB Yugoslavia

For addresses and further information on these, contact the Head Office address in Whitstable (see above).

TESOL: Teachers of English to Speakers of Other Languages is the largest association, with over 20,000 members and national affiliates running their own local organisations in a number of countries. Like IATEFL, TESOL has a network of special interest groups. It publishes reference books and two magazines, TESOL News and *TESOL Matters*, and holds an annual international conference, usually in March, at a major North American city and attended by up to 10,000 teachers. Membership details are available from: TESOL Central Office, 700 South Washington Street, Suite200, Alexandria, Virginia 22314, USA. Tel: 703 836 0774, Fax: 703 836 7864, e-mail: tesol@tesol.edu. There are TESOL affiliates in the following countries and states of America:

Alabama-Mississippi TESOL (AMTESOL); Alaska Association of Bilingual Education (AKABE); TESOL Arabia; Argentina TESOL; Arizona TESOL (AZ-TESOL); Arkansas TESOL (ARKTESOL); Armenia - Association of English Teachers of Armenia (AELTA); Australia New south Wales (ATES0L); Brazil TESOL (BRAZ-TESOL); British Columbia (BC TEAL); California TESOL (CATESOL); Carolina TESOL (North and South Carolina TESOL); TESOL Chile (ICNC); Columbia (ASOCOPI); Colorado TESOL (CoTESOL); Connecticut TESOL (ConnTESOL); Costa Rica (ACPI); Croatia: Croatian Association of TESOL (CRO-TESOL); Cuba (GELI); Czech Republic (ATE-CR); Dominican Republic (DATE); Ecuador (FENAPIUPE); England (NALDIC); Florida TESOL (FLATESOL); Florida: Sunshine State TESOL; TESOL France; Georgia TESOL (GATESOL); Republic of Georgia (ETAG); TESOL Greece; Guam TESOL; Hawaii TESOL; Hungary: Angoltanatok Nemzetkozi Egyesulete (IATEFL); Illinois TESOL/Bilingual Education (Illinois TESOL/BE); Indiana TESOL (INTESOL); Intermountain TESOL (I-TESOL); Israel TESOL (ISRATESOL); TESOL Italy; Japan Association of Language Teaching (JALT); Kansas TESOL (MATESOL); Kentucky TESOL (KYTESOL); Korea

TESOL; Louisiana TESOL (LaTESOL); Maryland TESOL (MDTESOL); Massachusetts Association of TESOL (MATSOL); Mexico TESOL (MEXTESOL); Michigan TESOL (MITESOL); Mid-America TESOL (MIDTESOL); Minnesota TESOL (MinneTESOL); New Jersey TESOL/New Jersey Bilingual Educators (NJTESOL/NJBE); New Mexico TESOL (NMTESOL): New York State TESOL (NYTESOL); New Zealand TESOL (TESOLANZ); Northern new England TESOL (NNETESOL); Ohio TESOL; Oklahoma TESOL (OKTESOL); Ontario (TESL Ontario); Oregon TESOL (ORTESOL); Pakistan (SPELT); Panama TESOL; Paraguay TESOL; Pennsylvania: Eastern Pennsylvania TESOL (PennTESOL - East); Pennsylvania Three Rivers TESOL (3-R TESOL); Peru TESOL; Portugal (APPI); Puerto Rico TESOL (P.R. TESOL); Quebec (SPEAQ); TESOL Russia; TESOL Scotland; Slovakia (SAUA/SATE); South Africa TESOL (SATESOL): Spain TESOL; St Petersburgh English Language Teachers Association (SPELTA); Sweden (Modern Language Society); Taiwan (ETAROC); Tennessee TESOL (TNTESOL); Texas El Paso area (TEXTESOL-1); Texas San Antonio area (TEXTESOL-II); Texas Houston area (TEXTESOL-IV); Texas Dallas area (TEXTESOL-V); Turkey (Inged-ELEA); TESOL Ukraine; Uruguay TESOL (URUTESOL); Venezuela TESOL (VENTESOL); Virginia Association of TESOL (VATESOL); Washington (WAESOL); Washington-Area TESOL (WATESOL); Wisconsin TESOL (WITESOL).

For addresses and further information on these, contact the Head Office address in Alexandria (see above).

JALT: Japan Association of Language Teachers is a non-profit organisation with 40 chapters located around Japan and 4,000 members and affiliates across Asia, the US and Europe. Publications include *The Language Teacher* and *JALT Journal*. Other JALT activities include annual international conferences and the biannual Pan Asian conferences.

Contact: JALT Central Office, Urban Edge Bldg, 5th Floor, 1-37-9 Taito, Taito-ku, Tokyo 110, Japan. Tel: 81 3 3837 1630, Fax: 81 3 3837 1631.

SEAL (Society for Effective Affective Learning): SEAL is an association for people interested in alternative approaches to language teaching, attracting teachers with a special interest in Suggestopaedia, Neuro Linguistic programming (NLP) and similar disciplines. It has a newsletter and biannual international conference. Details can be obtained from Emma Grant, SEAL, The Language Centre, University of Brighton, Falmer, Sussex BN1 9PH, UK. The US equivalent of SEAL is SALT, the Society for Alternative Learning and Teaching.

Wherever you are posted, there are likely to be a number of conferences or conventions nearby. The submission of conference papers is often encouraged by associations. If you want to present a paper, remember that the deadline may be up to ten months before the conference is set to take place. Keep an eye on the EL *Gazette* and specialist newsletters to stay notified of any changes to conference schedules.

Broadcasting and other media

The BBC World Service's English by Radio Department broadcasts some excellent regular programmes for teachers, such as its *Speaking of English* magazine programme, which includes interviews with key figures and reviews of the latest books. The US equivalent of the BBC World Service is Voice of America. Contact your local US embassy for details of programmes and scheduling.

Internet

Still feeling lonely and isolated? Plug in your computer and modem and access the massive virtual world of ELT which now exists on the Internet. Many associations and institutions have their own Web pages and there are a number of interactive bulletin boards where teachers are dying to get into virtual conversations. There are also plenty of well-organised pages with collections of links to help you get where you want to go more quickly. Below are a few Websites to get you started. Happy surfing!

Adult ESOL: http://www.wgbb.org
American University & ESL Information Services (AUSELIS): http://www.iac.net/"conversa/S_homepage.html
BBC World Service: http://bbc.co.uk/worldservice
Bilingual Education & ESL Resources: http://www.educ.wsu.edu80/esl/index.html
British Council: http://www.britishcouncil.org/english/index.htm
Central European Training Program: www.beloit.edu/-cetp
CIEE: www.ciee.org
CNN: http://www.cnn.com
Dave's ESL Café: http://www.pacifnet.net/"sperling/eslcafe.html
Digital Education Network: http://www.edunet.com
ECIS: www.ecis.org
Education Links: http://www.magic.ca/"geoftay/edlink.html
ESL Teacher connection: http://www.sils.umich.edu/"jarmour/etc/etchome.htm
FIELS: www.fiels.co.nz
IATEFL: http://www.man.ac.uk/IATEFL/
Internet TESL Journal: http://www.aitech.ac.jp/iteslj/ESL.3.html
Linguistic Funland: http://www.math.unt.edu/linguistics/tesl.html/teslmenu
NZEIL: www.nzeil.co.nz
Ohio University CALL: http://www.tcom.ohio.edu/OU_Language/
OZ Govt Education Services: www.aief.edu.au
Peace Corps: http://www.peacecorps.gov/
Project Trust: projecttrust.org.uk
Student Center: http://www.infomall.org/studententer
Teaching abroad: www.teaching_abroad.uk.com
TESOL: http://www.tesol.edu/
Useful Resources: http://www.ling.lancs.ac.uk/staff/visitors/kenji/
USIA: http://www.usia.gov/
Voice of America: http://www.usia.gov/
Voluntary Service Overseas: http://www.oneworld.org/vso/

Useful Addresses for Jobs

Chain Schools

AEON Intercultural USA, Wiltshire Bvd, Suite 202, Beverley Hills, CA 90210, USA

AEON Institute of Foreign Languages, 7f Nihonsimei Bldg, 1-1, 3 Shimoishii, Okayami-shi 700, Japan

American Language Academy, 1401 Rockville Pike, Suite 550, Rockville, MD 20852 A080, USA

Anglo-Continental Education Group, 29-35 Wimborne Rd, Bournemouth BH2 6NA, UK

Benedict Schools, Via Peri 9B, Lugano 6901, Switzerland

Berlitz Inc, 9-13 Grosvenor St, London W1A 3BZ, UK

Berlitz Inc, 400 Alexander Park Drive, Princeton, NJ 05440-6303, USA

Bell Language Schools, 5 Red Cross Lane, Cambridge CB2 2QX, UK

Cambridge Schools, Av de Linerdale 173, 1250 Lisboa, Portugal

ELS Language Centres, 3 Charing Cross Rd, London WC28 0HA, UK

ELS Language Centres, 5761-6 Buckingham Parkway, Culver City, California, CA 90230-6538, USA

Embassy Summer Schools, 44 Cromwell Rd, Hove, East Sussex BN3 3ER, UK

Eurocentres Head Office, Seestrasse 247, 8038 Zurich, Switzerland

Eurocentres, 21 Meadow Court Rd, Lee Green, London SE3 9EU, UK

GEOS Corporation, 55-61 Portland Rd, Hove, Sussex BN3 5DQ, UK

GEOS Corporation, 415 Yonge St, Suite 1609, Toronto, Ontario M5B QE7, Canada

inLingua, Rodney Lodge, Rodney Rd, Cheltenham, Gloucestershire GL50 1JF, UK. Tel: 01242 253 181

Interact Nova Group, 2 Oliver St, Suite 7, Boston, MA 02110, USA

Interact Nova Group, 601 California St, Suite 702, San Francisco, CA 94108, USA

Interact Nova Group, 1881 Yonge St, Suite 700, Toronto, Ontario M45 3C4, Canada

International House, 106 Piccadilly, London W1V 9FL, UK. Tel: 0171 491 2958, Fax: 0171 491 0959

Language Link, 21 Harrington Rd, South Kensington, London SW7 3EU, UK

Kaplan, Kaplan Educational Centres, 888 7th Ave, 22nd Floor, New York, NY 1016 K040, USA

Linguarama, Oceanic House, 89 High St, Alton, Hampshire GU34 1LG, UK

Multi Lingua, Administration Centre, Abbot House, Sydenham Rd, Guildford, Surrey GU1 3RL, UK

Nord-Anglia International, Head Office, 10 Eden Place, Cheadle, Stockport, Cheshire SK8 1AT, UK

Nova Corporation, 141 Queen St Mall 23F, Brisbane, 4001 QLD, Australia

Nova Group, Carrington House, 126-130 Regent St, London W1R 5FE, UK

Oxford School, San Marco 1513, Venice, Italy

Saxoncourt Recruitement, (Shane Schools), 59 South Moulton St, London W1Y 1HH, UK

YBM/ELSI Language Institutes, Yeoksam Heights Bldg, 2nd Floor 642-19, Yeoksam-Dong, Kangham-Gu, Seoul 135081, South Korea

Recruitment Agencies

Anglo-Pacific (Asia) Consultancy, Suite 32, Nevilles Court, Dollis Hill Lane, London NW2 6HG, UK. Tel: 0181 452 7836

English Worldwide, The Italian Building, Dockhead, London SE1 2BS, UK. Tel: 0171 252 1402, Fax: 0171 251 8002

Kingswood Group, (Summer schools), Linton House, 164-180 Union St, London SE1 0LH, UK

Nord-Anglia International, Overseas Recruitment Dept, 10 Eden Place, Cheadle, Stockport, Cheshire SK8 1AT, UK

International Placement Group, Jezkova 9, 130 000 Praha 3, Czech Republic

Key Language Services, P O Box 17, 07 9770 Quito, Ecuador

QTS Recruitment Consultants, 36 High Ash Drive, Leeds LS17 8RA, UK

Saxoncourt Recruitment, (Shane Schools), 59 South Moulton St, London W1Y 1HH, UK

Skola Recruitment, 21 Star St, London W2 1QB, UK

SLP Recruiting, Songang University, 1-1 Sinsu-dong, Mapogu, Seoul, Korea

Teacher Recruitment International, Box 177, Tumby Bay 5605, S Australia

Teacher Recruitment Unit, Ministry of Education, Kay Faing Rd, Singapore 248922

TESOL Placement Agency, 700 South Washington Street, Suite200, Alexandria, Virginia 22314, USA. Tel: 703 836 0774, Fax: 703 836 7864

Government and Voluntary Agencies, Employers

Anglo-Continental Education Group, 29-35 Wimborne Rd, Bournemouth BH2 6NA, UK

British Council, Teacher vacancies, 10 Spring Gardens, London SW1A 2BN, UK. Tel: 0171 389 4931, Fax: 0171 389 4140

Central European Training Program, Beloit College, 700 College St, Beloit W1 53511, USA

CfBT Education Services, 1 The Chambers, East St, Reading RG1 4JD, UK. Tel: 0118 952 3900, Fax: 0118 952 3924

Christians Abroad, 1 Stockwell Green, London SW9 9HP, UK. Tel: 0171 737 7811, Fax: 0171 737 3237

Council on International Education Exchange (CIEE) - Administrative Centre, (North America), International and North American Administrative Centre, 205 East 42nd St, New York, NY 10017, USA. Tel: 212 822 2600, Fax: 212 822 2699

Council on International Education Exchange (CIEE) - Administrative Centre, (Europe), European Regional Administrative Centre, 66 Champs-Elysees, Batiment E, 75008 Paris, France. Tel: 33 1 40 75 95 10, Fax: 33 1 40 56 65 27

Council on International Education Exchange (CIEE) - Administrative Centre, (Asia), Asian Regional Administrative Centre, Cosmos Aoyama, Gallery Floor, 5-53-67 Jingumae, Shibuya-ku, Tokyo 150, Japan. Tel: 81 3 5467 5501, Fax: 81 3 5467 7031

Council on International Education Exchange (CIEE) - Administrative Centre, UK Council Programme Office, 52 Poland St, London W1V 4JQ, UK. Tel: 0171 478 2000, Fax: 0171 734 7322 (Administers JET and Teach in China Programme in the UK)

EEP (East European Partnership), London SW16, UK. Tel: 0181 780 2841, Fax: 0181 780 7550

Embassy Summer Schools, 44 Cromwell Rd, Hove, East Sussex BN3 3ER, UK

ECIS (European Council of International Schools), (UK), 21b Lavant St, Petersfield, Hampshire GU32 3EL, UK. Tel: 44 1730 268244, Fax: 44 1730 267914

ECIS (European Council of International Schools), (North America), 105 Tuxford Terrace, Basking Ridge, New Jersey 07920, USA. Tel: 1 908 903 0552, Fax: 1 908 580 9381

ECIS (European Council of International Schools), (Iberia), P O Box 6066, 28070 Madrid, Spain. Tel: 34 1 562 6722, Fax: 34 1 563 6854

ECIS (European Council of International Schools), (Australasia), 'Cumburri' IEC, P O Box 367, Kilmore 3764, Victoria, Australia. Tel: 61 3 5781 1351, Fax: 61 3 5781 1151

Executive Language Services, 20 Rue Sainte Croix de Bretonnerie, 75004 Paris, France

Higher Colleges of Technology, Central Personnel Services, P O Box 25026, Abu Dhabi, United Arab Emirates

International House,
106 Piccadilly, London W1V 9FL, UK.

1 to 1 International Projects, One Cottage Rd, Headingly, Leeds LS6 4DD, UK

JET (Japan Exchange & Teaching) Programme, see CIEE (page 282)

League for the Exchange of Commonwealth Teachers, Commonwealth House, 7 Lion Yard, Tremadoc Rd, London SW4 7NQ, UK

Peace Corps, 1990 K St NW, Room 4100, Washington, DC 20526, USA. Tel: 202 606 3780

Project Trust, The Hebridean Centre, Ballyhough, Isle of Coll, Argyll PA78 6TE, UK. Tel: 01879 23044, Fax: 01879 230357

Right Hand Trust, Gelligason, Llanfair Caereinion, Powys, SY21 9HE, Wales, UK

Skillshare Africa, 3 Belvoir Rd, Leicester LE1 6SL, UK. Tel: 0116 254 0517

Soros Foundation, Open Society Institute, 400 West 59 St, New York, NY 10019, USA

Students Partnership Worldwide, 17 Dean's Yard, London SW1P 3PB, UK. Tel: 0171 222 0138, Fax: 0171 233 0008

Teaching Abroad/Projects Abroad, Gerrard House, Rustington, West Sussex BN16 1AW, UK. Tel: 01903 859911, Fax: 01903 785779

UNV (United Nations Volunteers), see VSO

USIA (United States Information Agency), 301 4th St SW, Washington, DC 20547-0001, USA. Tel: 202 485 2869

VSO (Voluntary Services Overseas), 317 Putney Bridge Rd, London SW15, UK. Tel: 0181 780 7527, Fax: 0171 608 3377

Winant Clayton Volunteers Association, Davenant Centre, 179 Whitechapel Rd, London E1 1DU, UK

Worldteach Inc, c/o Harvard Institute, International Development, 1 Eliot St, Cambridge, MA 021 138, USA. Tel: 001 617 495 5527, Fax: 001 617 495 1599

Worldwide Education Service (WES), Canada House, 272 Field End Rd, Eastcote, Middx HA4 9PE, UK. Tel: 0181 866 4400, Fax: 0181 429 4838

Useful Addresses

Below is a list of other useful addresses:

UNITED KINGDOM

ABLS (Association of British Language Schools), 217-9 Tottenham Court Rd, London W1P 9AF. Tel: 0171 631 0627, Fax: 0171 637 7291

ACTDEC (Accreditation Council for TESOL Distance Education Courses), 21 Wessex Gdns, Dore, Sheffield S17 3PQ

Africa Venture, 10 Market Place, Devizes, Wiltshire SN10 1HT

ARELS (Association of Recognised English Language Services), 2 Pontypool Place, Valentine Place, London SE1. Tel: 0171 242 3136, Fax: 0171 928 9378

BALEAP (British Association of Lecturers in English for Academic Purposes), English Lang Unit, Huw Owen Bldg, OCW, Penglais, Aberyswyth, Dyfed, Wales

BASELT (British Association of State English Language Teaching), Cheltenham and Gloucester College of Higher Education, Francis Close Hall, Swindon Rd, Cheltenham, Glos. Tel: 01242 227099, Fax: 01242 227055

BATQI (British Association of TESOL Qualifying Institutions), School of Education, University of Leeds, LS2 9AJ

BBC World Service, Bush House, London WC2B 4PH. Tel: 0171 257 8305, Fax: 0171 257 8311

BELNATE, King Charles St, London SW1A 2AH

Berlitz Publishing, Berlitz House, Peterley Rd, Oxford OX4 2TX

British Council, 10 Spring Gardens, London SW1A 2BN; Information Centre, Medlock St, Manchester M15 4AA (see also Central Bureau and OAS)

British Universities North America Club, 16 Bowling Green Lane, London EC1R 0BD. Tel: 0171 251 2372

Cambridge University Press, The Edinburgh Building, Shaftesbury Rd, Cambridge CB2 2RU

Central Bureau for Educational Visits & Exchanges, 10 Spring Gardens, London SW1A 2BN. Tel: 0171 389 4004, Fax: 0171 389 4426

Christians Abroad, 1 Stockwell Green, London SW9 9HP. Tel: 0171 737 7811, Fax: 0171 737 3237

Collins Cobuild, 77/85 Fulham Palace Rd, London W8 8JB

Concern Worldwide, 248-250 Lavender Hill, London SW11 1LJ

Contributions Agency International Services, see Social Security. (page 286 & DSS below)

Department of Health, Intnl Relations 2C, Room 512, Richmond House, 79 Whitehall, London SW1A 2NS. Tel: 0171 210 5318

DSS Benefits Agency, Pensions and Overseas Benefits Directorate (MED), Tyneview Park, Whitley Rd, Newcastle-upon-Tyne NE98 1BA

DynEd International, Tree Tops, Watts Green, Chearsley, Bucks HP13 0DD. Tel: 01844 208 495, Fax: 01844 201 329

English Contacts Abroad, P O Box 126, Oxford OX2 6UB

EL*Gazette*/EL*Prospects*, Dilke House, 1 Malet St, London WC1E 7JA. Tel: 0171 255 1969, Fax: 0171 255 1972

English Speaking Board, 26a Princes St, Southport PR8 1EQ. Tel: 01704 501730, Fax: 01704 539637

Gabbitas, 126-130 Regent St, London W1R 6EE

GAP Activity Projects, 44 Queen's Rd, Reading, Berks RG1 4BB.
Tel: 0118 959 4914, Fax: 0118 959 6634

Georgian Press, 56 Sandy Lane, Leyland, Preston, Lancashire PR5 1ED.
Tel: 01772 431 790, Fax: 01772 431 378

IATEFL (International Association of Teachers of English as a Foreign Language), 3 Kingsdown Park, Tankerton, Whitstable, Kent CT5 2DJ. Tel: 01277 276528

ICD (International Co-operation for Development), Unit 3, Canonbury Yard, 190a New North Rd, London N1 7BJ

ICELS, Oxford Brookes University, Headington, Oxford OX3 6BP

ICL Recruitment, 1 Riding House St, London W1A 3AS

Inland Revenue, (General Enquiries), Room G1, West Wing, Somerset House, Strand, London WC1R 1LB. Tel: 0171 438 6420

Institute of Education, University of London, TESOL Dept, 20 Bedford Way, London WC1 0AL

Institute for International Communication, 56 Eccleston Square, London SW1V 1PQ.
Tel: 0171 233 9888

KELTIC Bookshop, 25 Chepstow Corner, Chepstow Place, London W2 4XE.
Tel: 0171 229 8560

Language Link, 45 High St Kensington, London S8 5EB

Language Matters, 2 Rookery Rd, Selly Oak B29 7DQ

Language Teaching Publications, 35 Church Rd, Hove, East Sussex BN3 2BE.
Tel: 01273 736 344, Fax: 01273 720 898

LCCI (London Chamber of Commerce & Industry) Exam Board, Marlow House, Station Rd, Sidcup, Kent DA15

Link Africa, Orwell House, Orwell Rd, Cambridge CB4 4WY. Tel: 01223 426665, Fax: 01223 426960

Macmillan Heinemann ELT, Macmillan Oxford, Between Towns Road, Oxford OX4 3PP. Tel: 44 (0) 1865 405700. Fax: 44 (0) 1865 405701. Email: elt@mhelt.com Website: http://www.mhelt.com International leaders in language teaching. 40 companies with offices worldwide. School publishers throughout the world

MASTA (Medical Advisory Service for Travellers Abroad), Keppel St, London WC1E 7HT

NATFHE (National Association of Teachers in Further and Higher Education), 27 Britannia St, London WC1X 9JP

NUT (National Union of Teachers), Hamilton House, Mabledon Place, London WC1

OAS (Overseas Appointment Service), Medlock St, Manchester M15 4PR. Tel: 0161 957 7000

OCTAB (The Overseas Contract Teachers and Advisors Branch of the IPS), The Secretary, 24 Ashford Rd, Manchester

ODA (Overseas Development Agency),
94 Victoria St, London SW1E 5JL.
Tel: 0171 917 7000

OMS (Overseas Missionary Service),
1 Sandleigh Ave, Manchester M20 3LN

Oxford University Press,
Great Clarendon St, Oxford OX2 6DP

Pearson Education, Edinburgh Gate, Burnt Mill,
Harlow, Essex CM20 2JE.
Tel: 01279 623 623, Fax: 01279 623 947

Pitman Qualifications,
1 Giltspur St, London EC1A 9DD.
Tel: 0171 331 4021, Fax: 0171 331 4022

Returned Volunteer Action,
1 Amwell St, London EC1R 1UL

Routledge, 11 New Fetter Lane,
London EC4P 3EE.
Tel: 0171 842 2098, Fax: 0171 842 2306

RSA/Cambridge Certificates & Diplomas,
see UCLES

**SEAL (Society for Effective Affective
Learning),** The Language Centre, University of
Brighton, Falmer, Sussex BN1 9PH

**(Social Security) Contributions Agency
International Services,** Longbenton,
Newcastle-upon-Tyne NE98 1YX.
Tel: 0645 1 54811. See also DSS Benefits Agency

SWELTA, c/o College of St Mark & St John,
Derriford, Plymouth, Devon PL6 8BH

TEFLNet Recruitment, The Lang Works,
41 Low Petergate, York YO1 2HT

TOEIC, TOEIC House, 129 Wendell Rd, London
W12 9SD. Tel: 0181 740 6282, Fax: 0181 740 5207

Trinity College London External Exam Board,
16 Park Crescent, London W1N 4AH.
Tel: 0171 323 2328, Fax: 0171 323 5201

**UCLES (University of Cambridge Local
Examinations Syndicate),**
1 Hills Rd, Cambridge CB1 2EU.
Tel: 01223 553311

UNA (United Nations Association),
UNA International Service, 3 Whitehall Court,
London SW1A 2EL

**ULEAC (University of London Examinations
and Assessment Council),** Stewart House,
32 Russell Square, London WC1B 5DN.
Tel: 0171 331 4121, Fax: 0171 331 4022

**UODLES (University of Oxford Delegacy of
Local Examinations),** Ewart House, Ewart
Place, Summertown, Oxford OX2 7BZ.
Tel: 01865 554291, Fax: 01865 510085

Verulam Publishing, 152a Park St Lane, Park St,
St Albans, Herts AL2 2AU.
Tel: 01272 872 770, Fax: 01272 873 866

Worldwide Education Service, 272 Field End
Rd, Eastcote, Middlesex HA4 9NA.
Tel: 0181 866 4400, Fax: 0181 429 4838

AUSTRALIA
Australia TESOL,
P O Box 296, Rozelle, NSW 2039

**ELICOS (English Lang Intensive Courses to
Overseas Students) Association,**
P O Box 30 Murray St, Pyrmont, NSW 2009.
Tel: 2 9660 6455, Fax: 2 9566 2230

National Curriculum Resource Centre, 5th
Floor, 197 Rundall Mall, Adelaide 5000

NCELTR (National Centre for English Language Teaching & Research), School of English & Linguistics, Macquarie University, Sydney, NSW 2109. Tel: 2 850 7673, Fax: 2 850 7849

Overseas Service Bureau, P O Box 350, 71 Argyle St, Fitroy, Victoria 3065

AUSTRIA
TEA (Teachers of English in Austria), TEA Office, Kleine Neugasse 7/2a, A-1050 Vienna

BRAZIL
BATE (British Association for Teacher Education), Rua Vinicius De Moraes 179, Ipanema 22411, Rio

Brazil TESOL, Rua Julia da Costa 1500, 80430 Curitba PR

IATEFL Brazil, Rua Antonio Ataide 515, Vila Velha, ES-29100-290

LAURELS (Latin American Union of Registered English Language Schools), c/o International House, Rua 4, No 80, Setor Oeste, Goiania GO 74110-140. Tel: 62 224 0478, Fax: 41 262 1738

Sociedad Cultural Brasiliera da Cultura, Inglese Av Graca Aranha, 327-7CP Caixa Postal 821, Rio de Janeiro

CANADA
Canadian Association of Private Language Schools (CAPLS), 12871 Carluke

Canadian Council of Second Langs, 151 Slater St, Ottawa, Ontario T1P

Canadian Education and Accreditation Commission, P O Box 340, 403-233 Colborne St, Brandford, ON N3T 5N3

Canadian Education Centre Network, Asia-Pacific Foundation of Canada, 666-999 Canada Place, Vancouver, BC V6C 3E1

Council of Second Language Programs in Canada (CSLPC), 355 Don Mills Rd, Suite 6, Box 202, Willowdale, ON M2H 3N3

Private English Language School Association (PELSA), c/o Pacific Language Institute, 3rd Floor, 755 Burrard St, Vancouver, BC V6Z 1X6

SWAP Scheme, CFS, 243 College St, Toronto, ON M5T 2Y1

TESL Canada, P O Box 44105, Burnaby, BC V5B 4Y2

CHILE
LABCI (Latin American-British Cultural Institutes), Mirian Rabinovitch (Chair), Instituto Chileno-Britanico De Cultura, Chile. Tel: 562 638 2156, Fax: 562 632 6637

CHINA
CETRAC, Shanghai Jaio Tong University, 1854 Hua Shan Rd, Shanghai 200030

NFLTAESC, Dept of Foreign Languages, Tsingua University, 55 Shatanhou St, Beijing 100009

State Bureau of Foreign Experts, Friendship Hotel, 3 Bai Shi Qiao Rd, 100873 Beijing

COLOMBIA
Associacion Colombiana de Profesores de Lenguas, Centro Oxford, Apartado Aereo 102420, Unicentro, Bogota

ASOCOPI, Av 19, No 3-05, Bogota

DENMARK
EETAE (Association of English Teachers in Adult Education),
Toftegardsvej, 24 DK 3500 Vaerlose

ECUADOR
Ecuadorian English Teachers Society,
P O Box 10935, Guayaquil

FINLAND
ATEF (Association of Teachers of English in Finland), Rautatielaisenkatu 6A 00520, Helsinki

FRANCE
ELTAF, Darmstaedter Landstr 109, 60958, Frankfurt am Main

FBCCI (Franco-British Chamber of Commerce & Industry), 41 rue de Turenne, 75003 Paris

FIPLV, 217 Ave Pierre-Brossolette, BP 710-F10002 Troyes

TESOL France, 15 rue Daguerre, 92500 Ruell-Malmaison

GERMANY
ELTA-Rhine, Erich Muller Strasse 20, 40597 Dusseldorf

ELTA Stuttgart, Westliche 271, D 75172, Pforzheim

MELTA (Munich English Lang Teachers' Association), Cramer Klett Str 2, 85579 Neubiberg

HELTA, Hanssensweg 1, 22303 Hamburg

RELTA e V, Uhlandweg 37, D-8829 Wangen

GREECE
PEKADE, 80 Evangelistrias St, Malithea 17671

TESOL Greece, 87 Academis St, Athens

HONG KONG
Hong Kong University Press, 139 Pokfulam Rd. Tel: 852 2550 2703, Fax: 852 2875 0734

HUNGARY
English Teachers Association of Hungary, Dozsa Gyorgy ut 104.II. 15, 068 Budapest. Tel: 1 132 8688, Fax: 1 131 9376

Kecskemet Association for Teachers of English Akademia,
Korut, 20.1.31 Kecsemet 6000

IRELAND
ATT (Association for Teacher Training in TEFL), P O Box 3384, Dublin 6

NATEFL (National Association of Teachers of English as a Foreign Language in Ireland,
P O Box 1917, Dublin 6

RESLA (Recognised English Language Schools Association), 17 Camden St Lower, Dublin 2. Tel: 353 475 3122, Fax: 353 475 3088

JAPAN
AJET (Association for Japan Exchange and Teaching), AJET Drop Box, 4F Nissaykojimachi Bldg, 3-3-6 Kudan Machi, Chiyoda-ku, Tokyo 102

JALT (The Japan Association of Lang Teachers), Central Office, Urban Edge Bldg, 5th Floor, 1-37-9 Taito, Taito-ku, Tokyo 110. Tel: 3 3837 1630, Fax: 3 3837 1630

**JET (Japan Exchange & Teaching)
Programme,** (see CIEE in Useful Addresses for
Jobs section and separate entry in USA sections)

KOREA
American Citizens Services Branch,
82 Sejong Rd, Chongro Ku. Tel: 2 397 4603

KOSETA, 901-903 Dong-A Apt, Muzlgae Maul
Guim-Dong, Bundang-gu Seongnam-si,
Kyonggi-do 463-500

Korea TESOL, Joo-kung Park, Dept of English,
Honam University, 59-1 Seobong-dong,
Kwangszan-gu, Kwanglu 506-090

LUXEMBOURG
**Association Luxembourgeoise des
Ensiegnants d'Anglais,**
BP 346, L-2013 Luxembourg

MALTA
**FELTOM (Federation of English Language
Teaching Organisations Malta),** Foundation for
International Studies, Old University Bldg,
St Paul St, Valletta VT 607

NETHERLANDS
CITO-TOEFL, P O Box 1203, 6801 BE Arnhem

VLLT, Schoutstraat 35, Nijmegen 6525 XS

NEW ZEALAND
**FIELS (Federation of Independent English
Language Schools),** P O Box 2577, Auckland

**NZEIL (New Zealand Education International
Ltd),** P O Box 10500, Wellington

NORWAY
**LMS (Modern Languages Association of
Norway),** Jonas Liesvei, 1B 1412 Sofiemyr

POLAND
FIPLV, Adam Micklewickz University,
28 Czerwca 1956 nr 198, PL-61-485 Poznan

Ministry of National Education,
Al J Ch Szucha 25, 00918 Warsaw.
Tel: 2 628 0461, Fax: 2 628 8561

Soros Foundation, Batory Foundation,
9 Flory St, 4th Floor, 00-586 Warsaw

PORTUGAL
**APPI (Associaco Portuguese de Professores de
Ingles),** Apartado 2885, 1122 Lisbon

RUSSIA
NLELTA, 31a Minin St, Nizhny Novgorod 603155

SPELTA, No 31 Ordzonikiolze Str, Corp 1,
Flat 133, St Petersburg 196158

SINGAPORE
Simon and Schuster Pte,
317 Alexandra Rd, 04-01 IKEA Bldg, Singapore.
Tel: 65 476 4688, Fax: 65 378 0378

SOUTH AFRICA
Education & Culture Service,
Private Bag 9008, Cape Town 8000

SPAIN
**APAC (Associaco de Professors d'Angles de
Catalunya),** Apartado 2287, 08080 Barcelona

Associacion de Professors de Ingles de Galicia, Apartado de Correo 1078, Santiago de Compostela

APIGA, 125-IoE, 15700 Santiago de Compostela

SWEDEN
LMS Sweden (Modern Languages Association of Sweden), Eriksdalsgatan 1, S-652-62 Karistad

SWITZERLAND
ETAS (English Teachers Association Switzerland), Gurzeingasse 25, 4500 Solothurn

TURKEY
METU, Dept of Basic English, Ankara 06531

THAILAND
Thai TESOL, 204/77 Phasukasem 3, Phatanakarn Rd, Parawet, Bangkok 10250

UNITED ARAB EMIRATES
TESOL Arabia, University of UAE, English Unit, P O Box 17172, Al Ain

UNITED STATES OF AMERICA
Abaca Books, P O Box 1028, Normal, IL 61761. Tel/Fax: 309 454 7141

Addison Wesley Longman, 10 Banks St, White Plains, New York, NY 10606. Tel: 914 993 5000, Fax: 914 997 8115

Alliances Abroad, 2830 Alameda, San Francisco, CA 94103. Fax: 415 621 1609

Andujar Communication Technologies, 7946 Ivanhoe Ave, Suite 302, La Jolla, California CA 92037. Tel: 619 459 2673, Fax: 619 459 9768

AASA (Association of American Schools in South America), 14750 NW 77 Court, Suite 210, Miami Lakes, Florida, FL 33016

Barron's Educational Service, 250 Wireless Blvd, Hauppauge, New York, NY 11788. Tel: 516 434 3311, Fax: 516 4434 3723

Center for Interim Programs, P O Box 2347, Cambridge, MA 02238. Tel: 617 547 0980, Fax: 617 661 2864

Dominie Press, 5945 Pacific Center Blvd, Suite 505, San Diego, CA 92121. Tel: 619 546 8899, Fax: 619 546 8822

Dymon Publications, 209 North 775 East, American Fork, Utah, UT 84003. Tel: 801 756 5171, Fax: 801 253 2915

English for Everybody, 655 Powell St, Suite 505, San Francisco, CA 94108

Fullbright Senior Scholar Program, 3007 Tilden St NW, Suite 5M, Washington, DC 20008-3009. Tel: 202 686 7877

Georgetown University, Center for Language Education & Development, 3607 'O' St NW, Washington, DC 20007

Heinemann, 361 Hanover St, Portsmouth, NH 03801. Tel: 603 431 7894, Fax: 603 431 7840

Heinle and Heinle Publishers, 20 Park Plaza, Boston, Massachusetts, MA 02116. Tel: 617 451 1940, Fax: 617 426 4379

InterExchange, 161 Sixth Ave, New York, NY 10012. Tel: 212 924 0466, Fax: 212 924 0575

International Educator, International Educators Institute, P O Box 103 West Bridgewater, Massachusetts, MA 02379

International Organization for Migration,
Latin American Programs, 1750 K St NW, Suite
1110, Washington, DC 20006

International Schools Services,
P O Box 5910, Princeton, NJ 08543.
Tel: 609 452 0990, Fax: 609 452 2690

JET (Japan Exchange & Teaching) Program,
Japanese Embassy, 2520 Massachusetts Ave NW,
Washington, DC 20008.
Tel: 202 939 6722

McGraw-Hill, 1221 Ave of the Americas,
New York, NY 10020. Tel: 212 512 228,
Fax: 212 512 4878

Michigan University Press, 839 Greene St,
P O Box 1104, Ann Abor, MI 48106.
Tel: 313 764 4392, Fax: 313 936 0456

University of Northern Iowa,
Overseas Placement Service for Educators,
UNI, Cedar Falls, Iowa, IO 50614-0390.
Tel: 319 273 2083

Ohio State University, Educ Careers Service,
110 Arps Hall, 1945 N High St,
Columbus, OH 43201-1172.
Tel: 614 292 2581

Overseas Missionary Service (OMS),
P O Box A, Greenwood, IN 46142-6599

Peace Corps, Room 8500, 1990 K St NW,
(P O Box 941), Washington, DC 20526.
Tel: 202 606 3780

Santillana Publishing,
2043 NW 87th Ave, Miami, FL 33172.
Tel: 305 591 9522, Fax: 305 591 9145
Scott Foresman, 1900 East Lake Ave, A-240,
Glenview, IL 60025.
Tel: 708 486 2419, Fax: 847 729 3065

Search Associates, P O Box 636,
Dallas, Philadelphia, PA 18612

**SPELT (Soros Professional English Language
Teaching Program),** 888 Seventh Ave,
31st Floor, New York, NY 10106.
Tel: 212 757 2323

Taking Off,
P O Box 104, Newton Highlands, MA 02161.
Tel: 617 630 1606

TESOL Association and Publications,
700 South Washington Street, Suite200,
Alexandria, Virginia 22314, USA. Tel: 703 836
0774, Fax: 703 836 7864
Time Out Associates, P O Box 503, Milton,
MA 02186. Tel: 617 698 8977

**TOEIC Service International, Educational
Testing Service,** 508 Carnegie Center,
Princetown, New Jersey, NJ 08541.
Tel: 609 951 1600, Fax: 609 520 1093

Townsend Press,
1038 Industrial Drive, Berlin, NJ 08009. Tel: 609
753 0554, Fax: 609 753 0649
United States Public Health Service,
Washington, DC 20402-9325

Worldwide Teachers Development Institute,
266 Beacon St, Boston, MA 02116.
Tel: 617 262 5722

URUGUAY
AUPPI, Las Heras 1832, Montevideo 11600

URUTESOL, Colonia 1342 Piso 7,
Montevideo 11100

Index

Index of Advertisers